THE INFANT MIND

The Infant Mind

Origins of the Social Brain

EDITED BY

MARIA LEGERSTEE
DAVID W. HALEY
MARC H. BORNSTEIN

THE GUILFORD PRESS
New York   London

© 2013 The Guilford Press
A Division of Guilford Publications, Inc.
72 Spring Street, New York, NY 10012
www.guilford.com

Printed in the United States of America

This book is printed on acid-free paper.

Last digit is print number: 9   8   7   6   5   4   3   2   1

Library of Congress Cataloging-in-Publication Data

The infant mind : origins of the social brain / [edited by] Maria Legerstee, David W.
Haley, Marc H. Bornstein.
   p. cm.
  Includes bibliographical references and index.
  ISBN 978-1-4625-0817-4 (cloth)
  1. Social perception in children.   2. Social interaction in children.   3. Cognition in
children.   4. Infants—Development.   I. Legerstee, Maria Theresia.   II. Haley, David
W.   III. Bornstein, Marc H.
  BF723.S6I54 2013
  155.42′23—dc23
                                 2012030158

About the Editors

Maria Legerstee, PhD, is Professor in the Department of Psychology and Director of the Infancy Centre for Research at York University in Toronto, Ontario, Canada. She is the recipient of a 5-year Canada University Research Fellowship from the Social Sciences and Humanities Research Council and a Dean's Award for Outstanding Research from York University. Dr. Legerstee is a member of the editorial boards of *Infant Behavior and Development* and *Infant and Child Development.* Her research focuses on behavioral and neurological correlates of social-cognitive development during early childhood.

David W. Haley, PhD, is Associate Professor of Psychology at the University of Toronto, where he serves as Principal Investigator in the Parent–Infant Research Lab and as Co-Organizer of the Centre for Parenting Research. His research examines the development of infant stress, learning, and memory in the context of the parent–infant relationship. Dr. Haley is currently examining the neural correlates of attention regulation in infants and parents.

Marc H. Bornstein, PhD, is Senior Investigator and Head of Child and Family Research at the Eunice Kennedy Shriver National Institute of Child Health and Human Development in Bethesda, Maryland. He has published in experimental, methodological, comparative, developmental, and cultural science, as well as neuroscience, pediatrics, and aesthetics. Dr. Bornstein is Founding Editor of the journal *Parenting: Science and Practice.*

Contributors

Patricia J. Bauer, PhD, Department of Psychology, Emory University, Atlanta, Georgia

Jay Belsky, PhD, Department of Human and Community Development, University of California, Davis, Davis, California; Department of Psychology, King Abdulaziz University, Jedda, Saudi Arabia; Institute for the Study of Children, Families, and Social Issues, Birkbeck, University of London, London, United Kingdom

Jeannette E. Benson, MA, Department of Psychology, Queen's University, Kingston, Ontario, Canada

Marc H. Bornstein, PhD, Eunice Kennedy Shriver National Institute of Child Health and Human Development, Bethesda, Maryland

Leslie J. Carver, PhD, Department of Psychology, University of California, San Diego, La Jolla, California

Carrie Coffield, PhD, The Boggs Center on Developmental Disabilities, Robert Wood Johnson Medical School, University of Medicine and Dentistry of New Jersey, New Brunswick, New Jersey

Michelle de Haan, PhD, Centre for Developmental Cognitive Neuroscience, Institute of Child Health, University College London, London, United Kingdom

Jonathan Delafield-Butt, PhD, Department of Psychology, University of Copenhagen, Copenhagen, Denmark; Faculty of Humanities and Social Science, University of Strathclyde, Glasgow, United Kingdom

Robin I. M. Dunbar, PhD, Department of Experimental Psychology, Institute of Cognitive and Evolutionary Anthropology, University of Oxford, Oxford, United Kingdom

Shaun Gallagher, PhD, Department of Philosophy, University of Memphis, Memphis, Tennessee; Department of Philosophy, University of Hertfordshire, Hertfordshire, United Kingdom

Vittorio Gallese, MD, Brain Center for Social and Motor Cognition, Italian Institute of Technology, and Department of Neuroscience, University of Parma, Parma, Italy

David W. Haley, PhD, Department of Psychology, University of Toronto, Toronto, Ontario, Canada

Ariel Knafo, PhD, Department of Psychology, The Hebrew University, Jerusalem, Israel

Sheila Krogh-Jespersen, PhD, Infant Learning and Development Laboratory, Department of Psychology, University of Chicago, Chicago, Illinois

Valerie A. Kuhlmeier, PhD, Department of Psychology, Queen's University, Kingston, Ontario, Canada

Maria Legerstee, PhD, Department of Psychology, York University, Toronto, Ontario, Canada

Estelle Mayhew, PhD, Department of Psychology, Rutgers, The State University of New Jersey, Piscataway, New Jersey

Peter Mundy, PhD, MIND Institute and Department of Psychiatry, University of California, Davis, Davis, California

Michael Pluess, PhD, Social, Genetic and Developmental Psychiatry Centre, Institute of Psychiatry, King's College London, London, United Kingdom

Magali Rochat, PhD, Department of Neuroscience, University of Parma, Parma, Italy

Mark A. Sabbagh, PhD, Department of Psychology, Queen's University, Kingston, Ontario, Canada

Suzanne E. Stevens, PhD, Department of Psychological Medicine, Faculty of Medical and Health Sciences, University of Auckland, Auckland, New Zealand

Colwyn Trevarthen, PhD, Department of Psychology, University of Edinburgh, Edinburgh, United Kingdom

Florina Uzefovsky, MA, Department of Psychology, The Hebrew University, Jerusalem, Israel

Arlene Walker-Andrews, PhD, Department of Psychology, University of Montana, Missoula, Montana

Preface

The study of the biological mechanisms that subserve social interaction is based on the idea that identifying biological, cognitive, and social levels of analysis contribute to more comprehensive explanations of human social-cognitive development. Consequently, research that focuses on collaborations between traditional social-cognitive developmental theory and social-cognitive developmental neuroscience (the empirical study of the neural mechanisms underlying development of social and cognitive processes) promises a more detailed account of the relative contributions that innate and environmental components make to social cognition, and advances an understanding of child development and behavior.

However, until now, many of the studies addressing the developing mind have relied on clever experimentation and the collection of behavioral data. Only recently have developmental scientists begun to merge with social neuroscientists. This collaboration is beginning to shed new light on important aspects of the infant brain. As a consequence, behavioral data of social phenomena are being elucidated by their biological foundations, thereby revealing the roles that various neural structures, genes, and neurotransmitter systems play in social cognition. Specifically, it has been shown that "cortical regions in the temporal lobe participate in perceiving socially relevant stimuli, whereas the amygdala, right somatosensory cortices, orbitofrontal cortices, and cingulate cortices all participate in linking perception of such stimuli to motivation, emotion, and cognition" (Adolphs, 2001, p. 231). Nonetheless, questions remain about the domain specificity of social cognition (emotions and thought) and the roles the environment plays in development.

A generous grant from the Office of the Vice President, Research and Innovation at York University, in Toronto, made it possible to invite colleagues from various disciplines who study the multiple domains that contribute to social and cognitive neuroscience development to come to York and discuss their exciting and groundbreaking research and subsequently contribute a chapter to the present volume.

As a result of these collaborations, we edited the *The Infant Mind: Origins of the Social Brain*. The book provides new insights into the development of the human child. The work is guided by extensive research into the reciprocal role of infant core abilities and social relationships in neural and behavioral development. The interdisciplinary scientists who contribute to this volume are using the latest behavioral, hormonal, genetic, and brain imaging technologies to discover how infants' sensory, perceptual, cognitive, emotional, and social capacities interact in social-cognitive development. Brought together in this volume for the first time, the work of these scientists provides a dynamic and holistic picture of early social-cognitive development that will constitute a major advance in the field. As such, we hope it will be an important teaching resource as well as an academic guide for those who work in the area of developmental social neuroscience and beyond.

The book is divided into five parts. To see how current understanding of the social mind has been formulated, it is important to put it into context. Consequently, Part I, "Evolutionary, Neural, and Philosophical Approaches to the Social Mind," includes three chapters that have given rise to the integration of developmental science and social neuroscience and to the recognition of the field of developmental social neuroscience. In Chapter 1, Dunbar proposes an evolutionary basis for social cognition. He argues that the social brain hypothesis owes its origin to an attempt to explain why primates have significantly larger brains for body size than all other mammals. Essentially, the claim is that primates live in unusually complex social systems, and it is the need to manage and manipulate a great deal of constantly changing information about the state of this social world that is computationally so demanding. Initially referred to as the social intelligence hypothesis (Humphrey, 1976) and the Machiavellian intelligence hypothesis (Byrne & Whiten, 1988), consensus has now settled on the term "social brain hypothesis" as being less tendentious and descriptively more neutral. In the end, what needs to be explained is the fact that primates have very large brains, both absolutely and relatively compared with other mammals, with most of this increase being attributed to an exponential growth in neocortex size. Although some mammals (e.g., elephants and many members of the whale and dolphin family) have volumetrically larger brains even than humans, the substantive issue lies in the size of the neocortex. Large neocortices are essentially a primate evolutionary novelty: In mammals in general, the neocortex accounts for 10–40% of total brain volume, whereas in primates, it accounts for 50–80%. In Chapter 2, Gallese and Rochat describe the role of mirror neurons in the development of social cognition. The authors propose that the motor cortical system, typically thought to merely enable movement programming and execution, plays a crucial role in complex cognitive abilities such as understanding motor goals and basic actions and intentions. They qualify such abilities as motor cognition. The authors present neuroscientific evidence relating the existence and functions of a neural mechanism—the mirror neuron mechanism—with action and intention understanding in macaque monkeys and humans. The possible contribution of this mechanism to the development of social-cognitive abilities in nonhuman primates and human infants is discussed. The authors address the relevance of motor cognition for the understanding of important aspects of autism spectrum disorder. Finally, in Chapter 3, Gallagher's interaction theory offers an intriguing "third" option that reconciles the works of major philosophers, particularly Merleau-Ponty, reemphasizing the embodiment of experience and the directedness of perceiving and acting in a social context. This way of contextualizing the reading-of-mind problem in the directedness of interaction is stimulating, and the chapter offers a platform for further reflection and discussion on this central problem.

Part II, "Social Experience and Epigenetic Mechanisms of Gene–Environment Interactions," includes two chapters that investigate the relation between early experience and later development. As we learn about the genetic contribution to brain development, we also learn about the impact of the environment on gene expression. The authors provide some of the most compelling evidence in the field showing that early experience has long-term implications for gene expression, which, in turn, affects the regulation of the neural systems underlying social cognition. In addition, the authors present new evidence of the unique contribution and changing roles of genes and experience on social behavior in infants and children. In Chapter 4, Pluess, Stevens, and Belsky elaborate on Belsky's theory in child development that individuals are differentially susceptible to the environment depending on genetic background. The main argument presented is that individuals with susceptible genes may fare better or worse depending on the environment. The chapter includes a new development of ideas and questions concerned with when these genetic susceptibilities are produced in the prenatal and postnatal context. In Chapter 5, Knafo and Uzefovsky provide new insights into genetic and environmental effects that influence cognitive and affective components of empathy in young children. The authors describe the development of empathy, and then conduct a meta-analysis of the extant literature on genetic and environmental contributions to individual differences in empathy. In affective empathy, genetics accounted for 30% of the variance, with the rest of the variance accounted for by nonshared environment and error. A different pattern was found for cognitive empathy, with the genetic effect estimated at 26%, all shared-environment effects estimated at 17%, and the rest of the variance (57%) attributable to the nonshared environment and error. The authors go beyond separating variation into genetic and environmental effects. They show that economic risk moderates the genetic influence on empathy. Furthermore, medical risk in infancy is associated with lower importance for genetic effects on empathy at age 3. Finally, the authors show a gene–parenting interaction between a genetic polymorphism, the exon III repeat region of the DRD4 receptor gene, and maternal negativity. Negativity relates negatively to observed empathy toward an examiner at 3½ years, but only among children carrying the 7-repeat allele of the polymorphism. The findings demonstrate the importance of gene–environment interactions in the early development of empathy.

Research on the types of early experiences that influence visual, memory, language, and the integration of multimodal stimuli is discussed in Part III, "The Dynamic Role of Early Social Experience in Vision, Memory, and Language." In Chapter 6, de Haan and Carver provide an integrative overview of the contributions of innate predispositions, brain maturation, and experience to the development of face-processing skills during infancy. The authors focus on infants' abilities to detect and orient to faces, recognize the faces of familiar people, perceive where a person is directing his or her gaze, and register emotions shown in the face. Their discussion makes clear that the development of face processing involves the combination of innate predispositions, brain maturation, and experience. Infants have innate biases that guide their visual exploration of faces, but both the maturation of the cortex and the structure of the visual environment modulate how these biases are expressed. In Chapter 7, Bauer shows that the development of explicit memory is possible as early as 6 months of age, and that by the end of the second year of life long-term recall is reliable and robust. She explores the developmental changes in memory that occur for past events, including socially relevant events, relying on a nonverbal imitation-based method and the recording of the brain's activity or event-related potentials to assess the developmental changes in neural processing that occur as infants and children develop memory. In Chapter 8, Trevarthen and Delafield-Butt discuss the importance of the creative musicality of play with voice, gestures, and facial expressions. They also propose that language exists for the purpose of communication and can be learned only in the context of interaction with people who want to communicate intimately in responsive engagement with the impulses of young children from infancy. In this chapter, the authors draw on their work on developmental brain science of human movement and detailed analyses of intersubjective games between parents and babies who are too young to speak. They conclude that conversations begin in story-making games of nonverbal communication, which have powerful rhythmic, musical properties long before actual words are uttered. They conclude that the "communicative musicality" of play through vocalizations, gestures, and facial expressions, linking the dynamic motives and complementary feelings of infants and their companions in pleasurable rituals, are essential for the development of symbolic communication in collaborative communities. In Chapter 9, Walker-Andrews, Krogh-Jespersen, Mayhew, and Coffield argue that perception develops optimally when stimulus information is dynamic, naturalistic, and multimodal (i.e., when faces, speech, and corresponding emotional characteristics are combined). The authors discuss how social interaction affects the development of awareness of the self, drawing on examples from their work on infants' perception of expressions of emotion and infants' intermodal percepts. The perspective presented is consistent with the Gibsonian notion that the brains of most organisms evolved in a reciprocal relationship to their environment.

In Part IV, "The Role of Early Experience in Social Development," authors present research on the types of early experiences that influence the role of interpersonal motives in the early emergence of social percepts and concepts as well as the specific types of parenting that seem to provide optimal social-cognitive outcomes. Evidence now reveals that the child's social-emotional development requires sensitive and attuned social responsiveness from sympathetic people, and that biology, perception, and cognition will not develop properly without such responsive social interactions. In Chapter 10, Legerstee addresses the existence of the social brain in infants by proposing a neuroconstructivist model. She argues that infants are born with early predispositions that allow for the construction of intersubjective transactions with others, which play a crucial role in subsequent regulation of early brain development. Intersubjectivity enables infants not only to connect with the social world and bond with their caregivers but also to become anxious about being separated from them and disturbed when being excluded in triadic contexts. She supports her argument by presenting behavioral and neurological data showing the development of jealousy between 3 and 6 months of age. In Chapter 11, Haley discusses how stress and learning affect memory consolidation. He argues that contingent and mutual interactions in the parent–infant dyad are linked to better infant stress regulation (stress hormones and autonomic activity), and that their disruption can have immediate effects on infant learning and memory by presenting new data demonstrating that individual differences in stress reactivity are linked to differences in learning novel information and memory consolidation. Further, he examines whether the infants' ability to detect the goals of others plays a role in their ability to imitate and remember those actions by providing new evidence for the early development of the mirror neuron system in young infants. In Chapter 12, Bornstein adopts a multilevel approach to attunement in mother–infant interactions. He discusses how specific aspects of parenting coordinate with changes in the developing child, first examining how parenting expresses itself in coordination with infant behavior in several different cultures. He then reports new data demonstrating that parents neurally and physiologically regulate and change their parenting behavior in response to the developing and changing needs of their child. Attunement at the hormonal, the autonomic nervous system, and the central nervous system levels appears to constitute critical determinants of positive social and cognitive outcomes in children. This research has several facets, including family life, parenting, and the effects of maternal depression.

Part V, "Neural Processes of Mental Awareness," presents work based on the notion that changes in brain activity parallel changes in attention regulation, joint attention, theory of mind, memory, and language development. Each author addresses these domains of social-cognitive development, providing an account of age-related changes that are known to occur when these different social-cognitive systems "come online." Although we are still in the rudimentary stages of understanding how early experience affects specific cognitive mechanisms, authors in Part V also speculate on the social antecedents and specific experiences that are thought to affect the development of the biological mechanisms examined. In Chapter 13, Sabbagh, Benson, and Kuhlmeier argue that the unique complexity of human social lives stems, at least in part, from having a sophisticated "theory of mind"—an understanding that human behavior is caused by internal, unseeable mental states such as beliefs, desires, and intentions. In all cultures that have been examined, preschool children go through a remarkable transition in their theory-of-mind capacity. During this time, they gain the ability to recognize that epistemic mental states (such as knowledge and belief) are person-specific representations that can differ in content from some true state of affairs. Yet recent research suggests that the beginnings of such an understanding may be in place in children during the late infancy period. In this chapter, the authors critically evaluate the evidence from infancy and use a burgeoning literature within the area of developmental cognitive neuroscience to better understand the nature of both early and later developments. In Chapter 14, Mundy elaborates on the different mechanisms that regulate the ability to share attention with others and the brain areas that are activated during social-cognitive tasks involving joint attention. Mundy argues that some forms of joint attention skills that emerge in infancy may be associated with activity in a cortical system that itself may be associated with social-cognitive processes in adults. This chapter provides new insights into specific brain regions that are involved in two key aspects of joint attention (initiating and responding to joint attention), which are clearly illustrated in children with autism.

The overarching goal of this book is to highlight how the social antecedents and biological mechanisms of social-cognitive development interact and jointly inspire the mind's self-organizing capacities to integrate early experience and to regulate the neural correlates of social-cognitive behavior. Each contributor to this volume has conducted groundbreaking research examining the developmental interplay among multiple domains of child development with a focus on infancy. Together, the lines of research pursued by these distinguished scientists form the new frontier in the study of social-cognitive development.

In short, two topics currently of critical importance in the psychological sciences are (1) the dynamic development of core abilities (i.e., the social and biological inter-actions that influence multiple domains of human development) and (2) the neural correlates of social-cognitive processes. However, these topics have rarely been con-sidered in relation to one another. *The Infant Mind* contributes to an emerging and new synthesis between these two lines of research to provide an integrated and novel perspective. At present, only a handful of individual investigators in the field are pursuing integrated models of social-cognitive development using methodologies and analytical frameworks that permit greater cross-fertilization of ideas and research perspectives. The scholars who have contributed to this book provide a fascinating overview of behavioral and neurological underpinnings of the developing infant mind during the first years of life, identifying the roles that genes, brain, and the environ-ment play in shaping development of the whole human child.

References

Adolphs, R. (2001). The neurobiology of social cognition. *Current Opinion in Neurobiology,* *11*, 231–239.

Byrne, R., & Whiten, A. (Eds.). (1988). *Machiavellian intelligence.* Oxford, UK: Oxford University Press.

Humphrey, N. K. (1976). The social function of intellect. In P. Bateson & R. Hinde (Eds.), *Growing points in ethology* (pp. 303–317). Cambridge, UK: Cambridge University Press.

Contents

IV. The Role of Early Experience on Social Development

V. Neural Processes of Mental Awareness

PART I

Evolutionary, Neural, and Philosophical Approaches to the Social Mind

CHAPTER 1

An Evolutionary Basis for Social Cognition

ROBIN I. M. DUNBAR

The social brain hypothesis owes its origin to an attempt to explain why primates have significantly larger brains for body size compared with all other mammals. Essentially, the claim is that primates live in unusually complex social systems, and it is the need to manage and manipulate a great deal of constantly changing information about the state of this social world that is computationally so demanding. Initially referred to as the social intelligence hypothesis (Humphrey, 1976) and the Machiavellian intelligence hypothesis (Byrne & Whiten, 1988), the consensus has now settled on the term "social brain hypothesis" as being less tendentious and descriptively more neutral. In the end, what we have to explain is the fact that primates have very large brains, both absolutely and relatively compared with other mammals, with most of this increase being attributed to an exponential growth in neocortex size (Finlay, Darlington, & Nicastro, 2001). Although some mammals do have volumetrically larger brains than even humans (e.g., elephants and many members of the whale and dolphin family), the substantive issue lies in the size of the neocortex. Large neocortices are essentially a primate evolutionary novelty: In mammals in general, the neocortex accounts for 10–40% of total brain volume, whereas in primates it accounts for 50–80%.

The crucial driver behind the relationship between neocortex (or brain) volume and sociality seems to have been the evolution of bondedness, which refers to the extent to which females (in particular) are bound to each other with deep social ties (Dunbar & Shultz, 2010). Bondedness is difficult to define precisely independently of its functional consequences, in part because it seems to have a deeply emotional component that we cannot easily register and dissect in the conscious, linguistic parts of our brains (Dunbar & Shultz, 2010). Nonetheless, in primates at least, the ties of bondedness are expressed in terms of the extent to which females maintain close spatial proximity, groom preferentially with each other, and support each other during conflicts. We have been able to show that the rate at which the major families of mammals evolved large brains through geological time correlates with the proportion of living species that have bonded social groups (Shultz & Dunbar 2010). However, in addition to the purely cognitive component to bondedness, there is also an important emotional element, almost certainly mediated by the endorphin system (Dunbar, 2010a; Machin & Dunbar, 2011), reflecting the fact that primate social bonding is a dual-component process (Dunbar, 2010b). Importantly, the endorphin system is known also to play an important role in mother–offspring bonding in mammals (Broad, Curley, & Keverne, 2006; Curley & Keverne, 2005).

While the social brain hypothesis offers a functional (i.e., evolutionary) explanation for the evolution of unusually large brains in some species, it inevitably slides over the fact that developmental processes must play an important role in this. Unless it is the case that behavior is genetically fixed (something that would be radically incompatible with the view that large brains evolved to confer phenotypic flexibility), learning and social experience must play an important role in fine-tuning the underlying brain-based cognitive processes involved in social cognition. In a very crude sense, genetics may provide the computer (i.e., brain), but a large computer without software has no benefit. The developmental processes provide the equivalent of the software programming. Thus, there is an inevitable and important developmental aspect to the social brain hypothesis that has, as yet, received very little attention. There are issues here not just about the development of the social-cognitive skills involved in mediating our trajectories through a complex social world but also about the development of the process of bonding itself.

I first review the current state of the social brain hypothesis and the evidence for it, and then explore some of the developmental issues that arise from it. The developmental implications of the social brain hypothesis have so far received very little attention. In some ways, this is surprising because the whole emphasis of the hypothesis is on managing complex social environments. We would not expect these kinds of capacities to be neurologically hard-wired because the social world is both complex and dynamic. While it might seem reasonable for the neurological machinery for perceptual processing (e.g., pattern recognition, color recognition) to be modular and hard-wired (after all, the properties of the physical world remain more or less constant), this makes much less sense for something that is inevitably both more serendipitous and more likely to change through time. Who knows how many brothers and sisters you might end up having, and yet the balance between them can radically affect an individual's optimal social strategy: Sisters might normally be the best allies to have, but if you happen not to have any, then you need to find an alternative substitute among what is available to you (presumably brothers). Similarly, even if you begin life with some sisters, they might not survive thanks to the vagaries of development and accident, or they might be drawn away from you by social rivals for their attention. If you live in a social world where alliances of this kind are important to either your survival or your ability to reproduce successfully (for evidence of the latter in primates, see Silk, Alberts, & Altmann, 2003), then you need to be phenotypically more flexible, and this in turn rests on having a brain capable of integrating information about the social world and making plausible projections about its future state. Because it would be impossible to legislate for this (the future is too uncertain to provide natural selection with the traction it needs), the only sensible solution is to use experience as a guide for behavior—and since this involves learning, it necessarily implies a balance between hardware and programmed software.

Evolutionary Background

The first definitive evidence to support the claim that primate brain evolution was driven by social complexity was provided by plotting social group size against neocortex ratio (Dunbar, 1992b). Social group size was taken to be a proxy for social complexity on the reasonable grounds that the number of dyadic and triadic relationships increases exponentially with group size; neocortex ratio (the ratio of the neocortex to the rest of the brain) offered a simple way of controlling for absolute brain volume. Subsequently, a number of analyses looked at various indices of *behavioral* complexity (the size of grooming cliques, the use of coalitions, the use of tactical deception, the correlation between dominance rank and male reproductive success) and showed that all these also correlate with neocortex ratio (Dunbar, 2008; Dunbar & Shultz, 2007). These relationships are an important reminder that the social brain is really about behavioral complexity and thus about individual relationships; the group size effect may, in fact, be an emergent property of the capacity to maintain complex social relationships with individuals. In Old World monkeys, for example, Lehmann and Dunbar (2009) found that the size of grooming cliques declines with neocortex ratio: This seems to be because, as species become smarter (i.e., evolve larger neocortices), they are able to develop increasingly intense relationships with a core set of intimates that act as an alliance to buffer them from the pressures of living in large groups. This is a very fine-tuned balancing act and is, I suspect, the reason why social life in large primate social groups is cognitively taxing.

However, this quantitative relationship between social group size and brain (or neocortex) volume appears to be more or less unique to the primates. When we have tried to extend the same analysis to other bird and mammals, we have generally failed to find a quantitative relationship between social group size and neocortex size (or any other measure of brain size). Instead, the social brain hypothesis takes a qualitative form in these taxa: Pair-bonded species have significantly larger brains/neocortices than polygamously or promiscuously mating species (Shultz & Dunbar, 2007). We interpret this as reflecting the heavy computational demands of pair-bonded relationships, in particular lifelong pair bonds. Pair-bonded mating systems are usually about the provision of biparental care, and I have argued elsewhere that the key issue here is the need to ensure equitable division of labor: Individuals need to be able to factor in their mate's demands and needs when scheduling their own activities in order to ensure that they achieve their common goal of successfully rearing offspring (Dunbar, 2011). One plausible suggestion is that adopting another individual's perspective may be sufficiently demanding in computational terms that it was this that kicked off the social brain. Later, primates extended this effect by applying the same cognitive mechanism to relationships with other nonreproductive individuals, thereby creating "friendships" (Dunbar & Shultz, 2010) and the quantitative relationships between group size and brain size that we see in this family.

One of the problems we face in undertaking comparative analyses of brain evolution is that the data sets we have are often relatively crude: In particular, they do not often partition down brain regions into the kind of fine-grained scale we really need. This is particularly problematic with the neocortex: Partly because the neocortex is (relatively) undifferentiated in terms of neural structure, there has been a tendency not to partition it. This becomes problematic because there is some evidence to suggest that the critical brain region may not be the neocortex as a whole but the more frontal elements. Joffe and Dunbar (1997) found a better fit between group size and non-V1[1] neocortex ratio than to total neocortex ratio. Similarly, an analysis of group size and frontal lobe volume, albeit for a small sample of species, produces a further improvement in the variance explained over that obtained by an analysis of the whole neocortex (Dunbar, 2011). This suggests that the more frontal regions of the brain, and the frontal lobes in particular, may be more heavily implicated in sociality (and hence group size) than other regions. This is significant for two reasons. First, the frontal lobes are widely assumed to be central to executive function cognition (Miller & Cohen, 2001; Thompson et al., 2001), and there are good arguments for suggesting that social-cognitive skills might be derivative of executive function competences rather than specialized skills in their own right (Barrett, Henzi, & Dunbar, 2003). Second, the brain has evolved (and develops) from back to front (Gogtay et al., 2004), so if any region is likely to differentiate between species in terms of newly evolving social skills, then it is most likely to be the more frontal cortex.

When we extend the social brain relationship to modern humans, the ape regression equation for group size as a function of neocortex (the most appropriate, as humans belong to the ape family) gives us a predicted social group size for humans of about 150 (Dunbar, 1992a). This turns out to be both a common group size in humans' institutional organization and the typical size of personal egocentric social networks (Hill & Dunbar, 2003; Roberts, Dunbar, Pollet, & Kuppens, 2009; Zhou, Sornette, Hill, & Dunbar, 2005). We interpret this as implying that, on average, there is a cognitively determined upper limit on the number of individuals with whom you can maintain relationships. As noted shortly, there is, in fact, considerable individual variation around this value, but as a generality it holds good, and perhaps because of that it sets an upper limit on the functional size of human communities or organizations (because larger organizations become increasingly unstable).

Individual Differences and the Social Brain

We have shown that although mean social network size in normal adults is about 150, there is considerable variance around that: The typical range is about 100–250 (Hill & Dunbar, 2003; Roberts et al., 2009; Stiller & Dunbar, 2007). Individual differences of this magnitude imply that a range of factors are likely to be involved. We know from our own analyses that these differences are, in part, explained by gender (women are, on average, better on intentionality tasks than men, and so usually have slightly larger networks) and, not surprisingly perhaps, by personality differences (Dunbar & Spoors, 1995; Roberts, Wilson, Fedurek, & Dunbar, 2008). More importantly, however, they are also related to individual differences in social-cognition competences (such as theory of mind) (Stiller & Dunbar, 2007).

These correlated differences in network size and social-cognition competences also turn out to correlate in a three-way relationship with the volumes of neural material in key regions of the brain (notably the prefrontal cortex) (Lewis, Rezaie,

Brown, Roberts, & Dunbar, 2011; Powell, Lewis, Dunbar, Garcia-Fiñana, & Roberts, 2010; Powell, Lewis, Roberts, & Dunbar, 2012). This suggests that there are likely to be neurobiological constraints involved. These effects might, of course, be the outcome of either inherited effects or developmental effects or both. Although it is surely inevitable that social-cognitive competence and limits on social network size have a significant genetic component (as we know to be the case for theory of mind: Hughes, 2005), we should probably interpret these more as developmental set points around which experience finetunes individuals' final positions (Meltzoff, Gopnik, & Repacholi, 1999). We know, for example, that the speed at which children achieve developmental benchmarks such as theory of mind depends on the size of their sibling group (and hence their social experiences) (Lewis, Freeman, Kyriakidou, Maridaki-Kassotaki, & Berridge, 1996; Perner, Ruffman, & Leekan, 1994). It is, therefore, possible (although as far as I know this has not yet been tested) that the final level of social intentional competence that individuals achieve and the size of social network they can manage as adults may also be determined by sibling cohort size and other social experiences. Testing this suggestion is likely to be difficult, since it would presumably require us to know individuals' personal social experiences over perhaps as much as the first 15 years of life. Nonetheless, these are clearly issues that deserve more extensive investigation.

My assumption is that these are actually causally related: Brain region volume determines competences in social cognition, and these, in turn, limit the size of the individual's social network. Although individual differences of this kind can be expected to have some kind of genetic basis, differences in neuroanatomy may also reflect both rearing circumstances (nutritional stress at any of the key neuronal developmental way points could result in less neurogenesis or a failure of crucial neuronal pruning) and social experiences (the number of siblings, or the opportunities to interact with peers).

Development and the Social Brain

The suggestion that some aspects of brain organization are relatively hard-wired in the modular sense is widely recognized as plausible for many aspects of low-level cognitive processing. This is modularity in the sense originally envisaged by Fodor (1983). Although this has sometimes been interpreted as applying more widely by some (but not all) evolutionary psychologists (i.e., to modules for every aspect of behavior), there is no particular reason to assume that this is so from an evolutionary point of view. Indeed, there are good reasons for assuming that the reverse may hold: The environment we live in is simply too unstable to make such tightly defined modules an evolutionarily worthwhile strategy for anything other than those low-level processes that are invariant because of the nature of physics. This is *a fortiori* the case with the social world, which is particularly unpredictable. That being so, learning and experience have to play an important role. In short, the cognitive mechanisms need to be open to fine-tuning in the light of circumstances.

It has been appreciated for some time that the best predictor of total brain volume in mammals is the length of gestation (or gestation and lactation combined). This follows from the fact that (1) brain size at birth is roughly a constant proportion of maternal body mass across mammalian species and (2) the rate of brain growth itself is constant across time and species (neural tissue gets laid down at a constant rate, and hence the only way to grow a bigger brain is to do it for longer: Finlay et al., 2001). Despite this, the best predictor of *neocortex* volume (and especially non-V1 neocortex volume) is the length of the juvenile period (defined as the time between weaning and first reproduction) (Joffe, 1997). Joffe (1997) argued that this reflected a sharp distinction between the constraints on what we might think of as the hardware (the time needed to grow a brain at all, a function of the duration of gestation-plus-lactation) and the constraints acting on the software (the learning processes needed to get the hardware functional, which are more likely to depend on the length of the period available for socialization). The fact that the best predictor for the more frontal regions of the neocortex (i.e., those most involved in active cognition as opposed to routinized perceptual processing) was the length of the juvenile period, whereas the gross hardware was better predicted by the period of primary parental investment, implies that socialization plays a critical role in respect of those regions of the brain that are most involved in what I term "active cognition" (e.g., executive function). This claim receives some indirect support from the fact that, for an admittedly modest sample of six primate species, the proportion of juvenile play that is social (as opposed to solitary or strictly object play) also correlates significantly with neocortex ratio (Lewis, 2000), suggesting that socialization might play an important role in those species that have relatively larger neocortices.

These findings are significant in the light of the fact that the brain (and specifically the neocortex) develops and matures from back (the visual areas in the occipital cortex) to front (the frontal lobes with their involvement in executive function) (Gogtay et al., 2004). This inevitably means that the frontal regions will be more heavily influenced by experience compared with those regions that mature early in life. It may thus be no coincidence that the prefrontal cortex is the last part of the brain to be myelinized (i.e., acquire the fatty insulation sheaths to the neurons that optimizes their capacity to transmit signals without loss from leakage across membranes) (Fuster, 2002; Shaw et al., 2008).

Figure 1.1 refines Joffe's analysis by focusing explicitly on frontal lobe gray matter volume for a sample of primate genera (including humans). Frontal lobe gray matter volume is plotted first against the length of the period of parental care (gestation-plus-lactation) (Figure 1.1A) and then against the length of the period of socialization (weaning to first reproduction) (Figure 1.1B). In both cases, the correlation is significant (Figure 1.1A: $r = .545$, $N = 17$, $p = .024$; Figure 1.1B: $r = .940$, $N = 16$, $p < .001$), but that for gestation-plus-lactation explains only about a third as much of the variance as that for socialization ($r^2 = .30$ vs. $r^2 = .88$, respectively). Partialling out the effect of gestation-plus-lactation has no effect on the correlation between frontal lobe gray matter and the socialization period ($r_{s[xy.z]} = .934$, $N = 11$, $p < .001$), but partialling out socialization period renders the correlation with primary parental investment nonsignificant *and* negative ($r_{[xz.y]} = -.319$, $N = 11$, $p = .287$). Thus, it seems that socialization (the opportunity to learn from a range of social experiences) plays a significant role in the social brain process, emphasizing once again the fact that the hardware alone is not sufficient.

This is a plausible argument, given that behavior-like tactical deception correlates with neocortex size (see Byrne & Corp, 2004). Tactical deception is complex behavior that depends crucially on being able to evaluate another individual's

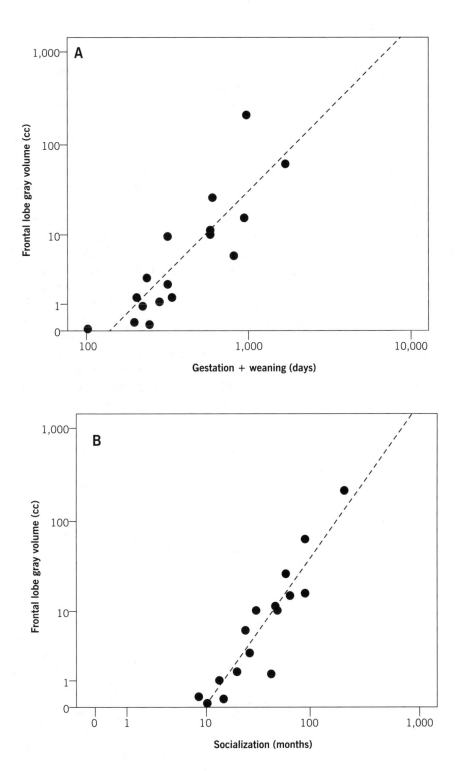

FIGURE 1.1. Frontal lobe gray matter volume plotted against (A) period of parental investment (gestation-plus-lactation) and (B) period of socialization (age at first reproduction minus age at weaning) for individual primate genera. Humans are the extreme right-hand data point in each case. Brain data from Bush and Allman (2004); life-history data from Harvey, Martin, and Clutton-Brock (1997).

perspective on a moment-by-moment basis, and that cannot be something that is hard-wired or instinctive. The social world is too complex and dynamic for its outcomes to be predicted in any consistent way. Learning is, therefore, bound to play an important role.

Some indirect evidence for the importance of learning is offered by a neuroimaging study of emotion recognition. Deeley and colleagues (2008) scanned 40 male subjects, ages 8–50 years, while performing a pictorial emotion recognition task (correctly identifying pictures of faces expressing disgust or fear). They found that there was a significant age-related shift in the areas activated during this task, with activation in Brodmann areas BA6 (right middle frontal gyrus) and BA10 (right superior frontal gyrus) correlating negatively with subject age, and activation in BA19 (right fusiform gyrus) correlating positively with age, while areas classically associated with emotional cuing (e.g., the amygdala) remained constant in their activation. This was interpreted as implying that processing emotional cues requires much more focused attention and conscious cognitive activity in younger people, but that from about the mid-20s onward these processes become automated. This is likely to be the outcome of learning and experience. This might explain why teenagers find relationships such hard work: They are literally having to work hard at processing the cues associated with others' internal states in order to interpret them correctly. With experience, we automate this process, and social life becomes (relatively) easier. It seems that this is not an easy thing to learn: The results obtained by Deeley and colleagues that this transition does not happen until the mid-20s, long after the individual has achieved physical adulthood. Similar results were obtained by Burnett and colleagues (2009), who noted that the regions processing social emotions (i.e., guilt and embarrassment as opposed to basic emotions such as disgust or fear) shifted increasingly from the medial prefrontal cortex to the left temporal pole between the ages of 11 and 32 years (see also Dumontheil, Hassan, Gilbert, & Blakemore, 2010).

This may be a general pattern. Blakemore (2008) reviewed a number of studies showing that the processing of social-cognitive tasks shifted from the medial prefrontal cortex in 8- to 10-year-old children to a more posterior locus (e.g., the superior temporal sulcus) in adulthood. These tasks involved not only emotion recognition but also a variety of mentalizing tasks. The relative lateness of this switch might be related to the fact that the frontal lobes are still undergoing significant neuroanatomical changes until well into the third decade of life. Not only does myelinization occur much later in the frontal lobes than elsewhere, but synaptic pruning and the decline in gray matter volume occur much later in the frontal lobe than elsewhere (Blakemore, 2008). There are even significant differences in the developmental patterns of gene expression in different brain regions: Genes that have their greatest influence on the sensory and motor cortices do so during childhood, whereas those that have most influence in the frontal and temporal regions do so during adolescence (Lenroot et al., 2009). Blakemore suggests that the changes in cognitive processing might be associated with increasing neuronal efficiency consequent on synaptic pruning. The signal-to-noise ratio is known to be low when there is an excess of "untuned" synapses, and this is likely to be a particular problem during the period of rapid synaptogenesis during childhood. Synaptic pruning might be associated with the creation of more specialized task-related neural circuits that result in less extravagant neuronal activity during task performance.

It has been suggested that this developmental trajectory corresponds to a shift in cognitive strategy from simulation (based on reference to the self and involving the ventral medial prefrontal cortex) to a more objective strategy (based on the dorsal medial prefrontal cortex) (Moriguchi, Ohnishi, Mori, Matsuda, & Komaki, 2007), the dorsal prefrontal cortex being more associated with reasoning and higher cognitive functions (Ardila, 2008). This may relate to the ongoing dispute between the simulation theory and the theory theory explanations for mentalizing skills, and especially for the fact that the evidence for the first of these appears earlier (about age 2 years) than evidence for the second (about age 4 years). Indeed, Frith (2009) has suggested that simulation theory may relate to the involvement of the mirror neuron system (see Gallese & Rochat, Chapter 2, this volume) and theory theory may relate to the more conventional theory of mind circuit (involving the prefrontal cortex and the temporal lobe). Belief/desire psychology would then presumably provide a convenient bridge between the two.

Development and Social Skills

If social-cognitive skills underpin the size of social group that an individual can cope with, it follows that we should see social network size growing in parallel to a child's developing social-cognitive skills. Some evidence for this is provided in Figure 1.2, which plots the number of children that an individual child was interacting with during school playtime as a function of their performance on extended intentionality tasks (similar to the classic false-belief tasks used to test for theory of mind in children [see Wimmer & Perner, 1983], but with more minds, and thus orders of intentionality, involved). The rather anomalous blip at intentionality level 2 notwithstanding, there is a significant correlation across individuals ($r = .241$, $N = 120$, $p = .008$). Figure 1.3 suggests that the anomalous blip at intentionality score 2 is mainly due to a number of older (12-year-old) boys who scored poorly on the intentionality tasks (as indicated by the unusually high variance in this group) but had "normal" playgroup sizes. We suspected at the time that the 12-year-old boys we sampled were not taking the task as seriously as the other children.

This developmental shift in the size of the group that an individual can manage is further highlighted in Figure 1.4, which plots the total number of individuals engaged in the game that the focal subject was part of (as opposed to the number of individuals with whom the focal subject was actively interacting, as shown in Figure 1.2). The distributions are significantly different across the age classes ($F_{4,115} = 40.38$, $p < .001$), with Scheffé multiple comparison tests indicating two separate clusters (4- and 6-year-olds on the one hand and 8- to 12-year-olds on the other). These data thus suggest that there is significant phase shift between 6 and 8 years of age in the size of playgroup that a child can handle. There was no effect due to sex ($F_{1,110} = 0.43$, $p = .845$), but there was a significant sex × age interaction ($F_{4,110} = 3.73$, $p = .007$), which seemed mainly to be due to an anomalously high range in group size among 8-year-old boys.

This pattern parallels the changes in weighted intentionality score: Although mean score increases with age (Figure 1.3), it is clear that there is considerable variance at each stage. Some 10- and 12-year-olds are able to perform at level 5 intentionality

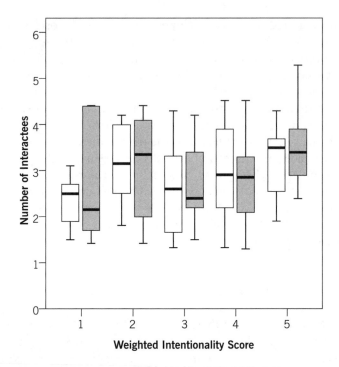

FIGURE 1.2. Median (± 50% and 95% ranges) number of children with whom a focal child was actively interacting plotted against achievable intentionality score, for a sample of 120 children (ages 4–12 years). An individual child was randomly selected from the school playground during playtime, and the number of other children with whom he or she was actively interacting was recorded at 60-second intervals over a 15-minute period; the focal individual was then removed from the playground to a quiet room where a multilevel intentionality task was administered. The intentionality task consisted of a set of story vignettes followed by a series of questions about the mind states of the story characters at levels 1–5 intentionality, inclusive. Intentionality score is a weighted average of the number of correct answers at each intentionality level, rescaled to a 0–5 range (see Stiller & Dunbar, 2007). White bars: males; gray bars: females. The data derive from two primary schools and one secondary school (see Henzi et al., 2007)

(the standard adult level: Kinderman, Dunbar, & Bentall, 1998; Stiller & Dunbar, 2007), but by no means are all able to do so, suggesting that, as an age cohort, even 12-year-olds are not fully fifth-order intentionally competent. Unfortunately, as yet, there has been no detailed testing of the developmental sequence by which adult competences in this respect are acquired, mainly perhaps because the great bulk of the work on social cognition has focused on theory of mind (level 2 intentionality), which children acquire at about age 5. However, if we take complete success at passing a given level of intentionality as the criterion, then Figure 1.3 strongly suggests that these data represent only two levels of social-cognitive competence: 4- to 6-year-olds who are competent at level 2 intentionality (formal theory of mind) and 8- to 12-year-olds who are competent at level 3 intentionality. This suggests that level 4 intentionality is reached sometime about 12 years, with the full adult-level competence at level 5 sometime during the later teens. Liddle and Nettle (2006) provide evidence that, in addition to age, socioeconomic context may be important: They found a significant

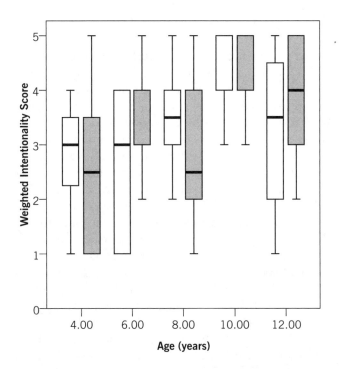

FIGURE 1.3. Median (± 50% and 95% ranges) in weighted intentionality score for males (open bars) and females (gray bars) as a function of age class. Data from Henzi et al. (2007).

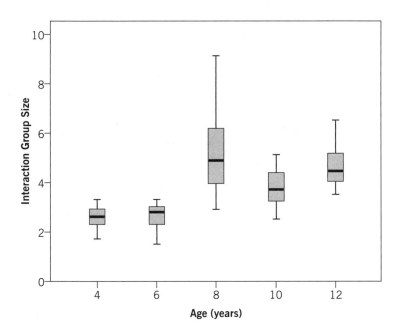

FIGURE 1.4. Median (± 50% and 95% ranges) in the size of group (excluding adults) that children of different ages were interacting with. In contrast to the data in Figure 1.2 (which show the number of active interactants), this graph plots all the children involved in the game in which the focal individual was taking part, even if the subject was not actively interacting with them. Data from Henzi et al. (2007).

effect of affluent versus deprived areas on performance on the same tasks among 10- to 11-year-olds. Thus, at the developmental level, social environment may play an important role in determining mentalizing competences. This might in turn, of course, be related to the well-known effect of environmental enrichment on brain development: At least in rats, pups raised in an enriched environment in which they acquire new skills exhibit a 25% increase in synapse number and a 3–7% increase in cortical thickness compared with rats raised in an impoverished environment (Diamond, Krech, & Rosenzweig, 1964; Diamond et al., 1966).

This raises an obvious question: How does social network size vary across time during the developmental sequence from childhood to adulthood? Presumably, infants have rather small social networks confined to the handful of carers and family members who they see every day. Somehow this increases through time to reach the adult network size of about 150 individuals (Hill & Dunbar, 2003; Roberts et al., 2009). Our analyses of social networks in normal adults suggest that these typically consist of a series of hierarchically embedded circles of acquaintanceship of rather characteristic size (5, 15, 50, 150 individuals—see Figure 1.5; Hill & Dunbar, 2003; Zhou et al., 2005). In a study of 30 teenagers (18-year-olds), we found that average network size was 51.7 (Roberts & Dunbar, 2011), and thus significantly smaller than the 150 recorded for a large sample of normal adults (ages 18–60 years). Combining this observation with the phase shift in playgroup size between 6 and 8 years in Figure 1.4 suggests that social networks grow with age by accruing levels in successive phase shifts. In relation to the structure of adult networks illustrated in Figure 1.5,

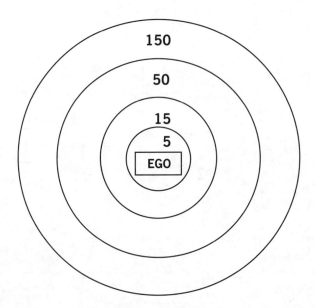

FIGURE 1.5. The "circles of acquaintanceship." Egocentric social networks consist of a series of hierarchically embedded layers of acquaintanceship that scale in a very consistent way (5 intimates, 15 best friends, 50 good friends, and 150 friends, with each layer including everyone from the inner circles within it) (Hill & Dunbar, 2003; Zhou et al., 2005). Average relationship quality (indexed by a simple analogue scale of emotional closeness) and interaction frequency both decline as one proceeds out through the layers. Data from Roberts and Dunbar (2011).

this might suggest a series of steps at key developmental points. Network sizes of about five individuals would be typical of young children over the period spanning 4 to 6 years of age once they have mastered formal theory of mind (second-order intentional competence), followed by the addition of the second layer (bringing network size to 15) once they have graduated onto third-order intentionality; this might then be followed by the addition of a further layer (bringing total network size up to 50) during the early teens when they acquire fourth-order intentional competence, and then the final layer during the later teens or early 20s once they acquire full adult competency at the fifth order.

This seems at least to be a plausible hypothesis, but at present it is at best only informed speculation and it needs testing in detail. There are some challenges to this because obtaining data on social network size is notoriously difficult. Adults can be relatively realistic about listing the number of individuals they know and specifying the kind of relationship they have with each, but children are not. Instead, when asked whom they are friends with, they commonly list all the people they know and seem unable to differentiate between friends and acquaintances. It is important to bear in mind that the circles of acquaintanceship in our adult social world extend far beyond the 150 that form our core egocentric network. Zhou and colleagues (2005) identified at least two additional layers at 500 and 1,500 that extend the circles of acquaintanceship into a world where relationships are less reciprocal and more formalized. Thus, the 1,500 layer seems to consist of all the individuals whom we can recognize by sight and name.

This issue, however, brings us back to the question of bondedness that I raised at the outset of this chapter and the strategies we use to include others in our social networks. At one level, bondedness does not extend equally to all members of the network. In older adolescents and adults, indices of emotional closeness decline with network layer (Roberts et al., 2009). By the same token, as total network size increases, average emotional closeness to its members declines, in part because individuals can devote less time to individual network members as their number increases. In our sample of 251 complete women's networks from Belgium and the United Kingdom, those between 18 and 25 years of age had significantly smaller total network sizes than older individuals ages 25–65 (means of 71.7 and 83.8, respectively; $F_{1,249} = 4.46$, $p = .036$). In contrast, this younger age group had contacted significantly more people during the previous week than the older ones ($F_{1,249} = 5.23$, $p = 0.023$), suggesting that while younger individuals may be more socially active, they are able to maintain fewer individuals in their outer network layers. In part, that may reflect age-dependent differences in the skills needed to manage large social networks, but it may also reflect growing opportunities for meeting new individuals who can be added into one's set of known individuals.

Note

1. The primary visual area, V1, is a large, structurally relatively homogeneous area in the back of the occipital lobe that is devoted almost entirely to processing visual input from the retina. In the Stephan, Frahm, and Baron (1981) brain database, V1 is the only region of the neocortex given separately.

References

Ardila, A. (2008). On the evolutionary origins of executive functions. *Brain and Cognition*, *68*, 92–99.

Barrett, L., Henzi, S. P., & Dunbar, R. I. M. (2003). Primate cognition: From "what now?" to "what if?" *Trends in Cognitive Sciences, 7*, 494–497.

Blakemore, S.-J. (2008). The social brain in adolescence. *Nature Reviews Neuroscience, 19*, 267–277.

Broad, K. D., Curley, J. P., & Keverne, E. B. (2006). Mother–infant bonding and the evolution of mammalian social relationships. *Philosophical Transactions of the Royal Society: B. Biologial Sciences, 361*, 2199–2214.

Burnett, S., Bird, G., Moll, J., Frith, C. D., & Blakemore, S.-J. (2009). Development during adolescence of the neural processing of social emotion. *Journal of Cognitive Neuroscience, 21*, 1736–1750.

Bush, E. C., & Allman, J. M. (2004). The scaling of frontal cortex in primates and carnivores. *Proceedings of the National Academy of Sciences USA, 101*, 3962–3966.

Byrne, R. W., & Corp, N. (2004). Neocortex size predicts deception rate in primates. *Proceedings of the Royal Society: B. Biological Sciences, 271*, 1693–1699.

Byrne, R. W., & Whiten, A. (Eds.). (1988). *Machiavellian intelligence*. Oxford, UK: Oxford University Press.

Curley, J. P., & Keverne, E. B. (2005). Genes, brains and mammalian social bonds. *Trends in Ecology and Evolution, 20*, 581–587.

Deeley, Q., Daly, E., Asuma, R., Surguladze, S., Giampietro, V., Brammer, M., et al. (2008). Changes in male brain responses to emotional faces from adolescence to middle age. *NeuroImage, 40*, 389–397.

Diamond, M. C., Krech, D., & Rosenzweig, M. R. (1964). The effects of an enriched environment on the histology of the rat cerebral cortex. *Journal of Comparative Neurology, 123*, 111–120.

Diamond, M. C., Law, F., Rhodes, H., Lindner, B., Rosenzweig, M. R., Krech, D., et al. (1966). Increases in cortical depth and glia numbers in rats subjected to enriched environment. *Journal of Comparative Neurology, 128*, 117–125.

Dumontheil, I., Hassan, B., Gilbert, S. J., & Blakemore, S.-J. (2010). Development of the selection and manipulation of self-generated thoughts in adolescence. *Journal of Neuroscience, 30*, 7664–7671.

Dunbar, R. I. M. (1992a). Coevolution of neocortex size, group size and language in humans. *Behavioral and Brain Sciences, 16*, 681–735.

Dunbar, R. I. M. (1992b). Neocortex size as a constraint on group size in primates. *Journal of Human Evolution, 22*, 469–493.

Dunbar, R. I. M. (2008). Mind the gap: Or why humans aren't just great apes. *Proceedings of the British Academy, 154*, 403–423.

Dunbar, R. I. M. (2010a). Brain and behaviour in primate evolution. In P. H. Kappeler & J. Silk (Eds.), *Mind the gap: Tracing the origins of human universals* (pp. 315–330). Berlin: Springer-Verlag.

Dunbar, R. I. M. (2010b). The social role of touch in humans and primates: Behavioural function and neurobiological mechanisms. *Neuroscience and Biobehavioral Reviews, 34*, 260–268.

Dunbar, R. I. M. (2011). Evolutionary basis of the social brain. In J. Decety & J. Cacioppo (Eds.), *Oxford handbook of social neuroscience* (pp. 28–38). Oxford, UK: Oxford University Press.

Dunbar, R. I. M., & Shultz, S. (2007). Understanding primate brain evolution. *Philosophical Transactions of the Royal Society: B. Biological Sciences, 362*, 649–658.

Dunbar, R. I. M., & Shultz, S. (2010). Bondedness and sociality. *Behaviour, 147,* 775–803.

Dunbar, R. I. M., & Spoors, M. (1995). Social networks, support cliques and kinship. *Human Nature, 6,* 273–290.

Finlay, B. L., Darlington, R. B., & Nicastro, N. (2001). Developmental structure in brain evolution. *Behavior and Brain Sciences, 24,* 263–308.

Fodor, J. A. (1983). *The modularity of mind.* Cambridge, MA: Bradford Books.

Frith, C. D. (2009). *The neuroscience of human social cognition: An overview.* Paper presented at the Nobel symposium for the 200th Anniversary of the Karolinska Institute, Stockholm.

Fuster, J. (2002). Frontal lobe and cognitive development. *Journal of Neurocytology, 31,* 373–385.

Gogtay, N., Giedd, J. N., Lusk, L., Hayashi, K. M., Greenstein, D., Vaituzis, A. C., et al. (2004). Dynamic mapping of human cortical development during childhood through early adulthood. *Proceedings of the National Academy of Sciences USA, 101,* 8174–8179.

Harvey, P. H., Martin, R. D., & Clutton-Brock, T. H. (1997). Life histories in comparative perspective. In B. B. Smuts, D. Cheney, R. M. Seyfarth, T. T. Struhsaker, & R. W. Wrangham (Eds.), *Primate societies* (pp. 181–196). Chicago: Chicago University Press.

Henzi, P., de Sousa Pereira, L., Hawker-Bond, D., Stiller, J., Dunbar, R. I. M., & Barrett, L. (2007). Look who's talking: Developmental trends in the size of conversational cliques. *Evolution and Human Behavior, 28,* 66–74.

Hill, R. A., & Dunbar, R. I. M. (2003). Social network size in humans. *Human Nature, 14,* 53–72.

Hughes, C. (2005). Genetic and environmental influences on individual differences in language and theory of mind: Common or distinct? In J. Astington & J. Baird (Eds.), *Why language matters for theory of mind* (pp. 319–339). Oxford, UK: Oxford University Press.

Humphrey, N. K. (1976). The social function of intellect. In P. Bateson & R. Hinde (Eds.), *Growing points in ethology* (pp. 303–317). Cambridge, UK: Cambridge University Press.

Joffe, T. H. (1997). Social pressures have selected for an extended juvenile period in primates. *Journal of Human Evolution, 32,* 593–605.

Joffe, T. H., & Dunbar, R. I. M. (1997). Visual and socio-cognitive information processing in primate brain evolution. *Proceedings of the Royal Society: B. Biological Sciences, 264,* 1303–1307.

Kinderman, P., Dunbar, R. I. M., & Bentall, R. P. (1998). Theory-of-mind deficits and causal attributions. *British Journal of Psychology, 89,* 191–204.

Lehmann, J., & Dunbar, R. I. M. (2009). Network cohesion, group size and neocortex size in female-bonded Old World primates. *Proceedings of the Royal Society: B. Biological Sciences, 276,* 4417–4422.

Lenroot, R. K., Schmitt, J. E., Ordaz, S. J., Wallace, G. L., Neale, M. C., Lerch, J. P., et al. (2009). Differences in genetic and environmental influences on the human cerebral cortex associated with development during childhood and adolescence. *Human Brain Mapping, 30,* 163–174.

Lewis, C., Freeman, N. H., Kyriakidou, C., Maridaki-Kassotaki, K., & Berridge, D. M. (1996). Social influences on false belief access: specific sibling influences or general apprenticeship. *Child Development, 67,* 2930–2947.

Lewis, K. (2000). A comparative study of primate play behaviour: Implications for the study of cognition. *Folia Primatologica, 71,* 417–421.

Lewis, P., Rezaie, R., Brown, R., Roberts, R., & Dunbar, R. I. M. (2011). Ventromedial prefrontal volume predicts understanding of others and social network size. *NeuroImage, 57,* 1624–1629.

Liddle, B., & Nettle, D. (2006). Higher-order theory of mind and social competence in school-age children. *Journal of Cultural and Evolutionary Psychology, 4*, 231–246.

Machin, A., & Dunbar, R. I. M. (2011). The brain opiod theory of social attachment: A review of the evidence. *Behaviour, 148*, 985–1025.

Meltzoff, A. N., Gopnik, A., & Repacholi, B. M. (1999). Toddlers' understanding of intentions, desires and emotions: Explorations of the dark ages. In P. D. Zelazo, J. W. Astington, & D. R. Olson (Eds.), *Developing theories of intention: Social understanding and self-control* (pp. 14–71). Mahwah, NJ: Erlbaum.

Miller, E. K., & Cohen, J. D. (2001). An integrative theory of prefrontal cortex function, *Annual Review of Neuroscience, 24*, 167–202.

Moriguchi, Y., Ohnishi, T., Mori, T., Matsuda, H., & Komaki, G. (2007). Changes of brain activity in the neural substrates for theory of mind during childhood and adolescence. *Psychiatry and Clinical Neurosciences, 61*, 355–363.

Perner, J., Ruffman, T., & Leekam, S. R. (1994). Theory of mind is contagious; you catch it from your sibs. *Child Development, 65*, 1224–1234.

Powell, J., Lewis, P. A., Dunbar, R. I. M., García-Fiñana, M., & Roberts, N. (2010). Orbital prefrontal cortex volume correlates with social cognitive competence. *Neuropsychologia, 48*, 3554–3562.

Powell, J., Lewis, P. A., Roberts, N., & Dunbar, R. I. M. (2012). Orbitomedial prefrontal cortex volume predicts social network size: An imaging study of individual differences in humans. *Proceedings of the Royal Society: B. Biological Sciences, 367*, 2192–2201.

Roberts, S. B. G., & Dunbar, R. I. M. (2011). Communication in social networks: Effects of kinship, network size, and emotional closeness. *Personal Relationships, 18*, 439–452.

Roberts, S. B. G., Dunbar, R. I. M., Pollet, T., & Kuppens, T. (2009). Exploring variations in active network size: Constraints and ego characteristics. *Social Networks, 31*, 138–146.

Roberts, S. B. G., Wilson, R., Fedurek, P., & Dunbar, R. I. M. (2008). Individual differences and personal social network size and structure. *Personality and Individual Differences, 44*, 954–964.

Shaw, P., Kabani, N. J., Lerch, J. P., Eckstrand, K., Lenroot, R., Gogtay, N., et al. (2008). Neurodevelopmental trajectories of the human cerebral cortex. *Journal of Neuroscience, 28*, 3586–3594.

Shultz, S., & Dunbar, R. (2010). Encephalization is not a universal macroevolutionary phenomenon in mammals but is associated with sociality. *Proceedings of the National Academy of Sciences USA, 107*, 21582–21586.

Shultz, S., & Dunbar, R. I. M. (2007). The evolution of the social brain: Anthropoid primates contrast with other vertebrates. *Proceedings of the Royal Society: B. Biological Sciences, 274*, 2429–2436.

Silk, J. B., Alberts, S. C., & Altmann, J. (2003). Social bonds of female baboons enhance infant survival. *Science, 302*, 1232–1234.

Stephan, H., Frahm, H., & Baron, G. (1981). New and revised data on volumes of brain structures in insectivores and primates. *Folia Primatologica, 35*, 1–29.

Stiller, J., & Dunbar, R. (2007). Perspective-taking and social network size in humans. *Social Networks, 29*, 93–104.

Wimmer, H., & Perner, J. (1983). Beliefs about beliefs: Representation and constraining function of wrong beliefs in young children's understanding of deception. *Cognition, 13*, 103–128.

Zhou, W.-X., Sornette, D., Hill, R. A., & Dunbar, R. I. M. (2005). Discrete hierarchical organization of social group sizes. *Proceedings of the Royal Society: B. Biological Sciences, 272*, 439–444.

CHAPTER 2

The Evolution of Motor Cognition

Its Role in the Development of Social Cognition and Implications for Autism Spectrum Disorder

VITTORIO GALLESE
MAGALI ROCHAT

The essence of social cognition is related to the comprehension of others' behavior. In our daily life, we constantly, thus not always consciously, attribute a meaning to the behavior of our social partners. We ascribe dispositions, intentions, desires, beliefs, emotions, and sensations to others, most of the time on the basis of their overt behavior. Classic cognitive science has traditionally emphasized that intersubjectivity mainly consists of the ability to represent and reflect upon the mental states of others, and that as such it uniquely pertains to the human realm. Such ability would ontogenetically develop following universal maturational steps, reaching its final stage in coincidence with the acquisition of full-blown linguistic competence. This account basically equates human social cognition with social metacognition. According to the same view, all other social species, including nonhuman primates, would exclusively rely upon the visible aspects of behavior and its statistical recurrence in a certain context.

The claim according to which behavior reading and mind reading constitute two autonomous realms has theoretically contributed to create an evolutionary gap, which has been radically questioned by recent findings in both animal and infant social-cognition research. On the phylogenetic side, a series of experiments have demonstrated that nonhuman primates can infer others' intentions on the basis of the observable cues of their behavior (Buttelmann, Carpenter, Call, & Tomasello, 2007; Call, Hare, Carpenter, & Tomasello, 2004; Flombaum & Santos, 2005; Hare, Call, & Tomasello, 2001; Santos, Nissen, & Ferrugia, 2006; Tomasello, Carpenter, Call, Behne, & Moll, 2005), while on the ontogenetic side experimental evidence has shown that the ability to understand others' goals and false beliefs develops well before the complete maturation of language (Falck-Ytter, Gredeback, & von Hofsten, 2006; Kovács, Téglás, & Endress, 2010; Onishi & Baillargeon, 2005; Sommerville & Woodward, 2005; Woodward, 1998). This evidence demonstrates that crucial aspects of social cognition and intersubjectivity appear both in phylogeny and ontogeny much earlier than previously thought. The same evidence highlights the potential heuristic value of a bottom-up approach to the development of social cognition, by empirically investigating its preverbal and non-meta-representational aspects (Gallese, 2007).

Recent findings in cognitive neuroscience revealed the existence of a neural mechanism, the mirror neuron mechanism (MNM), matching action perception on action execution. It has been proposed that this mechanism could account for direct understanding of action and intention both in humans and in nonhuman primates (Gallese, Fadiga, Fogassi, & Rizzolatti, 1996; Rizzolatti, Fadiga, Gallese, & Fogassi, 1996). We posit that a fundamental ingredient of social cognition—that is, the ability to predict and understand the motor goals and motor intentions of the actions of others—is intrinsically embodied in the organization of the cortical motor system. We qualify this ability as motor cognition (see Gallese & Rochat, 2009; Gallese, Rochat, Cossu, & Sinigaglia, 2009). A consequence of our hypothesis is that action understanding is tightly related to the motor expertise individuals acquire during their development.

The aim of the present chapter is to challenge the classical dichotomous view of social cognition by proposing that the development in phylogeny and ontogeny of action and intention understanding both rely upon a common neurophysiological substrate: the MNM. Our stance on the study of human social cognition embraces an evolutionary perspective, capitalizing upon the neurophysiological and psychological investigation of the mechanisms and processes implicated in nonhuman primates' social cognition. By doing so, a different picture emerges: Apparently different social-cognitive abilities and strategies adopted by different species of primates appear to be the product of a similar functional mechanism, which, in the course of evolution, acquired increasing complexity.

We first consider the neuroscientific evidence relating the existence and functions of a neural mechanism—the MNM—with action-understanding abilities in macaque monkeys and humans. The possible contribution of this mechanism to the development of social-cognitive abilities in nonhuman primates and human infants is discussed. Finally, we address the relevance of motor cognition for the understanding of important aspects of autistic spectrum disorder.

Motor Goals and Motor Intentions
Are Embodied in the Motor System: Mirror Neurons

The neurophysiological investigation of the motor system of nonhuman primates conducted during the last three decades enabled a radical revision of the role of the motor cortex in social cognition. The cortical motor system, typically thought to enable mere movement programming and execution, plays, in fact, a crucial role in complex cognitive abilities, such as the understanding of the motor goals and intentions of actions. It was demonstrated that motor neurons in the anterior part of the macaque monkey's ventral premotor cortex (area F5) do not discharge in association with simple hand or mouth movements but rather during the execution of motor acts leading to a specific goal, like grasping an object, tearing it apart, or holding it (Rizzolatti et al., 1988). A consistent percentage of these motor neurons discharge during a specific goal-related motor act, like grasping, independently of the effectors used to accomplish it (Rizzolatti et al., 1988; Rizzolatti, Fogassi, & Gallese, 2000).

Furthermore, Umiltà and colleagues (2008) showed that F5 grasping-related neurons specifically discharge during goal achievement independently of the particular sequence of movements required to grasp the object. Altogether, these data demonstrate that part of the macaque monkey motor system goes beyond the kinematic description of movement (e.g., force, amplitude, direction) and supports a more abstract representation of action in terms of its goal (see also Alexander & Crutcher, 1990; Crutcher & Alexander, 1990; Kakei, Hoffman, & Strick, 1999, 2001).

Besides motor neurons, F5 contains two specific classes of visuomotor neurons: canonical neurons and mirror neurons. Canonical neurons, the first class, respond both to the observation of objects of particular size and shape and during the execution of a motor act corresponding to that suggested by the object's affordances (Murata et al., 1997; Raos, Umiltà, Murata, Fogassi, & Gallese, 2006; Rizzolatti et al., 2000; Umiltà, Brochier, Spinks, & Lemon, 2007). In other terms, canonical neurons translate the visual features of the external world in terms of potential motor acts; three-dimensional objects are coded not in relation to their mere physical appearance but in relation to the effect of the interaction with an acting agent (Gallese, 2000, 2009).

The second class—mirror neurons—discharges not only when the monkey executes goal-related hand movements like grasping objects but also when observing others executing similar acts (Gallese et al., 1996; Gallese, Keysers, & Rizzolatti, 2004; Rizzolatti et al., 1996; Rizzolatti & Craighero, 2004; Rizzolatti, Fogassi, & Gallese, 2001). Neurons with similar properties were later discovered in a sector of the posterior parietal cortex reciprocally connected with area F5 (Bonini et al., 2010; Fogassi et al., 2005; Gallese, Fogassi, Fadiga, & Rizzolatti, 2002) and in the primary motor cortex (Dushanova & Donoghue, 2010; Tkach, Reimer, & Hatsopoulos, 2007). The principal triggering element to elicit the neural discharge during both action execution and observation is the interaction between object and body effectors like the hand or the mouth: Mirror neurons in monkeys do not respond to the observation of an object alone, and they do not respond, or respond much less, to the sight of a hand mimicking an action without a target (Gallese et al., 1996).

For about one-third of mirror neurons in F5, the effective executed and observed motor actions coincide in terms of both goal (e.g., grasping) and how the goal is achieved (e.g., grasping with a particular handgrip). However, for the majority of mirror neurons, this congruence appears to be broader, linking observed and executed motor acts on the basis of the achievement of a similar goal rather than on the similarity of movement kinematics. These broadly congruent mirror neurons seems to be endowed with a more abstract level of action coding, which allows them to map the motor goal of the observed action across many instances of it (Rizzolatti et al., 2001).

Recently, an electrophysiological study examined the extent to which hand-grasp mirror neurons respond to the observation of a motor act having the same goal (taking possession of the object) but achieved with artificial effectors (Rochat et al., 2010). F5 mirror neurons were recorded from two monkeys trained to use a pair of reverse pliers to grasp food. Reverse pliers require one to reverse the sequence of hand movements naturally executed to grasp objects: One has to first operate a pressure on the handles to open the pliers tips and then release the pressure by opening one's hand in order to close the tips around the object. The results showed that virtually all neurons responding to the observation of handgrasping also responded to the observation of grasping with pliers, with the peak of their discharge coinciding with the moment of goal achievement.

Of particular interest is the fact that many of these mirror neurons were also activated by the observation of spearing with a stick, a motor act that monkeys never learned to execute and never observed outside the experimental sessions. The intensity and pattern of the response differed, however, among conditions. The earliest and strongest discharge was determined by handgrasp observation, while pliers grasping and spearing observation triggered weaker responses at longer latencies. These results demonstrate that F5 grasping mirror neurons respond to the observation of a *family* of stimuli leading to the same goal. However, the response pattern depends on the similarity between the observed motor act and the one contained in the natural motor repertoire of the observer.

The discovery of the existence of a shared neural substrate coding perceived and executed actions provides a parsimonious solution to the problem of translating the results of the visual analysis of observed motor behavior into something that the observer is able to understand to the extent that the observer "experientially owns" it already. It was proposed that this "direct-matching" mechanism could be at the basis of a direct form of action understanding where the observer's motor knowledge is used to understand others' goal-directed behavior (Gallese et al., 1996; Rizzolatti et al., 1996; Rizzolatti & Gallese, 1997).

The proposal that mirror neurons' activity reflects an internal description of the meaning of the perceived action rather than a mere visual description of its features has been demonstrated in two studies. In the first study, Umiltà and colleagues (2001) found that a subset of F5 mirror neurons code the action outcome even in the absence of complete visual information about it. Macaque monkeys' mirror neurons map observed motor acts not exclusively on the basis of their visual description but also on the basis of the anticipation of their final goal state, simulated through the activation of its motor neural "representation" in the observer's premotor cortex.

Of course, these data do not exclude the coexistence of a system that visually analyzes and describes the motor acts of others. However, such "pictorial" analysis per se is most likely insufficient to provide an understanding of the observed act. Without reference to the observer's internal "motor knowledge," this description is devoid of experiential meaning for the observing individual (Gallese & Rochat, 2009).

Successively, Kohler and colleagues (2002) demonstrated that F5 mirror neurons also code the meaning of a motor act on the basis of its related sound. A particular class of F5 mirror neurons ("audio-visual mirror neurons") responds not only when the monkey *executes* and *observes* a given hand motor act, like breaking a peanut, but also when it just *hears* the sound the motor act typically produces. These neurons selectively respond to the sound of actions and discriminate between the sounds of different actions. Mirror neurons' activity reveals the existence of a mechanism through which perceived events as different as sounds, images, or voluntary acts of the body are nevertheless coded as similar to the extent that they represent the assorted sensory aspects of the motor act's goal state.

A major step forward in the research on the MNM lays in the discovery that premotor and parietal mirror neurons not only code the goal of an executed/observed motor act, like grasping an object, but they also discriminate identical motor acts (like grasping) according to the final goal of the action in which the act is embedded (e.g., grasping an object to bring it to the mouth or into a container; Bonini et al., 2010; Fogassi et al., 2005). The MNM maps integrated sequences of goal-related motor acts (grasping, holding, bringing, placing) to obtain different and chained-in-parallel sequences of motor acts properly assembled to accomplish a more distal goal state. Each embedded motor acts appears to be facilitated by the previously executed one, reorganizing itself as to map the fulfillment of the overarching motor goal of the action. These results suggest, at least at the level of basic actions, that the motor intention of eating or placing the food is also coded by mirror neurons.

Bonini and colleagues (2010) recently compared the neuronal properties of premotor area F5 and inferior parietal area PFG during the same grasp-to-eat and grasp-to-place motor tasks. Results indicated that while the vast majority of parietal neurons discharged differently during grasping when this act was embedded into actions aimed at different goals, the proportion of this type of neurons was lower in area F5, where the majority of the recorded neurons were not differentially activated in the two grasping conditions. The authors suggest that parietal area PFG would play a more important role in organizing motor acts into actions with different distal goals (e.g., to eat vs. to place), whereas area F5 would be more devoted to code the goal of single motor acts in an abstract fashion, independently of the used effector or even of the executed sequence of movements. However, when comparing F5 and parietal mirror neurons, the results showed that a conspicuous percentage of these neurons in both areas responded during the execution and observation of grasping according to the overarching goal of the action in which it was embedded: Some neurons only responded when grasping led to bringing the object to the mouth but not when it led to placing the object into a container, and vice versa. Parietal and premotor mirror neurons, by virtue of this functional characteristic, might allow the observing monkey to anticipate the agent's next motor act, henceforth its core motor intention.

What is the relevance of the mirror mechanism for macaque monkeys' social cognition? The studies just reviewed demonstrate that the MNM has the functional properties that could enable monkeys to understand what others are doing and for what basic purpose. These aspects, though, even if crucial, do not exhaust the realm of social cognition. Empirical evidence shows that macaque monkeys are capable of shared-attention behaviors (Ferrari, Coudé, Gallese, & Fogassi, 2008; Ferrari, Kohler, Fogassi, & Gallese, 2000). Shepherd, Klein, Deaner, and Platt (2009) discovered a class of neurons in the posterior parietal area LIP, known to be involved in oculomotor control, that fired both when the monkey looked in a given direction and when it observed another monkey looking in the same direction. Shepherd and colleagues suggested that LIP mirror neurons for gaze might contribute to sharing of observed attention, thus playing a role in imitative behavior.

The relevance of mirror neurons for monkeys' social cognition is also evident from the study by Caggiano, Fogassi, Rizzolatti, Thier, and Casile (2009), showing that F5 mirror neurons activity is modulated by the distance at which the observed action takes place. About half of the recorded mirror neurons responded only when the observed agent acted either inside or outside monkey's peripersonal space. Such modulation, however, did not simply measure the physical distance between agent and observer. A consistent percentage of mirror neurons not responding to the experimenter's grasping actions carried out near the monkey resumed their discharge when a transparent barrier was interposed between the object target of the action and the observing monkey. Blocking the monkey's potentiality for action on the target of the action of another remaps the spatial location of the observed agent according to a system of coordinates dictated by and expressing the monkey's relational potentiality for interaction.

Given that the MNM, as we show in the next section, is not unique to monkeys but has also been detected in the human brain, a new evolutionary scenario emphasizing the crucial role of motor cognition for the emergence of human social cognition is becoming progressively evident (Gallese et al., 2009; Gallese & Rochat, 2009).

The Mirror Mechanism in Humans

Several studies have documented the presence of a common neural activation during action observation and execution in the human brain by using different experimental methodologies and techniques (for review, see Gallese, 2003a, 2003b, 2006; Gallese et al., 2004; Rizzolatti et al., 2001; Rizzolatti & Craighero, 2004; Rizzolatti & Sinigaglia, 2010).

A series of studies using transcranial magnetic stimulation (TMS) provided direct evidence that the motor system in humans is endowed with mirror properties. Fadiga, Fogassi, Pavesi, and Rizzolatti (1995) showed that when participants observed transitive and intransitive hand and arm movements, increased motor evoked potentials (MEPs) were registered in the very same muscles involved in the observed movements. Those results were confirmed by other TMS studies (Maeda, Kleiner-Fisman, & Pascual-Leone, 2002; Patuzzo, Fiaschi, & Manganotti, 2003) and successively extended by Gangitano, Mottaghy, and Pascual-Leone (2001), who demonstrated that the time course of motor cortical excitability during action observation follows that of movement execution. Altogether, TMS studies indicate that a motor resonance mechanism exists in the human brain, and that it can be also activated by the observation of intransitive and meaningless movements, a mirroring property that was never observed in monkeys (Rizzolatti & Craighero, 2004).

More recently, coherently with the goal relatedness of mirror neurons in monkeys demonstrated by Rochat and colleagues (2010), a TMS study on humans showed that the amplitude of MEPs recorded from participants' opponens pollicis muscle during the observation of grasping performed with normal and reverse pliers was modulated by the goal of the observed motor act, regardless of the movements required to accomplish it (Cattaneo, Caruana, Jezzini, & Rizzolatti, 2009). Finally, a recent TMS adaptation study confirms the specific role of the motor system in generating a context-independent mapping of motor goal relatedness. Such property appears to be absent in extrastriate visual areas sensitive to the observation of biological motion, demonstrating that a visual description of motor behavior falls short of accounting for its goal relatedness (Cattaneo, Sandrini, & Schwarzbach, 2010). The intentional character of behavior as it is mapped by the cortical motor system enables a direct appreciation of purpose without relying on explicit inference.

Brain-imaging techniques allowed researchers to localize the brain areas activated by action perception and execution (Buccino et al., 2001; Decety, Chaminade, Grèzes, & Meltzoff, 2002; Grafton, Arbib, Fadiga, & Rizzolatti, 1996; Grèzes, Armony, Rowe, & Passingham, 2003; Grèzes, Costes, & Decety, 1998; Grèzes et al., 2001; Iacoboni et al., 1999, 2001; Koski, Iacoboni, Dubeau, Woods, & Mazziotta, 2003; Koski, Wohlschläger, Bekkering, Woods, & Dubeau, 2002; Manthey, Schubotz, & von Cramon, 2003; Nishitani & Hari, 2000, 2002; Perani et al., 2001; Rizzolatti et al., 1996). According to all of these studies, the likely human homologues of macaque monkey mirror areas include the ventral part of the precentral gyrus, the posterior part of the inferior frontal gyrus, the rostral part of the inferior parietal lobule, and regions within the intraparietal sulcus and the superior temporal sulcus (Cattaneo & Rizzolatti, 2009).

Just like the homologue monkey areas, human cortical areas displaying the MNM present a somatotopic organization, with an activation of specific regions within the premotor and posterior parietal cortices during the observation/execution of motor acts involving different parts of the body (Aziz-Zadeh, Wilson, Rizzolatti, & Iacoboni, 2006; Buccino et al., 2001).

The existence of shared neural representations of one's own and other's action could at least partially account for the human ability to imitate actions. Functional magnetic resonance imaging (fMRI) evidence shows that mirror areas in humans are selectively activated during simple-movement imitation (Iacoboni et al., 1999) and during imitation learning of complex skills (Buccino, Vogt, et al., 2004; Vogt et al., 2007). Buccino, Vogt, and colleagues (2004) proposed that during learning of new motor patterns by imitation the observed actions are decomposed into elementary motor acts that automatically activate the corresponding motor maps. The prefrontal cortex would then recombine the activated motor maps according to the observed model.

The MNM seems to be also involved in the detection of the motor intentions of basic actions. In their fMRI study, Iacoboni and colleagues (2005) demonstrated that human mirror areas respond differently to the observation of the same grasping actions if the actions are embedded in different contexts that suggest different motor intentions associated with the grasping actions, such as drinking or cleaning up. Another fMRI study by Brass, Schmitt, Spengler, and Gergely (2007) shows that the observed goal-related motor act, even when unusual—like switching on the light with a knee—and whether plausible (hands occupied) or not (hands free), always leads to MNM activation.

This high level of motor abstraction generates the possibility of executing, hence also of recognizing in the perceptual domain, an orderly sequence of motor acts appropriately chained to accomplish a distal goal. When such level of motor mapping is present, motor behavior can be described at a higher level of abstraction, without implying an explicit language-mediated conceptualization. From the single motor goal (e.g., grasping), we move up to the level of the goal hierarchy (e.g., grasping for eating) characterizing a whole motor action as such. Thus, premotor mirror areas—areas active during the execution and the observation of motor acts and previously thought to be involved only in action recognition—are actually also involved in understanding the motor intentions of basic actions, by relying on the context to infer a forthcoming new goal.

These results suggest that even humans do not need to explicitly represent intentions as such when understanding them in others. Action motor intentions are embedded within the intrinsic intentionality of action—that is, its intrinsic relatedness to an end state, a motor goal. Most of the time we do not explicitly ascribe intentions to others, we simply detect them. When witnessing others' behaviors, their motor intentional content can be directly grasped without the need to represent it in propositional format.

Motor Cognition

We challenge the traditional purely mentalistic and disembodied view of intersubjectivity and social cognition heralded by classic cognitive science by positing that the capacity to understand others' intentional behavior—from both a phylogenetic and an ontogenetic point of view—relies on a more basic functional mechanism, which exploits the intrinsic organization of primates' motor system. As reviewed in the preceding sections, abilities like goal detection, action anticipation, and hierarchical representation of action with respect to a distal goal can all be viewed as the direct consequence of the peculiar functional architecture of the motor system, organized in terms of goal-directed motor acts (Rizzolatti & Gallese, 1997; Rizzolatti et al., 1988, 2000). We qualify such abilities as *motor cognition* (Gallese & Rochat, 2009; Gallese et al., 2009). An important corollary of our hypothesis is that the correct development of such a mechanism is required to scaffold more cognitively sophisticated social-mental abilities.

Goal coding is a distinctive functional feature of the organization of the cortical motor system of primates, humans included. This functional principle can also shed light on the debate of the relative importance of motor and perceptual experience to grasp the meaning of an observed action. The results of Umiltà (2008) and Rochat (2010) and their colleagues show at the single-neuron level the impact of motor experience on action coding. The same data also show that when the observed action performed by others becomes part of the observer's motor experience, it leads to a more anticipated and stronger response of mirror neurons. Indeed, coherently with these data, several brain-imaging studies conducted on human beings have shown that the intensity of the MNM activation during action observation depends on the similarity between the observed actions and the participants' action repertoire (Aglioti, Cesari, Romani, & Urgesi, 2008; Buccino, Lui, et al., 2004; Calvo-Merino, Glaser, Grèzes, Passingham, & Haggard, 2005; Cross, Hamilton, & Grafton, 2006; Haslinger et al., 2006). In particular, one fMRI study (Calvo-Merino, Grèzes, Glaser, Passingham, & Haggard, 2006) focused on the distinction between the relative contribution of visual and motor experience in processing an observed action. The results revealed greater activation of the MNM when the observed actions were frequently performed with respect to those that were only perceptually familiar but never practiced.

These discoveries emphasize the crucial role played by the motor system in providing the building blocks upon which more sophisticated social-cognitive abilities can be built. The earliest indirect evidence available to date on the MNM in human infants is provided by Shimada and Hiraki (2006), who showed with near-infrared spectroscopy the presence of an action execution/observation matching system in 6-month-old human infants. Southgate, Johnson, and Csibra (2008) showed with high-density electroencephalography (EEG) that 9-month-old infants exhibit alpha-band attenuation over central electrodes (a sign of motor resonance) both during hand action execution and observation. Moreover, Southgate, Johnson, El Karoui, and Csibra (2010) showed a similar effect in 13-month-old infants during prediction of others' motor goals using an experimental paradigm modeled on that of Umiltà and colleagues (2001), in which monkeys' mirror neurons were tested during the observation of a handgrasp behind an occluding surface. Finally, van Elk, van Schieb, Hunnius, Vesperc, and Bekkering (2008) recorded 14- to 16-month-old infants' EEG during observation of action videos. Their findings indicate stronger mu- and beta-desynchronizations during observation of crawling compared with walking videos. The size of the effect was strongly related to the infants' own crawling experience. As the authors conclude, these data suggest that when observing others' actions, infants' perception is influenced by their previous action experience.

We do not yet know when and how the MNM appears. We do not know whether mirror neurons are innate and how they are shaped and modeled during development. It has been proposed that mirror neurons are the outcome of a simple associative mechanism binding the motor commands enabling action execution with the visual perception of the same action (Heyes, 2010; Keysers & Perrett, 2004). This hypothesis, though, does not account for mirroring mechanisms pertaining to motor acts performed with body parts to which neither monkeys nor humans have direct visual access, like the mouth and the face. Second, this hypothesis, for the same reasons, is forced to downplay or even deny plausibility to compelling evidence about neonatal imitation both in nonhuman primates (Ferrari et al., 2006; Myowa-Yamakoshi, Tomonaga, Tanaka, & Matsuzawa, 2004) and humans (Meltzoff & Moore, 1977). Third, this hypothesis falls short of explaining empirical evidence showing that motor experience without any visual feedback boosts perceptual ability when directed to human biological motion (see Casile & Giese, 2006). Del Giudice, Manera, and Keysers (2009) proposed that mirror neurons might initially develop through experiential canalization of Hebbian learning, allowing for the possibility of some genetic preprogramming. According to this hypothesis, infants view themselves while acting. Then visual neurons in the temporal cortex that respond *selectively* to the observed action as it unfolds reinforce the premotor neurons controlling the action and thereby induce Hebbian potentiation. This hypothesis bears the burden of explaining how visual selectivity for specific actions is achieved by temporal cortex visual neurons. Furthermore, similarly to the just-mentioned associative hypothesis, Del Giudice and colleagues could not account for neonatal facial imitation and for the motor bias of perceptual recognition of biological motion.

Gallese provided an alternative account of the ontogenesis of the MNM (Gallese, 2009; Gallese et al., 2009). It has been shown that the prenatal development of hand motor control is remarkably sophisticated (Castiello et al., 2010; Myowa-Yamakoshi & Takeshita, 2006; Zoia et al., 2007). According to Gallese, before birth, specific connections develop between the motor centers controlling mouth and hand movements and brain regions that will be the recipient of visual inputs after birth. Such connectivity, likely genetically predetermined, tunes the visual areas for spatiotempo-ral patterns of neural firing that correspond to the spatiotemporal patterns in motor areas during the execution of the mouth and hand movements. This tuning acts as a functional template. Once visual information is provided, the neonate would be ready to respond to the observation of hand or facial gestures that produce spatiotemporal patterns of activity matching the templates, thus enabling neonatal imitation and the reciprocal behaviors characterizing our postnatal life since its very beginning. A similar motor tuning of visual processing could also account for the advantages offered by motor experience, with respect to visual familiarity, observed in a variety of perceptual tasks performed by adults. When the relative contribution of visual and motor experience in processing an observed action is investigated, the results reveal greater activation of the mirror mechanism when the observed actions are frequently performed by the observers compared with those only perceptually familiar but never practiced (see Calvo-Merino et al., 2006).

It can be hypothesized that an innate rudimentary MNM might be already present at birth, to be subsequently and flexibly modulated by motor experience and gradually enriched by visuomotor learning. According to Lepage and Théoret (2007), the development of the MNM can be conceptualized as a process whereby the child learns to refrain from acting out the automatic mapping mechanism link-ing action perception and execution. This scenario found more recent support from data obtained both in monkeys (Kraskov, Dancause, Quallo, Shepherd, & Lemon, 2010) and in humans (Mukamel, Ekstrom, Kaplan, Iacoboni, & Fried, 2010). In fact, both studies presented neurophysiological evidence of mirror neurons activated dur-ing action execution but inhibited during the observation of actions by others. The development of cortical inhibitory mechanisms likely leads the gradual transition from mandatory reenactment to mandatory embodied motor simulation.

The discovery of the MNM provided a neurofunctional basis to interpret the ever-growing evidence from comparative psychology and developmental psychology research on the role of experience-based motor knowledge in shaping the ontogenetic development of social-cognitive skills.

The Phylogeny of Motor Cognition in Primates

Nonhuman primates, similarly to humans, are social beings living in highly cohesive groups. During their social interactions, nonhuman primates exhibit several com-plex behaviors such as gaze following, deception, or reconciliation that are appar-ently very similar to human behavior. These similarities notwithstanding, a crucial difference between human and nonhuman primates' social cognition lies in their intentional understanding, that is, the understanding of what causes a goal-directed action. According to a mainstream view, humans would have the unique ability to go beyond a behavior's surface, to infer mental states such as intentions, beliefs, and desires supposedly driving the current or future agent's behavior (Povinelli & Eddy, 1996; Tomasello & Call, 1997). In contrast, nonhuman primates' social knowledge is thought to rely on the extraction of procedural rules from observable environ-mental regularities (Köhler, 1927; Povinelli, 2000; Visalberghi & Tomasello, 1998). However, evidence in comparative psychology has recently challenged the traditional conception of nonhuman primates as mere behavior readers.

Chimps' inability to understand others as intentional agents is only apparent in particular *cooperative* contexts. Recent evidence showed that when engaged in a *competitive* setting chimps understand what others know on the basis of where they are looking (Hare et al., 2001; Tomasello et al., 2005). Further evidence shows that apes understand what others intend (Buttelman et al., 2007; Call et al., 2004). More importantly, it has been shown that rhesus monkeys can establish a cognitive link between seeing and knowing, as evidenced by their systematically choosing to steal food from a human competitor, who could not see the food, but refraining from stealing it when the human competitor could see it (Flombaum & Santos, 2005). Similarly, it has been shown that rhesus monkeys choose to obtain food silently only in situations in which silence is crucial in order to remain undetected by a human competitor (Santos et al., 2006).

Krachun, Carpenter, Call, and Tomasello (2009) compared the performance of 5-year-old children with that of chimpanzees and bonobos in a nonverbal false-belief task where participants were in direct competition with another individual. In this task, participants and a human competitor witnessed the experimenter hiding a reward in one of two containers. The location of the containers was then switched when the competitor could not see it. The 5-year-old children successfully chose the other container after the competitor reached toward the incorrect one, while great apes did not demonstrate a similar understanding of the competitor's false belief. Interestingly though, in conditions that heavily enhanced the competitor's false belief, apes tended to look more often at the not-chosen container so as to indicate some implicit or uncertain understanding of the competitor's belief.

Although, for a long time, nonhuman primates have been considered better emulators than imitators, achieving the same goal of a model by following their own strategy (Tomasello, Davis-Dasilva, Camak, & Bard, 1987), recent experiments showed that apes and macaque monkeys actually display unexpected abilities in imitation tasks. Horner and Whiten (2005) demonstrated that, similarly to 14-month-old children (Gergely, Bekkering, & Kiràly, 2002), wild-born chimpanzees could solve a tool-using task by flexibly switching from emulation to imitation strategy when causal information was insufficient. In an observational learning task, rhesus macaques learned to respond in a particular sequence to items that were simultaneously displayed on a touch screen. Results showed that monkeys did not acquire new sequences by simple motor imitation but by detecting and copying a cognitive rule underlying the demonstrator motor's behavior (Subiaul, Cantlon, Holloway, & Terrace, 2004).

Imitation is not only a matter of cultural transmission but also a fundamental tool to establish an emotional bond between interaction partners. Paukner, Suomi, Visalberghi, and Ferrari (2009) showed that capuchin monkeys recognize when their own behavior is being imitated, thus preferring to look at, sit next to, and interact with imitator partners. Yawning has been demonstrated to be highly contagious both in human and in nonhuman anthropomorphic primates *(Pan troglodytes)*. Studies have shown this phenomenon also in monkeys (*Macaca arctoides*: Paukner & Anderson, 2006; *Theropithecus gelada*: Palagi, Leone, Mancini, & Ferrari, 2009), confirming the evolutionary origin of this behavior. Although the exact function of yawning—a physiological way to maintain attention at a good level or a social way to synchronize group behavior, thus promoting social cohesion—is still debated, a recent study drew an interesting link between yawn contagion and empathy. In gelada baboons

(Theropithecus gelada), Palagi and colleagues (2009) found that the contagiousness of yawning was highly correlated with the degree of bonding between individuals. Moreover, adult females were more accurate in reproducing the exact type of yawning seen or heard, suggesting an enhanced emotional tuning toward companions.

These findings suggest an original interpretation of yawn contagion, a stereotyped behavior likely promoted by a mirroring mechanism (Arnott, Singhal, & Goodale, 2009), as a revelator of the emotional connection between individuals, possibly a rudimental version of the empathy observed among humans and some great apes. Altogether, these data suggest that behavior matching, be it voluntary imitation or passive contagion, might be based on a mirroring mechanism that has been preserved throughout phylogeny to promote affiliation in nonhuman and human primates.

Since several studies have demonstrated the existence of neonatal imitation in nonhuman primates (Bard, 2007; Ferrari et al., 2006; Myowa-Yamakoshi et al., 2004), the mirroring mechanism could provide the neural underpinning of this ability (see Gallese et al., 2009). Neonatal imitation in macaque monkeys shows the same transitory nature and large interindividual variability described in human infants. Ferrari, Paukner, Ionica, and Suomi (2009) connected the differential imitative responses of newborn macaque monkeys to the development of sensory, motor, and cognitive skills during their first month of life. Results showed that precocious imitators are also the most skilled in performing early goal-directed motor acts such as reaching and grasping objects. These authors suggest that cortical motor organization of imitators is at a more advanced stage of development than in nonimitators, thus proposing that neonatal imitation abilities are predictive of future neurobehavioral development.

Rochat, Serra, Fadiga, and Gallese (2008) investigated the phylogenetic origin of the ability to evaluate and predict the goal-directed action of others. Nonhuman primates' ability to discriminate between means and end and to use contextual cues to evaluate the ecological validity of a chosen mean has been tested by adapting a looking-time paradigm previously used with human infants (Gergely, Nádasdy, Csibra, & Bíró, 1995). Results showed that macaque monkeys, similarly to 9- to 12-month-old human infants, detect the goal of an observed motor act and, according to the physical characteristics of the context, construe expectancies about the most likely action the agent will execute in a given context. This, however, is true only when observed motor acts are consonant with the observer's motor repertoire. Inadequate motor acts, non-goal-related movements, or unfamiliar goal-related motor acts do not allow any simulation and prediction. Although this study does not provide direct evidence about the neural mechanisms underpinning the results, Rochat and colleagues hypothesized that monkeys evaluate the observed acts by mapping them on their own motor neural substrate through the activation of the MNM.

These results reveal that nonhuman primates are endowed with the ability to understand the intentional meaning of others' behavior by relying upon visible behavioral cues; hence, they seriously argue against the traditional dichotomous account of primate social cognition based on a sharp evolutionary discontinuity between behavior and mind readers (Gallese, 2007; Gallese & Umiltà, 2006). These results further corroborate the notion that motor behavior contains elements that can be detected and used to understand it and construe predictions about it without necessarily relying on mental representations in propositional format, certainly precluded to nonhuman primates.

The Ontogeny of Motor Cognition in Humans

Human beings are social creatures, and action represents the earliest means to express their social inclination. Very early in life, human social cognition is anchored to action at an interindividual level (von Hofsten, 2007). Already at birth humans engage in interpersonal mimetic relations by means of neonatal imitation. Since the seminal study of Meltzoff and Moore (1977), the innate presence of imitative abilities in human infants is a well-known transitory phenomenon, extensively investigated and confirmed by different studies. Newborns are able to reproduce facial gestures (Legerstee, 2005; Meltzoff & Moore, 1992), facial expressions (Field, Woodson, Greenberg, & Cohen, 1982) and to a certain extent hand gestures (Fontaine, 1984; Nagy et al., 2005). It is worth noticing that 5- to 8-week-old infants imitate the tongue protrusion behavior of a human model only, and not the one of a nonbiological agent (Legerstee, 1991). This finding shows that neonatal imitation behavior is selective for conspecifics. Neonates are innately prepared to link to their caregivers through imitation and affective attunement, clarifying yet another of the various capacities that locate human infants in the social world from the very beginning of life.

Infants very early on participate in social interaction sequences. As aptly put by Legerstee (2009, p. 2), "Infants communicate with eye contact, facial expression, vocalizations, and gestures while assimilating the rhythm of their interactions to that of their caretakers." They actively solicit their caregivers' attention and engage themselves in body activity displaying "protoconversational" turn-taking structure, that is, characterized by a structure similar to adult conversations (see Braten 1988, 1992, 2007; Meltzoff & Brooks, 2001; Meltzoff & Moore, 1977, 1998; Stern, 1985; Trevarthen, 1979, 1993; Tronick, 1989). Furthermore, as shown by Reddy (2008), few-months-old preverbal infants, when participating in social interactions, show signs of so-called self-conscious emotions like embarrassment, pride, and coyness. They display these behaviors at a developmental age preceding the onset of self-reflective consciousness, definitely well before being capable of self-recognition when looking at their reflection in a mirror. Reddy writes, "[Self-conscious emotions,] rather than derive from conceptual development in the second year of human infancy, exist in simple forms as ways of managing the exposure of self to other from early in the first year and are crucial for shaping the infant's emerging conception of self and other" (p. 41).

We proposed that from a functional perspective cognitive development has to do with expanding the prospective control of actions (Gallese et al., 2009). Indeed, in humans motor skills mature much earlier than previously thought. At birth the primary somatosensory and motor cortex show an advanced maturation compared with other brain areas (Chiron et al., 1992). Newborns are already endowed with a rudimentary form of eye–hand coordination (von Hofsten, 1982) and can purposely control their arm movements to meet external demands (van der Meer, 1997).

Even more interestingly, there is evidence that motor control is remarkably sophisticated well before birth. Fetuses at week 22 of gestation show anticipatory opening movement of the mouth preceding the arrival of the hand (Myowa-Yamakoshi & Takeshita, 2006), and display hand movements with different kinematic patterns depending on where they are aimed (Zoia et al., 2007). Thus, the kinematic study of prenatal twin fetuses behavior offers a unique opportunity to investigate the dawning of social interactions in our species. A recent study (Castiello et al., 2010) showed that fetal twins already at the 14th week of gestation display upper limb movements with different kinematic profiles according to whether they target their own body or the body of the twin. Furthermore, between 14 and 18 weeks of gestation, the proportion of self-directed movements decreases, while that of the movements targeting the sibling increases. These data clearly show that the human motor system, well before birth, is already instantiating functional properties enabling social interactions, and that such social interactions are expressed obeying to different motor potentialities. The dawning of the *interpersonal self* (Neisser, 1988) appears to occur before birth. When the context enables it, as in the case of twin pregnancies, bodily otherness is mapped on one's own motor potentialities, similarly to the basic social interactions taking place after birth.

What is the relevance of motor cognition for the development of social cognition? According to a widely held opinion, such role is marginal. As we argued in introduction, the dominant view is still equating intersubjectivity and social cognition with explicit mind reading. Mind reading, in turn, is viewed by many as a mainly theoretical enterprise—theory of mind (ToM; Premack & Woodruff, 1978)—grounded on metarepresentational abilities like the ascription to others of the propositional attitudes of folk psychology. The achievement of a full-blown ToM is considered to occur when infants pass the false-belief task (Baron-Cohen, Leslie, & Frith, 1985), that is, when they understand others' behavior as being driven by their own representation of the world, which might not accurately reflect reality (Baron-Cohen et al., 1985; Wimmer & Perner, 1983).

Solid experimental evidence, though, shows that during the first year of life infants' action understanding is already fairly well developed. It is clear that these early forms of action understanding do not imply any meta-representational capacity, nor can they be interpreted in terms of mind reading. Gergely and Csibra's teleological stance hypothesis (Csibra, Birò, Koòs, & Gergely, 2003; Csibra, Gergely, Birò, Koòs, & Brockbank, 1999; Gergely et al., 1995) posits that by 9 months of age infants are equipped with an inferential system applied to factual reality (action, goal state, and current situational constraints) for generating nonmentalistic goal-directed action representations. According to these authors, an action is represented as teleological only if it satisfies a "principle of rational action," stating that an action can be explained by its goal state if the agent reaches its goal through the most efficient means given the contextual constraints.

A different theoretical view on the emergence of infants' goal-directed action interpretation, stresses the intrinsic link between action understanding and motor experience. Several scholars emphasize the constructional effect of self-agentive experience on infants' understanding of actions' goal relatedness (see Sommerville & Woodward, 2005). Infant research by means of habituation/dishabituation paradigms showed that previous motor experience facilitates 3-month-old infants' perception of goal-directed actions performed by others (Sommerville, Woodward, & Needham, 2005). Moreover, 10-month-old infants' ability to construe an action representation as hierarchically organized toward a distal goal strictly depends on their ability to perform similarly structured action sequences (Sommerville & Woodward, 2005).

It must be stressed that the congruency between the observed action and the observer's motor repertoire is crucial for goal prediction. In a recent study, it has been shown that infants produce proactive goal-directed eye movements when observing an agent placing balls into a bucket, only to the extent they can perform the same action (Falck-Ytter et al., 2006). Furthermore, it has been shown that infants' early goal discrimination is initially confined to actions executed by conspecifics. Six-month-old infants are sensitive to the action's goal of others only when performed by a human agent (Woodward, 1998). Meltzoff (1995) showed that older infants imitate the unseen motor goal of a human model but not of an inanimate object.

Goal detection forms the core ability of action understanding and social learning through imitation. Both adults (Baird & Baldwin, 2001) and children represent actions as constituted by units hierarchically organized with respect to an overarching goal. Ten-month-old children share with adults the ability to parse actions in units whose boundaries correspond to the completion of a goal (Baldwin, Baird, Saylor, & Clark, 2001). Imitation tasks reflect children's ability to represent actions' units as organized toward a distal goal. When asked to imitate the action of another person, preschoolers reproduce the higher order goal of the action (Bekkering, Wohlschläger, & Gattis, 2000). Eighteen-month-old infants reproduce the goal they inferred from the failed attempts of a human demonstrator (Meltzoff, 1995). Carpenter, Call, and Tomasello (2005) showed that infants could flexibly interpret the goal of an observed sequence of movements according to the context and therefore reenact either the goal of an observed action or the means by which it had been produced. Underlying this cognitive flexibility is the fundamental ability to discriminate between means and ends.

We showed in the previous section that when facing the actions of others, non-human primates can discriminate between means and ends and use contextual cues to evaluate the ecological validity of a chosen mean. Furthermore, we showed that goal relatedness is the functional organizing principle of primates' motor system. Altogether, we believe that this evidence provides a possible phylogenetic explanatory framework lending support to a deflationary motor account of the development of important aspects of social cognition in humans.

Of course, this is only one part of the story. We provided a new account of the role played by the cortical motor system in social cognition without taking into account sensations, emotions, and affects. Our actions are almost never divorced by the sense of emotionally charged personal involvement with the situation. However, we posit that emotions and affects can be fully understood only when considering the role of the cortical motor system in making sense of our and others' behavior. Indeed, as recently pointed out by Daniel Stern (2010), the pervasive affective quality of mother–infant interactions can be captured by the notion of "forms of vitality." According to Stern, forms of vitality consist of a gestalt of movement, force, temporal flow, and intentionality. Such action-related gestalt leads to a subjective globality carrying along a sense of vitality or aliveness. As Stern writes:

> Vitality forms are associated with a content. More accurately, they carry content along with them. Vitality forms are not empty forms. They give a temporal and intensity contour to the content, and with it a sense of an alive performance. The content can be a shift in emotion, a train of thoughts, physical or mental movements, a memory, a fantasy, a means–end action. . . . The vitality dynamic gives the content its form as a dynamic experience. (p. 23)

Dynamic forms of vitality would developmentally precede the domain of feelings and emotions and represent the primary manner in which infants experience the human world. It will be very interesting to investigate how these different dimensions interact at the level of the brain.

In the next section, we explore the possible role of motor cognition in shedding light on autism spectrum disorder.

Motor Cognition and Autism Spectrum Disorder

Autism spectrum disorder (ASD) is a disorder of neurodevelopment occurring with a frequency of 1:150 children. Clinical manifestations can vary both in their nature and in intensity all through the ontogenetic development and are also extremely variable among individuals. Albeit consistent differences in their clinical profiles, individuals with autism share a constant impairment in three specific domains: social interactions, verbal and nonverbal communication, and the repertory of behaviors and field of interests. In other words, in ASD basically all behaviors necessary to successfully establish and regulate social interactions seem to be impaired.

For many years a dominant paradigm in the study of ASD characterized it as the consequence of a defective theory of mind, as a sort of "mindblindness" (Baron-Cohen, 1995). Recent advances in neurophysiology, however, challenge this view and shed new light on the relationship between ASD and impaired motor cognition. A clarification, though, is in order. Being a spectrum disorder, it is unlikely that autism can be exclusively reduced to a deficit of motor cognition. Even less likely, autism can be simply equated to a mere malfunctioning of the MNM. Both views appear too simplistic and fall short of capturing the multilayered and diversified aspects characterizing ASD. Our point is different. We posit that many of the social-cognitive impairments manifested by individuals with ASD are rooted in their incapacity to organize and directly grasp the intrinsic goal-related organization of motor behavior.

Several studies aimed to define the neurological causes underpinning the impairments in social relationships of individuals with ASD. Some have suggested an abnormal neural organization and connectivity during cerebral growth. An increase of white matter seems to be at the origin of the anomalous head and brain dimension most frequently observed in infants with ASD (Courchesne, Carper, & Akshoomoff, 2003; Dawson et al., 2007; Redcay & Courchesne, 2005). Cerebral peak overgrowth involves regions mediating the high-order social, emotional, cognitive, and language functions. Courchesne and Pierce (2005) proposed that a surplus of neurons within frontal and temporal cortices would produce an imbalance in the ratio of local (and potentially poorly inhibited and organized) connectivity to long-distance corticocortical connections. Imbalance of short-distance over long-distance connectivity would disrupt the formation of large-scale neural assemblies, thus altering integrative information processing between brain regions (Brock, Brown, Boucher, & Rippon, 2002; Just, Cherkassky, Keller, & Minshew, 2004; Minshew & Williams, 2007). According to the theory of neural maldevelopment, early brain development in autism is characterized by two phases of brain growth pathology (Courchesne et al., 2003; Courchesne & Pierce, 2005): an early brain overgrowth at the beginning of life and a slowing or arrest of growth during early childhood. In some individuals, a third phase, degeneration, may occur during preadolescence in some brain regions.

Hadjikhani, Joseph, Snyder, and Tager-Flusberg (2006) found that the cerebral thickness of superior parietal, temporal, and frontal cortices is particularly reduced in adolescents with autism. Interestingly, these regions include areas involved in social cognition, those involved in facial expression and recognition, and those displaying the MNM.

Several authors have proposed that abnormalities in MNM functioning could be critical in autism (Dapretto, 2006; Gallese, 2003b, 2006; Hadjikhani et al., 2006; Oberman et al., 2005; Oberman & Ramachandran, 2007; Théoret et al., 2005; Williams, Whiten, Suddendorf, & Perrett, 2001; Williams et al., 2006). Moreover, it is reasonable to hypothesize that the malfunctioning of shared representation for perceived and executed actions would impair the capacity to translate others' perspective into their own, thus potentially shedding light on difficulties that children with ASD have in imitation (Gallese, 2003a, 2006; Rogers, Hepburn, Stackhouse, & Wehner, 2003; Rogers & Pennington, 1991; Williams, Whiten, & Singh, 2004).

The relationship between the MNM and ASD is controversial (see Dinstein et al., 2010; Fan, Decety, Yang, Liu, & Cheng, 2010; Hamilton, Brindley, & Frith, 2007; Southgate & Hamilton, 2008). However, it must be added that critics of the relationship between ASD and the MNM are not always fully consistent. For example, Dinstein, Hasson, Rubin, and Heeger (2007) and Dinstein and colleagues (2010) first concluded that mirror neurons likely do not exist in the human brain, but later concluded that individuals with ASD have normal mirror neurons showing repetition suppression (Dinstein et al., 2010).

Children with ASD regularly show motor coordination problems that might be associated with cerebellar disfunctions (Mostofky, Reiss, Lockhart, & Denckla, 1998). Unlike typically developing children, children with autism use motor strategies basically relying on feedback information rather than on feedforward modes of control. Such motor disturbance prevents children with ASD from adopting anticipatory postural adjustments (Schmitz, Martineau, Barthélemy, & Assaiante, 2003). The theoretical relevance of these findings was clarified by a series of experiments documenting that children with ASD fail to activate a specific action chain from its very outset, thus being deprived of an internal copy of the whole action before the execution thereof. An electromyographic experiment (Cattaneo et al., 2008) has documented that high-functioning children with ASD are unable to organize their own motor acts in the intentional motor chains shown by typically developing children. Participants' mouth-opening mylohyoid muscle (MH) was recorded while they executed and observed two actions: grasping a strawberry to eat it and grasping an object to place it into a container. Results showed that during the execution and observation conditions, a sharp increase of MH was recorded in typically developed (TD) children, starting well before the food was grasped. No increase of MH activity was present during the execution and observation of the placing action. This means that one of the muscles responsible for the action final goal (opening the mouth to eat a piece of food) is already activated during the initial phases of the action. The motor system anticipates the motor consequences of the action final goal (to eat), thus directly mapping the action intention, both when the action is executed and observed when done by others. In contrast, high-functioning children with ASD showed a much later activation of the MH muscle during eating action execution and no activation at all during eating action observation.

The results of Cattaneo and colleagues (2008) reveal that children with ASD are impaired in smoothly chaining sequential motor acts within a reaching-to-grasp-to-eat intentional action. This impairment is mirrored in the action observation condition, and most likely accounts for their difficulty in directly understanding the intention of the observed action when executed by others. The presence of an atypical organization in action chaining has been further demonstrated by Boria and Rizzolatti (2009) in their investigation of the kinematics of intentional actions in children with ASD. In this study, children with autism and TD children were asked to execute two actions, each of which consisted of three motor acts: grasping a small object, lifting it, and placing it in a large or a small container. In both actions, the first motor act (grasping) was identical, while the last one varied for its difficulty (placing an object in a small container requires a more cautious oculomotor coordination than throwing it in a large receptacle). The result showed that in children with autism, unlike in TD children, the kinematics of the first motor act was not modulated by task difficulty. This finding suggests that children with autism have problems in chaining motor acts into a global action.

Carpenter (2006) stressed that children with autism may understand others' goals toward objects, but they relatively lack understanding of others' communicative intentions (including those relevant for highlighting what is to be copied in tests of imitation) and are less motivated to collaborate and share experiences with others. Boria and colleagues (2009) demonstrated that when presented with pictures showing hand–object interactions and asked *what* the individual was doing and *why*, children with ASD have no deficit in recognizing the kind *(what)* of goal-related action they observed. However, in contrast with TD children, autistic children have severe difficulties in understanding others' intentions *(why)* when they have to rely exclusively on motor cues. These results show that in the absence of a context suggesting the use of the object, children with ASD guess others' intention by using functional information derived from the object's semantics exemplifying its standard use.

Additional aspects of motor cognition, such as action simulation, mimicry, and imitation, have been explored in a number of studies, all confirming an impairment of its core mechanisms in children with ASD. Hobson and Hobson (2008) investigated two potentially dissociable aspects of imitation: copying goal-directed actions on the one hand and imitating the "style" with which a person demonstrates those actions on the other. Results showed that participants with and without autism were similar in their ability to copy relatively complex goal-directed actions but were significantly different in imitating the style with which simpler goal-directed actions were executed, especially when style was incidental to accomplishing the goal. In line with their theoretical position (see Hobson, 1989, 1993, 2002; Hobson & Lee, 1999), the authors explained the failure of children with ASD in incorporating aspects of the style into their own repertoire in light of their specifically weak propensity to identify with others. Several authors have suggested that the imitation impairment in autism would result from impaired self–other representation or difficulties in detecting commonality in body movements between self and other (Hobson & Meyer, 2006; Meltzoff & Gopnik, 1993; Rogers & Bennetto, 2000; Rogers & Pennington, 1991).

Several studies using different techniques suggest that individuals with ASD might be suffering an action simulation deficit induced by a dysfunction of their MNM. Théoret and colleagues (2005) using TMS demonstrated that in participants with ASD observation of hand movement in the egocentric view failed to properly activate motor structures of the brain, while they were normally activated by the observation in an allocentric view. The authors argue that the difference between toward–away conditions in individuals with ASD may be explained by a self-consciousness deficit resulting in faulty self–other representation. EEG studies showed that individuals with ASD, compared with healthy controls, did not show mu frequency attenuation over the sensorimotor cortex during action observation, a sign of MNM activation (Oberman et al., 2005; Oberman & Ramachandran, 2007; Martineau, Cochin, Magné, & Barthélémy, 2008). Bernier, Dawson, Webb, and Murias (2007) demonstrated imitative deficits in individuals with ASD and a positive correlation between the severity of such deficits and the reduced attenuation of mu rhythm over the motor cortex during action observation, thus suggesting a relationship between imitation deficits and a malfunctioning MNM in individuals with ASD.

However, it has been shown that mu attenuation is sensitive to the degree of familiarity between agent and observer: When a sibling or someone related to the individual with ASD performed the observed action, mu attenuation could be detected (Oberman, Ramachandran, & Pineda, 2008). In fact, as pointed out by Oberman and colleagues (2008), children with ASD display improved communication skills, increased rate of physical contact and eye contact, as well as improved social interaction skills when they interact with familiar as opposed to unfamiliar individuals. This suggests that the MNM is not necessarily absent in individuals with ASD, and that its functionality is somehow modulated by the possibility for the observer to identify with the agent. Such findings point to an emotional gating of the MNM still to be thoroughly explored in both TD individuals and those with ASD.

Further evidence on the relationship between impaired motor cognition and ASD comes from the neuroimaging study by Dapretto and collaborators (2006). The results showed that activity in a premotor MNM region (pars opercularis) was diminished or absent for participants with autism during observation and imitation of the facial expression of basic emotions. The more that activation in the pars opercularis was reduced, the more severe the symptoms of children with ASD. Williams and colleagues (2006) found a diminished activation of MNM activity in individuals with autism during the imitation of finger movements. Finally, a magnetoencephalography study conducted by Nishitani, Avikainen, and Hari (2004) revealed the presence of an abnormal imitation-related cortical activation sequence in patients with Asperger syndrome. The authors proposed that the delay in the temporal progression of activation in MNM areas suggests a deficit of connectivity between these areas.

All of these findings, although far from conclusive, strongly point to a relationship between impaired motor cognition and several aspects characterizing social cognition in individuals with ASD. They also suggest that a possible successful therapeutic strategy could capitalize upon fostering active interactions by means of dance and reciprocal imitation. Several reports provide preliminary evidence of a beneficial effect of imitation-based interventions in children with ASD (Escalona, Field, Nadel, & Lundy, 2002; Field, Sanders, & Nadel, 2001; Ingersoll & Gergans, 2007; Ingersoll, Lewis, & Kroman 2007; Ingersoll & Schreibman, 2006).

Conclusion

In the present chapter, we challenge the traditional classic cognitive view of intersubjectivity and social cognition by positing that the capacity to understand others' basic actions and motor intentions—both from a phylogenetic and an ontogenetic point of view—relies on a basic functional mechanism, which exploits the intrinsic functional organization of primates' motor system in terms of goal-directed motor acts. We propose that goal detection, action anticipation, the hierarchical representation of action with respect to a distal goal, and the possibility of detecting motor intentions in the behavior of others might be enabled in the first place by the MNM. All of these abilities qualify as motor cognition. We hypothesize that the correct development of motor cognition is required to scaffold more cognitively sophisticated social-mental abilities, and that pathological neural development causing an impaired and defective motor cognition might be the basis of several aspects of social cognition in individuals with ASD.

Acknowledgments

This work was supported by MIUR (Ministero Italiano dell'Università e della Ricerca) and by EU grants ROSSI and TESIS.

References

Aglioti, S. M., Cesari, P., Romani, M., & Urgesi, C. (2008). Action anticipation and motor resonance in elite basketball players. *Nature Neuroscience, 11*(9), 109–116.

Alexander, G. E., & Crutcher, M. D. (1990). Neural representations of the target (goal) of visually guided arm movements in three motor areas of the monkey. *Journal of Neurophysiology, 64,* 164–178.

Arnott, S. R., Singhal, A., & Goodale, M. A. (2009). An investigation of auditory contagious yawning. *Cognitive, Affective and Behavioral Neuroscience, 9*(3), 335–342.

Aziz-Zadeh, L., Wilson, S. M., Rizzolatti, G., & Iacoboni, M. (2006). Congruent embodied representations for visually presented actions and linguistic phrases describing actions. *Current Biology, 16,* 1818–1823.

Baird, J. A., & Baldwin, D. A. (2001). Making sense of human behavior: Action parsing and intentional inferences. In B. F. Malle, L. J. Moses, & D. A. Baldwin (Eds.), *Intentions and intentionality* (pp. 193–206). Cambridge, MA: MIT Press.

Baldwin, D. A., Baird, J. A, Saylor, M. M., & Clark, M. A. (2001). Infants parse dynamic action. *Child Development, 72,* 708–717.

Bard, K. A. (2007). Neonatal imitation in chimpanzees (Pan troglodytes) tested with two paradigms. *Animal Cognition, 10*(2),233–242.

Baron-Cohen, S. (1995). *Mindblindness.* Cambridge, MA: MIT Press.

Baron-Cohen, S., Leslie, A. M., & Frith, U. (1985). Does the autistic child have a "theory of mind"? *Cognition, 21,* 37–46.

Bekkering, H., Wohlschläger, A., & Gattis, M. (2000). Imitation of gestures in children is goal-directed. *Quarterly Journal of Experimental Psychology, 53A,* 153–164.

Bernier, R., Dawson, G., Webb, S., & Murias, M. (2007). EEG mu rhythm and imitation impairments in individuals with autism spectrum disorder. *Brain and Cognition, 64*(3), 228–237.

Bonini, L., Rozzi, S., Serventi, F. U., Simone, L., Ferrari, P. F., & Fogassi, L. (2010). Ventral premotor and inferior parietal cortices make distinct contribution to action organization and intention understanding. *Cerebral Cortex, 20*(6),1372–1385.

Boria, S., Fabbri-Destro, M., Cattaneo, L., Sparaci, L., Sinigaglia, C., Santelli, E., et al. (2009). Intention understanding in autism. *PLoS ONE, 4*(5), 5596.

Brass, M., Schmitt, R. M., Spengler, S., & Gergely, G. (2007). Investigating action understanding: Inferential processes versus action simulation. *Current Biology, 17*, 2117–2121.

Braten, S. (1988). Dialogic mind: The infant and the adult in protoconversation. In M. Carvallo (Ed.), *Nature, cognition and system* (Vol. 1, pp. 187–205). Dordrecht, The Netherlands: Kluwer Academic.

Braten, S. (1992). The virtual other in infants' minds and social feelings. In H. Wold (Ed.), *The dialogical alternative* (pp. 77–97). Oslo, Norway: Scandinavian University Press.

Braten, S. (2007). *On being moved: From mirror neurons to empathy.* Amsterdam: John Benjamins.

Brock, J., Brown, C. C., Boucher, J., & Rippon, G. (2002). The temporal binding deficit hypothesis of autism. *Development and Psychopathology, 14*(2), 209–224.

Buccino, G., Binkofski, F., Fink, G. R., Fadiga, L., Fogassi, L., Gallese, V., et al. (2001). Action observation activates premotor and parietal areas in a somatotopic manner: An fMRI study. *European Journal of Neuroscience, 13*, 400–404.

Buccino, G., Lui, F., Canessa, N., Patteri, I., Lagravinese, G., Benuzzi, F., et al. (2004). Neural circuits involved in the recognition of actions performed by nonconspecifics: An fMRI study. *Journal of Cognitive Neuroscience, 16*, 114–126.

Buccino, G., Vogt, S., Ritzl, A., Fink, G. R., Zilles, K., Freund, H.-J., et al. (2004). Neural circuits underlying imitation learning of hand actions: An event-related fMRI study. *Neuron, 42*, 323–334.

Buttelmann, D., Carpenter, M., Call, J., & Tomasello, M. (2007). Enculturated chimpanzees imitate rationally. *Developmental Science, 10*(4), 31–38.

Caggiano, V., Fogassi, L., Rizzolatti, G., Thier, P., & Casile, A. (2009). Mirror neurons differentially encode the peripersonal and extrapersonal space of monkeys. *Science, 324*, 403–406.

Call, J., Hare, B., Carpenter, M., & Tomasello, M. (2004). "Unwilling" versus "unable": Chimpanzees' understanding of human intentional action. *Developmental Science, 7*(4), 488–498.

Calvo-Merino, B., Glaser, D. E., Grèzes, J., Passingham, R. E., & Haggard, P. (2005). Action observation and acquired motor skills: An fMRI study with expert dancers. *Cerebral Cortex, 15*, 1243–1249.

Calvo-Merino, B., Grèzes, J., Glaser, D. E., Passingham, R. E., & Haggard, P. (2006). Seeing or doing?: Influence of visual and motor familiarity in action observation. *Current Biology, 16*(19), 1905–1910.

Carpenter, M. (2006). Instrumental, social, and shared goals and intentions in imitation. In S. J. Rogers & J. H. G. Williams (Eds.), *Imitation and the social mind: Autism and typical development* (pp. 48–70). New York: Guilford Press.

Carpenter, M., Call, J., & Tomasello, M. (2005). Twelve- and-18-months-old copy actions in terms of goals. *Developmental Science, 8*, F13–F20.

Casile, A., & Giese, M. A. (2006). Nonvisual motor training influences biological motion perception. *Current Biology. 16*, 69–74.

Castiello, U., Becchio, C., Zoia, S., Nelini, C., Sartori, L., Blason, L., et al. (2010). Wired to be social: The ontogeny of human interaction. *PLoS ONE, 5*(10), e13199.

Cattaneo, L., Caruana, F., Jezzini, A., & Rizzolatti, G. (2009). Representation of goal and movements without overt motor behavior in the human motor cortex: A transcranial magnetic stimulation study. *Journal of Neuroscience, 29*, 11134–11138.

Cattaneo, L., Fabbi-Destro, M., Boria, S., Pieraccini, C., Monti, A., Cossu, G., et al. (2008). Impairment of actions chains in autism and its possible role in intention understanding. *Proceedings of the National Academy of Sciences USA, 104,* 17825–17830.

Cattaneo, L., & Rizzolatti, G. (2009). The mirror neuron system. *Archives of Neurology 5,* 557–560.

Cattaneo, L., Sandrini, M., & Schwarzbach, J. (2010). State-dependent TMS reveals a hierarchical representation of observed acts in the temporal, parietal, and premotor cortices. *Cerebral Cortex, 20*(9), 2252–2258.

Chiron, C., Raynaud, C., Mazière, B., Zilbovicius, M., Laflamme, L., Masure, M. C., et al. (1992). Changes in regional cerebral blood flow during brain maturation in children and adolescents. *Journal of Nuclear Medicine, 33,* 696–703.

Courchesne, E., Carper, R., & Akshoomoff, N. (2003). Evidence of brain overgrowth in the first year of life in autism. *Journal of American Medical Association, 290,* 337–344.

Courchesne, E., & Pierce, K. (2005). Brain overgrowth in autism during a critical time in development: implications for frontal pyramidal neuron and interneuron development and connectivity. *International Journal of Developmental Neuroscience, 23,* 153–170.

Cross, E. S., Hamilton, A. F., & Grafton, S. T. (2006). Building a motor simulation de novo: Observation of dance by dancers. *NeuroImage, 31*(3), 1257–1267.

Crutcher, M. D., & Alexander, G. E. (1990). Movement-related neuronal activity selectively coding either direction or muscle pattern in three motor areas of the monkey. *Journal of Neurophysiology, 64,* 151–163.

Csibra, G., Birò, S., Koòs, O., & Gergely, G. (2003). One-year-old infants use teleological representations of actions productively. *Cognitive Science, 27,* 111–133.

Csibra, G., Gergely, G., Birò, S., Koòs, O., & Brockbank, M. (1999). Goal attribution without agency cues: The perception of "pure reason" in infancy. *Cognition, 72,* 237–267.

Dapretto, M., Davies, M. S., Pfeifer, J. H., Scott, A. A., Sigman, M., Bookheimer, S. Y., et al. (2006). Understanding emotions in others: Mirror neuron dysfunction in children with autism spectrum disorders. *Nature Neuroscience, 9,* 28–30.

Dawson, G., Munson, J., Webb, S. J., Nalty, T., Abbott, R., & Toth, K. (2007). Rate of head growth decelerates and symptoms worsen in the second year of life in autism. *Biological Psychiatry, 61,* 458–464.

Decety, J., Chaminade, T., Grèzes, J., & Meltzoff, A. N. (2002). A PET exploration of the neural mechanisms involved in reciprocal imitation. *NeuroImage, 15,* 265–272.

Del Giudice, M., Manera, V., & Keysers, C. (2009). Programmed to learn?: The ontogeny of mirror neurons. *Developmental Science, 12*(2), 350–363.

Dinstein, I., Hasson, U., Rubin, N., & Heeger, D. J. (2007). Brain areas selective for both observed and executed movements. *Journal of Neurophysiology, 98,* 1415–1427.

Dinstein, I., Thomas, C., Humphreys, K., Minshew, N., Behrmann, M., & Heeger, D. J. (2010). Normal movement selectivity in autism. *Neuron, 66*(3), 461–469.

Dushanova, J., & Donoghue, J. (2010). Neurons in primary motor cortex engaged during action observation. *European Journal of Neuroscience, 31*(2), 386–398.

Escalona, A., Field, T., Nadel, J., & Lundy, B. (2002). Brief report: Imitation effects on children with autism. *Journal of Autism and Developmental Disorders, 32,* 141–144.

Fabbri-Destro, M., Cattaneo, L., Boria, S., & Rizzolatti, G. (2009). Planning actions in autism. *Experimental Brain Research, 192*(3), 521–525.

Fadiga, L., Fogassi, L., Pavesi, G., & Rizzolatti, G. (1995). Motor facilitation during action observation: A magnetic stimulation study. *Journal of Neurophysiology, 73,* 2608–2611.

Falck-Ytter, T., Gredeback, G., & von Hofsten, C. (2006). Infants predict other people's action goals. *Nature Neuroscience, 9*(7), 878–879.

Fan, Y. T., Decety, J., Yang, C. Y., Liu, J. L., & Cheng, Y. (2010). Unbroken mirror neurons in autism spectrum disorders. *Journal of Child Psychology and Psychiatry, 51,* 981–988.

Ferrari, P. F., Coudé, G., Gallese, V., & Fogassi, L. (2008). Having access to others' mind through gaze: The role of ontogenetic and learning processes in gaze-following behavior of macaques. *Society for Neuroscience, 3*(3–4), 239–249.

Ferrari, P. F., Kohler, E., Fogassi, L., & Gallese, V. (2000). The ability to follow eye gaze and its emergence during development in macaque monkeys. *Proceedings of the National Academy of Sciences USA, 97*(25), 13997–14002.

Ferrari, P. F., Paukner, A., Ionica, C., & Suomi, S. J. (2009). Reciprocal face-to-face communication between rhesus macaque mothers and their newborn infants. *Current Biology, 19*(20), 1768–1772.

Ferrari, P. F., Visalberghi, E., Paukner, A., Fogassi, L., Ruggiero, A., & Suomi, S. J. (2006). Neonatal imitation in rhesus macaques. *PLoS Biology, 4*(9), e302.

Field, T., Woodson, R. W., Greenberg, R., & Cohen, C. (1982). DIscrimination and imitation of facial expressions by neonates. *Autism, 5*, 317–323.

Flombaum, J. L., & Santos, L. R. (2005). Rhesus monkeys attribute perceptions to others. *Current Biology, 15*, 447–452.

Fogassi, L., Ferrari, P. F., Gesierich, B., Rozzi, S., Chersi, F., & Rizzolatti, G. (2005). Parietal lobe: from action organization to intention understanding. *Science, 308*, 662–667.

Fontaine, R. (1984). Imitative skills between birth and six months. *Infant Behavior and Development, 7*, 323–333.

Gallese, V. (2000). The inner sense of action: Agency and motor representations. *Journal of Consciousness Studies, 7*, 23–40.

Gallese, V. (2003a). The manifold nature of interpersonal relations: The quest for a common mechanism. *Philosophical Transactions of the Royal Society: B. Biological Sciences, 358*, 517–528.

Gallese, V. (2003b). The roots of empathy: The shared manifold hypothesis and the neural basis of intersubjectivity. *Psychopathology, 36*(4), 171–180.

Gallese, V. (2006). Intentional attunement: A neurophysiological perspective on social cognition and its disruption in autism. *Brain Research, 1079*, 15–24.

Gallese, V. (2007). Before and below theory of mind: Embodied simulation and the neural correlates of social cognition. *Philosophical Transactions of the Royal Society: B. Biological Sciences, 362*, 659–669.

Gallese, V. (2009). Motor abstraction: A neuroscientific account of how action goals and intentions are mapped and understood. *Psychological Research, 73*(4), 486–498.

Gallese, V., Fadiga, L., Fogassi, L., & Rizzolatti, G. (1996). Action recognition in the premotor cortex. *Brain, 119*, 593–609.

Gallese, V., Fogassi, L., Fadiga, L., & Rizzolatti, G. (2002). Action representation and the inferior parietal lobule. In W. Prinz & B. Hommel (Eds.), *Attention and performance XIX* (pp. 247–266). Oxford, UK: Oxford University Press.

Gallese, V., Keysers, C., & Rizzolatti, G. (2004). A unifying view of the basis of social cognition. *Trends in Cognitive Science, 8*(9), 396–403.

Gallese, V., & Rochat, M. (2009). Motor cognition: The role of the motor system in the phylogeny and ontogeny of social cognition and its relevance for the understanding of autism. In P. D. Zelazo, M. Chandler, & E. Crone (Eds.), *Developmental social cognitive neuroscience* (pp. 13–42). New York: Psychology Press.

Gallese, V., Rochat, M., Cossu, G., & Sinigaglia, C. (2009). Motor cognition and its role in the phylogeny and ontogeny of action understanding. *Developmental Psychology, 45*(1), 103–113.

Gallese, V., & Umiltà, M. A. (2006). Cognitive continuity in primate social cognition. *Biological Theory, 1*(1), 25–30.

Gangitano, M., Mottaghy, F. M., & Pascual-Leone, A. (2001). Phase specific modulation of cortical motor output during movement observation. *NeuroReport, 12*, 1489–1492.

Gergely, G., Bekkering, H., & Kiràly, I. (2002). Rational imitation in preverbal infants. *Nature, 415*, 755.

Gergely, G., Nádasdy, Z., Csibra, G., & Bíró, S. (1995). Taking the intentional stance at 12 months of age. *Cognition, 56*(2), 165–193.

Grafton, S. T., Arbib, M. A., Fadiga, L., & Rizzolatti, G. (1996). Localization of grasp representations in humans by PET: 2. Observation compared with imagination. *Experimental Brain Research, 112*, 103–111.

Grèzes, J., Armony, J. L., Rowe, J., & Passingham, R. E. (2003). Activations related to "mirror" and "canonical" neurones in the human brain: An fMRI study. *NeuroImage 18*, 928–937.

Grèzes, J., Costes, N., Decety, J. (1998). Top-down effect of strategy on the perception of human biological motion: A PET investigation. *Cognitive Neuropsychology, 15*, 553–82.

Grèzes, J., Fonlupt, P., Bertenthal, B., Delon-Martin, C., Segebarth, C., & Decety, J. (2001). Does perception of biological motion rely on specific brain regions? *NeuroImage, 13*(5), 775–785.

Hadjikhani, N., Joseph, R. M., Snyder, J., & Tager-Flusberg, H. (2006). Anatomical differences in the mirror neuron system and social cognition network in autism. *Cerebral Cortex, 16*, 1276–1282.

Hamilton, A. F., Brindley, R. M., & Frith, U. (2007). Imitation and action understanding in autistic spectrum disorders: How valid is the hypothesis of a deficit in the mirror neuron system? *Neuropsychologia, 45*, 1859–1868.

Hare, B., Call, J., & Tomasello, M. (2001). Do chimpanzees know what conspecifics know? *Animal Behaviour, 61*(1), 139–151.

Haslinger, B., Erhard, P., Altenmuller, E., Schroeder, U., Boecker, H., & Ceballos-Baumann, A. O. (2006). Transmodal sensorimotor networks during action observation in professional pianists. *Journal of Cognitive Neuroscience, 17*, 282–293.

Heyes, C. (2010). Where do mirror neurons come from? *Neuroscience and Biobehavioral Reviews, 34*, 575–583.

Hobson, P., & Meyer, J. (2006). Imitation, identification, and the shaping of mind: Insights from autism. In S. J. Rogers & J. H. G. Williams (Eds.), *Imitation and the social mind: Autism and typical development* (pp. 198–224). New York: Guilford Press.

Hobson, R. P. (1989). Beyond cognition: A theory of autism. In G. Dawson (Ed.), *Autism: Nature, diagnosis and treatment* (pp. 22–48). New York: Guilford Press.

Hobson, R. P. (1993). *Autism and the development of mind.* Hove, UK: Erlbaum.

Hobson, R. P. (2002). *The cradle of thought.* London: Macmillan.

Hobson, R. P., & Hobson, J. A. (2008). Dissociable aspects of imitation: A study in autism. *Journal of Experimental Child Psychology, 101*(3), 170–185.

Hobson, R. P., & Lee, A. (1999). Imitation and identification in autism. *Journal of Child Psychology and Psychiatry, 40*(4), 649–59.

Horner, V., & Whiten, A. (2005). Causal knowledge and imitation/emulation switching in chimpanzees *(Pan troglodytes)* and children *(Homo sapiens). Animal Cognition, 8*, 164–181.

Iacoboni, M., Koski, L. M., Brass, M., Bekkering, H., Woods, R. P., Dubeau, M. C., et al. (2001). Reafferent copies of imitated actions in the right superior temporal cortex. *Proceedings of the National Academy of Sciences USA, 98*, 13995–13999.

Iacoboni, M., Molnar-Szakacs, I., Gallese, V., Buccino, G., Mazziotta, J., & Rizzolatti, G. (2005). Grasping the intentions of others with one's owns mirror neuron system. *PLoS Biology, 3*, 529–535.

Iacoboni, M., Woods, R. P., Brass, M., Bekkering, H., Mazziotta, J. C., & Rizzolatti, G. (1999). Cortical mechanisms of human imitation. *Science, 286*, 2526–2528.

Ingersoll, B., & Gergans, S. (2007). The effect of a parent-implemented imitation intervention on spontaneous imitation skills in young children with autism. *Research in Developmental Disabilities, 28*, 163–175.

Ingersoll, B., Lewis, E., & Kroman, E. (2007). Teaching the imitation and spontaneous use of descriptive gestures in young children with autism using a naturalistic behavioral intervention. *Journal of Autism and Developmental Disorders, 37*(8), 1446–1456.

Ingersoll, B., & Schreibman, L. (2006). Teaching reciprocal imitation skills to young children with autism using a naturalistic behavioral approach: Effects on language, pretend play, and joint attention. *Journal of Autism and Developmental Disorders, 36*, 487–505.

Just, M. A., Cherkassky, V. L., Keller, T. A., & Minshew, N. J. (2004). Cortical activation and synchronization during sentence comprehension in high-functioning autism: Evidence of underconnectivity. *Brain, 127*, 1811–1821.

Kakei, S., Hoffman, D. S., & Strick, P. L. (1999). Muscle and movement representations in the primary motor cortex. *Science, 285*, 2136–2139.

Kakei, S., Hoffman, D. S., & Strick, P. L. (2001). Direction of action is represented in the ventral premotor cortex. *Nature Neuroscience, 4*, 1020–1025.

Keysers, C., & Perrett, D. I. (2004). Demystifying social cognition: A Hebbian perspective. *Trends in Cognitive Science, 8*, 501–507.

Kohler, E., Keysers, C., Umiltà, M. A., Fogassi, L., Gallese, V., & Rizzolatti, G. (2002). Hearing sounds, understanding actions: Action representation in mirror neurons. *Science, 297*, 846–848.

Köhler, W. (1927). *The mentality of apes*. Vintage: New York.

Koski, L., Iacoboni, M., Dubeau, M. C., Woods, R. P., & Mazziotta, J. C. (2003). Modulation of cortical activity during different imitative behaviors. *Journal of Neurophysiology, 89*, 460–471.

Koski, L., Wohlschläger, A., Bekkering, H., Woods, R. P., & Dubeau, M. C. (2002). Modulation of motor and premotor activity during imitation of target-directed actions. *Cerebral Cortex, 12*, 847–855.

Kovács, A. M., Téglás, E., & Endress, A. D. (2010). The social sense: Susceptibility to others' beliefs in human infants and adults. *Science, 330*, 1830–1834.

Krachun, C., Carpenter, M., Call, J., Tomasello, M. (2009). A competitive nonverbal false belief task for children and apes. *Developmental Science, 12*(4), 521–535.

Kraskov, A., Dancause, N., Quallo, M. M., Shepherd, S., & Lemon, R. N. (2010). Corticospinal neurons in macaque ventral premotor cortex with mirror properties: A potential mechanism for action suppression? *Neuron, 64*, 922–930.

Legerstee, M. (1991). The role of person and object in eliciting early imitation. *Journal of Experimental Child Psychology, 51*(3), 423–433.

Legerstee, M. (2005). *Infants' sense of people: Precursors to a theory of mind*. Cambridge, UK: Cambridge University Press.

Legerstee, M. (2009). The role of dyadic communication in social cognitive development. *Advances in Child Development and Behavior, 37*, 1–53.

Lepage, J. F., & Théoret, H. (2007). The mirror neuron system: Grasping other's actions from birth? *Developmental Science, 10*(5), 513–529.

Maeda, F., Kleiner-Fisman, G., & Pascual-Leone, A. (2002). Motor facilitation while observing hand actions: Specificity of the effect and role of observer's orientation. *Journal of Neurophysiology, 87*(3), 1329–1335.

Manthey, S., Schubotz, R. I., & von Cramon, D. Y. (2003). Premotor cortex in observing erroneous action: An fMRI study. *Cognitive Brain Research, 15*, 296–307.

Martineau, J., Cochin, S., Magné, R., Barthélémy. C. (2008). Impaired cortical activation in autistic children: is the mirror neuron system involved? *International Journal of Psychophysiology, 68*(1), 35–40.

Meltzoff, A. N. (1995). Understanding the intentions of others: Re-enactment of intended acts by 18-month-old children. *Developmental Psychology, 31*, 838–850.

Meltzoff, A. N., & Brooks, R. (2001). "Like me" as a building block for understanding other minds: Bodily acts, attention, and intention. In B. F. Malle, L. J. Moses, & D. A. Baldwin (Eds.), *Intentions and intentionality: Foundations of social cognition* (pp. 171–191). Cambridge, MA: MIT Press.

Meltzoff, A. N., & Gopnik, A. (1993). The role of imitation in understanding persons and developing a theory of mind. In S. Baron-Cohen, H. Tager-Flusberg, & D. J. Cohen (Eds.), *Understanding other minds: Perspectives from autism* (pp. 335–366). London: Oxford University Press.

Meltzoff, A. N., & Moore, M. K. (1977). Imitation of facial and manual gestures by human neonates. *Science, 198*, 75–78.

Meltzoff, A. N., & Moore, M. K. (1992). Early infant imitation within a functional framework: The importance of person identity, movement, and development. *Infant Behavior and Development, 15*, 479–505.

Meltzoff, A. N., & Moore, M. K. (1998). Infant inter-subjectivity: Broadening the dialogue to include imitation, identity and intention. In S. Braten (Ed.), *Intersubjective communication and emotion in early ontogeny* (pp. 47–62). Paris: Cambridge University Press.

Minshew, N. J., & Williams, D. L. (2007). The new neurobiology of autism: cortex, connectivity, and neuronal organization. *Archives of Neurology, 64*(7), 945–950; erratum 64(10), 1464.

Mostofky, S. H., Reiss, A. L., Lockhart, P., & Denckla, M. B. (1998). Evaluation of cerebellar size in attention-deficit hyperactivity disorder. *Journal of Child Development, 17*, 83–99.

Mukamel, R., Ekstrom, A. D., Kaplan, J., Iacoboni, M., & Fried, I. (2010). Single-neuron responses in humans during execution and observation of actions. *Current Biology, 20*(8), 750–756.

Murata, A., Fadiga, L., Fogassi, L., Gallese, V., Raos, V., & Rizzolatti, G. (1997). Object representation in the ventral premotor cortex (area F5) of the monkey. *Journal of Neurophysiology, 78*(4), 2226–2230.

Myowa-Yamakoshi, M., & Takeshita, H. (2006). Do human fetuses anticipate self-directed actions?: A study by four-dimensional (4D) ultrasonography. *Infancy, 10*(3), 289–301.

Myowa-Yamakoshi, M., Tomonaga, M., Tanaka, M., & Matsuzawa, T. (2004). Imitation in neonatal chimpanzees *(Pan troglodytes)*. *Developmental Science, 7*(4), 437–442.

Nagy, E., Compagne, H., Orvos, H., Pal, A., Molnar, P., Janszky, I., et al. (2005). Index finger movement imitation by human neonates: Motivation, learning, and left-hand preference. *Pediatric Research, 58*(4), 749–753.

Neisser, U. (1988). Five kinds of self-knowledge. *Philosophical Psychology, 1*, 35–59.

Nishitani, N., Avikainen, S., & Hari, R. (2004). Abnormal imitation-related cortical activation sequences in Asperger's syndrome. *Annals of Neurology, 55*(4), 558–562.

Nishitani, N., & Hari, R. (2000). Temporal dynamics of cortical representation for action. *Proceedings of the National Academy of Sciences USA, 97*, 913–918.

Nishitani, N., & Hari, R. (2002). Viewing lip forms: Cortical dynamics. *Neuron, 36*, 1211–1220.

Oberman, L. M., Hubbard, E. M., McCleery, J. P., Altschuler, E. L., Ramachandran, V. S., & Pineda, J. A. (2005). EEG evidence for mirror neuron dysfunction in autism spectrum disorders. *Cognitive Brain Reseach, 24*, 190–198.

Oberman, L. M., & Ramachandran, V. S. (2007). The simulating social mind: The role of the mirror neuron system and simulation in the social and communicative deficits of autism spectrum disorders. *Psychological Bulletin, 133*, 310–327.

Oberman, L. M., Ramachandran, V. S., & Pineda, J. A. (2008). Modulation of mu suppression in children with autism spectrum disorders in response to familiar or unfamiliar stimuli: The mirror neuron hypothesis. *Neuropsychologia, 46*(5), 1558–1565.

Onishi, K. H., & Baillargeon, R. (2005). Do 15-month-old infants understand false beliefs? *Science, 308,* 255–258.

Palagi, E., Leone, A., Mancini, G., & Ferrari, P. F. (2009). Contagious yawning in gelada baboons as a possible expression of empathy. *Proceedings of the National Academy of Sciences USA, 17, 106*(46), 19262–19267.

Patuzzo, S., Fiaschi, A., & Manganotti, P. (2003). Modulation of motor cortex excitability in the left hemisphere during action observation: A single and paired-pulse transcranial magnetic stimulation study of self- and non-self action observation. *Neuropsychologia, 41,* 1272–1278.

Paukner, A., & Anderson, J. R. (2006). Video-induced yawning in stumptail macaques *(Macaca arctoides). Biology Letters, 2*(1), 36–38.

Paukner, A., Suomi, S. J., Visalberghi, E., & Ferrari, P. F. (2009). Capuchin monkeys display affiliation toward humans who imitate them. *Science, 325,* 880–883.

Perani, D., Fazio, F., Borghese, N. A., Tettamanti, M., Ferrari, S., Decety, J., et al. (2001). Different brain correlates for watching real and virtual hand actions. *NeuroImage, 14,* 749–758.

Povinelli, D. J. (2000). *Folk physics for apes: A chimpanzee's theory of how the world works.* Oxford, UK: Oxford University Press.

Povinelli, D. J., & Eddy, T. J. (1996). What young chimpanzees know about seeing. *Monographs of the Society for Research in Child Development, 61,* 1–152.

Premack, D., & Woodruff, G. (1978). Does the chimpanzee have a theory of mind? *Behavioral and Brain Sciences, 1,* 515–526.

Raos, V., Umiltà, M. A., Murata, A., Fogassi, L., & Gallese, V. (2006). Functional properties of grasping-related neurons in the ventral premotor area F5 of the macaque monkey. *Journal of Neurophysiology, 95*(2), 709–729.

Redcay, E., & Courchesne, E. (2005). When is the brain enlarged in autism?: A meta-analysis of all brain size reports. *Biological Psychiatry, 58,* 1–9.

Reddy, V. (2008). *How infants know minds.* Cambridge, MA: Harvard University Press.

Rizzolatti, G., Camarda, R., Fogassi M., Gentilucci M., Luppino G., & Matelli M. (1988). Functional organization of inferior area 6 in the macaque monkey: II. Area F5 and the control of distal movements. *Experimental Brain Research, 71,* 491–507.

Rizzolatti, G., & Craighero, L. (2004). The mirror-neuron system. *Annual Review of Neuroscience, 27,* 169–192.

Rizzolatti, G., Fadiga, L., Gallese, V., & Fogassi, L. (1996). Premotor cortex and the recognition of motor actions. *Cognitive Brain Research, 3*(2), 131–141.

Rizzolatti, G., Fogassi, L., & Gallese, V. (2000). Mirror neurons: Intentionality detectors? *International Journal of Psychology, 35,* 205.

Rizzolatti, G., Fogassi, L., & Gallese, V. (2001). Neurophysiological mechanisms underlying the understanding and imitation of action. *Nature Review of Neuroscience, 2,* 889–901.

Rizzolatti, G., & Gallese, V. (1997). From action to meaning. In J.-L. Petit (Ed.), *Les neurosciences et la philosophie de l'action* (pp. 217–229). Paris: Librairie Philosophique J. Vrin.

Rizzolatti, G., & Sinigaglia, C. (2010). The functional role of the parieto-frontal mirror circuit: Interpretations and misinterpretations. *Nature Review Neuroscience, 11,* 264–274.

Rochat, M. J., Caruana, F., Jezzini, A., Escola, L., Intskirveli, I., Grammont, F., et al. (2010). Responses of mirror neurons in area F5 to hand and tool grasping observation. *Experimental Brain Research, 204*(4), 605–616.

Rochat, M. J., Serra, E., Fadiga, L., & Gallese, V. (2008). The evolution of social cognition: Goal familiarity shapes monkeys' action understanding. *Current Biology, 18*(3), 227–232.

Rogers, S. J., & Bennetto, L. (2000). Intersubjectivity in autism: The roles of imitation and executive function. In A. M. Wetherby & B. M. Prizant (Eds.), *Autism spectrum disorders: A transactional developmental perspective* (pp. 79–107). Baltimore: Brookes.

Rogers, S. J., Hepburn, S. L., Stackhouse, T., & Wehner, E. (2003). Imitation performance in toddlers with autism and those with other developmental disorders. *Journal of Child Psychology and Psychiatry, 44*(5), 763–781.

Rogers, S. J., & Pennington, B. F. (1991). A theoretical approach to the deficits in infantile autism. *Development and Psychopathology, 3*, 137–162.

Santos, L. R., Nissen, A. G., & Ferrugia, J. A. (2006). Rhesus monkeys, *Macaca mulatta*, know what others can and cannot hear. *Animal Behavior, 71*, 1175–1181.

Schmitz, C., Martineau, J., Barthélemy, C., & Assaiante, C. (2003). Motor control and children with autism: Deficit of anticipatory function? *Neuroscience Letter, 348*, 17–20.

Shepherd, S. V., Klein, J. T., Deaner, R. O., &Platt, M. L. (2009). Mirroring of attention by neurons in macaque parietal cortex. *Proceedings of the National Academy of Sciences USA, 106*(23), 9489–9494.

Shimada, S., & Hiraki, K. (2006). Infant's brain responses to live and televised action. *NeuroImage, 32*, 930—939.

Sommerville, J. A., & Woodward, A. (2005). Pulling out the intentional structure of action: The relation between action processing and action production in infancy. *Cognition, 95*(1), 1–30.

Sommerville, J. A., Woodward, A., & Needham, A. (2005). Action experience alters 3-month-old perception of other's actions. *Cognition, 96*(1), 1–11.

Southgate, V., & Hamilton, A. F. (2008). Unbroken mirrors: Challenging a theory of autism. *Trends in Cognitive Science, 12*, 225–229.

Southgate, V., Johnson, M. H., & Csibra, G. (2008). Infants attribute goals even to biomechanically impossible actions. *Cognition, 107*(3), 1059–1069.

Southgate, V., Johnson, M. H., El Karoui, I., & Csibra, G. (2010). Motor system activation reveals infants' on-line prediction of others' goals. *Psychological Science, 21*(3), 355–359.

Stern, D. N. (1985). *The interpersonal world of the infant.* London: Karnac Books.

Stern, D. N. (2010). *Forms of vitality: Exploring dynamic experience in psychology, the arts, psychotherapy, and development.* Oxford, UK: Oxford University Press.

Subiaul, F., Cantlon, J. F., Holloway, R. L., & Terrace, H. S. (2004). Cognitive imitation in rhesus macaques. *Science, 305*, 407–410.

Théoret, H., Halligan, E., Kobayashi, M., Fregni, F., Tager-Flusberg, H., & Pascual-Leone, A. (2005). Impaired motor facilitation during action observation in individuals with autism spectrum disorder. *Current Biology, 15*(3), 84–85.

Tkach, D., Reimer, J., & Hatsopoulos, N. G. (2007). Congruent activity during action and action observation in motor cortex. *Journal of Neuroscience, 27*, 13241–13250.

Tomasello, M., & Call, J. (1997). *Primate cognition.* New York: Oxford University Press.

Tomasello, M., Carpenter, M., Call, J., Behne, T., & Moll, H. (2005). Understanding and sharing intentions: The origins of cultural cognition. *Behavioral and Brain Science, 28*, 675–691.

Tomasello, M., Davis-Dasilva, M., Camak, L., & Bard, K. (1987). Observational learning of tool-use by young chimpanzees. *Journal of Human Evolution, 2*, 175–183.

Trevarthen, C. (1979). Communication and cooperation in early infancy: A description of primary intersubjectivity. In M. Bullowa (Ed.), *Before speech: The beginning of interpersonal communication* (pp. 321–347). New York: Cambridge University Press.

Trevarthen, C. (1993). The self born in intersubjectivity: An infant communicating. In U. Neisser (Ed.), *The perceived self* (pp. 121–173). New York: Cambridge University Press.

Tronick E. (1989). Emotion and emotional communication in infants. *American Psychologist, 44*, 112–119.

Umiltà, M. A., Brochier, T., Spinks, R. L., & Lemon, R. N. (2007). Simultaneous recording of macaque premotor and primary motor cortex neuronal populations reveals different functional contributions to visuomotor grasp. *Journal of Neurophysiology, 98*(1), 488–501.

Umiltà, M. A., Escola, L., Intskirveli, I., Grammont, F., Rochat, M., Caruana, F., et al. (2008). How pliers become fingers in the monkey motor system. *Proceedings of the National Academy of Sciences USA, 10*, 2209–2213.

Umiltà, M. A., Kohler, E., Gallese, V., Fogassi, L., Fadiga, L., Keysers, C., et al. (2001). I know what you are doing: A neurophysiological study. *Neuron, 31*(1), 155–165.

van der Meer, A. L. H. (1997). Keeping the arm in the limelight: Advanced visual control of arm movements in neonates. *European Journal of Paediatric Neurology, 4*, 103–108.

van Elk, M., van Schieb, H. T., Hunnius, S., Vesperc, C., & Bekkering, H. (2008). You'll never crawl alone: Neurophysiological evidence for experience-dependent motor resonance in infancy. *NeuroImage, 43*(4), 808–814.

Visalberghi, E., & Tomasello, M. (1998). Primates causal understanding in the physical and psychological domains. *Behavioural Process, 42*, 189–203.

Vogt, S., Buccino, G., Wohlschläger, A. M., Canessa, N., Shah, N. J., Zilles, K., et al. (2007). Prefrontal involvement in imitation learning of hand actions: Effects of practice and expertise. *NeuroImage, 37*(4), 1371–1383.

von Hofsten, C. (1982). Eye–hand coordination in newborns. *Developmental Psychology, 18*, 450–461.

von Hofsten, C. (2007). Action in development. *Developmental Science, 10*(1), 54–60.

Williams, J. H., Waiter, G. D., Gilchrist, A., Perrett, D. I., Murray, A. D., & Whiten, A. (2006). Neural mechanisms of imitation and "mirror neuron" functioning in autistic spectrum disorder. *Neuropsychologia, 44*, 610–621.

Williams, J. H., Whiten, A., & Singh, T. (2004). A systematic review of action imitation in autistic spectrum disorder. *Journal of Autism and Developmental Disorders, 34*(3), 285–299.

Williams, J. H., Whiten, A., Suddendorf, T., & Perrett, D. I. (2001). Imitation, mirror neurons and autism. *Neuroscience and Biobehavioral Review, 25*, 287–295.

Wimmer, H., & Perner, J. (1983). Beliefs about beliefs: Representation and constraining function of wrong beliefs in young children's understanding of deception. *Cognition, 13*, 103–128.

Woodward, A. L. (1998). Infants selectively encode the goal object of an actor's reach. *Cognition, 69*, 1–34.

Zoia, S., Blason, L., D'Ottavio, G., Bulgheroni, M., Pezzetta, E., Scabar, A., et al. (2007). Evidence of early development of action planning in the human foetus: A kinematic study. *Experimental Brain Research, 176*, 217–226.

CHAPTER 3

When the Problem of Intersubjectivity Becomes the Solution

Shaun Gallagher

To philosophers it may sound strange to say that there is no problem of other minds, just as it would to psychologists to say that there is no problem of social cognition. People have been thinking about these problems for a long time. Yet in a certain way we should say that there is no problem, if we take the problem to be defined in the standard way, as follows: We have a problem understanding others because we lack any access to the other person's mental states. Since we cannot directly perceive the other's thoughts, feelings, or intentions, we need some extraperceptual cognitive process that will allow us to infer what they are.

I don't think this is the problem, or at least not the central problem of social cognition. And recognizing that this is not the problem becomes part of the solution to the extent that it motivates us to think differently about the phenomenon of intersubjectivity. To be precise, I think the *real problem* (let's call it that) is that standard approaches think inaccessibility *is* the problem. If, in fact, we do have access to the other person's mind, then this problem dissipates. So the solution to the real problem is to show that there is no problem defined in terms of access to the other's mind.

I realize that this will be a hard sell, precisely because people have been trying to solve the problem of social cognition, understood as inaccessibility, for a long time. I first briefly review how things are understood in the standard approaches. I then point out a number of problems in these standard approaches. Finally, I offer an alternative account that avoids these problems.

Standard Theory-of-Mind Solutions to the Problem of Social Cognition

In psychology, in philosophy-of-mind, and more recently in the neurosciences, studies of how one person understands and interrelates with another person, so-called "theory of mind" (ToM), have been dominated by two main approaches: theory theory (TT) and simulation theory (ST). The major tenets of TT are based on scientific experiments showing that children develop an understanding of other minds at about the age of 4. One version of TT claims that this understanding is based on an innately specified, domain-specific mechanism designed for "reading" other minds (e.g., Baron-Cohen, 1995; Leslie, 1991). An alternative version claims that children attain this ability through a course of development in which they test and learn from the social environment (e.g., Gopnik & Meltzoff, 1997). Common to both versions is the idea that children attain their understanding of other minds through the use of folk or commonsense psychology, which they use to make theoretical inferences about certain entities to which they have no access, namely, the mental states of other people. Taking this theoretical stance involves postulating the existence of mental states in others and using such postulations to explain and predict another person's behavior. When we make such inferences and attribute specific mental states to others, we are said to be *mentalizing* or *mindreading.*

The second approach, ST, argues that rather than theorizing or making inferences about the other person's mind, we use our own mental experience as an internal model for the other mind (e.g., Gordon, 1986, 1995; Heal, 1986, 1998). To understand the other person, I simulate the thoughts or feelings that I would experience if I were in the situation of the other, exploiting my own motivational and emotional resources. I imagine what must be going on in the other person's mind; or I create in my own mind pretend beliefs, desires, or strategies that I use to understand the other's behavior. My source for these simulations is not a theory that I have. Rather, I have a real model of the mind at my immediate disposal; that is, I have *my own mind*, and I can use it to generate and run simulations. I simply run through the sequence or pattern of behavior or the decision-making process that I would engage in if I were faced with the situation in question. I do it "offline," however. That is, my imaginary rehearsal does not lead to actualizing the behavior on my part. Finally, I attribute this pattern to the other person, who is actually in that situation. According to some versions of ST, this process may remain nonconscious, with only an awareness of the resulting understanding or prediction. The nonconscious process itself, however, is structured as an internal, representational simulation (Gordon, 1986). On other versions of ST, the simulation is explicit or conscious, perhaps even a matter of introspection. This was Goldman's original "introspectionist ST" view (1995, p. 216), for example, and is now relegated to what he calls high-level mindreading (Goldman, 2006, p. 245ff).[1]

Despite the clear distinction between the TT and ST accounts of mindreading, and the fact that for the last 25 years the dominant debate in the field of social cognition has been between proponents of TT and the proponents of ST, any neat division is an oversimplification, not only because of the existence of several hybrid theories that combine TT and ST without contradiction but also because TT and ST share some basic suppositions. The first one is precisely the problem just mentioned.

1. The problem of social cognition is due to the lack of access that we have to the other person's mental states. Since we cannot directly perceive the other's thoughts, feelings, or intentions, we need some extraperceptual cognitive process (mindreading or mentalizing) that will allow us to infer or simulate what they are.[2]

2. Our normal everyday stance toward other people is a third-person, observational stance. On the basis of what we observe, we use mindreading to
   explain or *predict* their behaviors.[3]
3. These mentalizing processes constitute our primary and pervasive way of
   understanding others.

The third supposition is a strong one and goes against a possible pluralism that
contends that when it comes to understanding others we may have many different
resources at our disposal, and we may do it differently in different situations. In
the pluralist view, mindreading would be one specialized ability that allows us to
attribute mental states to others in specific circumstances where we need to explain
their behavior, for example, when we are puzzled by their behavior or when we try
to justify (give reasons for) their behavior. Theory theorists and simulation theorists
alike support the third supposition and deny the idea that mindreading is a specialized capacity. Here are sample claims:

> Mind-reading and the capacity to negotiate the social world are not the same thing,
> but the former seems to be necessary for the latter. . . . our basic grip on the social
> world depends on our being able to see our fellows as motivated by beliefs and
> desires we sometimes share and sometimes do not. (Currie & Sterelny, 2000, p. 145)

> The strongest form of ST would say that all cases of (third-person) mentalization
> employ simulation. A moderate version would say, for example, that simulation is
> the *default* method of mentalization . . . I am attracted to the moderate version . . .
> Simulation is the primitive, root form of interpersonal mentalization. (Goldman,
> 2002, pp. 7–8).[4]

The Science behind ToM

According to supposition 2, TT and ST assume that our relations with others are
characterized by an observational stance. The best way to see what this means
(besides looking at the various statements made in characterizing mindreading by
theory theorists and simulation theorists) is to look at some of the science that is cited
in support of these views. The observational stance is very clearly seen in almost all
standard false-belief tests. For example, a subject (often a child) is asked to observe
the behavior of two other children (or sometimes puppets). Sally puts a marble in a
basket and leaves the room; another child, Anne, moves the marble from the basket
to a box. Sally comes back in the room, and the subject is asked where Sally will look
for the marble. Four-year-olds tend to answer correctly that Sally will look in the basket; 3-year-olds tend to answer incorrectly that Sally will look in the box, where the
marble actually is. This is taken as evidence that the 3-year-old subjects (and some
autistic subjects) are unable to appreciate that having a different perspective could
lead to Sally's false belief; 4-year-old children apparently have developed a theory of
mind that can deal with false beliefs (Leslie & Frith, 1988; Wimmer & Perner, 1983).
   Notice that such experiments are designed so that the subject is simply a third-
person observer of events; the subject never participates in the events or interacts

with Sally or Anne. The child is in an observational relation to the person (or puppet) being asked about; that is, the child is observing, but not interacting with, that person. Although it is never noted by those who appeal to these experiments as supporting of ToM accounts, the child is also in a *second-person* relation to the experimenter to whom the child is responding when asked the questions. The child is *interacting* with the experimenter but not with the third person (or puppet). The test is not about that interaction, however. So one question is whether false-belief experiments are actually telling us anything about our everyday interactions with others rather than about a set of more specialized observational mindreading abilities we might have.

Theory theorists have traditionally appealed to the standard false-belief experiments. They take such experiments to demonstrate that at about age 4 the nonautistic child comes to have a theory of mind, that is, starts to employ folk psychology at a level sophisticated enough to be able to recognize that the other person has a false belief. Children younger than 4 years, on average, and autistic children, lack this ability. This view has been challenged by experiments showing that much younger children, indeed about age 13–15 months, are capable of passing false-belief tests (Onishi & Baillargeon, 2005; Surian, Caldi, & Sperber, 2007). One can look at this evidence in various ways. On the one hand, Carruthers (2009), for example, takes it to be evidence that children much younger than first thought have ToM abilities. The experiments suggest to him that 13-month-olds already have meta-representational abilities, so he sees this as completely consistent with TT. On the other hand, others doubt that infants of that age have a concept of belief, and they give an ST interpretation of the experiments (e.g., Herschbach, 2008). Others, however, are not so quick to see them as supporting either of the ToM interpretations. Perner and Ruffman (2005), for example, suggest that the infants' performance can be explained by a disappointment of expected contextualized behavior—a violation of *behavior rules* already known by the infants (e.g., "People look for objects where they last saw them") gained via statistical learning abilities.

Baillargeon, Scott, and He (2010) suggest that the behavioral rules explanation fails because of the large number of rules that would be needed in a variety of situations involving false beliefs. It is not clear whether they mean a variety of different belief contents, where the false belief may be about identity, properties, number, and so on, or a variety of belief-determining situations where agents are guided by knowledge gained in different ways. For example, infants are not surprised that agents, who do not know that the toy has been shifted from A to B, look in A; but they are surprised if the agent looks in A after being informed by word or gesture that the toy is in B (Song, Onishi, Baillargeon, & Fisher, 2008) or are informed not by vision but some other modality or action of their own (Träuble, Marinovič, & Pauen, 2010). It is not clear, however, why infants should not be able to apply perception and action principles to different features of the objects involved or to apply them flexibly to different sensory or motor modalities that inform the agent, especially if they spend their entire first year interacting with others and begin to engage in joint attention and joint actions starting about 9–12 months. As Träuble and colleagues (2010) suggest, the behavior rules view cannot yet be ruled out, since the rule may be formulated more flexibly or more generally: "Infants might well use a rule whereupon people search for objects according to their perceptual access in a more general sense, including various forms like visual, auditory, and tactile access" (pp. 442–443). It is also possible to model the infants' performance on enactive perception without appealing explicitly to behavioral rules (see later discussion). Although this remains an open question, the performance of the infants clearly starts to push against the first supposition—that the mind of the other is hidden away.

The appeal to ST in this regard presents another possibility if we consider what Goldman calls low-level simulation, a form of simulation that is fast and automatic and does not require the use of conscious imagination or introspection. This view of simulation has received important support from the neuroscience of mirror neurons (MNs).

MNs are neurons that are activated in two conditions: (1) when we engage in intentional actions and (2) when we see others engage in intentional actions. MNs in the premotor cortex, in Broca's area, and in the parietal cortex of the human brain, for example, are activated both when the subject engages in specific instrumental actions and when the subject observes someone else engage in those actions (Rizzolatti, Fogassi, & Gallese, 2001). In effect, one's motor system reverberates or resonates in a way that seems to mimic our own action when we encounter others acting. For neural ST, these subpersonal processes themselves just are a simulation of the other's intentions. Gallese summarizes this position clearly in his claim that activation of MNs involves "automatic, implicit, and nonreflexive simulation mechanisms" (Gallese, 2005, p. 117; also see Gallese, 2007; Jeannerod & Pacherie, 2004). Goldman (2006) distinguishes between simulation as a high-level (explicit) mindreading and simulation as a low-level (implicit) mindreading where the latter is "simple, primitive, automatic, and largely below the level of consciousness" (p. 113), and the prototype for which is "the mirroring type of simulation process" (p. 147). That MN activation is a simulation not only of the goal of the observed action but of the intention of the acting individual, and therefore a form of mindreading, is suggested by research that shows MNs discriminate identical movements according to the intentional action and contexts in which these movements are embedded (Fogassi et al., 2005; Iacoboni et al., 2005; Kaplan & Iacoboni, 2006). Neural simulation has also been extended as an explanation of how we grasp emotions and pain in others (Avenanti & Aglioti, 2006; Gallese, Eagle, & Migone, 2007; Minio-Paluello, Avenanti, & Aglioti 2006). Evidence of dysfunction in "simulator neurons" has suggested an explanation for the social problems found in autism (Oberman & Ramachandran, 2007).

Seven Problems for the ToM Solutions

There are a number of problems with the ToM solutions. Some of them are logical-conceptual, others are phenomenological, and still others concern the interpretation of the science. I'll start with one of the logical problems.

The Starting Problem

The starting problem is a version of what cognitive scientists call the frame problem. For TT and ST it comes at the very beginning of the mindreading process. Neither theory has a good explanation of how the process gets off the ground—or more precisely what ground we stand on as we engage in the process.

The theory theorist will claim that we simply apply our folk psychological theory by appealing to some specific rule that will explain the other person's behavior. But that seems to assume that we already know what the appropriate rule is for the specific situation. For example, as I drive down the road, I see my neighbor raise his hand as I approach. I somehow interpret this as a wave of hello from someone I know. My neighbor *wants* to say hello. I wave back. In another case, however, as I drive down the road, I see a police officer hold up her hand. I know that if I simply waved back I would likely get a traffic ticket, since it is quite apparent that she *wants* me to stop and *believes* that waving her hand will signal that I should stop. How do I know which rule to apply to interpret this signal? After all, the rules of folk psychology are rather abstract: They supposedly apply to human behavior in general and, in part, that is what makes them theoretical. The application of such rules may be especially troublesome in ambiguous situations, for example, when my neighbor is the police officer. Does she want to say hello, or does she want me to stop? The issue is this: Faced with a particular situation, how do we know which rule to apply?

The situation is no easier for the simulationist. One can see this, for example, in Alvin Goldman's description of the very first step involved in running a simulation routine: "First, the attributor creates in herself pretend states intended to match those of the target. In other words, the attributor attempts to put herself in the target's 'mental shoes'" (Goldman, 2005, p. 80). The first step seems tricky. How do I know which pretend state (belief or desire) matches what the other person has in mind? Indeed, isn't this what simulation is supposed to explain? If I already knew what state matched the target, then the problem, as defined by ST, would already be solved.

Starting the process seems to be a problem for both TT and ST. To address this, some theorists have pursued a hybrid version of theory of mind, that is, a combination of TT and ST. For example, I am in a position to take the first step in the simulation process precisely because I already have a folk psychology that allows me to make a supposition about what the other person is thinking. Hybrid theorists thus suggest that folk psychology provides not a sense of what is going on with the other person, but some general rules about how people think and behave in certain situations, and that this is what the simulationist can use to generate the pretend mental states needed for the simulation process (e.g., Currie & Ravenscroft, 2002). Theory helps me to get my simulation off the ground. But how does theory get off the ground in any particular case? Perhaps it can go the other way. I know what rule of folk psychology to apply because I begin by simulating the other person's situation. But then, again, how do I start the simulation? It seems to me that these hybrid approaches simply push the problem back a step; one ends up in a circle of starting problems, which turns from abstract rules to unsure suppositions and then returns to abstract rules. What seems to be lacking is an account of how we get the right kind of particularistic or contextual knowledge that would be the ground for getting things off the ground.

To be clear, I am not suggesting that theorists of TT and ST would deny that both folk psychology and simulation depend on what I call, following terminology suggested by Bruner and Kalmar (1998), a *massive hermeneutical background* (see Gallagher, 2011). But neither theory says much about it; they don't explain how we get this background, what sort of thing it is, or how precisely it comes into play when we attempt to use folk psychology or simulation.

The Diversity Problem

Diversity is a problem that pertains to various versions of ST. It is reflected in the starting problem for simulation, but is directly tied to the supposed nature of simulation. Simulation depends specifically on one's own first-person experience as the basis for what goes into the simulation. Thus, one possible response to the starting problem for simulation is that we depend on our own prior experience to have a sense of what the other person may be thinking in a particular situation. We start with our own experience and project some tentative empathic conception of what must be going on in the other's mind. Even at the level of neural simulation there is evidence that our MNs activate only if we have previously done the sort of action that we see being done by the other (see, e.g., Sommerville, Woodward, & Needham, 2005). The question is, when we project ourselves imaginatively into the perspective of the other, when we put ourselves in his or her shoes, do we really attain an understanding of the other, or are we merely reiterating ourselves? Goldman describes simulation in the following way: "In all cases, observing what other people do or feel is transformed into an inner representation of what we would do or feel in a similar, endogenously produced, situation" (Goldman, 2008, p. 27). But how does knowing what we would do help us know what someone else would do? Indeed, many times we are in a situation where we see what someone is doing, and know that we would do it differently or perhaps not do it at all.

Given the vast variety of actions, beliefs, experiences, and feelings that people experience, it seems presumptuous to suggest that one's own limited first-person experience is capable of capturing that diversity. If I project the results of my own simulation onto the other, I understand only myself in that other situation, but I don't necessarily understand the other. The issue, then, is whether a process of simulation will ever allow for a true understanding of the *other* or merely let me attain an understanding of myself in a different situation.

The Developmental Problem

An objection mentioned by Scheler (1954) can be raised against both TT and the more explicit versions of ST. The kind of inferential or simulation processes found in explicit versions of TT and ST are too cognitively complex to account for the infant's ability to understand the intentions of others. As demonstrated later, there is a large amount of evidence to support the idea that young infants are able to grasp intentions in others. For now we can mention Onishi and Baillargeon's (2005) false-belief experiment with young infants. Here the debate on how to interpret the results raises the developmental problem. It is almost standard to simply assume a ToM framework for interpreting the results of this experiment. Are infants actually capable of meta-representational processes that would involve having a conception of belief, as Carruthers suggests? Or is it possible for them to run a mentalistic simulation routine? On this score, perhaps a neural ST would have an advantage. Assuming that MNs are already functioning in young infants, then simulation would be automatic and they would be capable of something like an intuitive mindreading. But this interpretation motivates a number of other questions that are not fully resolved. Does the MN system register mental states? That is, can we say that neural simulation is a form of mindreading, or is it primarily a form of action recognition, which requires further cognitive processing to reach the level of mindreading? If it is the latter, then the neural simulation account indicates nothing about the concept of false belief. And in any case, there are questions about how MNs would function if the infants did not first have an experience of what they saw. We mentioned this in connection with the diversity problem, but it actually sends us back to a version of the starting problem. A strict version of this would say that the infants cannot understand anyone's actions until they do such actions themselves and tune up their MNs. In any event, there are a number of unanswered questions here.

The Simple Phenomenological Objection

This is an objection directed only at versions of TT and ST that maintain that theoretical inference or simulation is (1) explicit or conscious and (2) pervasive and characteristic of our everyday understandings of others. Goldman's original position of introspectionist ST may be a good example of this, if we combine it with his contention that simulation is the default mechanism for social cognition. Since the claim is that these processes are both explicit and pervasive, then we should have some awareness of the different steps that we go through as we simulate the other's mental states. But there is no phenomenological evidence for this. When I interact with or come to understand another person, there is no experiential evidence that I use such conscious (imaginative, introspective) simulation routines or, as TT might suggest, theoretical inferences. That is, when we consult our own common experience of how we understand others, we don't find such processes. Of course, this is not to say that we never use simulations, but that in itself is telling. It may be the case that confronted with some strange or unaccountable behavior I do try to understand the other person by running a simulation routine (or by appealing to theory). I think this is the rare case, however. Moreover, it tends to stand out in its rarity. I can easily become aware that I am, in fact, taking this approach, and it is all the more apparent when I do this, simply because it tends to be the exception. Indeed, it may be the unusual practice motivated when something goes wrong with our normal everyday processes. But this tells against the idea that I employ simulation or theory in the usual everyday circumstance. Most of our encounters are not third-person puzzles solved by first-person introspective procedures or third-person inferences.

A possible defense of TT and ST is to make it less explicit and more implicit. Perhaps explicit simulation can be made so habitual that it becomes implicit, so that we do it without being aware that we do it, in the same way that we drive a car without being explicitly aware of all of our driving habits, or in the same way that an expert may employ cognitive strategies that become so habitual that the expert is no longer aware of how she does what she does. The simple phenomenological objection would be that if such implicit processes stay at the personal level, they would remain accessible to conscious reflection, or at least they would become apparent, as unworkable habits, in problematic situations when our habitual strategies break down. We can become aware of a habit that we are not usually aware of in such circumstances. This simply does not seem to be the case for the sort of processes described by TT or ST. Again, it seems to go the other way: We may find ourselves initiating simulation processes or appealing to folk psychology precisely in the odd cases where our ordinary abilities and habitual practices for understanding others break down.

To be clear, the simple phenomenological objection does not say anything about processes that may be subpersonal.

The Integration Problem

Another problem for explicit versions of TT and ST involves the temporal aspects of high-level conscious cognitive processes. If the processes described by TT and ST are conscious and involve multistep routines, as in Goldman's description of introspectionist or high-level simulation, it would be difficult to see how they integrate into our normal experiences of intersubjective interactions with others, where things often seem to flow smoothly in quick back-and-forth responses that depend on anticipatory processes. In regard to the issue of temporal integration, high-functioning individuals with autism who have difficulty understanding others often report using explicit theoretical inference and purely intellectual mentalizing to figure out what others mean by their behavior (Sacks, 1995, p. 258; Zahavi & Parnas, 2003). In this regard, however, they complain that this is a slow process and that frequently they only figure things out after relatively long delays when the interaction is already completed.

The Problem of Pretense and Instrumental Control

The remaining problems pertain to the ST interpretation of the neuroscience of mirror neurons. There are several things wrong with calling mirror system processes simulations (for more detailed arguments, see Gallagher 2007, 2008). Consider, first, the meaning of *simulation* as defined by ST. Specifically, two aspects are of importance here: (1) Simulation involves pretense; (2) simulation has an instrumental character (i.e., it is characterized in terms of a mechanism or model that we manipulate or control in order to understand something to which we do not have instrumental access). We find both aspects discussed in the ST literature; indeed, they are ubiquitous and considered essential to the concept of simulation (see, e.g., Adams, 2001; Bernier, 2002; Dokic & Proust, 2002, p. viii; Goldman, 2002, p. 7; Gordon, 2004, p. 1). The aspect of pretense seems essential for simulation if it is to be distinguished from a theoretical model or a simple practice of reasoning (see Fisher, 2006).

It seems clear, however, that neither of these conditions is met by MNs. First, in regard to the instrumental aspect, if simulation is characterized as a process that I (or my brain) instrumentally use, manipulate, or control, then it seems clear that what is happening in the neuronal processes of motor resonance is not simulation. We, at the personal level, do not manipulate or control the activated brain areas. In fact, we have no instrumental access to neuronal activation, and we cannot use it as a model. Nor does it make sense to say that at the subpersonal level the brain itself is *using* a model or methodology, or that one set of neurons makes use of another set of neurons as a model in order to generate an understanding of something else. Indeed, in precisely the intersubjective circumstances that we are considering, these neuronal systems do not take the initiative; they do not activate themselves. Rather, they are activated by the other person's action. The other person *has an effect on us* and *elicits* this activation. It is not us (or our brain) *initiating* a simulation; it is the other who does this to us via a perceptual elicitation.

Second, in regard to pretense, in subpersonal mirror processes there is no pretense. Obviously, as vehicles or mechanisms, neurons either fire or don't fire. They don't pretend to fire. More to the point, portrayed as representations, what these neurons represent or register cannot involve pretense in the way required by ST. It is the common understanding that since MNs are activated both when I engage in intentional action and when I see you engage in intentional action, the mirror system is neutral with respect to the agent; no first- or third-person specification is involved (deVignemont, 2004; Gallese, 2004, 2005; Hurley, 2005; Jeannerod & Pacherie, 2004). In that case, it is not possible for them to register *my* intentions as pretending to be *your* intentions; there is no "as if" of the sort required by ST because there is no "I" or "you" represented. I note that things are more complicated than this since there may be other ways to understand MN activation as nonneutral with respect to who the agent is. For example, there are temporal differences, and intrinsic differences in firing rates between MN activation for my action versus perception of your action, as well as differences in the rest of the motor system (e.g., presence or absence of efference signals; also see the concept of the "who system" in Georgieff & Jeannerod, 1998). But even if this means that we can discern self–other differentiation in the system, self–other differentiation (self *versus* other) still does not add up to pretense, which would have to involve something more: self *as if* other.

The Matching Problem

In response to just these kinds of worries, one could argue that the instrumental and pretense conditions are not necessary conditions for simulation, and that a necessary condition for simulation is something more minimal. Goldman (2006; Goldman & Sripada, 2005), for example, with respect to the concept of neural simulation, acknowledges a discrepancy between the ST definition of simulation and the working of subpersonal mirror processes: "Does [the neural simulation] model really fit the pattern of ST? Since the model posits unmediated resonance, it does not fit the usual examples of simulation in which pretend states are created and then operated upon by the attributor's own cognitive equipment (e.g., a decision-making mechanism), yielding an output that gets attributed to the target" (Goldman & Sripada, 2005, p. 208). To address this discrepancy, Goldman and Sripida (2005) propose a generic definition of simulation, and what we can call the "matching hypothesis":

> However, we do not regard the creation of pretend states, or the deployment of cognitive equipment to process such states, as essential to the generic idea of simulation. The general idea of simulation is that the simulating process should be similar, in relevant respects, to the simulated process. Applied to mindreading, a minimally necessary condition is that the state ascribed to the target is ascribed as a result of the attributor's instantiating, undergoing, or experiencing, that very state. In the case of successful simulation, the experienced state matches that of the target. This minimal condition for simulation is satisfied [in the neural model]. (p. 208)

The original MN researchers at University of Parma also embrace the matching hypothesis. The "direct matching hypothesis" involves an automatic neural resonance of the MN system when observing the actions of others. Matching means "mapping the visual representation of the observed action onto the motor representation of the same action" (Rizzolatti et al., 2001, p. 661).

Let me suggest, however, against any version of ST that makes matching the primary requirement, that the minimal condition of matching, or any simulation that one can build on this, cannot be the pervasive or default way of attaining an under-standing of others. There are many cases of encountering others in which we simply do not adopt, or find ourselves in, a matching state. Furthermore, with respect to neural ST, if simulation were as automatic as MNs firing, then it would seem that we would not be able to attribute a state different from our own to someone else. But we do this all the time. Also consider the difficulties involved if we were interacting with more than one other person or trying to understand others who are interacting with each other. Is it possible to enter into the same, or what are likely different states, and thereby simulate the neural/motor/mental/emotional states of more than one person at the same time? Or can we alternate quickly enough, going back and forth from one person to the other, if in fact our simulations must be such that we instantiate, undergo, or experience the states in question? How complicated does it get if there is a small crowd in the room? Would there not be an impossible amount of cognitive work or subpersonal matching required to predict or to understand the interactions of several people if the task involves simulating their mental states, especially if in such interpersonal interactions the actions and intentions of each person are affected by the actions and intentions of the others? (Morton, 1996, makes a similar point.)

In addition to such examples, in a recent experiment, Dinstein, Thomas, Behrmann, and Heeger (2008) have shown that, in fact, in certain areas of the brain where MNs are thought to exist, specifically the *anterior intraparietal sulcus* (aIPS), areas activated for producing a particular hand action are not activated for perceiving that hand action in another (vs. intrasystemic matching). They use the rock–paper–scissors game, asking subjects to alternate executing a specific hand gesture and view-ing a specific hand gesture. They show that for matching gestures "distinctly different fMRI response patterns were generated by executed and observed movements in aIPS . . . aIPS exhibits movement-selective responses during both observation and execu-tion of movement, but . . . the representations of observed and executed movements are fundamentally different from one another" (Dinstein et al., 2008). That is, even for matching gestures, there were no neuronal matching patterns found across action condition versus observation of action condition in the MN area (also see Catmur, Walsh, & Heyes, 2007).

Further empirical research on MNs suggests good reasons to think that MN acti-vation does not always or even usually involve a precise match between motor system execution and observed action. Csibra (2005) points out that, conservatively, between 21 and 45% of neurons identified as MNs are sensitive to multiple types of action; of those activated by a single type of observed action, that action is not necessarily the same action defined by the motor properties of the neuron; approximately 60% of MNs are "broadly congruent," which means there may be some relation between the observed action(s) and their associated executed action, but not an exact match. Only about one-third of MNs show a one-to-one congruence. Newman-Norlund,

Noordzij, Meulenbrock, and Bekkering (2007, p. 55) suggest that activation of the broadly congruent MNs may represent a complementary action rather than a similar action. In that case, they could not be simulations defined on the matching hypothesis.

Interaction Theory

It is not enough to criticize TT and ST without offering something in their place. The alternative that I propose is interaction theory (IT), which contends that understanding other people is primarily neither theoretical nor based on an internal simulation but rather a form of embodied practice. The standard and dominant approaches to social cognition rarely emphasize intersubjective *interaction* per se, and even when they do mention interaction, they frame the problem, as we saw, in terms of two minds that have to communicate across the seemingly thin air of an unbridgeable gap. On this view, interaction is not a solution but simply another way to state the problem of other minds. Consider, for example, the following formulation:

> The study of social interaction . . . is concerned with the question of how two minds shape each other mutually through reciprocal interactions. To understand interactive minds we have to understand how thoughts, feelings, intentions, and beliefs can be transmitted from one mind to the other. (Singer, Wolpert, & Frith, 2004, p. xvii)

The problem is posed in terms of the meeting of minds, where one of the minds is inaccessible to the other. It is one mind speculating on another mind. Traditional ToM accounts make little mention of how the body might fit into the process of understanding others. At best, the other's bodily behavior is what we observe and the source of evidence for constructing the inference or initiating a simulation routine. Only neural ST suggests a more important role for embodied processes, but even here the central processes are just the *central* processes that take place in the brain.

IT defines interaction in the following way (see De Jaegher, Di Paolo, & Gallagher 2010); I refer to this as "strong interaction" to distinguish it from other definitions or more common uses of the term:

> *Strong Interaction*: a mutually engaged coregulated coupling between at least two autonomous agents where the coregulation and the coupling mutually affect each other, constituting a self-sustaining organization in the domain of relational dynamics.

IT draws on evidence from developmental studies to show that a pragmatic understanding of others is generated in the intersubjective interaction that begins long before a child reaches the age of 4. IT also offers an alternative (i.e., nonsimulationist), enactive, interpretation of the neuroscience of MNs. It further draws on phenomenological evidence and theories of embodied cognition to argue that the various embodied processes that characterize interaction from the earliest age do not disappear, to be replaced by ToM mechanisms or simulationist talents; rather, they mature and continue to characterize our adult interactions. Moreover, with respect to the more sophisticated and nuanced understanding found in those interactions, IT emphasizes the role of communicative and narrative practices.

Developmentally, one can think of IT as building on three sets of abilities, taking as its point of departure the notion of primary intersubjectivity (Trevarthen, 1979).

- *Primary intersubjectivity* (starting from birth): sensory–motor abilities—enactive perceptual capacities in processes of strong interaction.
- *Secondary intersubjectivity* (starting from 1 year): joint attention, shared contexts, pragmatic engagements, acting *with* others.
- *Communicative and narrative competencies* (starting from 2–4 years): communicative and narrative practices that represent intersubjective interactions, motives, and reasons and provide a more nuanced and sophisticated social understanding (Gallagher & Hutto, 2008).

Appealing to these features of intersubjectivity, IT challenges the three suppositions associated with ToM approaches. In their place, IT argues for the following propositions.

1. Other minds are not hidden away and inaccessible.[5] The other person's intentions, emotions, and dispositions are expressed in their embodied behavior. In most cases of everyday interaction, no inference or projection to mental states beyond those expressions and behaviors is necessary.
2. Our normal everyday stance toward the other person is not third-person, detached observation; it is second-person interaction. We are not primarily spectators or observers of other people's actions; for the most part, we are interacting with them in some communicative action, on some project, in some predefined relation; or we are treating them as others with whom we can potentially interact.
3. Our primary and pervasive way of understanding others does not involve mentalizing or mindreading; in fact, these are rare and specialized abilities that we develop only on the basis of a more embodied engagement with others.

In the rest of this chapter, I summarize some scientific evidence that supports these statements, and I argue that IT is able to address or avoid all of the problems found in the ToM approaches.

Primary Intersubjectivity

Primary intersubjectivity consists of the innate or early-developing sensory–motor capacities that bring us into relation with others and allow us to interact with them. These capacities are manifested at the level of perceptual experience: We see or more generally perceive in the other person's bodily movements, gestures, facial expressions, eye direction, and so on what they intend and what they feel, and we respond with our own bodily movements, gestures, facial expressions, gaze, and so on. On this view, in second-person interactions, the "mind" of the other is not entirely hidden or private, but is given and manifest in the other person's embodied comportment.[6] The basis for human interaction and for understanding others can be found already at work in early infancy in certain embodied practices that are emotional, sensory–motor, perceptual, and nonconceptual. Interaction theory contends that these embodied practices constitute our primary access for understanding others, and continue to do so through adulthood.

In most of our ordinary and everyday intersubjective situations, we have a perception-based understanding of another person's intentions because their intentions are explicitly expressed in their embodied actions. This kind of primary understanding does not require us to postulate some belief or desire that is hidden away in the other person's mind. To put it most succinctly, with respect to the issue of intersubjective understanding in most of our everyday interactions, the mind conceived as a set of mental states, or inner representations, or propositional attitudes simply does not come into it. What we might reflectively or abstractly call a person's belief or desire or mental state is, with respect to intersubjective interaction, expressed directly in their contextualized behavior, their actions, and communicative practices.

This is not a return to behaviorism or a denial that we have phenomenal consciousness or an inner experiential life. Rather, it is to treat such phenomena as continuous with, and indeed as accomplished in, embodied processes and practices. The bodily expressions are not externalizations of something hidden in the mind, however; they are the continuance of or, in some cases, the accomplishment of what we, in reflective consideration, come to call mental states.

In brief, the developmental evidence for primary intersubjectivity suggests that sensory–motor capabilities for understanding others already exist in very young children. Infants already have a sense from their own proprioception and movement of what it means to be an experiencing subject-agent. They can sense that certain kinds of entities (but not others) in the environment are indeed subject-agents like themselves, and that in some way these entities are similar to and in other ways different from themselves. This sense is implicit in the very early behavior of newborns. Infants from birth are capable of perceiving and imitating facial gestures presented by another (Meltzoff & Moore, 1977, 1994). Infants are able to distinguish between inanimate objects and agents. They can respond in a distinctive way to human faces, that is, in a way in which they do not respond to other objects (Legerstee, 1991; Johnson, 2000; Johnson, Slaughter, & Carey, 1998).

The evidence suggests that from birth the action of the infant and the perceived action of the other person are coded in the same "language," a cross-modal sensorimotor system that is directly attuned to the actions and gestures of other humans (Gallagher & Meltzoff, 1996; Meltzoff & Moore, 1994). Accordingly, we can say that there is a common bodily intentionality that is shared across the perceiving subject and the perceived other. Merleau-Ponty calls this "intercorporeity," and characterizes it in this way: "Between this phenomenal body of mine and that of another as I see it from the outside, there exists an internal relation which causes the other to appear as the completion of the system" (1962, p. 352). As Gopnik and Meltzoff put it, "We innately map the visually perceived motions of others onto our own kinesthetic sensations" (1997, p. 129).

Primary intersubjectivity can be specified in more detail. At 2 months, second-person interaction is evidenced by the timing and emotional response of infants' behavior. Infants "vocalize and gesture in a way that seems [affectively and tem-porally] 'tuned' to the vocalizations and gestures of the other person" (Gopnik & Meltzoff, 1997, p. 131). Still-face experiments with infants from 3–6 months of age by Tronick, Als, Adamson, Wise, and Brazelton (1978) and others (for review, see Adamson & Frick, 2003; Muir & Lee, 2003) and the video contingency studies conducted by Murray and Trevarthen (1985) provide good evidence for both the temporal and the emotional aspects of interaction. Both types of studies show that if ongoing interactions between mother and child are interrupted because the mother becomes passive, or a recorded videotape is substituted for a live video interaction, the child quickly notices and becomes upset. At 5–7 months, infants are able to detect correspondences between visual and auditory information that specify the expression of emotions (Hobson, 1993, 2002; Walker, 1982). At 6 months, infants start to perceive grasping as goal directed, and at 10–11 months infants are able to parse some kinds of continuous action according to intentional boundaries (Baird & Baldwin 2001; Baldwin & Baird, 2001; Woodward & Sommerville, 2000). They start to perceive various movements of the head, the mouth, the hands, and more general body movements as meaningful, goal-directed movements (Senju, Johnson, & Csibra, 2006).

Buckner, Shriver, Crowley, and Allen (2009) have referred to these different capacities as a "weakly integrated swarm of first-order mechanisms." It is important, however, to highlight the strongly *interactive* nature of the infant's relations with others in precisely these primary sensorimotor processes. First, it is not a matter of simply specifying a mechanism or capacity in the individual agent. This is why the term "mechanism" may not be the most appropriate. For example, imitation is con-sidered to be an important element of primary intersubjectivity. Yet this kind of imi-tation is not an automatic or mechanical procedure; Csibra and Gergely (2009) have shown, for example, that the infant is more likely to imitate only if the other person is attending to it. The quest for underlying mechanisms, which motivates much of the developmental ToM literature, is misguided insofar as it overlooks the essential contribution of interaction itself in order to focus on individual capacities. Second, I want to discount the idea that the infant is simply a passive spectator trying to figure out what is going on. As noted, studies show the very early appearance of, and impor-tance of, the timing and coordination of interaction. Across the various processes of primary intersubjectivity, at a very basic bodily level, agents unconsciously coordi-nate their movements, gestures, and facial and vocal expressions (Issartel, Marin, & Cadopi, 2007; Kendon, 1990; Lindblom, 2007; Lindblom & Ziemke, 2007), entering into synchronized resonance with others, with slight temporal modulations (Gergely, 2001), in either in-phase or phase-delayed rhythmic covariation (Fuchs & De Jaegher, 2009). The key idea of strong interaction is that in some cases interaction itself plays an essential role in constituting social cognition.

The concept of strong interaction can best be explained from an enactive per-spective. On the enactive view, as embodied agents, we do not passively receive infor-mation from our environment and then create internal representations of the world in our heads; rather, we actively participate in the generation of meaning, which is the result of pragmatic and dynamic interchanges between agent and environment (Varela, Thompson, & Rosch, 1991). In the intersubjective context, strong interac-tion has a certain autonomy that goes beyond what individuals bring to the process (De Jaegher et al., 2010). Indeed, much like dancing the tango, the interaction is not reducible to a set of mechanisms contained within the individual; it requires at least two embodied individuals who are dynamically coupled in the right way.

Primary intersubjectivity and the strong interaction that goes with it are not phenomena that disappear after the first year of life. It is not a stage that we leave behind, and it is not, as Greg Currie suggests, a set of precursor states "that underpin early intersubjective understanding, and *make way* for the development of later theorizing or simulation" (2008, p. 212, emphasis added; cf. Baron-Cohen, 1991, 1995). Rather, citing both behavioral and phenomenological evidence, IT argues that we do not leave primary intersubjectivity behind; these embodied processes do not "make way" for the purportedly more sophisticated mindreading processes, but rather continue to characterize our everyday encounters even as adults. That is, we continue to understand others in strong interactional terms, facilitated by our recognition of facial expressions, gestures, postures, and actions as meaningful.

Scientific experiments bear this out. Point-light experiments (actors in the dark wearing point lights on their joints, presenting abstract outlines of emotional and action postures), for example, show that not only children (although not autistic children) but also adults perceive emotion even in movement that offers minimal information (Dittrich, Troscianko, Lea, & Morgan, 1996; Hobson & Lee, 1999). Close analysis of facial expression, gesture, and action in everyday contexts shows that as adults we continue to rely on embodied interactive abilities to understand the intentions and actions of others and to accomplish interactive tasks (Lindblom, 2007; Lindblom & Ziemke, 2007). It is well known that intentions shape action kinematics. For example, positions are different in grasping an apple when you are going to eat it, or offer it to someone, or throw it, respectively (Jeannerod, 1997). Recent studies by Becchio, Manera, Sartori, Cavallo, and Castiello (2012) show that perceivers are sensitive to differences in visual kinematics and are able to discriminate between cooperative, competitive, and individual-oriented actions (Sartori et al., 2011). Subjects are even able to discriminate these differences without specific contextual information—in the dark with point-lights on the wrist and fingers of the agent (Manera, Becchio, Cavallo, Sartori, & Castiello, 2011).

We noted a number of problems associated with the interpretation of MNs in terms of simulation. Here is an alternative interpretation that avoids those problems. Rather than simulation, which involves instrumental control, pretense, or matching, MN activation can easily be viewed as part of the neuronal processes that underlie an enactive intersubjective perception that functions within the interactional context. That is, the articulated neuronal processes that include activation of MNs or shared representations may underpin a nonarticulated immediate perception of the other person's intentional actions and emotional expressions rather than a distinct process of simulating. This claim requires that we conceive of perception as a temporal phenomenon and as an enactive process.

MNs fire 30–100 milleseconds after appropriate visual stimulation. This short amount of time between activation of the visual cortex and activation of the MN system raises the question of where precisely to draw the line between perceptual processes and something that would count as a subpersonal simulation. Even if it is possible to distinguish at the neuronal level between activation of the visual cortex and activation of the premotor cortex, this certainly does not mean that this constitutes a distinction between processes that are purely perceptual and processes that involve something more than perception.

If we think of perception as an enactive process (Hurley, 1998; Varela et al., 1991), that is, as involving embodied sensorimotor skills rather than as just sensory input/processing—thus, as an active, skillful, embodied engagement with the world rather than as the passive reception of information from the environment—then it is more appropriate to think of mirror resonance processes as part of the structure of the perceptual process when it is a perception of another person's actions. Fogassi and Gallese, despite their simulationist interpretation, put this point clearly: "Perception, far from being just the final outcome of sensory integration, is the result of senso-rimotor coupling" (2002, p. 27). Mirror activation, on this interpretation, is not the initiation of simulation; it is part of an enactive intersubjective perception of what the other is doing.

This interpretation of MN activation provides a tight fit with IT. On this account, the capacities for human interaction and intersubjective understanding are already operative in infancy in embodied, enactive practices—practices that are sensorimo-tor, perceptual, emotional, and nonconceptual. These embodied practices constitute our primary way of understanding others, and they continue to do so even after we attain our more sophisticated abilities in this regard.

This kind of perception-based understanding, therefore, is not a form of mind-reading or mentalizing. In seeing the actions and expressive movements of the other person, one already sees their meaning in the context of the surrounding world; no inference to a hidden set of mental states (e.g., beliefs, desires) is necessary. At the phenomenological level, when I see the other's action or gesture, I see (I *immediately perceive*) the meaning in the action or gesture. I see the joy or I see the anger, or I see the intention in the face or in the posture or in the gesture or action of the other. I see it. No simulation of what is readily apparent is needed, and no simulation of something more than this is required in the majority of contexts.

From Secondary Intersubjectivity to Narrative Competency

In secondary intersubjectivity, interaction is shaped by joint attention and the sur-rounding environment. Trevarthen shows that infants, starting at 9 months to 1 year, go beyond the person-to-person immediacy of primary intersubjectivity and enter into *contexts* of shared attention—shared situations—in which they learn what things mean and what they are for (see Hobson, 2002; Trevarthen & Hubley, 1978). The contextualized objects and events of the world become a focus between people, the references for communication and further interaction.

Children are not passive observers. Rather, they interact with others, and in doing so they develop further capabilities in the contexts of those interactions. At 18 months, children can comprehend what another person intends to do with an object. They are able to reenact to completion the goal-directed behavior that an observed subject does not complete. The child, seeing an adult who tries to manipulate a toy in the right way and who appears frustrated about being unable to do so, quite read-ily picks up the toy and shows the adult how to do it (Meltzoff, 1995; Meltzoff & Brooks, 2001). Just as we understand our own actions on the highest pragmatic level possible (see, e.g., Gallagher & Marcel, 1999; Jeannerod, 1997), we understand the actions of others in the same way. That is, we understand actions at the most relevant pragmatic (intentional, goal-oriented) level, ignoring possible subpersonal or lower-level descriptions, and also ignoring ideational or mentalistic interpretations. We do not need to make an inference to what the other person is intending, starting by observing the movements of his or her hands on the toy and moving thence to the level of desires and beliefs. If I see you reach for a glass and a bottle of water, I know what your intentions are as much from the glass and the bottle of water as from your reach. We interpret the actions of others in terms of their goals and intentions set in contextualized situations rather than abstractly in terms of either their muscular performance or their mental states.

An explanation of the false-belief experiments in early infancy can be modeled on enactive perception without appealing explicitly to behavioral rules. Consider, for example, some of the more interactive experimental designs that are starting to appear. In a study by Buttelmann, Carpenter, and Tomasello (2009), 18-month-olds try to help an agent retrieve a toy while taking into account the fact that the agent does not know about a switched location (the false-belief situation). In that situation, when the agent focuses on the wrong container (the original location, A), the infant is ready to lead him to the correct box (B), but not in the situation when the agent does know about the switch—the true-belief situation—and still goes to A. In the latter case, the infant goes to assist the agent at A. In this study, when the agent goes to box A, the infant sees exactly the same thing in the case of true belief (when the agent knows there has been a shift from A to B) as in the case of false belief (when the agent does not know about the shift). Again, the fact that the infant knows either that the agent has seen the switch or not, plus the agent's behavior with respect to A (e.g., moving to A and attempting to open it), is enough to specify the difference in the agent's intention. For the infant, that signals a difference in affordance, that is, a difference in how the infant can act and thereby interact with the agent. The infant does not have to make inferences to mental states, since all of the information needed to understand the other and to interact is already available in what the infant has seen of the situation.

In a further study by Southgate, Chevallier, and Csibra (2010), the agent hides two toys in separate boxes and then leaves. Infants then watch as another person switches the contents of the two boxes. When the agent returns, she (the agent) points to one of the boxes (A), announcing that the toy hidden inside is a "sefo." When the infants are then asked to retrieve the "sefo," most of them approach the other box (B), indicating that they must have understood that the agent intended to name the toy that was now in B, unaware of the toy's changed location. The infant sees the agent's original action and sees the switch that the agent does not see. There is interaction when the agent communicates in this situation and when the infant is invited to act. It is not at all clear that the infant has to engage in mindreading, since all of this information is available in the behavioral situation and is sufficient to inform the infant's action.

These results can be easily interpreted within the framework of interaction theory. Generally, they suggest that the capacity for understanding social situations complicated by an agent's lack of information is closely intertwined with the ability to deploy social competences that engage with those situations. Whether an explanation in terms of behavioral rules (Ruffman & Perner, 2005) can be vindicated or not, it seems likely that the more parsimonious explanation will have to build on the relevant resources developed in processes that are closer to the perceptual and interaction processes of primary and secondary intersubjectivity than to meta-representational and mentalizing abilities, the purported presence of which in young infants continues to surprise even theory theorists (see Gallagher & Povinelli, 2012).

Language development adds both communicative and narrative competencies to our resources for understanding others. These processes are helped along and in some way transformed by our ability for generating and comprehending vocal communications. As behaviors and environments become more complex, the child relies on communication to sort out the ambiguities of various situations. Infants have been caught up in what Merleau-Ponty (1962) calls the "whirlwind of language" from the very beginning, and things and people start to fall into place linguistically through the various and pervasive practices of reading and telling stories to children and then eliciting their own stories. Through such processes, we begin to represent the pragmatic and social contexts for action already encountered in secondary intersubjectivity, and new contexts, more nuanced and more sophisticated, begin to open up via narrative practices. These practices are shaped not only by our own experiences, but by culture, which defines the limitations and possibilities of narrative, by the expectations of others, and by our own initiatives.

Much more can be said about all of these topics, but I think I have said a sufficient amount to briefly indicate how IT can solve or avoid the various problems encountered in TT and/or ST approaches. Let me start at the bottom of that list. For IT there are no problems in regard to matching or pretense and instrumental control. These are problems with the simulationist interpretation of MNs. For IT and the enactivist interpretation of MNs, these problems simply do not arise since on the enactive view our motor systems do not match and do not involve pretense or instrumental control. The problem of integration is solved because interaction is online and real time. If we take strong interaction to involve enactive perception in a second-person framework rather than third-person observation, the interaction view is consistent with our everyday phenomenology. It is also consistent with what infants do and indeed points to developmental studies for support. In regard to the diversity problem, interaction is not reducible to drawing on only first-person experiential resources (which is the basis for simulation). The other, in his or her diversity, is already included in the basic unit of explanation—that is, the interaction itself.

My claim here is not that IT solves all problems of communication and diversity. I am only talking about avoiding the theoretical problems involved with TT and IT. Understanding others in their diversity is one of the main problems of human relations, and one of the things a good account of social cognition needs to do is give a good account of the limitations and significant amount of misunderstandings encountered in human communication and understanding. In this regard, we can only say that even strong interaction is imperfect.

Conclusion: Of Three Minds

Placing emphasis on social interaction rather than mindreading leads to a conception of the mind as a second-person phenomenon. The mind of the other person is "out there" in their actions and interactions, in their gestures and communications, constituted as they engage with the world and with others. The mind in this sense is extended into and supported by context, situation, and the social roles in which we, as agents, are engaged. In most of our everyday situations, we need go no further for an understanding of the other person.

This is not to deny that there is also an important first-person dimension of the mind. As I engage in actions and interactions with others, I enter into ecological relations with the world and with others that generate my embodied, pre-reflective first-person experience. In developmental terms, at first, this sensorimotor experience is all there is in my phenomenal, first-order awareness. Bodily processes and second-person interactions combine to shape this awareness and to move us through a stream of experience, from one thing to the next. This is indubitably *my* experience that *you* have no access to. But that is not a problem for social cognition; it is not the problem of other minds. You do not need to access or mindread my first-person experience in order to understand me; much of that first-person experience is being shaped and driven as we interact in second-person relations that already give you access to my bodily movements, facial expressions, gestures, and epistemic and communicative actions, and thereby to my "second-person mind," or what Sartre (1956) might call my existence-for-others.

Still less do we need to worry about the mind as it is conceived in standard ToM approaches—that is, in terms of belief-desire psychology, as a set of propositional attitudes or mental states. This is what we might call the third-person mind. As we experience the world and enter into second-person interactions, we form dispositions and habits. As we *reflect* on these dispositions and habits, and on our first-order experiences, using concepts developed in linguistic and cultural practices, we formulate a shorthand way of describing ourselves in terms of our beliefs and desires, and because they are already linguistically formed, we can communicate what they are. Such propositional attitudes derive significantly from our second-person interactions, but in every case they are derivative, the product of reflection and/or linguistic practice. This is the conception of the mind that standard ToM approaches worry about. It is the mind that seems hidden away—the private mind of beliefs and desires—when, in fact, it is the mind that is most easily expressible in terms of language. To the extent that such mental states enter back into our second-person interactions, it is through the fact that we communicate about them. In this regard, they are not really hidden away and they present no real problem of social cognition.

This is not to deny that we are all capable of deception. And if you set out to deceive me, you may well succeed. The only way I may be able to discover that is through your actions, your facial expressions, your gestures, and so on. I may also be able to reason some things out, such as inconsistencies between what you say and what you do. Unless I am constantly suspicious of you, however, I don't think that this would be my usual practice. If and when I do engage in this mindreading practice, or in cases where I am puzzled by your behavior or in some other unusual circumstances, I may put myself in the observational stance described by TT and ST. I may try to work out, through inferences or simulations, what your beliefs and desires might be. The abilities I have for this are quite specialized, and they require that I take a third-person perspective on this derivative conception of the mind as a set of mental states. Thus, when TT and ST describe the problem of social cognition as this kind of problem, I suggest that this is only one specialized kind of problem, which really tells us of the broader solution. In most cases of social cognition, we have no need to engage in this type of thing since we have ready access to the other person's behaviors, movements, actions, expressions, and so on.

Once we understand that just such second-person interactional processes have priority over third-person observational processes, we can see a clear resolution to the starting problem. The starting problem is a problem for TT and ST approaches, that is, for approaches that describe only the specialized cases that call for mindreading inferences and simulations. How do such processes get off the ground? How do we know what bits of folk psychology to apply or what beliefs and desires to push into our pretense mechanisms? The answer can be found in our constant and everyday interactions with others. What sets us on the right track and gets social cognition off the ground, even in these rare and specialized cases, are the embodied and contextualized practices of interaction. We arrive on the scene already attuned to other people's faces and their emotional expressions; and we come prepared to interact with others. These are precisely the strong interactive processes that IT points to, not only as the starting point developmentally but as the continuous starting point for our everyday engagements with others. To whatever extent we do actually engage in mindreading, whether by theory or simulation, these strong interactive processes solve the starting problem. They provide the minimal embodied skills and—together with the rich, worldly contextualization that comes along with secondary intersubjectivity and the even richer social and cultural contexts that come along with communicative and narrative practices—they form the "massive hermeneutical background" (see Gallagher, 2011) that in every instance continues to get social cognition off the ground.

Acknowledgments

I thank the École Normale Supérieure de Lyon and CNRS for their support on this project during a stay as visiting professor at the Centre d'Epistémologie des Sciences Cognitives, ENS in Lyon (2010).

Notes

1. Thus, for example, Goldman writes: "'High-level' mindreading is mindreading with one or more of the following features: (a) it targets mental states of a relatively complex nature, such as propositional attitudes; (b) some components of the mindreading process are subject to voluntary control; and (c) the process has some degree of accessibility to consciousness" (2006, p. 147).
2. Here are some exemplary statements of this idea. "One of the most important powers of the human mind is to conceive of and think about itself and other minds. Because the mental states of others (and indeed of ourselves) are completely hidden from the senses, they can only ever be inferred" (Leslie, 1987, p. 139). And again: "Normal humans everywhere not only 'paint' their world with color, they also 'paint' beliefs, intentions, feelings, hopes, desires, and pretenses onto agents in their social world. They do this despite the fact that no human has ever seen a thought, a belief, or an intention" (Tooby & Cosmides, in Baron-Cohen, 1995, p. xvii).
3. Carruthers (2009) has taken issue with my claim with regard to this supposition. He writes: "In particular, it is simply false that theory-theorists must (or do) assume that

mentalizing usually involves the adoption of a third-person, detached and observational, perspective on other people. On the contrary, theory theorists have always emphasized that the primary use of mindreading is in interaction with others (which Gallagher calls 'second-personal')" (p. 167). Yet Carruthers himself characterizes mindreading as observational. The task of mindreading is just this: "'to provide fine-grained intentionalistic predictions and explanations' based on 'inferences from *observation*'" (Carruthers, 1996, p. 26, emphasis added). Carruthers, characterizes mindreading as something done by "a third-party observer" (2009, p. 134), and indicates that "we surely use our mind-reading system, for example, when processing a *description* of someone's state of mind as well as when *observing* their behavior" (2002, p. 666, emphasis added).

4. There are many examples that could be cited here. See, for example, Baron-Cohen (1995, pp. 3–4), Frith and Happé (1994, p. 2), Jeannerod and Pacherie (2004, p. 128), Karmiloff-Smith (1992, p. 117), Leslie (2000, p. 1236), and Wellman (1993, pp. 31–32).

5. For a Wittgensteinian version of this idea, see Carpendale and Lewis (2004).

6. This is not to deny that there is some private aspect to mental experience. The possibility of deception attests to the fact that we do not always have complete access to the other person's mind. The argument here is simply that we do not appeal to a hidden mind when we interact with others in this primary way.

References

Adams, F. (2001). Empathy, neural imaging, and the theory versus simulation debate. *Mind and Language, 16*(4), 368–392.

Adamson, L. B., & Frick, J. E. (2003). The still face: A history of a shared experimental paradigm. *Infancy, 4,* 451–473.

Avenanti, A., & Aglioti, S.M. (2006). The sensorimotor side of empathy for pain. In M. Mancia (Ed.), *Psychoanalysis and neuroscience* (pp. 235–256). Milan: Springer.

Baillargeon, R., Scott, R. M., & He, Z. (2010). False-belief understanding in infants. *Trends in Cognitive Sciences, 14*(3), 110–118.

Baird, J. A., & Baldwin, D. A. (2001). Making sense of human behavior: Action parsing and intentional inference. In B. F. Malle, L. J. Moses, & D. A. Baldwin (Eds.), *Intentions and intentionality: Foundations of social cognition* (pp. 193–206). Cambridge, MA: MIT Press.

Baldwin, D. A., & Baird, J. A. (2001). Discerning intentions in dynamic human action. *Trends in Cognitive Science, 5*(4), 171–178.

Baron-Cohen, S. (1991). Precursors to a theory of mind: Understanding attention in others. In A. Whiten (Ed.), *Natural theories of mind: Evolution, development and simulation of everyday mindreading* (pp. 233–251). Cambridge, MA: Basil Blackwell.

Baron-Cohen, S. (1995). *Mindblindness: An essay on autism and theory of mind*. Cambridge, MA: MIT Press.

Becchio, C., Manera, V., Sartori, L., Cavallo, A., & Castiello, U. (2012). Grasping intentions: From thought experiments to empirical evidence. *Frontiers in Human Neuroscience, 6,* 1–6.

Bernier, P. (2002). From simulation to theory. In J. Dokic & J. Proust (Eds.), *Simulation and knowledge of action* (pp. 33–48). Amsterdam: John Benjamins.

Bruner, J., & Kalmar, D. A. (1998). Narrative and metanarrative in the construction of self. In M. Ferrari & R. J. Sternberg (Eds.), *Self-awareness: Its nature and development* (pp. 308–331). New York: Guilford Press.

Buckner, C., Shriver, A., Crowley, S., & Allen, C. (2009). How 'weak' mindreaders inherited the earth. *Behavioral and Brain Sciences, 32*(2), 140–141.

Buttelmann, D., Carpenter, M., & Tomasello, M. (2009). Eighteen-month-old infants show false belief understanding in an active helping paradigm. *Cognition, 112*, 337–342.

Carpendale, J. L. M., & Lewis, C. (2004). Constructing an understanding of the mind: The development of children's social understanding within social interaction. *Behavioural and Brain Sciences, 27*, 79–151.

Carruthers, P. (1996). Simulation and self-knowledge: A defence of the theory-theory. In P. Carruthers & P. K. Smith (Eds.), *Theories of theories of mind* (pp. 22–38). Cambridge, UK: Cambridge University Press.

Carruthers, P. (2002). The cognitive functions of language. *Behavioral and Brain Sciences, 25*, 657–726.

Carruthers, P. (2009). How we know our own minds: The relationship between mindreading and metacognition. *Behavioral and Brain Sciences, 32*(2), 121–182.

Catmur, C., Walsh, V., & Heyes, C. (2007). Sensorimotor learning configures the human mirror system. *Current Biology, 17*(17), 1527–1531.

Csibra, G. (2005). Mirror neurons and action observation. Is simulation involved? *ESF Interdisciplines.* Retrieved from *www.cdcb.bbk.ac.uk/people/scientificstaff/gergo/publ/.../mirror.pdf.*

Csibra, G., & Gergely, G. (2009). Natural pedagogy. *Trends in Cognitive Sciences, 13*, 148–153.

Currie, G. (2008). Some ways of understanding people. *Philosophical Explorations, 11*(3), 211–218.

Currie, G., & Ravenscroft, I. (2002). *Recreative minds.* Oxford, UK: Oxford University Press.

Currie, G., & Sterelny, K. (2000). How to think about the modularity of mind-reading. *Philosophical Quarterly, 50*, 145–160.

De Jaegher, H., Di Paolo, E., & Gallagher, S. (2010). Does social interaction constitute social cognition? *Trends in Cognitive Sciences, 14*(10), 441–447.

de Vignemont, F. (2004). The co-consciousness hypothesis. *Phenomenology and the Cognitive Sciences, 3*(1), 97–114.

Dinstein, I., Thomas, C., Behrmann, M., & Heeger, D. J. (2008). A mirror up to nature. *Current Biology, 18*(1), R13–R18.

Dittrich, W. H., Troscianko, T., Lea, S. E. G., & Morgan, D. (1996). Perception of emotion from dynamic point-light displays represented in dance. *Perception, 25*, 727–738.

Dokic, J., & Proust, J. (2002). Introduction. In J. Dokic & J. Proust (Eds.), *Simulation and knowledge of action* (pp. vii–xxi). Amsterdam: John Benjamins.

Fisher, J. C. (2006). Does simulation theory really involve simulation? *Philosophical Psychology, 19*(4), 417–432.

Fogassi, L., Ferrari, P. F., Gesierich, B., Rozzi, S., Chersi, F., & Rizzolatti, G. (2005). Parietal lobe: From action organization to intention understanding. *Science, 308*, 662–667.

Fogassi, L., & Gallese, V. (2002). The neural correlates of action understanding in non-human primates. In M. I. Stamenov & V. Gallese (Eds.), *Mirror neurons and the evolution of brain and language* (pp. 13–35). Amsterdam: John Benjamins.

Frith, U., & Happé, F. (1994). Autism: Beyond "theory of mind." *Cognition, 50*, 115–132.

Fuchs, T., & De Jaegher, H. (2009). Enactive intersubjectivity: Participatory sense-making and mutual incorporation. *Phenomenology and the Cognitive Sciences, 8*, 465–486.

Gallagher, S. (2007). Simulation trouble. *Social Neuroscience, 2*(3–4), 353–365.

Gallagher, S. (2008). Neural simulation and social cognition. In J. A. Pineda (Ed.), *Mirror neuron systems: The role of mirroring processes in social cognition* (pp. 355–371). Totowa, NJ: Humana Press.

Gallagher, S. (2011). Narrative competence and the massive hermeneutical background. In P. Fairfield (Ed.), *Education, dialogue and hermeneutics* (pp. 221–38). New York: Continuum.

Gallagher, S., & Hutto, D. (2008). Understanding others through primary interaction and narrative practice. In J. Zlatev, T. Racine, C. Sinha, & E. Itkonen (Eds.), *The shared mind: Perspectives on intersubjectivity* (pp. 17–38). Amsterdam: John Benjamins.

Gallagher, S., & Marcel, A. J. (1999). The self in contextualized action. *Journal of Consciousness Studies, 6*(4), 4–30.

Gallagher, S., & Meltzoff, A. N. (1996). The earliest sense of self and others. *Philosophical Psychology, 9,* 213–236.

Gallagher, S., & Povinelli, D. (2012). Enactive and behavioral abstraction accounts of social understanding in chimpanzees, infants, and adults. *Review of Philosophy and Psychology, 3*(1), 145–169.

Gallese, V. (2004). Intentional attunement: The mirror neuron system and its role in interpersonal relations. *ESF Interdisciplines.* Retrieved February 16, 2011, from *www.interdisciplines.org/medias/confs/archives/archive_8.pdf.*

Gallese, V. (2005). "Being like me": Self–other identity, mirror neurons and empathy. In S. Hurley & N. Chater (Eds.), *Perspectives on imitation I* (pp. 101–118). Cambridge, MA: MIT Press.

Gallese, V. (2007). Before and below "theory of mind": Embodied simulation and the neural correlates of social cognition. *Philosophical Transactions of the Royal Society: Biological Sciences, 362,* 659–669.

Gallese V., Eagle M.N., & Migone, P. (2007). Intentional attunement: Mirror neurons and the neural underpinnings of interpersonal relations. *Journal of the American Psychoanalytic Association, 55*(1), 131–176.

Georgieff, N., & Jeannerod, M. (1998). Beyond consciousness of external events: A "who" system for consciousness of action and self-consciousness. *Consciousness and Cognition, 7,* 465–477.

Gergely, G. (2001). The obscure object of desire: "Nearly, but clearly not, like me": Contingency preference in normal children versus children with autism. *Bulletin of the Menninger Clinic, 65,* 411–426.

Goldman, A. I. (1995). Desire, intention and the simulation theory. In B. F. Malle, L. J. Moses, & D. A. Baldwin (Eds.), *Intentions and intentionality: Foundations of social cognition* (pp. 207–224). Cambridge, MA: MIT Press.

Goldman, A. I. (2002). Simulation theory and mental concepts. In J. Dokic & J. Proust (Eds.), *Simulation and knowledge of action* (pp. 1–19). Amsterdam: John Benjamins.

Goldman, A. I. (2005). Imitation, mind reading, and simulation. In S. Hurley & N. Chater (Eds.), *Perspectives on imitation II* (pp. 80–91). Cambridge, MA: MIT Press.

Goldman, A. I. (2006). *Simulating minds: The philosophy, psychology, and neuroscience of mindreading.* New York: Oxford University Press.

Goldman, A. I. (2008). Does one size fit all?: Hurley on shared circuits. *Behavioral and Brain Sciences, 31*(1), 27–28.

Goldman, A. I., & Sripada, C. S. (2005). Simulationist models of face-based emotion recognition. *Cognition, 94,* 193–213.

Gopnik, A., & Meltzoff, A. N. (1997). *Words, thoughts, and theories.* Cambridge, MA: MIT Press.

Gordon, R. M. (1986). Folk psychology as simulation. *Mind and Language, 1,* 158–171.

Gordon, R. M. (1995, December 27). *Developing commonsense psychology: Experimental data and philosophical data.* Paper presented at the APA Eastern Division Symposium on Children's Theory of Mind, New York.

Gordon, R. M. (2004). Folk psychology as mental simulation. In N. Zalta (Ed.), *The Stanford encyclopedia of philosophy.* Retrieved February 16, 2011, from *http://plato.stanford.edu/archives/fall2004/entries/folkpsych-simulation.*

Heal, J. (1986). Replication and functionalism. In J. Butterfield (Ed.), *Language, mind, and logic* (pp. 45–59). Cambridge, UK: Cambridge University Press.

Heal, J. (1998). Co-cognition and off-line simulation: Two ways of understanding the simulation approach. *Mind and Language, 13,* 477–498.

Herschbach, M. (2008). Folk psychological and phenomenological accounts of social perception. *Philosophical Explorations, 11,* 223–235.

Hobson, P. (1993). The emotional origins of social understanding. *Philosophical Psychology, 6,* 227–249.

Hobson, P. (2002). *The cradle of thought.* London: Macmillan.

Hobson, P., & Lee, A. (1999). Imitation and identification in autism. *Journal of Child Psychology and Psychiatry, 40,* 649–659.

Hurley, S. L. (1998). *Consciousness in action.* Cambridge, MA: Harvard University Press.

Hurley, S. L. (2005). Active perception and perceiving action: The shared circuits model. In T. Gendler & J. Hawthorne (Eds.), *Perceptual experience* (pp. 205–259). New York: Oxford University Press.

Iacoboni, M., Molnar-Szakacs, I., Gallese, V., Buccino, G., Mazziotta, J.C., & Rizzolatti, G. (2005). Grasping the intentions of others with one's own mirror neuron system. *PLoS Biology, 3*(3), 529–535.

Issartel, J., Marin, L., & Cadopi, M. (2007). Unintended interpersonal coordination: 'Can we march to the beat of our own drum'? *Neuroscience Letters, 411,* 174–179.

Jeannerod, M. (1997). *The cognitive neuroscience of action.* Oxford, UK: Blackwell.

Jeannerod, M., & Pacherie, E. (2004). Agency, simulation, and self-identification. *Mind and Language, 19*(2), 113–146.

Johnson, S.C. (2000). The recognition of mentalistic agents in infancy. *Trends in Cognitive Science, 4,* 22–28.

Johnson, S. C., Slaughter, S., & Carey, S. (1998). Whose gaze will infants follow?: The elicitation of gaze-following in 12-month-old infants. *Developmental Science, 1,* 233–238.

Kaplan, J. T., & Iacoboni, M. (2006). Getting a grip on other minds: Mirror neurons, intention understanding, and cognitive empathy. *Social Neuroscience, 1*(3–4), 175–183.

Karmiloff-Smith, A. (1992). *Beyond modularity: A developmental perspective on cognitive science.* Cambridge, MA: MIT Press.

Kendon, A. (1990). *Conducting interaction: Patterns of behavior in focused encounters.* Cambridge, UK: Cambridge University Press.

Legerstee, M. (1991). The role of person and object in eliciting early imitation. *Journal of Experimental Child Psychology, 51,* 423–433.

Leslie, A. (1991). The theory of mind impairment in autism: Evidence for a modular mechanism of development? In A. Whiten (Ed.), *Natural theories of mind: Evolution, development and simulation of everyday mindreading* (pp. 63–78). Oxford, UK: Blackwell.

Leslie, A. (2000). "Theory of mind" as a mechanism of selective attention. In M. Gazzaniga (Ed.), *The cognitive neurosciences* (2nd ed., pp. 1235–1247). Cambridge, MA: MIT Press.

Leslie, A. M. (1987). Children's understanding of the mental world. In R. L. Gregory (Ed.), *The Oxford companion to the mind* (pp. 139–142). Oxford, UK: Oxford University Press

Leslie, A. M., & Frith, U. (1988). Autistic children's understanding of seeing, knowing and believing. *British Journal of Developmental Psychology, 6,* 315–324.

Lindblom, J. (2007). *Minding the body: Interacting socially through embodied action.* Unpublished doctoral dissertation, Linköping University.

Lindblom, J., & Ziemke, T. (2007). Embodiment and social interaction: Implications for cognitive science. In T. Ziemke, J. Zlatev, & R. Frank (Eds.), *Body, language, and mind: Embodiment* (pp. 129–162). Berlin: Mouton de Gruyter.

Manera, V., Becchio, C., Cavallo, A., Sartori, L., & Castiello, U. (2011). Cooperation or competition?: Discriminating between social intentions by observing prehensile movements. *Experimental Brain Research, 211,* 547–556.

Meltzoff, A. N. (1995). Understanding the intentions of others: Re-enactment of intended acts by 18–month-old children. *Developmental Psychology, 31,* 838–850.

Meltzoff, A. N., & Brooks, R. (2001). "Like me" as a building block for understanding other minds: Bodily acts, attention, and intention. In B. F. Malle, L. J., Moses, & D. A. Aldwin (Eds.), *Intentions and intentionality: Foundations of social cognition* (pp. 171–191). Cambridge, MA: MIT Press.

Meltzoff, A. N., & Moore, M. K. (1977). Imitation of facial and manual gestures by human neonates. *Science, 198,* 75–78.

Meltzoff, A. N., & Moore, M. K. (1994). Imitation, memory, and the representation of persons. *Infant Behavior and Development, 17,* 83–99.

Merleau-Ponty, M. (1962). *Phenomenology of perception.* New York: Routledge & Kegan Paul.

Minio-Paluello, I., Avenanti, A., & Aglioti, S. M. (2006). Left-hemisphere dominance in reading the sensory qualities of others' pain? *Social Neuroscience, 1*(3–4), 320–333.

Morton, A. (1996). Folk psychology is not a predictive device. *Mind, 105,* 119–137.

Muir, D., & Lee, K. (2003). The still-face effect: Methodological issues and new applications. *Infancy, 4*(4), 483–491.

Murray, L., & Trevarthen, C. (1985). Emotional regulations of interactions between two-month-olds and their mothers. In T. M. Field & N. A. Fox (Eds.), *Social perception in infants* (pp. 177–197). Norwood, NJ: Ablex.

Newman-Norlund, R. D., Noordzij, M. L., Meulenbroek, R. G. J., & Bekkering, H. (2007). Exploring the brain basis of joint attention: Co-ordination of actions, goals and intentions. *Social Neuroscience, 2*(1), 48–65.

Oberman, L. M., & Ramachandran, V. S. (2007). The simulating social mind: The role of the mirror neuron system and simulation in the social and communicative deficits of autism spectrum disorders. *Psychological Bulletin, 133*(2), 310–327.

Onishi, K.H., & Baillargeon, R. (2005). Do 15–month-old infants understand false beliefs? *Science, 308,* 255–258.

Perner, J., & Ruffman, T. (2005) Infants' insight into the mind: How deep? *Science, 308,* 214–216.

Rizzolatti, G., Fogassi, L., & Gallese, V. (2001). Neurophysiological mechanisms underlying the understanding and imitation of action. *Nature Reviews Neuroscience, 2,* 661–670.

Ruffman, T., & Perner, J. (2005). Do infants really understand false belief?: Response to Leslie. *Trends in Cognitive Sciences, 9*(10), 462–463.

Sacks, O. (1995). *An anthropologist on Mars.* New York: Vintage Books.

Sartori, L., Becchio, C., & Castiello, U. (2011). Cues to intention: The role of movement information. *Cognition, 119,* 242–252.

Sartre, J.-P. (1956). *Being and nothingness.* (H. E. Barnes, Trans.). New York: Philosophical Library.

Scheler, M. (1954). *The nature of sympathy* (P. Heath, Trans.). London: Routledge & Kegan Paul.

Senju, A., Johnson, M. H., & Csibra, G. (2006). The development and neural basis of referential gaze perception. *Social Neuroscience, 1*(3–4), 220–234.

Singer, W., Wolpert D., & Frith, C. (2004). Introduction: The study of social interactions. In C. Frith & D. Wolpert (Eds.), *The neuroscience of social interaction* (pp. xii–xxvii). Oxford, UK: Oxford University Press.

Sommerville, J. A., Woodward, A. L., & Needham, A. (2005). Action experience alters 3–month-old infants' perception of others' actions. *Cognition, 96,* B1–B11.

Song, H-J., Onishi, K. H., Baillargeon, R., & Fisher, C. (2008). Can an agent's false belief be corrected by an appropriate communication?: Psychological reasoning in 18-month-old infants. *Cognition, 109*(3), 295–315.

Southgate, V., Chevallier, C., & Csibra, G. (2010). Seventeen-month-olds appeal to false beliefs to interpret others' referential communication. *Developmental Science, 13*(6), 907–912.

Stack, J., & Lewis, C. (2008). Steering towards a developmental account of infant social understanding. *Human Development, 51*, 229–234.

Surian, L., Caldi, S., & Sperber, D. (2007). Attribution of beliefs by 13-month-old infants. *Psychological Science, 18*(7), 580–586.

Träuble, B., Marinovič, V., & Pauen, S. (2010). Early theory of mind competencies: Do infants understand others' beliefs? *Infancy, 15*(4), 434–444.

Trevarthen, C. B. (1979). Communication and cooperation in early infancy: A description of primary intersubjectivity. In M. Bullowa (Ed.), *Before speech* (pp. 321–348). Cambridge, UK: Cambridge University Press.

Trevarthen, C., & Hubley, P. (1978). Secondary intersubjectivity: Confidence, confiding and acts of meaning in the first year. In A. Lock (Ed.), *Action, gesture and symbol: The emergence of language* (pp. 183–229). London: Academic Press.

Tronick, E., Als, H., Adamson, L.,Wise, S., & Brazelton, T. B. (1978). The infants' response to entrapment between contradictory messages in face-to-face interactions. *Journal of the American Academy of Child Psychiatry, 17*, 1–13.

Varela, F., Thompson, E., & Rosch, E. (1991). *The embodied mind*. Cambridge, MA: MIT Press.

Walker, A. S. (1982). Intermodal perception of expressive behaviors by human infants. *Journal of Experimental Child Psychology, 33*, 514–535.

Wellman, H. M. (1993). Early understanding of mind: The normal case. In S. Baron-Cohen, H. Tager-Flusberg, & D.J. Cohen (Eds.), *Understanding other minds: Perspectives from autism* (pp. 10–39). Oxford, UK: Oxford University Press.

Wimmer, H., & Perner, J. (1983). Beliefs about beliefs: Representation and constraining function of wrong beliefs in young children's understanding of deception. *Cognition, 13*, 103–128.

Woodward, A. L., & Sommerville, J. A. (2000). Twelve-month-old infants interpret action in context. *Psychological Science, 11*, 73–77.

Zahavi, D., & Parnas, J. (2003). Conceptual problems in infantile autism research: Why cognitive science needs phenomenology. *Journal of Consciousness Studies, 10*(9–10), 53–71.

PART II

Social Experience and Epigenetic Mechanisms of Gene–Environment Interactions

CHAPTER 4

Differential Susceptibility

Developmental and Evolutionary Mechanisms of Gene–Environment Interactions

MICHAEL PLUESS
SUZANNE E. STEVENS
JAY BELSKY

Central to much thinking about human development is the presumption that experiences in the early years of life influence individual differences in later development. This is reflected in the large number of studies investigating how environmental experiences encountered early in life relate to functioning later in life. Consider in this regard studies chronicling links between prenatal maternal stress and temperament in infancy (Huizink, de Medina, Mulder, Visser, & Buitelaar, 2002), between maternal sensitivity in the first year and attachment security thereafter (Bakermans-Kranenburg, van IJzendoorn, & Juffer, 2003), between quality of child care in the preschool years and vocabulary scores at age 10 years (Belsky et al., 2007), between parental divorce/separation in early adolescence and school grades later in adolescence (Lansford et al., 2006), and between early family environment and depression symptomatology in early adulthood (Taylor et al., 2006).

Even though a great deal of effort has been spent trying to elucidate *whether, how much*, and *how* early experiences affect later functioning, the evolutionary ultimate question as to *why* any relation should exist between early experience and later development has rarely been considered by developmentally minded thinkers. Consider in this regard research on the (proximate) determinants of infant attachment security. Despite the fact that Bowlby (1969) drew heavily on evolutionary reasoning when formulating his attachment theory, his concern with ultimate causation has been more or less abandoned in developmental studies of individual differences in attachment (for exceptions, see Belsky, Steinberg, & Draper, 1991; Chisholm, 1996; Simpson & Belsky, 2008). Although an abundance of evidence supports Bowlby's

(1969) thesis that a secure attachment lays the foundation for general well-being and Ainsworth's (1973) proposition that it is maternal sensitivity that fosters security, developmentalists fascinated with the attachment bond rarely wonder *why* development operates this way rather than some other.

What has been widely investigated and appreciated, though, is that individuals vary in whether and/or the degree to which they are affected, over the shorter and longer term, by developmental experiences as a result of their personal characteristics. Perhaps the most striking evidence that this is the case and that person characteristics condition or moderate environmental effects is found in research on gene–environment interaction (G×E) (Burmeister, McInnis, & Zollner, 2008). Much such work chronicles the fact that early as well as recent experiences seem to exert a stronger effect on development in the case of individuals carrying certain genetic variants, whereas others carrying different ones are much less affected or not at all influenced when exposed to the very same experiences. Yet again, though, the evolutionary question of *why* this should be the case in the first place is rarely addressed.

It is the purpose of this chapter to consider these rarely discussed but fundamental questions as to why early experiences should prove influential for the later functioning and why this should be more so for some people than for others. After presenting three different evolutionary-inspired theoretical arguments as to why individuals should differ in their susceptibility to environmental influences, we review a selection of empirical evidence of G×E findings consistent with these theoretical arguments. In a concluding section, questions regarding differential susceptibility are raised, focusing on, among others, the roles of nature and nurture and potential mediating mechanisms.

Evolutionary Perspective

Two distinct, though by no means mutually exclusive, evolutionary-inspired theoretical arguments challenge the idea that early experiences should prove influential for all: (1) Belsky's (1997a, 1997b, 2005) differential-susceptibility (DS) hypothesis and (2) Boyce and Ellis's (2005; Ellis, Essex, & Boyce, 2005; Ellis, Jackson, & Boyce, 2006) biological-sensitivity-to-context (BSC) thesis. Importantly, both models predict that some children and perhaps adults will be more susceptible than others to not only adverse but also beneficial effects of, respectively, unsupportive and supportive contextual conditions.

The following two sections delineating each perspective are largely based on a more extensive discussion of evolutionary aspects of the DS hypothesis and the BSC thesis by Ellis, Boyce, Belsky, Bakermans-Kranenburg, and van IJzendoorn (2011).

Differential Susceptibility

The question "*Why* should childhood experiences influence later development?" was the origin of DS theory. It arose when the behavior genetic critique of much socialization research was specifically directed at Belsky and colleagues' (1991) evolutionary theory of socialization, which attempted to recast thinking about early experience in terms of the developmental regulation of reproductive strategy (Rowe, 2000; Rowe,

Vazsonyi, & Figueredo, 1997). Central to the theory was the conditional adaptation-based claim that stressful and supportive extrafamilial environments *influence* family dynamics, most especially parent–child and parent–parent relationships, thereby *shaping* children's early emotional and behavioral development and, through it, subsequent reproductive development and fitness. Behavior genetic analyses suggested, instead, that variation in children's emotional and behavioral development and subsequent reproductive strategies was attributable not so much to family experiences but rather to genes shared by parents and children and thus genetic mediation.

This challenge led Belsky (1997a, 1997b, 2000, 2005) to reflect on why, from an evolutionary perspective, there would even be the expectation that later development would be influenced by earlier experiences. This would seem to make biological sense only if the future was tolerably related to the past, at least within generations. Only then could there be reliable fitness payoffs in using developmental experiences in childhood to regulate reproductive functioning in adolescence and adulthood. The fact that the future is inherently uncertain, however, meant that natural selection for a developmental mechanism that used early experiences to functionally match organisms to expected future environments (i.e., conditional adaptation) was theoretically problematic.

This realization led Belsky (1997a, 1997b, 2000, 2005) to propose that, while genes common to parents and their progeny could, in the case of some, shape both environmental conditions early in life (e.g., hostile parenting) and components of reproductive strategy in adolescence and adulthood (e.g., opportunistic/advantage-taking social orientation, early puberty and sexual debut), this might not be so in the case of others. Indeed, it would be evolutionarily strategic, he theorized, for "conditional" and "alternative" reproductive strategies to evolve (Rowe et al., 1997). Whereas conditional strategies would be shaped by environmental factors to better fit the organism to the future environment in a manner consistent with Belsky and colleagues' (1991) original formulation, alternative strategies would, in a manner consistent with behavior genetic thinking, be largely fixed and less subject to environmental influence. Consequently, natural selection would have shaped parents to bear children varying in *developmental plasticity* as a fitness-optimizing strategy involving the hedging of bets (Belsky, 2005). This way, if environmental effects (e.g., parenting) proved counterproductive in fitness terms, those children not affected by it would not have incurred the cost of developing in ways that ultimately proved "misguided" when it came to passing on genes to future generations. Importantly, in light of inclusive-fitness considerations, these less malleable children's reduced susceptibility to environmental influences would have benefited not only themselves directly but their more malleable sibs as well but indirectly, given that sibs, like parents and children, share 50% of their specific alleles. By the same token, had the parenting influenced children in ways that enhanced fitness, then not only would more plastic or malleable offspring have benefited directly by virtue of parental influence, but so, too, would their parents and even their less malleable sibs who did not benefit from the parenting they received, again for inclusive-fitness reasons (i.e., shared genes).

Although Belsky's theorizing stipulated that children should vary in their susceptibility to environmental influences, it did not specify what might distinguish those children who were more susceptible from those who were less. Belsky (1997a, 1997b,

2005) presumed that individuals varied for genetic reasons in their developmental plasticity without denying the possibility of environmental influences on malleability. Early attempts to identify potential susceptibility factors or markers called attention, somewhat surprisingly, to negative emotionality or difficult temperament (Belsky, 1997a, 2005; Belsky, Hsieh, & Crnic, 1998), whereas G×E work, as well as theory and research on physiological reactivity by Boyce and Ellis (Boyce et al., 1995; Boyce & Ellis, 2005), called attention to genetic and physiological markers of variation in susceptibility (e.g., Bakermans-Kranenburg & van IJzendoorn, 2007; Belsky & Pluess, 2009a).

Biological Sensitivity to Context

The concept of BSC has its roots in a 1995 *Psychosomatic Medicine* report by Boyce and colleagues, presenting two studies of naturally occurring environmental adversities and stress reactivity as predictors of respiratory illnesses in 3- to 5-year-old children. Results revealed, first, that children showing low cardiovascular or immune reactivity to stressors had approximately equal rates of respiratory illnesses in both low- and high-adversity settings. Second, and consistent with the prevailing diathesis-stress model, highly biologically reactive children exposed to high-adversity child care settings or home environments had substantially higher illness incidences than all other groups of children. Third, and unexpectedly, highly reactive children living in lower adversity conditions (i.e., more supportive child care or family settings) had the *lowest* illness rates, significantly lower than even low-reactivity children in comparable settings. Boyce and colleagues thus advanced what would later become known as the *differential-susceptibility hypothesis* (and which Belsky, 1997a, 1997b, promulgated on a purely theoretical basis, without awareness of the work of Boyce et al.): that children differ in their susceptibility to environmental influence in a "for-better-and-for-worse" manner. Furthermore, the initial Boyce and colleagues research, together with subsequent work (Boyce & Ellis, 2005), identified a physiological mechanism of environmental susceptibility—autonomic, adrenocortical, or immune reactivity to psychosocial stressors—and proposed that psychobiological reactivity moderated the effects of early environmental exposures on physical and mental health outcomes in a bivalent manner. More reactive children displayed heightened sensitivity to both positive and negative environmental influences and thus were given the shorthand designation of *orchid* children, signifying their special susceptibility to both highly stressful and highly nurturing environments. Children low in reactivity, on the other hand, were designated as *dandelion* children, reflecting their relatively high capacity for thriving in species-typical circumstances of all varieties (Boyce & Ellis, 2005).

Boyce and Ellis (2005) further argued that for adaptive reasons children in both especially supportive and especially unsupportive developmental contexts should develop or maintain high levels of physiological stress reactivity, which they regard as a susceptibility factor and thus plasticity mechanism, that is, the endophenotypic instantiation of susceptibility to environmental influence. Thus, they expect a curvilinear, U-shaped relation between levels of supportiveness versus stressfulness in early childhood environments and the development of stress-reactive profiles, with high reactivity disproportionately emerging in both highly stressful and highly protected social environments. In the case of children fortunate enough to grow up in particularly supportive contexts, Boyce and Ellis contend that it would be adaptive to be maximally influenced by the developmental environment. Indeed, the physical, behavioral, and psychological embodiment of the rich resource base provided by the family and the broader ecology would enhance the social competitiveness of the individual through the development of a broad range of competencies, thereby increasing his or her mate value and eventual reproductive fitness. In contrast, those growing up under harsh and dangerous conditions would increase their chances of survival and eventual reproduction if they developed heightened vigilance to threat and proved highly prepared to actively combat risks that they might face. For them, too, heightened physiological reactivity is presumed to be the vehicle for getting this developmental job done. Thus, it is Boyce and Ellis's thesis that the stress–response system operates as a conditional adaptation, selected to enable individuals to fit environments that, starting early in life, would enhance their fitness prospects.

Central to all evolutionary arguments under consideration is the claim that individual differences in plasticity have evolved. In fact, a 2008 simulation study by Wolf, van Doorn, and Weissing seeking to determine whether plasticity could evolve clearly showed this to be the case, with some individuals being more responsive to environmental conditions than others.

For Better and for Worse?

Both DS and BSC arguments define individual differences in developmental plasticity to mean that some children and even adults will be more susceptible than others to both the adverse *and* beneficial effects of, respectively, unsupportive and supportive contextual conditions. This view contrasts markedly with traditional dual-risk/diathesis-stress frameworks, on which most GxE studies are based, that regard certain putatively "vulnerable" individuals as more likely than others to be adversely affected by unsupportive contextual conditions, while stipulating nothing about differential responsiveness to supportive conditions (Monroe & Simons, 1991; Sameroff, 1983; Zuckerman, 1999). Therefore, diathesis-stress thinking does not propose, as the DS and BSC theories explicitly do, that the very individual attributes that make some individuals disproportionately susceptible to adversity simultaneously make them disproportionately likely to benefit from supportive ones (Belsky & Pluess, 2009a). Throughout the next section, we present illustrative GxE evidence of differential susceptibility to environmental influence that is consistent with the view that individuals differ in their plasticity, with some being more affected than others by experiential influences in a for-better-*and*-for-worse manner.

Empirical Evidence for DS

This selective review of GxE findings consistent with the DS hypothesis concentrates on those between early environmental experiences (e.g., early adversity, parenting competence) and three well-known genetic polymorphisms: monoamine oxidase A (MAOA), serotonin transporter (5-HTTLPR), and dopamine receptor D4 (DRD4); for a more comprehensive review, see Belsky and Pluess (2009a).

Monoamine Oxidase A

The MAOA gene is located on the X chromosome. It encodes the MAOA enzyme, which metabolizes neurotransmitters such as norepinephrine, serotonin, and dopamine, rendering them inactive. Two sets of evidence—one linking the low-activity MAOA allele to antisocial behavior and another linking abuse and neglect in childhood to the same developmental outcome—led Caspi and associates (2002) to hypothesize that inconsistency in findings in both literatures could be a result of the fact that maltreatment effects are moderated by genotype; and this is exactly what they discovered in their groundbreaking G×E research carried out on a New Zealand birth cohort followed into young adulthood. More specifically, it was principally young men—females were not studied—with one form of the gene that is associated with low MAOA activity who proved most violence prone when subject to child maltreatment. For those children with the high-MAOA-activity allele, a substantially smaller effect of child maltreatment emerged.

Although most have interpreted these findings, not unreasonably, in diathesis-stress terms, few seem to have noticed that those most vulnerable to the adverse effects of maltreatment actually scored lowest in antisocial behavior when not exposed to maltreatment, suggesting perhaps greater plasticity rather than just greater vulnerability to adversity. This interpretation is buttressed by results of a reasonably large number of studies seeking to replicate the Caspi and colleagues (2002) findings. For example, Kim-Cohen and colleagues (2006) found that at age 7 boys with the low-MAOA-activity variant were rated by mothers and teachers as having more mental health problems, and specifically attention-deficit/hyperactivity disorder symptoms, if they had been victims of abuse, but fewer problems if they had not, compared with boys with the high-MAOA-activity genotype. In a large longitudinal study of adolescent twin boys ages 8–17 years, Foley and colleagues (2004) observed that those with the low-MAOA-activity allele were more likely to be diagnosed with conduct disorder if exposed to higher levels of childhood adversity and less likely if exposed to lower levels of adversity compared with boys with the high-MAOA-activity allele. Similar results emerged in Nilsson and associates' (2006) cross-sectional investigation of adolescent boys when the predictor was psychosocial risk, operationalized in terms of maltreatment experience and living arrangement, and the outcome to be explained was criminal behavior (composite of vandalism, violence, stealing).

Four additional studies provide more evidence of the heightened susceptibility to environmental influences of individuals carrying the low-MAOA allele. One was a prospective investigation of the long-term effects of (court-substantiated) child abuse and neglect on white male and female violent and antisocial behavior in adolescence and through the early 40s (Widom & Brzustowicz, 2006). The second was a retrospective study of adult psychiatric outpatients and healthy controls linking trauma experienced in childhood with physical aggression in adulthood (Frazzetto et al., 2007). The third was a retrospective study of female American Indians investigating effects of childhood sexual abuse on symptoms of antisocial personality disorder (Ducci et al., 2008). The fourth was a large longitudinal study of prospectively measured stressful life events in infancy and early childhood and their relation to hyperactivity at ages 4 and 7 years. The pattern of differential susceptibility was apparent in the results presented for the girls but not for the boys (Enoch, Steer, Newman, Gibson, & Goldman, 2009).

Serotonin Transporter

Far more studied than G×E interactions involving MAOA have been those involving 5-HTTLPR. The serotonin transporter–linked polymorphic region (5-HTTLPR) is a degenerate repeat polymorphic region in SLC6A4, the gene that codes for the serotonin transporter. Most research focuses on two variants—those carrying at least one short allele (s/s, s/l) and those homozygous for the long allele (l/l)—though more variants than these have been identified (Nakamura, Ueno, Sano, & Tanabe, 2000). The short allele has generally been associated with reduced expression of the serotonin transporter molecule, which is involved in the reuptake of serotonin from the synaptic cleft, and thus considered to be related to depression, either directly or in the face of adversity.

Although our focus in the current chapter is on the effects of early experience, the majority of the G×E research on the *5-HTTLPR* has been done in relation to life events in adulthood, including the seminal work in this area carried out by Caspi and associates (2003) on depressive symptoms, probability of suicide ideation/attempts, and major depressive episodes. With relevance for our focus on early experience, Taylor and associates (2006) reported that young adults homozygous for the short allele (s/s) manifested greater depressive symptomatology than individuals with other allelic variants when they retrospectively reported a problematic childrearing history (as well as, independently, many recent negative life events), yet the fewest symptoms when they experienced a supportive early environment (or, independently, recent positive experiences).

The effect of 5-HTTLPR in moderating environmental influences in a manner consistent with differential susceptibility is not restricted to depression and its symptoms, affecting a wide range of other behavioral outcomes, including negative emotionality in infancy (Pauli-Pott, Friedel, Hinney, & Hebebrand, 2009); ADHD, particularly that which persists into adulthood (Retz et al., 2008); anxiety (Gunthert et al., 2007; Stein, Schork, & Gelernter, 2008); and posttraumatic stress disorder (Xie et al., 2009). In all this research, whether examining effects of childhood emotional abuse (Stein et al., 2008), maternal attachment (Pauli-Pott et al., 2009), or adverse childrearing environment (Retz et al., 2008), it proved to be those individuals carrying one or two copies of the short allele who responded to developmental or concurrent experiences in a for-better-*and*-for-worse manner, depending on the nature of the experience in question.

Dopamine Receptor D4

Moving from the serotonergic to the dopaminergic system, which is engaged in attentional, motivational, and reward mechanisms, a polymorphism of the DRD4 gene has also stimulated much G×E research. Variants of the DRD4 differ by the number of 48-base pair tandem repeats in exon III, ranging from 2 to 11. The 7-repeat variant has been identified as a *vulnerability* factor because of its links to ADHD (Faraone,

Doyle, Mick, & Biederman, 2001), high novelty-seeking behavior (Kluger, Siegfried, & Ebstein, 2002), and low dopamine-reception efficiency (Robbins & Everitt, 1999), among other correlates.

Yet a number of studies indicate that not only are individuals carrying this putative risk allele more adversely affected than others by poor environmental conditions but, broadly conceived, they also benefit more from good-quality ones (van IJzendoorn & Bakermans-Kranenburg, 2006). Four related inquiries focused on parenting are considered particularly important because a "good" environment was operationalized not just as the absence of adversity, as is common in psychiatric genetic research (Belsky et al., 2009), but in terms of high-quality parenting. In a longitudinal investigation, maternal sensitivity observed when children were 10 months old predicted externalizing problems reported by mothers more than 2 years later, but only for children carrying the 7-repeat DRD4 allele (Bakermans-Kranenburg & van IJzendoorn, 2006). Whereas such children displayed the most externalizing behavior of all children when mothers were judged insensitive, they also manifested the least externalizing behavior when mothers were highly sensitive (but see, for contradictory results, Propper, Willoughby, Halpern, Carbone, & Cox, 2007). A cross-sectional study of sensation seeking in 18- to 21-month-old children generated results in line with those just summarized. Toddlers with the 7-repeat allele, compared with those without, were rated by parents as showing less sensation-seeking behavior when parenting quality was high but more of this behavior when parenting quality was low (Sheese, Voelker, Rothbart, & Posner, 2007). Likewise, in a cross-sectional study on the effect of maternal attachment security on altruistic, prosocial behavior (operationalized as amount of money provided by an experimenter subsequently donated to UNICEF following exposure to UNICEF promotional film clips of poor children) among 7-year-old twins, it was found that children with the DRD4 7-repeat allele donated the most coins of all when they had a secure attachment and the least coins of all when their attachment was insecure (Bakermans-Kranenburg & van IJzendoorn, 2011).

Experimental intervention research designed to enhance parenting also reveals a moderating effect of the 7-repeat allele. When Bakermans-Kranenburg, van IJzendorn, Pijlman, Mesman, and Juffer (2008) looked at change over time in parenting—from before to well after a video-feedback parenting intervention was provided on a random basis to mothers of 1- to 3-year-olds who scored high on externalizing problems—they found that the intervention succeeded in promoting more sensitive parenting and positive discipline. Moreover, this intervention effect translated into improvements in child behavior but only for those children carrying the DRD4 7-repeat allele.

Discussion

The preceding summary of G×E studies provides extensive, although illustrative and selective, empirical evidence for the evolutionary-based theoretical claim that some individuals should be more affected by early experiences than others. More specifically, some individuals appear more susceptible to both the adverse effects of unsupportive contextual conditions *and* the beneficial effects of supportive ones as a function of genotype. Given the diathesis-stress focus of much of the available G×E research, most reviewed studies measure both a restricted range of environments, typically emphasizing the negative end of the spectrum and failing to measure at all the positive (except for the absence of adversity), and a restricted range of psychological and behavioral outcomes, also typically emphasizing the negative, thereby failing to assess competent functioning (except for the absence of dysfunction). Of course, there are exceptions (e.g., Kaufman et al., 2004, 2006; Wilhelm et al., 2006). This raises the possibility that studies are actually poorly designed to differentiate differential susceptibility from diathesis-stress and that the former may go undetectable in studies designed to test the latter.

Qualitative or Quantitative Trait?

The fact that some single-gene variants appear to influence whether an individual is more or less susceptible to both negative and positive environmental influences seems to indicate that differences in plasticity are best conceptualized in qualitative rather than quantitative terms. Adopting evolutionary terminology pertaining to reproductive strategy, this would mean that there exist "plastic and fixed strategists" who are and are not, respectively, susceptible to environmental experiences, thereby following "conditional" and "alternative" pathways of development as previously mentioned (Belsky, 2000). However, the observation that different and unrelated gene polymorphisms are associated with developmental plasticity means that an individual can carry more or less of these plasticity alleles (e.g., the 5-HTTLPR short allele *and* the DRD4 7-repeat allele); this raises the possibility that the more plasticity alleles an individual carries, the more susceptible to environmental influences he or she will prove to be. Consequently, genetic developmental plasticity may be better understood as a quantitative trait that involves a multitude of different gene variants (Plomin, Haworth, & Davis, 2009) and in terms of a "plasticity gradient," with individuals varying in degree of susceptibility to environmental influences as a function of the sum of plasticity alleles (see Figure 4.1) (Belsky et al., 2009; Belsky & Pluess, 2009a).

Some evidence consistent with this proposition comes from two recent studies, one addressing this issue in a post hoc fashion and the other on an a priori basis. In the former, in their study of 5- to 17-year-olds diagnosed with ADHD, Sonuga-Barke and associates (2009) discovered, after identifying two separate G×E interactions, that children carrying alleles other than 10R/10R in the case of DAT1 *and* other than two long alleles in the case of 5-HTTLPR proved most susceptible to the anticipated adverse effects of high levels of maternal expressed (negative) emotion on conduct disorder. In the second study, individuals were scored in terms of whether they carried 0/1, 2, 3, or 4/5 putative plasticity alleles—5-HTTLPR short allele, MAOA 2R/3R, DRD4 7-repeat, DRD2 A1, and DAT1 10R—to test the hypothesis that those with more plasticity alleles would be more affected by parenting quality than those carrying fewer when the outcome to be explained was self-control in adolescence (Belsky & Beaver, 2011); this is exactly what was found in the case of males. More than anything else, what these two preliminary inquiries suggest is that individuals carrying more plasticity alleles do appear more susceptible to at least some environmental influences than those carrying fewer. Indeed, the Belsky and Beaver (2011) work

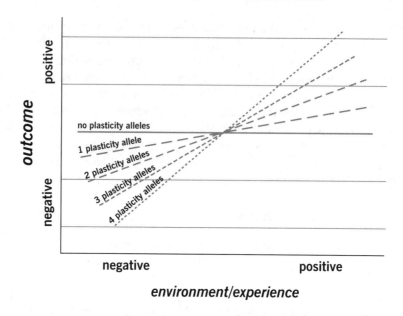

FIGURE 4.1. Plasticity gradient as a function of plasticity allele frequency.

suggests that further efforts should be made to measure cumulative genetic plasticity by creating a composite score based on multiple plasticity alleles—in much the same way as multiple environmental risk factors are often combined to create indices of cumulative contextual risk (e.g., Belsky & Fearon, 2002).

Nature or Nurture?

The G×E evidence cited in this chapter certainly suggests that differences in developmental plasticity are primarily a function of genotype. Also consistent with, but by no means confirming, this view is animal research showing that plasticity is heritable in many species (Bashey, 2006; Pigliucci, 2007). But just because G×E studies are replete with evidence, often unnoticed, of differential susceptibility should not lead to the presumption that plasticity is only a function of genetics. Central to Boyce and Ellis's (2005) thinking, it will be recalled, is the role of extremely supportive and unsupportive environments in fostering physiological reactivity and, thereby, developmental plasticity. Especially notable, in this regard, is recent research on the putatively adverse effects of maternal stress during pregnancy. This is because "prenatal programming" appears to predict both physiological (e.g., cortisol reactivity) and behavioral (e.g., infant negative emotionality) characteristics found in work cited elsewhere (Belsky & Pluess, 2009b; Pluess & Belsky, 2011) to demarcate heightened susceptibility to environmental influences. For example, in the National Institute of Child Health and Human Development (NICHD) study of early child care, low birth weight—a marker for adverse prenatal environment—predicted infant difficult temperament (Pluess & Belsky, 2011), an empirically established marker within the NICHD study of heightened susceptibility to both negative and positive effects of early rearing experience (Bradley & Corwyn, 2008; Pluess & Belsky, 2009, 2010).

It also seems appropriate to hypothesize that some fetuses, because of their genetic makeup, will prove more susceptible to prenatal stress effects, including those on physiological and behavioral susceptibility factors and, thereby, on postnatal plasticity (Belsky & Pluess, 2009b). First evidence of genetic susceptibility to prenatal experiences emerged in a reanalysis of data from Neuman and associates' (2007) G×E study of effects of maternal smoking during pregnancy on ADHD in childhood (Pluess, Belsky, & Neuman, 2009). Children carrying the dopamine receptor D4 7-repeat allele proved most *and* least likely of all studied, including those not carrying this allele, to develop ADHD, depending on whether their mothers did and did not smoke during pregnancy. A recent G×E study based on data from a large Dutch cohort study chronicled first empirical evidence for the just-stated hypothesis that some fetuses will be more affected by prenatal stress vis-à-vis postnatal plasticity factors as a function of genes (Pluess et al., 2011). Maternal anxiety during pregnancy significantly predicted negative emotionality at 6 months in infants carrying one or more copies of the 5-HTTLPR short allele, but not in those homozygous for the long allele, suggesting that individuals carrying certain genotypes who are exposed to specific prenatal environments are more likely than those not carrying such alleles or not so exposed to prove susceptible to postnatal environmental influences. Hence, developmental plasticity is a function not just of nature or nurture but also of their interaction (Belsky & Pluess, 2009b).

Not to be ignored in this discussion of the determinants of developmental plasticity is evidence that physiological and behavioral susceptibility factors are also shaped by postnatal experiences (e.g., Heim et al., 2000; Kaplan, Evans, & Monk, 2008). Figure 4.2 represents a schematic model outlining multiple means and pathways by which developmental plasticity is likely regulated, including (1) genetic contributions to susceptibility; (2) genetic contributions mediated by behavioral and physiological susceptibility factors; (3) prenatal and (4) postnatal environmental effects on behavioral and physiological susceptibility factors; (5) G×E interactions involving the prenatal and (6) postnatal environment; and (7) interactions between the prenatal and postnatal environment in shaping susceptibility factors.

Empirical evidence for the moderating effect of postnatal experiences can be found in Bergman, Sarkar, Glover, and O'Connor's (2008) longitudinal study of 123 mother–child dyads. The association between prenatal stress (i.e., stressful life events during pregnancy) and observed child fearfulness at 17 months postpartum—a behavioral susceptibility factor—proved to be itself moderated by attachment security, which can be considered a marker for quality of the rearing environment given the well-established, even causal, connection between maternal sensitivity and attachment security (Belsky & Fearon, 2008). The effect of prenatal stress on child fearfulness was strongest in children with an insecure/resistant attachment, suggesting that prenatal experiences interact with early postnatal experiences in regulating developmental plasticity. Relatedly, although focusing on the prediction of depression, Costello, Worthman, Erkanli, and Angold (2007) found that low birth weight, an indicator for prenatal adversity, predicted adolescent depression more strongly in girls with a history of adverse postnatal experiences, suggesting that effects of prenatal experiences are conditional on the postnatal environment.

Pre- and postnatal programming of developmental plasticity is likely a function of epigenetic mechanisms, as suggested in Figure 4.2. Oberlander and colleagues'

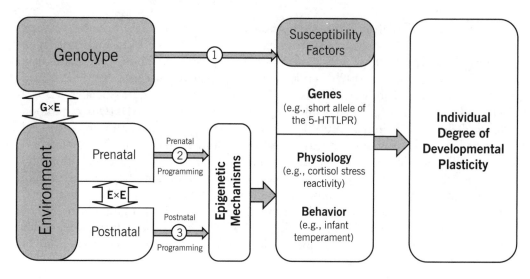

FIGURE 4.2. Nature, nurture, and differential susceptibility: A process model. 1, genetic contribution to general susceptibility partially mediated by susceptibility factors (nature); 2, prenatal environment shapes susceptibility factors (nurture); 3, postnatal environment shapes susceptibility factors (nurture). In addition, genotype interacts with both prenatal and postnatal environment, and prenatal and postnatal environments interact with each other to shape susceptibility factors. GxE, gene–environment interaction; ExE, environment–environment interaction.

(2008) findings that maternal depressed mood in pregnancy predicts increased methylation of the human glucocorticoid receptor gene (NR3C1, measured in neonatal cord blood), which itself forecasts elevated cortisol stress reactivity at age 3 months, a physiological susceptibility factor, provide empirical evidence for epigenetic mechanisms that may be central to the programming of developmental plasticity, in fact the very one that Boyce and Ellis (2005) heralded in their BSC thesis.

Developmental Perspective

The different pathways in the prediction of developmental plasticity (see Figure 4.2) suggest that the capacity for developmental plasticity is a function of nature, nurture, and manifold interactions between the two. Additionally, the observation that later environmental factors moderate effects of earlier ones in the prediction of behavioral susceptibility factors (e.g., Bergman et al., 2008) suggests that susceptibility to environmental influences develops across childhood/adolescence —and potentially even during adulthood—as a function of genes and different environmental experiences. As illustrated in the developmental model in Figure 4.3, developmental plasticity in early infancy (A) can be considered a function of genes, the prenatal environment, and the interaction between both. Developmental plasticity in childhood (B), then, is a function of genes, the postnatal environment, and the interaction between prenatally programmed plasticity (A) and the postnatal environment. This postnatally programmed plasticity (B) interacts further with consequent environmental factors throughout childhood/adolescence and predicts, together with main effects of genes and environmental factors, the developmental plasticity in adulthood (C). According

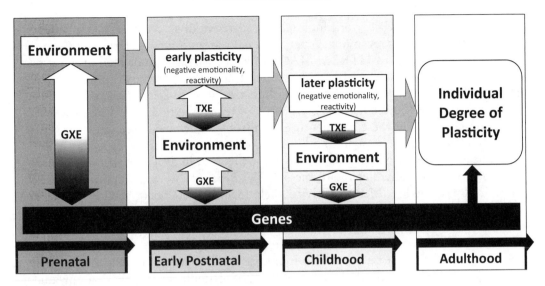

FIGURE 4.3. Developmental model of developmental plasticity across childhood; G×E = gene–environment interaction; T×E, temperament–environment interaction.

to this developmental model, plasticity can be understood as a primarily genetic potential that unfolds to different degrees dependent on successive environmental factors. Furthermore, as illustrated in Figure 4.3, early experiences are expected to have stronger effects on developmental plasticity than later ones.

Mediating Mechanisms

Although G×E findings chronicling differential susceptibility effects are being reported in growing numbers, knowledge regarding underlying biological mechanisms remains very limited. One of the primary reasons why some individuals are more responsive to environmental conditions than others may be because they have a more sensitive nervous system (Aron & Aron, 1997). More specifically, they may have lower thresholds for experiencing pleasure and/or displeasure, thus being more sensitive and responsive than others to, respectively, rewards and/or punishments, very broadly conceived (Gray, 1981, 1982). Although it is rather easy to see how having a lower threshold for discomfort might make one more likely to respond in a negative, problematic way to adverse and displeasure-inducing experiences, maybe by becoming depressed, anxious, and/or antisocial, it is perhaps more difficult to see why such individuals would also be more likely to prove susceptible, as the DS viewpoint presupposes, to the benefits of positive environments. By the same token, although it is easy to imagine how having a low threshold for pleasure might increase an individual's responsiveness to rewards and thus enable one to benefit more from positive, supportive experiences, it is difficult to imagine how this proclivity could translate into being more adversely affected by negative experiences. Perhaps, though, this conundrum is more apparent than real, if only because the reduction of discomfort and the loss or denial of a rewarding experience may register most powerfully on those who have low thresholds for, respectively, displeasure and pleasure.

Intriguingly, the G×E work highlighting differential susceptibility may be consistent with this line of reasoning. After all, it calls attention to both the serotonergic system (i.e., 5-HTTLPR, HTR2A, MAOA, THP1), which is implicated in the experience of displeasure (e.g., depression, anxiety), and the dopaminergic system (i.e., DRD4, DRD2, MAOA), which has been linked to reward sensitivity and sensation seeking (Robbins & Everitt, 1999). Our line of reasoning, along with the G×E evidence, implicates that these two neurotransmitter systems would seem not unrelated to Gray's (1981, 1982) behavioral inhibition and behavioral activation systems.

The amygdala also seems very likely to be involved in differential susceptibility–related processes. Individuals with the 5-HTTLPR short allele (Munafo, Brown, & Hariri, 2008), the low MAOA activity allele (Meyer-Lindenberg et al., 2006), and the *COMT* met allele (Smolka et al., 2005)—all putative plasticity markers—are the ones who manifest the greatest amygdala activity/reactivity. Interestingly, according to recent research, individuals with greater amygdala reactivity are not only more responsive to fearful stimuli but also more affected by neutral (Heinz et al., 2007) and positive (Sergerie, Chochol, & Armony, 2008) stimuli, suggesting that amygdala reactivity might be a mediating central nervous mechanism of genetic susceptibility to environmental influences.

Effects of genetic susceptibility may be mediated not only by amygdala reactivity but also by other endophenotypic factors such as physiological stress reactivity and by phenotypic factors (e.g., negative emotionality). For example, negative emotionality, which has been found to moderate effects of early parenting and child care quality in a for-better-and-for-worse manner (Bradley & Corwyn, 2008; Pluess & Belsky, 2009), has also been associated with two plasticity alleles: the 5-HTTLPR short allele and the DRD4 7R allele (Holmboe, Nemoda, Fearon, Sasvari-Szekely, & Johnson, 2011). Cortisol reactivity, an endophenotypic susceptibility factor that has been found to moderate early adversity (Obradovic, Bush, Stamperdahl, Adler, & Boyce, 2010), has recently been linked to the 5-HTTLPR short allele (Mueller, Brocke, Fries, Lesch, & Kirschbaum, 2010).

The observation that the same putative plasticity genes are associated with a more reactive amygdala, negative emotionality in infancy, and also physiological stress reactivity suggests that the very children who are characterized by these traits could often be one and the same. This lends empirical support to the hypothesis that heightened susceptibility to environmental influences—demarcated by genetic, physiological, and behavioral factors—may be characterized and driven by a more sensitive central nervous system (Aron & Aron, 1997).

In conclusion, two different yet related evolutionary-inspired theoretical arguments assert that individuals should vary in their developmental plasticity in order to increase inclusive fitness. A large number of G×E studies indicate that individuals with specific gene variants—so-called plasticity alleles—are more affected by early experiences, importantly both negative and positive, suggesting that the widely embraced diathesis-stress/dual-risk model of development may seriously misrepresent some developmental processes, especially how developmental plasticity operates: Some children may not simply be more vulnerable to adverse environments but, in fact, more susceptible to both negative and positive experiences. One reason this possibility has rarely been discussed in the literature is probably a result of psychology's disproportionate focus on the *adverse* effects of *negative* experiences on *problems* in development and thus the identification of individuals, including children, who, for organismic reasons, are particularly "vulnerable" to contextual risks or "protected" from them. What the DS hypothesis postulates, in contrast, is that the very individuals who are putatively vulnerable to adversity vis-à-vis problems in development may be equally and disproportionately susceptible to the developmentally beneficial effects of supportive environments.

This fundamentally different understanding may actually require the recasting of common concepts like "vulnerability" and "resilience." Vulnerability may represent just one side of plasticity—the negative one—and therefore reflect only half of the story. The observation that "vulnerable" children will also benefit disproportionately from positive environments calls for a different, more neutral, term: susceptibility, plasticity, or malleability. "Resilience," generally understood as the advantageous ability to withstand negative effects of adverse environments, may, in fact, represent a general immunity to environmental influences of all kinds, including positive ones, not just to adversity. To the extent that this is the case, resilience, typically regarded as an advantage (in adverse environments), would seem to be disadvantageous, too— in supportive environments. In these latter contexts, the malleable will reap developmental benefits, whereas the less malleable, including perhaps the resilient, will not or will do so to a far less extent.

Acknowledgments

Preparation of this chapter was supported by a grant of the Swiss National Science Foundation awarded to Michael Pluess (Grant No. PBBSP1-130909).

References

Ainsworth, M. D. S. (1973). The development of infant–mother attachment. In B. M. Caldwell & H. N. Ricciuti (Eds.), *Review of child development research* (Vol. 3, pp. 1–94). Chicago: University of Chicago Press.

Aron, E. N., & Aron, A. (1997). Sensory-processing sensitivity and its relation to introversion and emotionality. *Journal of Personality and Social Psychology, 73*(2), 345–368.

Auerbach, J., Geller, V., Lezer, S., Shinwell, E., Belmaker, R. H., Levine, J., et al. (1999). Dopamine D4 receptor (D4DR) and serotonin transporter promoter (5-HTTLPR) polymorphisms in the determination of temperament in 2–month-old infants. *Molecular Psychiatry, 4*(4), 369–373.

Bakermans-Kranenburg, M. J., & van IJzendoorn, M. H. (2006). Gene-environment interaction of the dopamine D4 receptor (DRD4) and observed maternal insensitivity predicting externalizing behavior in preschoolers. *Developmental Psychobiology, 48*(5), 406–409.

Bakermans-Kranenburg, M. J., & van IJzendoorn, M. H. (2007). Research Review: Genetic vulnerability or differential susceptibility in child development: The case of attachment. *Journal of Child Psychology and Psychiatry and Allied Disciplines, 48*(12), 1160–1173.

Bakermans-Kranenburg, M. J., & van IJzendoorn, M. H. (2011). Differential susceptibility to rearing environment depending on dopamine-related genes: New evidence and a meta-analysis. *Development and Psychopathology, 23*(1), 39–52.

Bakermans-Kranenburg, M. J., van IJzendoorn, M. H., & Juffer, F. (2003). Less is more: Meta-analyses of sensitivity and attachment interventions in early childhood. *Psychological Bulletin, 129*(2), 195–215.

Bakermans-Kranenburg, M. J., van IJzendoorn, M. H., Pijlman, F. T., Mesman, J., & Juffer, F. (2008). Experimental evidence for differential susceptibility: Dopamine D4 receptor polymorphism (DRD4 VNTR) moderates intervention effects on toddlers' externalizing behavior in a randomized controlled trial. *Developmental Psychology, 44*(1), 293–300.

Bashey, F. (2006). Cross-generational environmental effects and the evolution of offspring size in the Trinidadian guppy Poecilia reticulata. *Evolution: International Journal of Organic Evolution, 60*(2), 348–361.

Belsky, J. (1997a). Theory testing, effect-size evaluation, and differential susceptibility to rearing influence: The case of mothering and attachment. *Child Development, 68*(4), 598–600.

Belsky, J. (1997b). Variation in susceptibility to rearing influences: An evolutionary argument. *Psychological Inquiry, 8*, 182–186.

Belsky, J. (2000). Conditional and alternative reproductive strategies: Individual differences in susceptibility to rearing experience. In J. Rodgers, D. Rowe, & W. Miller (Eds.), *Genetic influences on human fertility and sexuality: Theoretical and empirical contributions from the biological and behavioral sciences* (pp. 127–146). Boston: Kluwer.

Belsky, J. (2005). Differential susceptibility to rearing influence: An evolutionary hypothesis and some evidence. In B. J. Ellis & D. F. Bjorklund (Eds.), *Origins of the social mind: Evolutionary psychology and child development* (pp. 139–163). New York: Guilford Press.

Belsky, J., & Beaver, K. M. (2011). Cumulative-genetic plasticity, parenting and adolescent self-control/regulation. *Journal of Child Psychology and Psychiatry, 52*(5), 619–626.

Belsky, J., & Fearon, R. M. (2002). Infant–mother attachment security, contextual risk, and early development: A moderational analysis. *Development and Psychopathology, 14*(2), 293–310.

Belsky, J., & Fearon, R. M. P. (2008). Precursors of attachment security. In J. Cassidy & P. R. Shaver (Eds.), *Handbook of attachment: Theory, research, and clinical applications* (2nd ed., pp. 295–316). New York: Guilford Press.

Belsky, J., Hsieh, K. H., & Crnic, K. (1998). Mothering, fathering, and infant negativity as antecedents of boys' externalizing problems and inhibition at age 3 years: Differential susceptibility to rearing experience? *Development and Psychopathology, 10*(2), 301–319.

Belsky, J., Jonassaint, C., Pluess, M., Stanton, M., Brummett, B., & Williams, R. (2009). Vulnerability genes or plasticity genes? *Molecular Psychiatry, 14*, 746–754.

Belsky, J., & Pluess, M. (2009a). Beyond diathesis–stress: Differential susceptibility to environmental influences. *Psychological Bulletin, 135*(6), 885–908.

Belsky, J., & Pluess, M. (2009b). The nature (and nurture?) of plasticity in early human development. *Perspectives on Psychological Science, 4*(4), 345–351.

Belsky, J., Steinberg, L., & Draper, P. (1991). Childhood experience, interpersonal development, and reproductive strategy: An evolutionary theory of socialization. *Child Development, 62*(4), 647–670.

Belsky, J., Vandell, D. L., Burchinal, M., Clarke-Stewart, K. A., McCartney, K., & Owen, M. T. (2007). Are there long-term effects of early child care? *Child Development, 78*(2), 681–701.

Bergman, K., Sarkar, P., Glover, V., & O'Connor, T. G. (2008). Quality of child–parent attachment moderates the impact of antenatal stress on child fearfulness. *Journal of Child Psychology and Psychiatry and Allied Disciplines, 49*(10), 1089–1098.

Bowlby, J. (1969). *Attachment and loss: Vol. 1. Attachment.* New York: Basic Books.

Boyce, W. T., Chesney, M., Alkon, A., Tschann, J. M., Adams, S., Chesterman, B., et al. (1995). Psychobiologic reactivity to stress and childhood respiratory illnesses: Results of two prospective studies. *Psychosomatic Medicine, 57*(5), 411–422.

Boyce, W. T., & Ellis, B. J. (2005). Biological sensitivity to context: I. An evolutionary-developmental theory of the origins and functions of stress reactivity. *Development and Psychopathology, 17*(2), 271–301.

Bradley, R. H., & Corwyn, R. F. (2008). Infant temperament, parenting, and externalizing behavior in first grade: A test of the differential susceptibility hypothesis. *Journal of Child Psychology and Psychiatry and Allied Disciplines, 49*(2), 124–131.

Burmeister, M., McInnis, M. G., & Zollner, S. (2008). Psychiatric genetics: Progress amid controversy. *Nature Reviews. Genetics, 9*(7), 527–540.

Caspi, A., McClay, J., Moffitt, T. E., Mill, J., Martin, J., Craig, I. W., et al. (2002). Role of genotype in the cycle of violence in maltreated children. *Science, 297*, 851–854.

Caspi, A., Sugden, K., Moffitt, T. E., Taylor, A., Craig, I. W., Harrington, H., et al. (2003). Influence of life stress on depression: Moderation by a polymorphism in the 5-HTT gene. *Science, 301*, 386–389.

Chisholm, J. S. (1996). The evolutionary ecology of attachment organization. *Human Nature: An Interdisciplinary Biosocial Perspective, 7*(1), 1–37.

Costello, E. J., Worthman, C., Erkanli, A., & Angold, A. (2007). Prediction from low birth weight to female adolescent depression: A test of competing hypotheses. *Archives of General Psychiatry, 64*(3), 338–344.

Ducci, F., Enoch, M. A., Hodgkinson, C., Xu, K., Catena, M., Robin, R. W., et al. (2008). Interaction between a functional MAOA locus and childhood sexual abuse predicts alcoholism and antisocial personality disorder in adult women. *Molecular Psychiatry, 13*(3), 334–347.

Ellis, B. J., Boyce, W. T., Belsky, J., Bakermans-Kranenburg, M. J., & van IJzendoorn, M. H. (2011). Differential susceptibility to the environment: An evolutionary-neurodevelopmental theory. *Development and Psychopathology, 23*(1), 7–28.

Ellis, B. J., Essex, M. J., & Boyce, W. T. (2005). Biological sensitivity to context: II. Empirical explorations of an evolutionary–developmental theory. *Development and Psychopathology, 17*(2), 303–328.

Ellis, B. J., Jackson, J. J., & Boyce, W. T. (2006). The stress response systems: Universality and adaptive individual differences. *Developmental Review, 26*(2), 175–212.

Enoch, M. A., Steer, C. D., Newman, T. K., Gibson, N., & Goldman, D. (2009). Early life stress, MAOA, and gene–environment interactions predict behavioral disinhibition in children. *Genes, Brain, and Behavior, 9*(1), 65–74.

Faraone, S. V., Doyle, A. E., Mick, E., & Biederman, J. (2001). Meta-analysis of the association between the 7–repeat allele of the dopamine D(4) receptor gene and attention deficit hyperactivity disorder. *American Journal of Psychiatry, 158*(7), 1052–1057.

Foley, D. L., Eaves, L. J., Wormley, B., Silberg, J. L., Maes, H. H., Kuhn, J., et al. (2004). Childhood adversity, monoamine oxidase A genotype, and risk for conduct disorder. *Archives of General Psychiatry, 61*(7), 738–744.

Frazzetto, G., Di Lorenzo, G., Carola, V., Proietti, L., Sokolowska, E., Siracusano, A., et al. (2007). Early trauma and increased risk for physical aggression during adulthood: The moderating role of MAOA genotype. *PLoS ONE, 2*(5), e486.

Gray, J. A. (1981). A critique of Eysenck's theory of personality. In H. J. Eysenck (Ed.), *A model for personality* (pp. 246–276). Berlin: Springer-Verlag.

Gray, J. A. (1982). *The neuropsychology of anxiety: An enquiry into the functions of the septo-hippocampal system*. New York: Oxford University Press.

Gunthert, K. C., Conner, T. S., Armeli, S., Tennen, H., Covault, J., & Kranzler, H. R. (2007). Serotonin transporter gene polymorphism (5-HTTLPR) and anxiety reactivity in daily life: A daily process approach to gene–environment interaction. *Psychosomatic Medicine, 69*(8), 762–768.

Heim, C., Newport, D. J., Heit, S., Graham, Y. P., Wilcox, M., Bonsall, R., et al. (2000). Pituitary-adrenal and autonomic responses to stress in women after sexual and physical abuse in childhood. *Journal of the American Medical Association, 284*(5), 592–597.

Heinz, A., Smolka, M. N., Braus, D. F., Wrase, J., Beck, A., Flor, H., et al. (2007). Serotonin transporter genotype (5-HTTLPR): Effects of neutral and undefined conditions on amygdala activation. *Biological Psychiatry, 61*(8), 1011–1014.

Holmboe, K., Nemoda, Z., Fearon, R. M., Sasvari-Szekely, M., & Johnson, M. H. (2011). Dopamine D4 receptor and serotonin transporter gene effects on the longitudinal development of infant temperament. *Genes, Brain, and Behavior, 10*(5), 513–522.

Huizink, A. C., de Medina, P. G., Mulder, E. J., Visser, G. H., & Buitelaar, J. K. (2002). Psychological measures of prenatal stress as predictors of infant temperament. *Journal of the American Academy of Child and Adolescent Psychiatry, 41*(9), 1078–1085.

Kaplan, L. A., Evans, L., & Monk, C. (2008). Effects of mothers' prenatal psychiatric status and postnatal caregiving on infant biobehavioral regulation: Can prenatal programming be modified? *Early Human Development, 84*(4), 249–256.

Kaufman, J., Yang, B. Z., Douglas-Palumberi, H., Grasso, D., Lipschitz, D., Houshyar, S., et al. (2006). Brain-derived neurotrophic factor-5-HTTLPR gene interactions and environmental modifiers of depression in children. *Biological Psychiatry, 59*(8), 673–680.

Kaufman, J., Yang, B. Z., Douglas-Palumberi, H., Houshyar, S., Lipschitz, D., Krystal, J. H., et al. (2004). Social supports and serotonin transporter gene moderate depression in maltreated children. *Proceedings of the National Academy of Sciences USA, 101*(49), 17316–17321.

Kim-Cohen, J., Caspi, A., Taylor, A., Williams, B., Newcombe, R., Craig, I. W., et al. (2006). MAOA, maltreatment, and gene-environment interaction predicting children's mental health: New evidence and a meta-analysis. *Molecular Psychiatry, 11*(10), 903–913.

Kluger, A. N., Siegfried, Z., & Ebstein, R. P. (2002). A meta-analysis of the association between DRD4 polymorphism and novelty seeking. *Molecular Psychiatry, 7*(7), 712–717.

Lansford, J. E., Malone, P. S., Castellino, D. R., Dodge, K. A., Pettit, G. S., & Bates, J. E. (2006). Trajectories of internalizing, externalizing, and grades for children who have and have not experienced their parents' divorce or separation. *Journal of Family Psychology, 20*(2), 292–301.

Meyer-Lindenberg, A., Buckholtz, J. W., Kolachana, B., Hariri, A. R., Pezawas, L., Blasi, G., et al. (2006). Neural mechanisms of genetic risk for impulsivity and violence in humans. *Proceedings of the National Academy of Sciences USA, 103*(16), 6269–6274.

Monroe, S. M., & Simons, A. D. (1991). Diathesis-stress theories in the context of life stress research: Implications for the depressive disorders. *Psychological Bulletin, 110*(3), 406–425.

Mueller, A., Brocke, B., Fries, E., Lesch, K. P., & Kirschbaum, C. (2010). The role of the serotonin transporter polymorphism for the endocrine stress response in newborns. *Psychoneuroendocrinology, 35*(2), 289–296.

Munafo, M. R., Brown, S. M., & Hariri, A. R. (2008). Serotonin transporter (5-HTTLPR) genotype and amygdala activation: A meta-analysis. *Biological Psychiatry, 63*(9), 852–857.

Nakamura, M., Ueno, S., Sano, A., & Tanabe, H. (2000). The human serotonin transporter gene linked polymorphism (5-HTTLPR) shows ten novel allelic variants. *Molecular Psychiatry, 5*(1), 32–38.

Neuman, R. J., Lobos, E., Reich, W., Henderson, C. A., Sun, L. W., & Todd, R. D. (2007).

Prenatal smoking exposure and dopaminergic genotypes interact to cause a severe ADHD subtype. *Biological Psychiatry, 61*(12), 1320–1328.

Nilsson, K. W., Sjoberg, R. L., Damberg, M., Leppert, J., Ohrvik, J., Alm, P. O., et al. (2006). Role of monoamine oxidase A genotype and psychosocial factors in male adolescent criminal activity. *Biological Psychiatry, 59*(2), 121–127.

Oberlander, T. F., Weinberg, J., Papsdorf, M., Grunau, R., Misri, S., & Devlin, A. M. (2008). Prenatal exposure to maternal depression, neonatal methylation of human glucocorticoid receptor gene (NR3C1) and infant cortisol stress responses. *Epigenetics, 3*(2), 97–106.

Obradovic, J., Bush, N. R., Stamperdahl, J., Adler, N. E., & Boyce, W. T. (2010). Biological sensitivity to context: The interactive effects of stress reactivity and family adversity on socio-emotional behavior and school readiness. *Child Development, 81*(1), 270–289.

Pauli-Pott, U., Friedel, S., Hinney, A., & Hebebrand, J. (2009). Serotonin transporter gene polymorphism (5-HTTLPR), environmental conditions, and developing negative emotionality and fear in early childhood. *Journal of Neural Transmission, 116*(4), 503–512.

Pigliucci, M. (2007). Do we need an extended evolutionary synthesis? *Evolution: International Journal of Organic Evolution, 61*(12), 2743–2749.

Plomin, R., Haworth, C. M., & Davis, O. S. (2009). Common disorders are quantitative traits. *Nature Reviews. Genetics, 10*(12), 872–878.

Pluess, M., & Belsky, J. (2009). Differential susceptibility to rearing experience: The case of childcare. *Journal of Child Psychology and Psychiatry and Allied Disciplines, 50*(4), 396–404.

Pluess, M., & Belsky, J. (2010). Differential susceptibility to parenting and quality child care. *Developmental Psychology, 46*(2), 379–390.

Pluess, M., & Belsky, J. (2011). Prenatal programming of postnatal plasticity? *Development and Psychopathology, 23*(1), 29–38.

Pluess, M., Belsky, J., & Neuman, R. J. (2009). Prenatal smoking and attention-deficit/hyperactivity disorder: DRD4-7R as a plasticity gene. *Biological Psychiatry, 66*(4), e5–e6.

Pluess, M., Velders, F. P., Belsky, J., van IJzendoorn, M. H., Bakermans-Kranenburg, M. J., Jaddoe, V. W., et al. (2011). Serotonin transporter polymorphism moderates effects of prenatal maternal anxiety on infant negative emotionality. *Biological Psychiatry, 69*(6), 520–525.

Propper, C., Willoughby, M., Halpern, C. T., Carbone, M. A., & Cox, M. (2007). Parenting quality, DRD4, and the prediction of externalizing and internalizing behaviors in early childhood. *Developmental Psychobiology, 49*(6), 619–632.

Retz, W., Freitag, C. M., Retz-Junginger, P., Wenzler, D., Schneider, M., Kissling, C., et al. (2008). A functional serotonin transporter promoter gene polymorphism increases ADHD symptoms in delinquents: Interaction with adverse childhood environment. *Psychiatry Research, 158*(2), 123–131.

Robbins, T. W., & Everitt, B. J. (1999). Motivation and reward. In M. J. Zigmond, F. W. Bloom, S. C. Landis, J. L. Roberts, & L. R. Squire (Eds.), *Fundamental neuroscience* (pp. 1245–1260). San Diego, CA: Academic Press.

Rowe, D. C. (2000). Environmental and genetic influences on pubertal development: Evolutionary life history traits? In J. L. Rodgers, D. C. Rowe, & W. B. Miller (Eds.), *Genetic influences on human fertility and sexuality: Recent empirical and theoretical findings* (pp. 147–168). Boston: Kluwer.

Rowe, D. C., Vazsonyi, A. T., & Figueredo, A. J. (1997). Mating-effort in adolescence: A conditional or alternative strategy. *Personality and Individual Differences, 23*, 105–115.

Sameroff, A. J. (1983). Developmental systems: Contexts and evolution. In P. Mussen (Ed.), *Handbook of child psychology* (Vol. 1, pp. 237–294). New York: Wiley.

Sergerie, K., Chochol, C., & Armony, J. L. (2008). The role of the amygdala in emotional processing: A quantitative meta-analysis of functional neuroimaging studies. *Neuroscience and Biobehavioral Reviews, 32*(4), 811–830.

Sheese, B. E., Voelker, P. M., Rothbart, M. K., & Posner, M. I. (2007). Parenting quality interacts with genetic variation in dopamine receptor D4 to influence temperament in early childhood. *Development and Psychopathology, 19,* 1039–1046.

Simpson, J. A., & Belsky, J. (2008). Attachment theory within a modern evolutionary framework. In J. Cassidy & P. R. Shaver (Eds.), *Handbook of attachment: Theory, research, and clinical applications* (2nd ed., pp. 131–158). New York: Guilford Press.

Smolka, M. N., Schumann, G., Wrase, J., Grusser, S. M., Flor, H., Mann, K., et al. (2005). Catechol-O-methyltransferase val158met genotype affects processing of emotional stimuli in the amygdala and prefrontal cortex. *Journal of Neuroscience, 25*(4), 836–842.

Sonuga-Barke, E. J., Oades, R. D., Psychogiou, L., Chen, W., Franke, B., Buitelaar, J., et al. (2009). Dopamine and serotonin transporter genotypes moderate sensitivity to maternal expressed emotion: The case of conduct and emotional problems in attention deficit/hyperactivity disorder. *Journal of Child Psychology and Psychiatry and Allied Disciplines, 50*(9), 1052–1063.

Stein, M. B., Schork, N. J., & Gelernter, J. (2008). Gene-by-environment (serotonin transporter and childhood maltreatment) interaction for anxiety sensitivity, an intermediate phenotype for anxiety disorders. *Neuropsychopharmacology, 33*(2), 312–319.

Taylor, S. E., Way, B. M., Welch, W. T., Hilmert, C. J., Lehman, B. J., & Eisenberger, N. I. (2006). Early family environment, current adversity, the serotonin transporter promoter polymorphism, and depressive symptomatology. *Biological Psychiatry, 60*(7), 671–676.

van IJzendoorn, M. H., & Bakermans-Kranenburg, M. J. (2006). DRD4 7–repeat polymorphism moderates the association between maternal unresolved loss or trauma and infant disorganization. *Attachment and Human Development, 8*(4), 291–307.

Widom, C. S., & Brzustowicz, L. M. (2006). MAOA and the "cycle of violence": Childhood abuse and neglect, MAOA genotype, and risk for violent and antisocial behavior. *Biological Psychiatry, 60*(7), 684–689.

Wilhelm, K., Mitchell, P. B., Niven, H., Finch, A., Wedgwood, L., Scimone, A., et al. (2006). Life events, first depression onset and the serotonin transporter gene. *British Journal of Psychiatry, 188,* 210–215.

Wolf, M., van Doorn, G. S., & Weissing, F. J. (2008). Evolutionary emergence of responsive and unresponsive personalities. *Proceedings of the National Academy of Sciences USA, 105*(41), 15825–15830.

Xie, P., Kranzler, H. R., Poling, J., Stein, M. B., Anton, R. F., Brady, K., et al. (2009). Interactive effect of stressful life events and the serotonin transporter 5-HTTLPR genotype on posttraumatic stress disorder diagnosis in 2 independent populations. *Archives of General Psychiatry, 66*(11), 1201–1209.

Zuckerman, M. (1999). *Vulnerability to psychopathology: A biosocial model.* Washington, DC: American Psychological Association.

CHAPTER 5

Variation in Empathy

The Interplay of Genetic and Environmental Factors

ARIEL KNAFO
FLORINA UZEFOVSKY

Empathy, the experience of others' emotional, physical, or psychological states (Zahn-Waxler, Robinson, & Emde, 1992), is considered the emotional state underlying prosocial behavior (Batson, 1991; de Waal, 2008) and facilitating human communication and cooperation (Eisenberg & Miller, 1987; Marcus, Telleen, & Roke, 1979; Stiff, Dillard, Somera, Kim, & Sleight, 1988; Vaish, Carpenter, & Tomasello, 2009). It involves experiencing an affective state that is partially congruent with that of another person (e.g., Decety & Meyer, 2008; Preston & de Waal, 2003; Spinrad et al., 2006). Although there is evidence for some sort of empathy in other animals, ranging from rodents (Chen, Panksepp, & Lahvis, 2009; Langford et al., 2006) to chimpanzees (Anderson, Myowa-Yamakoshi, & Matsuzawa, 2004; de Waal, 2008, 2009; O'Connell, 1995), humans' empathic ability is remarkable (de Waal, 2009). But there are vast individual differences, too, from impaired empathy as in autism (Baron-Cohen, 1997; Smith, 2009) or callous-unemotional behavior (de Wied, Gispen-de Wied, & van Boxtel, 2010; Frick & White, 2008) to the damages caused by excessive caring in the case of empathic distress fatigue (Klimecki & Singer, 2012). Evidently, there is great variability also in the normal range of empathy in adults (Lawrence, Shaw, Baker, Baron-Cohen, & David, 2004), children (Bryant, 1982), and infants (Knafo, Zahn-Waxler, Van Hulle, Robinson, & Rhee, 2008).

Where do individual differences in children's empathy come from? Assuming that children are socialized to be empathic, can we account for individual differences in empathy by parenting? And what about other environmental variables such as schooling or life events? Because empathy has a strong biological component (Barraza & Zak, 2009; Chapman et al., 2006; de Waal, 2009; Preston & de Waal, 2003), to what extent do genes account for individual differences? We address the relative contributions of genetics and the environment by meta-analyzing the extant litera-ture. However, genetic and environmental effects cannot be seen as truly independent (Plomin, DeFries, & Loehlin, 1977), and a wide range of ways in which the two work together in affecting empathy are described using data from our study of young chil-dren's empathic development.

Before delving into the genetic, environmental, and joint contributions to empa-thy, we need to describe what we mean by it. We do not fully discuss the definition of empathy, which has been hotly debated elsewhere (Baron-Cohen & Wheelwright, 2004; Batson, Fultz, & Schoenrade, 2006; Blair, 2005; Decety & Jackson, 2004; Preston & de Waal, 2003). Instead, we describe in the following sections the pro-cesses that have been proposed to underlie empathy and the cognitive and affective components of this complex construct.

Empathic Processes

Philosophers and theorists have long been searching for an explanation and a frame of reference for humans' ability to understand each other, an ability that does not have to rely on verbal communication. Two main theories emerged to account for the process of empathy and to explain its development (Carruthers & Smith, 1996).

Theory Theory

According to this view, children's experiences in the world teach them rules, gen-eralizations, and laws that govern social cause and effect, something akin to an implicit scientific theory (Wellman, 1990). However, there is no single theory, but a constantly evolving and changing set of theories (Gopnik & Wellman, 1994). For instance, children learn either through personal experience or through observation that when one falls, hurts her knee, and cries, she is upset. Thus, the context of the behavior (falling) is used to infer the meaning of the behavior (crying). Accord-ing to this view there is an ever growing, yet finite, set of causality laws that is used to infer the meaning, intention, and feelings of an object. Before the age of 2, infants already have an underdeveloped sense of others' representational states, as evidenced by occurrences of joint attention and coordination of interactions with others (Gopnik & Wellman, 1994). Infants at this age have basic representations of desires, understanding others' behaviors through attribution of simple desires (Well-man & Woolley, 1990). As children grow older, the attributions and representations become increasingly complex.

Simulation Theory

Simulation theory suggests that we understand others' feelings, beliefs, and desires by putting ourselves in their shoes. The person imagines himself under the same circumstances, and attributes to the object what would arise in him. Importantly, this process is not necessarily a conscious one; rather, it is a mechanism employed to understand and predict others' behavior (Gordon, 1992). The theory states that the simulation mechanism is innate and is refined through development (Harris, 1992).

Components of Empathy

Reflecting the multiple theories that have tried to explain what empathy is and how it came to be, from a cognitive versus physical simulation perspective, empathy has been acknowledged as a multifaceted concept. It is important to further elucidate this concept in order to understand the development of empathy. Empathy is considered to contain a *cognitive* component, namely an understanding of what others feel or think, and an *affective* component, that is, sharing the feelings of another, while maintaining a self–other distinction (Davis, 1983; Zahn-Waxler, Radke-Yarrow, Wagner, & Chapman, 1992). For example, in children's reactions to simulated pain, the cognitive aspect of empathy is indexed by behaviors of *hypothesis testing* or inquisitiveness, in which the child actively tries to understand the other's problem, while the affective aspect of empathy, *empathic concern*, is observed in emotional expressions of concern for the victim (Zahn-Waxler et al., 1992). Several researchers (e.g., Blair, 2005) refer to a third component: *motor* empathy (involving behaviors such as mimicking others' expression). While motor empathy may be seen as an important precursor of affective empathy (Preston & de Waal, 2003), it is less central to the current report and is not discussed here.

Adam Smith (1759) was among the first to distinguish between an automatic response of emotional resonance with another person and an understanding of another's feelings, devoid of any emotional response. This view was later supported by findings from developmental psychology (Knafo, Zahn-Waxler, et al., 2008; Zahn-Waxler et al., 1992) and neuroscience (Decety & Jackson, 2004; Shamay-Tsoory & Aharon-Peretz, 2007; Shamay-Tsoory, Aharon-Peretz, & Perry, 2009). It has been suggested that while some brain regions, such as the superior temporal cortex, are involved in all aspects of the empathic process, others are unique to a specific component (Blair, 2005; Shamay-Tsoory et al., 2009). For example, the cognitive and affective aspects of empathy are differentially impaired in individuals with schizophrenia (Shamay-Tsoory et al., 2007), those with Asperger syndrome (Shamay-Tsoory, Tomer, Yaniv, & Aharon-Peretz, 2002), and patients with localized brain damage (Shamay-Tsoory & Aharon-Peretz, 2007). The conclusion stemming from these findings is that the components of empathy have a common basis (Blair, 2005), and yet we can explore the differences between them in brain anatomy and function, in behavior, and throughout development.

Another important issue concerns whether the response to others' affective states involves a distinction between the other's state and that of the self. A few hours after birth, infants respond in crying to the sound of another infant's cry (Sagi & Hoffman, 1976). Thus, the most basic aspect of *affect sharing* or *emotional resonance* is present early on. Preston and de Waal (2003) suggest that the developmental default is an automatic response to others' emotions, which is later moderated through development of knowledge and regulatory mechanisms (such as the possibility of responding differently to the plight of friends and foes). The end of this process is a relatively governed response to others. Neuroscientific evidence supports the notion that empathy has a component of emotional resonance (Decety & Meyer, 2008). Witnessing another person's plight involves activation of brain processes overlapping with those activated when the self experiences pain (Singer et al., 2004). The overlap between self and others may be using the mirror neuron system, which involves activation of the same brain processes in behavior and when observing others' goal-directed behavior (Lepage & Théoret, 2007), though evidence for this comes mainly from studies of motor empathy.

Stages of Empathy Development

Despite many years of research, there is still no consensus about the sequence in which empathy, in general, develops. However, an important account has been proposed by Hoffman (1982), who argued that empathy, at its mature form, co-develops with other cognitive-based functions. Thus, empathy development is seen as following a route from purely emotional to cognitively controlled, from an intuitive and automatic response to a complex process that relies on top-down control and regulation.

According to this account, *self–other differentiation* is the driving force behind the maturation of empathic responses from early infancy through early childhood. In Hoffman's view, we are born with a rudimentary ability to feel others but no ability to distinguish between self and other. This stage of "global empathy," lasts for most of the first year of life. A typical response to another's suffering during this stage is self-distress. The second stage begins at about 11–12 months, when the infant starts to develop an immature sense of self. At that point, her response is one of "egocentric empathic distress," that is, seeking comfort for herself upon encountering another's distress. The third stage, "quasi-egocentric empathic distress," begins in the second year of life, during which toddlers develop self–other differentiation but are still unaware of the possibility that others might have different internal states. Therefore, a toddler will offer to help or comfort others, but in a way that would be comforting to herself (e.g., by giving her teddy bear to an upset adult).

The next stage, "veridical empathic distress," has been described as developing in the second year. With mental maturation, the toddler not only becomes aware of others' feelings but also develops the ability to comprehend that these might be different than her own. Thus, children can now abandon the egocentric view and be more attuned to another's feeling and needs, developing emotional and cognitive empathy. Furthermore, as their language skills develop, children are able to understand and empathize with a broader range of emotions than before. With further cognitive development (including abstract thought), they are able to empathize with others even when they are not physically present, and later on (in adolescence) with an entire, even abstract, group of people, such as the survivors of the Haiti earthquake (Eisenberg, Fabes, & Spinrad, 1998).

Although this theory is intuitively compelling, there is lack of systematic evidence to support these claims: There has been almost no research on empathy in the first year of life (beyond studies of very early affective resonance), and to the best of our knowledge no study has longitudinally studied empathic development from early infancy to early childhood. In addition, there is some evidence for self–other differentiation as early as the first months of life (Dondi, Simion, & Caltran, 1999; Legerstee, Anderson, & Schaffer, 1998; Rochat & Hespos, 1997). Finally, there is evidence for other-focused empathic responses as early as 6 or 8 months of age (Hay, Nash, & Pedersen, 1981; Roth-Hanania & Davidov, 2009). Although the theory may not account for all early forms of empathy, it does offer the important idea that some empathic reactions are self focused rather than other focused.

Children's capacity for *emotional regulation* is also important in empathic development. When faced with others' distress, there is a tendency to experience a degree of discomfort, referred to as empathic arousal (Eisenberg, 2000). This tendency, as reflected in emotional resonance, emerges very early on (Ungerer et al., 1990). Although it is clear that an infant will respond to another's suffering, the nature of that response is not. The ability to regulate negative emotions is a key factor in determining the reaction to others' distress. Children can channel this arousal either by attending to the other person, showing *empathic concern,* or by a self-oriented response, referred to as *empathic distress* (Zahn-Waxler & Radke-Yarrow, 1990). The former entails an other-oriented process in which one identifies with the other's feeling but to a limited extent. This preservation of the outward view is possible when one is not overwhelmed with the other's feeling. The latter occurs when the other's situation exceeds one's capacity for self-regulation, and it involves a self-focused distress (Wood, Saltzberg, & Goldsamt, 1990), in which others' suffering yields feelings of anxiety and distress. This process will often involve a self-preserving reaction or behavior (e.g., looking the other way, leaving the situation) and decrease frequency of helping behaviors (Eisenberg & Fabes, 1990).

One study showed that the ability to emotionally self-regulate at 4 months predicts whether a 12-month-old infant will become distressed (as seen by an increase in self-soothing behavior) by another infant's distress. Interestingly, even at this young age there were individual differences among infants in emotion regulation, resulting in a response similar to that exhibited by adults (Ungerer et al., 1990). The importance of emotional regulation is evident in older children as well. At ages 5 and 7, children high on emotional regulation have responded more sympathetically to a distressing videotape (Eisenberg et al., 1996). Children highly knowledgeable of others' emotions were more likely to show empathy toward an experimenter in pain, if they were low in emotional problems, but the same level of affective knowledge was associated with *lower* empathy in those high in emotional problems (Knafo et al., 2009).

A third factor relevant to developmental changes in empathy involves *sociocognitive abilities.* Infants and children become increasingly capable of *affective knowledge* (i.e., recognition and differentiation among others' emotional states). Advanced affective knowledge can account for children's improved abilities to detect subtler and more complex emotions compared with "simple" distress. It is not clear when infants are first able to distinguish among facial expressions. Evidence has been found for rudimentary discrimination among emotional expressions in neonates at the age of 36 hours, as evidenced by increased visual fixation to a new expression and mimicry of the expression (Young-Browne, Rosenfeld, & Horowitz, 1977). Later, 3-month-old infants have been shown to be able to discriminate between facial expressions of surprise and happiness (Young-Browne et al., 1977). In sum, affective knowledge abilities improve substantially during early childhood (Knafo et al., 2009; Wellman, Harris, Banerjee, & Sinclair, 1995).

Another aspect of the sociocognitive ability involved in empathy has been referred to as *theory of mind* (ToM)—or the ability to take others' perspective and understand their beliefs and desires, often necessitating a suppression of the beliefs and desires of the self (Wellman, 1990). Developmental disorders of empathy, such as autism, have been described as involving low ToM abilities (Baron-Cohen, 1997). As with affective knowledge, precursors of ToM develop dramatically from infancy through early childhood (Flavell, 1999) and may account for the observed maturation of empathic ability within this time frame.

Taken together, these processes suggest that empathy should increase from infancy to middle childhood, perhaps through to adulthood. Indeed, in a study that followed children throughout the second year of life, both the frequency and range of other-oriented responses have increased steadily (Zahn-Waxler et al., 1992). In the largest developmental study of empathy to date, twins' affective empathy (empathic concern) increased during the 14- to 20-month age period. The cognitive aspect of empathy (hypothesis testing) further increased at 24 months and then again at 36 months, possibly reflecting the cognitive and linguistic maturation that takes place in this life period.

It is important to note that the same processes that influence the development of empathy into its mature form may be the ones regulating adult manifestations of empathy. For example, whether others' distress is experienced as distressing to the self to the extent that it becomes a self-focused experience affects adults' likelihood of providing support to the other person in distress (Batson, 1991). Thus, the behavioral repertoire for empathy may vary little across the lifespan, although the relative likelihood of different responses in specific conditions may vary greatly with maturation.

Genetic and Environmental Influences on Empathy

Up to this point, we discussed empathy as a behavioral characteristic present, at least in rudimentary forms, in normally functioning humans since the first days of life, and described age-related changes that may occur for all normally developing children as they grow up. It is also important to note, however, that there are meaningful individual differences in the extent of children's empathy. Knafo, Zahn-Waxler, and colleagues (2008) reported that different measurements of children's empathic response correlated positively with each other, whether one was looking at the affective and cognitive aspects of empathy, at children's behavior at the lab and at home, at their responses toward their mother and an unfamiliar examiner, or at children's responses at 14, 20, 24, or 36 months of age. Knafo, Zahn-Waxler, and colleagues saw these stable, consistent, individual differences as evidence for a broad empathy disposition. This disposition can be part of a prosocial personality disposition (Eisenberg et al., 1999), which may be proposed as a separate, hitherto neglected temperamental dimension (Knafo & Israel, 2012).

Where do individual differences in this disposition come from? Research is typically divided along the nature-versus-nurture dimension. Although currently most would agree that the contributions of nurture and nature, separately and jointly, are both important (Plomin, DeFries, McClearn, & McGuffin, 2008), a great deal of the literature is organized along this dimension, which roughly parallels the distinction between genetic and environmental factors.

Environmental Factors

Environmental factors may include both biological factors such as hormonal levels during pregnancy (Cohen-Bendahan, van de Beek, & Berenbaum, 2005; Petridou,

Panagiotopoulou, Katsournni, Spanos, & Trichopoulos, 1990; Reinisch & Sanders, 1992) and social factors. The social factors associated with empathy include parenting, educational settings, and the effects of peers and siblings. Parent behavior can become integrated as part of the child's self via mechanisms of social learning and modeling (Eisenberg, Fabes, Schaller, Carlo, & Miller, 1991) and through an encouragement of the development of specific characteristics (Davidov & Grusec, 2006a, 2006b; Grusec, Goodnow, & Kuczynski, 2000). Both modes of parental influence have been described as having an influence on empathy development. As such, supporting parenting styles and dispositional empathy of parents (Barnett, King, Howard, & Dino, 1980), and an emphasis on coping strategies and parental sympathy levels (Eisenberg et al., 1991), have all been linked to higher empathy levels in young children and in adolescents (Soenens, Duriez, Vansteenkiste, & Goossens, 2007).

Educational studies have shown that schools can influence social behavior through focused interventions. Some interventions promote and encourage prosocial behavior and diminish antisocial behavior (Cooke et al., 2007; Peng, 2008); others increase social competence and diminish externalizing problems (Holsen, Smith, & Frey, 2008). In addition to having these positive effects on social functioning, educational programs that focus on empathy can yield positive results in educational achievement and positive self-concept (Feshbach & Feshbach, 2009). The third important environmental aspect in relation to empathy is peer relationships. Social adjustment, acceptance, and functioning are very much linked to a child's ability to empathize with others (Dodge, McClaskey, & Feldman, 1985; Eisenberg, Fabes, Guthrie, & Reiser, 2000; Gleason, Jensen-Campbell, & Ickes, 2009), and emotional intelligence (i.e., an understanding of the emotions of self and other, a concept closely linked to empathy) is positively correlated to the amount of social support and the satisfaction with it (Ciarrochi, Chan, & Bajgar, 2001). In their 2009 study of adolescents with poor empathic accuracy (a kind of cognitive empathy), Gleason and colleagues found a relationship between worse peer relationship and lower adjustment. In sibling relationships, closer adult relationships have been characterized by increased empathic accuracy in both siblings (Shortt & Gottman, 2006).

Genetic Effects

Genetic effects can be estimated through two major methods. The more straightforward method addresses the relationship between empathy and variability in observed DNA sequences. Although exciting in its prospects, this line of research is relatively new, and we are aware of only two published studies on the topic. Baron-Cohen's group examined 68 candidate genes in two groups of subjects: a population sample and a case-control sample of subjects with Asperger syndrome. In this study, 19 genes showed nominally significant associations with self-report measures of empathy and autistic tendencies (Chakrabarti et al., 2009). The second study focused on a gene coding for the oxytocin receptor and found it to be significantly correlated with empathy (Rodrigues, Saslow, Garcia, John, & Keltner, in press).

A more established approach uses genetically informative research designs (e.g., the adoption design) to estimate genetic and environmental effects on a trait through partitioning variance by looking at differences in how similar family members of different levels of genetic and/or environmental relatedness are behaviorally (Plomin et al., 2008). All such genetically informative studies of empathy have used the twin design, comparing identical (monozygotic [MZ]) twins, who share all of their genetic sequence, with fraternal (dizygotic [DZ]) twins, who share, on average, 50% of their genes. Assuming that MZ and DZ twins growing up in their biological families are equal in terms of how similar their environments are, greater similarity of MZ twins indicates *heritability* (the relative influence of genetic factors within a specific population in a specific context). Similarity beyond this genetic effect is attributed to the *shared environment*, and any further twin differences indicate effects of the *nonshared environment* and measurement error (Plomin et al., 2008). The twin design cannot indicate the exact genes involved, and only gives a rough estimate of environmental effects that include factors ranging from neighborhood effects to parenting to childhood infections. On the other hand, it is very powerful in simultaneously pointing to the importance of genetic and environmental influences and estimating their relative contributions to individual differences.

Meta-Analysis

To date, eight twin studies have addressed the genetic and environmental influences on empathy (see reviews by Knafo & Israel, 2009; Knafo, Zahn-Waxler, et al., 2008). All of these studies except one (Ando et al., 2004) found a meaningful genetic influence on empathy, in at least one of the age groups studied. Most studies found little evidence for shared-environment effects on empathy.

For the purposes of this chapter, we conducted a meta-analysis of the results from published studies (located through the databases of ISI Web of Knowledge, SSRN, PubMed, and Google scholar) that used twin models to evaluate the genetic and environmental contributions to individual variance in empathy. We screened out studies that focused on clinical aspects of empathy, such as very low empathy, and studies that used partial samples that were later analyzed more comprehensively. Additionally, one outlier study (Saudino, Carter, Purper-Ouakil, & Gorwood, 2008) in which both MZ and DZ correlations were unusually high ($r \geq .80$) was dropped from the analysis. When information was missing, it was retrieved through direct contact with the corresponding author. Table 5.1 presents a summary description of the studies used in this meta-analysis and details how multiple data points from the same study were treated.

Averaging across studies, the effect size was calculated at $r = .20$ for DZ twins and $r = .37$ for MZ twins. Model fitting in Mx (Neale, Boker, Xie, & Maes, 1999) tested genetic and environmental effects using the aggregated similarity scores. The genetic effect on empathy was estimated at .35 (with a 95% confidence interval [CI] ranging from .21 to .41). A very small shared-environment effect was estimated at .02 (CI: .0–.14), and the remaining variance (.63, CI: .59–.67) was accounted for by nonshared environment and error (NSE). It was possible to drop the weak shared-environment component without affecting model fit, $\Delta\chi^2(df = 1) = 0.17$, ns. Model fit was excellent, as indicated by several fit indices: $\chi^2(df = 4) = 0.18$, ns; Akaike's information criterion (AIC) = –7.82; root mean square error of approximation (RMSEA) = .00. The resulting model estimated a significant genetic effect at 37% (CI: .33–.41), with the remaining variance (.63, CI: .59–.67) accounted for by NSE.

TABLE 5.1. Studies and Main Statistics Included in the Meta-Analysis

Study	Facet of empathy	Type of empathy	Age (years)	Measure	rMZ (n)	rDZ (n)
Davis, Luce, & Kraus (1994)	Emotional	Empathic concern	17	Questionnaire	0.22 (509)	0.08 (330)
	Cognitive	Perspective taking	17	Questionnaire	0.19 (509)	0.09 (330)
Knafo, Zahn-Waxler, et al. (2008)	Emotional	Empathic concern	1.2	Behavioral	0.215 (222)	0.11 (171)
	Emotional	Empathic concern	1.8	Behavioral	0.19 (196)	0.205 (158)
	Emotional	Empathic concern	2	Behavioral	0.225 (194)	0.1 (162)
	Emotional	Empathic concern	3	Behavioral	0.185 (187)	0.085 (155)
	Cognitive	Hypothesis testing	1.2	Behavioral	0.48 (222)	0.52 (171)
	Cognitive	Hypothesis testing	1.8	Behavioral	0.4 (196)	0.455 (158)
	Cognitive	Hypothesis testing	2	Behavioral	0.47 (194)	0.35 (162)
	Cognitive	Hypothesis testing	3	Behavioral	0.34 (187)	0.29 (155)
	Emotional	Empathic concern	3.5	Behavioral	0.25 (33)	0.03 (49)
Knafo et al. (2009)	Cognitive	Hypothesis testing	3.5	Behavioral	0.59 (33)	−0.01 (49)
Ando et al. (2004)	Overall	Overall empathy	20 (m)	Questionnaire	0.29 (414)	0.24 (203)
Matthews et al. (1981)	Emotional	Empathic concern	48 (m)	Questionnaire	0.41 (114)	0.05 (116)
Rushton et al. (1986)	Emotional	Emotional empathy	30 (m)	Questionnaire	0.54 (296)	0.2 (179)
Volbrecht et al. (2007)	Emotional	Empathic concern	1.1 (m)	Behavioral	0.48 (67)	0.35 (140)
	Cognitive	Hypothesis testing	1.1 (m)	Behavioral	0.57 (67)	0.38 (140)

Note. (m), mean age. In the longitudinal study (Knafo, Zahn-Waxler, et al., 2008), participant number was decreased in each time point by a factor calculated in the following manner: At each time point, participants have dropped from the study. The number of participants at the final time point was divided by the number of time points, and this was used as the new N for that time point. At each additional time point, the number of participants who withdrew from the next session was divided by the number of sessions they participated in. Two methods (funnel plot and classic fail-safe N) showed a very small likelihood for publication bias.

Different Types of Empathy

As previously described, empathy is a complex construct, consisting of both emotional and cognitive aspects, with evidence that the two are influenced by both similar and different underlying anatomical brain structures (Blair, 2005). It is, therefore, important to consider whether the two empathy components are influenced by genes and environment through similar or separate developmental factors. Toward this end, we considered separately the genetic and environmental influences on these two aspects of empathy. For all of the studies (except for Ando et al., 2004, where an overall score of empathy was used), outcome measures were grouped into these two main categories. In affective empathy, the correlation between DZ twins was .13 and between MZ twins .31. A genetic effect accounted for 30% of the variance (CI: .24–.35), with the rest of the variance accounted for by NSE (.70, CI: .65–.76). A different pattern was found for cognitive empathy, for which the pulled DZ correlation was .30 and that of MZ twins was .43. For cognitive empathy, the genetic effect was estimated at .26 (CI: .10–.43). A meaningful shared-environment effect was estimated at .17 (CI: .03–.31), with the remaining variance (.57, CI: .52–.63) attributable to NSE.

Variation by Distress Levels

When the ability to self-regulate reaction to others' suffering fails, one is overwhelmed with one's emotions and turns inward to reestablish self-control and deal with the emotions. Obviously, in this situation one becomes unable to focus on others, leaving few resources for empathy or sympathy (Eisenberg & Fabes, 1992). Many studies have looked into the various implications of high negative emotionality (i.e., emotional overarousal, feelings of negative emotions) (Eisenberg et al., 2000) on social functioning in general (Eisenberg et al., 2000) and on psychopathologies (Cole, Zahn-Waxler, Fox, Usher, & Welsh, 1996; Stice & Gonzales, 1998). Additionally, negative emotionality has been directly associated to the ability to feel and express empathy in both infants (Young, Fox, & Zahn-Waxler, 1999) and children (Eisenberg et al., 2009). Decety led an interesting study (Cheng et al., 2007) that looked at the effect of expertise in protecting against overarousal when encountered with another's pain. In this study, both physicians and naive participants watched short clips of needles inserted into various body parts while their brain activity was measured using functional magnetic resonance imaging. While naive participants responded with an activation of the pain brain matrix (feeling others' pain), doctors' response was an activation of areas related to regulation and theory of mind (Cheng et al., 2007). Importantly, distress has been shown to have a significant heritable component in addition to environmental influences (Emde et al., 1992). It is, therefore, important to study the role of children's tendency to regulate negative emotions.

We thus addressed the issue of the interplay of genes and emotional negativity in relation to empathy. We analyzed data from 1,353 pairs of 3-year-old twins from the Longitudinal Israeli Study of Twins (LIST). Mothers described twins' birth and medical history, and reported twins' emotional symptoms (Goodman, 1997) and empathy (Kochanska, DeVet, Goldman, Murray, & Putnam, 1994). Details of sampling, measures, and zygosity assessment are described elsewhere (Knafo, 2006).

We tested genetic and environmental effects on mother-rated empathy separately for same-sex pairs in which twins were either both high (upper third) or low (bottom third) in mother-rated emotional symptoms. The cutoffs yielded small groups of 45 low-symptom MZ pairs (twin correlation, $r = .95$, $p < .001$), 48 low-symptom DZ pairs ($r = .89$, $p < .001$), 65 high-symptom MZ pairs ($r = .92$, $p < .001$), and 78 high-symptom DZ pairs ($r = .57$, $p < .001$). As in the other study of mother-reported empathy (Saudino et al., 2008), MZ and DZ correlations were both very high, which could reflect a strong shared-environment effect but also a reporter bias, which has not been observed with mothers rating the same twins on other traits (Benish-Weisman, Steinberg, & Knafo, 2010; Saudino et al., 2008). Thus, shared-environment results should be taken with caution.

The high correlations for both MZ and DZ twins among low-symptom twins indicate no genetic effect for this group and high shared-environmental effects. The substantially higher correlations among high-symptom MZ compared with DZ twins indicate a genetic effect in this group. Among low-symptom twins, model fitting found a small, nonsignificant genetic effect on empathy (.08, CI: .0–.21), a large shared-environment effect (.86, CI: .73–.93), with some variance accounted for by NSE (.06, CI: .04–.10). An opposite effect was found for high-symptom twins (heritability: .65, CI: .41–.93; shared environment: .26, CI: .00–.50; NSE: .08, CI: .06–.13). It was not possible to equate the genetic and shared-environment components in the two groups without affecting model fit, $\Delta\chi^2(df = 2) = 23.75$, $p < .0001$, and thus a model with separate estimates was preferred, which had an excellent model fit,

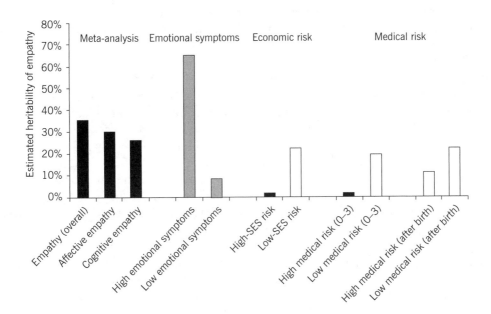

FIGURE 5.1. Different estimates of the heritability of empathy. Symptoms, mother-reported negative emotionality; SES, socioeconomic status (mother-rated family income relative to the national average that was presented to them on a 5-point scale—families scoring "much below average" [25%] were identified as under high economic risk); medical risk, hospitalization in the first 3 years of life; NICU, admittance to a neonatal intensive care unit.

$\chi^2(df = 6) = 2.42$, ns; AIC = –9.59; RMSEA = .00. The different heritability estimates are illustrated in Figure 5.1.

Dynamic Development of Genetic and Environmental Influences

Age has been previously shown (e.g., Scourfield, John, Martin, & McGuffin, 2004) to interact with the genetic effects on prosocial behavior, with heritability increasing from 2 to 3, 4, and then 7 years of age (Knafo & Plomin, 2006). Despite the small number of studies, we used our meta-analysis to explore this possibility for empathy. For DZ twins ($b = -0.045$, $p = .035$), age was a negative predictor of the twin correlation, so that as the twins grow older they become less similar to each other. On the other hand, as MZ twins grow older, they become more similar to one another ($b = .0042$, $p = .047$), indicating that the heritability effect does indeed strengthen as people age.

This cross-study age comparison is problematic because the childhood studies used observational methods while adult studies used self-reports. It is, therefore, important to look at the moderating effect of age with a comparable—preferably the same—sample. The only published longitudinal, genetically informative study of empathy showed that the relative influences of genetics and the environment on empathy were age dependent. Knafo, Zahn-Waxler, and colleagues (2008), who studied a Colorado twin sample (part of which was studied by Zahn-Waxler, Schiro, Robinson, Emde, & Schmitz, 2001), found no heritability for a common empathy factor at 14 and 20 months. However, by 24 months, genetics accounted for 34% of the variance, further increasing toward a 47% estimate at 36 months. In contrast, for shared-environmental influences, strong effects were observed at the younger ages, but these effects decreased from .69 at 14 months to .00 at 36 months. A large part of the variance (31–53%) was accounted for by the NSE (Knafo, Zahn-Waxler, et al., 2008).

The longitudinal design enabled Knafo, Zahn-Waxler, and colleagues (2008) to use multivariate genetic analyses to explore the contributions of genetics and the environment to *stability and change*. In late infancy (14 months), no genetic effects were apparent. The main change in the genetic components of empathy occurred from 20 to 24 months, which was followed by stability in the genetic effect, so that the same effect carried on to explain all genetic variance at 36 months. Thus, genetics accounted for both change (20–24 months) and continuity (24–36 months) in empathy. In contrast, shared-environment effects accounted for continuity, and the same effects were carried on toward 36 months (though they increasingly accounted for a smaller part of the variance). Finally, new NSE effects emerged at each age, indicating that NSE contributed to change in empathy.

It is tempting to consider age only from an ontogenetic perspective, focusing, for example, on developing infants' increased sociocognitive abilities. However, it is important to note that infants' social world changes dramatically as they progress toward early childhood. Thus, while many 14-month-olds will have the majority of their social experiences within the family context, by 36 months most children are already involved with a peer group outside the family. Watching and interacting with a variety of children is likely to elicit a variety of behavioral responses that have not been present at earlier ages. Thus, age can be considered as a social context as well, and the increase in heritability with age may be one kind of gene–environment interaction (GxE).

Gene–Environment Interactions

In developmental research, there is an increasing awareness that genetic and environmental influences on development are in many cases not independent of each other (e.g., Caspi et al., 2002; Plomin et al., 1977). One way to show the presence of G×E is by comparing the genetic contributions with individual differences across different levels of a measured environmental variable (e.g., Turkheimer, Haley, Waldron, D'Onofrio, & Gottesman, 2003). When the relative influence of genetic effects varies depending on the environmental variable, a G×E is indicated.

Heritability estimates are only meaningful in the specific context in which they are measured. While questionnaire studies usually seek to measure a trait trans-situationally, observational studies can provide some evidence for the specific influences that genes and the environment can have in different contexts. We are aware of only one study that partially addressed this issue. In a study that assessed empathy toward mothers and unknown examiners, a common empathy factor emerged, but there was additional, target-specific variance. The genetic influences on these unique variance components were found mainly for responses toward the examiner compared with the mother (Knafo, Zahn-Waxler, et al., 2008). Thus, there may be genetic aspects of empathy that emerge only when children encounter a stranger compared with a well-known adult, a clear indication of a G×E.

Gene–Environmental Risk Interaction

It has been shown previously that levels of heritability can be affected by the level of socioeconomic status, that is, the specific environment in which the child is raised. Specifically, heritability estimations for intelligence are lower for impoverished families and higher for affluent families, both for young children (Turkheimer et al., 2003) and for adolescents (Harden, Turkheimer, & Loehlin, 2007). Exploratory analyses showed a similar pattern: of more meaningful heritability in low-economic-risk families (Figure 5.1).

We next tested the role of environmental risk as indicated by twins' hospitalization during their early years (0–3). We note that disease could result from both genetic and environmental factors effects; however, hospitalization itself represents an environmental risk factor due to, for example, separation from parents or painful interactions with the medical staff. We focused the analyses on same-sex pairs in which both twins shared the hospitalization status (both hospitalized or both not). Preliminary analyses found no main effects of medical risk on children's mother-rated empathy.

In low-risk families, MZ twins correlated more highly ($r = .88$, $p < .001$, $N = 134$) than DZ twins ($r = .81$, $p < .001$, $N = 222$), suggesting a small yet significant genetic effect on empathy (.19, CI: .10–.29), a large shared-environment effect (.70, CI: .61–.78), and some variance accounted for by NSE (.11, CI: .08–.14). In contrast, in high-risk pairs, MZ ($r = .80$, $p < .001$, $N = 42$) and DZ ($r = .85$, $p < .001$, $N = 55$) correlations were both very high, indicating no genetic effect in this group. The variance was fully accounted for by the shared environment (.82, CI: .69–.88) and NSE (.18, CI: .12–.25). It was not possible to equate the genetic components in the two groups without affecting model fit, $\Delta\chi^2(df = 1) = 4.62$, $p < .05$, and thus a model with separate estimates was preferred, which had a very good model fit, $\chi^2(df = 6) = 6.181$, ns; AIC = –5.82; RMSEA = .036. In sum, like economic risk, medical risk was associated with lower heritability. A similar finding with regard to twins' stay in a neonatal intensive care unit is also illustrated in Figure 5.1.

Gene–Parenting Interactions

A more direct indication of G×E uses measured genes and measured environments rather than broad estimates of heritability. This relatively novel approach compares the association between a phenotype and a measured environmental variable in individuals with different genetic profiles (e.g., Caspi et al., 2002). In this respect, it is interesting to note that some children may be genetically more susceptible to parental influence (Belsky, 1997). Several polymorphic genes that regulate the serotonin and dopamine brain systems may underlie such differential susceptibility to parental influence (Belsky, Bakermans-Kranenburg, & van IJzendoorn, 2007; Belsky & Pluess, 2009; Propper & Moore, 2006).

To date, no study of G×E in empathy has been published. For current purposes, we studied the role of the DRD4-III polymorphism, a DNA sequence ranging from 2 to 10 repeats (2, 4, and 7 are the most common) of a 48-bp sequence (Asghari, Sanyal, Buchwaldt, Paterson, & Jovanovic, 1995). Several studies (e.g., (Bakermans-Kranenburg & van IJzendoorn, 2006; DiLalla, Elam, & Smolen, 2009) have provided evidence that the DRD4-III polymorphism may be associated with susceptibility to parental influence (see Belsky & Pluess, 2009; Knafo, Israel, & Ebstein, 2010, for discussion). All of these studies have shown stronger associations between parenting and child outcomes in children with the 7-repeat allele of DRD4-III. Here we sought to explore such DRD4-III–parenting interactions with regard to empathy. Specifically, we predicted that the relationships between parenting and empathy would be stronger among children who carry the 7-repeat allele than among noncarriers.

A subset of LIST families also participated at age 3.5 years in a lab session measuring empathy toward an examiner's simulated pain (Knafo et al., 2009). When preparing this chapter, we had full data on parenting, DNA, and observed empathy from 120 individual twins. For current purposes, and because data from twins in the same family are not independent, we randomly selected one twin in pairs with full data, leaving a total of 67 independent children. Empathic concern and hypothesis testing were observed from children's reactions to an unknown examiner's simulated pain (Zahn-Waxler et al., 1992). The investigators measured parenting based on mothers' reactions toward each twin (Knafo & Schwartz, 2003; Robinson, Mandleco, Olsen, & Hart, 1995). This yielded a factor of parental *positivity* (warmth, induction and reasoning, autonomy support) and *negativity* (verbal hostility, physical coercion, love withdrawal) (see Knafo et al., 2010, for details).

There were no significant relationships between empathy and parental positivity or negativity. However, our goal was to test separately for these relationships in the presence and absence of the DRD4 7-repeat allele. Among children without the 7-repeat allele, no relationship was found between parenting and empathy. In contrast, among children with the 7-repeat allele, a negative relationship was found between empathic concern and maternal negativity, $r = -.42$, $p < .05$. As a formal test of the interaction, we regressed children's empathic concern on their DRD4-III polymorphism (where 7-repeat allele present was coded 1 and 7-repeat allele absent 0) and

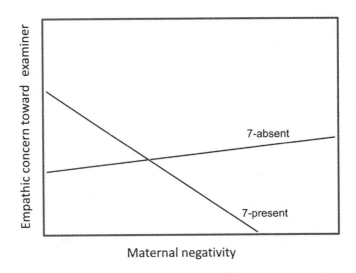

FIGURE 5.2. Relationship between maternal negativity and children's empathic concern toward an examiner based on the presence of the DRD4-III 7-repeat allele.

on maternal negativity as well as their interaction term. Neither negativity ($\beta = .08$, $t = .50$, ns) nor DRD4-III ($\beta = -.17$, $t = -1.42$, ns) predicted empathic concern, yet their interaction did ($\beta = -.30$, $t = 1.99$, $p < .05$). Figure 5.2 presents the regression slopes predicting empathic concern with maternal negativity based on the presence or absence of the DRD4-III 7-repeat allele.

Discussion

We reanalyzed the extant body of evidence on the genetic and environmental influences on individual differences in empathy. Our small-scale meta-analysis shows that genetic factors are moderately important for both affective and cognitive empathy. Note that these pulled heritability estimates are somewhat lower than those found for other variables, such as personality traits (Jang, Livesley, & Vernon, 1996) and antisocial behavior (Mason & Frick, 1994), leaving room for the influence of environmental effects and for G×E. Importantly, although one study found that a correlation of .41 between affective and cognitive aspects of empathy was accounted for mainly (67%) by overlapping genetic factors (Knafo et al., 2009), our results show that cognitive empathy, but not affective empathy, is significantly influenced by shared environment. Perhaps this reflects a stronger influence of socializing agents on the more cognitive aspect of empathy, but more research is needed to address this possibility. Thus, although they are related, the two components of empathy have quite different etiologies.

All studies but one were consistent in showing both genetic and non-shared-environmental effects on empathy. The substantial genetic effects on empathy suggest the need to account for this heritability by specific polymorphisms and the psychobiological endophenotypes underlying their influence (Knafo, Israel, et al., 2008). In this nascent field of inquiry, candidate genes involved in empathy could be divided into several groups. The first includes genes related to the oxytocin–vasopressin system, which has been implicated in influencing prosocial behavior (Israel et al., 2008, 2009; Knafo, Israel, et al., 2008), trust (Kosfeld, Heinrichs, Zak, Fischbacher, & Fehr, 2005; Zak, Kurzban, & Matzner, 2005), mother–infant bond (Levine, Zagoory-Sharon, Feldman, & Weller, 2007), and romantic relationships (Gordon et al., 2008). The second includes genes that were previously implicated in autism, such as the brain-derived neurotrophic factor (e.g., Nishimura et al., 2007; Tsai, 2005). The third includes genes such as the androgen receptor, which might explain some of the consistent gender difference in empathy (Auyeung et al., 2009; Chapman et al., 2006). The last group includes genes that were previously shown to affect various personality traits and psychopathologies such as the dopamine D4 receptor gene (DRD4) (e.g., Ebstein et al., 1996) or the serotonin transporter gene (5-HTTLPR) (e.g., Melke et al., 2001).

Nevertheless, genetics do not operate in isolation in affecting children's empathy. First, the increase in heritability estimates with age may indicate the differential social environments encountered by children and adults in different ages, a sort of GxE. It can also indicate the accumulated effect of gene–environment *correlations* in which children's environment (e.g., parenting) is associated with their own genetic tendencies (e.g., Jaffee & Price, 2007; Knafo & Plomin, 2006). With age, and with children's increased agency, long-standing parent–child–parent reciprocal influences are expected to increasingly reflect children's genetic influences, showing up as larger heritabilities.

Second, the effects of genetics may be moderated by those of environmental factors. We provided the first, to our knowledge, evidence for differential heritability depending on environmental stressors with regard to empathy. Despite the limitations we offered for parent reports on empathy, it is noteworthy that, as with IQ (Turkheimer et al., 2003), no heritability was found in the poorer families for empathy, while modest genetic effects were found for families with better economic standing.

We also looked at health risk as a potential moderator of genetic effects on empathy. Both hospitalization in the neonate stage and hospitalization within the next 3 years were associated with lower genetic influences on empathy. Further analyses showed no differences between children growing up in medical or economic risk environments and other children either in the means or variances of mother-reported empathy. However, risk did interact with genetics. Possibly in low-risk contexts environmental interventions are less needed, and children grow up to their genetic potential. In contrast, in high-risk contexts, interventions (e.g., changes in parenting or day care) may be more efficient, increasing the importance of environmental factors. Obviously, more research is needed in order to understand how risk and genetics interact with regard to empathy.

One way in which environmental factors moderate genetic influences concerns epigenetic processes. Thus, there is now growing evidence that DNA expression is affected by environmental factors (e.g., Meaney & Szyf, 2005). Even MZ twins, whose DNA sequence is virtually identical, show differences in DNA methylation, associated with twin differences in life events (Fraga et al., 2005), including genomic imprinting, and gene expression regulation (Haque, Gottesman, & Wong, 2009). It is important to note that stress, in particular, can have an enduring effect through epigenetic mechanisms (Jaenisch & Bird, 2003). Our finding that heritability of empathy is much higher in twins who show high degrees of emotional symptoms (reflecting either genetic influences on distress or the effects of environmental variables, such as negative life events) demonstrates the complexity of genetic and environmental influences in children of different dispositions.

Third, genetic factors can moderate the effect of the environment, particularly parenting. In our study, parenting did not directly relate to empathy in the whole sample. In contrast, we found a meaningful correlation between empathy and parental negativity in DRD4-III 7-repeat allele carriers. To our knowledge, this is the first study of a significant gene–parenting interaction affecting empathy. It joins the first studies on prosociality suggesting that children with 7-repeat allele are more susceptible to parental influence (Bakermans-Kranenburg & van IJzendoorn, 2010; Knafo, Israel, & Ebstein, 2011). Although strong evidence has emerged for DRD4-III as a susceptibility gene, additional genes are likely to be important too (Belsky & Pluess, 2009). Finally, although evidence shows that parenting and other measured environmental factors are more strongly correlated with children's development, in children with the putative susceptibility allele (i.e., 7-repeat allele) there exists the possibility that other environmental factors not measured hitherto in this line of research predict individual differences in children *lacking* this allele.

In sum, both genetic and environmental influences are found for empathy. However, this overall conclusion is to be qualified. The relative contributions of genetics and the environment vary by kind of empathy (affective and cognitive), by age, and by children's emotional symptoms. Genetic effects are stronger in low-risk environments, and parenting is more strongly related to observed empathy in children with a specific genetic heritage. The picture is of a complex, dynamic process, where genes, environmental risks, parenting, and age interact in affecting individual differences in empathy.

Acknowledgments

We are indebted to the parents and twins in the Longitudinal Israeli Study of Twins (LIST) for making the study possible. We also thank the research assistants who collected and coded the data. LIST is supported by Grant No. 31/06 from the Israel Science Foundation and a grant by the Notre Dame Science of Generosity Project funded by the Templeton Foundation to Ariel Knafo. Genotyping was done with the help of Professor Richard P. Ebstein and supported by a grant from the National Institute for Psychobiology in Israel to Ariel Knafo.

References

Anderson, J., Myowa-Yamakoshi, M., & Matsuzawa, T. (2004). Contagious yawning in chimpanzees. *Proceedings of the Royal Society of London: Series B. Biological Sciences, 271*(Suppl. 6), S468.

Ando, J., Suzuki, A., Yamagata, S., Kijima, N., Maekawa, H., Ono, Y., et al. (2004). Genetic and environmental structure of Cloninger's temperament and character dimensions. *Journal of Personality Disorders, 18*(4), 379–393.

Asghari, V., Sanyal, S., Buchwaldt, S., Paterson, A., & Jovanovic, V. (1995). Modulation of intracellular cyclic AMP levels by different human dopamine D4 receptor variants. *Journal of Neurochemistry, 65*(3), 1157–1165.

Auyeung, B., Baron-Cohen, S., Ashwin, E., Knickmeyer, R., Taylor, K., & Hackett, G. (2009). Fetal testosterone and autistic traits. *British Journal of Psychology, 100*(Pt. 1), 1–22.

Bakermans-Kranenburg, M. J., & van IJzendoorn, M. (2006). Gene–environment interaction of the dopamine D4 receptor (DRD4) and observed maternal insensitivity predicting externalizing behavior in preschoolers. *Developmental Psychobiology, 48*(5), 406–409.

Bakermans-Kranenburg, M. J., & van IJzendoorn, M. H. (2010). *The role of dopamine related genes in GxE interaction in human development.* Paper presented at the biennial meeting of the Society for Research of Child Development, Montreal.

Barnett, M., King, L., Howard, J., & Dino, G. (1980). Empathy in young children: Relation to parents' empathy, affection, and emphasis on the feelings of others. *Developmental Psychology, 16*(3), 243–244.

Baron-Cohen, S. (1997). *Mindblindness: An essay on autism and theory of mind.* Cambridge, MA: MIT Press.

Baron-Cohen, S., & Wheelwright, S. (2004). The empathy quotient: An investigation of adults with Asperger syndrome or high functioning autism, and normal sex differences. *Journal of Autism and Developmental Disorders, 34*(2), 163–175.

Barraza, J. A., & Zak, P. J. (2009). Empathy toward strangers triggers oxytocin release and subsequent generosity. *Annals of the New York Academy of Sciences, 1167,* 182–189.

Batson, C. (1991). *The altruism question: Toward a social psychological answer.* Hillsdale, NJ: Erlbaum.

Batson, C., Fultz, J., & Schoenrade, P. (2006). Distress and empathy: Two qualitatively distinct vicarious emotions with different motivational consequences. *Journal of Personality, 55*(1), 19–39.

Belsky, J. (1997). Theory testing, effect-size evaluation, and differential susceptibility to rearing influence: The case of mothering and attachment. *Child Development, 68*(4), 598–600.

Belsky, J., Bakermans-Kranenburg, M. J., & van IJzendoorn, M. H. (2007). For better *and* for worse: Differential susceptibility to environmental influences. *Current Directions in Psychological Science, 16*(6), 300–304.

Belsky, J., & Pluess, M. (2009). Beyond diathesis stress: Differential susceptibility to environmental influences. *Psychological Bulletin, 135*(6), 885–908.

Benish-Weisman, M., Steinberg, T., & Knafo, A. (2010). Genetic and environmental links between children's temperament and their problems with peers. *Israel Journal of Psychiatry, 47,* 144–151.

Blair, R. (2005). Responding to the emotions of others: Dissociating forms of empathy through the study of typical and psychiatric populations. *Consciousness and Cognition, 14*(4), 698–718.

Bryant, B. (1982). An index of empathy for children and adolescents. *Child Development, 53,* 413–425.

Carruthers, P., & Smith, P. (1996). *Theories of theories of mind.* Cambridge, UK: Cambridge University Press.

Caspi, A., McClay, J., Moffitt, T., Mill, J., Martin, J., Craig, I., et al. (2002). Role of genotype in the cycle of violence in maltreated children. *Science, 297,* 851–854.

Chakrabarti, B., Dudbridge, F., Kent, L., Wheelwright, S., Hill-Cawthorne, G., Allison, C., et al. (2009). Genes related to sex steroids, neural growth, and social-emotional behavior are associated with autistic traits, empathy, and Asperger syndrome. *Autism Research, 2*(3), 157–177.

Chapman, E., Baron-Cohen, S., Auyeung, B., Knickmeyer, R., Taylor, K., & Hackett, G. (2006). Fetal testosterone and empathy: Evidence from the empathy quotient (EQ) and the "reading the mind in the eyes" test. *Social Neuroscience, 1*(2), 135–148.

Chen, Q., Panksepp, J., & Lahvis, G. (2009). Empathy is moderated by genetic background in mice. *PLoS ONE, 4*(2), e4387.

Cheng, Y., Lin, C.-P., Liu, H.-L., Hsu, Y.-Y., Lim, K.-E., Hung, D., et al. (2007). Expertise modulates the perception of pain in others. *Current Biology, 17*(19), 1708–1713.

Ciarrochi, J., Chan, A., & Bajgar, J. (2001). Measuring emotional intelligence in adolescents. *Personality and Individual Differences, 31*(7), 1105–1119.

Cohen-Bendahan, C., van de Beek, C., & Berenbaum, S. (2005). Prenatal sex hormone effects on child and adult sex-typed behavior: Methods and findings. *Neuroscience and Biobehavioral Reviews, 29*(2), 353–384.

Cole, P., Zahn-Waxler, C., Fox, N., Usher, B., & Welsh, J. (1996). Individual differences in emotion regulation and behavior problems in preschool children. *Journal of Abnormal Psychology, 105,* 518–529.

Cooke, M., Ford, J., Levine, J., Bourke, C., Newell, L., & Lapidus, G. (2007). The effects of city-wide implementation of "Second Step" on elementary school students' prosocial and aggressive behaviors. *Journal of Primary Prevention, 28*(2), 93–115.

Davidov, M., & Grusec, J. E. (2006a). Multiple pathways to compliance: Mothers' willingness to cooperate and knowledge of their children's reactions to discipline. *Journal of Family Psychology, 20*(4), 705–708.

Davidov, M., & Grusec, J. E. (2006b). Untangling the links of parental responsiveness to distress and warmth to child outcomes. *Child Development, 77*(1), 44–58.

Davis, M. (1983). Measuring individual differences in empathy: Evidence for a multidimensional approach. *Journal of Personality and Social Psychology, 44*(1), 113–126.

Davis, M. H., Luce, C., & Kraus, S. J. (1994). The heritability of characteristics associated with dispositional empathy. *Journal of Personality, 62*(3), 369–391.

de Waal, F. (2008). Putting the altruism back into altruism: The evolution of empathy. *Annual Review of Psychology, 59,* 279–300.

de Waal, F. (2009). *The age of empathy: Nature's lessons for a kinder society.* New York: Crown.

de Wied, M., Gispen-de Wied, C., & van Boxtel, A. (2010). Empathy dysfunction in children and adolescents with disruptive behavior disorders. *European Journal of Pharmacology, 626*(1), 97–103.

Decety, J., & Jackson, P. (2004). The functional architecture of human empathy. *Behavioral and Cognitive Neuroscience Reviews, 3*(2), 71–100.

Decety, J., & Meyer, M. (2008). From emotion resonance to empathic understanding: A social developmental neuroscience account. *Developmental Psychopathology, 20*(4), 1053–1080.

DiLalla, L., Elam, K., & Smolen, A. (2009). Genetic and gene–environment interaction effects on preschoolers' social behaviors. *Developmental Psychobiology, 51*(6), 451–464.

Dodge, K., McClaskey, C., & Feldman, E. (1985). Situational approach to the assessment of social competence in children. *Journal of Consulting and Clinical Psychology, 53*(3), 344–353.

Dondi, M., Simion, F., & Caltran, G. (1999). Can newborns discriminate between their own cry and the cry of another newborn infant? *Developmental Psychology, 35*(2), 418–426.

Ebstein, R. P., Novick, O., Umansky, R., Priel, B., Osher, Y., Blaine, D., et al. (1996). Dopamine D4 receptor (D4DR) exon III polymorphism associated with the human personality trait of novelty seeking. *Nature Genetics, 12*(1), 78–80.

Eisenberg, N. (2000). Emotion, regulation, and moral development. *Annual Review of Psychology, 51,* 665–697.

Eisenberg, N., & Fabes, R. (1990). Empathy: Conceptualization, measurement, and relation to prosocial behavior. *Motivation and Emotion, 14*(2), 131–149.

Eisenberg, N., & Fabes, R. (1992). Emotion, regulation, and the development of social competence. *Review of Personality and Social Psychology, 14,* 119–150.

Eisenberg, N., Fabes, R., Guthrie, I., Murphy, B., Maszk, P., Holmgren, R., et al. (2009). The relations of regulation and emotionality to problem behavior in elementary school children. *Development and Psychopathology, 8,* 141–162.

Eisenberg, N., Fabes, R., Guthrie, I., & Reiser, M. (2000). Dispositional emotionality and regulation: Their role in predicting quality of social functioning. *Journal of Personality and Social Psychology, 78*(1), 136–157.

Eisenberg, N., Fabes, R., Murphy, B., Karbon, M., Smith, M., & Maszk, P. (1996). The relations of children's dispositional empathy-related responding to their emotionality, regulation, and social functioning. *Developmental Psychology, 32*(2), 195–209.

Eisenberg, N., Fabes, R., Schaller, M., Carlo, G., & Miller, P. (1991). The relations of parental characteristics and practices to children's vicarious emotional responding. *Child Development, 62*(6), 1393–1408.

Eisenberg, N., Fabes, R., & Spinrad, T. (1998). Prosocial development. In W. Damon & N. Eisenberg (Eds.), *Handbook of child psychology: Vol. 3. Social, emotional, and personality development* (5th ed., pp. 701–778). New York: Wiley.

Eisenberg, N., Guthrie, I., Murphy, B., Shepard, S., Cumberland, A., & Carlo, G. (1999). Consistency and development of prosocial dispositions: A longitudinal study. *Child Development, 70*(6), 1360–1372.

Eisenberg, N., & Miller, P. (1987). The relation of empathy to prosocial and related behaviors. *Psychological Bulletin, 101*(1), 91–119.

Emde, R. N., Plomin, R., Robinson, J. A., Corley, R., DeFries, J., Fulker, D. W., et al. (1992). Temperament, emotion, and cognition at fourteen months: The MacArthur Longitudinal Twin Study. *Child Development, 63*(6), 1437–1455.

Feshbach, N. D., & Feshbach, S. (2009). Empathy and education. In J. Decey & W. Ickes (Eds.), *The social neuroscience of empathy* (pp. 85–98). Cambridge, MA: MIT Press.

Flavell, J. (1999). Cognitive development: Children's knowledge about the mind. *Annual Review of Psychology, 50*(1), 21–45.

Fraga, M. F., Ballestar, E., Paz, M., Ropero, S., Setien, F., Ballestar, M., et al. (2005). Epigenetic differences arise during the lifetime of monozygotic twins. *Proceedings of the National Academy of Sciences USA, 102*(30), 10604–10609.

Frick, P., & White, S. (2008). The importance of callous-unemotional traits for developmental models of aggressive and antisocial behavior. *Journal of Child Psychology and Psychiatry, 49*(4), 359–375.

Gleason, K., Jensen-Campbell, L., & Ickes, W. (2009). The role of empathic accuracy in adolescents' peer relations and adjustment. *Personality and Social Psychology Bulletin, 35*(8), 997–1011.

Goodman, R. (1997). The Strengths and Difficulties Questionnaire: A research note. *Journal of Child Psychology and Psychiatry, 38*(5), 581–586.

Gopnik, A., & Wellman, H. M. (1994). The theory theory. In L. A. Hirschfeld & S. A. Gelman (Eds.), *Mapping the mind: Domain specificity in cognition and culture* (pp. 257–293). New York: Cambridge University Press.

Gordon, I., Zagoory-Sharon, O., Schneiderman, I., Leckman, J., Weller, A., & Feldman, R. (2008). Oxytocin and cortisol in romantically unattached young adults: Associations with bonding and psychological distress. *Psychophysiology, 45*(3), 349–352.

Gordon, R. M. (1992). The simulation theory: Objections and misconceptions. *Mind and Language, 7*(1–2), 11–34.

Grusec, J. E., Goodnow, J. J., & Kuczynski, L. (2000). New directions in analyses of parenting contributions to children's acquisition of values. *Child Development, 71*(1), 205–211.

Haque, F., Gottesman, I., & Wong, A. (2009). Not really identical: Epigenetic differences in monozygotic twins and implications for twin studies in psychiatry. *American Journal of Medical Genetics: Part C. Seminars in Medical Genetics, 151,* 136–141.

Harden, K., Turkheimer, E., & Loehlin, J. (2007). Genotype by environment interaction in adolescents' cognitive aptitude. *Behavior Genetics, 37*(2), 273–283.

Harris, P. (1992). From simulation to folk psychology: The case for development. *Mind and Language, 7*(1–2), 120–144.

Hay, D., Nash, A., & Pedersen, J. (1981). Responses of six-month-olds to the distress of their peers. *Child Development, 52*(3), 1071–1075.

Hoffman, M. (1982). Development of prosocial motivation: Empathy and guilt. In N. Eisenberg (Ed.), *The development of prosocial behavior* (pp. 281–313). New York: Academic Press.

Holsen, I., Smith, B., & Frey, K. (2008). Outcomes of the social competence program second step in Norwegian elementary schools. *School Psychology International, 29*(1), 71–88.

Israel, S., Lerer, E., Shalev, I., Uzefovsky, F., Reibold, M., Bachner-Melman, R., et al. (2008). Molecular genetic studies of the arginine vasopressin 1a receptor (AVPR1a) and the oxytocin receptor (OXTR) in human behavior: From autism to altruism with some notes in between. *Progress in Brain Research, 170*, 435–449.

Israel, S., Lerer, E., Shalev, I., Uzefovsky, F., Riebold, M., Laiba, E., et al. (2009). The oxytocin receptor (OXTR) contributes to prosocial fund allocations in the Dictator Game and the Social Value Orientations Task. *PLoS ONE, 4*(5), e5535.

Jaenisch, R., & Bird, A. (2003). Epigenetic regulation of gene expression: How the genome integrates intrinsic and environmental signals. *Nature Genetics, 33*, 245–254.

Jaffee, S., & Price, T. (2007). Gene–environment correlations: A review of the evidence and implications for prevention of mental illness. *Molecular Psychiatry, 12*(5), 432–442.

Jang, K., Livesley, W., & Vernon, P. (1996). Heritability of the big five personality dimensions and their facets: A twin study. *Journal of Personality, 64*, 577–592.

Klimecki, O., & Singer, T. (2012). Empathic distress fatigue rather than compassion fatigue?: Integrating findings from empathy research in psychology and social neuroscience. In B. Oakley, A. Knafo, G. Madhavan, & D. S. Wilson (Eds.), *Pathological altruism* (pp. 368–384). Cambridge, UK: Oxford University Press.

Knafo, A. (2006). The Longitudinal Israeli Study of Twins (LIST): Children's social development as influenced by genetics, abilities, and socialization. *Twin Research and Human Genetics, 9*(6), 791–798.

Knafo, A., & Israel, S. (2009). Genetic and environmental influences on prosocial behavior. In M. Mikulincer & P. R. Shaver (Eds.), *Prosocial motives, emotions, and behavior: The better angels of our nature* (pp. 149–167). Washington, DC: American Psychological Association.

Knafo, A., & Israel, S. (2012). Empathy, prosocial behavior, and other aspects of kindness. In M. Zentner & R. L. Shiner (Eds.), *The handbook of temperament* (pp. 168–179). New York: Guilford Press.

Knafo, A., Israel, S., Darvasi, A., Bachner-Melman, R., Uzefovsky, F., Cohen, L., et al. (2008). Individual differences in allocation of funds in the dictator game associated with length of the arginine vasopressin 1a receptor (AVPR1a) RS3 promoter-region and correlation between RS3 length and hippocampal mRNA. *Genes, Brain and Behavior, 7*(3), 266–275.

Knafo, A., Israel, S., & Ebstein, R. P. (2012). Heritability of children's prosocial behavior and differential susceptibility to parenting by variation in the dopamine receptor D4 gene. *Development and Psychopathology, 23*(1), 53–67.

Knafo, A., & Plomin, R. (2006). Parental discipline and affection and children's prosocial behavior: Genetic and environmental links. *Journal of Personality and Social Psychology, 90*(1), 147–164.

Knafo, A., & Plomin, R. (2006). Prosocial behavior from early to middle childhood: Genetic and environmental influences on stability and change. *Developmental Psychology, 42*(5), 771–786.

Knafo, A., & Schwartz, S. (2003). Parenting and adolescents' accuracy in perceiving parental values. *Child Development, 74*(2), 595–611.

Knafo, A., Zahn-Waxler, C., Davidov, M., Van Hulle, C., Robinson, J., & Rhee, S. (2009).

Empathy in early childhood: Genetic, environmental, and affective contributions. *Annals of the New York Academy of Sciences, 1167*(1), 103–114.

Knafo, A., Zahn-Waxler, C., Van Hulle, C., Robinson, J. L., & Rhee, S. H. (2008). The developmental origins of a disposition toward empathy: Genetic and environmental contributions. *Emotion, 8*(6), 737–752.

Kochanska, G., DeVet, K., Goldman, M., Murray, K., & Putnam, S. (1994). Maternal reports of conscience development and temperament in young children. *Child Development, 65*(3), 852–868.

Kosfeld, M., Heinrichs, M., Zak, P. J., Fischbacher, U., & Fehr, E. (2005). Oxytocin increases trust in humans. *Nature, 435*, 673–676.

Langford, D., Crager, S., Shehzad, Z., Smith, S., Sotocinal, S., Levenstadt, J., et al. (2006). Social modulation of pain as evidence for empathy in mice. *Science, 312*, 1967–1970.

Lawrence, E., Shaw, P., Baker, D., Baron-Cohen, S., & David, A. (2004). Measuring empathy: Reliability and validity of the empathy quotient. *Psychological Medicine, 34*(5), 911–920.

Legerstee, M., Anderson, D., & Schaffer, A. (1998). Five-and eight-month-old infants recognize their faces and voices as familiar and social stimuli. *Child Development, 69*(1), 37–50.

Lepage, J. F., & Théoret, H. (2007). The mirror neuron system: Grasping others' actions from birth? *Developmental Science, 10*(5), 513–523.

Levine, A., Zagoory-Sharon, O., Feldman, R., & Weller, A. (2007). Oxytocin during pregnancy and early postpartum: Individual patterns and maternal-fetal attachment. *Peptides, 28*(6), 1162–1169.

Marcus, R., Telleen, S., & Roke, E. (1979). Relation between cooperation and empathy in young children. *Developmental Psychology, 15*(3), 346–347.

Mason, D., & Frick, P. (1994). The heritability of antisocial behavior: A meta-analysis of twin and adoption studies. *Journal of Psychopathology and Behavioral Assessment, 16*(4), 301–323.

Matthews, K., Batson, C., Van Hulle, C., Robinson, J. L., & Rhee, S. H. (1981). "Principles in his nature which interest him in the fortune of others...": The heritability of empathic concern for others. *Journal of Personality, 49*(3), 237–247.

Meaney, M., & Szyf, M. (2005). Environmental programming of stress responses through DNA methylation: Life at the interface between a dynamic environment and a fixed genome. *Dialogues in Clinical Neuroscience, 7*(2), 103–123.

Melke, J., Landén, M., Baghei, F., Rosmond, R., Holm, G., Björntorp, P., et al. (2001). Serotonin transporter gene polymorphisms are associated with anxiety-related personality traits in women. *American Journal of Medical Genetics: Part B. Neuropsychiatric Genetics, 105*(5), 458–463.

Neale, M., Boker, S., Xie, G., & Maes, H. (1999). *Mx: Statistical modeling*. Unpublished data, Virginia Commonwealth University.

Nishimura, K., Nakamura, K., Anitha, A., Yamada, K., Tsujii, M., Iwayama, Y., et al. (2007). Genetic analyses of the brain-derived neurotrophic factor (BDNF) gene in autism. *Biochemical and Biophysical Research Communications, 356*(1), 200–206.

O'Connell, S. (1995). Empathy in chimpanzees: Evidence for theory of mind? *Primates, 36*(3), 397–410.

Peng, Y. (2008). *Children's prosocial behavior and its relationships with parenting styles and rainbow life education*. Unpublished manuscript.

Petridou, E., Panagiotopoulou, K., Katsournni, K., Spanos, E., & Trichopoulos, D. (1990). Tobacco smoking, pregnancy estrogens, and birth weight. *Epidemiology, 1*(3), 247–250.

Plomin, R., DeFries, J., & Loehlin, J. (1977). Genotype-environment interaction and correlation in the analysis of human behavior. *Psychological Bulletin, 84*(2), 309–322.

Plomin, R., DeFries, J., McClearn, G., & McGuffin, P. (2008). *Behavioral genetics.* New York: Worth.

Preston, S., & de Waal, F. (2003). Empathy: Its ultimate and proximate bases. *Behavioral and Brain Sciences, 25,* 1–20.

Propper, C., & Moore, G. A. (2006). The influence of parenting on infant emotionality: A multi-level psychobiological perspective. *Developmental Review, 26*(4), 427–460.

Reinisch, J., & Sanders, S. (1992). Effects of prenatal exposure to diethylstilbestrol (DES) on hemispheric laterality and spatial ability in human males. *Hormones and Behavior, 26*(1), 62–75.

Robinson, C., Mandleco, B., Olsen, S., & Hart, C. (1995). Authoritative, authoritarian, and permissive parenting practices: Development of a new measure. *Psychological Reports, 77,* 819–830.

Rochat, P., & Hespos, S. (1997). Differential rooting response by neonates: Evidence for an early sense of self. *Early Development and Parenting, 6*(34), 105–112.

Rodrigues, S. M., Saslow, L. R., Garcia, N., John, O. P., & Keltner, D. (2009). Oxytocin receptor genetic variation relates to empathy and stress reactivity in humans. *Proceedings of the National Academy of Sciences USA, 106,* 21437–21441.

Roth-Hanania, R., & Davidov, M. (2009, April). *Early development of empathy: A new perspective.* Paper presented at the biennial meeting of the Society for Research in Child Development, Denver, CO.

Sagi, A., & Hoffman, M. (1976). Empathic distress in the newborn. *Developmental Psychology, 12*(2), 175–176.

Saudino, K., Carter, A., Purper-Ouakil, D., & Gorwood, P. (2008). The etiology of behavioral problems and competencies in very young twins. *Journal of Abnormal Psychology, 117*(1), 48–62.

Scourfield, J., John, B., Martin, N., & McGuffin, P. (2004). The development of prosocial behaviour in children and adolescents: A twin study. *Journal of Child Psychology and Psychiatry, 45*(5), 927–935.

Shamay-Tsoory, S. G., & Aharon-Peretz, J. (2007). Dissociable prefrontal networks for cognitive and affective theory of mind: A lesion study. *Neuropsychologia, 45*(13), 3054–3067.

Shamay-Tsoory, S. G., Aharon-Peretz, J., & Perry, D. (2009). Two systems for empathy: A double dissociation between emotional and cognitive empathy in inferior frontal gyrus versus ventromedial prefrontal lesions. *Brain, 132*(3), 617–627.

Shamay-Tsoory, S. G., Shur, S., Barcai-Goodman, L., Medlovich, S., Harari, H., & Levkovitz, Y. (2007). Dissociation of cognitive from affective components of theory of mind in schizophrenia. *Psychiatry Research, 149*(1–3), 11–23.

Shamay-Tsoory, S. G., Tomer, R., Yaniv, S., & Aharon-Peretz, J. (2002). Empathy deficits in Asperger syndrome: A cognitive profile. *NeuroCase, 8*(3), 245–252.

Shortt, J., & Gottman, J. (2006). Closeness in young adult sibling relationships: Affective and physiological processes. *Social Development, 6*(2), 142–164.

Singer, T., Seymour, B., O'Doherty, J., Kaube, H., Dolan, R. J., & Frith, C. D. (2004). Empathy for pain involves the affective but not sensory components of pain. *Science, 303,* 1157–1162.

Smith, A. (1759). *The theory of the moral sentiments.* London: A. Millar.

Smith, A. (2009). The empathy imbalance hypothesis of autism: A theoretical approach to cognitive and emotional empathy in autistic development. *Psychological Record, 59*(2), 22.

Soenens, B., Duriez, B., Vansteenkiste, M., & Goossens, L. (2007). The intergenerational transmission of empathy-related responding in adolescence: The role of maternal support. *Personality and Social Psychology Bulletin, 33*(3), 299–311.

Spinrad, T., Eisenberg, N., Cumberland, A., Fabes, R., Valiente, C., Shepard, S., et al. (2006). Relation of emotion-related regulation to children's social competence: A longitudinal study. *Emotion, 6*(3), 498–510.

Stice, E., & Gonzales, N. (1998). Adolescent temperament moderates the relation of parenting to antisocial behavior and substance use. *Journal of Adolescent Research, 13*(1), 5–31.

Stiff, J., Dillard, J., Somera, L., Kim, H., & Sleight, C. (1988). Empathy, communication, and prosocial behavior. *Communication Monographs, 55*(2), 198–213.

Tsai, S. (2005). Is autism caused by early hyperactivity of brain-derived neurotrophic factor? *Medical Hypotheses, 65*(1), 79–82.

Turkheimer, E., Haley, A., Waldron, M., D'Onofrio, B., & Gottesman, I. (2003). Socioeconomic status modifies heritability of IQ in young children. *Psychological Science, 14*(6), 623–628.

Ungerer, J., Dolby, R., Waters, B., Barnett, B., Kelk, N., & Lewin, V. (1990). The early development of empathy: Self-regulation and individual differences in the first year. *Motivation and Emotion, 14*(2), 93–106.

Vaish, A., Carpenter, M., & Tomasello, M. (2009). Sympathy through affective perspective taking and its relation to prosocial behavior in toddlers. *Developmental Psychology, 45*(2), 534–543.

Volbrecht, M. M., Lemery-Chalfant, K., Aksan, N., Zahn-Waxler, C., & Goldsmith, H. H. (2007). Examining the familial link between positive affect and empathy development in the second year. *Journal of Genetic Psychology, 168*(2), 105–129.

Wellman, H. (1990). *The child's theory of mind.* Cambridge, MA: MIT Press.

Wellman, H. M., Harris, P. L., Banerjee, M., & Sinclair, A. (1995). Early understanding of emotion: Evidence from natural language. *Cognition and Emotion, 9*(2), 117–149.

Wellman, H., & Woolley, J. (1990). From simple desires to ordinary beliefs: The early development of everyday psychology. *Cognition, 35*(3), 245–275.

Wood, J., Saltzberg, J., & Goldsamt, L. (1990). Does affect induce self-focused attention? *Journal of Personality and Social Psychology, 58*(5), 899–908.

Young, S. K., Fox, N. A., & Zahn-Waxler, C. (1999). The relations between temperament and empathy in 2-year-olds. *Developmental Psychology, 35*(5), 1189–1197.

Young-Browne, G., Rosenfeld, H., & Horowitz, F. (1977). Infant discrimination of facial expressions. *Child Development, 48*(2), 555–562.

Zahn-Waxler, C., & Radke-Yarrow, M. (1990). The origins of empathic concern. *Motivation and Emotion, 14*(2), 107–130.

Zahn-Waxler, C., Radke-Yarrow, M., Wagner, E., & Chapman, M. (1992). Development of concern for others. *Developmental Psychology, 28*(1), 126–136.

Zahn-Waxler, C., Robinson, J., & Emde, R. (1992). The development of empathy in twins. *Developmental Psychology, 28*(6), 1038–1047.

Zahn-Waxler, C., Schiro, K., Robinson, J. L., Emde, R. N., & Schmitz, S. (2001). Empathy and prosocial patterns in young MZ and DZ twins: Development and genetic and environmental influences. In R. N. Emde & J. K. Hewitt (Eds.), *Infancy to early childhood: Genetic and environmental influences on developmental change* (pp. 141–162). New York: Oxford University Press.

Zak, P. J., Kurzban, R., & Matzner, W. T. (2005). Oxytocin is associated with human trustworthiness. *Hormones and Behavior, 48*(5), 522–527.

PART III

The Dynamic Role of Early Social Experience in Vision, Memory, and Language

CHAPTER 6

Development of Brain Networks for Visual Social-Emotional Information Processing in Infancy

MICHELLE DE HAAN
LESLIE J. CARVER

Faces are key components of everyday social interactions and provide emotionally significant signals, such as the warning of danger in a fearful face or the rewarding value of a familiar, smiling face. Even for very young infants, identifying faces in the visual environment and recognizing familiar social partners are valuable skills that contribute to the formation of early social relationships, including attachment to caregivers. Thus, faces are a key source of visual social-emotional information beginning in infancy and continuing throughout adult life. In this chapter, we discuss the contribution of innate predispositions, brain maturation, and experience to the development during infancy of face-processing skills, including the abilities to detect and orient to faces within the visual environment, to recognize the faces of familiar people, to perceive where a person is directing his or her gaze, and to register emotions shown in the face. From this discussion, it will become clear that the development of face processing involves the combination of innate predispositions, brain maturation, and experience. For example, infants have innate biases that guide their visual exploration toward faces, but both the maturation of the cortex and the structure of the visual environment itself modulate how these biases are expressed. Scientists are only just beginning to understand these types of complex interactions among innate predispositions, brain maturation, and experience, but the domain of face processing provides a useful model for exploring these issues.

Brain Networks for Face Processing in Adults

The neural systems underlying face processing must be able to rapidly and reliably register and react to complex and dynamic facial displays. At the same time, they must be able to learn from experience and be amenable to cognitive control. Evidence from a variety of sources suggests that to deliver a face-processing system that is rapid and reliable but still flexible, the mature brain uses multiple pathways, with subcortical routes providing quick but less detailed processing of faces and cortical pathways providing slower but more detailed and controlled processing of faces. Before describing how the brain pathways involved in face processing emerge in infancy, we first set the context by presenting a brief overview of the neurocognitive system for face processing in adults. Processing of faces can be divided into perceptual processing, which involves distinguishing different facial configurations, and conceptual processing, which involves understanding meanings linked to particular configurations. In adults, these processes are mediated by a distributed neural network involving subcortical and cortical areas. Visual information about faces is initially passed along two neural pathways: (1) a subcortical pathway that is involved in detecting faces and directing visual attention to them and (2) a core cortical pathway that is involved in the detailed visual-perceptual analysis of faces. Both of these components interact with (3) an extended cortical–subcortical pathway involved in further processing of faces, such as the conscious processing of emotional intentions of others (Gobbini & Haxby, 2007; Haxby, Hoffman, & Gobbini, 2000; Johnson, 2005). See Figure 6.1.

In the subcortical pathway for face processing, information travels from the retina directly to the superior colliculus, then to the pulvinar, and on to the amygdala (de Gelder, Frissen, Barton, & Hadjikhani, 2003; Johnson, 2005). This route is believed to process facial information quickly and automatically and to rely primarily on low spatial frequency information (reviewed in Johnson, 2005). Existence of such a pathway in humans is supported by studies showing that the emotional valence of facial expressions can be reliably discriminated even following lesions to the primary visual cortex that abolish conscious visual experience (Morris, de Gelder, Weiskrantz, & Dolan, 2001; Morris, Ohman, & Dolan, 1999), and that emotional expressions not consciously registered because of brief presentations and use of backward masking can still activate the amygdala (Whalen, Rauch, Etcoff, McInerney, Lee, & Jenike, 1998; but see Pessoa, Japee, Sturman, & Ungerleider, 2006). The subcortical pathway could allow an initial rapid processing of basic features to be carried out before slower, conscious cortical processing is completed and might also modulate this slower cortical processing (reviewed in Tamietto & de Gelder, 2010). For example, projections from the amygdala to the occipital cortex may enhance visual processing of emotionally salient stimuli (Morris et al., 1999; Vuilleumier & Pourtois, 2007).

The core pathway for visual analysis of faces receives input from the retina via the geniculostriate pathway and includes the inferior occipital gyrus (encompassing the lateral occipital area, of which the occipital face area is a subregion), fusiform gyrus (including the fusiform face area), and posterior superior temporal sulcus/gyrus. The inferior occipital gyrus mediates the early perception of faces and passes this information to two areas: the fusiform gyrus and the superior temporal sulcus/gyrus. There is evidence that the fusiform gyrus is primarily involved in the interpretation of the static components of facial expressions and identity (Kanwisher, McDermott, & Chun, 1997), and the superior temporal gyrus contributes to the recognition of dynamic properties of facial expressions and eye gaze (Allison, Puce, & McCarthy, 2000). The N170 elicited by faces in the adult event-related potential (ERP) is thought to be generated by regions in the core cortical system, which themselves are also modulated by other components of the face-processing network such as the amygdala.

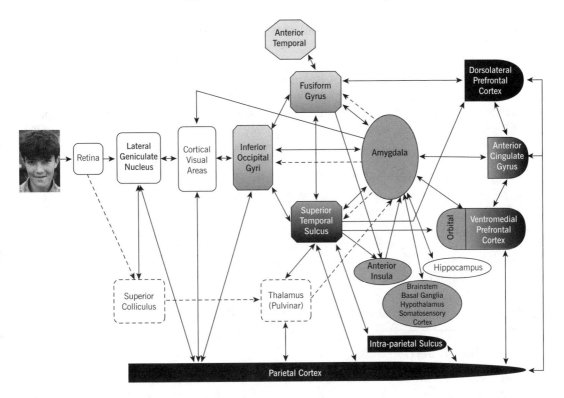

FIGURE 6.1. Face perception and attention systems. The three rectangles with beveled edges indicate the core system for face perception (Haxby et al., 2000). Areas shaded in light gray represent regions involved in processing identity and associated semantic information, areas in dark gray represent regions involved in emotion analysis (Adolphs, 2002), and those in black reflect the frontoparietal cortical network involved in spatial attention. Solid lines indicate cortical pathways and dashed lines represent the subcortical route for rapid and/or coarse emotional expression processing. This model is highly simplified and excludes many neural areas and connections. In addition, processing is not strictly hierarchical (i.e., from left to right) but involves multiple feedback connections (Bullier, 2001). Based on Palermo and Rhodes (2007).

The extended pathway receives input from, and in return communicates with, both the subcortical pathway and the core cortical pathway. It encompasses a variety of regions involved in the further processing of these inputs to allow activities necessary for normal social processing, such as conscious emotional appraisal and interpretation of the intentions of others. The paralimbic and higher cortical areas, such as the medial prefrontal cortex, somatosensory cortices, and anterior cingulate, are involved in longer latency processing of conscious representations of emotional states, in controlling behavior in social situations, and in planning actions and goals.

Development of Face Detection

To take advantage of the social content of faces, infants must be able to detect that a face is present in the visual environment. There is evidence that this basic ability to detect faces begins to operate from very early in postnatal life. Newborns preferentially orient and attend to faces in the visual environment from just minutes to hours after birth (e.g., Johnson, Dziurawiec, Ellis, & Morton, 1991). According to one influential hypothesis, this early ability is mediated by the subcortical pathway, which thereby provides a "face-biased" input to the developing cortex and enhances cortical activation to faces (Morton & Johnson, 1991; see also Leppanen & Nelson, 2009). This face-based input may ultimately play a role in establishing the specialization of cortical regions for face processing observed in the mature brain. According to a different view, newborns' preferential orienting to faces is instead the consequence of more general perceptual biases. For example, the eyes–nose–mouth configuration of the face is "top-heavy," having a greater density of elements in the top of the display than the bottom, and studies have shown that young infants generally prefer top-heavy patterns (Simion, Valenza, Macchi Cassia, & Turati, 2002; but see Chien, Hsu, & Su, 2010). In spite of the debate as to the best way to describe the visual biases that lead newborns to preferentially look to faces (for further discussion, see de Haan, Humphreys, & Johnson, 2002; Lepannen & Nelson, 2009), the different views concur that such a bias exists, that it is likely to be mediated subcortically, and that experience plays a minimal, if any, role in establishing the response.

Is Early Face Detection Subcortical?

The subcortical and cortical (geniculostriate) visual pathways differ in their retinal inputs, and researchers have exploited these differences to examine whether face-processing abilities differentially rely on the two pathways. One such difference is the representation of the visual field. The input to the subcortical pathway favors representation of the temporal visual field compared with the nasal visual field (Rafal, Henik, & Smith, 1991; Sylvester, Josephs, Driver, & Rees, 2007), whereas the input to the geniculostriate pathway does not. Thus, the presence of temporal–nasal field asymmetries in favor of the temporal hemi-field has been used as evidence of subcortical involvement in face processing (but see Bompas, Sterling, Rafal, & Sumner, 2008).

Investigators have used temporal–nasal asymmetries to probe whether newborns' preferential orienting to faces is mediated by subcortical pathways. If it is mediated subcortically, then it should be more prominent in the temporal than nasal visual field, whereas if it is cortically mediated the opposite pattern should occur. Human newborns show preferential orienting to a face-like arrangement of three blobs (two "eye" blobs above a "mouth" blob) compared with the same arrangement inverted only in the temporal visual field and not the nasal visual field (Simion, Valenza, Umiltà, & Dalla Barba, 1998). This result is not due to a general failure to orient discriminately in the nasal visual field, as newborns preferentially orient to stripes equally well in both visual fields (Simion et al., 1998). This finding suggests that newborns' preferential orienting to faces is mediated by the subcortical pathway, and there is some evidence that the same pathway is also functioning in adults (Tomalski, Johnson, & Csibra, 2009). Some caution, however, in interpreting this result is warranted. Data supporting the anatomic asymmetry in retinal projections are strong in cats but less striking in primates, and functional magnetic resonance imaging (fMRI) studies that have reported the asymmetry in humans (Sylvester et al., 2007) are not conclusive, as they cannot discriminate between feedforward and feedback inputs to subcortical structures.

Although such findings are consistent with a role for subcortical structures in the detection of faces in the first postnatal months, a role for the cortex cannot be ruled out because it has not been directly evaluated in very young infants. For example, in infants born preterm, magnetic resonance imaging measures of the integrity of the geniculostriate pathway obtained at term age are related to basic visual function (Bassi et al., 2008), suggesting that cortical areas could be contributing to visual abilities like face detection in newborns. Moreover, one positron emission topography study in 2-month-olds showed activation of a core cortical network, including areas interpreted as the fusiform gyrus and occipital "face area" when the infants viewed a female face compared with a control stimulus of small lights (Tzourio Mazoyer et al., 2002). However, because all six infants tested had suffered from hypoxic-ischemic encephalopathy, and older individuals were not tested with the same procedure, such interpretations must be taken with caution. The study also did not find evidence of activation in the superior temporal suclus, which could be due to the use of static, neutral faces or could reflect a developmental change in the configuration of the core cortical network.

ERP studies from infants at 3–4 months also suggest a role for the cortex by this time in development. ERPs are changes in brain electrical activity that can be recorded in response to a brief event (e.g., a face appearing on a screen for 1 second) by electrodes placed on the scalp. ERPs are generally thought to reflect primarily cortical activity and can provide some information about the spatial distribution of the brain's response and precise information about the timing of the response. A large body of ERP studies of face perception in adults has identified the N170, a negative deflection peaking about 170 milliseconds after stimulus onset over occipitotemporal regions (Bentin, Allison, Puce, Perez, & McCarthy, 1996). The N170 is described as a "face-sensitive" component because it is typically of larger amplitude and shorter latency to faces than other objects (Bentin et al., 1996; Rossion et al., 2000). In addition, just as turning a face upside down disrupts face recognition, the same manipulation affects the latency and amplitude of the N170 to faces (Bentin et al., 1996; Rossion et al., 2000).

In infants, an ERP component called the N290 is generated by regions within the core cortical pathway similar to those identified for the adult N170, including the lateral occipital area bilaterally and the fusiform gyrus and superior temporal sulcus, particularly on the right (Johnson et al., 2005). The N290 in 3-month-olds is larger for faces than visual noise (Halit, Csibra, Volein, & Johnson, 2004) but does not differ for canonical faces compared with ones with features scrambled (Macchi Cassia, Kuefner, Westerlund, & Nelson, 2006; Parise, Handl, & Striano, 2010). By 4 months (Parise et al., 2010), infants do show an adult-like pattern of larger N290 for scrambled versus canonical faces, even when the scrambled faces retain a top-heavy arrangement. These findings suggest that infants' representation of faces becomes more refined by 3–4 months, a result consistent with behavioral studies showing that infants by 3 months, but not before, are able to relate information from different faces they have seen to form a mental representation of a face prototype (de Haan, Johnson, Maurer, & Perrett, 2001).

Near-infrared spectroscopy (NIRS) has also been used to investigate face processing in infants. NIRS is an optical imaging technique that can noninvasively measure changes in blood oxygenation, which is a correlate of brain activation. Studies indicate that the right superior temporal sulcus is involved in processing the basic structure of the face by 5–8 months of age because this region shows increases in activation for canonical compared with scrambled faces (Honda, Nakato, Otsuka, Kanazawa, Kojima, Yamaguchi, & Kakigi, 2010) and upright compared with inverted faces (Otsuka et al., 2007). However, the role of other key core pathway cortical regions, notably the fusiform gyrus, remains unclear from the NIRS studies because this technique is not sensitive to the activity of areas that, like the fusiform gyrus, lie on the bottom surface of the brain.

Although a cortical response to the face is seen in ERPs by 3 months, the youngest age tested, the response is still immature. For example, the N290 in infants does not show an inversion effect specific to human faces until 12 months of age, even though upright and inverted faces can be discriminated much earlier (de Haan et al., 2002; Halit et al., 2004). These results have been interpreted to reflect the influence of experience: As infants gain more and more experience viewing human faces in their social environments, the core cortical pathway becomes more tuned to respond selectively to such inputs.

Is the Young Infant's Natural Experience Biased toward Seeing Faces?

If one role of the subcortical system is to provide a "face-biased" input to the developing cortex, two questions arise: (1) Do infants actually focus on faces in more natural settings? (2) What faces do infants usually experience?

One study used eye tracking to examine development of infants' attention to faces in complex, dynamic scenes to examine the first question ("Peanuts" cartoon; Frank, Vul, & Johnson, 2009). Results indicated that 3-month-olds' looking was better predicted by low-level perceptual salience than by face location, 6-month-olds' looking was not well predicted by either factor, and 9-month-olds' looking was best predicted by face location. The authors suggest that the difference across age could reflect either a specific increase in interest in faces, a general increase in attentional control and the ability to inhibit response to distraction, and/or increased processing of intermodal information.

Another set of studies examined infants' memories for faces in scenes with women performing natural actions (e.g., brushing teeth) and found that 5.5- month-olds did not show discrimination or memory for the faces after a 1-minute or 7-week delay, even though they did show evidence of remembering the actions at both delays (Bahrick, Gogate, & Ruiz, 2002). Follow-up experiments showed that discrimination of the faces in this context was possible by 7 months of age and also possible for 5.5-month-olds if they were given more familiarization time (Bahrick & Newell, 2008). Overall, discrimination of actions was more robust and occurred earlier in processing time than discrimination of faces.

Another study (Rennels & Davis, 2008) used parent rating scales to address the question of what types of faces are typically in infants' visual environment. Results showed that 2-, 5-, 8-, and 11-month-olds have the majority of their facial experience with their primary caregiver, females, and other individuals of the same race and age as their primary caregiver. Infant age and the stranger's gender were predictive of the amount of time spent interacting with one another, and the stranger's gender was also predictive of the amount of attention infants allocated during the social encounter. The general results of this study are consistent with findings of studies investigating the development of infants' preferences among faces of different genders and races. Generally, researchers have found that infants at birth do not exhibit preferences among faces varying on these variables. Preferences emerge by around 3–4 months, with infants preferring faces of the same gender and race as the primary caregiver (Kelly et al., 2005; Quinn, Yahr, Kuhn, Slater, & Pascalis, 2002)

Together, the results of these studies suggest that faces are not necessarily the most salient stimuli in infants' visual environment. It is necessary to remember, as discussed further later, that factors in addition to visual information might help orient infants to faces in naturalistic settings. Over the first postnatal months, infants typically do begin to show a bias toward focusing more on particular kinds of faces (e.g., according to gender and race) both when this is assessed in their natural environment (as indicated by parents' ratings) and in laboratory settings (using measures such as fixation time).

The Role of Additional Sensory Information

Information from sources other than vision may also contribute to early face detection. For example, although newborns cannot see their own face and its movements, they can perceive their unseen facial movements through proprioception. It has been suggested that this sensory information received by the infants about their own bodies and body movements may be a route through which they acquire a mental representation about the basic structure of faces (Sugita, 2009).

Vocal or olfactory cues may also help orient infants to social partners, and the multisensory information present could facilitate perceptual detection and further processing. Studies examining multisensory processing of faces have generally addressed the question not of face detection but of processing facial information such as identity or emotion. For example, the voice may facilitate facial identity recognition. Studies show that newborn infants prefer the mother's voice: In de Casper and Fifer (1980), infants "nursed" more frequently on a nonnutritive nipple to produce the mother's voice versus a stranger's voice. The mother's voice may also facilitate young infants' processing of her face: When looking time measures are used, both 1- and 3-month-olds show more robust looking time evidence of a preference for mother's face when the voice is also present. When observers' forced-choice judgments of the positioning of stimuli based on infants' behaviors are used, 1-month-olds show evidence of mother–stranger face discrimination only when the voice is present, whereas 3-month-olds do so even when only visual cues are present (Burnham, 1993).

Early odor-based recognition may also play a role in facilitating early recognition of the caregiver's identity (Porter, 2004). Human infants are particularly responsive to olfactory cues emanating from their mother's nipple/areola region. Beginning within minutes after birth, maternal breast odors elicit preferential head orientation by neonates and help guide them to the nipple. Newborns are generally attracted to breast odors produced by lactating women, and breast-fed infants rapidly learn their mother's characteristic olfactory signature while nursing at her breast (reviewed in Porter & Winberg, 1999). To some extent, the chemical profile of breast secretions overlaps with that of amniotic fluid. Therefore, early postnatal attraction to odors associated with the nipple/areola may even reflect prenatal exposure and familiarization. Early odor-based recognition could thus contribute to recognition of the mother's familiar face and formation of the infant–caregiver bond.

Summary of the Development of Face Detection

Indirect evidence supports the idea that the subcortical pathway underlies face detection in the first postnatal months, but a contribution of the cortical pathway cannot be ruled out because it has not been directly tested. Evidence from PET, NIRS, and ERP studies converge to show cortical activation to faces by 2–8 months of age, with the functioning of each component of the core cortical pathway identified. Behavioral studies suggest that when faces are viewed in more naturalistic contexts (moving and in scenes with other objects and actions), factors such as movement or low-level perceptual salience have a strong influence on infants' visual attention until 8–9 months. At the same time, when tested in the laboratory, infants from 3 months of age show evidence of tuning in to the facial characteristics of the caregiver in terms of species, gender, and race. Overall, these results are consistent with the idea that infants' main learning about faces in the first half of the first postnatal year is in face-to-face social interactions, with less influence of "incidental" faces presented in the background or in the context of a busy environment. The role of additional sensory factors in facilitating orienting to/learning about basic facial structure could be significant but has not been well studied.

Processing Social Information from the Eyes

The direction of another person's eye gaze is a social cue that can provide information both about that person's intentions and about significant events in the environment. In fact, it has been argued that one factor contributing to the development of infants' abilities to process direction of gaze is their learning that monitoring their caregiver's direction of gaze allows them to predict the locations of interesting objects or events in their environment (Moore & Corkum, 1994). Shifts in eye gaze are such a powerful cue that they can influence the viewer's attention even in an automatic, reflexive manner (Driver et al., 1999; but see Vecera & Rizzo, 2006).

Infants are sensitive to direction of eye gaze from the first days of life, preferring to look at faces with direct, versus averted, gaze (Farroni, Csibra, Simion, & Johnson, 2002). Viewing faces with direct gaze also influences how infants process and react to them. For example, 4-month-old infants can only effectively use a gaze shift to guide their own looking if it is preceded by at least a brief period of mutual eye contact (Farroni, Mansfield, Lai, & Johnson, 2003). In addition, 4-month-olds (Farroni, Massaccesi, Menon, & Johnson, 2007), like adults (Mason, Hood, & Macrae, 2004), are better at recognizing facial identity when they have studied faces with direct gaze than with averted gaze (see Blass & Camp, 2001, for a similar type of result).

Several ERP studies have examined the neural correlates of processing eye gaze in infants, comparing conditions with direct and averted gaze and with manipulation of facial expression and presence of an object target for the averted gaze. These studies have focused mainly on the Nc, a frontally maximal component linked to allocation of attention and the N290/P400 components linked to activation of the core cortical pathway. These studies have found that the N290/P400 components are influenced by gaze in 4- to 7-month-olds, with a larger amplitude response to direct compared with averted gaze if faces are presented alone, but only if the faces are neutral (Farroni et al., 2004) and not if they are displaying happy, angry, or fearful emotional expressions (Hoehl & Striano, 2008; Rigato, Farroni, & Johnson, 2010). In this same age group, if neutral faces are presented with objects alongside, there is a larger N290/P400 response to faces gazing at objects compared with faces gazing away from objects (Parise et al., 2010; Senju, Johnson, & Csibra, 2006). Responses to faces looking toward or away from objects while displaying emotion have not been tested for these components. Together, these results suggest that for neutral faces (but not emotional faces) the direction of eye gaze is detected early in processing, and there is enhancement of early perceptual processing for direct gaze from a social partner or gaze averted to look at an object.

Early-latency detection of eye gaze may be carried out in part by the fusiform region because the infant N290 response to direction of eye gaze in neutral faces appears to be generated there (Johnson et al., 2005). This enhanced early processing of faces with direct gaze may contribute to the better recognition of identity from faces with direct gaze just mentioned. It would be interesting to see whether the behavioral advantage in recognition of faces with direct gaze would be absent for emotional faces, just as the enhancement of the N290 for direct gaze is absent for emotional faces. This difference in the N290's sensitivity to gaze in the context of neutral versus emotional faces may reflect immaturity of connections with the amygdala, a structure known to modulate fusiform activity to emotional stimuli in adults.

For the later-latency Nc and positive slow wave (PSW), when no objects are present, amplitudes do not differ for direct and averted gaze in happy, fearful, or neutral faces (Hoehl & Striano, 2008; Rigato et al., 2010; Striano, Kopp, Grossmann, & Reid 2006), although for angry faces the Nc and PSW are enhanced for direct compared with averted gaze at 7 and 4 months, respectively (Hoehl & Striano, 2008; Striano, Kopp, et al., 2006). At 7 months, the Nc is larger for fearful faces with gaze averted toward an object than if the object is present but the gaze is direct, but there is no difference between these gaze conditions for neutral faces (Hoehl, Wiese, & Striano, 2008). Source localization studies suggest that the Nc has generators in the anterior cingulate cortex and the PSW has generators in the temporal lobes (Reynolds & Richards, 2005), suggesting that integrating differences in eye gaze with facial expressions of emotion might occur via the extended cortical–subcortical pathway. This conclusion is consistent with the results of a NIRS study showing greater right frontopolar cortex activation in 4-month-olds when viewing a smiling face with direct versus averted gaze (Grossmann et al., 2008).

In summary, ERP studies suggest that early in the processing stream the infant core cortical pathway reacts to direction of eye gaze in neutral faces, with enhanced processing of direct mutual gaze or gaze averted to a peripheral object. ERP source localization studies suggest that activity in the fusiform region may mediate the effects of eye gaze on processing of neutral faces, although future NIRS studies may help better define whether the STS also plays a role (as it does in adults). Later in processing, probably through their extended cortical–subcortical pathway, infants respond to negative emotions directed toward the self (angry) or to objects (fearful). Whether experience plays a role in helping infants to link eye gaze with emotional information in the face remains a question for further study.

Recognizing Familiar Social Partners

The ability to recognize familiar social partners is a foundation on which social relationships are built and maintained. The initial role of the face-detection system may not be about seeking faces in general but rather to learn about the caregiver. With time and as the infant's social world expands, he or she will increasingly need to identify specific individuals, and the processing involved helps to drive the "perceptual narrowing" or tuning of the face-processing system to the types of faces common to that infant's environment (Scott & Monesson, 2010). In this section, we review evidence regarding the development and neural bases of recognition of familiar faces, focusing on studies looking at recognition of personally familiar faces, such as the parent.

In adults, familiar faces activate the extended pathway, including the anterior cingulate, temporal cortex, and frontal cortex involved in processing episodic, semantic, and emotional knowledge linked to the face. One fMRI study in adults examining responses to mothers' faces, fathers' faces, and male and female celebrities' or strangers' faces showed that mothers' faces overall elicited more activation in core and extended brain regions involved in familiar face processing than fathers' faces or any other female faces (Arsalidou Barbeau, Bayless, & Taylor 2010; see Gobbini, Leibenluft, Santiago, & Haxby, 2004, for a similar pattern of results). Specifically, mothers' faces elicited more activity in the superior temporal gyrus than fathers' faces and more activity in the inferior frontal and middle temporal gyri than stranger or celebrity faces. There were no effects on the fusiform area in this study and, generally, effects of familiarity on activation of the fusiform are not always consistent across studies (Gobbini et al., 2004). The absence of effects may be because activation in the fusiform region is influenced not only by face familiarity but also by the perceiver's social profile: Shy adults showed greater activation of the fusiform for personally familiar versus stranger faces, whereas social adults show the opposite pattern (Beaton et al., 2009). In addition, adults with autism spectrum disorders, who might be thought of as on the extreme end of a continuum of shyness, also show greater fusiform responses to familiar than to unfamiliar faces (Pierce, Haist, Sedaght & Courchesne, 2004). Shy adults also show greater right amygdala activation for strangers' faces compared with personally familiar faces (Beaton et al., 2008, 2009). The latter result is similar to those of other studies showing greater amygdala activation to strangers' faces, a finding thought to be linked to their social salience rather than only to their novelty per se (Gobbini et al., 2004).

The one fMRI study that has examined responses to personally familiar faces in children found that both 3- to 8-year-olds and adults showed greater activation in the left genual anterior cingulate for mothers compared with strangers (Todd, Evans, Morris, Lewis, & Taylor, 2011). In adults, findings suggest a graded response, in which genual anterior cingulate cortex is activated more for self than mothers and more for mothers than familiar others. Such results are often interpreted in terms of overlapping self–other representations or person-knowledge networks. There was no effect of familiarity on activation of the amygdala, fusiform, or superior temporal regions in this study at either age. The difference from the previous study with adults may be because the adult-only study used neutral faces (Arsalidou et al., 2010), whereas the study with children and adults used happy and angry emotional expressions (Todd et al., 2011).

There is little information about the neural bases of processing personally familiar faces in infants. Existing behavioral data indicate that newborns are able to learn and recognize individual faces, including the mother's face as well as faces experienced only during the experiment (Pascalis & de Schonen, 1994; Pascalis, de Schonen, Morton, Deruelle, & Fabre-Grenet, 1995). Newborns appear to rely more on the outer features of the face for recognition, with the inner features less reliably linked to recognition (Pascalis et al., 1995; Turati, Macchi Cassia, Simion, & Leo, 2006).

NIRS studies provide some further information about the neural bases of familiar face processing in infants. One study involving 6- to 9-month-olds found increased activation to mothers' faces compared with baseline, but not to strangers' faces compared with baseline, over right frontotemporal regions (F4/T4 in 10-20 coordinates; Carlsson, Lagercrantz, Olson, Printz, & Bartocci, 2008). This study did not record over the left hemisphere. A second study recording over more posterior temporal regions (T5/6) found that both mothers' and strangers' faces showed an increased response relative to baseline in the right side, but only the mothers' faces did so on the left (Nakato et al., 2011)

The possible right-hemisphere bias for recognizing familiar faces has also been observed in ERP studies. Six-month-old infants showed a larger Nc response to the mother's face than to a stranger's face over the right hemisphere (T4/6) but a bilateral recognition response for toys (de Haan & Nelson, 1997, 1999).

The ERP response to the mother's face changes over the toddler period: Children 18–24 months show a larger Nc to mother than to stranger, children 24–45 months show no differential response, and children 45–54 months show a larger Nc response to stranger than to mother (Carver et al., 2003). This change was driven by a developmental change in the ERP to mother, with the response to stranger remaining stable over this period. The authors suggest that this may relate to the changing salience of the mother's face as the relationship between mother and child develops over this period. Another study examined 6-month-old infants' behaviors during separation from the mother in relation to ERPs to the mother's face and to a stranger's face (Swingler, Sweet, & Carver, 2010). Distress during separation was associated with larger amplitude P400 and Nc responses to the mother's face, and visual search for mother was associated with longer P400 and Nc latencies to the stranger's face. These studies suggest that longer latency ERP responses to faces may also reflect more general aspects of the developing social relationship.

How Are Familiar Faces Learned?

How do faces become familiar to infants? One study examined the role of infant state (calm or crying), social engagement, and sweet taste in familiar face learning (Blass & Carsp, 2001). The confluence of sweet taste and eye contact was necessary and sufficient for calm 9- and 12-week-olds to form a preference for the researcher after a 3.5-minute exposure. Crying infants never did so, even though eye contact and sweet taste arrested crying.

Another study with 4-month-olds supports the role for eye contact in establishing familiarity. Four-month-old infants were shown faces with both direct and averted gaze and subsequently given a preference test involving the same face and a novel one. A novelty preference during test was found only after initial exposure to a face with direct gaze. Furthermore, face recognition was also generally enhanced for faces both with direct and with averted gaze when the infants started the task with the direct gaze condition (Farroni, Massaccesi, et al., 2007).

Studies have also focused on the role of neuropeptides in the acquisition of face familiarity. This type of work raises the possibility that the neuropeptide oxytocin plays a role in face learning in infants. Oxytocin is a key component in regulating social behavior in mammals (reviewed in MacDonald & MacDonald, 2010). It is thought that oxytocin enhances perception of cues relevant for social interaction and bonding and also reduces the impact of socially aversive and threatening cues (Heinrichs, Meinlschmidt, Wippich, Ehlert, & Hellhammer, 2004). Among its effects, oxytocin has been shown to enhance memory for familiar faces. For example, in one study adults were given intranasal oxytocin or placebo and then familiarized with a set of faces and a set of nonsocial images (landscapes, sculptures .and houses) in a task where they had to judge how approachable each image was (Rimmele, Hediger, Heinrichs, & Klaver, 2009). In a surprise recognition test 24 hours later, the group that received oxytocin showed better recognition of faces compared with the placebo group, whereas both groups showed similar levels of recognition for the nonsocial stimuli. These findings parallel those obtained in animal studies, which have further shown that the effects of oxytocin seem to be specific to encoding: Injection of oxytocin in oxytocin knockout mice before, but not after, an initial social encounter restores social recognition (Ferguson et al., 2000). Oxytocin may bias the viewer to focus on the eye region of faces, which may in itself also facilitate recognition (Gustella, Mitchell, & Dadds, 2008). Oxytocin is released when young infants are nursing, a context that often involves face-to-face contact, so it may also play a role in acquisition of the caregiver's face as familiar.

The areas of the brain mediating oxytocin's enhancement of familiar face recognition are not entirely clear. In rodents, oxytocin is essential in the medial amygdala for establishing a social memory via olfactory cues (Ferguson, Young, & Insel, 2002). The medial amygdala projects to the bed nucleus of the stria terminalis and via the lateral septum to hippocampus, a brain region that is crucial for the storage and retrieval of memories and that also contains oxytocin receptors. In humans, fMRI studies have focused mainly on the amygdala, showing a specific modulation of amygdala activity during face processing after administration of oxytocin (Domes et al., 2007; Petrovic, Kalisch, Singer, & Dolan, 2008) as well as modulations in the fusiform gyrus, a part of the core cortical pathway that communicates with the amygdala (Petrovic et al., 2008).

These data suggest that oxytocin may play a role in enhancing memory for familiar and socially relevant faces. Salivary oxytocin levels in 4- to 6-month-old infants increase after playful interactions with their caregivers, with higher levels related to greater affective synchrony and infant social engagement (Feldman, Gordon, & Zagoory-Sharon, 2010). However, the link with face learning should be interpreted with caution; there is still much to be learned about how oxytocin systems develop in humans.

Does Learning about Faces in Infancy Have a Lasting Impact on the Nature of the Mature System?

There may be an experience-expectant sensitive period in the development of face emotion processing, starting from 5–7 months of life and continuing for several years

(Leppannen & Nelson, 2009). There is evidence consistent with the view that early experience has a lasting impact on face-processing abilities. For instance, patients with congenital cataracts who were deprived of patterned visual input from birth until 2–6 months of age show deficits in particular aspects of face processing even after at least 9 years of "normal" visual input. These patients show normal processing of featural information in the face (e.g., subtle differences in the shape of the eyes and mouth) but impairments in processing configural information (i.e., the spacing of features within the face; Le Grand, Mondloch, Maurer, & Brent, 2001). Studies with such patients also indicate that input to the right hemisphere plays a special role (Le Grand, Mondloch, Maurer, & Brent, 2003). These studies suggest that visual input during early infancy is necessary for the normal development of at least some aspects of face processing.

Some studies have also considered how the inherent structure in the typical infant environment might shape infants' experience with faces and subsequent face-processing skills. Feeding is a frequently occurring situation in which young infants repeatedly have exposure to faces. Young infants spend a large part of their waking time in this context—for example, 4 hours a day for the average 10-week-old (St. James-Roberts et al., 2006). Infant-holding preferences have also been examined in relation to development of face processing. Adult children whose mothers had a right-arm preference for holding infants have a reduced left-side bias for recognizing faces, suggesting that they are less well right-hemisphere lateralized for perceiving faces (Vervloed, Hendriks, & van den Eijnde, 2011). Results from a study in which mothers picked up dolls with built-in facial cameras suggested that this might be because early visual exposure to faces is suboptimal for right-arm held infants: Less area of the face was visible of mothers who held the doll in their right arm compared with those who held the doll in their left arm (Hendriks, van Rijswijk, & Omtzigt, 2010).

One study has also considered how exposure to siblings early in life may influence later face-processing skills (Macchi Cassia, Kuefner, Picozzi, & Vescovo, 2009). This study used the inversion effect as an index of face expertise, with better processing of upright than inverted faces considered a sign of expertise and the lack of such difference a sign of lack of expertise. The idea of the study was to examine the "other-age" effect, to see whether individuals with exposure to infants'/children's faces showed expertise with faces of this age; all participants were expected to show expertise for adults' faces. A comparison of 3-year-olds with and without younger siblings confirmed that the former showed inversion effects (expertise) for both infant and adult faces but the latter only for adult faces. First-time mothers only showed expertise with infant faces if they themselves had a younger sibling, and adult woman who were not mothers but who had younger siblings did not show expertise for the infant faces. The pattern of results suggested that exposure to younger siblings' faces leads to expertise in processing infant faces, but that this expertise lays dormant going into adulthood until it is reactivated by exposure to infant faces as occurs when becoming a mother. The fact that mothers who had not had younger siblings did not show the effect again points to a sensitive time for learning in the first postnatal years.

Summary of Development of Recognition of Familiar Faces

Studies of infants' responses to socially familiar faces have established many interesting patterns. Infants quickly recognize familiar faces and may use multisensory mechanisms to do so. Development of the extended cortical–subcortical pathway likely plays a key role in establishing faces as familiar, as may operation of psychobiological systems such as the oxytocin pathways. Experiential factors such as extended exposure to the caregiver's face during holding and feeding, having a sibling, and the status of infants' attachment relationships may also contribute to how infants respond to socially familiar faces. While several studies using different populations and methods suggest that early experience with faces may have a lasting impact on operation of the mature face-processing system, the neural bases of these effects have not been established.

Recognizing Emotions

Although there is evidence that newborn infants can detect faces and direct eye gaze and recognize caregivers' identities, studies of their abilities to detect emotion in the face have yielded conflicting results. Studies examining whether newborns can imitate the facial expressions they see have yielded both positive (Field, Woodson, Greenberg, & Cohen, 1982) and negative (Kaitz, Meschulach-Sarfaty, Auerbach, & Eidelman, 1988) findings. One looking time study found no evidence that newborns could discriminate fearful and neutral expressions, but did find that they looked longer at happy than fearful expressions (Farroni, Menon, et al., 2007). It is possible that these studies underestimate newborns' abilities because they used static stimuli, whereas natural facial expressions involve movement. Studies with infants 6–7 months of age have generally reported more positive findings even with static images, with infants being capable of perceptual discrimination and categorization of many of the basic emotions (reviewed in de Haan & Matheson, 2010) but with improvements in abilities continuing throughout infancy.

In adults, the superior temporal sulcus is thought to be needed for processing the dynamic information conveyed in natural expressions, and the amygdala for emotion recognition (Adolphs, 2002). There is limited direct information about the involvement of the core or extended cortical–subcortical pathways in infants' processing of facial expressions. Studies examining 7-month-old infants' responses to fearful compared with happy or angry expressions (de Haan, Belsky, Reid, Volein, & Johnson, 2004; Nelson & de Haan, 1996) demonstrated that ERPs differ for happy compared with fearful faces by approximately 140–260 milliseconds after stimulus onset, but ERPs to angry and fearful faces do not differ at any latency up to 1,700 milliseconds after stimulus onset. Another study comparing ERPs to angry and fearful faces at the same age but using longer stimulus exposure (1,000 vs. 500 milliseconds) found that the Nc response was larger for angry compared with fearful faces (Kobiella, Grossman, Reid, & Striano, 2008). With respect to early-latency components, the infant P400 component response, like the adult N170, is larger to fearful faces compared with happy faces (Leppannen, Moulson, Vogel-Farley, & Nelson, 2007). Another study found a larger N290, but smaller P400, response for angry compared with fearful faces (Kobiella et al., 2008). However, because the effects of emotion on these components were measured at sites (P3/4) where they did not appear maximal and where grand averages appeared affected by slow drifts, this result should be interpreted with caution.

An NIRS study investigated responses to happy and angry facial expressions in 6- to 7-month-olds over the T5/6 positions (Nakato, Otsuka, Kanazawa, Yamaguchi,

& Kaigi, 2011). The response to happy expressions increased slowly and persisted even after the stimulus disappeared, whereas the response to angry expressions peaked quickly and disappeared quickly after stimulus offset. In addition, prominent responses were noted over the left hemisphere (T5) for happy expressions and over the right (T6) for angry expressions compared with a baseline condition of pictures of vegetables.

Studies of patients with amygdala injury related to mesial temporal sclerosis also provide some evidence regarding this structure's role in early emotion recognition. In patients with temporal lobe epilepsy resulting from mesial temporal sclerosis, the amgydala is often damaged together with the hippocampus. Studies of such patients suggest that onset of right mesial temporal sclerosis before the age of 5–6 years is associated with particular difficulty in recognition of fearful faces compared with left mesial temporal lobe sclerosis, temporal lobe epilepsy from other causes, or epilepsy outside the temporal lobes (Hlobil, Rathore, Alexander, Sarma, & Radhakrishnan, 2008; McClelland et al., 2006; Meletti, Benuzzi, Nichelli, & Tassinari, 2003). In patients with early-onset right mesial temporal sclerosis requiring surgical treatment, emotion recognition difficulties remain following surgery (Hlobil et al., 2008; McClelland et al., 2006). These results have led investigators to argue that normal early development of the right amygdala plays a critical role in establishing the normal circuitry for emotion recognition, and that other brain mechanisms are unable to compensate for injury occurring in the first years of life (McClelland et al., 2006; Meletti et al., 2003). The amgydala is not the only brain structure damaged in patients with mesial temporal sclerosis, and some have argued that the co-occurring damage to the hippocampus also plays a critical role in the observed deficits in emotion recognition (Meletti et al., 2003).

Summary of Development of Emotion Recognition

By 6–7 months infants show perceptual categorization of several of the basic emotions from static pictures, but further study is needed to clarify abilities before this age. There is limited NIRS and ERP evidence, and studies have tended to compare different emotions rather than emotional faces with neutral faces. One NIRS study suggests involvement of the superior temporal sulcus in the processing of angry and happy expressions. ERP studies generally show enhanced attention to fear compared with happy by 7 months of age, but results for comparisons of fear versus angry expressions or for early-latency components are less consistent.

Using Social Information to Guide Learning and Behavior

In the previous sections, we reviewed and discussed infants' abilities to perceive different types of information from faces and how the interplay between emerging brain systems and environmental inputs might be involved in the development of such skills. In this final section, we briefly discuss the small number of studies aimed at investigating the neural correlates of how infants use this information to comprehend their social world, focusing first on studies examining the neural correlates of processing objects cued by social signal and then raising questions about the role of associative learning.

Joint attention requires monitoring another person's attention in relation to the self, an external object, and the other person's attention toward the same external object. The studies reviewed previously show that infants are able to detect faces and eye gaze early on. Several ERP studies have examined whether infants use this information to guide their processing of objects in a triadic context. Generally, infants show more negative ERP activity, with variable scalp topography, to objects when infant and adult first establish a mutual eye gaze and then the adult's eye gaze shifts to the object compared with various comparison conditions (e.g., shift away from object, no initial mutual gaze). This is seen as a larger Nc response to such objects in 5-month-olds (left side; Parise, Reid, Stets, & Striano, 2008) and 9-month-olds (central; Striano, Reid, & Hoehl, 2006), more negative occipitotemporal (~300 milliseconds) and frontal (N200, N400) activity in 9-month-olds (Senju et al., 2006), and less positive slow wave in 4-month-olds (Reid, Striano, Kaufman, & Johnson, 2004). In addition, 3-month-olds (Hoehl et al., 2008) and 12-month-olds (Vaccaro & Carver, 2007) show a larger Nc response to objects that have been cued by negative emotion compared with those cued by positive or neutral emotions. One possibility is that more negative ERP activity to cued objects indicates enhanced processing of the cued objects. These effects may be similar to results of ERP studies in adults showing that a reflexive shift of attention following the observation of a dynamic or static eye gaze cue enhances and speeds up early visual processing of a target presented at the gazed-at location (Schuller & Rossion, 2004). Another possibility is that the negative shifts represent a form of a negative slow wave that is related to response preparation, as the infant may see the interaction as a cue for action.

Several questions remain about how infants achieve the ability to relate social cues conveyed in the face to different stimuli. How do infants learn the association between shared attention and the attention-sharing stimulus (in the case of enhanced processing of co-attended objects), or between emotional information and emotion-eliciting objects, in the case of learning from another's emotional displays? Do early gaze-following abilities and later shared attention influence other things infants might learn about the target object? For example, if attention is drawn to a stimulus through a medium other than the face, are objects processed in the same enhanced way? Research is beginning to address these types of questions. One study examined how social cues, like a face, might help infants learn about the statistical properties of objects. In two experiments, Wu, Gopnik, Richardson, and Kirkham (2011) first showed that 9-month-olds make the inference that co-occurring visual features should remain fused, but do so only if the spatial layout remains the same between study and test trials. However, social cues helped infants make the inference about object properties even under the more difficult condition when the spatial layout changed at test, and helped infants choose patterns among distractors during learning and test. The authors argued that social cues may be important for helping the infant learn in naturalistic environments, which are filled with competing, distracting information.

Summary and Conclusions

Faces are a salient part of infants' environments, providing them with a connection to familiar caregivers and with cues that can facilitate their comprehension of the complex world around them and guide their behavior within it. From birth, infants appear able to detect faces, as evidenced by their preferential orienting to face-like patterns. There is evidence to support the idea that this ability is subcortically mediated; however, this evidence is not conclusive, and the possibility that the cortical mechanisms are also active from birth and contribute to this or other early-appearing face-processing skills has not yet been ruled out.

Cortical mechanisms of the core system are clearly active by 3–4 months of age, and development of this, and the extended, system likely contributes to subsequent gains in abilities to process familiar faces, recognize emotional expressions, and perceive eye gaze. There is evidence from PET and ERP source localization studies that the fusiform gyrus is activated during infants' face processing and from ERP and NIRS studies that the superior temporal sulcus is also involved. It is possible that the relative contributions of these two regions of the core cortical pathway to various face-processing skills is different in infants and adults; for example, the superior temporal sulcus was not activated to faces in the infant PET study and did not play a prominent role in eye gaze processing in the infant ERP source localization study, even though it is known to be important for processing eye gaze in adults. Future studies will help determine whether these results reflect true functional differences of the fusiform and superior temporal sulcus over development or are related to methodological issues (e.g., limits in accurate source localization in infants).

The amygdala, a prominent link between the subcortical and cortical systems, may play a key early role in organizing brain emotion-processing systems. More speculatively, oxytocin actions involving the amygdala may also facilitate learning familiar faces, such as of caregivers.

There is increasing evidence that infants' experience with faces shapes the development of their brain face-processing systems. It is relevant to note, however, that studies that have specifically examined whether infants are actually biased to look at faces suggest that in the first half of the first postnatal year, other factors such as low-level visual salience or motion are as good or better at attracting attention. Future studies examining the multisensory information that might normally be presented to help orient infants to faces and learn about their content may be informative. Results from visual studies also suggest that visual experience in infancy and early childhood may have a lasting impact on how faces are processed as adults. This evidence comes from a variety of sources, including studies of healthy children and adults and those who experienced pediatric visual deprivation. How the mechanisms involved in this type of learning are instantiated in the brain remains unknown.

From a neuroscience perspective, less is known about the mechanisms involved in infants using cues from the face to guide their attention and learning about cued objects and whether faces play a special role in this regard. Research supports the idea that faces support learning about objects in the environment, possibly through enhancing attention to the objects. These effects would likely be mediated through the extended cortical–subcortical system. However, detailed comparisons of the effectiveness of faces compared with other cues or of what components of the facial signal are critical remain to be carried out.

In conclusion, visual biases are present at birth that, probably together with cues from other modalities, help orient newborns to faces. Over the next months, infants begin to learn about the faces present in their environment, come to prefer faces with those characteristics, and start to seek out more clearly faces in the complex visual environment. This early process is most likely mediated by the fusiform cortex, superior temporal sulcus, and amygdala, and as these regions and their connections to other cortical regions develop, more complex processing of facial cues also emerges. While the face-processing system remains flexible and able to learn new faces throughout life, the learning that takes place during these first postnatal years appears to have a lasting imprint on how the mature face-processing system ultimately functions. The brain mechanisms underlying the long-lasting influence of infant learning, as well as questions about how facial information influences more generally what and how infants learn about the world, are important topics for future work. For now, it is clear that innate perceptual biases, brain maturation, and the social environment that the infant experiences all play a role in the process.

References

Adolphs, R. (2002). Recognizing emotions from facial expressions: Psychological and neurological mechanisms. *Behavioral and Cognitive Neuroscience Reviews, 1,* 21–62.

Allison, T., Puce, A., & McCarthy, G. (2000). Social perception from visual cues: Role of the STS region. *Trends in Cognitive Sciences, 4,* 267–278.

Arsalidou, M., Barbeau, E. J., Bayless, S. J., & Taylor, M. H. (2010). Brain responses differ to faces of mothers and fathers. *Brain and Cognition, 74,* 47–51.

Bahrick, L. E., Gogate, L. J., & Ruiz, I. (2002). Attention and memory for faces and actions in infancy: The salience of actions over faces in dynamic events. *Child Development, 73,* 1629–1643.

Bahrick, L. E., & Newell, L. C. (2008). Infant discrimination of faces in naturalistic events: Actions are more salient than faces. *Developmental Psychology, 44,* 983–996.

Bassi, L., Ricci, D., Volzone, A., Allsop, J. M., Srinivasan, L., Pai, A., et al. (2008). Probabilistic diffusion tractography of the optic radiations and visual function in preterm infants at term equivalent age. *Brain, 131,* 573–582.

Beaton, E. A., Schmidt, L. A., Schulkin, J., Antony, M. M., Swinson, R. P., & Hall, G. B. (2008). Different neural responses to stranger and personally familiar faces in shy and bold adults. *Behavioral Neuroscience, 122,* 704–709.

Beaton, E. A., Schmidt, L. A., Schulkin, J., Antony, M. M., Swinson, R. P., & Hall, G. B. (2009). Different fusiform activity to stranger and personally familiar faces in shy and social adults. *Social Neuroscience, 4,* 308–316.

Bentin, S., Allison, T., Puce, A., Perez, E., & McCarthy, G. (1996). Electrophysiological studies of face perception in humans. *Journal of Cognitive Neuroscience, 8,* 551–565.

Blass, E. M., & Camp, C. A. (2001). The ontogeny of face recognition: Eye contact and sweet taste induce a preference in 9- and 12-month-old infants. *Developmental Psychobiology, 42,* 312–316.

Bompas, A., Sterling, T., Rafal, R. D., & Sumner, P. (2008). Naso-temporal asymmetry for signals invisible to the retinotectal pathway. *Journal of Neurophysiology, 100,* 412–421.

Bullier, J. (2001). Feedback connections and conscious vision. *Trends in Cognitive Sciences, 5,* 369–370.

Burnham, D. (1993). Visual recognition of mother by young infants: Facilitation by speech. *Perception, 22,* 1133–1153.

Carlsson, J., Lagercrantz, H., Olson, L., Printz, G., & Bartocci, M. (2008). Activation of the right front-temporal cortex during maternal face recognition in young infants. *Acta Pediatrica, 97.* 1221–1225.

Carver, L. J., Dawson, G., Panagiotides, H., Meltzoff, A. N., McPartland, J., Gray, J., et al. (2003). Age-related differences in neural correlates of face recognition during toddler and preschool years. *Developmental Psychobiology, 42,* 148–159.

Chin, S. H., Hsu, H. Y., & Su, B. H. (2010). Discriminating "top-heavy" versus "bottom-heavy" geometric patterns in 2- to 4.5-month-old infants. *Vision Research, 50,* 2029–2036.

de Casper, A. J., & Fifer, W. P. (1980). Of human bonding: Newborns prefer their mothers' voices. *Science, 208,* 1174–1176.

de Gelder, B., Frissen, I., Barton, J., & Hadjikhani, N. (2003). A modulatory role for facial expressions in prosopagnosia. *Proceedings of the National Academy of Sciences USA, 100,* 12105–12110.

de Haan, M., Belsky, J., Reid, V., Volein, A., & Johnson, M. H. (2004). Maternal personality and infants' neural and visual responsivity to facial expressions of emotion. *Journal of Child Psychology and Psychiatry, 45,* 1209–1218.

de Haan, M., Humphreys, K., & Johnson, M. H. (2002). Developing a brain specialized for face perception: A converging methods approach. *Developmental Psychobiology, 40,* 200–212.

de Haan, M., Johnson, M. H., Maurer, D., & Perrett, D. I. (2001). Recognition of individual faces and average face prototype by 1- and 3-month-old infants. *Cognitive Development, 16,* 1–20.

de Haan, M., & Matheson, A. (2010). The development and neural bases of processing emotion in faces and voices. In M. de Haan & M. R. Gunnar (Eds.), *Handbook of developmental social neuroscience* (pp. 107–121). New York: Guilford Press.

de Haan, M., & Nelson, C. A. (1999). Brain activity differentiates face and object processing in 6-month-old infants. *Developmental Psychology, 35,* 1113–1121.

de Haan, M., & Nelson, C. A. (1997). Recognition of the mother's face by six-month-old infants: A neurobehavioral study. *Child Development, 68,* 187–210.

de Haan, M., Pascalis, O., & Johnson, M. H. (2002). Specialization of neural mechanisms underlying face recognition in humans infants. *Journal of Cognitive Neuroscience, 14,* 199–209.

Domes, G., Heinrichs, M., Glascher, J., Buchel, C., Braus, D. F., & Herpertz, S. C. (2007). Oxytocin attenuates amygdala responses to emotional faces regardless of valence. *Biological Psychiatry, 62,* 1187–1190.

Driver, J., Davis, G., Ricciardelli, P., Kidd, P., Maxwell, E., & Baron-Cohen, S. (1999). Gaze perception triggers reflexive visuospatial orienting. *Visual Cognition, 6,* 509–540.

Farroni, T., Csibra, G., Simion, F., & Johnson, M. H. (2002). Eye contact detection in humans from birth. *Proceedings of the National Academy of Sciences USA, 99,* 9602–9605.

Farroni, T., Mansfield, E. M., Lai, C., & Johnson, M. H. (2003). Infants perceiving and acting on the eyes: Tests of the evolutionary hypothesis. *Journal of Experimental Child Psychology, 85,* 199–212.

Farroni, T., Massaccesi, S., Menon, E., & Johnson, M. H. (2007). Direct gaze modulates face recognition in young infants. *Cognition, 102,* 396–404.

Farroni, T., Menon, E., & Johnson, M. H. (2006). Factors influencing newborns' preferences for faces with eye contact. *Journal of Experimental Child Psychology, 95,* 298–308.

Farroni, T., Menon, E., Rigato, S., & Johnson, M. H. (2007). The perception of facial expressions in newborns. *European Journal of Developmental Psychology, 4,* 2–13.

Feldman, R., Gordon, I., & Zagoory-Sharon, O. (2010). The cross-generation transmission of oxytocin in humans. *Hormones and Behavior, 58,* 669–676.

Ferguson, J. N., Young, L. J., Hearn, E. F., Matzuk, M. M., Insel, T. R., & Winslow, J. T. (2000). Social amnesia in mice lacking the oxyotcin gene. *Nature Genetics, 25,* 284–288.

Ferguson, J. N., Young, L. J., & Insel, T. R. (2002). The neuroendocrine basis of social recognition. *Frontiers in Neuroendocrinology, 23,* 200–224.

Field, T., Woodson, R., Greenberg, R., & Cohen, D. (1982). Discrimination and imitation of facial expressions by neonates. *Science, 218,* 179–181.

Frank, M. C., Vul, E., & Johnson, S. P. (2009). Development of infants' attention to faces during the first year. *Cognition, 110,* 160–170.

Gobbini, M. H., Leibenluft, E., Santiago, N., & Haxby, J. (2004). Social and emotional attachment in the neural representation of faces. *NeuroImage, 22,* 1628–1635.

Gobbini, M. I., & Haxby, J. V. (2007). Neural systems for recognition of familiar faces. *Neuropsychologia, 45,* 32–41.

Grossmann, T., Johnson, M. H., Lloyd-Fox, S., Blasi, A., Deligianni, F., Elwell, C., et al. (2008). Early cortical specialization for face-to-face communication in human infants. *Proceedings of the Royal Society: B. Biological Sciences, 275,* 2803–2811.

Gustella, A. J., Mitchell, P. B., & Dadds, M. R. (2008). Oxytocin increases gaze to the eye region of human faces. *Biological Psychiatry, 63,* 3–5.

Halit, H., Csibra, G., Volein, A., & Johnson, M. H. (2004). Face-sensitive cortical processing in early infancy. *Journal of Child Psychology and Psychiatry, 45,* 1228–1234.

Haxby, J. V., Hoffman, E. A., & Gobbini, M. I. (2000). The distributed human neural system for face perception. *Trends in Cognitive Sciences, 4,* 223–233.

Heinrichs, M., Meinlschmidt, G., Wippich, W., Ehlert, U., & Hellhammer, D. H. (2004). Selective amnesic effects of oxytocin on human memory. *Physiology and Behavior, 83,* 31–38.

Hendriks, A. W., van Rijswijk, M., & Omtzigt, D. (2010). Holding-side influences on infant's view of mother's face. *Laterality, 5,* 1–15.

Hlobil, U., Rathore, C., Alexander, A., Sarma, S., & Radhakrishnan, K. (2008). Impaired facial emotion recognition in patients with mesial temporal lobe epilepsy associated with hippocampal sclerosis (MTLE-HS): Side and age of onset matters. *Epilepsy Research, 80,* 150–157.

Hoehl, S., & Striano, T. (2008). Neural processing of eye gaze and threat-related emotional facial expressions in infancy. *Child Development, 79,* 1752–1760.

Hoehl, S., & Striano, T. (2010). Infants' neural processing of positive emotion and eye gaze. *Social Neuroscience, 5,* 30–39.

Hoehl, S., Wiese, L., & Striano, T. (2008). Young infants' neural processing of objects is affected by eye gaze direction and emotional expression. *PLoS ONE, 3,* e2389.

Honda, Y., Nakato, E., Otsuka, Y., Kanazawa, S., Kojima, S., Yamaguchi, M. K., et al. (2010). How do infants perceive scrambled face?: A near-infrared spectroscopic study. *Brain Research, 1308,* 137–146.

Johnson, M. H. (2005). Subcortical face processing. *Nature Reviews Neuroscience, 6,* 766–774.

Johnson, M. H., Dziurawiec, S., Ellis, H., & Morton, J. (1991). Newborns' preferential tracking of face-like stimuli and its subsequent decline. *Cognition, 40,* 1–19.

Johnson, M. H., Griffin, R., Csibra, G., Halit, H., Farroni, T., de Haan, M., et al. (2005). The emergence of the social brain network: Evidence from typical and atypical development. *Developmental Psychopathology, 17,* 599–619.

Kaitz, M., Meschulach-Sarfaty, O., Auerbach, J., & Eidelman, A. (1988). A re-examination of newborns' ability to imitate facial expressions. *Developmental Psychology, 24,* 3–7.

Kanwisher, N., McDermott, J., & Chun, M. M. (1997). The fusiform face area: A module in human extrastriate cortex specialized for face perception. *Journal of Neuroscience, 17,* 4302–4311.

Kelly, D. J., Quinn, P. C., Slater, A. M., Lee, K., Gibson, A. Smith, M., et al. (2005). Three-month-olds, but not newborns, prefer own-race faces. *Developmental Science, 8,* F31–F36.

Kobiella, A., Grossman, T., Reid, V. M., & Striano, T. (2008). The discrimination of angry and fearful facial expressions in 7-month-old infants: An event-related potential study. *Cognition and Emotion, 22*, 134–146.

Le Grand, R., Mondloch, C. J., Maurer, D., & Brent, H. P. (2001). Neuroperception: Early visual experience and face processing. *Nature, 410*, 890.

Le Grand, R., Mondloch, C. J., Maurer, D., & Brent, H. P. (2003). Expert face processing requires visual input to the right hemisphere during infancy. *Nature Neuroscience, 6*, 1108–1112.

Leppanen, J. M., Moulson, M. C., Vogel-Farley, V. K., & Nelson, C. A. (2007). An ERP study of emotional face processing in the adult and infant brain. *Child Development, 78*, 232–245.

Leppanen, J. M., & Nelson, C. A. (2009). Tuning the developing brain to social signals of emotions. *Nature Reviews Neuroscience, 10*, 37–47.

Macchi Cassia, V., Kuefner, D., Westerlund, A., & Nelson, C. A. (2006). Modulation of face-sensitive event-related potentials by canonical and distorted human faces: The role of vertical symmetry and up-down featural arrangements. *Journal of Cognitive Neuroscience, 18*, 1343–1358.

Macchi Cassia, V. M., Kuefner, D., Picozzi, M., & Vescovo, E. (2009). Early experience predicts later plasticity for face processing: Evidence for the reactivation of dormant effects. *Psychological Science, 20*, 853–859.

MacDonald, K., & MacDonald, T. M. (2010). The peptide that binds: A systematic review of oxytocin and its prosocial effects in humans. *Harvard Review of Psychiatry, 18*, 1–21.

Mason, M. F., Hood, B. M., & Macrae, C. N. (2004). Look into my eyes: Gaze direction and person memory. *Memory, 12*, 637–643.

McClelland, S., Garcia, R. E., Peraza, D. M., Shih, T. T., Hirsch, L. J., Hirsch, J., et al. (2006). Facial emotion recognition after curative nondominant temporal lobectomy in patients with mesial temporal sclerosis. *Epilepsia, 47*, 1337–1342.

Meletti, S., Benuzzi, F., Nichelli, P., & Tassinari, C. A. (2003). Damage to the right hippocampal-amygdala formation during early infancy and recognition of fearful faces: Neuropsychological and fMRI evidence in subjects with temporal lobe epilepsy. *Annals of the New York Academy of Sciences, 1000*, 385–388.

Moore, C., & Corkum, V. (1994). Social understanding at the end of the first year of life. *Developmental Review, 14*, 349–372.

Morris, J. S., de Gelder, B., Weiskrantz, L., & Dolan, R. J. (2001). Differential extrageniculostriate and amygdale responses to presentation of emotional faces in a cortically blind field. *Brain, 124*, 1241–1252.

Morris, J. S., Ohman, A., & Dolan, R. J. (1999). A subcortical pathway to the right amygdala mediating "unseen" fear. *Proceedings of the National Academy of Sciences USA, 96*, 1680–1685.

Morton, J., & Johnson, M. H. (1991). CONSPEC and CONLERN: A two-process theory of infant face recognition. *Psychology Review, 98*, 164–181.

Nakato, E., Otsuka, Y., Kanazawa, S., Yamaguchi, M. K., Honda, Y., & Kakigi, R. (2011). I know this face: Neural activity during mother's face perception in 7- to 8-month-old infants as investigated by near-infrared spectroscopy. *Early Human Development, 87*, 1–7.

Nakato, E., Otsuka, Y., Kanazawa, S., Yamaguchi, M. K., & Kakigi, R. (2011). Distinct differences in the pattern of hemodynamic response to happy and angry facial expressions in infants. *NeuroImage, 54*, 1600–1606.

Nelson, C. A., & de Haan, M. (1996). Neural correlates' of infants' visual responsiveness to facial expressions of emotion. *Developmental Psychobiology, 29*, 577–595.

Otsuka, Y., Nakato, E., Kanazawa, S., Yamaguchi, M. K., Watanabe, S., & Kakigi, R. (2007). Neural activation to upright and inverted faces in infants measured by near infrared spectroscopy. *NeuroImage, 34,* 399–406.

Palermo, R., & Rhodes, G. (2007). Are you always on my mind?: A review of how face perception and attention interact. *Neuropsychologia, 45,* 75–92.

Parise, E., Handl, A., & Striano, T. (2010). Processing faces in dyadic and triadic contexts. *Neuropsychologia, 48,* 518–528.

Parise, E., Reid, V. M., Stets, M., & Striano, T. (2008). Direct eye contact influences the neural processing of objects in 5-month-old infants. *Social Neuroscience, 3,* 141–150.

Pascalis, O., & de Schonen, S. (1994). Recognition memory in 3- to 4-day old human neonates. *NeuroReport, 5,* 1721–1724.

Pascalis, O., de Schonen, S., Morton, J., Deruelle, C., & Fabre-Grenet, M. (1995). Mother's face recognition by neonates. *Infant Behavior and Development, 18,* 79–85.

Pessoa, L., Japee, S., Sturman, D., & Ungerleider, L. G. (2006). Target visibility and visual awareness modulate amygdale response to fearful faces. *Cerebral Cortex, 16,* 366–375.

Petrovic, P., Kalisch, R., Singer, T., & Dolan, R. J. (2008). Oxytocin attenuates affective evaluations of conditioned faces and amygdala activity. *Journal of Neuroscience, 28,* 6607–6615.

Pierce, K., Haist, F., Sedaghat, F., & Courchesne, E. (2004). The brain response to personally familiar faces in autism: Findings of fusiform activity and beyond. *Brain, 127,* 2703.

Porter, R. H. (2004). The biological significance of skin-to-skin contact and maternal odours. *Acta Paediatrica, 93,* 1560–1562.

Porter, R. H., & Winberg, J. (1999). Unique salience of maternal breast odors for newborn infants. *Neuroscience and Biobehavioral Reviews, 23,* 439–449.

Quinn, P. C., Yahr, J., Kuhn, A., Slater, A. M., & Pascalis, O. (2002). Representation of the gender of human faces by infants: A preference for female. *Perception, 31,* 1109–1121.

Rafal, R., Henik. A., & Smith, J. (1991). Extrageniculate contribution to reflex visual orienting in normal humans: A temporal hemifield advantage. *Journal of Cognitive Neuroscience, 3,* 322–328.

Reid, V. M., Striano, T., Kaufman, J., & Johnson, M. H. (2004). Eye gaze cueing facilitates neural processing of objects in 4-month-olds. *NeuroReport, 15,* 2552–2555.

Rennels, J. L., & Davis, R. E. (2008). Facial experience during the first year. *Infant Behavior and Development, 31,* 665–678.

Reynolds, G. D., & Richards, J. F. (2005). Familiarization, attention and recognition memory in infancy. *Developmental Psychology, 41,* 598–615.

Rigato, S., Farroni, T., & Johnson, M. H. (2010). The shared signal hypothesis and neural responses to expressions and gaze in infants and adults. *Scan, 5,* 88–97.

Rimmele, U., Hediger, K., Heinrichs, M., & Klaver, P. (2009). Oxytocin makes a face familiar in memory. *Journal of Neuroscience, 29,* 38–42.

Rossion, B., Gauthier, I., Tarr, M. J., Despland, P., Bruyer, R., Linotte, S., et al. (2000). The N170 occipito-temporal component is delayed and enhanced to inverted faces but not to inverted objects: An electrophysiological account of face-specific processes in the human brain. *NeuroReport, 11,* 69–74.

St. James-Roberts, I., Alvarez, M., Csipke, E., Abramsky, T., Goodwin, J., & Sorgenfrei, E. (2006). Infant crying and sleeping in London, Copenhagen when parents adopt a "proximal" form of care. *Pediatrics, 117,* 1146–1155.

Schuller, A. M., & Rossion, B. (2004). Perception of static eye gaze direction facilitates subsequent early visual processing. *Clinical Neurophysiology, 115,* 1161–1168.

Scott, L., & Monesson, A. (2010). Experience-dependent neural specialization during infancy. *Neuropsychologia, 48,* 1857–1861.

Senju, A., Johnson, M. H., & Csibra, G. (2006). The development and neural basis of referential gaze perception. *Social Neuroscience, 1*, 220–234.

Simion, F., Valenza, E., Macchi Cassia, V., & Turati, C. (2002). Newborns'preference for up-down asymmetrical configurations. *Developmental Science, 5*, 427–434.

Simion, F., Valenza, E., Umiltà, C., & Dalla Barba, B. (1998). Preferential orienting to faces in newborns: A temporal-nasal asymmetry. *Journal of Experimental Psychology Human Perception and Performance, 24*, 1399–1405.

Striano, T., Kopp, F., Grossmann, T., & Reid, V. M. (2006). Eye contact influences neural processing of emotional expressions in 4-month-old infants. *Scan, 1*, 87–94.

Striano, T., Reid, V. M., & Hoehl, S. (2006). Neural mechanisms of joint attention in infancy. *European Journal of Neuroscience, 23*, 2819–2823.

Sugita, Y. (2009). Innate face processing. *Current Opinion Neurobiology, 19*, 39–44.

Swingler, M. M., Sweet, M. A., & Carver, L. J. (2010). Brain-behavior correlations: Relationships between mother–stranger face processing and infants' behavioural responses to separation from mother. *Developmental Psychology, 46*, 669–680.

Sylvester, R., Josephs, O., Driver, J., & Rees, G. (2007). Visual fMRI responses in human superior colliculus show a temporal-nasal asymmetry that is absent in lateral geniculate and visual cortex. *Journal of Neurophysiology, 97*, 1495–1502.

Tamietto, M., & de Gelder, B. (2010). Neural bases of the non-conscious perception of emotional signals. *Nature Reviews Neuroscience, 11*, 697–709.

Todd, R. M., Evans, J. W., Morris, D., Lewis, M. D., & Taylor, M. J. (2011). The changing face of emotion: Age related patterns of amygdala activation to salient faces. *Social Cognitive and Affective Neuroscience, 6*, 12–23.

Tomalski, P., Johnson, M. H., & Csibra, G. (2009). Temporal-nasal asymmetry of rapid orienting to face-like stimuli in adults. *NeuroReport, 20*, 1309–1312.

Turati, C., Macchi Cassia, V., Simion, F., & Leo, I. (2006). Newborns' face recognition: Role of inner and outer features. *Child Development, 77*, 297–311.

Tzourio-Mazoyer, N., de Schonen, S., Crivello, F., Reutter, B., Augard, Y., & Mazoyer, B. (2002). Neural correlates of woman face processing by 2-month-old infants. *NeuroImage, 15*, 454–461.

Vaccaro, B. G., & Carver, L. J. (2007). 12-month-olds allocate increased neural resources to stimuli associated with negative adult emotion. *Developmental Psychology, 43*, 54–69.

Vecera, S. P., & Rizzo, M. (2006). Eye gaze does not produce reflexive shifts of attention: Evidence from frontal-lobe damage. *Neuropsychologia, 44*, 150–159.

Vervloed, M. P., Hendriks, A. W., & van den Eijnde, E. (2011). The effects of mothers' past holding preferences on their adult children's face processing lateralisation. *Brain and Cognition, 75*, 248–254.

Vuilleumier, P., & Pourtois, G. (2007). Distributed and interactive brain mechanisms during emotion face perception: Evidence from functional neuroimaging. *Neuropsychologia, 45*, 174–194.

Whalen, P. J., Rauch, S. L., Etcoff, N. L., McInerney, S. C., Lee, M. B., & Jenike, M. A. (1998). Masked presentations of emotional facial expressions modulate amygdala activity without explicit knowledge. *Journal of Neuroscience, 18*, 411–418.

Wu, R., Gopnik, A., Richardson, D. C., & Kirkham, N. (2001). Infants learn about objects from statistics and people. *Developmental Psychology, 47*, 1220–1229.

CHAPTER 7

Event Memory

Neural, Cognitive, and Social Influences on Early Development

PATRICIA J. BAUER

$\mathbf{H}$ow long is your life story? How far back into your own past are you able to remember? Most adults remember few, if any, events from the first 3 to 4 years of life. The years between ages 4 and 7 (Pillemer & White, 1989) to as late as age 11 (Bauer, Burch, Scholin, & Güler, 2007) are marked by fewer event memories than would be expected based on forgetting alone. Until the mid-1980s, this "amnesia of child-hood" (Freud, 1905/1953) was widely attributed to the inability of infants and very young children to recall the past. This provided a ready explanation for the sparse representation in adults' corpora of memories from the first years of life. Changing perspectives on the nature of the infant mind (Mandler, 2004) and brain (Nelson, de Haan, & Thomas, 2006), coupled with methodological advances (Bauer, 2004), challenged the prevailing view. Twenty years of research using a nonverbal analogue to verbal report has made clear that, before their first birthdays, infants remember past events. Nevertheless there are pronounced changes in event memory throughout infancy and beyond (e.g., Bauer, 2004; Hayne, 2004). Ultimately, explanation of the changes will entail multiple levels of analysis, from neurons, neural systems, and basic memory processes to familial and cultural influences on remembering. In this chapter, the primary focus is on lower levels of analysis, including neural systems and basic cognitive processes, with attention to social influences on their development.

Event Memory: What Is Remembered?

The term "event" is broad, encompassing anything from water dripping from a faucet to something as complex and temporally extended as the Renaissance. For purposes of this chapter, I borrow a definition from K. Nelson (1986): Events "involve people in purposeful activities, and acting on objects and interacting with each other to achieve some result" (p. 11). This definition excludes simple physical transformations such as water dripping because they do not involve actors engaged in purposeful activity. In contrast, the definition includes the activities in which individuals engage as they move through a typical day as well as the unique experiences that ultimately define us as individuals. This definition also specifies what there is to be remembered about events, namely actors, actions, objects, and the orders in which the elements combine to achieve specific goals.

It has long been clear that infants learn and otherwise benefit from past experience and thus evidence memory of some sort (e.g., Piaget, 1952). In fact, DeCasper and Spence (1986) suggested that even prenatal experiences later may manifest themselves in changes in behavior toward stimuli: Mere hours after birth, infants distinguish between a novel story passage and one that their mothers read aloud during the last weeks of pregnancy. Other examples of robust memory in very young infants come from visual paired comparison and habituation (Bahrick & Pickens, 1995; Rose, Feldman, & Jankowski, 2007; Rose, Gottfried, Melloy-Carminar, & Bridger, 1982) and operant conditioning paradigms such as mobile conjugate reinforcement (Rovee-Collier & Cuevas, 2009, for a review). Yet, as described in Bauer (2006), these findings were not what prompted revision of the suggestion that the first years of life were devoid of the ability to mentally represent objects or events and thereby recall them. They did not have that effect because they do not necessarily demonstrate the type of memory required to remember actors, actions, objects, and the orders in which the elements combine to achieve specific goals. Because the distinction between types or forms of memory is critical to adequate description and explanation of developmental change, I discuss it before continuing with explication of the course of development of early event memory.

Distinguishing Types of Memory: Declarative and Nondeclarative

Although not universally accepted by either developmental cognitive scientists or adult cognitive scientists, it is widely believed that memory is not a unitary trait but rather is composed of different systems or processes, which serve distinct functions and are characterized by fundamentally different rules of operation (e.g., Squire, 1992). The type of memory termed "declarative" (or explicit) captures most of what we think of when we refer to "memory" or "remembering" (Zola-Morgan & Squire, 1993). It involves the capacity for explicit recognition or recall of names, places, dates, events, and so on. In contrast, the type of memory termed "nondeclarative" represents a variety of nonconscious abilities, including the capacity for learning habits and skills, priming, and some forms of conditioning (see Lloyd & Newcombe, 2009, for a review). A defining feature of nondeclarative memory is that the impact of experience is made evident through a change in behavior or performance, but that the experience leading to the change is not consciously accessible (Zola-Morgan & Squire, 1993). Declarative memory is characterized as fast (e.g., supporting one-trial learning), fallible (e.g., memory traces degrade, retrieval failures occur), and flexible (i.e., not tied to a specific modality or context). Nondeclarative memory is characterized as slow (i.e., with the exception of priming, it results from gradual or incremental learning), reliable, and inflexible (Squire, Knowlton, & Musen, 1993).

The distinction between different types of memory originally was derived from the adult cognitive and neuroscience literatures. Yet it is vitally important for developmental scientists because declarative and nondeclarative memory types rely on different neural substrates that have different courses of development. Several brain regions are implicated in support of nondeclarative memory, including neocortex (priming), striatum (skill learning), and cerebellum (conditioning) (see Toth, 2000, for review). These regions are thought to develop early and, as a result, to support early emergence of nondeclarative memory (see Nelson, 1997, for a review). In contrast, as described in more detail later, declarative memory depends on a multicomponent neural network, including temporal and cortical structures (e.g., Zola & Squire, 2000). Whereas most of the medial temporal lobe components of declarative memory develop early, other aspects of the network undergo a protracted developmental course. The entire circuit begins to coalesce near the end of the first year of life and continues to develop for years thereafter, contributing to pronounced changes in declarative memory (see Bauer, 2007, 2009a; Bachevalier & Mishkin, 1994; Nelson et al., 2006; Richman & Nelson, 2008, for reviews).

Measuring Declarative Memory Nonverbally

Because a primary distinction between types of memory is whether the experiencer has conscious access to mental content, distinguishing between types of memory presents challenges for research with infants, who, by definition, are unable to verbally comment on the contents of their conscious minds. One cannot present them with a list of words and then ask them to recall the words or respond to a question of whether a particular word was on the list. On the surface, techniques such as visual paired comparison and habituation appear to be nonverbal analogues to explicit recognition. They involve exposing infants to pictures of a stimulus and then introducing a novel one and observing at which of these infants look (e.g., Bahrick & Pickens, 1995; Rose et al., 1982, 2007). Whereas attentional preference techniques measure changes in infants' responses to previously encountered stimuli, it is unclear whether they measure the same type of recognition evidenced when adults explicitly affirm that they have seen a particular stimulus before. Mandler (1998) suggested that infant recognition memory experiments are most analogous to studies of priming in adults (a form of nondeclarative memory). Consistent with this suggestion, adults suffering from amnesia show normal priming even as they evidence pronounced deficits in recognition memory (Warrington & Weiskrantz, 1974; see also Snyder, 2007, for discussion). Thus, although changes in the distribution of infant attention as a result of prior exposure *may* be based on recognition memory, because explicit judgments are not required to produce the response (e.g., McKee & Squire, 1993), it should not be assumed that such responses are explicit, especially in light of alternative candidate explanations (see Bauer, Larkina, & Deocampo, 2010, for elaboration of this argument and extension of it to another major technique used in the infant memory literature, namely operant conditioning as measured by the mobile conjugate reinforcement (see, e.g., Rovee-Collier & Cuevas, 2009, for a review).

In contrast to visual paired comparison, which has high surface similarity to adult measures of declarative recognition (though low deep-structure similarity, as just discussed), another infant memory technique—deferred imitation—does not immediately appear to be analogous to verbal measures of recall and recognition.

Yet it has emerged as the paradigm of choice for measuring infant event memory. Deferred imitation originally was suggested by Piaget (1952) as a hallmark of the development of symbolic thought. Beginning in the mid-1980s, the technique was developed as a test of mnemonic ability in infants and young children (e.g., Bauer & Mandler, 1989; Bauer & Shore, 1987; Meltzoff, 1985). It involves using props to produce a single action or a multistep sequence and then, either immediately (elicited imitation), after a delay (deferred imitation), or both, inviting the infant or young child to reproduce the sequence.

As discussed in detail elsewhere (e.g., Bauer, 2007; Bauer, DeBoer, & Lukowski, 2007; Carver & Bauer, 2001; Mandler, 1990; Meltzoff, 1990; Squire et al., 1993), the conditions of learning and later testing in deferred imitation are conducive to the formation of declarative but not nondeclarative memories, and the resulting mnemonic behaviors share characteristics of declarative memories. First, although performance is facilitated by multiple experiences (e.g., Bauer, Hertsgaard, & Wewerka, 1995), infants learn and remember on the basis of a single experience (e.g., Bauer & Hertsgaard, 1993). Rapid learning is characteristic of declarative memory. Second, the contents of memories formed in imitation-based tasks are accessible to language. Once children acquire the linguistic capacity to do so, they talk about multistep sequences they experienced as preverbal infants (e.g., Bauer, Kroupina, Schwade, Dropik, & Wewerka, 1998; Cheatham & Bauer, 2005; although see Simcock & Hayne, 2002, for a suggestion to the contrary, and Bauer et al., 2004, for a discussion of possible reasons for the negative findings in Simcock & Hayne).

Third, imitation-based tasks pass the "amnesia test." McDonough, Mandler, McKee, and Squire (1995) tested adults with amnesia (in whom declarative memory processes are impaired) and control participants in an imitation-based task using multistep sequences. Whereas normal adults produced the model's actions even after a delay, patients with amnesia did poorly, performing no better than control participants who had never seen the events demonstrated. Older children and young adults who were rendered amnesic as a result of pre- or perinatal insults also show decreased performance on imitation-based tasks (Adlam, Vargha-Khadem, Mishkin, & de Haan, 2005). These findings strongly suggest that although imitation-based tasks are behavioral rather than verbal, they tap declarative memory.

Developments in Event Memory in Infancy

Using elicited and deferred imitation, researchers have documented early emergence and pronounced changes in event memory in infancy. One of the most salient changes is in the length of time over which event memory is observed. The length of time over which events are remembered increases dramatically over the first 2 years of life. Importantly, because like any complex behavior the length of time an event is remembered is multiply determined, there is no "growth chart" function that specifies that children of a given age will remember for a particular length of time. Nevertheless, by comparing across studies with similar methodologies, it is possible to discern developmental trends.

Early in the first year of life, the temporal extent of declarative memory is limited. For example, at 6 months of age, infants remember an average of one action of a three-step sequence (taking a mitten off a puppet's hand; shaking the mitten, which, at the time of demonstration, held a bell that rang; and replacing the mitten) for 24 hours (Barr, Dowden, & Hayne, 1996). Collie and Hayne (1999) found that 6-month-olds remembered an average of one of five unique actions over a 24-hour delay.

By 9 to 11 months of age, the length of time over which memory for events is apparent has increased substantially. Nine-month-olds remember individual actions over delays from 24 hours (Meltzoff, 1988) to 5 weeks (Carver & Bauer, 1999, 2001). By 10 to 11 months, infants remember over delays of 3 months (Carver & Bauer, 2001). Thirteen- to 14-month-olds remember actions over delays of 4 to 6 months (Bauer, Wenner, Dropik, & Wewerka, 2000; Meltzoff, 1995). By 20 months, children remember the actions of event sequences for as many as 12 months (Bauer et al., 2000). Thus, over the first 2 years of life, there is a steady age-related increase in the length of time events are remembered.

Sources of Age-Related Change in Event Memory

As already noted, a full explanation of developmental changes in event memory will involve multiple levels of analysis, from proteins and synapses, to neural systems, to cultural influences on memory and its expression (Bauer, 2006b, 2007; Nelson & Fivush, 2004). At present, powerful leverage is being gained by adopting an inter-mediate level of analysis—one connecting behavior with the processes and neural systems that support it (e.g., Bachevalier & Vargha-Khadem, 2005; Nelson et al., 2006). Perhaps because of their salience, changes in prefrontal cortex and associated changes in retrieval are frequent nominees for "what develops" in early memory. For example, Liston and Kagan (2002) invoked more effective retrieval to explain the observation that infants 17 and 24 months of age at the time of the experience of events remembered them 4 months later, whereas infants only 9 months old did not. Yet attribution of change to retrieval processes implies that memory storage did not differ between the older and younger infants. Equivalent storage, in turn, implies no age-related differences in encoding. Consideration of the processes of memory trace construction and maintenance (Squire, 2004), and of the development of the struc-tures and network that support them (Bachevalier, 2001), suggests that the assump-tions of age-related similarities in encoding and storage are not "safe." After review of the relevant literatures, an emerging alternative conceptualization that places the locus of age-related differences in long-term recall early in life not at the "rear end" of retrieval but at the "front end" of encoding and consolidation is discusssed (Bauer, 2006a, 2008). In this framework, age differences associated with retrieval are later to develop.

Memory Traces "under Construction"

In adult humans, the formation, maintenance, and subsequent retrieval of memo-ries of events depends on a multicomponent network involving medial temporal and cortical structures (e.g., Eichenbaum & Cohen, 2001; Markowitsch, 2000; Zola & Squire, 2000). Upon experience of an event, sensorimotor inputs from multiple brain regions distributed throughout the cortex converge on parahippocampal structures within the temporal lobes (e.g., entorhinal cortex). The work of binding the elements together to create a durable, integrated memory trace is carried out by another temporal lobe structure: the hippocampus. Cortical structures are the long-term storage sites for memories. Prefrontal structures are implicated in their retrieval after a delay. Thus, long-term recall requires multiple cortical regions, including prefrontal cortex, temporal structures, and intact connections between them.

In the human, aspects of the temporal structures in the temporal-cortical declarative memory network develop early. For instance, as reviewed by Seress and Abraham (2008), the cells that make up most of the hippocampus are formed in the first half of gestation, and virtually all are in their adult locations by the end of the prenatal period. The neurons in most of the hippocampus also begin to connect early in development, with the adult number and density of synapses reached by approximately 6 postnatal months. Lagging behind in development is the dentate gyrus of the hippocampus (Seress & Abraham, 2008). At birth, this critical bridge between cortex and the hippocampus includes only about 70% of the adult number of cells, and it is not until 12–15 postnatal months that the morphology of the structure appears adultlike. Maximum density of synaptic connections in the dentate gyrus also is delayed. Synaptic density increases dramatically (to well above adult levels) beginning at 8 to 12 postnatal months and reaching its peak at 16 to 20 months. After a period of relative stability, excess synapses are pruned until adult levels are reached at about 4 to 5 years of age (Eckenhoff & Rakic, 1991). As discussed elsewhere (e.g., Bauer, 2007, 2009a; Nelson, 1995, 1997, 2000), development of the dentate gyrus of the hippocampus may be a rate-limiting variable in memory early in life. Even beyond the preschool years, there are increases in hippocampal volume and myelination that continue into adolescence (e.g., Arnold & Trojanowski, 1996; Benes, Turtle, Khan, & Farol, 1994; Giedd et al., 1999; Gogtay et al., 2004; Utsunomiya, Takano, Okazaki, & Mistudome, 1999).

The association areas also undergo a protracted course of development. It is not until the 7th prenatal month that all six cortical layers are apparent. The density of synapses in prefrontal cortex increases dramatically at 8 postnatal months and peaks between 15 and 24 months. Pruning to adult levels does not begin until late childhood; adult levels are not reached until late adolescence or early adulthood (Huttenlocher, 1979; Huttenlocher & Dabholkar, 1997; see Bourgeois, 2001, for discussion). In the years between, some cortical layers undergo changes in the size of cells and the lengths and branching of dendrites (Benes, 2001). There also are changes in glucose utilization and blood flow over the second half of the first year and into the second year (Chugani, Phelps, & Mazziotta, 1987). Other maturational changes in prefrontal cortex, such as myelination, continue into adolescence, and adult levels of some neurotransmitters are not seen until the second and third decades of life (Benes, 2001).

Changes in Basic Mnemonic Processes

Developmental changes in the declarative memory network have implications for the efficiency and efficacy with which information is encoded and stabilized for long-term storage, in the reliability with which it is stored, and in the ease with which it is retrieved (see Bauer, 2004, 2006b, 2007, 2008, 2009a, 2009b, for expanded versions of this discussion). Late development of prefrontal cortex can be expected to impact all phases of the life of a memory trace from its initial encoding through consolidation to retrieval. Late development of the dentate gyrus is significant because it may lead to less efficient and effective consolidation of new information. That is, less information may make its way into the hippocampus, and that which is projected to the structure may be lost before it is stabilized and integrated into a long-term memory trace. As discussed in Bauer (2006a; see also Bauer et al., 2010), the consequences of less efficient and effective early-stage processing are profound: If encoding is compromised, there is less to be consolidated. If consolidation is compromised and/or the information available for consolidation is degraded, less information will be stored. If less information is stored, there will be less to retrieve. Differences in the amount available for retrieval will become more apparent with the passage of time as interference and decay take their toll, further depleting the already degraded trace.

Encoding

Although encoding cannot be directly observed, we can test for age differences in memory shortly after learning. Both behavioral and electrophysiological measures indicate age-related changes in the first 2 years of life. When they are tested immediately after a single experience of an event, 16-month-olds remember fewer actions and less information about temporal order than 20-month-olds (Bauer & Dow, 1994). Studies in which children are brought to a criterion level of learning—implying complete encoding—reveal that 12-month-olds require more learning trials than 15-month-olds, who, in turn, require more trials than 18-month-olds (Howe & Courage, 1997).

Event-related potentials (ERPs) also suggest age-related changes in encoding. ERPs are electrical oscillations in the brain that are time-locked to presentation of a stimulus. Differences in the activity recorded to different classes of stimuli (e.g., familiar and novel events) can be interpreted as differential neural processing and recognition. In a longitudinal study of relations between encoding and long-term event memory, my colleagues and I (Bauer et al., 2006) recorded infants' ERPs as they looked at photographs of props used in multistep events to which they had just been exposed interspersed with photographs of props from novel events. The amplitudes of responses to newly encoded stimuli at 10 months were larger than those of the same infants at 9 months; there were no differences in responses to novel stimuli. The differences at encoding were related to differences in long-term event memory. One month after each ERP, imitation was used to test long-term recall of the events. The infants had higher rates of recall of the events to which they had been exposed at 10 months compared with those to which they had been exposed at 9 months. In contrast, their performance on novel, control events did not differ.

Consolidation and Storage

Age-related differences in encoding are not the sole source of age trends in long-term event memory. Even with levels of encoding controlled statistically (Bauer et al., 2000), by matching (Bauer, 2005), or by bringing children of different ages to the same learning criterion (Howe & Courage, 1997), older children have higher levels of event memory than younger children. This suggests, for younger children in particular, that even once a memory has been successfully encoded, it remains vulnerable to forgetting. Greater vulnerability likely stems from the relative immaturity of the structures and connections required to consolidate memories for long-term storage (see Bauer, 2006a, 2009b, for discussion).

Consolidation is the process by which an initially labile memory trace is stabilized and integrated into long-term storage. It originally was hypothesized by Müller and Pilzecker (1900) to account for retroactive interference. In laboratory tests, they observed that new material learned shortly after (but not long after) old material produced deficits in memory for the old material. Consider two testing situations, both of which involve learning and remembering lists of words. In one situation, List 1 is learned, time is allowed to pass, and then List 2 is learned. In this situation, Müller and Pilzecker observed high levels of memory of both lists. In the other situation, List 1 is learned, and then very shortly thereafter List 2 is presented. In this case, they observed good recall of List 2 but poor recall of List 1. It seemed that in the short-delay situation List 2 retroactively interfered with List 1. Müller and Pilzecker advanced the hypothesis that there was retroactive interference because at the time List 2 was learned, List 1 had not yet been stabilized or integrated into storage, a process they termed *consolidation*. The work illustrated a critical principle about memory, namely that processes that take place after encoding influence later remembering.

A clear indication that consolidation and storage processes are a source of variance in long-term event memory in the first year of life comes from another study in which we combined ERP and behavior. Bauer, Wiebe, Carver, Waters, and Nelson (2003) used ERPs and behavior to test (1) encoding of events via an immediate ERP, (2) consolidation and storage via an ERP 1 week later, and (3) long-term recall via deferred imitation 1 month later. We exposed 9-month-old infants to different sequences (A, B, and C) at each of three sessions. At the third session, we assessed encoding via ERP (old Sequence A vs. new Sequence D). One week later, we tested consolidation and storage by administering another ERP test (Sequences B and E). We tested long-term recall of the sequences 1 month later. As a group, the infants showed evidence of encoding (differential responses to the old and new stimuli: Sequences A and D), yet there was differential long-term recall that, in turn, related to differential consolidation and storage. Infants who did not recall the events after 1 month also did not recognize the familiar props after 1 week (similar responses to Sequences B and E). In contrast, infants who recalled the events after 1 month showed successful consolidation and storage after 1 week (differential responses to Sequences B and E). The two subgroups of infants did not differ at encoding, and individual variability in encoding was not a significant predictor of long-term recall. In contrast, successful consolidation and storage over 1 week accounted for 28% of the variance in recall 1 month later. As discussed in the next section, differential savings in relearning suggests that the less successful group experienced storage failure as opposed to retrieval failure.

Retrieval

Evidence that encoding and consolidation and storage processes account for age-related and individual variability in long-term recall makes clear that we cannot explain developmental changes only by examining end-stage processes such as retrieval. In fact, the observation that together encoding and consolidation and storage processes account for as much as 70% of the variance in long-term recall (Bauer, Cheatham, Cary, & Van Abbema, 2002) begs the question of whether retrieval processes explain *any* age-related variance in long-term recall in infancy. The role of age-related variance in retrieval processes in long-term recall is surprisingly difficult to evaluate because in most studies there is no experimental means of determining whether age effects occur because younger infants experience retrieval failure (memory traces remain intact but become inaccessible) or storage failure (memory traces lose their integrity and become unavailable).

One means of distinguishing storage from retrieval failure is to provide multiple test trials without intervening study trials (Howe & O'Sullivan, 1997). The logic is that since each retrieval attempt entails re-encoding (Markowitsch, 2000), even though the material is not presented again overtly, the associated strengthening of the memory and route to retrieval can render an intact trace more accessible on a subsequent trial. Conversely, lack of improvement across trials implies that the trace is not available. Relearning also can distinguish between an inaccessible trace and one that has disintegrated. Classically, when the number of trials required to relearn a stimulus was smaller than the number required for initial learning, savings in relearning was said to have occurred (Ebbinghaus, 1885/1913). Savings presumably accrue because the products of relearning are integrated with an existing (though not necessarily accessible) trace. Conversely, the absence of savings is attributed to storage failure: There is no residual trace upon which to build. Age-related differences in relearning would suggest that the residual traces available to children of different ages are differentially intact.

Because the strategy of examining the constituent processes of memory is new to the infancy literature, means of differentiating storage and retrieval failure rarely have been invoked. When they are, they suggest storage, rather than retrieval, as the major source of age-related change. In Bauer (2005), 13- to 20-month-olds were matched for levels of encoding prior to imposition of 1- to 6-month delays. In spite of the matching, age-related differences in memory loss were apparent. At the longer delays in particular, younger infants showed more forgetting than older infants; the differences were apparent on two test trials, the second of which also featured additional retrieval cues (thus further reducing retrieval demands). Storage processes also were implicated by age-related differences in relearning. In each case, older children evidenced greater preservation of memory traces in storage relative to younger children. Similarly, group differences in relearning were apparent in Bauer and colleagues (2003): Infants with apparently more successful consolidation and storage as indexed by an ERP test 1 week after exposure to events also had higher levels of relearning.

Does the relative paucity of evidence of variance explained by retrieval processes early in life imply that the dramatic postnatal changes in prefrontal cortex have no implications for developments in long-term recall? Certainly not. For one thing, the variance associated with retrieval processes has yet to be systematically identified. Much additional research is needed to map age-related changes associated with each phase of memory trace construction, storage, and subsequent retrieval. Second, prefrontal cortex plays many roles in memory, only one of which is retrieval. Cortical and medial temporal structures interact during encoding and consolidation. As a consequence, developments in both loci may contribute to age-related changes.

Third, the ultimate storage sites for long-term memories are the association cortices (Takehara, Kawahara, & Kirino, 2003). Prefrontal cortex plays an especially significant role in storage of the *where* and *when* of events and experiences (Cabeza et al., 2004), the very features that locate memories in specific place and time. Thus, even if not through retrieval processes, changes in prefrontal cortex no doubt will be found to make substantial contributions to developments in long-term event memory (e.g., Bauer, 2004).

Shift in the Locus of Forgetting

Although the approach of parsing memory into its constituent processes is new in the literature on early development of event memory, it already has permitted refinements of our perspective on the source(s) of age-related change and thus the mechanisms of change. Together, the data suggest that over development, as medial temporal structures reach maturity, the locus of age-related differences in forgetting may shift from the initial phases of memory trace construction to the later phases of trace retrieval (e.g., Bauer, 2006a, 2007). Consistent with this suggestion, storage failure rates decline over childhood (Howe & O'Sullivan, 1997). Additional research is necessary to determine the time course and rate of changes in the variance accounted for by encoding, consolidation and storage, and retrieval processes over development.

The Broader Context of Memory Development

The discussion thus far has made clear that adopting a level of analysis that connects behavior with the processes and neural systems that support it is useful in understanding developmental change in event memory in infancy. But, of course, development takes place in a context. By virtue of the fact that development of the neural substrate and cognitive processes involved in event memory is protracted, there is ample opportunity for it to be impacted by context, both negatively and positively. Indeed, scholars have proposed that the hippocampus, in particular, is open to negative postnatal environmental influence (e.g., Seress & Mrzljak, 1992; Webb, Monk, & Nelson, 2001). The hypothesized susceptibility of this neural structure, coupled with evidence that its major role, namely consolidation and storage of memory traces, is a primary source of developmental change in the first years of life, suggests that there may be developmental populations in whom consolidation and/or storage functions are compromised. In this section, I describe some of the results from the study of children from one such population, namely children who spent their first months of life in institutional care. I end the section with discussion of a social developmental context that has proven supportive and conducive to event memory.

Event Memory in Children from Institutional Care

As discussed by Kroupina, Bauer, Gunnar, and Johnson (2010), there are a number of reasons to expect compromised development in children who spent their early months in an institutional care environment. Perhaps chief among them is deprivation, both cognitive and social. Thankfully, at the end of the 20th century, conditions in most orphanages (almost all of which are in the developing world and Eastern Europe) are significantly better than those observed under the Ceauçescu regime in Romania (which fell in the early 1990s; see the 1998 report by Rutter and the English and Romanian Adoptees Study Team for a description), for example. Nevertheless, relative to the "expected" environment, institutions invariably fall short. Even when adequate nutrition and health care are available, children rarely are provided with levels of stimulation and support sufficient to ensure normative development. Ratios of children to staff often are high; the staff frequently turns over; and because of concerns about transmission of disease, children are given few toys to manipulate and explore (see Gunnar, 2001, for a discussion). These conditions virtually ensure that children receive suboptimal levels of social and cognitive interaction. As a consequence, institutionalized children frequently exhibit sensorimotor, cognitive, and language delays. The longer children remain institutionalized, the more pronounced the effects (see Gunnar, 2001, for a review).

Animal models of early deprivation provide some insight into one potential source of cognitive delay, namely compromised hippocampal function. For example, primates deprived of normal rearing conditions exhibit elevated levels of glucocorticoids in response to stressors (e.g., Higley, Suomi, & Linnoila, 1992). High levels of glucocorticoids are not healthy for hippocampal neurons. In addition, there are suggestions that the licking and grooming that rodent mothers provide to their pups support the development of the hippocampus (Caldji et al., 1998). Removal of this source of stimulation results in levels of hippocampal cell death as much as 50% higher than normal (Zhang, Xing, Levine, Post, & Smith, 1997). The combination of these effects could be profound indeed. On the basis of nonhuman primate models, we may expect infants deprived of social-emotional support and stimulation to mount exaggerated responses to stressors, which could contribute to cell death in the hippocampus. Because these same infants also experience relative social deprivation, the exaggerated response may impact a hippocampus that already has fewer than the expected numbers of neurons. Coupled with a lack of cognitive stimulation, compromised hippocampal function is a distinct logical possibility.

To determine whether early deprivation is associated with deficits in event memory function, we tested a group of children adopted into the state of Minnesota from orphanages in China and Russia (Kroupina et al., 2010). The children—ranging in age from 4 to 18 months at adoption—were recruited through the International Adoption Clinic based in Minneapolis. On average, the children were tested 8 months postadoption. Most of the children were around 20 months at the time of test. To obtain a measure of general intellectual development, we tested the children on the Bayley Scales of Infant Development. We also tested their performance on immediate and 10-minute deferred imitation tasks and compared it with that of a group of home-reared children matched for age and gender, although not on race and ethnicity (the home-reared children were all white, reared in the upper midwestern United States). Measures of immediate recall provide an opportunity to determine whether groups of children differ in encoding processes.

Measures of 10-minute delayed recall permit determination of whether groups of children differ in the formation of memory traces that would survive for long-term storage. Although 10 minutes may not seem a long time, we had three reasons to believe that performance after this period would be diagnostic of consolidation processes. First, adults suffering from medial temporal lobe amnesia exhibit deficits in performance on tasks such as diagram recall, in which they are required to reproduce a diagram from memory after a 5- to 10-minute delay (e.g., Reed & Squire, 1998). Second, medial temporal lesions inflicted on nonhuman primates produce deficits in delayed-nonmatching-to-sample performance after delays as brief as 10 minutes (e.g., Zola-Morgan, Squire, Rempel, Clower, & Amaral, 1992). Third, in normally developing children, recall after a 10-minute delay is correlated with recall after a 48-hour delay (Bauer et al., 1999). These observations suggest that performance after a 10-minute delay provides information as to the integrity of medial temporal function.

On the test of immediate recall, the home-reared children and the children adopted from institutional care did not differ from one another. Thus, the ability to encode the events was intact in the latter group. Whereas the 10-minute delay had no observable effect on the performance of the home-reared children (i.e., immediate and 10-minute delayed recall did not differ), for the children who spent their early months in institutional care, the 10-minute delay produced a decrement in performance. The resulting difference between the groups remained even after children's Bayley scores were taken into account. Thus, as many as 8 months after adoption out of an impoverished environment into what, by comparison, would be described as "enriched," children who spent their first months of life in institutional care exhibited decrements in delayed event memory. Given that they exhibited adequate encoding of sequences in the immediate-recall condition, the most likely source of the decrement was compromised initial consolidation.

Maternal Narrative Style and Development of Event Memory

Just as there are contexts that prove suboptimal for the development of event memory, so too are there contexts that facilitate it. One such context is that of an elaborative style of reminiscing about past events. Mothers who provide rich descriptive information about previous experiences and invite their children to "join in" on the construction of stories about the past are said to use an *elaborative* style. In contrast, mothers who provide fewer details about past experiences and instead pose specific questions to their children (e.g., "What was the name of the restaurant where we had breakfast?") are said to use a *repetitive* or *low-elaborative* style.

Maternal narrative stylistic differences have implications for children's event memory. Specifically, children of mothers whose language more closely approximates the elaborative style report more about past events than children of mothers whose language more closely resembles the repetitive style (e.g., Fivush & Fromhoff, 1988; Tessler & Nelson, 1994). Relations between maternal language style and children's memory narratives are observed concurrently and over time (Reese, Haden, & Fivush, 1993).

Most of the research on maternal narrative style has been conducted with preschool-age and older children. There are a smaller number of studies with pre- and early-verbal children. For example, Hudson (1990) reported effects of differential degrees of maternal verbal elaboration on 24- to 30-month-olds' participation in memory conversations. Farrant and Reese (2000) extended this finding to children as young as 19 months. In Bauer and Burch (2004), we sought to expand this small literature into the context of the elicited-imitation paradigm. Examining possible relations between maternal verbal behavior and children's performance in the elicited-imitation task allows us to forge a link between the literatures on verbal and nonverbal recall. It also permits us to examine a naturally occurring behavior—that of variability in maternal style—under the conditions of greater experimental control afforded by a specific laboratory task.

Typically, in the elicited- or deferred-imitation paradigm, to-be-remembered events are modeled by an experimenter and children are encouraged to imitate. However, in Bauer and Burch (2004), to permit examination of possible effects of variability in maternal style on young children's recall, we had mothers, rather than experimenters, test their 24-month-old children. During the baseline period, children explored the event-related props. Mothers then demonstrated the test events for their children and elicited their children's imitation (i.e., immediate recall) of the events. One week later, the dyads returned to the laboratory and mothers tested their children's delayed recall. To prepare them for their task, mothers were exposed to a silent videotape on which the events were demonstrated. Beyond the instruction that they were to "talk naturally," mothers were given no guidelines regarding how to verbally communicate as they demonstrated and then tested their children's memories for the events.

Maternal Narrative Variability

Mothers exhibited variability in their language both when teaching the events and when testing their 24-month-old children's memories, with some providing fewer than 30 verbal elaborations and others providing more than 80. Similarly, affirmations of children's behaviors ranged from fewer than 15 to more than 60. Thus, even though we used a nonverbal task, we observed the same type of maternal language variability with 24-month-olds that has been reported in the literature on verbal narrative production with preschool-age and older children.

Relations between Mothers' Language and Children's Event Memory

Having observed variability in measures related to maternal style, we explored whether it was related to children's immediate or 1-week delayed event memory. Maternal verbal behavior during the spontaneous, child-controlled baseline period was related to the total number of target actions that the children produced both immediately and after the delay. Thus, mothers who were engaged in the task had children who were engaged in the task. Maternal verbal behavior also was related to children's engagement during immediate recall of the events. Mothers who produced relatively more verbal elaborations during the immediate-recall period had children who produced a larger number of both total target actions and different target actions. Maternal affirmations during the immediate-recall period also had a cross-lagged relation to children's performance after the delay: Children whose mothers provided affirmation during immediate recall were more engaged in the task at delayed recall. The children also did their part to keep the system going: Children who produced a larger number of target actions during immediate recall had mothers who produced both a large number of affirmations and more total category tokens during delayed recall.

These data make clear that by 24 months of age the interaction of factors that heretofore has been observed in the domain of verbal expression of event memory extends into the domain of nonverbal expression of memory: Variability in maternal verbal behavior relates to differences in children's nonverbal recall performance. Systematic variability in maternal language was apparent in the baseline phase, before any memory behavior was observed, and was related to children's levels of engagement in the task. These relations are reflective of the cascade of factors that influence the development of event memory in infancy and beyond.

Summary and Conclusions

Memory for events is fundamental to mental life. It allows us to find our car in the parking lot at the end of the day and to remember the significant events that shape who we are and how we perceive and conceive of the world. For much of the history of developmental psychology, human infants and very young children were thought to lack the ability to recall and reflect on the past (Piaget, 1952). With the development of a nonverbal analogue to verbal report, this assumption was challenged and found wanting. It now is apparent that by the end of the second year of life the ability to remember past events is relatively well established. There are pronounced changes in event memory as the ability is becoming established, and although they were not discussed here, developmental change continues well beyond infancy.

Adoption of a neurodevelopmental perspective suggests that major sources of developmental differences in event memory early in life are changes in encoding and consolidation. This implies that these early-stage processes are a primary locus for age-related differences in event memory. If we elaborate this implication, we are led to conclude that, rather than setting in as time goes by or as memories age, age-related differences in event memory begin virtually at the beginning of the life of a memory. Over developmental time, as the neural structures and networks on which they rely develop, encoding and consolidation processes become less vulnerable. As a result, more memories will survive their "infancy" and thus be available for recall after long delays. Logically, this means that the source of age-related differential vulnerability of event memories shifts from early-stage processes to the later-stage processes of storage and retrieval. Tests of this suggestion require that we examine the variance accounted for by each stage in the life of a memory (encoding, consolidation, storage, retrieval) at different points in developmental time. The expectation is that we will observe a shift in the "responsibility" for age-related differences in mnemonic success and failure. The specific expectation is that early in life encoding and consolidation process will account for the most variance in explaining age-related differences in event memory, whereas later in development storage and retrieval will begin to explain greater variance.

Importantly, neither brain nor cognitive development take place in a vacuum. Research with special populations may be especially revealing of the impact of environmental factors such as social and cognitive deprivation and stimulation. Infants who experience relative deprivation, such as occurs under conditions of institutional care, seemingly are at risk for negative consequences to the developing event memory system. In the sample reported here (Kroupina et al., 2010), children adopted from international orphanages did not differ from their home-reared peers in the encoding of new event memories. They did, however, evidence impaired retention of them over a brief delay, implying that the memories were especially vulnerable in the early stages of consolidation. The deficits were apparent even with levels of general cognitive ability taken into account.

Individual differences in event memory are associated with factors far less dramatic than institutional rearing. Children of mothers who use a more elaborative style of language as their children learn laboratory events are more engaged in the process both concurrently and over a 1-week delay. Greater engagement went hand-in-hand with better memory for the actions of the events the children learned. Children's memory also contributed to maternal behavior, such that children who produced more event-related actions at Session 1 had mothers who were more elaborative at Session 2. The work nicely illustrates the system that both pushes and pulls the development of event memory.

Finally, we may use the findings reported in this chapter to speculate on the implications of social factors not only for event memory but for development of the neural structures and networks that support it. In the case of institutionally reared children, there is reason to believe that hippocampal function may have been compromised as a result of elevated levels of glucocorticoids in response to stressors, coupled with less readily available social sources of facilitation of hippocampal development (i.e., in rodents, licking and grooming by dams). Infants deprived of social-emotional support could be expected to mount exaggerated responses to stressors. This, in turn, could lead to cell death in an already compromised hippocampus. The result would be increased vulnerability of memories as they undergo consolidation, a process subserved by the hippocampus (in concert with association cortices). Under these circumstances, the hypothesized "shift" from early- to later-stage processes as the locus of variability in long-term event memory may be slower to occur.

Fortunately, relations between structure and function work in the positive as well as the negative direction. The facilitating effects that maternal elaborative styles have on young children's event memory may be expected to provide optimal conditions for development of the neural structures that are "exercised" each time they are engaged. It may be going too far to suggest that maternal elaborative style is the equivalent of narrative licking and grooming, but the principle may be sufficiently similar to derive some benefit from their alignment. Maternal elaborative style may provide the optimal stimulation of the temporal-cortical declarative memory system, thus facilitating its development. Better neural structures contribute to better memory performance, which, in turn, engenders yet more maternal support for memory. The "big picture" result may be that more "early" event memories survive their most vulnerable period, with a resulting earlier "shift" from early- to later-stage processes as the locus of variability in long-term event memory. These speculations await systematic empirical test.

Acknowledgments

I gratefully acknowledge the National Institute of Child Health and Human Development (Grant Nos. HD-28425 and HD-42483) and Emory University for support of the work reported in this chapter. I also extend my appreciation to the many colleagues who have contributed to the work and to the infants and families who have participated in it.

References

Adlam, A.-L. R., Vargha-Khadem, F., Mishkin, M., & de Haan, M. (2005). Deferred imitation of action sequences in developmental amnesia. *Journal of Cognitive Neuroscience, 17*, 240–248.

Arnold, S. E., & Trojanowski, J. Q. (1996). Human fetal hippocampal development: I. Cytoarchitecture, myeloarchitecture, and neuronal morphologic features. *Journal of Comparative Neurology, 367*, 274–292.

Bachevalier, J. (2001). Neural bases of memory development: Insights from neuropsychological studies in primates. In C. A. Nelson & M. Luciana (Eds.), *Handbook of developmental cognitive neuroscience* (pp. 365–379). Cambridge, MA: MIT Press.

Bachevalier, J., & Mishkin, M. (1994). Effects of selective neonatal temporal lobe lesions on visual recognition memory in rhesus monkeys. *Journal of Neuroscience, 14*, 2128–2139.

Bachevalier, J., & Vargha-Khadem, F. (2005). The primate hippocampus: Ontogeny, early insult and memory. *Current Opinion in Neurobiology, 15*, 168–174.

Bahrick, L. E., & Pickens, J. N. (1995). Infant memory for object motion across a period of three months: Implications for a four-phase attention function. *Journal of Experimental Child Psychology, 59*, 343–371.

Barr, R., Dowden, A., & Hayne, H. (1996). Developmental change in deferred imitation by 6- to 24-month-old infants. *Infant Behavior and Development, 19*, 159–170.

Bauer, P. J. (2002). Early memory development. In U. Goswami (Ed.), *Blackwell handbook of childhood cognitive development* (pp. 127–146). Oxford, UK: Blackwell.

Bauer, P. J. (2004). New developments in the study of infant memory. In D. M. Teti (Ed.), *Blackwell handbook of research methods in developmental science* (pp. 467–488). Oxford, UK: Blackwell.

Bauer, P. J. (2005). Developments in declarative memory: Decreasing susceptibility to storage failure over the second year of life. *Psychological Science, 16*, 41–47.

Bauer, P. J. (2006a). Constructing a past in infancy: A neuro-developmental account. *Trends in Cognitive Sciences, 10*, 175–181.

Bauer, P. J. (2006b). Event memory. In D. Kuhn & R. Siegler (Vol. Eds.), W. Damon & R. M. Lerner (Eds.-in-Chief), *Handbook of child psychology: Vol. 2. Cognition, perception, and language* (6th ed., pp. 373–425). Hoboken, NJ: Wiley.

Bauer, P. J. (2007). *Remembering the times of our lives: Memory in infancy and beyond.* Mahwah, NJ: Erlbaum.

Bauer, P. J. (2008). Toward a neuro-developmental account of the development of declarative memory. *Developmental Psychobiology, 50*, 19–31.

Bauer, P. J. (2009a). The cognitive neuroscience of the development of memory. In M. L. Courage & N. Cowan (Eds.), *The development of memory in infancy and childhood* (2nd ed., pp. 115–144). New York: Psychology Press.

Bauer, P. J. (2009b). Neurodevelopmental changes in infancy and beyond: Implications for learning and memory. In O. A. Barbarin & B. H. Wasik (Eds.), *Handbook of child development and early education: Research to practice* (pp. 78–102). New York: Guilford Press

Bauer, P. J., & Burch, M. M. (2004). Developments in early memory: Multiple mediators of foundational processes. In J. Lucariello, J. A. Hudson, R. Fivush, & P. J. Bauer (Eds.), *Development of the mediated mind: Culture and cognitive development. Essays in honor of Katherine Nelson* (pp. 101–125). Mahwah, NJ: Erlbaum.

Bauer, P. J., Burch, M. M., Scholin, S. E., & Güler, O. E. (2007). Using cue words to investigate the distribution of autobiographical memories in childhood. *Psychological Science, 18*, 910–916.

Bauer, P. J., Cheatham, C. L., Cary, M. S., & Van Abbema, D. L. (2002). Short-term forgetting: Charting its course and its implications for long-term remembering. In S. P. Shohov (Ed.), *Advances in psychology research* (pp. 53–74). Huntington, NY: Nova Science.

Bauer, P. J., DeBoer, T., & Lukowski, A. F. (2007). In the language of multiple memory systems, defining and describing developments in long-term declarative memory. In L. M. Oakes & P. J. Bauer (Eds.), *Short- and long-term memory in infancy and early childhood: Taking the first steps toward remembering* (pp. 240–270). New York: Oxford University Press.

Bauer, P. J., & Dow, G. A. A. (1994). Episodic memory in 16– and 20-month-old children: Specifics are generalized, but not forgotten. *Developmental Psychology, 30*, 403–417.

Bauer, P. J., & Hertsgaard, L. A. (1993). Increasing steps in recall of events: Factors facilitating immediate and long-term memory in 13.5– and 16.5-month-old children. *Child Development, 64*, 1204–1223.

Bauer, P. J., Hertsgaard, L. A., & Wewerka, S. S. (1995). Effects of experience and reminding on long-term recall in infancy: Remembering not to forget. *Journal of Experimental Child Psychology, 59*, 260–298.

Bauer, P. J., Kroupina, M. G., Schwade, J. A., Dropik, P., & Wewerka, S. S. (1998). If memory serves, will language? Later verbal accessibility of early memories. *Development and Psychopathology, 10*, 655–679.

Bauer, P. J., Larkina, M., & Deocampo, J. (2010). Early memory development. In U. Goswami (Ed.), *Blackwell handbook of childhood cognitive development* (2nd ed., pp. 153–199). Oxford, UK: Blackwell.

Bauer, P. J., & Mandler, J. M. (1989). One thing follows another: Effects of temporal structure on one- to two-year-olds' recall of events. *Developmental Psychology, 25*, 197–206.

Bauer, P. J., & Shore, C. M. (1987). Making a memorable event: Effects of familiarity and organization on young children's recall of action sequences. *Cognitive Development, 2*, 327–338.

Bauer, P. J., Van Abbema, D. L., & de Haan, M. (1999). In for the short haul: Immediate and short-term remembering and forgetting by 20-month-old children. *Infant Behavior and Development, 22*, 321–343.

Bauer, P. J., Van Abbema, D. L., Wiebe, S. A., Strand Cary, M., Phill, C., & Burch, M. M. (2004). Props, not pictures, are worth a thousand words: Verbal accessibility of early memories under different conditions of contextual support. *Applied Cognitive Psychology, 18*, 373–392.

Bauer, P. J., Wenner, J. A., Dropik, P. L., & Wewerka, S. S. (2000). Parameters of remembering and forgetting in the transition from infancy to early childhood. *Monographs of the Society for Research in Child Development, 65*(4, Serial No. 263).

Bauer, P. J., Wiebe, S. A., Carver, L. J., Lukowski, A. F., Haight, J. C., Waters, J. M., et al. (2006). Electrophysiological indices of encoding and behavioral indices of recall: Examining relations and developmental change late in the first year of life. *Developmental Neuropsychology, 29*, 293–320.

Bauer, P. J., Wiebe, S. A., Carver, L. J., Waters, J. M., & Nelson, C. A. (2003). Developments in long-term explicit memory late in the first year of life: Behavioral and electrophysiological indices. *Psychological Science, 14*, 629–635.

Benes, F. M. (2001). The development of prefrontal cortex: The maturation of neurotransmitter systems and their interaction. In C. A. Nelson & M. Luciana (Eds.), *Handbook of developmental cognitive neuroscience* (pp. 79–92). Cambridge, MA: MIT Press.

Benes, F. M., Turtle, M., Khan, Y., & Farol, P. (1994). Myelination of a key relay zone in the hippocampal formation occurs in the human brain during childhood, adolescence, and adulthood. *Archives of General Psychiatry, 51,* 477–484.

Bourgeois, J.-P. (2001). Synaptogenesis in the neocortex of the newborn: The ultimate frontier for individuation? In C. A. Nelson & M. Luciana (Eds.), *Handbook of developmental cognitive neuroscience* (pp. 23–34). Cambridge, MA: MIT Press.

Cabeza, R., Prince, S. E., Daselaar, S.M., Greenberg, D. L., Budde, M., Dolcos, F., et al. (2004). Brain activity during episodic retrieval of autobiographical and laboratory events: An fMRI study using a novel photo paradigm. *Journal of Cognitive Neuroscience, 16,* 1583–1594.

Caldji, C., Tannenbaum, B., Sharma, S., Francis, D., Plotsky, P. M., & Meaney, M. J. (1998). Maternal care during infancy regulates the development of neural systems mediating the expression of fearfulness in the rat. *Proceedings of the National Academy of Sciences USA, 95,* 534–544.

Carver, L. J., & Bauer, P. J. (1999). When the event is more than the sum of its parts: Nine-month-olds' long-term ordered recall. *Memory, 7,* 147–174.

Carver, L. J., & Bauer, P. J. (2001). The dawning of a past: The emergence of long-term explicit memory in infancy. *Journal of Experimental Psychology: General, 130,* 726–745.

Cheatham, C. L., & Bauer, P. J. (2005). Construction of a more coherent story: Prior verbal recall predicts later verbal accessibility of early memories. *Memory, 13,* 516–532.

Chugani, H. T., Phelps, M., & Mazziotta, J. (1987). Positron emission tomography study of human brain functional development. *Annals of Neurology, 22,* 487–497.

Collie, R., & Hayne, H. (1999). Deferred imitation by 6- and 9-month-old infants: More evidence of declarative memory. *Developmental Psychobiology, 35,* 83–90.

DeCasper, A. J., & Spence, M. J. (1986). Prenatal maternal speech influences newborns' perceptions of speech sounds. *Infant Behavior and Development, 9,* 133–150.

Ebbinghaus, H. (1913). *On memory* (H. A. Ruger & C. E. Bussenius, Trans.). New York: Teachers' College. (Original work published 1885)

Eckenhoff, M., & Rakic, P. (1991). A quantitative analysis of synaptogenesis in the molecular layer of the dentate gyrus in the rhesus monkey. *Developmental Brain Research, 64,* 129–135.

Eichenbaum, H., & Cohen, N. J. (2001). *From conditioning to conscious recollection: Memory systems of the brain.* New York: Oxford University Press.

Farrant, K., & Reese, E. (2000). Maternal style and children's participation in reminiscing: Stepping stones in children's autobiographical memory development. *Journal of Cognition and Development, 1,* 193–225.

Fivush, R., & Fromhoff, F. (1988). Style and structure in mother-child conversations about the past. *Discourse Processes, 11,* 337–355.

Freud, S. (1953). Three essays on the theory of sexuality. In J. Strachey (Ed. & Trans.), *The standard edition of the complete psychological works of Sigmund Freud* (Vol. 7, pp. 135–243). London: Hogarth Press. (Original work published 1905)

Giedd, J. N., Blumenthal, J., Jeffries, N. O., Castellanos, F. X., Liu, H., Zijdenbos, A., et al. (1999). Brain development during childhood and adolescence: A longitudinal MRI study. *Nature Neuroscience, 2,* 861–863.

Gogtay, N., Giedd, J. N., Lusk, L., Hayashi, K. M., Greenstein, D., Vaituzis, A. C., et al. (2004). Dynamic mapping of human cortical development during childhood through early adulthood. *Proceedings of the National Academy of Sciences USA, 101,* 8174–8179.

Gunnar, M. R. (2001). Effects of early deprivation: Findings from orphanage-reared infants and children. In C. A. Nelson & M. Luciana (Eds.), *Handbook of developmental cognitive neuroscience* (pp. 617–629). Cambridge, MA: MIT Press.

Hayne, H. (2004). Infant memory development: Implications for childhood amnesia. *Developmental Review, 24*, 33–73.

Higley, L. D., Suomi, S. J., & Linnoila, M. (1992). A longitudinal study of CSF monoamine metabolite and plasma cortisol concentrations in young rhesus monkeys: Effects of early experience, age, sex, and stress on continuity of individual differences. *Biological Psychiatry, 32*, 127–145.

Howe, M. L., & Courage, M. L. (1997). Independent paths in the development of infant learning and forgetting. *Journal of Experimental Child Psychology, 67*, 131–163.

Howe, M. L., & O'Sullivan, J. T. (1997). What children's memories tell us about recalling our childhoods: A review of storage and retrieval processes in the development of long-term retention. *Developmental Review, 17*, 148–204.

Hudson, J. A. (1990). The emergence of autobiographical memory in mother-child conversation. In R. Fivush & J. A. Hudson (Eds.), *Knowing and remembering in young children* (pp. 166–196). Cambridge, UK: Cambridge University Press.

Huttenlocher, P. R. (1979). Synaptic density in human frontal cortex: Developmental changes and effects of aging. *Brain Research, 163*, 195–205.

Huttenlocher, P. R., & Dabholkar, A. S. (1997). Regional differences in synaptogenesis in human cerebral cortex. *Journal of Comparative Neurology, 387*, 167–178.

Kroupina, M. G., Bauer, P. J., Gunnar, M. R., & Johnson, D. E. (2010). Institutional care as a risk for declarative memory development. In P. J. Bauer (Ed.), *Advances in child development and behavior: Vol. 38. Varieties of early experience: Implications for the development of declarative memory in infancy* (pp. 138–160). London: Elsevier.

Liston, C., & Kagan, J. (2002). Memory enhancement in early childhood. *Nature, 419*, 896.

Lloyd, M. E., & Newcombe, N. S. (2009). Implicit memory in childhood: Reassessing developmental invariance. In M. L. Courage & N. Cowan (Eds.), *The development of memory in infancy and childhood* (pp. 93–113). New York: Taylor & Francis.

Mandler, J. M. (1990). Recall of events by preverbal children. In A. Diamond (Ed.), *The development and neural bases of higher cognitive functions* (pp. 485–516). New York: New York Academy of Science.

Mandler, J. M. (1998). Representation. In D. Kuhn & R. Siegler (Vol. Eds.), W. Damon (Ed.-in-Chief), *Handbook of child psychology: Vol. 2. Cognition, perception, and language* (pp. 255–308). New York: Wiley.

Mandler, J. M. (2004). Two kinds of knowledge acquisition. In J. M. Lucariello, J. A. Hudson, R. Fivush, & P. J. Bauer (Eds.), *Development of the mediated mind: Culture and cognitive development. Essays in honor of Katherine Nelson* (pp. 13–32). Mahwah, NJ: Erlbaum.

Markowitsch, H. J. (2000). Neuroanatomy of memory. In E. Tulving & F. I. M. Craik (Eds.), *The Oxford handbook of memory* (pp. 465–484). New York: Oxford University Press.

McDonough, L., Mandler, J. M., McKee, R. D., & Squire, L. R. (1995). The deferred imitation task as a nonverbal measure of declarative memory. *Proceedings of the National Academy of Sciences USA, 92*, 7580–7584.

McKee, R. D., & Squire, L. R. (1993). On the development of declarative memory. *Journal of Experimental Psychology: Learning, Memory, and Cognition, 19*, 397–404.

Meltzoff, A. N. (1985). Immediate and deferred imitation in fourteen- and twenty-four-month-old infants. *Child Development, 56*, 62–72.

Meltzoff, A. N. (1988). Infant imitation and memory: Nine-month-olds in immediate and deferred tests. *Child Development, 59*, 217–225.

Meltzoff, A. N. (1990). The implications of cross-modal matching and imitation for the development of representation and memory in infants. In A. Diamond (Ed.), *The development and neural bases of higher cognitive functions* (pp. 1–31). New York: New York Academy of Science.

Meltzoff, A. N. (1995). What infant memory tells us about infantile amnesia: Long-term recall and deferred imitation. *Journal of Experimental Child Psychology, 59*, 497–515.

Müller, G. E., & Pilzecker, A. (1900). Experimentalle Beitrage zur Lehre vom Gedachtnis. *Zeitschrift fur Psychologie, 1*, 1–300.

Nelson, C. A. (1995). The ontogeny of human memory: A cognitive neuroscience perspective. *Developmental Psychology, 31*, 723–738.

Nelson, C. A. (1997). The neurobiological basis of early memory development. In N. Cowan (Ed.), *The development of memory in childhood* (pp. 41–82). Hove East Sussex, UK: Psychology Press.

Nelson, C. A. (2000). Neural plasticity and human development: The role of early experience in sculpting memory systems. *Developmental Science, 3*, 115–136.

Nelson, C. A., de Haan, M., & Thomas, K. (2006). Neural bases of cognitive development. In D. D. Kuhn & R. Siegler (Vol. Eds.), W. Damon & R. M. Lerner (Eds.-in-Chief), *Handbook of child psychology: Vol. 2. Cognition, perception, and language* (6th ed., pp. 3–57). Hoboken, NJ: Wiley.

Nelson, K. (1986). *Event knowledge: Structure and function in development.* Hillsdale, NJ: Erlbaum.

Nelson, K., & Fivush, R. (2004). The emergence of autobiographical memory: A social cultural developmental theory. *Psychological Review, 111*, 486–511.

Piaget, J. (1952). *The origins of intelligence in children.* New York: International Universities Press.

Pillemer, D. B., & White, S. H. (1989). Childhood events recalled by children and adults. In H. W. Reese (Ed.), *Advances in child development and behavior* (Vol. 21, pp. 297–340). Orlando, FL: Academic Press.

Reed, J. M., & Squire, L. R. (1998). Retrograde amnesia for facts and events: Findings from four new cases. *Journal of Neuroscience, 18*, 3943–3954.

Reese, E., Haden, C. A., & Fivush, R. (1993). Mother-child conversations about the past: Relationships of style and memory over time. *Cognitive Development, 8*, 403–430.

Richman, J., & Nelson, C. A. (2008). Mechanisms of change: A cognitive neuroscience approach to declarative memory development. In C. A. Nelson & M. Luciana (Eds.), *Handbook of developmental cognitive neuroscience* (2nd ed., pp. 541–552). Cambridge, MA: MIT Press.

Rose, S. A., Feldman, J. F., & Jankowski, J. J. (2007). Developmental aspects of visual recognition memory in infancy. In L. M. Oakes & P. J. Bauer (Eds.), *Short- and long-term memory in infancy and early childhood: Taking the first steps toward remembering* (pp. 153–178). New York: Oxford University Press.

Rose, S. A., Gottfried, A. W., Melloy-Carminar, P., & Bridger, W. H. (1982). Familiarity and novelty preferences in infant recognition memory: Implications for information processing. *Developmental Psychology, 18*, 704–713.

Rovee-Collier, C., & Cuevas, K. (2009). The development of infant memory. In M. L. Courage & N. Cowan (Eds.), *The development of memory in infancy and childhood* (2nd ed., pp. 11–41). New York: Psychology Press.

Rutter, M., and the English and Romanian Adoptees (ERP) Study Team. (1998). Developmental catch-up, and deficit, following adoption after severe global early privation. *Journal of Child Psychology and Psychiatry, 39*, 465–476.

Seress, L., & Abraham, H. (2008). Pre- and postnatal morphological development of the human hippocampal formation. In C. A. Nelson & M. Luciana (Eds.), *Handbook of developmental cognitive neuroscience* (2nd ed., pp. 187–212). Cambridge, MA: MIT Press.

Seress, L., & Mrzljak, L. (1992). Postnatal development of mossy cells in the human dentate gyrus: A light microscopic Golgi study. *Hippocampus, 2*, 127–142.

Simcock, G., & Hayne, H. (2002). Breaking the barrier? Children fail to translate their pre-verbal memories into language. *Psychological Science, 13*, 225–231.

Snyder, K. A. (2007). Neural mechanisms of attention and memory in preferential looking tasks. In L. M. Oakes & P. J. Bauer (Eds.), *Short- and long-term memory in infancy and early childhood: Taking the first steps toward remembering* (pp. 179–208). New York: Oxford University Press.

Squire, L. R. (1992). Memory and the hippocampus: A synthesis from findings with rats, monkeys, and humans. *Psychological Review, 99*, 195–231.

Squire, L. R. (2004). Memory systems of the brain: A brief history and current perspective. *Neurobiology of Learning and Memory, 82*, 171–177.

Squire, L. R., Knowlton, B., & Musen, G. (1993). The structure and organization of memory. *Annual Review of Psychology, 44*, 453–495.

Takehara, K., Kawahara, S., & Kirino, Y. (2003). Time-dependent reorganization of the brain components underlying memory retention in trace eyeblink conditioning. *Journal of Neuroscience, 23*, 9897–9905.

Tessler, M., & Nelson, K. (1994). Making memories: The influence of joint encoding on later recall by young children. *Consciousness and Cognition, 3*, 307–326.

Toth, J. P. (2000). Nonconscious forms of human memory. In E. Tulving & F. I. M. Craik (Eds.), *The Oxford handbook of memory* (pp. 245–261). New York: Oxford University Press.

Utsunomiya, H., Takano, K., Okazaki, M., & Mistudome, A. (1999). Development of the temporal lobe in infants and children: Analysis by MR-based volumetry. *American Journal of Neuroradiology, 20*, 717–723.

Warrington, E. K., & Weiskrantz, L. (1974). The effect of prior learning on subsequent retention in amnesic patients. *Neuropsychologia, 12*, 419–428.

Webb, S. J., Monk, C. S., & Nelson, C. A. (2001). Mechanisms of postnatal neurobiological development: Implications for human development. *Developmental Neuropsychology, 19*, 147–171.

Zhang, L. X., Xing, G. O., Levine, S., Post, R. M., & Smith, M. A. (1997, October). Maternal deprivation induces neuronal death. *Society of Neuroscience Abstracts*, p. 1113.

Zola, S. M., & Squire, L. R. (2000). The medial temporal lobe and the hippocampus. In E. Tulving & F.I.M. Craik (Eds.), *The Oxford handbook of memory* (pp. 485–500). New York: Oxford University Press.

Zola-Morgan, S., & Squire, L. R. (1993). Neuroanatomy of memory. *Annual Review of Neuroscience, 16*, 547–563.

Zola-Morgan, S., Squire, L. R., Rempel, N. L., Clower, R. P., & Amaral, D. G. (1992). Enduring memory impairment in monkeys after ischemic damage to the hippocampus. *Journal of Neuroscience, 9*, 4355–4370.

CHAPTER 8

Biology of Shared Experience and Language Development

Regulations for the Intersubjective Life of Narratives

COLWYN TREVARTHEN
JONATHAN DELAFIELD-BUTT

Language exists for the purpose of communicating intentions and knowledge, and it is learned in dialogue from infancy. It can only be passed on by people who respond to the sociable impulses of young children, engaging intimately with their eager expressions of intention, awareness, and affection (Bateson, 1979; Bruner, 1983; Papoušek, 1994; Trevarthen, 1979). Human expressive movement depends on unique developments in the brain and body before birth (Trevarthen, 2011b), and detailed analyses of intersubjective games between parents and infants who are too young to speak show that conversations begin as story-making games of nonverbal communication. In these games, powerful, rhythmic, "musical" stories are played out long before actual words are uttered (Dissanayake, 2000; Gratier & Trevarthen, 2008; Malloch, 1999; Trevarthen, 1999, 2005a).

The sympathetic enjoyment of play with the "communicative musicality" of vocalizations, hand gestures, and facial expressions, transmitting the dynamic motives and complementary feelings that all human beings are born with, is essential for "social bonding," for sharing experience and the development of symbolic communication, and for cultural "common sense." As was clear to Thomas Reid (1764) a century before Darwin, our artificial tools of communication, including speech, depend on the sympathy of a "natural language":

> It is by natural signs chiefly that we give force and energy to language; and the less language has of them, it is the less expressive and persuasive. (pp. 106–107)

Artificial signs signify, but they do not express; they speak to the understanding, as algebraical characters may do, but the passions, the affections, and the will, hear them not: these continue dormant and inactive, till we speak to them in the language of nature, to which they are all attention and obedience. (p. 108)

The vitality of human creativity and cooperation finds a voice before words are mastered, and learns to hear the poetry of cultural meaning.

Being Human and Becoming Intelligent in the Human Way

We have, at first, two stories to tell: one about the postnatal life and development in the individual of this human communication leading to language, and the other about the growth and functions of body and brain before birth. Both demonstrate anticipations for human habits of sociable life, and for the ritual and symbolic communication of intentions and affects on which human habits depend. A need for language and culture is innate in the body and sociable motives of a child (Trevarthen, 2011b, in press).

Behind these events that take place in each and every human lifetime, there is a third, more ancient creative process of "environment expectancy," demonstrating that we have shared principles of vitality with other species and how new expectations have evolved. Over millions of years, animals have gained ways of acting intelligently and surviving. They possess rhythms of prospective conscious control of whole-body movements and affective visceral systems that estimate how life in movement must be paced and regulated by affective appraisals, to gain benefits from the environment and protect that life from harm. It is these systems of vital movement and emotion that are at the heart of the sympathetic, experience-sharing processes that regulate cooperation in any animal community—that bond offspring to their parents and that inspire the parents to feed and protect their family (Freeman, 2000a; Keltner, 2003, 2009; Porges, 2001) . Animal social life depends on sharing the adaptive motives that serve the survival of individuals and that set the goals for cooperative ways of life. Human social life has these motives, but also a unique epigenetic power to invent cultural practices and knowledge that grow through hundreds of generations and that are transmitted symbolically in evolving language (Trevarthen, in press).

We seek to explain, as biologists, the special adaptations of human beings that show expectancy for participating in the rituals, techniques, and languages of culture, drawing on evidence about how infants actively take part in the telling of stories of adventure and discovery from birth, and how young children learn skillful practices with the artifacts of a meaningful world by intent participation in tasks with companions. We give special attention to the expressions of intention and affection within early *narratives of vitality*, and consider how "propositional" regulation of internally generated motives and self-awareness shared intimately between human beings may determine the syntax and semantics of language—what words are *about* and how they actively designate those purposes, objects, or events. The innate motivating dynamics of human action and self-regulation, and their unique story-making communicative musicality, which infants appreciate from before birth, remain vital even in the most artificial, most technical, and most ritualized symbolic practices and messages of our diverse cultures (Malloch & Trevarthen, 2009). Our task is to demystify how the motivating impulses of animals gave rise to the special human motives for making shared cultural meanings—to explain how our actions are adapted to "make sense."

Prevailing theories of cognitive programs for discrimination and generation of the rich syntactical resources of language, and their possible evolution as uniquely human, ignore the motivating and affective roots (Hauser, Chomsky, & Fitch, 2002). They do not adequately reflect either the knowledge we have about vocal and postural communication in animals and its learning or the development of unique vocal and gestural communication skills in human beings before they are able to speak (Merker, 2009a; Trevarthen, Delafield-Butt, & Schögler, 2011). They neglect the functional social space of meaning (Halliday & Matthiessen, 2004) and the poetic/emotional "languages within language" (Fónagy 2001), which motivate and guide the mastery of communication between minds in early childhood (Bråten 2009). They regard emotional expression as a manifestation of stresses in regulation of the body and of information processing, not as integral with the causal motivators of adaptive action and experience. But there are alternative views of the life and brains of animals and humans that give both intentions and emotions powerful causal roles in the creation of shared experience, without which referential signs are meaningless (Freeman, 2008; Panksepp, 2003; Panksepp & Trevarthen, 2009; Trevarthen, 2009). Infants demonstrate these intentional and emotional factors of meaning making.

The Need to Define the Motives and Affects of Movement that Serve Complex Representational Skills

It is fair to say that human beings, if we are animals, are of the most mobile, ambitious, imaginative, and intimately cooperative kind. Our bodies have super-complex motor capacities and many senses. We are also the most "talkative," or "demonstrative," species, with the most extravagant semiosis, and share by far the most elaborate fantasies and largest retentive memories with the aid of language. But is that a "total" difference? How far do animals show related talents?

Many authorities in both philosophy and science, especially in psychology and linguistics, think the gap between ourselves and our closest animal relatives is so great the comparison has little meaning. They find scientific study of animals and their behavior useful for discovery of the essential biological foundations of our bodily needs and instincts, but believe other species have no rationality, no language, and a restricted imagination and memory of what the world can hold. Animals are assumed by many philosophers and psychologists to have no consciousness and, of course, no moral capacities—their emotions thought to be simply unconscious regulators of individual or group survival.

Indeed, modern psychology would rather turn to computational machines to find models for human intelligence. It is as if the human species has stepped off the ladder of biological evolution to make a completely unnatural ecology of learned knowledge, in which a supernatural intelligence flourishes by processing, storage, and elaboration of information, turning the urges of our essential vitality into frivolous extras, vestiges of a less intelligent past that require "civilizing" by education.

It is our intention to describe the dynamic patterns of cooperative life between human beings of all ages and stages. Our first goal is to challenge the idea that our conscious spiritual, artistic, problem-solving, and moral life is essentially unrelated to the life of other animals, especially those species of birds and mammals that are complex in their mobility and intensely cooperative in societies. Our second goal is to identify what is new in human motility and its adaptations for social use.

We believe that we must acknowledge the creativity and cooperation that other animals share with us. The sciences of comparative psychobiology and ethology also clarify the exceptional life processes of our *morphogenesis*—how the form of the human body and its organs are adapted in special ways from the embryo stage to serve future functions in human society. They describe the environment-expectant *epigenesis*, by which each individual person and every human community grows through stages of development and sustains its survival and well-being while mastering new knowledge and skills, being changed by it. This account is inspired by the thinking of natural scientists, who have given due credit to animals both for their intelligent awareness of their world and for their powers of signaling their intentions and emotions for social cooperation. Two whose works continue to be inspiring and challenging are Charles Darwin (1872) and Jocob von Uexküll (1957).

Attention to fundamental principles of animal phenomenology will lead to a cautionary tale about the future of a mechanistic psychology that thinks we are just our educated intelligence—with intelligent and impressionable single heads with greatly expanded cerebral cortex and with obedient bodies that strive to keep in good health, we perceive, learn, invent, manufacture, and sell to one another. The assumption we are not animals appears to be linked to a self-congratulatory attention to the inanimate "products" of human invention—in politics, law, art, science, and industry—a restricted attention that obscures the "life process" that makes that culture possible, including the creation of languages that serve as tools and products of culture and that speed its evolution.

Brain science proves our motives and emotions have close relation to those of other species. It finds homologous neural systems, and intricately sustained functional states, across great ranges of life forms. The most persuasive support for Darwin's theory of human evolution is in comparative anatomy and comparative physiology. These show relationships between species adapted to different habitats and ways of life. The more we know about the elaborate anatomy and function of the human body and brain, the more it appears we share essential principles of life function with those of other birds and mammals, especially the primates, most like us in their motor skills and social life (Panksepp, 1998, 2003; Rizzolatti, Fogassi, & Gallese, 2001). And where we differ, we show special inherited adaptations for collaboration in an inventive and playfully cooperative community that strives to store memories learned in symbolic forms, which link many generations of discovery and enterprise.

When we see a crowd of birds flying about with perfect conscious mastery of space and awareness of its complexity as they navigate among the branches and over the houses, when we hear them call to one another and see them come at the appropriate time and place for a feed, bickering impatiently, what do they lack? They are sure masters of powerful motor coordination and the graceful rhythms of flight; they see the world to be flown in with their delicately engineered bodies. They hear one another's excitement, joy, and fear. They are sociable and rivalrous and very sharp to detect a meal. Some species of birds have capacities for vocal imitation comparable with those of at least young humans, though less imagination for making use of it (Merker, 2009a, 2009b). Chimpanzees, baboons, and rhesus monkeys live as known individuals in intimate bands with a precisely regulated sharing of knowledge and skills and a social order maintained by subtle rituals of emotional expression and "feeling" for each other as identified individuals (Cheney & Seyfarth, 2007; de Waal, 2006, 2009; Suomi, 2005). What innate talents are missing in these species from those that humans exhibit and share? That is what we seek to define by analyzing the special adaptations of the infant body and brain for learning the meaning of language. There is an urge already present in newborn infants that leads to an immediate sharing of imaginative purposes for their own sake, before they have locomotor capacity to explore and make use of the world outside the family and its social and technical conventions.

Infant Communication: Anticipations of Company and the Exchange of Ideas

Expectancy for the responsive company of other persons is, indeed, alive before birth. We recognize our mother as a special individual from the start (DeCasper & Prescott, 2009; DeCasper & Spence, 1986). Dramatic evidence of a readiness for communicating with another person by speech comes from observations of intimate engagements with infants just hours old (Trevarthen, 2011b) and even, in one case, with a newborn observed in dialogue with her father four weeks after her premature birth at 27 weeks gestation (Trevarthen, 1999). This case offers very detailed evidence of an inborn expectancy for human company, showing with what precision the innate rhythms of expression can be shared (Figure 8.1).

Infants sense the essential animacy of human movements by "amodal perception" (Michotte, 1962), translating between the senses of their own body and the expressive forms of another person who is seeking communication. Gunilla Preisler (Preisler & Palmer, 1986) has recorded subtle expressive communication between blind infants and their mothers. She filmed 5-month-old Maria, who was born totally blind, "conducting" her mother's singing (Trevarthen, 1999). Maria is lying on her back while her mother is bottle-feeding her and singing two Swedish baby songs, which the baby knows well. From time to time, baby Maria joins with the music by waving her left hand in graceful undulations. Her dancing hand points up toward her head as her mother's voice rises in pitch and drops at the wrist at the close of a stanza, making flowing gestures that resemble those of a trained conductor. Accurate measurement of the movements revealed that on several occasions, when there is an important lift of feeling in the melody, the baby's hand movements precede the changes of the mother's voice by approximately 300 milliseconds. She and her mother behave exactly like two dancers or improvising jazz musicians, and at key points the baby leads as if she were causing her mother's song. This exemplifies the human harmony of the embodied spirit with its future imagined in movement (Trevarthen, 1999, 2009).

Darwin studied the movements of infants and especially their expressions of emotion. He observed pleasurable emotions, distinguishing interpersonal and

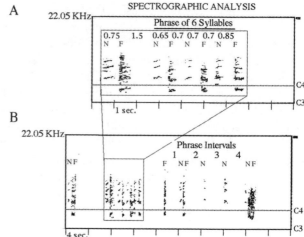

FIGURE 8.1. Innate "speech" rhythms. A 2-month premature newborn in an ICU in The Netherlands communicates with her father, who is "kangarooing" her under his shirt. She makes clear, simple calls, and her father imitates the sounds closely. Both pitch their sounds a little above middle C (C4). After the first exchange of one sound each, they generate a 4-second "phrase" of short (ca. 0.3 second) sounds alternating at a "syllable" frequency, with intervals between 650 and 850 millseconds, that is, around *andante* (spectrograph on lower right). Then a series of single utterances are made. When the father does not respond, the infant makes three sounds at phrase-length intervals (4 seconds), the first weak and the others louder, before he replies. The infant has an intrinsic time sense for syllables and phrases. N, infant; F, father.

"self-generated" signals. He saw his own children smile with pleasure when not even 2 months old:

> The smiles arose chiefly when looking at their mother, and were therefore probably of mental origin; but this infant [his son] often smiled then, and for some time afterwards, from some inward pleasurable feeling, for nothing was happening which could have in any way excited or amused him. When 110 days old he was exceedingly amused when a pinafore being thrown over his face and then suddenly withdrawn; and so he was when I suddenly covered my own face and approached his. (1877, pp. 288–289)

In these comments, Darwin describes evidence of two essential functions of human emotional expressions: They may establish and confirm an affectionate relationship, and they assist the negotiation of playful exchanges where intentions and expectations are provoked and "teased."

Reciprocal, Sympathetic Imitation with Newborns: A Test of Readiness for the Actions and Emotions of Human Company

There have been many reports that young infants imitate, although influential authorities, including Piaget and Skinner, convinced by a prejudice that very young humans can have no intentions, consciousness of external events, or self-awareness, have asserted that young infants do not imitate. However, formal tests since the 1970s have proved that newborns can imitate a range of discrete expressions of face, voice, and hands (Bråten, 1998; Meltzoff & Moore, 1977; Nadel & Butterworth, 1999) and that the similarities of expression are not coincidences or just products of physiological "arousal" that causes infants to move more in what appear to be "matching" ways. But controlled stimulus–response tests are not suitable for studying motives and affects for communication. The experiments have not clarified how imitating can evolve through tens of seconds as a "project" of communication in dialogue. To study dynamic interpersonal aspects and "prove" the baby has an *intention* to imitate and to collaborate in generation of narrations, descriptions of the detail of less constrained reciprocal encounters between the infant and another person, over a sequence of turns, have to be used. The "intersynchrony" of their mutual awareness and intention to act together (Condon, 1979), and the "serial ordering" of actions by the infant and partner together (Lashley, 1951), must be studied.

Close observation of how the newborn engages with the actions of an attentive person who "respects" the infant's initiatives and gives time for them, and descriptions of the emotional expressions the infant makes while attempting to imitate, reveal that the infant is being intentional and is expressing emotional appraisal of what the other person is doing (Als, 1979; Brazelton, 1979; Brazelton & Nugent, 1995; Nagy, 2011; Trevarthen, 2011b). Furthermore, the imitated acts may also be offered by the infant as "provocations" for an imitative response from the adult (Nagy & Molnár, 2004), and the infant is disturbed by the "still-face" test, in which the natural impulse of the adult is blocked (Nagy, 2008). The infant wants an *exchange*, is seeking imitative *dialogue*, and is responding with emotions that evaluate a "good" exchange, one that is courteously timed and intimately shared. This proves that a human child does not need to learn how to communicate "thoughtfully" in a human way.

The Miraculous Precocity of Protoconversation

Condon and Sander (1974) reported that a newborn infant may move arms in synchrony with the vocalizations of adult speech, demonstrating an intimate involvement of expressive timing of behaviors similar to that recorded between adults in ordinary intense conversation. "Conversational analysis" of films shows that the postures and gestures of a listener may become coupled in synchrony or alternation with the unconscious self-synchrony of movements of the parts of a speaker's body, and this intersynchrony can apply even when the listener is a newborn (Condon, 1979).

Further rich evidence that the human brain is built for participation in conversation by coordinating the timing of expressions between persons comes from study of slightly older infants, whose sight is more acute. Vision is one sense that must be comparatively "retarded" in development at birth. Whereas touch, taste, and hearing can already be exercised and take samples of experience from the world outside the body before birth, sight has very limited usefulness inside the mother's body, and we have no evidence of visual learning before birth. Correspondingly, although a newborn can direct gaze to look at and track a nearby object, and can see a person well enough to imitate face and hand movements, there is very rapid improvement in the alertness and discrimination of sight in the early weeks, and an expansion of the field of visual awareness away from the body.

After 6 weeks, with development of visual and auditory discrimination of human expressions, the infant is more ready to pay attention to another person a short distance away, to seek eye contact, and to share their changing interests and feelings, building stories of relationship. This is change that is deeply appreciated by an affectionate parent, who feels the baby is becoming more of a social person. The consequence of this change in mutual, intersubjective awareness is the emergence of a completely human behavior called "protoconversation." Its precocious readiness for showing mental processes and narrations of purpose and its particular anticipations of many features of living language have been explored in the past 40 years, transforming our ideas of what it takes to learn and use language. One of the discoverers, and the person who described the behavior as protoconversation, gave these descriptions of what she saw in a film of a mother chatting with her 9-week-old infant.

> A study of these sequences established that the mother and infant were collaborating in a pattern of more or less alternating, non-overlapping vocalization, the mother speaking brief sentences and the infant responding with coos and murmurs, together producing a brief joint performance similar to conversation, which I called "proto conversation." The study of timing and sequencing showed that certainly the mother and probably the infant, in addition to conforming in general to a regular pattern, were acting to sustain it or to restore it when it faltered, waiting for the expected vocalization from the other and then after a pause resuming vocalization, as if to elicit a response that had not been forthcoming. These interactions were characterized by a sort of delighted, ritualized courtesy and more or less sustained attention and mutual gaze. Many of the vocalizations were of types not described in the acoustic literature on infancy, since they were very brief and faint, and yet were crucial parts of the jointly sustained performances. (Bateson, 1979, p. 65)

> Language cannot be used for any other purpose unless some agreement is established that one is "in touch." (Bateson, 1979, p. 64)

> Here at the prelinguistic level we can see the child playing a "grammatical" game. This should cast new light on our data on games playing, imitation and mother–child interaction at later stages of development. Indeed, it provides an analogy for understanding a wide variety of interactions in which change or learning takes place, from psychotherapy to religious ritual to the ordinary pleasures of conversation, and the general phenomenon of active participatory learning. (Bateson, 1979, p. 76)

These detailed observations by an anthropologist and linguist with knowledge of the use of ritual in human communities present a revolutionary insight into the intense intimacy and intelligence of natural human communication at 2 months after birth, long before it has been enriched by the symbolic code of language.

Bateson's observations, and contemporary ones by other researchers who profited from the advantages of film for retrospective analysis, prove that the whole animated baby, with its human self-awareness and expressivity, is the language acquisition device (LAD) capable of acquiring language (Chomsky, 1957). But this natural LAD is not a special processing module of an intelligent brain set to master language with the logic of a universal grammar. It is a human person dependent on the companionship and inventive play of communication with the motives and feelings of other persons.

As Bruner says, the baby needs a language acquisition support system—at first the intimate skills of an affectionate mother who will help the baby build stories out of their play with expressions (Bruner, 1983). Mother and infant have matching needs for cooperation in affective rhythms of narration. A joy in relatedness of actions drives them to constantly discover and elaborate new forms of conversation in a human way.

The Narrative Musicality of Early Dialogue

Application of musical acoustic techniques to dialogues between infants and their mothers has transformed our knowledge of the dynamics of the movement, experience, and affect they share (H. Papoušek, 1996; M. Papoušek, 1994). Malloch (1999) used knowledge of the practice of playing Western classical music, and a training in composition and conducting, to detect, with the aid of spectrographs and pitch plots, intuitive patterns in the vocal behaviors of a mother and her 6-week-old daughter as they engaged in a 27-second chat. He concluded that they demonstrated "communicative musicality," that both were precisely regulating the parameters of pulse and quality to share the exchange, and that this exchange took the form of a "narrative." A plot of how the pitch of their voices changed through time revealed they were sharing meaning with a sense of purpose in passing time, making a coherent musical story with well-defined motor/affective or purposeful phases of *introduction, development, climax,* and *resolution* (see Figure 8.2).

Study of the expressive, prosodic features of mothers' talk in intimate address to their infants and their playful games and songs has revealed strong, melodic elements in a special affectionate form of discourse called "motherese," or infant-directed speech (Fernald, 1989, 1992). Tests of infants' preferential orientation to sounds of the human voice and of music confirm that they are born with strong awareness of human-made sounds, especially in the higher range of the female voice and its affectionate modulations (Trehub, 2000). Few-weeks-old infants make refined discriminations of pitch, harmony, and rhythm, and they prefer harmonious cords and melodic phrases to those that are dissonant and mechanical. The Papoušeks (1981) described these preferred features of a mother's speech as showing "musicality." With Bateson, they concluded that the intimate sharing of musical expressions serves to guide infants to learn language.

Musical analysis of baby songs, to which infants older than 4 months respond enthusiastically (Mazokopaki & Kugiumutzakis, 2009), has revealed both that their affective tone is detected and that young infants attend to, and move with, the rhythms and narrative patterns or melodies (Trainor, 1996; Trevarthen, 1993, 1999). Infants soon become influenced by certain cultural features of their parents' speech or music. They share and learn the ways the mother "belongs" to her family and its culture (Custodero & Johnson-Green, 2003; Gratier & Trevarthen, 2007, 2008). A universal time pattern and pitch range of the notes or syllables, phrases, and verses of baby songs indicates that they are adapted to engage with biochronological and affective principles of human movement and self-regulation, to which infants' listening is "attuned" (Figure 8.3). Innate properties of coordinated polyrhythmic body movement express the intrinsic-motive pulse (IMP) of a human brain, and these rhythms carry the emotionally charged messages of communication (Panksepp & Trevarthen, 2009; Trevarthen, 1999).

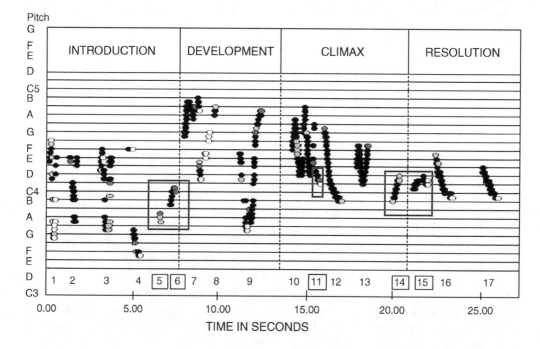

INTRODUCTION	DEVELOPMENT	CLIMAX	RESOLUTION
1 Come on	7 Oh yes!	10 Tell me some	15 Ch ch
2 Again	8 Is that right?	more then	With INFANT
3 Come on then	9 Well tell me	11 INFANT	16 Ahgoo
4 That's clever	some more then	12 Ooorrh	17 Goo
5 INFANT		13 Come on	
6 INFANT		14 Ch ch ch ch	
		With INFANT	

FIGURE 8.2. Acoustic analysis of a protoconversation. Photos show the expressions of a 6-week-old and her mother in dialogue. The pitch plot indicates how the narrative of their protoconversation demonstrates four parts: *introduction, development, climax,* and *resolution.* Finally, after the excited climax, the mother is no longer speaking, just making affectionate sounds, which bring this small shared experience to a close, before they start another story. Utterance numbers appear immediately above the time axis and in the table. Copyright 2009 by Oxford University Press, from Malloch and Trevarthen, 2009, Figure 1.2, page 5.

It appears that the infant acquires cognitive capacities for discriminating conventions of dancing gestures and musical art by adapting a set of dynamic-motive principles that arise in the intricate tissue of the brain as it generates and guides the movements of a complex human body with rhythmically coordinated intention and feeling (Bernstein, 1967; Buzsáki, 2006; Freeman, 2008). The infant's brain gives time to the movements while assimilating perceptual information that confirms and guides them, and uses them to move with the "moving" of other persons, engaging

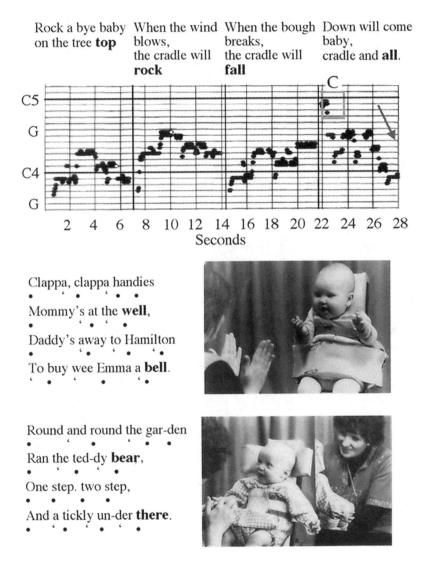

FIGURE 8.3. The narrative form of baby songs. *Top:* A pitch plot of "Rock a Bye Baby" showing the classic four-line stanza, with the melody in the octave above middle C (C4) and rhyming words on the ends of lines 1 and 2 and lines 2 and 4. The lines form the sections *introduction, development, climax* (C), and *resolution* (arrow). *Bottom:* Action songs "Clappa Clappa Handies" and "Round and Round the Garden" with 6-month-old infants, showing the four-line stanzas and iambic feet of the poetic recitation.

"compassionately" with their changing motives, vitality, and feelings (Freeman, 2000a; Keltner, 2003, 2009; Porges, 2001; Stern, 2010). As Dissanayake (2000) says, the arts of human communication are born in "intimacy" generated by the dynamics of movement and the vital affective states that mothers and infants demonstrate so clearly.

The Growth of Play and Provocative Games

The expressive vitality of infants' and mothers' talk and play is led to new developments by changes in the bodies and motive impulses of the infants, not just by the learning of the adults' care and the skills that are practiced with them. Gratier has, after Bourdieu (1984), named the special games or rituals that a mother and infant create a "proto-habitus," a world of expected occasions for sharing interests, actions, and roles (Gratier & Trevarthen, 2007). The infant does attend and become familiar with a mother's particular habits and the games she has learned, but this gift of learned ways of acting is received or expected "creatively" by the infant's active interest, which has strong innate dynamic purposes and aesthetic preferences. There are "rules" for a good game or action song with an infant, and they derive from how the baby wants to act and share the pleasure.

Stern (1971, 1974) pioneered film study of the dynamic creativity of play of a mother with her 3½-month-old twins. He defined "relational emotions" and their composition in "dynamic narrative envelopes" (Stern, 1985) or "vitality contours" (Stern, 1999), such as Malloch later called "narratives of musicality," and Stern, Hofer, Haft, and Dore (1985) introduced the idea that sharing of experience begins with "affect attunement," by which a mother joins with and confirms her infant's changing expressions of energy in play using "intermodal fluency" to translate between forms of expression, as in the case of Maria and her mother, described previously. Stern (2010) summarizes his experience of engagement with infant animacy and its relation to therapeutic dialogue and performance in art as "vitality dynamics." The feeling for time in life is an essential part of the brain's job to coordinate and regulate the muscular forces of a moving body (Buzsáki, 2006; Meissner & Wittmann, 2011; Wittmann, 2009). That "visceral" or "arousal" energy is channeled and enhanced by the "teasing" engagement between mother and baby is evident, as Darwin recorded when he played peekaboo with his son. As the baby becomes stronger and more alert, adult and infant both move in more challenging ways, increasing the fun they share. We celebrate and enjoy life together, building customs, by joining in expressive displays of intention (Freeman, 2000a; Merker, 2009b). The foundations for this convivial display of feelings in movement are evident in animal play (Panksepp, 2005), but the elaboration of ever new forms of art, and their preservation in complex forms of culture, is human (Trevarthen, in press).

Teasing: Testing the Will and Humor of the Other by Changing the Plot

Infants not only demonstrate prospective engagement in dialogue from birth, joining the story and its drama and then mastering the theatrical forms of action songs, but they develop the prospects enthusiastically, humorously, and provocatively in joyful games of teasing and joking (Reddy, 2008). They take an active part in the creative art of the games into which they are invited by the communicative musicality of baby songs, giving their excitement to the plot and celebrating the carnival, making jokes of meaning, testing what their partners have in mind, what their emotional expectations, and enthusiasm for action, are. Bruner used analysis of the game of peekaboo to illustrate the joy of story-making as a bridge to learning how to talk (Bruner & Sherwood, 1975).

In the middle of the first year, after the transformation of awareness and the capacity to manipulate objects at about 4 months of age, babies gain both a social self-consciousness and a lively playfulness that likes to tease and practice trickery and jokes. They learn customary expressions of their family, and they make fun of them, seeking appreciation of their wittiness. Reddy (2008) takes these convivial behaviors as proof of a self-and-other awareness or second-person intentionality, and she demonstrates its importance for the development of the "self-consciousness-in-the-eyes-of-the-other," the I–thou relationship of Buber (1923/1970), and the "social Me" of Mead (1934). From this intimacy and mutual appraisal develops the capacity to share practical attentions to the world and to participate in the purposes and emotions of "acts of meaning" before language.

Getting Technical: Sharing Tasks and Building Projects

In 1974 Penelope Hubley, a young researcher in the Infant Communication Laboratory at Edinburgh University who was analyzing video recordings of games developing between infants and their mothers, witnessed a major transformation at 9 months in one infant's capacities for a dialogue. The infant, Tracy, was starting to be curious about her mother's ideas and ways of using objects, and she took the initiative to "assist" her mother to complete her intentions (Trevarthen & Hubley, 1978). They began to exchange and build on ideas of how to use objects in systematic constructive ways, imitating one another, not just for fun, but more seriously to invent and collaborate in joint tasks. Up to then, Tracy had been a playful companion in games invented by the mother to amuse her. Now she began to be very willing to take "instructions" or "directions" of how to take part in a simple cooperative task, to accept initiatives to make combinations of objects or to move an object in a particular way. Most obvious was that the mother intuitively detected this new willingness, and she started to give indication how her part actions could be completed or her pointing movements could be complied with (Trevarthen & Marwick, 1986). She sensed the baby had become a confident coworker. In the preceding few months, Tracy had been a spirited and willful playmate, first in body movement *person–person games* her mother invented and then in *person–person–object games* involving chasing and teasing. Now she was a confident coworker in a "secondary intersubjectivity," where practical intentions and social gestures were shared in a cooperative and knowing "business-like" way. Hubley followed up her discovery with a longitudinal video study of five infant girls through the critical ages, from 8 to 12 months. All changed at 9 months just as Tracy had done: They began to be motivated to "share a task" (Hubley & Trevarthen, 1979).

The change is not just a development of "joint attention," but extension of the pleasure of predicting another's actions to take on or imitate their practical intentions and to enjoy the pride of acting on objects by "helping" the other's initiative (Trevarthen, 2011a). Child and parent take part in creative and constructive projects when the child has no words. They confide in purposes and projects in a totally cooperative way, exhibiting the "serious intent" Piaget (1954, 1962) had commented on in studying the individual child's "pleasure in mastery" of an "object concept." To cooperate in this way, two persons must pay attention "seriously" to the movements of another's head, eyes, and hands, to observe their acts of intention with imagination or "projicience" of understanding of the "affordances" of objects (Gibson, 1977; Sherrington, 1906), sometimes sharing affective appraisal of how the performance goes, participating together in the pleasure in mastery.

Piaget's self-motivated "little scientist" is not open to ideas of a community's culture, the conventions others have invented to do tasks in cooperative ways. Piaget did not believe infants had any reciprocal sympathy of understanding of others' purposes of feelings before developing an object concept after months of experiment with effects of their own moving, and neither did Freud. This step in the infant's imagination and intention recorded by Hubley is a development of the imitative dialogues, protoconversations, and games of younger stages in a particular relationship, and is essential preparation for naming actions and their objects in a symbolic community. It constitutes the "proto-language" of Halliday (1979), in which nonverbal acts of meaning are made with combinations of gestured intentions and affective vocalizations. The relationship between what is achieved at the end of the first year and mastery of a language code is best described as follows:

> Some cooperative behavior, like showing and pointing, giving and taking, have been observed in the course of studies of early steps in language development (Bates, 1976; Bruner, 1977). In such studies attempts have been made to show how syntax, semantics, and pragmatics, formally distinguished in linguistic analysis of dialogue, have important precursors in pre-language communication. Recent findings in prelinguistic communication of infants with their mothers show the presence of an underlying interpersonal comprehension which may be studied in its own right, independent of language development. This interpersonal comprehension is a larger psychological function than spoken language which develops within it, greatly extending its power of reference and categorization. We are directly concerned with the structure of cooperative understanding for its own sake at an age when there is no evidence that infants can comprehend the specific reference of any word. (Hubley & Trevarthen, 1979, p. 58)

Babies are born with many "anticipatory adaptations for cultural learning," of which a capacity for joint attention to share consciousness of objects is just one (Tomasello & Farrar, 1986)—and not the earliest or most beguiling. In the first year, children become more skilled at sharing both the purposes and the pleasures of tasks, and the people they prefer to work with become friends and collaborators, while strangers are greeted with care and suspicion, and their knowledge and trustfulness are tested cautiously. Right from the neonate stage, who you respond to and who responds to you are important, as is the sensitivity, respect, and spontaneity of their actions toward you, sharing feelings. This is made clear by studies of infants' preference for having fun or doing tasks with familiar persons, their withdrawal from strangers, and their confusion and distress when engagement with a known person is perturbed by nonresponse or by emotionally defensive or aggressive behavior. Learning meaning from others depends on "openness" to them with your feelings and a trust that they will be open with you, sympathetically (Trevarthen, 2011a).

Toddlers' "Child's Culture": Collaborative Imagining in Performance (Carnival)

Two-year-olds are famous for their imperious will and sensitivity to being imposed upon or instructed by adult authority, which they often challenge (Spitz, 1957). They are undergoing a change in zest for learning on the threshold of language as well as mastering new skills of the body in movement on two feet. They are also experiencing richer opportunities of creative communication with peers (Bjørkvold, 1992).

Nadel and her colleagues have observed that intricate imitative games can be created and elaborated to make theater-like narrations in small groups of toddlers 15 months of age who have little or no language (Nadel & Pezé, 1993). The desire to share meaningful projects and to act in sociable, inventive ways is very strong in human beings before the purposes or discoveries can be discussed.

Young infants, too, are capable of subtle sociability with other infants in the absence of adult support. Studies of infant trios by Selby and Bradley (2003) show that babies 6 to 9 months old who are unknown to each other and on their own, facing each other in a triangle of infant walkers, can engage in complex bouts of communication, each showing sensitivity to how their pronouncements addressed to their companions are received and reacting accordingly. These authors claim that babies are born with a "general relational capacity" or sociability, besides the dyadic program that generates attachment to the mother. The companionship with subtle moral regulations we find infants developing in play with their mothers clearly can be extended, not only to other members of the family but to other infants who are strangers. The infant trios show the same shared temporal and affective musicality in their exchanges as have been recorded for interactions of infants of this age with their mothers (Bradley, 2009).

In his theory of the environment of evolutionary adaptiveness, John Bowlby hypothesized that early human communities with their altricial offspring lived in small, highly sociable groups that shared the duties of mothering (Bowlby, 1969; Hrdy, 1999). Exclusive attachment to a mother for an early period of nursing does not preclude precocious development of human sociability and the exchange of inventive messages within a circle of companions of different ages.

These developments toward learning conventions and inventions of meaning before language manifest the eager growth of intersubjective motives in the infant person. They are motives that were already present at birth. To find the source or nature of this extraordinary preparation of the human organism for intimate intelligence and merging of wills and affections, and for accumulation of knowledge of a new world, we seek information about what happens in the 9 months before a baby is born.

Embryo and Fetal Human Beings: Development of a Self-Conscious Agent That Will Want to Talk with Others about the World

That the human brain is born prepared for awareness of people and for sharing their actions and consciousness is evident. The subcortical emotional brain and the limbic cortex motivate both emotional communication and a child's learning and its dependence on communicating with the interests and feelings in other persons' brains. The cortical tissue for cultural learning can be changed and functions can be increased, relocated, or weakened by experience, but how the human brain grows before birth, and what infants can do shortly after they are born, shows that basic rules—for object perception, for purposeful movement, and for motive states that construct time and space for action and that might become conscious of other bodies and their behaviors—all begin their differentiation without benefit of experience, and they have a program of development that expects human company. This program is laid down in the core of the brain in association with systems of autonomic self-regulation. The way the regulatory systems of the brain develop form and function from embryo stages proves that the essential preparation begins in the core of the brainstem before the neocortex appears, and the body develops organs adapted for human expressions of communication and for their perception in others in the fetus (Figure 8.4), before the central nervous system excites any movements (Trevarthen, 2001, 2004).

The mind of an active animal, with its feelings of organic integrity and impulses to move with prospective control, is generated and regulated within the upper brainstem and midbrain regions that Penfield and Jasper (1954) first identified as the "centrencephalic" seat of human consciousness. Its importance for autonomic function through the evolution of vertebrates was established by Paul MacLean (1990). Northoff and Panksepp (2008) define this as the core SELF (simple ego-type life form),

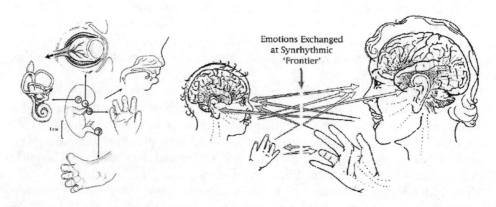

FIGURE 8.4. The organs of conversation, adapted for sharing states of mind. *Left:* An 8-week fetus has the special human organs for sight and hearing, oral organs for speaking, and hands and feet for gesturing, all of which move to express interests, intentions, and feelings to other persons, who may sense their expressions. *Right:* A young infant shares a protoconversation, exchanging interest and emotions with the mother. Each watches the eyes, face, mouth, and hands and listens to the voice of the other across a "synrhythmic frontier" of communication (Trevarthen, Aitken, Vandekerckhove, Delafield-Butt, & Nagy, 2006).

and Vandekerckhove and Panksepp (2011) confirm that, although this ancient system is *anatomically subcortical*, it is *functionally supracortical* in its role as the principal instigator of action and integrator of sensory information in primary "anoetic" (without knowledge) affective consciousness, and the driver for development of a more sophisticated "noetic" (knowledge-based) life experience. This core consciousness integrates the three regulatory systems of the self as agent, defined by Sherrington (1906) in his seminal work on the *Integrative Action of the Nervous System*: (1) *visceroceptive* information from the organs of the body that convey signals of vital need and enable the brain to control adjustment of the organs that sustain the body, including heartbeat and breathing; (2) *proprioceptive* information relayed by receptors and sensory nerves from the muscles, from the body surface, and from the organs sensitive to accelerations that feed back direct evidence of movement of the body and its parts; and (3) with greatest dependence on learning, the fate of the moving self in relation to the external world perceived through the *exteroceptive* distance receptors for sight, sound, and smell that detect surroundings and objects of action.

At birth a human infant has a body with self-sustaining awareness of its internal vitality and a capacity to make intricately coordinated patterns of body movement, both of which are adapted to support from a mother's body (Trevarthen, 2011b). Awareness of the world and its resources is rudimentary at this stage. Growth of world knowledge depends on affectively appraised use of the great retentive powers of the cerebral and cerebellar cortices as they grow for many years, accumulating experience and making new expectations (Trevarthen et al., 2006; Trevarthen & Aitken, 2003).

As Sherrington (1906) noted, the nervous system integrates many different actions and kinds of information with "foresight," enabling the organism to act with projicience, or knowledge of the subsequent effects of an action and the properties of its selected object. The primary importance of the motivating core of the human brain for building this knowledge is demonstrated by the mental life of children born without a cerebral cortex, who nevertheless are conscious, active to a certain degree, and emotionally responsive (Merker, 2007). In normal development of a child, new cortical capacities for associative learning, perceptual discriminations, motor planning, and creative imaginings are able to develop as elaborations of the subcortical core self, increasing the person's capacity for relating the present, emotionally appraised moment with a history of past knowledge and an imagined world of possible future experience, a process Tulving describes as "autonoesis" (Tulving, 2005).

The least developed parts of the human cerebral neocortex at birth are frontal, parietal, and temporal areas that receive massive input from motivating and affective systems of the brainstem, subcortical motor centers, and archaic midline and limbic systems, including the hypothalamus, amygdala and dorsomedial thalamus, and insula, the same core mechanism of self-related processing (Northoff & Panksepp, 2008; Wittmann, 2009). The late-developing neocortex areas are homologous with ancient territories of the early vertebrate brain that direct experience and actions to beneficial objects, or that prevent damaging experiences, and they are also ones that are proportionally elaborated in humans and that play essential roles in personal relationships and in learning of cultural skills, including language, through childhood.

Temporal, parietal, and frontal lobes of the hemispheres grow disproportionally after infancy, changing the shape of the brain (Trevarthen, 2004). Their periods of development correlate with changes in motivation for social life and for seeking experience. In early infancy, the right hemisphere and orbitofrontal and inferior temporal cortices develop in relation to the affective regulation of the mother–child relationship and developments in communication with other intimate companions. Developments in superior temporal and prefrontal cortex are both significant during the first weeks as the child's social awareness increases with recognition of others' intentions and interests. Lateral prefrontal cortex expands conspicuously in the last months of the first year and into the second year with developments both in intelligence for exploration and combining of objects and in *protolanguage*—the use of gesture and voice to make "acts of meaning." Alternating surges of hemisphere growth on right and left are observed throughout life: around birth, at the end of infancy, in middle childhood, in adolescence, in middle life, and in old age. These express changes in motivation and emotional self-regulation, which affect who becomes a friend and what is experienced, learned, and remembered (Davis & Panksepp, 2011; Keltner, Horberg, & Oveis, 2006).

The basis of this social perception is an innate capacity for expression and imitation of prosodic intonations and melodies of the voice and accompanying gestures and body movement, which is evident long before the words of a language are understood or imitated, and also before an infant has cognitive mastery of how to handle, perceive, or combine physical objects . Recent studies of neural activity in monkeys and humans demonstrate that when we move, or imagine moving, we do so with prospective perception of what James Gibson (1977) called the "affordances" for action among objects in our environment, the form of action being an intentional part of the process of perception (Gallese, 2000). Furthermore, we perceive the actions of others not through rationalistic, top-down processing of complex perceptual information, but in a more simple, eloquent, and intelligent method that reads their motor intention by direct neural resonance (see Chapter 1, this volume; Gallagher, 2008; Gallese, Rochat, Cossu, & Sinigaglia, 2009).

Initiation of consciousness for self or other action and its consequences excites certain neurons in the premotor area F5 of monkeys and in the equivalent but more elaborate motor cortex of humans sensitive to organism-object relations or goals of awareness and not to a particular perceptual modality or motor activity components that may realize the intended purpose (Gallese, 2000; Gallese & Sinigaglia, 2010). Furthermore, functional brain imaging of human subjects reveals that the same premotor areas become active when a person merely thinks about such an action without actually performing it (Chao & Martin, 2000; Grèzes, Armony, Rowe, & Passingham, 2003). Altogether, these recent neural data on the perceptual-motor system show a remarkable overlap in brain activity between (1) thinking about performing an act, (2) performing the act, and (3) observing another perform the act. Such "direct resonance" between preparation, execution, and observation confirms that there is a common "motor image," as was first demonstrated by Bernstein (1967), which is set up as the goal-directed intentionality by which the body of a subject gains mastery of its object. The neuromotor activity is not to obey input from any specific sensory modality or to activate any one motor mechanism by which the intention is carried out and guided. Such an amodal perception-action system, active to create the purpose and experience of moving with an integrated body-sense, becomes a powerful and robust means of communication across many channels (gesture, voice, posture, position, etc.), from one person's subjective purpose and experience to another, generating an embodied intersubjective relation that is given meaning by their shared intentions and shared goals.

With development, intentional motor acts become serially organized to make more distal goals possible (Fogassi et al., 2005; Lashley, 1951; Pezzulo & Castelfranchi, 2009). This "purposeful and propositional" organization allows complex thinking and the kinds of goal-directed actions that characterize creative human movement capable of reaching distal objectives by transforming the environment. Purposeful bodily projects give syntactic structure to human social worlds and generate contextual meaning. From the organization of intentional body movement and their sharing in the company of babies and others to the syntactic word structure of language, the actions and utterances of a person are always "going somewhere," "going to something," or "going away from something" and generating imaginative narrations (Bruner, 1990; Read & Miller, 1995; Stern, 1992). Body and language are always in movement and the intentions of the movement structure messages of communication, before and within language. The engagement of a newborn infant with another person, by controlled patterns of expressive movement that may involve the whole body or only the eyes, the face, or the hands, shows that the infant possesses an intentional motor system capable of experiencing the intention of expressions of another person in what Bråten (2009) calls "felt immediacy." A newborn infant may translate between the intention of a mother's voice and an attitude change of the head, a facial expression, or a subtle gesture of the hands. Moreover, the expressive movements of the infant's hands give evidence of cerebral asymmetry, the right hand being favored for "assertive" contribution to the exchange (Trevarthen, 1996, 2012). There is complementary evidence that a preferential perception of emotion in the mother's voice, serving to identify her, is "processed" by the right half of the infant's brain, which is more advanced in development than the left brain at this stage and responsible for "affect attunement" with the mother (De Casper & Prescott, 2009; Schore, 2000).

It is important to distinguish these infantile communicative or interpersonal behaviors from "prereaching" intentional movements that aim attention to selected objects and that direct limbs to take up objects in the environment. Rather, they are a special class of intentions for "intersubjective motor control" (Trevarthen, 1986a) with the kinematic features or "dynamic forms" of affective expression described by Stern (2010). They communicate emotions of "self-related processing" (Northoff & Panksepp, 2008), making it possible for the infant and caregiver to establish a shared "amphoteronomic" emotional attunement and attachment, with which "synrhythmic" communications of intentions and interests may develop (Trevarthen et al., 2006). These fundamental brain processes of human personhood are the foundation for acquisition of cultural skills, including language (Gratier & Trevarthen, 2008; Trevarthen, 2011b, 2012, in press). They represent adaptations of rhythmic activity in the whole human brain for inventive social life in movement (Freeman, 2000), but at present the methods of functional brain imaging are not sufficiently precise or sensitive to rapid temporal patterns of integrative activity to identify and locate the responsible neurons (Turner & Ioannides, 2009). They are surely of importance for the pre- and postnatal development of the neocortex tissues that are found to mediate motor images of conscious intentions and their intersubjective "mirroring" (Trevarthen, 2004).

Meeting the Voice of the Mother before Birth as First Language Teacher

Learning a language, dependent on the great learning capacities of the cerebral cortex with its persistent rhythmic activity, transforms all processes of thought and reasoning. Nevertheless, the cell masses of the left temporal and parietal lobes that become essential for language understanding are already asymmetric in a human fetus of 160 days gestational age—4 months before birth. The human brain is set in many ways to acquire some language long before it hears a single word and associates it with a defined experience. The right hemisphere, which is ahead of the left hemisphere in development during late fetal stages and early infancy, is more sensitive to emotion in the voice. The orbitofrontal cortex of the right hemisphere leads in the development of an affectionate attachment between infant and caregiver (Schore, 2000), and young babies recognize the affection of a caregiver's voice by its prosody with their left ears, connected to the right hemisphere (DeCasper & Prescott, 2009). In the last 3 months of gestation, a fetus can hear and learn to recognize the expressive rhythms and tones of the mother's voice, and even come to know songs she sings or music heard frequently near her. The baby can recognize and show preference for these particular human-made sounds immediately after birth. Then new stimuli that identify her by sight and communicate her feelings by the way she moves her face and hands are sought and actively taken up by a baby, guiding growth of the brain.

Remarkably, territories in temporoparietal and frontal cortices known to be critical in adults for recognizing who other individuals are, for perceiving their actions and expressions, and for sympathizing with their motives and emotions become active in a 2-month-old's brain when simply looking at a picture of a woman's face. This "mother/teacher-perceiving system" of a human baby is essential for the learning of speech and all other cultural skills (Tzourio-Mazoyer et al., 2002).

As soon as a baby is born and can breathe and move, the voice calls for a response and attempts to reply in a dialogue of simple phonemes, with intonations that express feelings of human need for live company and confirmation (Trevarthen, in press). An adult speaker in adult company uses similar modulations of rhythm and tonality of his or her voice to regulate intimate relationships and to cooperate in evaluating the practical uses of knowledge and skills. The manner or tone in which words are articulated to name things and to explain the importance of acquired knowledge and beliefs, the persons to whom they are directed, and how words are ordered in affecting narratives all determine what talking in conventional symbolic ways actually means (Fónagy, 2001).

How We Are Motivated to Narrate the Lifetime of a Moving Body in Sympathetic Dialogues: Beginning Our Autobiography

A human newborn, we have seen, is capable of being in touch with and responsive to the dynamic impulses of another person (see Figure 8.1). In early dialogues, long before language, expressions of intention and awareness are passed between infant and parent, creating proto-conversational "narratives" of vitality (see Figure 8.2). These dialogues with infants have the evolving structure of projects that may be shared, like the stories told later in the much more elaborate forms of language or in the melodies of music. Soon they are shared in baby songs (see Figure 8.3). The behaviors of engagement are both imaginative or creative and collaborative, generated by the capacity of adult and infant to perceive and respond with sensitivity to the dynamics of each other's signs of attentiveness and vitality (Gratier & Trevarthen, 2008; Stern, 1999, 2010). Each has the ability to anticipate the other's expressions as productive and emotional states of mind, and microanalysis of film recordings shows they take complementary parts in delicately controlled patterns of exchange with turn-taking and temporal intersynchrony (Condon & Sander, 1974; Stern, 1971). Infant and adult demonstrate the rhythm of "courtesy" that Bateson (1979) described or the "dyadic phases" that are organized into playful cycles of increasing and decreasing engagement (Tronick, Als, & Adamson, 1979). It is clear that infants hear the beat of human vitality in movement from birth (Winkler, Háden, Ladinig, Sziller, & Honing, 2009) and they move to the rhythms of music (Zentner & Eerola, 2010). They participate in communicative musicality, and may share its emotional benefits (Bernatzky, Presch, Anderson, & Panksepp, 2011; Malloch, 1999; Malloch & Trevarthen, 2009; Mazokopaki & Kugiumutzakis, 2009; Trevarthen, 1999; Van Puyvelde et al., 2010).

Human exchanges of purpose at all levels of elaboration are mediated by complexes of many different motor signals—of the head, the eyes, the face, the vocal system, the hands, and the whole body. The entire array is active from birth (see Figure 8.4) (Trevarthen, 1979; Tronick et al., 1979). They combine characteristic time-regulated gestural components (Trevarthen et al., 2012), which are organized into expressive phases of a few seconds, and the phrases are sequenced in larger complexes lasting tens of seconds (Trevarthen, 1999). The compound, narrative-like units that describe organized experiences have a characteristic contour of energy expressive of a regulatory tide of vitality (see Figures 8.2 and 8.5). Stern (1992, 1999, 2010) calls them "proto-narrative envelopes." These appear to express the ebb and flow of autonomic or visceral processes that function as a background "psychic time" in the organization of sequences of cognitive elements, intentional acts, and the affective, interpersonal quality of expressions in communication (Delamont, Julu, & Jamal, 1999; Keltner, 2003; Meissner & Wittmann, 2011; Wittmann, 2009).

When persons enter into an intimate exchange of actions and interests, periods of close mutual attention and growing intensity of engagement are separated by periods of disengagement. These cycles are experienced as spontaneous narrative units inviting dialogue. As Bruner observes, "Narrative structure is even inherent in the praxis of social interaction before it achieves linguistic expression" (1990, p. 77). Narrative episodes, of dramatic action, of speaking in conversation, or of music, appear to be essential in the emotional regulation of all forms of movement and to all forms of intersubjective co-creation of meaning in dyadic states of consciousness (Trevarthen, 2005a, 2005b; Tronick, 2005). They make predictable patterns of engagement and lead to mutual involvement in vocal and motor expressions of changes in feeling. As Adam Smith (1777/1982) said in his essay on music as one of the imitative arts, a melody lives between memory and imagination. Imagined worlds with their emotional appreciation are built out of the times experienced in familiar episodes, the vitality contours of which may be anticipated, recalled, and shared with companions.

Over the course of an extended communicative exchange, or through a lifetime of collaborative activity between people who know each other well, narrative structures, such as that diagramed in Figure 8.5, may arise many times. Those in enduring relationships and productive interactions are likely to pick up themes from earlier narratives, thus developing a memory or "habitus" of engagement that builds meaning and understanding between the actors (Bourdieu, 1990). This process is evident in the intense mutual interest of adult–infant protoconversations, and recurring ritualized games that are enjoyed between an infant and a mother (see Figure 8.3), which strengthen their affection and give them a sense of meaningful belonging, may be described as creating a "proto-habitus" (Gratier & Trevarthen, 2008).

The change in level of animation or energy of vitality in a narrative game with an infant normally takes the form of a skewed bell curve, the location of the climax varying depending on the interest, vigor, or provocation of the story or game. In animated encounters, such as a teasing game, the climax is pushed further toward the end, and is followed by a more dramatic resolution. For example, in "Round and Round the Garden," illustrated in Figure 8.3, the climax at the word *tickly* as the mother tickles the infant is reached by the steady, slowed steps of line 3, and line 4 is pronounced at a gallop, with *accelerando*. In lively teasing or competitive games, the regular narrative cycle may be broken into small episodes as the interactants move to change or interrupt the purposes of their partners.

It is clear that the narrative, with its internally programmed phases of vitality or animation, has a natural collaborative function in positive engagements of action and awareness. The *introduction* opens the transmission of energy between the two partners, drawing the interests of the "protagonists," present or imagined, together. Reciprocated expressive acts, enacted in a rhythmic exchange of turns, build the emotional, psychological, and physical intensity of the interaction through the *development*. The process of cooperative building and repair is eloquently described by Bateson in the prior quotation. The quality and timing of each expressive act are varied as the participants craft the feel, character, or tone of the interaction until they experience the *climax* at a point of maximal effort and excitement, often accompanied by

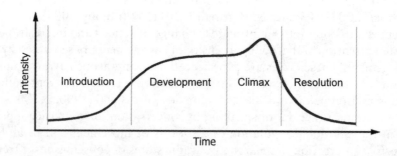

FIGURE 8.5. Intensity contour of engagement of impulses or movement energy in the time of a narrative over its four phases: (1) The "interest" of the narrative begins at a low intensity in the *introduction,* which "invites" participation in purposefulness; then (2) the coordination of the actions and interests of real and imagined agents intensifies over the *development,* as the "plan" or "project" is developed, until (3) a peak of coincident excitation and achievement of a goal in mutual intention is reached at the *climax,* after which (4) the intensity reduces as the purposes of the participants come to a *resolution,* and those who were closely engaged separate.

expressions of joy. Thereafter, their energy dissipates, and the narrative recedes to its *resolution* at a more relaxed level of effort and interest.

If a narrative episode is observed closely as a project of human bodies in movement, it becomes clear that, as the anticipated plot thickens, so too does the sensorimotor intensity of the actions. There is an increase in the number of modalities of expression and often greater force and size of component movements. The roles of actor and "audience" or co-performer change, showing alternating periods of attentive watching and listening or synchrony in performance. When the narrative is finished, the experience of its creation will remain with each of the partners, and between them they may hold its special memory—a memory of a unique, shared experience, the co-creation of which imbues the memory with meaning. The conclusion of a narrative episode is usually followed by a disengagement, which allows the two partners to consider renewing their mutual focus, ready to begin building a new narrative cycle, or they may separate. Read and Miller, social psychologists, consider narratives to be "universally basic to conversation and meaning making" (1995, p. 143). They can be regarded as the essential foundation for consciousness in a more elaborate purposeful social life, among animals, for infants, and for older human beings who have mastered language (Dautenhahn, 2002). Narratives of purpose and affective appraisal do not have to be linguistic.

Primary Narrative as Embodied Meaning-Making Inviting Sensorimotor Attunement between Imaginative and Sympathetic Agents

The creation of a narrative in dialogue requires that two individuals attend to and appreciate each other's expressive acts, following the path of their separate intentions with sympathetic engagement. From birth and through life, the messages are discrete actions of the body: facial expressions, bodily movements, hand gestures, and vocalizations performed rhythmically in sequences with precise synchrony (Bernstein, 1967; Condon, 1979; Lashley, 1951). Research on the coordination and regulation of infants' body movements and on engagements between infants and parents proves that human beings are born with *subjectivity*, or coherent self-awareness in movement, and a drive for *intersubjectivity*, or cooperation in intimate coordination with other persons (Trevarthen, 1979, 1984, 1986a, 1986b). The movements of the two partners become affectively attuned to one another as they respond in a reciprocal exchange (Stern et al., 1985). Parental speech, or "motherese" (Bateson, 1979; Fernald, 1989, 1992; Papoušek & Papoušek, 1981), shows enhanced expression that attracts interest and facilitates coordinated regulation of intentions and feelings, and that may clearly express loss of animation when a mother is depressed (Marwick & Murray, 2009). Successful, happy, or at least satisfying interactions have a shared tempo, with particular expressive acts usually occurring predictably, on a rhythmic beat (Malloch, 1999), and the whole progression modulated by a "proto-narrative envelope" or "melody" of emotional change, expressive of action-regulating changes in deep arousal and affective systems of the brain (Panksepp & Trevarthen, 2009; Stern, 1992, 2000, 2010). The sharing of the rhythm and affective tone of movement makes possible the co-creation of a meaningful experience, one with memorable and suggestive form or content (Gratier & Trevarthen, 2008). Lack of response to expressions of an infant seeking confirmation of intention and awareness causes distress and withdrawal (Murray & Trevarthen, 1985; Tronick, Als, Adamson, Wise, & Brazelton, 1978).

The primary psychological events, affective intentions given in body movement and voice, and their synthesis to generate mutual interest, shared excitement, and reflective satisfaction with another, give rise to the earliest form of dialogue between a newborn infant and his affectionate mother. Many forms of expression are used, and intersubjective contact is mediated by complementary modalities of sense as two human beings compensate for their very different levels of development, the mother coming close to her infant in rhythm and sympathy, and the infant animating his feelings in seductive ways in immediate response to her encouragements. These primary, intuitive motives create narrative awareness between human beings, generating the foundations for affective and embodied meaning-making.

Conclusion: How Human Beings Make Their Self-Conscious Agency Meaningful for Others

Infant–adult interactions, such as the ones we have described, display, in miniature, the essential motivations for sharing feelings creatively of all social engagements between persons, including the balancing of "deference" between pride and shame as adjustments are made with regard to claims of experience, skill, or social station (Scheff, 1988; Trevarthen, 2005b), the carnival celebrations of many voices meeting in excitement (Bakhtin, 1986), and the human seriousness of play in ritual and theatre (Turner, 1982). They make up a measured flow of intentions expressed in consciously monitored actions, signaling spontaneous attitudes and gestures of an animated consciousness, as well as affective appraisals in an inner, "visceral" time.

Of course, social displays of animation are seen among animals, and so are rituals that regulate cooperative habits and tasks for survival, but the human stories are different, even in infancy. When an infant and mother make a story, it is about thoughtfulness of agency for its own sake, about discovery of fantasies in imagined actions, of the kind that can become theories that either recall and explain nature scientifically or that are totally fantastic works of art and drama, for entertainment. The adaptive value of this motivation for thoughtful and moving stories is that it can invent elaborate cultural projects, and carry an inexhaustible code of meanings, including words of a language.

In a narrative, separate psychological events or actions become one evolving experience, a product of an integrative action of the brain and body joining separate moments of conscious commitment and emotional evaluation in sequence to make a single and new project. That is the job of a narrative. "It deals in human or human-like intention and action and the vicissitudes and consequences that mark their course. It strives to put its timeless miracles into the particulars of experience, and to locate the experience in time and place" (Bruner, 1986, p. 13). Bruner describes the narrative as a striving to put the richness of experience into body action, making contours of motor energy that express, or push out, the intentions of the experience that they serve. Stern (2010) calls these actions of feeling "forms of vitality" carried in the shape of the movement. Schögler, Pepping, and Lee (2008) have defined movements to make music as actions of the body that are patterned by prospective control. They have a form that reaches "forward in time" and can, therefore, serve as gestures that communicate intentions and hoped-for futures to other conscious agents (Trevarthen, 1986b; Trevarthen et al., 2011).

In a social engagement of any kind, the anticipating and predictable form of narration opens up prospects of a shared planning and use of energy. The rhythms and vital forms of movement that pattern human movements are tied into the physiology of arousal, distribution of energy, and social affordances for possible action (Stern, 2010; Trevarthen, 2007). In this way, narratives arise from the psychophysiological capacities and motor structures of the extravagantly mobile human body to make possible cooperations in an intersubjective space of consciousness, where two partners may organize their body actions, their intentions, and their feelings to share themselves with each other in acts of communion, making the present part of future imaginings and past rememberings. Our phenomenal reality of living is fresh with dynamic Gestalts expressed in forms of movement (Stern, 2010). These are perceived not by identification of separate sensory modalities, but according to the movements' intentions (Gallese, Rochat, Cossu, & Sinigaglia, 2009), with changes in their affective and motivational quality or manner expressed and perceived in fractions of a second, and in narrative projects shared over many seconds. The unfolding of these "present moments" in life experience come together in awareness of meaning between minds (Stern, 2004). Each is enabled to get to know the other and, ultimately, to "touch" or "emotionally transform" them in a peak moment of intimate agency and "common sense," often signaled by exclamations or laughter.

The play of a narrative gives form and structure to the process of building an intense intimate communion and shared belief. Co-creating shared narrative time also permits endless mischief, and is open to disruption that teases or deflects impulses and challenges expectations and emotions. Teasing play, of animal rough-and-tumble games, or absurd jokes about human intentions and ideal worlds, explores trust and mutual understanding with willing others, invigorating bodies and relationships, and this is how infants know minds and partake in the friendship of their knowing and acting (Reddy, 2008).

Mary Bateson's sensitive observations of one mother–infant protoconversation showed that both the mother and the infant "were acting to sustain [the conversation] or to restore it when it faltered" (Bateson, 1979, p. 65). Their mutual effort to create the communication reveals a fundamental *motive force* for intersubjective connection, for sharing what is in mind, and for making sense of existence in a human-made world.

References

Als, H. (1979). Social interaction: Dynamic matrix for developing behavioral organization. In I. Uzgiris (Ed.), *Social interaction during infancy: New directions for child development* (Vol. 4, pp. 21–39). San Francisco: Jossey-Bass.

Bakhtin, M. M. (1986). *Speech genres and other late essays.* Austin: University of Texas Press.

Bates, E. (1976). *Language and context: The acquisition of pragmatics.* New York: Academic Press.

Bateson, M. C. (1979). The epigenesis of conversational interaction: A personal account of research development. In M. Bullowa (Ed.), *Before speech: The beginning of human communication* (pp. 63–77). London: Cambridge University Press.

Bernatzky, G., Presch, M., Anderson, M., & Panksepp, J. (2011). Emotional foundations of music as a non-pharmacological pain management tool in modern medicine. *Neuroscience and Biobehavioral Reviews, 35*(9), 1989–1999.

Bernstein, N. (1967). *Coordination and regulation of movements.* New York: Pergamon.

Bjørkvold, J.-R. (1992). *The muse within: Creativity and communication, song and play from childhood through maturity.* New York: HarperCollins.

Bourdieu, P. (1984). *Distinction: A social critique of the judgement of taste.* Cambridge, MA: Harvard University Press.

Bourdieu, P. (1990). *The logic of practice.* Palo Alto, CA: Stanford University Press.

Bowlby J. (1969). *Attachment and loss: Vol. 1. Attachment.* London: Hogarth Press.

Bradley, B. S. (2009). Early trios: Patterns of sound and movement in the genesis of meaning between infants. In S. Malloch & C. Trevarthen (Eds.), *Communicative musicality: Exploring the basis of human companionship* (pp. 263–280). Oxford, UK: Oxford University Press.

Bråten, S. (1998). *Intersubjective communication and emotion in early ontogeny.* Cambridge, UK: Cambridge University Press.

Bråten, S. (2009). *The intersubjective mirror in infant learning and evolution of speech.* Amsterdam: John Benjamins.

Brazelton, T. B. (1979). Evidence of communication during neonatal behavioural assessment. In M. Bullowa (Ed.), *Before speech: The beginning of human communication* (pp. 79–88). London: Cambridge University Press.

Brazelton, T. B., & Nugent, J. K. (1995). *The Neonatal Behavioral Assessment Scale.* Cambridge, UK: Mac Keith Press.

Bruner, J. S. (1977). Early social interaction and language acquisition. In H. R. Schaffer (Ed.), *Studies in mother–infant interaction: The Loch Lomond symposium* (pp. 271–290). London: Academic Press.

Bruner, J. S. (1983). *Child's talk: Learning to use language.* New York: Norton.

Bruner, J. S. (1986). *Actual minds, possible worlds.* Cambridge, MA: Harvard University Press.

Bruner, J. S. (1990). *Acts of meaning.* Cambridge, MA: Harvard University Press.

Bruner, J. S., & Sherwood, V. (1975). Early rule structure: The case of peekaboo. In J. S. Bruner, A. Jolly, & K. Sylva (Eds.), *Play: Its role in evolution and development* (pp. 277–285). Harmondsworth, UK: Penguin Books.

Buber, M. (1970). *I and thou* (W. Kaufmann, Trans.). Edinburgh, UK: T. & T. Clark. (Original work published 1923)

Buzsáki, G. (2006). *Rhythms of the brain.* Oxford, UK: Oxford University Press.

Chao, L. L., & Martin, A. (2000). Representation of manipulable man-made objects in the dorsal stream. *NeuroImage, 12,* 478–484.

Cheney, D. L., & Seyfarth, R. M. (2007). *Baboon metaphysics: The evolution of a social mind.* Chicago: University of Chicago Press.

Chomsky, N. (1957). *Syntactic structures.* The Hague, The Netherlands: Mouton.

Condon, W. S. (1979). Neonatal entrainment and enculturation. In M. Bullowa (Ed.), *Before speech: The beginnings of human communication* (pp. 131–148). London: Cambridge University Press.

Condon, W. S., & Sander, L. S. (1974). Neonate movement is synchronized with adult speech: Interactional participation and language acquisition. *Science, 183,* 99–101.

Custodero, L. A., & Johnson-Green, E. A. (2003). Passing the cultural torch: Musical experience and musical parenting of infants. *Journal of Research in Music Education, 51*(2), 102–114.

Darwin, C. (1872). *The expression of emotion in man and animals*. London: Methuen.

Darwin, C. (1877). A biographical sketch of an infant. *Mind, 2*(7), 285–294.

Dautenhahn, K. (2002). The origins of narrative: In search of the transactional format of narratives in humans and other social animals. *International Journal of Cognition and Technology, 1*(1), 97–123.

Davis, K. L., & Panksepp, J. (2011). The brain's emotional foundations of human personality and the Affective Neuroscience Personality Scales. *Neuroscience and Biobehavioral Reviews, 35*(9), 1946–1958.

de Waal, F. B. M. (2006). *Primates and philosophers: How morality evolved*. Princeton, NJ: Princeton University Press.

de Waal, F. B. M. (2009). *The age of empathy: Nature's lessons for a kinder society*. New York: Harmony Books.

DeCasper, A. J., & Prescott, P. (2009). Lateralized processes constrain auditory reinforcement in human newborns. *Hearing Research, 255*, 135–141.

DeCasper, A. J., & Spence, M. J. (1986). Prenatal maternal speech influences newborns' perception of speech sounds. *Infant Behavior and Development, 9*, 133–150.

Delamont, R. S., Julu, P. O. O., & Jamal, G. A. (1999). Periodicity of a noninvasive measure of cardiac vagal tone during non-rapid eye movement sleep in non-sleep-deprived and sleep-deprived normal subjects. *Journal of Clinical Neurophysiology, 16*(2), 146–153.

Dissanayake, E. (2000). *Art and intimacy: How the arts began*. Seattle: University of Washington Press.

Fernald, A. (1989). Intonation and communicative interest in mother's speech to infants: Is the melody the message? *Child Development, 60*, 1497–1510.

Fernald, A. (1992). Meaningful melodies in mothers' speech to infants. In H. Papoušek, U. Jürgens, & M. Papoušek (Eds.), *Nonverbal vocal communication: Comparative and developmental aspects* (pp. 262–282). Cambridge, UK: Cambridge University Press.

Fónagy, I. (2001). *Languages within language: An evolutive approach*. Amsterdam: John Benjamins.

Fogassi, L., Ferrari, P. F., Gesierich, B., Rozzi, S., Chersi, F., & Rizzolatti, G. (2005). Parietal lobe: From action organization to intention understanding. *Science, 308*, 662–667.

Freeman, W. J. (2000a). Emotion is essential to all intentional behaviors. In M. D. Lewis & I. Granic (Eds.), *Emotion, development, and self-organisation: Dynamic systems approaches to emotional development* (pp. 209–235). Cambridge, UK: Cambridge University Press.

Freeman, W. J. (2000b). A neurological role of music in social bonding. In N. L. Wallin, B. Merker, & S. Brown (Eds.), *The origins of music* (pp. 411–424). Cambridge, MA: MIT Press.

Freeman, W. J. (2008). Nonlinear brain dynamics and intention according to Aquinas. *Mind and Matter, 6*(2), 207–234.

Gallagher, S. (2008). Direct perception in the intersubjective context. *Consciousness and Cognition, 17*, 535–543.

Gallese, V. (2000). The inner sense of action: Agency and motor representations. *Journal of Consciousness Studies, 7*, 23–40.

Gallese, V., Rochat, M., Cossu, G., & Sinigaglia, C. (2009). Motor cognition and its role in the phylogeny and ontogeny of action understanding. *Developmental Psychology, 45*(1), 103–113.

Gallese, V., & Sinigaglia, C. (2010). The bodily self as power for action. *Neuropsychologia, 48*, 746–755.

Gibson, J. J. (1977). The theory of affordances. In R. Shaw & J. Bransford (Eds.), *Perceiving, acting, and knowing: Toward an ecological psychology* (pp. 67–82). Hillsdale, NJ: Erlbaum.

Gratier, M., & Trevarthen, C. (2007). Voice, vitality and meaning: On the shaping of the infant's utterances in willing engagement with culture. Comment on Bertau's "On the notion of voice." *International Journal for Dialogical Science, 2*(1), 169–181.

Gratier, M., & Trevarthen, C. (2008). Musical narrative and motives for culture in mother-infant vocal interaction. *Journal of Consciousness Studies, 15*(10–11), 122–158.

Grèzes, J., Armony, J. L., Rowe, J., & Passingham, R. E. (2003). Activations related to "mirror" and "canonical" neurons in the human brain: An fMRI study. *NeuroImage, 18,* 928"937.

Halliday, M. A. K. (1979). One child's protolanguage. In M. Bullowa (Ed.), *Before speech: The beginning of human communication* (pp. 171–190). London: Cambridge University Press.

Halliday, M. A. K., & Matthiessen, C. M. I. M. (2004). *An introduction to functional grammar* (3rd ed.). London: Arnold.

Hauser, M. D., Chomsky, N., & Fitch, W. T. (2002). The faculty of language: What is it, who has it, and how does it evolve? *Science, 298,* 1569–1579.

Hrdy, S. H. (1999). *Mother nature: A history of mothers, infants, and natural selection.* New York: Pantheon.

Hubley, P., & Trevarthen, C. (1979). Sharing a task in infancy. *Social Interaction during Infancy: New Directions for Child Development, 4,* 57–80.

Keltner, D. (2003). Expression and the course of life: Studies of emotion, personality, and psychopathology from a social functional perspective. *Annals of the New York Academy of Sciences, 1000,* 222–243.

Keltner, D. (2009). *Born to be good: The science of a meaningful life.* New York: Norton.

Keltner, D., Horberg, E. J., & Oveis, C. (2006). Emotions as moral intuitions. In J. P. Forgas (Ed.), *Affect in thinking and social behavior* (pp. 161–175). New York: Psychology Press.

Lashley, K. S. (1951). The problems of serial order in behavior. In L. A. Jeffress (Ed.), *Cerebral mechanisms in behavior* (pp. 112–136). New York: Wiley.

MacLean, P. D. (1990). *The triune brain in evolution, role in paleocerebral functions.* New York: Plenum Press.

Malloch, S. (1999). Mother and infants and communicative musicality. In I. Deliège (Ed.), *Rhythms, musical narrative, and the origins of human communication* [Musicae Scientiae, Special Issue, 1999–2000] (pp. 29–57). Liège, Belgium: European Society for the Cognitive Sciences of Music.

Malloch, S., & Trevarthen, C. (Eds.). (2009). *Communicative musicality: Exploring the basis of human companionship.* Oxford, UK: Oxford University Press.

Marwick, H., & Murray, L. (2009). The effects of maternal depression on the "musicality" of infant-directed speech and conversational engagement. In S. Malloch & C. Trevarthen (Eds.), *Communicative musicality: Exploring the basis of human companionship* (pp. 281–300). Oxford, UK: Oxford University Press.

Mazokopaki, M., & Kugiumutzakis, G. (2009). Infant rhythms: Expressions of musical companionship. In S. Malloch & C. Trevarthen (Eds.), *Communicative musicality: Exploring the basis of human companionship* (pp. 185–208). Oxford, UK: Oxford University Press.

Mead, G. H. (1934). *Mind, self, and society.* Chicago: Chicago University Press.

Meissner, K., & Wittmann, M. (2011). Body signals, cardiac awareness, and the perception of time. *Biological Psychology, 86*(3), 289–297.

Meltzoff, A. N., & Moore, M. K. (1977). Imitation of facial and manual gestures by human neonates. *Science, 198,* 75–78.

Merker, B. (2007). Consciousness without a cerebral cortex: A challenge for neuroscience and medicine. *Behavioral and Brain Sciences, 30,* 63–134.

Merker, B. (2009a). Returning language to culture by way of biology. *Behavioral and Brain Sciences, 32*(5), 460.

Merker, B. (2009b). Ritual foundations of human uniqueness. In S. Malloch & C. Trevarthen (Eds.), *Communicative musicality: Exploring the basis of human companionship* (pp. 45–60). Oxford, UK: Oxford University Press.

Michotte, A. (1962). *Causalité, permanence et réalité phénomenales.* Louvain, Belgium: Publications Universitaires.

Murray, L., & Trevarthen, C. (1985). Emotional regulation of interactions between two-month-olds and their mothers. In T. M. Field & N. A. Fox (Eds.), *Social perception in infants* (pp. 177–197). Norwood, NJ: Ablex.

Nadel, J., & Butterworth, G. (Eds.). (1999). *Imitation in infancy.* Cambridge, UK: Cambridge University Press.

Nadel, J., & Pezé, A. (1993). Immediate imitation as a basis for primary communication in toddlers and autistic children. In J. Nadel & L. Camioni (Eds.), *New perspectives in early communicative development* (pp. 139–156). London: Routledge.

Nagy, E. (2008). Innate intersubjectivity: Newborns' sensitivity to communication disturbance. *Developmental Psychology, 44*(6), 1779–1784.

Nagy, E. (2011). The newborn infant: A missing stage in developmental psychology. *Infant and Child Development, 20,* 3–19.

Nagy, E., & Molnár, P. (2004). Homo imitans or homo provocans?: The phenomenon of neonatal initiation. *Infant Behavior and Development, 27,* 57–63.

Northoff, G., & Panksepp, J. (2008). The trans-species concept of self and the subcortical–cortical midline system. *Trends in Cognitive Sciences, 12*(7), 259–264.

Panksepp, J. (1998). The periconscious substrates of consciousness: Affective states and the evolutionary origins of the self. *Journal of Consciousness Studies, 5,* 566–582.

Panksepp, J. (2003). At the interface between the affective, behavioral and cognitive neurosciences: Decoding the emotional feelings of the brain. *Brain and Cognition, 52,* 4–14.

Panksepp, J. (2005). Beyond a joke: From animal laughter to human joy? *Science, 308,* 62–63.

Panksepp, J., & Trevarthen, C. (2009). The neuroscience of emotion in music. In S. Malloch & C. Trevarthen (Eds.), *Communicative musicality: Exploring the basis of human companionship* (pp. 105–146). Oxford, UK: Oxford University Press.

Papoušek, H. (1996). Musicality in infancy research: Biological and cultural origins of early musicality. In I. Deliège & J. Sloboda (Eds.), *Musical beginnings: Origins and development of musical competence* (pp. 37–55). Oxford, UK: Oxford University Press.

Papoušek, M. (1994). Melodies in caregivers' speech: A species specific guidance towards language. *Early Development and Parenting, 3,* 5–17.

Papoušek, M., & Papoušek, H. (1981). Musical elements in the infant's vocalization: Their significance for communication, cognition, and creativity. In L. P. Lipsitt & C. K. Rovee-Collier (Eds.), *Advances in infancy research* (Vol. 1, pp. 163–224). Norwood, NJ: Ablex.

Penfield, W., & Jasper, H. H. (1954). *Epilepsy and the functional anatomy of the human brain.* London: Little, Brown.

Pezzulo, G., & Castelfranchi, C. (2009). Thinking as the control of imagination: A conceptual framework for goal-directed systems. *Psychological Research, 73*(4), 559–577.

Piaget, J. (1954). *The construction of reality in the child* (M. Cook, Trans.). New York: Basic Books.

Piaget, J. (1962). *Play, dreams and imitation in childhood.* London: Routledge & Kegan Paul.

Porges, S. W. (2001). The polyvagal theory: Phylogenetic substrates of a social nervous system. *International Journal of Psychophysiology, 42,* 123–146.

Preisler, G., & Palmer, C. (1986). The function of vocalization in early parent-blind child interaction. In B. Lindblom & R. Zetterstrom (Eds.), *Precursors of early speech* (pp. 269–277). Basingstoke, UK: Macmillan.

Read, S. J., & Miller, L. C. (1995). Stories are fundamental to meaning and memory: For social creatures, could it be otherwise? In R. S. Wyer (Ed.), *Knowledge and memory: The real story* (pp. 139–152). Hillsdale, NJ: Erlbaum.

Reddy, V. (2008). *How infants know minds.* Cambridge, MA: Harvard University Press.

Reid, T. (1764). *An inquiry into the human mind: On the principles of common sense.* Edinburgh, UK: J. Bell.

Rizzolatti, G., Fogassi, L., & Gallese, V. (2001). Neurophysiological mechanisms underlying the understanding and imitation of action. *Nature Reviews. Neuroscience, 2,* 661–670.

Scheff, T. J. (1988). Shame and conformity: The deference-emotion system. *Sociological Review, 53,* 395–406.

Schögler, B., Pepping, G.-J., & Lee, D. N. (2008). TauG-guidance of transients in expressive musical performance. *Experimental Brain Research, 189*(3), 361–372.

Schore, A. N. (2000). The self-organization of the right brain and the neurobiology of emotional development. In M. Lewis & I. Granic (Eds.), *Emotion, development, and self-organization, dynamic systems approaches to emotional development* (pp. 155–185). New York: Cambridge University Press.

Selby, J. M., & Bradley, B. S. (2003). Infants in groups: A paradigm for study of early social experience. *Human Development, 46,* 197–221.

Sherrington, C. S. (1906). *The integrative action of the nervous system.* New Haven, CT: Yale University Press.

Smith, A. (1982). Of the nature of that imitation which takes place in what are called the imitative arts. In W. P. D. Wightman & J. C. Bryce (Eds.), *Essays on philosophical subjects* (pp. 176–213). Indianapolis, IN: Liberty Fund. (Original work published 1777)

Spitz, R. A. (1957). *No and yes: On the genesis of human communication.* New York: International Universities Press.

Stern, D. N. (1971). A micro-analysis of mother–infant interaction: Behaviors regulating social contact between a mother and her three-and-a-half-month-old twins. *Journal of American Academy of Child Psychiatry, 10,* 501–517.

Stern, D. N. (1974). Mother and infant at play: The dyadic interaction involving facial, vocal and gaze behaviours. In M. Lewis & L. A. Rosenblum (Eds.), *The effect of the infant on its caregiver* (pp. 187–213). New York: Wiley.

Stern, D. N. (1985). *The interpersonal world of the infant: A view from psychoanalysis and development psychology.* New York: Basic Books.

Stern, D. N. (1992). L'enveloppe prénarrative: Vers une unité fondamentale d'expérience permettant d'explorer la réalité psychique du bébé. *Revue Internationale de Psychopathologie, 6,* 13–63.

Stern, D. N. (1999). Vitality contours: The temporal contour of feelings as a basic unit for constructing the infant's social experience. In P. Rochat (Ed.), *Early social cognition: Understanding others in the first months of life* (pp. 67–90). Mahwah, NJ: Erlbaum.

Stern, D. N. (2000). *The interpersonal world of the infant: A view from psychoanalysis and development psychology* (2nd ed.). New York: Basic Books.

Stern, D. N. (2004). *The present moment: In psychotherapy and everyday life.* New York: Norton.

Stern, D. N. (2010). *Forms of vitality: Exploring dynamic experience in psychology, the arts, psychotherapy and development.* Oxford, UK: Oxford University Press.

Stern, D. N., Hofer, L., Haft, W., & Dore, J. (1985). Affect attunement: The sharing of feeling states between mother and infant by means of inter-modal fluency. In T. M. Field & N. A. Fox (Eds.), *Social perception in infants* (pp. 249–268). Norwood, NJ: Ablex.

Suomi, S. J. (2005). Mother–infant attachment, peer relationships, and the development of social networks in rhesus monkeys. *Human Development*, 48(1–2), 67–79.

Tomasello, M., & Farrar, M. J. (1986). Joint attention and early language. *Child Development*, 57(6), 1454–1463.

Trainor, L. J. (1996). Infant preferences for infant-directed versus non-infant-directed play songs and lullabies. *Infant Behavior and Development*, 19, 83–92.

Trehub, S. E. (2000). Human processing predispositions and music universal. In N. L. Wallin, B. Merker, & S. Brown (Eds.), *The origins of music* (pp. 427–448). Cambridge, MA: MIT Press.

Trevarthen, C. (1979). Communication and cooperation in early infancy. A description of primary intersubjectivity. In M. Bullowa (Ed.), *Before speech: The beginning of human communication* (pp. 321–347). London: Cambridge University Press.

Trevarthen, C. (1984). How control of movements develops. In H. T. A. Whiting (Ed.), *Human motor actions: Bernstein reassessed* (pp. 223–261). Amsterdam: North-Holland.

Trevarthen, C. (1986a). Development of intersubjective motor control in infants. In M. G. Wade & H. T. A. Whiting (Eds.), *Motor development in children: Aspects of coordination and control* (pp. 209–261). Dordrecht, The Netherlands: Martinus Nijhof.

Trevarthen, C. (1986b). Form, significance and psychological potential of hand gestures of infants. In J.-L. Nespoulous, P. Perron, & A. R. Lecours (Eds.), *The biological foundation of gestures: Motor and semiotic aspects* (pp.149–202). Hillsdale, NJ: Erlbaum.

Trevarthen, C. (1993). The function of emotions in early infant communication and development. In J. Nadel & L. Camaioni (Eds.), *New perspectives in early communicative development* (pp. 48–81). London: Routledge.

Trevarthen, C. (1996). Lateral asymmetries in infancy: Implications for the development of the hemispheres. *Neuroscience and Biobehavioral Reviews, 20*(4), 571–586.

Trevarthen, C. (1999). Musicality and the intrinsic motive pulse: Evidence from human psychobiology and infant communication. In I. Deliège (Ed.), *Rhythms, musical narrative, and the origins of human communication* [Musicae Scientiae, Special Issue, 1999–2000] (pp. 157–213). Liège, Belgium: European Society for the Cognitive Sciences of Music.

Trevarthen, C. (2001). The neurobiology of early communication: Intersubjective regulations in human brain development. In A. F. Kalverboer & A. Gramsbergen (Eds.), *Handbook on brain and behavior in human development* (pp. 841–882). Dordrecht, The Netherlands: Kluwer.

Trevarthen, C. (2004). Brain development. In R. L. Gregory (Ed.), *Oxford companion to the mind* (2nd ed.). Oxford, UK: Oxford University Press.

Trevarthen, C. (2005a). Action and emotion in development of the human self, its sociability and cultural intelligence: Why infants have feelings like ours. In J. Nadel & D. Muir (Eds.), *Emotional development* (pp. 61–91). Oxford, UK: Oxford University Press.

Trevarthen, C. (2005b). "Stepping away from the mirror: Pride and shame in adventures of companionship"—reflections on the nature and emotional needs of infant intersubjectivity. In C. S. Carter, L. Ahnert, K. E. Grossman, S. B. Hrdy, M. E. Lamb, S. W. Porges, et al. (Eds.), *Attachment and bonding: A new synthesis* (pp. 55–84). Cambridge, MA: MIT Press.

Trevarthen, C. (2007). Moving experiences: Perceiving as action with a sense of purpose. In G.-J. Pepping & M. Grealy (Eds.), *Closing the gap: The scientific writings of David N. Lee* (pp. 1–20). Mahwah, NJ: Erlbaum.

Trevarthen, C. (2009). The functions of emotion in infancy: The regulation and communication of rhythm, sympathy, and meaning in human development. In D. Fosha, D. J. Siegel, & M. F. Solomon (Eds.), *The healing power of emotion: Affective neuroscience, development, and clinical practice* (pp. 55–85). New York: Norton.

Trevarthen, C. (2011a). The generation of human meaning: How shared experience grows in infancy. In A. Seemann (Ed.), *Joint attention: New developments in philosophy, psychology, and neuroscience* (pp. 73–135). Cambridge, MA: MIT Press.

Trevarthen, C. (2011b). What is it like to be a person who knows nothing?: Defining the active intersubjective mind of a newborn human being. *Infant and Child Development, 20*(1), 119–135.

Trevarthen, C. (2012). Embodied human intersubjectivity: Imaginative agency, to share meaning. *Cognitive Semiotics, 4*(1), 6–56.

Trevarthen, C. (in press). Born for art, and the joyful companionship of fiction. In D. Narvaez, J. Panksepp, A. Schore, & T. Gleason (Eds.), *Evolution, early experience and human development: From research to practice and policy*. Oxford, UK: Oxford University Press.

Trevarthen, C., & Aitken, K. J. (2003). Regulation of brain development and age-related changes in infants' motives: The developmental function of "regressive" periods. In M. Heimann (Ed.), *Regression periods in human infancy* (pp. 107–184). Mahwah, NJ: Erlbaum.

Trevarthen, C., Aitken, K. J., Vandekerckhove, M., Delafield-Butt, J., & Nagy, E. (2006). Collaborative regulations of vitality in early childhood: Stress in intimate relationships and postnatal psychopathology. In D. Cicchetti & D. J. Cohen (Eds.), *Developmental psychopathology: Vol. 2. Developmental neuroscience* (2nd ed., pp. 65–126). New York: Wiley.

Trevarthen, C., Delafield-Butt, J., & Schögler, B. (2012). Psychobiology of musical gesture: Innate rhythm, harmony and melody in movements of narration. In A. Gritten & E. King (Eds.), *Music and gesture 2* (pp. 11–43). Aldershot, UK: Ashgate.

Trevarthen, C., & Hubley, P. (1978) Secondary intersubjectivity: Confidence, confiding and acts of meaning in the first year. In A. Lock (Ed.), *Action, gesture and symbol: The emergence of language* (pp. 183–229). London: Academic Press.

Trevarthen, C., & Marwick, H. (1986). Signs of motivation for speech in infants, and the nature of a mother's support for development of language. In B. Lindblom & R. Zetterstrom (Eds.), *Precursors of early speech* (pp. 279–308). Basingstoke, UK: Macmillan

Tronick, E. Z. (2005). Why is connection with others so critical?: The formation of dyadic states of consciousness: coherence governed selection and the co-creation of meaning out of messy meaning making. In J. Nadel & D. Muir (Eds.), *Emotional development*(pp. 293–315). Cambridge, MA: Oxford University Press.

Tronick, E. Z., Als, H., & Adamson, L. (1979). Structure of early face-to-face communicative interactions. In M. Bullowa (Ed.), *Before speech: The beginning of human communication* (pp. 349–372). London: Cambridge University Press.

Tronick, E. Z., Als, H., Adamson, L., Wise, S., & Brazelton, T. B. (1978). The infant's response to entrapment between contradictory messages in face-to-face interaction. *Journal of the American Academy of Child Psychiatry, 17*, 1–13.

Tulving, E. (2005). Episodic memory and autonoesis: Uniquely human? In H. S. Terrace & J. Metcalfe (Eds.), *The missing link in cognition: Self-knowing consciousness in man and animals* (pp. 3–56). New York: Oxford University Press.

Turner, R., & Ioannides, A. (2009). Brain, music and musicality: Inferences from neuroimaging. In S. Malloch & C. Trevarthen (Eds.), *Communicative musicality: Exploring the basis of human companionship* (pp. 147–181). Oxford, UK: Oxford University Press.

Turner, V. W. (1982). *From ritual to theatre: The human seriousness of play*. New York: PAJ Publications.

Tzourio-Mazoyer, N., De Schonen, S., Crivello, F., Reutter, B., Aujard, Y., & Mazoyer, B. (2002). Neural correlates of woman face processing by 2-month-old infants. *NeuroImage, 15*, 454–461.

Van Puyvelde, M., Vanfleteren, P., Loots, G., Deschuyffeleer, S., Vinck, B., Jacquet, W., et al. (2010). Tonal synchrony in mother–infant interaction based on harmonic and pentatonic series. *Infant Behavior and Development, 33,* 387–400.

Vandekerckhove, M., & Panksepp, J. (2011). A neurocognitive theory of higher mental emergence: From anoetic affective experiences to noetic and autonoetic awareness. *Neuroscience and Biobehavioral Reviews, 35*(9), 2017–2025.

von Uexküll, J. (1957). A stroll through the worlds of animals and men: A picture book of invisible worlds. In C. H. Schiller (Ed. & Trans.), *Instinctive behavior: The development of a modern concept* (pp. 5–80). New York: International Universities Press

Winkler, I., Háden, G. P., Ladinig, O., Sziller, I., & Honing, H. (2009). Newborn infants detect the beat in music. *Proceedings of the National Academy of Sciences USA, 106,* 2468–2471.

Wittmann, M. (2009). The inner experience of time. *Philosophical Transactions of the Royal Society of London: B. Biological Science, 364,* 1955–1967.

Zentner, M., & Eerola, T. (2010). Rhythmic engagement with music in infancy. *Proceedings of the National Academy of Sciences USA, 107,* 5768–5773.

CHAPTER 9

The Situated Infant

Learning in Context

ARLENE WALKER-ANDREWS
SHEILA KROGH-JESPERSEN
ESTELLE MAYHEW
CARRIE COFFIELD

> The proper unit for study is an organism in the environment
> in which it evolved, functioning in a reciprocal relationship.
> —ELEANOR J. GIBSON (1997, p. 25)

The title of this chapter refers to the "situated" infant, in recognition of human infants' discovery of the self through active engagement with the physical and interpersonal world. Infants are not merely observers, but they act on the world to produce fascinating events. In the social world, they smile as they engage others in rich, interactive episodes that include imitation, affective mirroring, turn-taking, and other coordinated behaviors (Rochat, 2003; Stern, 1985). To gain an understanding of what humans and other organisms perceive when they are faced with complicated, real-world events, including social interactions, demands that the investigator take an ecological approach. And nowhere is it more critical to take a broad, comparative view that looks at development in context than during the period of infancy. For human infants, perception is supported by dynamic and multimodal information. The infant is situated in relation to other persons and physical objects while interacting with the world (Garvey & Fogel, 2008), and the relationship between an organism and its environment is the appropriate object of study. Moreover, we assert that an informed understanding of an infant's perceptual capabilities and emotional development requires the use of ecologically valid stimulus materials and a strategy for combining multiple, converging methods. Others, most notably Gibson (1969) and Brunswik (1952), have made similar claims about the necessity of examining the relationship between the organism and the environment. In the present chapter, we argue that perception develops optimally when stimulation is dynamic, naturalistic, and multimodal. Several lines of research are used as examples, with an emphasis on the development of the perception of emotional expressions. The development of the perception of emotion is a singular example of the development of the perception of affordances because the emotional expressions of others can be defined as "experiences of *harm* or *benefit*, perceived as personally meaningful with respect to the individual's changing relationship with the environment" (Garvey & Fogel, 2008, p. 63). Studies of the development of perception of emotional expressions offer a window on infants' developing abilities to discover structure and meaning in the behaviors of others. Such expressive behaviors not only are signs of emotion, but they also convey information about another person's probable actions.

For the most part, investigators agree that for infants dynamic events afford a rich and varied source for learning about diverse properties of the environment (Bahrick, Gogate, & Ruiz, 2002). For example, it was demonstrated long ago that infants detect object shape more effectively when the object is moving rather than still (Kellman & Spelke, 1983) and that they use motion information in the perception of causality (Cohen & Oakes, 1993; Leslie & Keeble, 1987), changing distance (Walker-Andrews & Lennon, 1985), and, as revealed more recently, the recognition of faces (Otsuka et al., 2009). Consequently, the most appropriate strategy for understanding perception and its development is not studying an illusion or showing participants line drawings or monocular views of manipulated figures; rather, it lies in providing the observer real-world (or at least ecologically valid) stimulus materials and allowing for a response. At any one moment, we detect literally millions of objects, events, textures, colors, sounds, and other stimuli. To remain standing, locomote, and hold a conversation simultaneously requires the ability to monitor postural changes, optical movements, and acoustic signals simultaneously. Misperceiving is rare and leads to obvious consequences: In most cases, organisms experience unfortunate outcomes directly when they make a perceptual error. Although studying illusions is intriguing and provides data about what organisms do when information is insufficient for veridical perception, such studies are limited for understanding how perception proceeds and develops.

In this chapter, we review a number of experimental studies carried out over a period spanning nearly 30 years that examine infants' perception of the affordances of the world. Results from these studies converge to illustrate the critical role of dynamic, multimodal information in infants' perception. First, we review two experimental studies conducted in collaboration with Eleanor J. Gibson that investigated infants' perception of the physical world of objects and events, specifically infants' sensitivities to dynamic, multimodal information. Gibson (1969) argued that motion carries information about the properties of objects and that, through the detection of motion, infants abstract invariant patterns of stimulation that specify enduring properties of objects. She also emphasized that young infants do not differentiate modalities; rather, they detect information for objects and events that is abstract and amodal. Following review of these studies of infants' perception of physical objects and events, we turn to experiments on infants' perception of emotional expressions, including infants' perception of bimodally presented emotional expressions and their perception of emotional expressions posed by familiar persons. Finally, we briefly summarize findings from studies of infants' perception of speech, given the critical importance of context for speech perception. As indicated, the research on infants' perception of the physical world demonstrates the early development of perception of a complex, dynamic, and multimodal environment. Research on infants' perception of the expressions and speech of others demonstrates the decisive importance of context as a support for veridical perception. The perception of others' expressions and speech leads to a more informed understanding of others' intentions and the ability of the self to influence others' behavior. Many of the selected studies come from our laboratory and were designed with an ecological approach, but we include findings from other researchers that amplify the importance of contextual factors in perceptual development.

Intermodal Perception of Objects and Events

A discussion of two classic studies on infants' intermodal perception provides a starting point for appreciating infants' perception of objects and events in the world. We live in, and in fact are part of, a multimodal world. Most of the time, multiple objects and events are perceptible at the same time and often in the same general direction. We do not, however, experience any particular difficulty in dealing with this environment; rather, perceptual selection is straightforward and seems effortless. So, too, does the young infant encounter a world of objects, events, people, and places that are specified multimodally. Even the self is specified across modalities: We can see parts of our bodies, hear our own voices and growling stomachs, taste salty tears, and experience feedback when we stretch out an arm or touch one finger to another. Historically, researchers proposed that perceivers must learn to pair and integrate sense-specific information in order to interpret it as meaningful. The typical question was how perceivers bind together these disparate pieces of information. Dating back to the question put to Locke by Molyneux about whether a man born blind would recognize shapes if vision were restored, the mechanism of association has been invoked to explain how the perceiver comes to integrate information to yield a unified percept.

Conversely, consider the redundancy provided to an observer when an object is encountered, such as when an object strikes a surface, producing visual and acoustic information united by synchrony and co-location as well as correspondences between the type of sound made by a particular substance. This redundancy permits efficient exploration and the detection of higher order perceptual structure (Bahrick & Lickliter, 2002). Smith (2005), in a discussion of a dynamic systems approach to cognitive development, describes such redundancy as providing time-locked correlations that produce a powerful learning mechanism, by which perception is self-taught. According to Lewkowicz (2001), at least three processes are important to intermodal perception, including association, nonspecific effects of stimulation in one modality on responsiveness to stimulation in another, and the detection of amodal invariants.

Selective Attention of Intermodal Correspondences

Infants' ability to detect such higher order structure, given in visual and auditory information, was examined by Bahrick, Walker, and Neisser (1981) in a study of infants' selective attention to complex, multimodal events. Infants observed an event ostensibly impossible to follow visually: Films of two events (a hand-clapping game and the cascading motions of a plastic slinky) were superimposed, while the soundtrack to one of the events was played. The upshot was a sort of visual hodgepodge: two different actions and sets of objects moving through the same spatial location, a perfect exemplar of "great blooming, buzzing confusion" (James, 1890/1983, p. 462). The question was whether infants could exploit the relationship of the acoustic information to the objects' movements, allowing the infants to disentangle the events. An analogy might be drawn to the common experience of standing at a window and gazing straight ahead. The observer can focus on the windowpane itself, staring at his or her own reflection, or the observer can look through the window to the scene beyond. Adults perform this task easily by shifting their visual attention. In Bahrick and colleagues, 4-month-old infants observed the superimposed films, but at scheduled intervals the projectors were rotated so that the superimposed events were separated, resulting in the projection of two single events positioned side by side. The sound automatically cut off during the separation phase. Infants' looking to the two events during spatial separation was monitored. The authors predicted that if the infants used the soundtrack to follow one of the events during superimposition, looking patterns would be affected during the subsequent separation phase.

This prediction was upheld. Bahrick and colleagues (1981) found that infants looked about two-thirds of the time at the event that had been silent during the superimposition phase. Typically, the infants looked straight ahead at the overlapping events during the superimposition phase. During the separation, after an initial pause, infants turned their heads and eyes in the direction of the previously silent event. Using results from control experiments, Bahrick and colleagues demonstrated convincingly that infants visually followed a single, unified event during the superimposition. For example, in one experiment, infants viewed a single event during the superimposition phase and then observed two events side by side on the tests. Infants looked about two-thirds of the time to the previously unseen event. In another experiment, infants viewed superimposed events as before, but sufficiently defocused so that only blurred color and motion were discernible. In this case, no preferences were shown afterward to the focused events presented side by side, ruling out an alternative interpretation: that infants merely looked for something that did not coincide with the sounds they had heard previously during the superimposition phase. Instead, results supported the conclusion that in the original experiment infants used the intermodal correspondences characterizing the sight and sound of an event to follow it during the superimposition phase, looking to the unattended event during the separation.

This set of experiments illustrates infants' ability to use redundant information to disambiguate events, as an infant must do in real-world situations. When the infant is lying in the crib and grandma and grandpa enter the room, swooping down close, exclaiming excitably, and stroking the infant's face, the infant determines which person is talking by attending to myriad correspondences between speaker and voice. The infant does not hear a voice and see a face and somehow glue these together; rather, the infant experiences the interaction and responds accordingly. As in the Bahrick and colleagues (1981) study, the infant benefits from the amodal, invariant relationships and intermodal correspondences that serve to unify events. Common temporal patterns, rate of action, temporal synchrony relations, and even the appropriateness of the type of sound for the visual information is sufficient for infants as young as 4 months to attend selectively to a particular event. Ample evidence exists that infants can learn arbitrary relations as well, such as the sound of a particular person's voice with his or her face when intermodal correspondences are highlighted (e.g., Brookes et al., 2001; Walker-Andrews, Bahrick, Raglioni, & Diaz, 1991). Bahrick and others (e.g., Bahrick & Watson, 1985; Rochat & Hespos, 1997) have demonstrated that very young infants can detect proprioceptive–visual relations that unite a visual display of the felt motions, also using invariant intermodal correspondences.

Visual–Tactual Perception of Affordances

Smith (2005, p. 29) emphasizes the detection of such correspondences or amodal relations as a way to obtain "qualitatively different glosses on the world," which allow the infant to discern higher-order regularities that transcend the modalities involved. Investigations of infants' ability to recognize objects across modalities demonstrate that infants can use such regularities. Pioneering studies designed by Gibson examined 3-month-old infants' ability to differentiate visually rigid motions from deforming ones and the ability to recognize the shape of an object across such motions (Gibson, Owsley, Walker, & Megaw-Nyce, 1979; Walker, Gibson, Owsley, Megaw-Nyce, & Bahrick, 1980). The results demonstrated that infants could detect two invariant properties in the same event: substance, as specified by type of motion; and shape, as revealed by the continuous transformations during motion.

Later experiments investigated whether infants detected information about the substance of an object visually and haptically (Gibson & Walker, 1984; Walker-Andrews & Gibson, 1986). Meltzoff and Borton (1979; see also Bryant, Jones, Claxton, & Perkins, 1972) found that newborn infants recognized the shape of an object they had mouthed when they viewed it on a subsequent test. Using a similar procedure, Gibson and Walker provided 12-month-olds an opportunity to handle either a rigid or a pliable object. One group of infants sat in their mothers' laps in a dark room. The target object, marked by a spot of phosphorescent cream, was placed on a table in front of the infant for manipulation. After ensuring that each infant handled the object for 60 seconds, the experimenter removed the object and showed the infant films of two objects, one being deformed by squeezing motions and the other being moved rigidly. The direction of the infants' first looks and the duration of looking time to the films were recorded to determine whether the haptic experience affected the infants' visual preferences. The infants' handling behavior was also coded from (infrared) videotapes. Another group of infants (visual and haptic experience) participated under normal lighting conditions, so that they could both view and handle an object. These infants also viewed films to determine whether they had a preference based on their haptic and visual experience. In a companion experiment, much younger infants (1-month-olds) participated. In this experiment, the infant's mother held either a small cylinder made of Lucite or one carved from a sponge in her infant's mouth so the baby could mouth it for 60 seconds. Once the baby had done so, he or she saw a visual tableau composed of two sponge cylinders presented side by side. An experimenter simultaneously squeezed and rhythmically released one cylinder while moving the other in a nodding motion. The infants' looking preferences were monitored.

Across these experiments, 1- and 12-month-old infants showed systematic looking patterns following the haptic exploration. The 1-month-olds looked more to the novel object whatever the substance. The older infants, in both visual–haptic and haptic-only conditions, looked predominantly at the object composed of the familiar substance. An examination of how the 12-month-olds handled the objects in the dark also highlighted their different patterns of exploration. For example, the infants squeezed and dragged the soft object across the surface, but enthusiastically and frequently banged the rigid object against the table. These results show that infants detect intermodal information about substance, carried by differentiating motions of objects. The affordance of "elasticity" or "rigidity" is detected by the haptic system and appears to generalize to the visual system.

Summary of Intermodal Work

Data from electrophysiological studies are consistent with the kind of behavioral evidence for early intermodal perceptual organization discussed previously. At birth, animals have well-organized inputs from different sensory modalities converging on the same target structures in the brain (e.g., Roe, Pallas, Halm, & Sur, 1990). In fact, Stein and Meredith (1993) assert that the newborn's brain is actually more multisensory than that of adult animals, as experience may modify convergence patterns over development. A particularly striking example of the latter comes from a study by King, Hutchings, Moore, and Blakemore (1988). These investigators obstructed an ear or repositioned an eye of young ferrets during early postnatal development, which led to functional shifts in the auditory receptive fields. Early on, however, across a range of brain structures, spatial correspondence among the receptive fields of multisensory neurons appears to provide a neural substrate for ensuring responses to spatially and/or temporally linked multimodal information. Multimodal stimulus combinations produce significant increases over unimodal responses in a number of measures of neural activity (Stein & Meredith, 1993). In summary, neurophysiological research indicates that young animals are sensitive to redundant sensory information early on, with responsiveness to such information influenced by the physical, social, and temporal contexts in which development occurs.

What do the behavioral and neurophysiological findings say about the proposition that infants must be considered as active, integrated organisms participating in a dynamic and multimodal world? Results suggest that, for infants, perception functions well when the stimulus information is dynamic, naturalistic, and multimodal. Objects, events, and the layout of surfaces are specified by information in an ambient array (optical, acoustic, and haptic) available to an organism with perceptual systems that have evolved to detect that information. The infant obtains information via its perceptual systems, and that information not only specifies an object or an event but it also has the potential of specifying an affordance of the object or event, its utility for adaptive behavior. For example, in the Gibson and Walker study, not only did infants look differentially to objects of varying substances following haptic experience, but they also performed different actions with them during their haptic exploration.

In addition, these results speak to the intermodal capacities of the human infant and are generalizable to the experience of the self:

> A sense of self is multifaceted and achieved over time; some parts of it may be present at birth. The more one knows about an infant's earliest intermodal abilities, the less compelling are any arguments to wait until an arbitrary response or point in time ('removing rouge from the face') before attributing a sense of self to an infant. From his earliest hours, the infant detects information that potentially specifies the self. He brings a hand to his mouth and sucks on it, obtaining dynamic information about the texture of his skin and the shape of the hand; simultaneously, he detects information about his mouthing activity from changes in pressure on the skin itself. As he turns his head, albeit clumsily, objects in the environment are progressively occluded and disoccluded, but his position remains constant. He cries and as he hears his own cry and experiences the physiological arousal accompanying that cry, someone appears and alters the experience with soothing sounds and touches. In such a fashion, infants acquire self knowledge—information about the self as observer, as agent, as a participant in social interactions, and for continuity over time. (Walker-Andrews, 1992, p. 131)

Perception of Emotional Expressions

It is this part of the infants' perception of self as an interacting participant that we turn to now, as addressed in research on the development of infants' understanding of others' emotional expressions. Some of the richest information for the self is available to the infant in expressive behaviors, both through observation of others' behaviors and through the experience of one's own emotional expressions. Young infants detect information for vocal and facial expressions quite early, moving to recognition of those expressions. Current research indicates that by about 4 to 5 months, infants perceive facial/vocal expressions as meaningful configurations. In many respects, perceiving other persons is no different from perceiving objects and events; the infant perceives the affordances of others by observing their expressions, actions, and more permanent properties.

For several decades, we have been investigating infants' perception of the emotional expressions of others. Walker (1982) examined whether infants could detect meaning in expressions using an intermodal preference procedure. The objective was to determine whether infants perceived the intermodal correspondences between a facial expression and a vocal expression, perhaps detecting something abstract and amodal equivalent to the affordance of the expressive behaviors. To summarize the general procedure, infants observed two films presented side by side, each depicting the same woman but with two different expressions. A single vocal expression corresponding to one of the facial expressions was played from a central location. In a series of experiments, both 5- and 7-month-old infants looked more to facial expressions (happy, sad, angry, and neutral) when they were sound specified compared with when they were not. Even when the soundtrack was presented asynchronously, 7-month-old infants looked preferentially at the affectively concordant display, suggesting that synchrony is but one correspondence between facial and vocal expressions detected by infants.

To examine further the hypothesis that temporal correspondences drove infants' looking preferences, Walker conducted an additional experiment. Data obtained by others using smiling as the dependent measure suggested that infants might not easily detect emotional expressions in inverted faces. Watson, Hayes, Vietze, and Becker (1979) found that inversion of face stimuli disrupted infants' perception of those faces.[1] Therefore, 7-month-old infants were shown facial expressions presented in an inverted orientation along with one of the soundtracks. Infants failed to look appropriately to the sound-specified film, although synchrony relations were preserved, demonstrating that temporal relations or generalized arousal does not account for the infants' looking preferences in this set of experiments (Walker, 1982).

In a later study, Walker-Andrews (1986) investigated infants' perception of angry and happy emotional expressions with an added manipulation designed to minimize the relevance of temporal information. Infants viewed films of a happy facial expression and an angry facial expression, presented side by side, but a draped cloth concealed the lower part of the models' faces, thus attenuating the synchrony relations between lip movements and vocalizations. Seven-month-old infants (but not 5-month-olds) maintained preferential looking to the sound-specified emotion films. These findings demonstrate that, at least by 7 months, infants detect information that is invariant across optic and acoustic displays of a single affective expression, thereby perceiving the bimodally presented expressions as unitary, meaningful events, even when synchrony information is severely limited. The results, combined with those of Walker (1982), suggest that infants detect intermodal correspondences or invariants specific to emotion rather than using temporal synchrony or arousal matching to determine which face goes with the voice they are hearing.

Others have used the intermodal preference technique to investigate the variables that may contribute to infants' ability to match facial and vocal expressions. Soken and Pick (1992) found that 7-month-old infants could detect the emotion correspondence between facial and vocal expressions based on motion information alone (using point-light displays). In a subsequent study (Soken & Pick, 1999), 7-month-old infants showed intermodal matching for point-light displays of happy, sad, interested, and angry expressions. Very few studies have compared infants' responsiveness to multimodal and unimodal stimulus materials in the same experiment, but in 2007 Flom and Bahrick reported that by 4 months infants discriminate emotional expressions when those expressions are presented bimodally, although they do not when those expressions are presented unimodally. This result complements a comparison of two studies by Caron and colleagues. In Caron, Caron, and MacLean (1988), 7-month-olds could detect happy and angry emotional expressions in a dynamic audiovisual display, while in Caron, Caron, and Myers (1985), 9-month-old infants had difficulty distinguishing differences in happy and angry expressions presented in photographs. (For a review of facial expression research using photographs, see Nelson, 1987.) Similarly, Otsuka and colleagues (2009) found that 3- to 4-month-old infants were more successful on a recognition task when they had been familiarized to moving images than to static images; the authors argued that motion information facilitated infants' learning of faces. Grossman, Striano, and Friederici (2006) examined 7-month-old infants' responses to emotionally congruent or incongruent face–voice pairs but using event-related potentials (ERPs) rather than preferential looking, finding that infants integrate emotional information across modalities and recognize common affect in the face and voice. Work with adults underscores the significance of multimodal presentations of emotion. De Gelder, Vroomen, and Pourtois (1999) report that facial and vocal expressions of emotion are combined early (within 178 milliseconds after voice onset) as measured by ERPs.

Impressive as these findings may be, others have documented sensitivity by still younger infants. For the most part, these experiments have been those in which (1) infants are engaged in live interactions with their own mothers or other caregiver and (2) measures other than looking time are used. The findings of these studies underscore the critical importance of using converging methods and providing rich stimulus information. For example, Haviland and Lelwica (1987) examined the responses of 10-week-old infants to their own mothers' live presentations of happy, sad, and angry facial/vocal expressions. These infants responded differentially and contingently to maternal emotional signals. Haviland and her colleagues also documented early emotional responsiveness among mother–infant dyads, finding that mothers exploit this mode of interaction as a context for socialization of infants' expressiveness, bringing them into line with cultural expectations (Malatesta & Haviland, 1982). Both mothers and infants displayed imitative behaviors in the Haviland studies, in keeping with results from others (e.g., Field, Woodson, Greenberg, & Cohen, 1982; Kugiumutzakis, 1993; Montague & Walker-Andrews, 2001) that infants selectively imitate facial and vocal expressions. Studies that take a dynamic systems approach and use microgenetic designs in which children are studied repeatedly over a short time span to investigate the development of face-to-face communication also find imitation and entrainment by mother and infant beginning at the end of the second month (e.g., Lavelli & Fogel, 2005).

The review of literature thus far has focused on behavioral evidence for the development of infants' perception of emotion. Corroborating evidence for infants' abilities, however, is beginning to be found in studies that examine the perception of faces and emotional expression using measures such as ERPs and research that focuses on the neural bases of multimodal integration during infancy, often using emotion displays because of the attention-getting features of such stimuli. In general, investigators assert that, because of their limited visual capacities, young infants' perception of facial expressions is based on low spatial frequency (LSF) information. According to Vlamings, Jonkman, and Kemner (2010), adults use LSF information to categorize emotional expressions, while they rely on high spatial frequency information to judge the intensity of expressions. This suggests that the LSF information is sufficient to convey emotion to infants, although it neglects the importance of motion and multimodal information in the perception of emotion. Nelson and his colleagues have also examined whether specific patterns in infants' brain activity are evoked when infants look at different facial expressions. Nelson and de Haan (1996) found that 7-month-olds responded differentially to slides of happy and fearful facial expressions. The amplitudes of two positive ERP components were greater for the happy expression, and the amplitude of a middle-latency negative component was greater for the fearful expression. No such differences were found for angry compared with fearful expressions, however. Nelson and de Haan concluded that infants apportioned more attentional resources to the fearful face than to the happy one, although it is not clear whether the middle-latency ERP component represents an obligatory or a voluntary attentional response, or whether the greater attention is based on the threat-related nature of fear or on the novelty of fearful expressions for most infants. Peltola, Leppanen, Palokangas, and Hietanen (2008) found that 7-month-olds are less able to shift visual fixation from a fearful face compared with a happy face, a finding similar to adult responses to threat-related stimuli. In general, the electrophysiological evidence regarding infants' sensitivity to facial expressions indicates that the neural systems responsive to fearful, happy, and neutral faces are functional within the first few months of life, and that emotion itself may modulate infants' attention to such facial expressions. These findings support and augment the behavioral evidence for infants' discrimination and recognition of emotional expressions.

Effect of Context: Familiarity of Person

Given infants' early sensitivity to maternal expressions in live interactions as documented by looking time and other measures, the inference arises that person familiarity itself may influence infants' ability to extract meaning from emotional expressions. An ecological approach proposes that an organism responds differently in diverse contexts and changes in response to its own activity in the world. Therefore, we decided to investigate infants' perception of emotional expressions portrayed by familiar people.

In the first experiment examining the effects of person familiarity, Kahana-Kalman and Walker-Andrews (2001) compared 3-month-old infants' ability to detect correspondences between vocal and facial expressions when these were portrayed by their own mothers or an unfamiliar woman. The questions were (1) whether infants detect the correspondences between facial and vocal displays when the infants' mothers display the emotions; and (2) whether infants exhibit different patterns of affective responses across these displays. Infants viewed two videotapes side by side for four 25-second trials. In the familiar condition, infants viewed their own mothers acting out happy and sad expressions. For the unfamiliar condition, infants viewed an unfamiliar female expressing the selected emotions. In addition to looking times, two measures of infants' emotion, including an assessment of overall responsiveness and the outcomes of more specific affect coding, were collected.

Kahana-Kalman and Walker-Andrews (2001) found that, overall, looking preferences were influenced both by familiarity of the actress and the portrayed emotion. Proportions of looking time to the sound-specified facial expression were higher when infants viewed their own mothers. Also, for both groups, infants looked longer at happy facial expressions than sad facial expressions. Separate analyses showed that infants who saw their own mothers looked longer to the happy facial expression when it was sound specified and to the sad facial expression when it was sound specified. In contrast, infants who viewed the same two emotions portrayed by an unfamiliar woman did not demonstrate preferential looking based on the vocal expression they were hearing.   To determine whether infants were matching based on temporal synchrony rather than on affective correspondences, an additional group of infants was tested, but a temporal incongruity between the vocalizations and the facial movements was created by introducing a 5-second delay between maternal vocal and facial displays. Despite the temporal manipulation, infants looked longer at the maternal expressions that were accompanied by an affectively appropriate vocal expression.

With respect to infants' engagement and overall responsiveness, global affect measures showed that infants across groups were rated as experiencing more positive affect and as more interested and engaged when the sound-specified emotion was happy versus sad. More importantly, infants from the groups who observed their own mothers were more positive and more engaged when happy was the sound-specified emotion. The infants who observed the unfamiliar female did not show much variability across emotions, and their affect was less pronounced than that of infants who observed their own mothers.

Three measures gauging the overall quantity of infant facial expressions were compared also. Frame-by-frame analysis of infants' facial behavior yielded the following: (1) facial expression time (percent of the coding interval during which the infant expressed affect other than neutral); (2) number of alternating expressions; and (3) variability of expressions. When happy was the sound-specified emotion, infants expressed affect twice as often, alternated their expressions nearly twice as often, and showed increased variability of expressions relative to when sad was the sound-specified emotion. This overall pattern of results suggests that infants' expressions were both held longer and changed more often when happy was the sound-specified emotion.

Kahana-Kalman and Walker-Andrews (2001) evaluated several measures of smiles and distress also, including (1) total duration of smiling and (2) latency to emergence of the first smile. The findings mirrored the earlier ones using global ratings. When happy was the sound-specified emotion, infants who watched their own mothers spent more time smiling than infants who watched the unfamiliar female. Across groups, infants spent less time smiling when sad was sound specified, but groups did not differ in the duration of smiling in the sad condition. In addition, the shortest latency to the first smile occurred when infants watched their own mothers' synchronous happy expressions. The types of smiles (full, bright, faint) also differed as expected across groups and conditions (familiar, unfamiliar, asynchronous, happy, and sad). Corresponding measures described distress bouts: (1) the proportion of time spent in distress and (2) latency to the first distress bout. Overall, the mean duration of distress was significantly longer for infants who observed the unfamiliar female. Infants also tended to remain more composed (i.e., took longer to become distressed) when happy was the sound-specified emotion.

In summary, both real-time and frame-by-frame coding showed that infants who observed their own mothers expressed more positive affect and less distress, especially when maternal happy expressions were sound specified. Also, smiles directed at mothers were more intense and tended to occur earlier. In contrast, infants who watched the unfamiliar woman showed more distress overall, and they did not show the same increase in positive affect when the happy was sound specified. In addition, infants in this group did not exhibit many full or bright smiles, whereas distress bouts were more frequent. Infants' abilities to detect and respond to the emotion information in faces and voices clearly are affected by the familiarity of the person depicting those emotional expressions, at least for their primary caregiver.

Effect of Context: Familiarity of Parents

In another experiment, Montague and Walker-Andrews (2002) built on these findings to investigate whether infants recognize the emotional expressions of both mothers and fathers, two important and familiar people in their lives. The study used the same preference method, but included two pairs of expressions (happy and sad, happy and angry) for both mothers and fathers. Parents were asked also about their typical interactions to determine whether the amount and kind of interactions that infants have with each of their parents are related to infants' ability to recognize their parents' emotional expressions.

The most robust outcomes were for maternal facial and vocal expressions. When infants viewed maternal happy and sad facial expressions, they looked predominantly at the facial expression accompanied by its characteristic soundtrack. Surprisingly, infants looked longer at the discordant (non-sound-specified) expression when maternal happy and angry expressions were paired. When infants viewed maternal happy and angry facial expressions along with the happy soundtrack, they looked longer at the angry expression. When the expressions were accompanied instead by the angry soundtrack, the infants looked longer at the happy facial expression. For both sets of expressions, looking preferences were significant but, as indicated, preferences were in the opposite direction. Infants gazed longer at the affectively concordant (sound-specified) expression when the pair was happy and sad but the affectively discordant (non-sound-specified) when the pair was happy and angry. Infants did not show any sign of intermodal matching for the paternal or strangers' expressions.

Montague and Walker-Andrews (2002) looked to the parent–infant interaction data to interpret the infants' patterns of intermodal matching. As expected, on average, the amount of time mothers reported spending with their infants was double that reported by fathers (9 vs. 4.5 hours per day). Of more interest was the specific relationship between parent–infant interactions and infants' visual preferences. First, the amount of direct contact between mother and child and the infant's preference for the concordant, sound-specified sad expression were positively correlated. In contrast, the correlation between amount of direct mother–infant interaction and proportion of looking time to the concordant angry expression was negative. This pattern was repeated with information from a child care activity questionnaire: For both mothers and fathers, greater parental involvement in a number of activities was related to the infants' intermodal matching. There were positive correlations with infants' preferences for the sound-specified expression in the happy/sad combination and negative correlations with preferences for the happy/anger pairings. For the small subset of fathers who reported high involvement, infant responses to paternal expressions paralleled those for the maternal expressions. This group of infants demonstrated intermodal matching for the paternal expressions.

Results from these two studies suggest an early sensitivity to expressions, especially when these are experienced as dynamic, multimodal, and familiar events. What is particularly intriguing is that 3-month-old infants detected and responded to the affective correspondences in their own mothers' facial and vocal expressions even when synchrony relations between the face and voice were disrupted (Kahana-Kalman & Walker-Andrews, 2001). They did not demonstrate a comparable ability for the synchronous vocal and facial expressions of an unfamiliar woman. Such a pattern implies that what accounts for infants' ability to detect correspondences between facial and vocal displays is their ability to extract a common meaning from the affective displays portrayed by their own mothers. This explanation builds on and extends proposals with respect to intermodal perception of emotional expressions. Given infants' early ability to detect multimodal relations, we suggest that it is through the detection of intermodal invariants that infants discover the meaning of emotional expressions. Infants initially recognize the affective expressions of others as part of a unified multimodal event that has a unique communicative affordance. Only later do they recognize that affective information in vocal expressions alone or facial expressions alone. In addition, these results underscore how emotion perception and experience develop in interpersonal contexts. Infants observe emotional expressions in interactions with others and abstract the information that specifies the affordances of those emotions for continued interaction and communication.

Generalization of Familiar Expressions

An experiment using another method to examine infants' perception of the expressions of familiar persons also suggests that infants detect the meaning of expressions in dynamic, multimodal, and familiar contexts. This experiment (Walker-Andrews, Krogh-Jespersen, Mayhew, & Coffield, 2011) used a visual habituation procedure to investigate infants' understanding of emotional expressions. Others also have used this method to examine infants' generalization of emotional expressions, finding good evidence of such generalization by about 7 months when infants recognize emotion rather than only responding to feature differences (Caron et al., 1988; but see Widen & Russell, 2008). In this procedure, infants view a number of instances from a single category until they exhibit visual habituation, as indexed by a decline in looking time. Immediately following the habituation sequence, they are shown a novel instance from the familiar category and/or an instance from the novel category. Increases in looking time are interpreted as evidence that infants discriminate items based on membership in the selected categories.

In this experiment, we examined whether infants could categorize emotional expressions of familiar persons. We videotaped infants' own mothers and fathers acting out happy and sad facial/vocal expressions and then used these emotion events as the stimulus materials in the parental expressions condition. In the stranger expressions condition, another group of infants viewed the same emotion videotapes, but in this case the videotapes were of strangers. That is, each infant was "matched" to an infant who viewed his or her parents' expressions, so that every mother–father pair served as an unfamiliar man and woman to the second group of same-age infants. Infants were assigned to one of four groups across conditions that followed the habituation sequence of alternating expressions: group 1 (control) continued to see the same female (mother or female stranger, depending on condition) acting out the familiar expression; group 2 continued to see the same female, but she portrayed a novel expression (expression-only change); group 3 saw a novel female acting out the familiar expressions (person-only change); and group 4 saw a female stranger depicting the novel expression (both person and expression change). The question was whether infants would generalize the expressions across the persons (mom and dad or female and male stranger) and discriminate them from a new expression no matter who posed it. A between-subjects experimental design was used, rather than within subjects, because infants show especially strong preferences for some emotional expressions, and increases in looking times are often quite substantial and show order effects based on the emotional expression presented during the habituation phase (e.g., Caron et al., 1988; Walker & Grolnick, 1983).

As expected, overall looking time was quite high. On average, infants looked at the parental expressions for approximately 6½ minutes and at strangers' expressions for 4½ minutes before reducing their looking to the habituation criterion. Comparisons between looking time increases revealed that infants in the parental expressions condition who were presented a change in person, expression, or both increased their looking time relative to the control group. The change groups did not differ from one another. That is, infants who viewed parental happy expressions during the habituation sequence failed to increase their looking time when their mother continued to model the (now familiar) happy expression. Infants showed an increase in looking time when (1) their mother modeled a sad expression, (2) when the unfamiliar female modeled the happy expression, and (3) when the unfamiliar female modeled a sad expression. For all three change groups, increases in looking time averaged about 15 seconds. Infants in the parental expressions condition who viewed sad expressions during the habituation sequence showed similar, but much greater increases in looking time. Infants who continued to view their mother depicting a sad expression failed to increase their looking time. Those who viewed their mother depicting a novel happy expression, an unfamiliar female depicting the familiarized sad expression, or an unfamiliar female depicting a novel happy expression all showed sharp increases in looking time (mean increases of more than 1 minute). Infants who participated in the stranger expressions condition did not increase their looking time to any of the changes in person or expression.

In summary, infants who viewed parental expressions during habituation discriminated the facial and vocal expressions presented to them. They increased their looking time to a change in expression, a change in person, and a change in person and expression. They did not show significant increases in looking time in the control conditions in which their mothers continued to show the habituated expressions. Infants did not uniformly ignore changes in person while increasing their visual attention to changes in expression only or to changes in both person and expression. However, infants treated the change in expression from happy to sad differently from the change from sad to happy, and they responded especially strongly to a change in person after they viewed parental depictions of sadness during the habituation sequence. Perhaps the infants found the parental expressions of sadness aversive, which might influence their visual attention. Support for this conjecture comes from Agnihotri (2003) and Cassano (2003). They each examined infants' affective responses to their parents' expressions, finding that infants smiled more to maternal happy expressions, showed more negative affect to their mothers' sad expressions, and showed more positive affect and visual attention to maternal happy expressions as a function of overall intensity of those happy expressions. Overall, these results suggest that infants' perception of emotional expressions is strongly influenced by context: Infants categorized the happy and sad expressions of their own parents, but failed to discriminate the expressions of other infants' parents (because the adult actors were unknown to them).

Perception of Speech during Early Infancy

The voluminous literature on the development of the perception of speech underscores the thesis that infants' perception rests on dynamic, multimodal information encountered in context. Clearly, the audible and visible attributes of a talking person contribute to the perception of speech by adults and infants. Adults, for example, benefit from seeing the lip movements of a speaker especially in a noisy environment. Infants, too, code faces and speech as intermodal objects of perception early on (Meltzoff & Kuhl, 1994; Rosenblum, 2010). Brain regions once thought to be sensitive only to the sounds of speech have been found to be responsive to visual speech information as well (e.g., Calvert et al., 1997). As indicated by the classic McGurk effect (McGurk & MacDonald, 1976), visual and auditory speech information is integrated automatically. Specifically, when an auditory utterance is paired with a face conveying a different utterance, perceivers report hearing something influenced by the mismatched visual component. Synchronizing a video of a face saying /ga/ with an auditory /ba/ results in reports of a "heard" /da/. Sometimes the visual information will dominate the auditory information; other times the components will be fused so that the perceiver reports something in between. Infants, too, experience the McGurk effect (Burnham, 1998; Rosenblum, Schmuckler, & Johnson, 1997).

Gogate, Walker-Andrews, and Bahrick (2001) reviewed studies that underscore the importance of such intermodal influences in language acquisition. Gogate and Bahrick (1998) reported that infants as young as 7 months could learn the arbitrary relations between a spoken vowel and a moving object when the timing of the vocalizations coincided with that of the object's motions. Contextual information also plays a strong role. When they talk to young language learners, caregivers emphasize particular words in the speech stream through the use of exaggerated prosody, such as stress and pitch variation, abbreviated sentences, and placement of specific words. When they talk about objects, caregivers point to them or touch them. It is the co-action of these two systems (caregiver and infant) that contribute to the infants' impressive word-learning abilities (Gros-Louis, West, Goldstein, & King, 2006; Zukow-Goldring, 1997). Recent theories of language development (e.g., McCune, 2008) emphasize that linguistic skills are acquired in a sociocultural context.

Research on infants' acquisition of a language via statistical learning also demonstrates infants' reliance on structured information in the environment. Saffran, Aslin, and Newport (1996) found that 8-month-olds exposed to an artificial language containing no cues to word boundaries other than transitional probabilities between syllables demonstrated an ability to detect these probabilities and use them to recognize which configurations were actual "words" in the artificial language. With only 2 minutes of exposure, infants capitalized on the statistical probabilities modeled in the speech input, using "experience-dependent mechanisms to extract information from the environment" (p. 1926).

Learning and Perceiving in Context

Although selective, this review of studies that examined infants' perception of objects, events, and persons across the first year of life demonstrates the importance of rich, multimodal displays for obtaining information about infants' developing abilities to perceive and know the world. The experimental data, coupled with neurophysiological evidence, supports the hypothesis that the brain is configured for multimodal processing (e.g., Calvert, 2001; Foxe & Schroeder, 2005). Results of experiments that examine infants' perception of speech emphasizes the importance of multimodal information and the effects of context as well. What has not been described as fully is infants' experience of emotion, although the reactions of infants to facial and vocal expressions (e.g., Kahana-Kalman & Walker-Andrews, 2001) suggests affective attunement (Stern, 1985) with the expressions of others, especially those of familiar persons. It is in this arena that speculation about infants' experience of emotion and recognition of the self seems most suitable. As an infant observes a parent expressing joy by smiling, laughing, and tickling, the infant responds with an engaging smile, pumping arms, and vocalizations. These responses are

> coordinated, multimodal actions involving vocalizations, gaze, facial expressions, body movement, and gestures, which relay information to the other, as well as to the infants themselves . . . about internal states. . . . The interaction of baby and other provides multimodal, time-locked correlations that provide information about the appearance, actions, and internal states of the self and others. (Walker-Andrews, 2008, p. 372)

A major thesis of this chapter is that infants discover the self through active interaction with the physical and interpersonal world. Infants continually act on the environment to create interesting events that reveal much about the relationship of the infant to the world and objects and events to one another. The infant detects and acts on the affordances of the environment as specified by dynamic and intermodal properties. Studies of infants' perception of emotional expressions, in particular, provide an instructive vantage point from which to examine infants' developing abilities to detect structure and meaning in the world. Emotional expressions are part of a system of communication that functions as a guide to action. Expressions are not only signs of emotion but social signals that provide information about an individual's likely actions and, consequently, steer one's own behaviors. As anticipated, infants are most sensitive to the emotional expressions provided in dynamic, multimodal contexts, in familiar situations, and by significant others with whom the infant has established patterns of actions. Intentions are discovered first in intense, frequent, and organized interactions such as those encountered with caregivers. Caregivers respond sensitively and contingently to an infant's active overtures, creating a dynamic and self-organizing communication system. Young infants experience an organization in the social world via these early imitative exchanges and via the dialogue (or interlocution; Walker-Andrews, 2009) of "vitality affects" (Stern, 1985) that the partners share. The interplay between infant and another person is characterized by dynamic and reciprocal interaction between intermodal perception, selective attention, and learning by infants, coupled with the specific structure marking intentional communication, including language. As the infant participates in the interaction, the sense of self is reaffirmed with a cascade of information underscoring the infant's role as observer, agent, and participant in the world.

Note

1. Later research (e.g., Muir & Hains, 1993) supported Watson and colleagues. Muir and Hains (1993) reported that infants ranging in age between 3 and 6 months looked equally at upright and inverted faces, but rarely smiled at inverted faces of their mothers.

References

Agnihotri, V. (2003). *Infants' emotional reaction to viewing varying intensities of their parents' happy and sad expressions.* Unpublished thesis, Rutgers University.

Bahrick, L. E., Gogate, L. J., & Ruiz, W. E. (2002). Attention and memory for faces and actions in infancy: The salience of actions over faces in dynamic events. *Child Development, 73,* 1629–1643.

Bahrick, L. E., & Lickliter, R. (2002). Intersensory redundancy guides early perceptual and cognitive development. In R. V. Kail (Ed.), *Advances in child development and behavior* (Vol. 30, pp. 153–187). San Diego, CA: Academic Press.

Bahrick, L. E., Walker, A. S., & Neisser, U. (1981). Selective looking by infants. *Cognitive Psychology, 13,* 377–390.

Bahrick, L. E., & Watson, J. S. (1985). Detection of intermodal proprioceptive-visual contingency as a potential basis of self-perception in infancy. *Developmental Psychology, 21,* 963–973.

Brookes, H., Slater, A., Quinn, P. C., Lewkowicz, D. J., Hayes, R., & Brown, E. (2001). Three-month-old infants learn arbitrary auditory-visual pairings between voices and faces. *Infant and Child Development, 10,* 75–82.

Brunswik, E. (1952). *The conceptual framework of psychology.* Chicago: University of Chicago Press.

Bryant, P. E., Jones, P., Claxton, B., & Perkins, G. M. (1972). Recognition of shapes across modalities by infants. *Nature, 240,* 303–304.

Burnham, D. (1998). Language specificity in the development of auditory-visual speech perception. In R. Campbell, B. Dodd, & D. Burnham (Eds.), *Hearing by eye: II. Advances in the psychology of speechreading and auditory-visual speech* (pp. 27–60). Hove, UK: Psychology Press/Erbaum.

Calvert, G. A. (2001). Crossmodal processing in the human brain: Insights from functional neuroimaging studies. *Cerebral Cortex, 11,* 1110–1123.

Calvert, G. A., Bullmore, E., Brammer, M. J., Campbell, R., Iversen, S. D., & Woodruff, P. (1997). Silent lipreading activates the auditory cortex. *Science, 276,* 593–596.

Caron, A. J., Caron, R. F., & MacLean, D. J. (1988). Infant discrimination of naturalistic emotional expressions: The role of face and voice. *Child Development, 59,* 604–616.

Caron, A. J., Caron, R. F., & Myers, R. S. (1985). Do infants see emotion expressions in static faces? *Child Development, 56,* 1552–1560.

Cassano, K. A. (2003). *Infants' emotional reaction to viewing their parents happy or sad.* Unpublished thesis, Rutgers University.

Cohen, L. B., & Oakes, L. M. (1993). How infants perceive a simple causal event. *Developmental Psychology, 29,* 421–433.

de Gelder, B., Vrommen, J., & Pourtois, G. (1999). Seeing cries and hearing smiles: Crossmodal perception of emotional expressions. In G. Aschersleben & T. Bachmann (Eds.), *Cognitive contributions to the perception of spatial and temporal events: Advances in psychology* (pp. 425–438). Amsterdam: North-Holland.

Field, T. M., Woodson, R., Greenberg, R., & Cohen, D. (1982). Discrimination and imitation of facial expressions by neonates. *Science, 218,* 179–181.

Flom, R., & Bahrick, L. E. (2007). The development of infant discrimination of affect in multimodal and unimodal stimulation: The role of intersensory redundancy. *Developmental Psychology, 43,* 238–252.

Foxe, J. J., & Schroeder, C. E. (2005). The case for feedforward multisensory convergence during early cortical processing. *NeuroReport, 16,* 419–423.

Garvey, A., & Fogel, A. (2008). Emotions and communication as a dynamic developmental system. *Espaciotiempo, 2,* 62–73.

Gibson, E. J. (1969). *Principles of perceptual learning and development.* Englewood Cliffs, NJ: Prentice Hall.

Gibson, E. J. (1997). An ecological psychologist's prolegomena for perceptual development: A functional approach. In C. Dent-Read & P. Zukow-Goldring (Eds.), *Evolving explanations of development* (pp. 23–54). Washington, DC: American Psychological Association.

Gibson, E. J., Owsley, C. J., Walker, A. S., & Megaw-Nyce, J. (1979). Development of the perception of invariants: Substance and shape. *Perception, 8,* 609–619.

Gibson, E. J., & Walker, A. S. (1984). Development of knowledge of visual-tactual affordances of substance. *Child Development, 55,* 453–460.

Gogate, L. J., & Bahrick, L. E. (1998). Intersensory redundancy and 7-month-old infants' memory for arbitrary syllable-object relations. *Infancy, 2,* 219–231.

Gogate, L. J., Walker-Andrews, A. S., & Bahrick, E. (2001). The intersensory origins of word comprehension: An ecological-dynamic systems view. *Developmental Science, 4,* 1–37.

Gros-Louis, J., West, M. J., Goldstein, M. H., & King, A. P. (2006). Mothers provide differential feedback to infants' prelinguistic sounds. *International Journal of Behavioral Development, 30,* 509–516.

Grossman, T., Striano, T., & Friederici, A. D. (2006). Crossmodal integration of emotional information from face and voice in the infant brain. *Developmental Science, 9,* 309–315.

Haviland, J. M., & Lelwica, M. (1987). The induced affect response: 10-week-old infants' responses to three emotion expressions. *Developmental Psychology, 23,* 97–104.

James, W. (1983). *The principles of psychology.* Cambridge, MA: Harvard University Press. (Original work published 1890)

Kahana-Kalman, R., & Walker-Andrews, A. S. (2001). The role of person familiarity in young infants' perception of emotion expressions. *Child Development, 72,* 352–369.

Kellman, P. J., & Spelke, E. S. (1983). Perception of partly occluded objects in infancy. *Cognitive Psychology, 15,* 482–524.

King, A. J., Hutchings, M. E., Moore, D. R., & Blakemore, C. (1988). Developmental plasticity in the visual and auditory representation in the mammalian superior colliculus. *Nature, 332,* 73–76.

Kugiumutzakis, G. (1993). Intersubjective vocal imitation in early mother–infant interaction. In J. Nadel & L. Camaioni (Eds.), *New perspectives in early communicative development* (pp. 23–47). Cambridge, UK: Cambridge University Press.

Lavelli, M., & Fogel, A. (2005). Developmental changes in the relationship between the infants' attention and emotion during early face-to-face communication: The 2-month transition. *Developmental Psychology, 41,* 265–280.

Leslie, A. M., & Keeble, S. (1987). Do six-month-old infants perceive causality? *Cognition, 25,* 265–288.

Lewkowicz, D. J. (2001). Heterogeneity and heterochrony in the development of intersensory perception. *Cognitive Brain Research, 14,* 41–63.

Malatesta, C. Z., & Haviland, J. M. (1982). Learning display rules: The socialization of emotion expression in infancy. *Child Development, 53,* 991–1003.

McCune, L. (2008). *How children learn to learn language.* New York: Oxford University Press.

McGurk, H., & MacDonald, J. W. (1976). Hearing lips and seeing voices. *Nature, 264,* 746–748.

Meltzoff, A N., & Borton, R. W. (1979). Intermodal matching by human neonates. *Nature, 282,* 403–404.

Meltzoff, A. N., & Kuhl, P. K. (1994). Faces and speech: Intermodal processing of biologically relevant signals in infants and adults. In D. J. Lewkowicz & R. Lickliter (Eds.), *Development of intersensory perception: Comparative perspectives* (pp. 335–369). Hillsdale, NJ: Erlbaum.

Montague, D. P. F., & Walker-Andrews, A. S. (2001). Peekaboo: A new look at infants' perception of emotion expressions. *Developmental Psychology, 37,* 826–838.

Montague, D. P. F., & Walker-Andrews, A. S. (2002). Mothers, fathers, and infants: The role of familiarity and parental involvement in infants' perception of emotion expressions. *Child Development, 73,* 1339–1352.

Muir, D.W., & Hains, S.M. (1993). Infant sensitivity to perturbations in adult facial, vocal, tactile, and contingent stimulation during face-to-face interactions. In B. Boysson-Bardies, S. de Schonen, P. Jusczyk, P. McNeilage, & J. Morton (Eds.), *Developmental Neurocognition: Speech and face processing in the first year of life* (pp. 171–185). Dordrecht, The Netherlands: Kluwer Academic/Plenum.

Nelson, C. A. (1987). The recognition of facial expressions in the first 2 years of life: Mechanisms of development. *Child Development, 58,* 889–909.

Nelson, C. A., & de Haan, M. (1996). Neural correlates of infants' visual responsiveness to facial expressions of emotion. *Developmental Psychobiology, 29,* 577–595.

Otsuka, Y., Konishi, Y., Kanazawa, S., Yamaguchi, J. K., Abdi, H., & O'Toole, A. J. (2009). Recognition of moving and static faces by young infants. *Child Development, 80,* 1259–1271.

Peltola, M. J., Leppanen, J. M., Palokangas, T., & Hietanen, J. K. (2008). Fearful faces modulate looking duration and attention disengagement in 7-month-old infants. *Developmental Science, 11,* 60–68.

Rochat, P. (2003). Five levels of self-awareness as they unfold early in life. *Consciousness and Cognition, 12,* 717–731.

Rochat, P., & Hespos, S. J. (1997). Differential rooting response by neonates: Evidence for an early sense of self. *Early Development and Parenting, 6,* 105–112.

Roe, A. W., Pallas, S. L., Hahm, J. O., & Sur, M. (1990). A map of visual space induced in primary auditory cortex. *Science, 150,* 818–820.

Rosenblum, L. D. (2010). Speech perception as a multimodal phenomenon. *Current Directions in Psychological Science, 17,* 405–409.

Rosenblum, L. D., Schmuckler, M. A., & Johnson, J. A. (1997). The McGurk effect in infants. *Perception and Psychophysics, 59,* 347–357.

Saffran, J. R., Aslin, R. N., & Newport, E. L. (1996). Statistical learning by 8-month-old infants. *Science, 274,* 1926–1928.

Smith, L. B. (2005). Cognition as a dynamic system: Principles from embodiment. *Developmental Review, 25,* 278–298.

Soken, N. H., & Pick, A. D. (1992). Intermodal perception of happy and angry expressive behaviors by seven-month-old infants. *Child Development, 63,* 787–793.

Soken, N. H., & Pick, A. D. (1999). Infants' perception of dynamic affective expressions: Do infants distinguish specific expressions? *Child Development, 70,* 1275–1282.

Stein, B. E., & Meredith, M. A. (1993). *The merging of the senses.* Cambridge, MA: MIT Press.

Stern, D. N. (1985). *The interpersonal world of the infant.* New York: Basic Books.

Vlamings, P. H., Jonkman, L. M., & Kemner, C. (2010). An eye for detail: An event-related potential study of the rapid processing of fearful facial expressions in children. *Child Development, 81,* 1304–1319.

Walker, A. S. (1982). Intermodal perception of expressive behaviors by human infants. *Journal of Experimental Child Psychology, 33,* 514–535.

Walker, A. S., Gibson, E. J., Owsley, C. J., Megaw-Nyce, J., & Bahrick, L. E. (1980). Detection of elasticity as an invariant property of objects by young infants. *Perception, 9,* 713–718.

Walker, A. S., & Grolnick, W. (1983). Discrimination of vocal expressions by young infants. *Infant Behavior and Development, 6,* 491–498.

Walker-Andrews, A. S. (1986). Intermodal perception of expressive behaviors: Relation of eye and voice? *Developmental Psychology, 22,* 373–377.

Walker-Andrews, A. S. (1992). A developing sense of self. Commentary on G. Butterworth, Origins of self perception in infancy. *Psychological Inquiry, 3,* 131–133.

Walker-Andrews, A. S. (2008). Intermodal emotional processes in infancy. In M. Lewis, J. M. Haviland-Jones, & L. Feldman Barrett (Eds.), *Handbook of emotions* (3rd ed., pp. 364–375). New York: Guilford Press.

Walker-Andrews, A. S. (2009, May). *Development of communication in a social/emotional context.* Paper presented at the Interlocution Workshop, University of British Columbia, Vancouver.

Walker-Andrews, A. S., Bahrick, L. E., Raglioni, S. S., & Diaz, I. (1991). Infants' bimodal perception of gender. *Ecological Psychology, 3,* 55–75.

Walker-Andrews, A. S., & Lennon, E. M. (1985). Auditory-visual perception of changing distance by human infants. *Child Development, 56,* 544–548.

Walker-Andrews, A. S., & Gibson, E. J. (1986). What develops in bimodal perception? In L. P. Lipsitt & C. K. Rovee-Collier (Eds.), *Advances in infancy research* (Vol. 4, pp. 171–181). Norwood, NJ: Ablex.

Walker-Andrews, A. S., Krogh-Jespersen, S., Mayhew, E., & Coffield, C. (2011). Young infants' generalization of emotional expressions: Effects of familiarity. *Emotion, 11,* 842–851.

Watson, J. S., Hayes, L. A., Vietze, P., & Becker, J (1979). Discriminative infant smiling to orientations of talking faces of mother and stranger. *Journal of Experimental Child Psychology, 26,* 92–99.

Widen, S. C., & Russell, J. A. (2008). Young children's understanding of others' emotions. In M. Lewis, J. M. Haviland-Jones, & L. Feldman Barrett (Eds.), *Handbook of emotion* (3rd ed., pp. 348–363). New York: Guilford Press.

Zukow-Goldring, P. (1997). A social ecological realist approach to the emergence of the lexicon: Educating attention to amodal invariants in gesture and speech. In C. Dent-Read & P. Zukow-Goldring (Eds.), *Evolving explanations of development* (pp. 199–250). Washington, DC: American Psychological Association.

PART IV

The Role of Early Experience on Social Development

CHAPTER 10

The Developing Social Brain

Social Connections and Social Bonds, Social Loss,
and Jealousy in Infancy

MARIA LEGERSTEE

On social connections:

Before language takes over as the instrument of interaction one cannot
interact humanly with others without some proto-linguistic "theory of mind."
—JEROME BRUNER (1990, p. 75)

On social rejections:

According to an old Russian proverb, "jealousy and love are sisters." This
seems to suggest that both come from the same brain regions and because
love exists early in life, so might jealousy.

Over the last century, the psychology of infancy has become a major subject of study
and has answered many questions about infants' developing ability for social cognition. Social cognition is about understanding people. Although people are like objects
in that they have various physical characteristics (e.g., size and shape), they are different because only people communicate and have feelings and intentions (Gelman &
Spelke, 1981; Legerstee, Anderson, & Schaffer, 1998; Legerstee, Corter, & Kienapple,
1990; Legerstee & Markova, 2007; for reviews, see Legerstee, 1992, 2005). Thus,
whereas physical events can be specified because they present stable and predictable
reactions, social events are subtle as well as unpredictable. That is because, unlike
objects, people have minds and experiences that are not easily accessible.

Developmental research on representing the minds of people has found that
by 4 years of age, most children are aware that people have minds and that their
beliefs may be different from their own (Wellman & Lui, 2004). However, the way
preverbal children represent people's minds remains enigmatic (see Sabbagh et al.,
Chapter 13, this volume). Various scientists and philosophers have proposed that
the infant is born with a tabula rasa, and as a consequence their impression of the
world is a "great blooming, buzzing confusion" (James, 1890, p. 462; Piaget, 1954).

Accordingly, before infants develop a realistic view of the world and the people in it, they have to learn to distinguish between the mental and the physical through a lengthy domain-general process. Thus for the first 2 years, people are known behaviorally rather than psychologically. It is not until the end of the sensorimotor period (second year of life) that infants' actions turn into thoughts and that children become aware of other minds.

In contrast, others postulate that infants are born with a "social brain," containing domain-specific abilities that allow them to connect with the social world from the start. Theorists interested in domain specificity support either a neuroconstructivist view (Karmiloff-Smith, 1992, in press; Legerstee, 2005, 2009) or a nativist orientation. Nativists propose a kind of genetic predeterminism, arguing that infants are born with modules or neural mechanisms (Baron-Cohen, 1991) that mature at different developmental times as a function of neural maturation. According to Karmiloff-Smith (1992, p. 6), one should not confuse modules with domains. A domain consists of specific areas of knowledge (e.g., linguistics, physics), "but a module is an information processing unit that houses this knowledge as well as the computations on it."

Empirical evidence has shown that the mind and its intellectual processes have a large range of reaction to environmental input. This suggests that the ontogeny of the structure of the mind and its resulting products are much more variable than the modular position suggests. Modules are rigid and less plastic; as a consequence, modules provide the infants with more information at the onset but are less amenable to change. Thus, rather than proposing that infants are born with a module to perceive mental states in others, the neuroconstructivists propose that infants have domain-specific predispositions that direct them to the necessary social input. Subsequent development is a function of an interaction between this prespecification and plasticity for learning. Thus, for neuroconstructivists, nature (nativism) or nurture (domain-general development) is clearly a false dichotomy because "genes, brain, and environment play a dynamic, multidirectional role in shaping, not merely triggering, developmental outcomes" (Karmiloff-Smith, 2009, p. 60). For example, if one adopts a neuroconstructivist view rather than a domain-general or nativist position, then one should expect infants to be predisposed to perceive mental states of people and changes in the complexity of this awareness with development. Accordingly, neuroconstructivists propose that newborns are preadapted to the early structure of communication, and argue that initially intersubjective sharing can be observed during dyadic interactions between caregiver and infant (Bruner, 1999; Fogel, 1993; Legerstee, 2009; Stern, 1985; Trevarthen & Delafield-Butt, Chapter 8, this volume; Tronick, 1981) and subsequently during triadic interactions, which extends the communicative context to a third party or object (Legerstee, Markova, & Fisher, 2007). During the dyadic communication period (0–3 months), infants connect with the social world, share emotions, and bond with others. They also show anxiety about being separated from their loved ones. During the triadic communication period (3–5 months), infants begin to share interesting aspects of the environment with people, but also develop a fear of losing a loved one to a rival (jealousy). Because both dyadic and triadic abilities imply mentalist construals, there is a connection between prelinguistic dyadic communication during the first months of life and more complex triadic communication during the subsequent months. Bruner (1999) argues that the progression from primary to secondary intersubjectivity is facilitated through "narrative scaffolding" where caretakers treat infants as if "they have things in mind." Legerstee and colleagues (2007) supported this hypothesis by showing that mothers who were emotionally attuned to their infant's actions had infants who engaged in longer eye contact during dyadic communication and progressed sooner to triadic communication than infants of low-attuned mothers.

Until now, the investigation of infant core abilities as revealed during dyadic and triadic communication, their relation to later sociocognitive abilities, as well as the role the environment plays in this relation has relied on clever experimentation and the collection of behavioral data. As the result of methodological and technological advances and the merging with developmental social-cognitive neuroscience, new light has been shed on important aspects of the infant brain. As a consequence, the behavioral data of social-cognitive phenomena are being clarified by their neural foundations, thereby revealing the roles that various neural structures, genes, and neurotransmitter systems play in social cognition. For instance, cognitive neuroscience has shown that in adults "cortical regions in the temporal lobe participate in perceiving socially relevant stimuli, whereas the amygdala, right somatosensory cortices, orbitofrontal cortices, and cingulate cortices all participate in linking perception of such stimuli to motivation, emotion, and cognition" (Adolphs, 2001, p. 231). Developmental social neuroscience has similarly revealed a biological basis for the perception of social stimuli in infants, such as face and eye gaze processing, perception of emotion, biological motion, but also infant mental states such as attention and intention (for a review, see de Haan & Gunnar, 2009; Grossman & Johnson, 2007; Mundy, Chapter 14, this volume). In addition, factors that promote the perception and conception of social stimuli, such as temporally matched interactions between mothers and infants, are underpinned by biological rhythms (see Feldman, 2007, for a review). Thus, recent works support the idea that infants have a social brain that provides the biological basis for social interaction.

Methodological Considerations

Although there is increasing biological evidence for infants' sensitivity to social stimuli, as discussed earlier, questions remain about the domain specificity of social cognition (emotions and thought) and the role the environment plays in development. According to de Haan and Gunnar (2009, p. 5), "Although a reasonable amount is known about the function of this network in adults, very little is known about its *development* and how it supports the progressive emergence of complex social abilities." As a result, mature or complex social processes are best analyzed by focusing on their precursors or *subcomponents*. For example, Legerstee, Ellenbogen, Nienhuis, and Marsh (2010) recently examined the development of jealousy in infants during the first half year of life. Jealousy is defined as an aversive reaction that results from the fear of losing a loved one to a third party, a rival. In adults, jealousy is a complex emotion, and the way it is expressed varies depending the context. That is, jealousy may conjure up emotions such as sadness (loss), anger (betrayal), and fear/anxiety (loneliness). In addition, the intensity of the feeling may be linked to subcortical emotional networks, and variations in human jealousy may further be a function of different cognitive capacities and environmental situations (see Markova, Stieben, & Legerstee, 2010). Consequently, the accompanying coherent infrastructures in the brain vary in adults, and thus mapping jealousy onto a specific region is difficult (Panksepp, 2010). As a result, speculations about the nature of jealousy in adults are primarily drawn from secondary sources. For instance, neurochemicals that reduce the impact of jealousy (because they reduce the painful feelings of being excluded) may be found among those that strengthen social bonds such as endogenous opioids (endorphins—substances in the brain that attach to the same cell receptors as morphine) and the pituitary hormone oxytocin, which regulates separation distress in animals, as well as those chemicals that reduce anxiety/fear (cf. Panksepp, 2010), an emotion commonly associated with the feelings of jealousy.

Given the complexity of the mature social emotion of jealousy, Legerstee and colleagues (2010) have focused on subcomponents of jealousy that people and infants have in common, such as the existence of a social bond and the fear of losing this bond to a rival (social exclusion). The most important relationship that develops soon after birth is with the caregiver (Ainsworth, Blehar, Waters, & Wall, 1978; Bowlby, 1980). Consequently, it is plausible that infants are born with an innate desire to develop a social bond, and jealousy could be seen as a reaction to the presence of one who threatens this social bond (Fivaz-Depeursinge, Favez, Scaiola, & Lopes, 2010; Hart & Legerstee, 2010; Legerstee et al., 2010; Panksepp, 2010). If so, then jealousy is not purely a creation of human culture, but goes back into deeper ancestral regions of brain and mind, and hence behavioral reactions of jealousy in infants should have neurological underpinnings (Panksepp, 2010). Thus, the ability to experience jealousy likely develops early in infancy and might even vary as a function of the quality of the social bond infants have with their caregivers. This social learning is unlikely to start from nothing.

Nevertheless, there are debates whether the social emotion of jealousy might present itself in infants (see Hart & Legerstee, 2010). Domain-general theorists argue that to experience jealousy the child must have attained a certain level of cognition, which is not present during the first year of life, such as the ability to differentiate self and other (consciousness) and the ability to perceive triadic relationships (Lewis, 2010; Piaget, 1954). In order to decide the issue, an examination of the development of the behavioral and biological core processes that enable infants to experience jealousy is necessary, since it would show how these subcomponents coalesce and relate to mature complex social processes later on.

Sociocognition and Jealousy

The aim of this chapter is to address the existence of a social brain in infants by examining the behavioral and neurophysiological correlates of jealousy in 3- and 6-month-old infants. If, as earlier defined, jealousy is the fear of losing a loved one to a third party—a rival—then we need to show that they have the sociocognitive prerequisites to apprehend such triadic situations. What might this be? First, infants would need to recognize social stimuli and differentiate them from nonsocial stimuli. In addition, because jealousy-evoking situations rely on the perceived separation from a loved one, infants need to have established a social bond. The social bond is the primary relationship within the interpersonal system of jealousy. In order to experience jealousy, infants have to be aware of the secondary relationship (the one between their caregiver and the rival). Thus, infants need to have developed an understanding of triadic relationships (the self, the beloved, and the rival). Finally, infants need to understand why they are excluded (the goals underlying people's actions).

Through examining these intersubjective transactions, it should be possible to establish whether infants have a "social brain," in which case infants should be able to experience jealousy within the first months of life, or a tabula rasa, in which case the neonate would have to learn everything about people. In the next paragraphs, I document that infants have various sociocognitive abilities during the first months of life. "Such sophistications indicate that implicit social understandings exist long before children acquire language, and long before they are capable of theorizing that others might have different wants and false beliefs about the state of the world" (Rochat, 2010, p. 2). Before turning to the empirical evidence, it is important to examine the hypotheses about the social brain put forth by recent theoretical frameworks.

The Biological Basis of Social Interaction

Dunbar (Chapter 1, this volume) argues that the biological basis of social interaction is a result of the evolution of bondedness, which is the formation of a close emotional tie between primates, such as the establishment of a relationship between mother and child, but in particular between various members of a social group. That is because whereas the hardware of the brain might be better predicted by parental care and bonding, mental state awareness is better predicted by interactions with our complex and dynamic social world later in life, where interactions involve deceptions as well as perspective taking.

Thus, Dunbar does not believe that the specific abilities that make up the social brain are hard-wired or modular. Instead, he argues that maintaining social relationships demands flexible social-cognitive abilities because the social environment is complex and, in order to be successful in the social world, primates need to adjust and conform to others. To do that, they need to become competent in readings others' minds. As a result of this mentalizing, human primates have developed a social brain with a neocortex, which accounts for 50–80% of total brain volume. Interestingly, the important brain regions are the frontal lobe regions because they are primarily implicated in sociality and thus in the amount of people we regularly interact with (group size). Although individual differences in social cognition may have a genetic basis, social interaction plays an important role in species that have large neocortices.

In addition to having a large neocortex, Gallese and colleagues propose that the social brain has a mirror neuron system, which underpins intersubjectivity and social cognition (Gallese, 2009). These neurons, observed in regions corresponding to inferior frontal cortex and inferior parietal cortex in macaque monkeys (Gallese & Rochat, Chapter 2, this volume; Rizzolatti, Fadiga, Gallese, & Fogassi, 1996), fire when a specific action is executed (e.g., breaking a nut) but also perceived. Similar processes are hypothesized to take place when human infants reproduce facial gestures, such as proprioceptive behaviors (i.e., mouth openings and tongue protrusions)

(Legerstee, 1991; Meltzoff & Moore, 1992). "Thus, it is proposed that a common underlying functional mechanism mediates our capacity to share the meaning of actions, intentions, feelings, and emotions with others, thus grounding our identification with and connectedness to others" (Gallese, 2009, p. 520). Although some argue that the existence of mirror neurons has not been fully empirically validated (e.g., Lieberman, 2007), there are strong suggestions that mirror neurons play an important role in intersubjectivity in infancy (Gallagher, Chapter 3, this volume) and nonverbal communication such as gestures, facial expressions, posture, and goals (DePaulo, 1992; Lieberman, 2007, p. 271). For instance, when we observe others crying, areas in the brain associated with these feelings become activated. Such empathic sharing can be elicited in very young infants (Hoffman, 1975). Thus, mirror neurons do more than automatically reproduce surface actions. That is because when two agents socially interact with one another, the activation of mirror networks creates shared representations (i.e., representations simultaneously activated in the brains of two agents; Gallese & Rochat, Chapter 2, this volume). These shared representations allow people to understand not only *what* others are doing but also *why*, thereby revealing an awareness of their intentional state.

In a functional magnetic resonance imaging (fMRI) study, Iacoboni and colleagues (2005) demonstrated that human mirror areas respond differentially to the observation of the same grasping actions, if the actions are embedded in different contexts, which suggests different motor intentions associated with the grasping actions such as drinking or cleaning up. This finding supports data of an imitation study in which infants between 5 and 8 weeks of age, when presented with mouth openings and tongue protrusions, imitated the gestures presented by a person but not when the same actions were presented by inanimate objects (Legerstee, 1991). Similarly, in another imitation study, 10-month-olds imitated the actions of people when they successfully put a ball in a bowl. If the adult was unsuccessful, the infants *completed* the intended goal of the adult (i.e., put the object in the bowl). However, infants did not complete the unsuccessful actions of inanimate objects (Legerstee & Markova, 2008). Thus, mirror neurons encode not only movements but also the meaning behind them.

In overview, theoretical accounts as well as empirical findings favor a biological basis for our social behaviors and their evolution. However, if indeed human infants have a biological basis for social behavior in general, and for jealousy in particular, then they should possess certain prerequisites that promote their recognition of and subsequent interaction with conspecifics.

Recognizing Conspecifics: Behavioral and Neurological Correlates

Research shows that neonates discriminate between faces of their mother and a stranger while potential olfactory cues are masked (Bushnell, Sai, & Mullin, et al., 1989). Infants also begin to recognize their own faces and voices as familiar social stimuli, discriminate them from inanimate objects and sounds, and become better at it between 5 and 8 months (Legerstee et al., 1998). In general, infants smiled and vocalized more to the social (faces and sounds) versus nonsocial stimuli (see Figure 10.1).

FIGURE 10.1. Video capture of five-month-olds discriminating between the moving and immobile face of self, peer, and dolls. Copyright by Maria Legerstee.

Event-related potential methods support the finding that infants are sensitive to faces early on. By 6 months, infant brains react differently to upright and inverted faces in a way that is similar to the way adults process this difference (de Haan & Carver, Chapter 6, this volume).

It is not surprising that infants recognize their own voice by 5 months (Legerstee et al., 1998) because at birth they prefer their mother's voice (which they have heard in utero) over that of a female stranger (DeCasper & Fifer, 1980). More surprisingly, infants pay attention to both the auditory and the visual identifier of a vowel, such as /a/ and /u/. Infants will imitate the vowel if the components match, but not if they are incongruent (i.e., seeing /a/ but hearing /u/) (Legerstee, 1991). Interestingly, at 6 months, infants' phonetic perception predicts language development at 24 months (Tsao, Liu, & Kuhl, 2004). According to Kuhl (2007), this link between natural speech and language learning depends on children's awareness of the communicative intentions of others. Relating human language learning to a broader set of neurobiological cases of communicative development, Kuhl argued that the earliest phases of language acquisition—the developmental transition from an initial universal state of language processing to one that is language specific—require social interaction (see also Trevarthen & Delafield-Butt, Chapter 8, this volume). Kuhl proposed that the social brain "gates" the computational mechanisms involved in human language learning.

Infants' ability to recognize faces and voices documents their capacity for storing and recalling information from *memory*; however, until recently they were assumed to lack this ability (Bauer, Chapter 7, this volume). Recognizing faces and voices indicates that infants are familiar with these stimuli; this familiarity provides the opportunity for establishing social bonds with the mother.

Not only does the ability to recall information improve rapidly during infancy, but *emotionally salient* events are better remembered. For instance, Bornstein, Arterberry, and Mash (2004) revealed long-term memory in 20-month-olds who had participated in a social interaction where an adult looked at them but refrained from communicating (the still-face procedure, during which infants respond with increased negativity and gaze aversions and reduced positive responses) at 5 months.

These infants (experience group) fixated the face of the person who had instigated the still face significantly less than the faces of two other novel persons. Control 20-month-olds (no-experience group) looked longer overall and fixated on the target person equally or more than on the two novel persons. That 2-year-olds were able to remember something that happened when they were 5 months of age reveals their early *intersubjective nature* and how communication is represented during the first months of life.

Overall, these findings suggest that infants have an early specialization of the cortical network involved in the recognition of social cues and signals. This sensitivity, so early in life, familiarizes infants with their caregivers, promotes bonding, and prepares infants to engage in communication with conspecifics and to learn from them.

Person–Object and Self–Other Differentiation

If infants have a social brain and a mirror neuron system that are activated by social signals, then we should find that infants' responses to people are different from their responses to nonsocial objects. It is clear that from birth infants smile, vocalize, and alternate their gazes more when facing people than objects (for reviews, see Gelman & Spelke, 1981; Legerstee, 1992). An important question is whether this differential responsiveness is based on infants' *conceptual* rather than *perceptual* abilities. Studies introducing proper controls (for reviews, see Legerstee, 2005, Ch. 4; Legerstee, 2009) with typically developing infants as well as with infants with Down syndrome at approximately the same mental age or level of perceptual-cognitive sophistication as the nondelayed infants revealed the same pattern of differential responsiveness during the first year of life. In particular, already at 5 weeks, infants communicate with people and act on interactive dolls (Legerstee, Pomerleau, Malcuit, & Feider, 1987). Between 2 and 3 months, infants imitate mouth opening and tongue protrusion in people but not of inanimate objects that simulate these gestures (Legerstee, 1991). Infant imitative responsiveness to people and not physical objects supports Gelman and Spelke's (1981, p. 54) contention that "the infant implicitly 'knows' that he and another person can act in kind." Moreover, at that age, infants expect people to share their affective states with them, but they do not have such expectations of inanimate objects (Legerstee et al., 1987; Legerstee & Markova, 2007). Affect is relational by its very nature, and it is the earliest emotional information that is being shared between two communicative partners (Barrett, 1995; Stern, 1985). According to Stern, "Affect, more than cognition, seems to determine whether one is engaged with an 'it' or another human being" (p. 214). Already by 6 months, infants expect people to communicate from a distance, but not inanimate objects (Legerstee, Barna, & DiAdamo, 2000).

There is also evidence from behavioral neuroscience to support the notion that a global animate–inanimate distinction is deeply rooted in our categorical thinking because different neural mechanisms have been found to underlie the processing of the two classes of stimuli. Apparently, brains of 7- to 8-month-old infants respond differently when presented with animates and inanimates (Jeschonek, Marinovich, Hoehl, Elsner, & Pauen, 2010, p. 863). Infants' brain responses to both categories differed systematically regarding the negative central (Nc) component (400–600 msec) at anterior channels. In particular, the Nc was more activated for living things then for nonliving things in two groups of infants. Different brain mechanisms also underlie the processing of the two classes of stimuli in adults. Results of fMRI showed ventrolateral activation for animates and ventromedial activation for inanimate objects, supporting the idea that this distinction is fundamental to human cognition (Wiggett, Pritchard, & Downing, 2009). Thus, it appears that the social brain has systems for recognizing and understanding people and to discriminate these from inanimates.

Mental States: Attention–Intentions

Although by discriminating between the attributes of people and objects infants show various aspects of social intelligence, the question is, are infants aware that only people mentalize? Mentalizing refers to the ability to read the mental states of others; consequently, differentiating as a function of mental state is the sine qua non of the difference between people and objects (Frith & Frith, 2010; Kampe, Frith, & Frith, 2003; Legerstee, 1992, 1994; Legerstee & Barillas, 2003). Frith and Frith (2007) argued that it is a unique ability of the brain to represent the mental states of the self and the other; their connection enables communication of ideas.

For instance, infants soon after birth react to eye gaze of people as an intention to communicate, but they do not have such expectations of inanimate objects that are matched on stimulus configurations (Legerstee et al., 1987). Similarly, by 5 months, infants use social signals such as eye contact to share attention about interesting toys with people, but not with inanimate objects (Legerstee, 2005, Ch. 6; Legerstee, Markova, & Fisher, 2007; see Figure 10.2), and by 12 months, infants may follow the direction of gaze of people and head turns of objects, but they will only direct people's gazes through pointing to interesting sights (Legerstee & Barillas, 2003; see Figure 10.3).

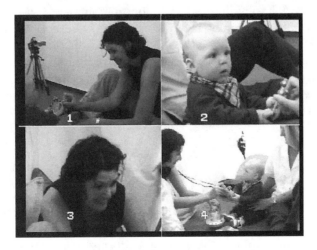

FIGURE 10.2. Video capture of five-month-old infant sharing attention over interesting toy with mother. Copyright by Maria Legerstee.

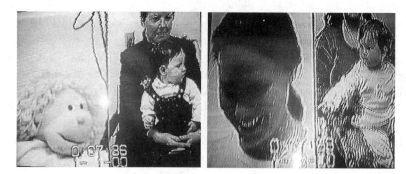

FIGURE 10.3. Twelve-month-old infants follow the direction of gaze of people and heads of objects, but only point to direct people's gazes to interesting sights. Copyright by Maria Legerstee.

Thus, infants are trying to "show" *people*, but never inanimate objects, something. That during the first year of life infants are expecting people to communicate with conspecifics, and their inclination to use declaratives with conspecifics of which the only reason is to share knowledge, suggests that neural mechanisms (Gallese & Rochat, Chapter 2, this volume) might underpin these deeply social interactions.

Grossman and Johnson (2010) examined 5-month-old infants' ability to follow the responses of the gazes of adults, and found that the prefrontal cortex was activated during triadic social interactions using near-infrared spectroscopy. It should be noted that infants in the Grossman and Johnson study responded only to the attention cues of the adult. Mundy (Chapter 14, this volume) reveals that responding to joint attention (RJA) and the actual initiation of joint attention (IJA) involves separate and distinguishable neural networks. Whereas frontal electroencephalographic (EEG) data are associated with IJA bids, RJA is associated with parietal EEG activation. It is not surprising that the two types of joint attention involve different neurological substrates. IJA is a more advanced ability than RJA because it involves an awareness that the play partner has some information about the object the infant initiates attention to, whereas RJA is simply a bid to follow the physical trajectory to the object (Camaioni, Perucchini, Bellagamba, & Colonnesi, 2004; Legerstee & Fisher, 2008).

In overview, infants are aware of the crucial distinctions between people and objects, which suggests that they develop a theory of mind differently from a theory of physical matters (Legerstee, 1992). These domain-specific predispositions serve as foundations on which infants further categorize and come to understand the distinctive properties of the social and nonsocial worlds (Legerstee, 1994; Legerstee, Anderson, & Schaffer, 1998).

Self–Other Differentiation: Consciousness

Although infants' differential responsiveness to people and objects lends credence to the idea that a concept of people has its roots in infancy, and hence is a result of early brain development, an important feature of a concept of a person is that it is distinguished from the concept of self. A sense of self is the result of the interactions infants have with other people during which representations are shared and the intersubjective nature of the self is formed. It is these interactions with other people that lead not only to subsequent changes in brain activity (Decety & Chaminade, 2003, p. 578) but to the development of a theory of mind (Dunbar, Chapter 1, this volume).

Evidence of dyadic social-emotional sharing (intersubjectivity) but also empathy (see Knafo & Uzefovsky, Chapter 5, this volume) is evidence of a concept of the self. Empathy involves an awareness of the other without necessarily involving a change in the self. To comprehend another person's mental state, it is important to be able to feel what they feel and to represent what they represent or feel. Lack of empathy is related to low theory of mind abilities in children with autism (Baron-Cohen, 1991).

Decety and Sommerville (2003) suggest that the right hemisphere, which is predominant early in life, is implicated in the ability for shared representations and thus may be responsible for the infant's feeling of empathy, namely that others are "with me" emotionally (Markova & Legerstee, 2006). Recent research suggests that empathy is largely biologically determined and is present in most mammals (Preston & deWaal, 2002), although the expression of empathy in human infants varies as a function of child rearing (Knafo & Uzefovsky, Chapter 5, this volume). Infants whose mothers empathize or are attuned to infants' emotions are infants who empathize with others (Ainsworth et al., 1978; Markova & Legerstee, 2006).

Gallese (2009) argues that our capacity to empathize with others is mediated by embodied simulation mechanisms—that is, by the activation of the same neural circuits underpinning our own emotional and sensory experiences. Thus, empathy is to be conceived as the outcome of our natural tendency to experience our interpersonal relations first and foremost at the implicit level of intercorporeity—"the mutual resonance of intentionally meaningful sensory-motor behaviors) as the main source of knowledge we directly gather about others" (Gallese, 2009, p. 523).

Connecting with the Social World

Thus far, the evidence suggests that newborns have predispositions that allow them to recognize conspecifics at birth: What are the mechanisms that allow them to *connect* with people? There are various theoretical opinions about this process. According to Piaget (1954), infants are born with reflexes that react to incoming stimulation. Others argue that infants connect with the social world because they are sensitive to movement, such as *social contingencies*. Specifically, these authors propose that from birth infants are only able to detect the effect their own actions have in the world, which is important for the development of an awareness of the self (e.g., "By kicking the sides of the crib I become aware of my feet"), but it is not until 3 months of age that infants begin to be sensitive to the type of contingent interactions provided by people (Gergely & Watson, 1999). Some suggest that infants establish intersubjective connections with people by detecting similarities between own and others' actions through imitation games. Imitation is an "attention-getter," and through it infants begin to perceive others to be "like me" (Meltzoff, 2007). Thus, according to these authors (Piaget included), infants for the first few months of life are not capable of connecting with their caregivers in a meaningful way.

According to Legerstee (2005, 2009), infants perceive others to be "like me" because they are born with an affect sharing device (AFS) that is made up of three components that act together: the ability to (1) recognize people as similar to themselves, (2) be sensitive to their own and others' emotions, and (3) perceive whether adults are attuned to their emotions and needs. The interplay among these three predispositions results in affectively attuned relationships that are important mechanisms for infants' sociocognitive development (Legerstee & Varghese, 2001; Markova & Legerstee, 2006). Thus, according to AFS theories, infants have an innate sense of people, which is activated through sympathetic emotions. Infants learn about themselves and other people through ongoing relationships, during which infants progress toward an increased consensus about shared meaning. Thus, AFS does not characterize others as providers of certain levels of temporal contingencies or of structurally similar responses to their actions but as beings with whom they can exchange intersubjective experiences and establish social attunement. As a consequence, infants not only perceive people to be "like me" physically but more importantly "with me" emotionally.

Markova and Legerstee (2006) assessed the predictions of the independent roles of contingency, imitation, and affect sharing in the development of social awareness. Infants were observed during natural (Figure 10.4a), imitative (Figure 10.4b), and yoked (Figure 10.4c) conditions with their mothers at 5 and 13 weeks of age. The dyads were divided into high- and low-attunement groups. Attunement was defined as (1) shared focus of attention (mothers would follow infants' attention), (2) social responsiveness (temporal coordination and contingent responsiveness), and (3) sensitivity (warm and appropriate behaviors) (see also Isabella & Belsky, 1991; Legerstee & Varghese, 2001). To determine whether infants enjoyed their mothers' responsiveness, their smiles, vocalizations, gazes, and negative emotions were observed. Results showed that at both ages infants of highly attuned mothers gazed longer, smiled, and vocalized positively more during the natural than the imitative and yoked conditions, whereas they increased negative vocalizations during the yoked conditions. In contrast, infants of less attuned (LA) mothers did not differentiate between the conditions, except at 13 weeks when the LA infants increased their gazes during the imitative condition. Thus, whereas contingencies and imitation draw infant attention to conspecifics, affective communication appears to lay the foundation for infants' social awareness and subsequent social relationships.

(a)   (b)   (c)

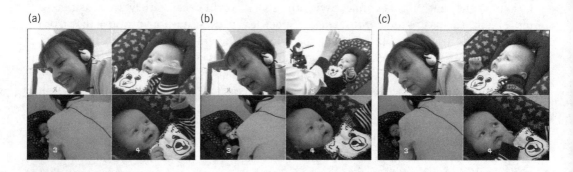

FIGURE 10.4. Mother and infant in (a) natural, (b) imitative, and (c) yoked interactions. Copyright by Maria Legerstee.

According to Gallese and Rochat (Chapter 2, this volume), the human neural system, well before birth, is already instantiating functional properties enabling social interactions, and such social interactions are expressed obeying different motor potentialities. They argue in support of Legerstee (2005; Markova & Legerstee, 2006) that neonates are innately prepared to connect to their caregivers not only through imitation but also affective attunement.

Social Bonds and the Development of Jealousy

So far, evidence for the existence of a social brain has been provided by focusing on the existence of prerequisite sociocognitive abilities of infants that enable them to experience jealousy: the ability to discriminate between (1) people and objects and 2) self and other and (3) an innate tendency to connect with the social world through attunement. It is clear that if jealousy is the fear of losing a loved one to a rival, then in order to experience jealousy, infants need to have formed a social bond, the one they fear to lose.

Social bonds are fundamental for human beings because social connections with others ensure the availability of not only physiological needs (e.g., food, shelter) but also social needs, such as the formation of relationships (see Bornstein, Chapter 12, this volume). However, as discussed earlier, maintaining dynamic social relationships is cognitively demanding because it involves an awareness of other minds. According to Dunbar (Chapter 1, this volume), "The social brain is really about behavioural complexity and thus about individual relationships." One reason why social relationships might increase brain size and promote subsequent cognitive and emotional development is that for successful bonding to take place, one needs to engage in perspective taking, which for mothers and infants means the reciprocal tuning in of each other's emotions. Variations in social experiences (high- or low-attuned interactions) may produce variations in intersubjectivity, bonding, and subsequent mental state awareness (Dunbar, Chapter 1, and Gallagher, Chapter 3, this volume; Legerstee, 2005).

Neurological evidence shows that social bonds have great adaptive value and are regarded as innate human predispositions (MacDonald & Leary, 2005). Biological rhythms (e.g., heart rate), hormonal levels, and activation in specific brain regions (i.e., superior temporal gyrus, anterior cingulate cortex, thalamus, and midbrain) underlie temporally matched interactions between mothers and infants (see Feldman, 2007). Because, in general, emotion reaction systems generate a sense of well-being with regard to important physiological and social needs (Panksepp, 1998), emotions that arise within relationships are essential and thus appear early in life (Markova et al., 2010). As a result of their inherent need for social connections, a great deal of an infant's life is spent interacting with others (Baumeister & Leary, 1995). During these interactions, infants as young as 1 week monitor people's gazes and exchange facial expressions, vocalizations, and movements in a reciprocal fashion. Such multimodal interactions (Walker-Andrews et al., Chapter 9, this volume) have been labeled protoconversations (Bateson, 1979) because they have a turn-taking structure that very much resembles adult-like verbal communication (Legerstee & Varghese, 2001;

Markova & Legerstee, 2006). As early as 5 weeks of age, infants recognize whether they are in tune with caregivers, since they get upset when mothers are not responsive to their signals (Legerstee et al., 1987; Markova & Legerstee, 2006). Chronically depressed mothers do not respond reliably to their infants' emotional states. As a result, infants generally show depressive states, expressed with lack of positive and negative responsiveness, because they have not developed expectations for affect sharing (Field et al., 1998; Legerstee & Markova, 2007; Legerstee & Varghese, 2001). Thus, infant–adult interactions are reciprocal in that infants perceive adults' acts as meaningful and adults interpret infant behavior as meaningful and communicative.

It is through the caregivers' attuned and empathic interactions that infants develop an increasingly sophisticated understanding of the minds of others. Recent works have elucidated the significance of epigenetic mechanisms of transmission that focus on the developmental outcomes of variations in parental care (Knafo & Uzefovsky, Chapter 5, and Pluess et al., Chapter 4, this volume; Meaney, 2001). For instance, Meaney and colleagues (Francis, Diorio, Liu, & Meaney, 1999; Parent et al., 2005; Szyf, Weaver, Champagne, Diorio, & Meaney, 2005) showed that harsh environmental conditions can contribute to stressful parent–offspring interactions in rats. This stress may affect gene expression in brain regions that are responsible for the proper regulation of behavioral, endocrine, and autonomic responses to stress, which may result in an increased risk for stress-related illness (Parent et al., 2005; Szyf et al., 2005). The authors studied epigenetic changes in rat pups. When rat mothers give birth, they will lick and groom (LG) their pups. However, not all mothers groom their young similarly. As a result of this variation in maternal care, adult offspring of high-LG mothers showed reduced corticotropin-releasing factor (CRF) production in the hypothalamus as well as reduced plasma adrenocorticotropin and glucocorticoid responses to acute stress compared with adult offspring of low-LG mothers (Liu et al., 1997). Thus, offspring of high-LG mothers demonstrated less fear and attenuated hypothalamus–pituitary–adrenal responses to stress than offspring of low-LG mothers. Furthermore, when pups born to high-LG mothers were raised by low-LG mothers (and vice versa), the adult offspring of high-LG mothers showed a significantly increased expression of specific proteins within the receptor that increase its function of inhibiting CRF expression (thereby increasing the fear response). The results of these cross-fostering studies indicate that individual differences in stress reactivity or in the expression of relevant genes can be directly altered by maternal behavior. Apparently, this effect is "particular to the amygdala and is reversed with cross-fostering" (Parent et al., 2005, p. 230).

Swain, Lorberbaum, Kose, and Strathearn (2007) studied how effects of environmental adversity on the emotional well-being of parents affected subsequent behavior in their infants. The authors examined human mother–infant pairs and found that their behaviors were influenced by infant signals that activated particular interacting neurotransmitters, such as oxytocin, prolactin, vasopressin, and dopamine. For instance, oxytocin released during breast-feeding was associated with reduced anxiety and stress in infants, which elicited more attuned behaviors of the mothers. However, when mothers became less attentive to infant social signals as a result of drug abuse or depression, it affected social bonding. Overall, the authors suggested that "infant stimuli activate basal forebrain regions, which regulate brain circuits that handle specific nurturing and caregiving responses and activate the brain's more general circuitry for handling emotions, motivation, attention, and empathy—all of which are crucial for effective parenting and bonding" (Swain et al., 2007, p. 262).

Social Loss

One way to examine the meaning infants assign to their relationships with others is to observe their reactions when they are faced with a possible loss of these relationships. According to Bowlby (1980), the deepest emotions surface during changes to the social bond. Changes that leave the social bond unchallenged elicit joy and security, whereas those that endanger the social bond engender anxiety and fear. Panksepp (2003) argues that two key brain areas are implicated in psychological pain in humans. Whereas the anterior cingulate cortex has been implicated in physical pain, the prefrontal cortex showed an opposite pattern of activity, becoming more active when the distress was least. Thus, both brain areas regulate the pain of social loss, suggesting that feelings of social exclusion might come from the same brain regions. He concludes: "Given the dependence of the mammalian young on their caregivers, it is not hard to comprehend the strong survival value conferred by common neural pathways that elaborate both social attachment and the affective qualities of physical pain" (Panksepp, 2003, p. 238).

Revisiting Jealousy

Throughout this chapter, I have defined jealousy as a fearful emotion that is being felt when one loses a loved one to a rival. This definition presupposes certain sociocognitive prerequisites such as the ability to distinguish between people and objects and being self-aware. In addition, the individual needs to have a primary bond with another person, and finally perceive that a third party is somehow a threat to this bond, to which one usually reacts with negative emotions, withdrawal, but also approach (Legerstee et al., 2010).

Thus, in addition to implicating these sociocognitive abilities, jealousy involves a variety of emotions. Jealousy has often been called a blended or mixed emotion (Plutchik, 1970), and has been suggested to include "a bewildering" array of emotions (Parrot, 1991, p. 15). In fact, jealousy is not really a distinct emotion such as fear, anger, sadness, disgust, and happiness. Social or moral emotions such as jealousy, shame, guilt, and embarrassment only have meaning within a social context and may have their foundation in the infants' feel of being with the other (Trevarthen & Aitken, 2001). According to Panksepp (2010), jealousy stands out as being the most "prepared" among the social-moral emotions in terms of their likelihood of being exhibited by practically everyone, at some stage of life, if the correct precipitating circumstances are present. Although jealousy is not a basic emotion, it is certainly evolutionarily prepared to emerge developmentally from the types of mind–brain dynamics that can be defensibly deemed basic emotions (Panksepp, 2010). An interesting way to categorize emotions is to focus on their functions. Barrett and Campos (1987) refer to emotions that are connected to the realization of an end state as "concurrent-goal/desire" emotions. Jealousy fits this definition because the infants' distress reactions during social exclusion from the loved one can be interpreted as aims to reinstate the social bond.

Onset of Jealousy

Research has revealed that infants as young as 5 months (Draghi-Lorenz, 2010) get upset when their mothers ignore them while paying attention to another child. This finding has since been replicated by others with 6-month-olds in paradigms where mothers pay exclusive attention to a doll (Hart, Carrington, Tronick, & Carroll, 2004; see Draghi-Lorenz, Reddy, & Costall, 2001, for a review). However, not all such reactions are the result of feelings of jealousy. To be certain that infants are not reacting to lack of attention, stimulation, and so on, when being excluded, infants need to be assessed in an experimental paradigm where their responses to the exclusion by a loved one are contrasted with their responses to someone with whom they do not have a social bond. Only if infants react with upset when excluded by the loved one in favor of a rival can one propose that their reactions are the result of jealousy.

To shed light on the development of jealousy in infants, Legerstee and colleagues (2010) recently studied 3- to 6-month-old infants under four triadic conditions during which a female experimenter and the mother were interacting with the infant, namely (1) natural, during which the female experimenter talked to the infants as one normally does when engaging babies; (2) still face, during which the experimenter looked at the baby but refrained from talking; and (3) two modified still faces, one during which the experimenter while looking at the infant drank from a water bottle and the other while the experimenter's looking and talking to the infant was interrupted by the mother, at which time the experimenter either began to talk to the mother about the experiment while the mother listened (monologue condition; Figure 10.5a) or engaged the mother in an active discussion about her baby (dialogue condition; Figure 10.5b and 10.5c). During the interrupted conditions both women excluded the infant.

It was expected that during the natural condition, infants would smile and vocalize. Based on evidence from the classic still-face research (Tronick, Als, Adamson, Wise, & Brazelton, 1978; Weinberg & Tronick, 1996), it was further expected that

(a)   (b)   (c)

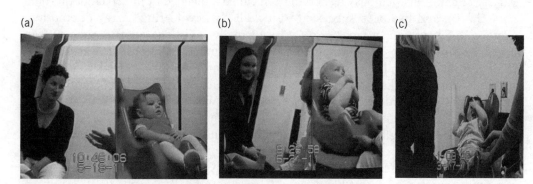

FIGURE 10.5. (a) Infant reactions in the Monologue condition—quiet interest. (b) Infant reactions in the Dialogue condition—increased looking/approach. (c) Infant reactions in the Dialogue condition—covering face/withdrawal. Copyright by Maria Legerstee.

during the still face when no reason for a break in contact was given, infants would respond with more sadness and gaze aversions than during the bottle condition and also during the interrupted conditions, where the break in contact was more salient. That is, if infants experienced the modified still-face conditions as instances where people for some apparent reason were unable to communicate with them because they either had a refreshment or were interrupted by someone, then fewer smiles and vocalizations were expected compared with the natural interaction and also fewer negative emotions compared with the still-face condition. However, if mothers engaged with the experimenter in a joyful and exciting dialogue while excluding the infants, a jealousy evocation situation was created to which infants were expected to react with intense agitation.

The results confirmed the hypotheses. Infants between 3 and 6 months perceived the actions of people who engaged in exciting dialogues with their mothers as a threat to the social bond they have with their mothers because they behaved with approach (Figure 10.5b) and protest (Figure 10.5c). Infants did not display these behaviors when mothers simply listened to others (monologue condition; Figure 10.5a). These findings suggested that the more cognitive aspects of the nervous system rapidly became highly attuned to precipitate jealousy when one's social resources were compromised (Panksepp, 2010).

Although this study provided behavioral evidence for the existence of the affective precondition for the emergence of human jealousy in infants ages 3–6 months, apart from very informative and stimulating theoretical models (see the various chapters in Hart & Legerstee, 2010), there are no studies that have examined what was happening in the infant brain. What might infants' neurophysiological reactions be during the social exclusion situations?

Neural Correlates of Jealousy

To investigate simultaneously infants' behavioral and neurophysiological reactions during their experiences of jealousy in triadic interactions, we replicated the Legerstee and colleagues (2010) study. Infants were observed during various triadic contexts where infants interacted with mothers and strangers, such as during the dialogue, monologue, still-face, and natural interactions. Each condition lasted 60 seconds. Infants' behavioral responses (gazes, facial expressions, vocalizations, protest, and approach behaviors) were recorded. Infants' EEG data were also collected continuously during the experimental conditions from 128 EEG electrodes using the Geodesic Sensor Net. EEG data were segmented into 1,000-millisecond epochs, and a continuous wavelet= transform was conducted in the 4–9 Hz range. Power was expressed as mean square microvolts, such that the lower number indicated greater cortical activation. EEG data were Ln transformed.

On the basis of earlier findings (Legerstee et al., 2010), we expected infants to show greater maternal gazing and positivity during the natural interaction compared with all other conditions, and also greater maternal gazing, negative affect, and protest behaviors during the dialogue compared with the monologue condition. We further expected infants to show differences in frontal EEG activation among all four conditions. That is because when adults are excluded from interactions (i.e., during a virtual tossing game, the other players stopped throwing the ball to them), fMRI showed that they experienced emotional distress during social exclusion, as measured by substantial blood flow in the dorsal anterior cingulate cortex, which is located in the prefrontal cortex, an area associated with physical pain (Eisenberger, Lieberman, & Williams, 2003; see also Panksepp, 2003). Because EEG can only provide information about hemispheric activation, it is hypothesized that during the experience of jealousy in infants, frontal regions of the brain will show greater activation compared with parietal regions.

The findings revealed that infants showed greater maternal gazing and more protest behaviors during the dialogue compared with the monologue condition and less positive affect compared with the natural interaction condition. These behavioral findings were consistent with the predictions of the study and the findings of Legerstee and colleagues (2010).

With respect to the neurophysiological correlates of jealousy, EEG results revealed both greater left- and right-hemisphere activations during the dialogue compared to the natural interaction and still-face conditions, supporting the behavioral data that infants showed more distress (protest) as well as approach (gazes at mother). There was also a difference between the dialogue and monologue conditions. Infants had greater left-hemisphere activation in the dialogue (approach) compared with the monologue condition. The findings of this study did not reveal a specific brain location of activity during jealousy-evocative situations. However, when back- and front-channel activation comparisons were performed, there was greater hemispheric activation in the frontal regions of the brain during the jealousy condition. Furthermore, there were equally high left- and right-hemispheric activations during the jealousy condition, suggesting that both hemispheres may be involved during the experience of this emotion.

Overall, the jealousy-like emotions appeared to be processed in the prefrontal cortex. Thus, when faced with the fear of losing a loved one to a rival, infants were protesting at losing exclusivity with their mother and used activities in order to try to regain her attention to reestablish their primary relationship (Avci, Legerstee, Haley, & Polyanski, 2011; see also Campos, Walle, & Dahl, 2010). Interestingly, there was no difference between the negative expressions during the jealousy condition compared with the natural interaction condition. In Markova and Legerstee (2006), discussed earlier, maternal interaction style was measured as a function of maternal attunement (maintaining attention, warm sensitivity, and social responsiveness). The results showed that infants of mothers who ranked high on attunement ranked high on social cognition (the infants discriminated between the various conditions) and on prosocial behaviors (the infants smiled more and gazed longer at the social stimuli) (see also Legerstee & Varghese, 2001). As suggested earlier, if jealousy is the fear of losing a loved one to a rival, then one can expect that infants of attuned mothers have stronger social bonds and may exhibit approach, whereas infants who are ambivalently or insecurely attached may feel anger and are more anxious in their expressions (see Fearon et al., 2010).

To examine the role of maternal attunement in the expression of jealousy, we examined individual differences in EEG activation during these different conditions as a function of maternal attunement. It was expected that infants of attuned mothers would protest more during the dialogue condition, as indicated by greater relative left frontal activation.

Maternal attunement was categorized as (1) warm sensitivity, (2) maintaining infant attention, and (3) responsiveness during the natural interaction condition (see Legerstee & Varghese, 2001; Markova & Legerstee, 2006). Infants were divided into high-attunement (HA) and low-attunement (LA) groups. If HA infants had stronger jealous reactions than LA infants, then we expected them to show greater maternal gazing and negative affect and also greater left frontal EEG activation during the jealousy condition compared with LA infants.

Analysis showed that there was greater maternal gazing in the dialogue condition compared with the monologue condition for both groups. In addition, infants of HA mothers showed greater positive affect in the natural interaction condition compared with all other conditions, confirming the Legerstee and Varghese (2001) data that infants of HA mothers overall ranked higher on prosocial behaviors.

Analyses of the EEG data indicated that infants of HA mothers showed significantly less frontal alpha power in the left hemisphere (i.e., greater activation) in the dialogue and natural interaction conditions and significantly greater activation in the right hemisphere during the monologue condition than infants of LA mothers.

Taken together, the studies reported here, including both behavioral and EEG data, confirmed the findings of Legerstee and colleagues (2010) that between 3 and 6 months of age infants showed greater maternal gazing during the jealousy condition. However, only infants with highly attuned mothers showed significantly greater positive affect during the natural interaction compared with all other conditions, including the jealousy condition. Furthermore, infants of highly attuned mothers showed greater left frontal activation during the jealousy condition, suggesting that they reacted more strongly when the bond they had with their mother was being threatened. Thus, the results support the socially precocious view of infant jealousy and indicate that social emotions are lateralized in the infant's developing brain. Finally, infants who received greater levels of maternal attunement showed greater lateralization of jealousy.

This is the first study showing that infants' brain reactions to jealousy-evocative situations are similar to those demonstrated by adults, suggesting that jealousy has its foundation early on in life. According to Panksepp (2010), separation anxiety is part of the old mammalian (social) brain. However, rejections (e.g., felt when experiencing the fear of losing a loved one to a rival) become manifest (albeit rapidly) through existential experiences of living in social worlds (Panksepp, 2010). Rejections and exclusions (as experienced during jealousy) is that social emotion whose adaptive value is to *counteract* severance of existing social bonds. Interestingly, the stronger the social bond, the more infants tried to reestablish this social bond through approach behaviors. An issue that needs to be addressed, however, is whether the feelings of the infants of the high-attuned mothers are more foundational than those of the low-attuned mothers. Variation in the expression of jealousy does not mean that jealousy is not based on a variety of primary, genetically ingrained, emotional processes (Panksepp, 2010).

Jealousy is an interesting phenomenon and fits the neuroconstructivist model well. Jealousy is founded on social loss, which is an aspect of the primate social brain (Panksepp, 2010). Both behavioral and neurological data show that jealousy becomes activated after infants have formed a social bond with a special person because they do not display jealousy with a stranger (Legerstee et al., 2010). Jealousy is also dependent on development because it is expressed differentially as a function of attuned interactions with the caretaker.

In this chapter, I have reviewed a range of studies to support the idea that infants have social brains that prepare them to interact with conspecifics. In particular, I have argued that infants are born with a social brain by providing behavioral and neurological evidence for the development of jealousy in infants ages 3–6 months. Infants show that they come prepared to manifest jealousy soon after birth because from birth infants are attracted to people, form social bonds, engage in triadic relationships, and have an awareness of goals. That infants are able—so early in life—to experience these intersubjective transactions suggests that love and loss are part of the primate social brain, and that through bonding with conspecifics infants develop an awareness of simple mental states such as emotions, attention, and intentions, which allows for experiences such as jealousy.

Although there has been some indication that infants get upset when their parents ignore them for each other (Fivaz-Depeursinge et al., 2010) or in favor of a book or a doll (Hart et al., 2004), these studies did not focus on the *reason* why infants got upset. To control for the possibility that infants are reacting to lack of attention rather than jealousy (fear of losing a loved one to a rival), infants' reactions while being ignored by a familiar person with whom they have developed a social bond (mother) versus one with whom they do not have a social bond (female stranger) need to be examined. The behavioral and neurological data we collected indicate that infants only become upset when they are excluded by a loved one in favor of someone else. Thus, it appears that already between 3 and 6 months infants feel the pain of social loss that adults speak of when being excluded by a loved one.

Increasingly, developmental research is beginning to address the ontogeny of sociocognitive development and to describe its function and developmental trajectory through examining the predispositions of the very young infant and relating them to later complex abilities. As the data revealed, infant sociocognitive development is complex, involving a multifactorial interplay between innate predispositions and environment. In addition, many social processes, including such complex constructs as emotions and theory of mind, are indirect and cannot be mapped directly onto neural systems (Pluess et al., Chapter 4, and Knafo & Uzefovsky, Chapter 5, this volume). For instance, an important developmental milestone occurs when infants change from sharing attention with others in dyadic (face-to-face) situations to coordinating attention between people and the environment during triadic interactions. Legerstee and colleagues (2007) showed that variability in maternal care introduced individual differences in this development. We replicated the influence of maternal care with our jealousy studies. However, this research does not make clear the individual contributions of the infants. If development is a complex, dynamic process, where genes, parenting, and age interact in affecting individual differences, then research addressing the brain structures of both mothers and infants that support such change needs to be conducted, allowing for an examination of this dynamic perception action coupling between interacting agents. The brain permits us to learn continuously. It is important to know how, with development, the brain changes as a function of environmental input and how subsequent learning changes the brain over time (Karmiloff-Smith, in press). This knowledge should enable us to contribute to the development of new theories of developmental social neuroscience and the elaboration of existing theories.

Acknowledgments

This chapter has been funded by the Vice President, Research and Innovation, York Seminar for Advanced Research, and the Social Sciences and Humanities Research Council (410-2010-2643) to Maria Legerstee.

References

Adolphs, R. (2001). The Neurobiology of Social Cognition. *Current Opinion in Neurobiology, 11,* 231–239.

Ainsworth, M. D. S., Blehar, M. C., Waters, E., & Wall, S. (1978). *Patterns of attachment: A psychological study of the strange situation.* Hillsdale, NJ: Erlbaum.

Avci, B., Legerstee, M., Haley, W. D., & Polyanski, V. (2011, June). *Infant frontal encephalogram (EEG) alpha power and behavioral response to jealousy.* Poster presented at the 41st annual meeting of the Jean Piaget Society, Berkeley, CA.

Baron-Cohen, S. (1991). Do people with autism understand what causes emotion? *Child Development, 62,* 385–395.

Barrett, F. J. (1995). Creating appreciative learning cultures. *Organizational Dynamics, 24,* 36–49.

Barrett, K., & Campos, J. (1987). Perspectives on emotional development: II. A functionalist approach to emotion. In J. Osofsky (Ed.), *Handbook of infant development* (pp. 555–578). New York: Wiley.

Bateson, G. (1979). *Mind and nature: A necessary unity.* New York: Bantam Books.

Baumeister, R. F., & Leary, M. R. (1995). The need to belong: Desire for interpersonal attachments as a fundamental human motivation. *Psychological Bulletin, 117,* 497–529.

Bornstein, M. H., Arterberry, M. E., & Mash, C. (2004). Long-term memory for an emotional interpersonal interaction occurring at 5 months of age. *Infancy, 6,* 407–416.

Bowlby, J. (1980). *Attachment and loss: Vol. 3. Loss, sadness and depression.* New York: Basic Books.

Bruner, J. (1990). *Acts of meaning.* Cambridge, MA: Harvard University Press.

Bruner, J. (1999). Narratives of aging. *Journal of Aging Studies, 13,* 7–9.

Bushnell, I. W. R., Sai, F., & Mullin, J. T. (1989). Neonatal recognition of the mother's face. *British Journal of Developmental Psychology, 7,* 3–15.

Camaioni, L., Perucchini, P., Bellagamba, F., & Colonnesi, C. (2004). The role of declarative pointing in developing a theory of mind. *Infancy, 5,* 291–308.

Campos, J. J., Walle, E. A., & Dahl, A. (2010). What is missing in the study of the development of jealousy? In S. L. Hart & M. Legerstee (Eds.), *Handbook of jealousy: Theory, research and multidisciplinary approaches* (pp. 312–328). Malden, MA: Wiley-Blackwell.

DeCasper, A. J., & Fifer, W. P. (1980). Of human bonding: Newborns prefer their mother's voice. *Science, 208,* 1174–1176.

Decety, J., & Chaminade, T. (2003). When the self represents the other: A new cognitive neuroscience view on psychological identification. *Consciousness and Cognition, 12,* 577–596.

Decety, J., & Sommerville, J. A. (2003). Shared representations between self and others: A social cognitive neuroscience view. *Trends in Cognitive Sciences, 7*, 527–533.

de Haan, M., & Gunnar, M. R. (Eds.). (2009). *Handbook of developmental social neuroscience*. New York: Guilford Press.

DePaulo, B. M. (1992). Nonverbal behavior and self-presentation. *Psychological Bulletin, 111*, 203–243.

Draghi-Lorenz, R. (2010). Parental reports of jealousy in early infancy: Growing tensions between evidence and theory. In S. L. Hart & M. Legerstee (Eds.), *Handbook of jealousy: Theory, research, and multidisciplinary approaches* (pp. 163–191). Malden, MA: Wiley-Blackwell.

Draghi-Lorenz, R., Reddy, V., & Costall, A. (2001). Re-thinking the development of "non-basic" emotions: A critical review of existing theories. *Developmental Review, 21*, 263–304.

Dunbar, R. I. M. (2003). The social brain: Mind, language, and society in evolutionary perspective. *Annual Review of Anthropology, 32*, 163–181.

Eisenberger, N. I., Lieberman, M. D., & Williams, K. D. (2003). Does social rejection hurt? An fMRI study of social exclusion. *Science, 302*, 290–292.

Fearon, R. M. P., van IJzendoorn, M. H., Fonagy, P., Bakermans-Kranenburg, M. J., Schuengel, C., & Bokhorst, C. L. (2010). In search of shared and nonshared environmental factors in security of attachment: A behavior-genetic study of the association between sensitivity and attachment security. *Developmental Psychology, 46*, 404–416.

Feldman, R. (2007). On the origins of background emotions: From affect synchrony to symbolic expression. *Emotion, 7*(3), 601–611.

Field, T., Healy, B., Goldstein, S., Perry, S., Bendell, D., Schanberg, S., et al. (1988). Infants of depressed mothers show "depressed" behaviors even with non-depressed adults. *Child Development, 59*, 1569–1579.

Fivaz-Depeursinge. E., Favez, N., Scaiola, L. C., & Lopes, F. (2010). Family triangular interactions in infancy: A context for the development of jealousy? In S. L. Hart & M. Legerstee (Eds.), *Handbook of jealousy: Theory, research and multidisciplinary approaches* (pp. 445–476). Malden, MA: Wiley-Blackwell.

Fogel, A. (1993). *Developing through relationships: Origins of communication, self, and culture*. Chicago: University of Chicago Press.

Francis, D., Diorio, J., Liu, D., & Meaney, M. J. (1999). Nongenomic transmission across generations of maternal behavior and stress responses in the rat. *Science, 286*, 1155–1158.

Frith, C., & Frith, U. (2007). Social cognition in humans. *Current Biology, 17*, 724–732.

Frith, U., & Frith, C. (2001). The biological basis of social interaction. *Current Directions in Psychological Science, 10*, 151–155.

Frith, U., & Frith, C. (2010). The social brain: Allowing humans to boldly go where no other species has been. *Philosophical Transactions of the Royal Society, B, 365*, 165–176.

Gallese, V. (2009). Mirror neurons, embodied simulation, and the neural basis of social identification. *Psychoanalytic Dialogues, 19*, 519–536.

Gelman, R., & Spelke, E. (1981). The development of thoughts about animate and inanimate objects: Implications for research on social cognition. In J. H. Flavell & L. Ross (Eds.), *Social cognition development: Frontiers and possible futures* (pp. 43–66). New York: Cambridge University Press.

Gergely, G., & Watson, J. S. (1999). Early social-emotional development: Contingency perception and the social-biofeedback model. In P. Rochat (Ed.), *Early socialization* (pp. 101–113). Mahwah, NJ: Erlbaum.

Grossmann, T., & Johnson, M. H. (2007). The development of the social brain in infancy. *European Journal of Neuroscience, 25*, 909–919.

Grossmann, T., & Johnson, M. H. (2010). Selective prefrontal cortex responses to joint attention in early infancy. *Biology Letters, 6,* 540–543.

Haley, D. W., Akano, A. J., & Dudek, J. (2011). Investigating social cognition in infants and adults using dense array electroencephalography (dEEG). *Journal of Visualized Experiments, 52,* 2759.

Hart, S., Carrington, H. A., Tronick, E. Z., & Carroll, S. R. (2004). When infants lose exclusive maternal attention: Is it jealousy? *Infancy, 6,* 57–78.

Hart, S., & Legerstee, M. (Eds.). (2010). *Handbook of jealousy: Theories, principles and multidisciplinary approaches.* Malden, MA: Wiley-Blackwell.

Hoffman, M. L. (1975). Developmental synthesis of affect and cognition and its implications of altruistic motivation. *Developmental Psychology, 23,* 97–104.

Iacoboni, M., Molnar-Szakacs, I., Gallese, V., Buccino, G., Mazziotta, J. C., & Rizzolatti, G. (2005). Grasping the intentions of others with one's own mirror neuron system. *PLoS Biology, 3,* e79.

Isabella, R. A., & Belsky, J. (1991). Interactional synchrony and the origins of infant–mother attachment. *Child Development, 62,* 373–384.

James, W. (1890). *The principles of psychology* Cambridge, MA: Harward University Press.

Jeschonek, S., Marinovic, V., Hoehl, S., Elsner, B., & Pauen, S. (2010). Do animals and furniture items elicit different brain responses in human infants? *Brain and Development, 32,* 863–871.

Kampe, K., Frith, C. D., & Frith, U. (2003). "Hey John": Signals conveying communicative intention towards the self activate brain regions associated with mentalising regardless of modality. *Journal of Neuroscience, 23,* 5258–5263.

Karmiloff-Smith, A. (1992). *Beyond modularity: A developmental perspective on cognitive science.* Cambridge, MA: MIT Press.

Karmillof-Smith, A. (2009). Nativism versus neuroconstructivism: Rethinking the study of developmental disorders. *Developmental Psychology, 45,* 56–63.

Karmiloff-Smith, A. (in press). Preaching to the converted?: From constructivism to neuro-constructivism. *Child Development Perspectives, 3*(2), 99–102.

Kuhl, P. K. (2007). Is speech learning "gated" by the social brain? *Developmental Science, 10,* 110–120.

Legerstee, M. (1991). Changes in the quality of infant sounds as a function of social and non-social stimulation. *First Language, 11,* 327–343.

Legerstee, M. (1992). A review of the animate/inanimate distinction in infancy: Implications for models of social and cognitive knowing. *Early Development and Parenting, 1,* 59–67.

Legerstee, M. (1994). Patterns of 4–month-old infant responses to hidden silent and sounding people and objects. *Early Development and Parenting, 3,* 71–80.

Legerstee, M. (2005). *Infants' sense of people: Precursors to a theory of mind.* Cambridge, UK: Cambridge University Press.

Legerstee, M. (2009). The role of dyadic communication in infant social-cognitive development. In P. Bauer (Ed.), *Advances in child development and behavior,* Volume 37 (pp. 1–53). Amsterdam: Elsevier.

Legerstee, M., Anderson, D., & Schaffer, M. (1998). Five- and eight-month-old infants recognize their faces and voices as familiar and social stimuli. *Child Development, 69,* 37–50.

Legerstee, M., & Barillas, Y. (2003). Sharing attention and pointing to objects at 12 months: Is the intentional stance implied? *Cognitive Development, 18,* 91–110.

Legerstee, M., Barna, J., & DiAdamo, C. (2000). Precursors to the development of intention: Understanding people and their actions at 6 months. *Developmental Psychology, 36,* 627–634.

Legerstee, M., Corter, C., & Kienapple, K. (1990). Hand, arm and facial actions of young infants to a social and nonsocial stimulus. *Child Development, 61,* 774–784.

Legerstee, M., Ellenbogen, B., Nienhuis, T., & Marsh, H. (2010). Social bonds, triadic relationships, and goals: Preconditions for the emergence of human jealousy. In S. L. Hart & M. Legerstee (Eds.), *Handbook of jealousy: Theories, principles and multidisciplinary approaches* (pp. 163–191). Malden, MA: Wiley-Blackwell.

Legerstee, M., & Fisher, T. (2008). Coordinated attention, imperative and declarative pointing in infants with and without Down syndrome: Sharing experiences with adults and peers. *First Language, 28,* 281–311.

Legerstee, M., & Markova, G. (2007). Intentions make a difference: Infant responses to still-face and modified still-face conditions. *Infant Behavior and Development, 30,* 232–250.

Legerstee, M., & Markova, G. (2008). Variations in 10–month-old infant imitation of people and things. *Infant Behavior and Development, 31,* 81–91.

Legerstee, M., Markova, G., & Fisher, T. (2007). The role of maternal affect attunement in dyadic and triadic communication. *Infant Behavior and Development, 2,* 296–306.

Legerstee, M., Pomerleau, A., Malcuit, G., & Feider, H. (1987). The development of infants' responses to people and a doll: Implications for research in communication. *Infant Behavior and Development, 10,* 81–95.

Legerstee, M., & Varghese, J. (2001). The role of maternal affect mirroring on socialexpectancies of three-month-old infants. *Child Development, 72,* 1301–1313.

Lewis, M. (2010). Loss, protest, and emotional development. In S. L. Hart & M. Legerstee (Eds.), *Handbook of jealousy: Theory, research and multidisciplinary approaches* (pp. 27–39). Malden, MA: Wiley-Blackwell.

Lieberman, M. D. (2007). Social cognitive neuroscience: A review of core processes. *Annual Review of Psychology, 58,* 259–289.

Liu, D., Diorio, J., Tannenbaum, B., Caldji, C., Francis, D., Freedman, A., et al. (1997). Maternal care, hippocampal glucocorticoid receptors, and hypothalamic–pituitary–adrenal responses to stress. *Science, 277,* 1659–1662.

MacDonald, G., & Leary, M. R. (2005). Roles of social pain and defense mechanisms in response to social exclusion: Reply to Panksepp (2005) and Corr (2005). *Psychological Bulletin, 131,* 237–240.

Markova, G., & Legerstee, M. (2006). Contingency, imitation, and affect sharing: Foundations of infants' social awareness. *Developmental Psychology, 42,* 132–141.

Markova, G., Stieben, J., & Legerstee, M. (2010). Neural structures of jealousy: Infants' experience of social exclusion with caregivers and peers. In S. L. Hart & M. Legerstee (Eds.), *Handbook of jealousy: Theory, research and multidisciplinary approaches* (pp. 83–100). Malden, MA: Wiley-Blackwell.

Meaney, M. J. (2001). Maternal care, gene expression, and the transmission of individual differences in stress reactivity across generations. *Annual Review of Neuroscience, 24,* 1161–1192.

Meltzoff, A. N. (2007). "Like me": A foundation for social cognition. *Developmental Science, 10,* 126–134.

Meltzoff, A. N., & Moore, M. K. (1983). Newborn infants imitate adult facial gestures. *Child Development, 54,* 702–709.

Miceli, M., & Castelfranchi, C. (2007). The envious mind. *Cognition and Emotion, 21,* 449–479.

Panksepp, J. (1998). *Affective neuroscience: The foundations of human and animal emotions.* New York: Oxford University Press.

Panksepp, J. (2003). Feeling the pain of social loss. *Science, 302,* 237–239.

Panksepp, J. (2010). The evolutionary sources of jealousy: Cross-species approaches to fundamental issues. In S. L. Hart & M. Legerstee (Eds.), *Handbook of jealousy: Theories, principles and multidisciplinary approaches* (pp. 101–120). Malden, MA: Wiley-Blackwell.

Parent, C., Zhang, T.-Y., Caldji, C., Bagot, R., Champagne, F. A., Pruessner, J., et al. (2005). Maternal care and individual differences. *Current Directions of Psychological Science, 14*(5), 229–233.

Parrot, W. G. (1991). The emotional experiences of envy and jealousy. In P. Salovey (Ed.), *The psychology of jealousy and envy* (pp. 3–28). New York: Guilford Press.

Piaget, J. (1954). *The construction of reality in the child.* New York: Basic Books.

Plutchik, R. (1970). Emotions, evolution and adaptive processes. In M. Arnold (Ed.), *Feelings and emotion* (pp. 384–402). New York: Academic Press.

Preston, S. D., & de Waal, F. B. M. (2002). Empathy: Its ultimate and proximate bases. *Behavioral Brain Sciences, 25,* 1–71.

Rizzolatti, G., Fadiga, L., Gallese, V., & Fogassi, L. (1996). Premotor cortex and the recognition of motor actions. *Cognitive Brain Research, 3,* 131–141.

Rochat, P. (2010). Is social cognition an oxymoron?: Comments on Astington and Edward, Miller, Moore and Sommerville. In R. E. Tremblay, R. G. Barr, R. D. Peters, & M. Boivin (Eds.), *Encyclopedia on early childhood development* (pp. 1–5). Montreal: Centre of Excellence for Early Childhood Develpment.

Stern, D. (1985). *The interpersonal world of the infant: A view from psychoanalysis and developmental psychology.* New York: Basic Books.

Swain, J. E., Lorberbaum, J. P., Kose, S., & Strathearn, L. (2007). Brain basis of early parent-infant interactions: Psychology, physiology, and in vivo functional neuroimaging studies. *Journal of Child Psychology and Psychiatry, and Allied Disciplines, 48,* 262–287.

Szyf, M., Weaver, I. C. G., Francis, A. Champagne, F. A., Diorio, J., & Meaney, M. J. (2005). Maternal programming of steroid receptor expression and phenotype through DNA methylation in the rat. *Frontiers in Neurendocrinology, 26,* 139–161

Trevarthen, C., & Aitken, K. J. (2001). Infant intersubjectivity: Research, theory and clinical applications. *Journal of Child Psychology and Psychiatry, 42,* 3–48.

Tronick, E., Als, H., Adamson, L., Wise, S., & Brazelton, T. B. (1978). The infant's response to entrapment between contradictory messages in face-to-face interaction. *Journal of the American Academy of Child Psychiatry, 17,* 1–13.

Tronick, E. Z. (1981). Infant communication intent: The infant's reference to social interaction. In R. E. Stark (Ed.), *Language behavior in infancy and early childhood* (pp. 5–16). New York: Elsevier.

Tsao, F. M., Liu, H. M., & Kuhl, P. K. (2004). Speech perception in infancy predicts language development in the second year of life: A longitudinal study. *Child Development, 75,* 1067–1084.

Wellman, H. N., & Lui, D. (2004). *Child Development, 75*(2), 523–541.

Weinberg, M. K. & Tronick, E. Z. (1996). Infant affective reactions to the resumption of maternal interaction after the still-face. *Child Development, 67,* 905–914.

Wiggett, A. J., Pritchard, I. C., & Downing, P. E. (2009). Animate and inanimate objects in human visual cortex: Evidence for task-independent category effects. *Neuropsychologia, 47,* 3111–3117.

CHAPTER 11

Infant Memory Consolidation

The Social Context of Stress, Learning, and Memory

DAVID W. HALEY

> It has often been assumed that animals were in the first place rendered
> social, and that they feel as a consequence uncomfortable when separated
> from each other, and comfortable while together; but it is a more probable
> view that these sensations were first developed, in order that those animals
> which would profit by living in society, should be induced to live together.
> —CHARLES DARWIN (1871, Vol. 1, Part 1, p. 80)

A question asked by psychologists and biologists alike is: What is the relationship between infant memory and attachment? The short answer is that attachment and memory are interrelated and intimately linked (Kraemer, 1992). To understand more fully the link between attachment and memory, however, we must ask more specific questions about the nature of their basic relationship: What types of learning and memory processes contribute to attachment formation? Once formed, how does attachment affect future learning and the formation of new memories? The first of these two questions has been examined extensively in animal models, which have provided a remarkable account of how early learning and memory processes, rather than simply instinct, play a critical role in the development of attachment behavior. One area of research has illuminated a developmentally coordinated set of reciprocal interactions among specific types of learning, their cellular and molecular and hormonal substrates, and the regulatory functions of the parent–infant dyad. This research demonstrates that biology has evolved "fail-safe" learning mechanisms for maintaining physical proximity to caregivers during critical periods of early bonding, in which learning to prefer and approach dominate and learning to fear and avoid are inhibited (Hofer, 2006).

The second question, which concerns how attachment affects learning and memory, has been examined extensively in human children and adults but very little in young human infants. Consistent with Bowlby's theory of attachment, it has been shown that more securely attached individuals have a greater cognitive flexibility, giving them the ability to recall both positive and negative events, than insecurely attached individuals (e.g., Belsky, Spritz, & Crnic, 1996; Mikulincer & Orbach, 1995). By focusing on specific constructs within the broader domain of attachment such as emotion regulation and self-regulation, we have been able to refine our questions further and make further progress on the neural mechanisms involved (e.g., Amini et al., 1996). In turn, this conceptual refinement has made it possible for researchers to more easily locate the neural structures underlying attachment representations and their presumed impact on the mind (e.g., Gillath, Bunge, Shaver, Wendelken, & Mikulincer, 2005). To further investigate physiological mechanisms that may link memory and attachment relationships more directly, we take up a third question: How does the parent–infant relationship in the first half year of life affect infant memory? To tackle this third question, we adopt the research strategy of attempting to titrate the stress of everyday parent–infant interactions and examine whether the stress physiology of brief relationship disruptions in these microsocial exchanges has an immediate impact on infant learning and memory processing. This approach contrasts with substantial research examining the long-term impact of parenting or attachment on social-cognitive development. After addressing this question, we consider how social learning in an attachment context contributes to memory development. Is the infant's capacity to understand others necessary for him or her to remember the actions of others? As a whole, then, this chapter examines the links among social context, relationship disruption, intentionality detection, and memory.

To start, we provide some background on what a physiological account of infant memory entails and how the parent–infant relationship may affect memory processing. First, however, we discuss two key claims about memory organization and memory consolidation that have motivated memory research for more than a century: (1) *Multiple memory systems* exist, and (2) memory processing is *time dependent*; that is, new memories are assumed to be fragile and to undergo a period of consolidation.

Multiple Memory Systems

The first claim is that learning and memory systems are mediated by multiple neural systems, which operate in parallel. This arrangement enables diverse types of information to either compete for neural representation or, perhaps, to become integrated into more complex neural representations. One of the specific neural structures associated with memory is the hippocampus, a seahorse-shaped structure located in the medial region of the brain, which is thought to serve long-term memory. More specifically, the hippocampus has been shown to mediate episodic memories within a spatial and/or temporal context (e.g., autobiographical memories) (O'Keefe & Nadel, 1978). A second important but less renowned structure is the amygdala, which is critical for forming associations between an emotional context and an individual stimulus (e.g., a neural stimulus and the context in which an electric shock was previously delivered) (LeDoux, 2000). There is some evidence in rodent studies that these structures are dissociated, but they also can interact and may do so in a competitive manner such that the removal of one structure can facilitate learning that is ordinarily dependent on the other. For instance, researchers have demonstrated that lesions to the amygdala cause rats to acquire a hippocampus-dependent spatial-reward learning task at a quicker rate than control groups, and lesions to the hippocampus cause rats to acquire an amygdala-dependent elemental cue-reward learning task at a faster rate (Ito & Canseliet, 2010). Similarly, administration of pharmacologocial agents that block long-term potentiation (LTP) or inhibit protein synthesis in these structures produces dissociation and/or competition among these structures. Within this multiple-memory-system framework, one can easily imagine how emotional experiences might facilitate memories for nonemotional events, such as the classic example of a flashbulb-like memory in which the details of the experience are remembered.

Memory under Construction

The second claim concerns the time-dependent nature of memory processing and theories of cellular or synaptic consolidation, which in a certain sense has been assumed since antiquity. For example, one of the metaphors Aristotle (384–322 B.C.) used to explain memory refers to the impressions made by putting a seal or ring signature on a layer of heated wax, which becomes hardened and fixed as the wax cools. Gradually, memories become less plastic and more permanent. This initial fragility suggests that multiple stages are involved in the formation of new memories: acquisition (encoding), storage (consolidation), and recall (retrieval). The plasticity of memory consolidation enables relatively distinct events and contextual cues to become associated or dissociated. Researchers over the past century have provided substantial evidence to support this view of memory, illuminating many cellular processes that are involved in memory consolidation. In short, it has been shown that immediately after learning there is a relatively brief temporal window during which the consolidation of a new memory can be disrupted or facilitated. However, beyond this temporal window, the memory becomes more fixed and is not easily affected. Thus, the memory is initially fragile and rapidly becomes stable. A variety of methods have been used to investigate the neural chemical changes that occur during the memory consolidation period, for example, introducing additional items to a list of to-be-remembered items, applying electrical shocks to the brain, and administering a stimulating pharmacological agent and protein inhibitors during the consolidation period.

Stress and Memory

Over 50 years of research on the neurobiology of stress and memory in animals and adult humans indicates that stress hormones play an important role in the formation of memories (i.e., memory consolidation) (McGaugh, 1966, 2000). New memories are temporarily fragile, disrupted, or enhanced by intense emotions or stress. For example, glucocorticoids (GC), or cortisol in humans, are the end product of the hypothalamic-pituitary-adrenal (HPA) axis, and are considered the gold standard of stress hormone research because they provide a noninvasive window for evaluating brain function. GC circulates in the body and may cross the blood–brain barrier, which allows it to act directly on central processes such as the hippocampus, a region highly populated with GC receptors (McEwen, Weiss, & Schwartz, 1968). Thus, GC has profound effects on cognition (Wolkowitz, Reus, Weingartner, & Thompson,

1990). An important feature of memory is that it is time dependent (McGaugh, 1966, 2000). Posttraining stress induction or stress treatment designs (e.g., social stress test or consumption of steroids) have shown that too little or too much stress impairs (Kirschbaum, Wolf, May, Wippich, & Hellhammer, 1996; Newcomer, Craft, Hershey, Askins, & Bardgett, 1994) but moderate stress facilitates (Abercrombie, Kalin, Thurow, Rosenkranz, & Davidson, 2003; Buchanan & Lovallo, 2001) memory consolidation. Given that most studies on infant memory have focused on age-related changes in retrieval, the issue of memory consolidation has received little, if any, systematic study in the context of stress physiology.

The neurobiological substrates of infant memory have been elucidated by examining measures of brain, autonomic, and neuroendocrine activity in conjunction with behavioral measures of memory. Substantial research has examined the relationship between GCs, which are produced endogenously by the activation of the HPA axis, and memory (Lupien, Maheu, Tu, Fiocco, & Schramek, 2007; McGaugh, 2000). GCs target GC receptors, which are expressed throughout the cortex and are densely populated in brain regions associated with memory encoding, consolidation, and retrieval such as the hippocampus and the prefrontal cortex, as well as with emotion, such as the amygdala. GCs target two specific types of GC receptors: mineralocorticoid (MR) and glucocorticoid receptors (GRs) (Gunnar & Quevedo, 2007; Sapolsky, Romero, & Munck, 2000). The ratio between the occupation of MR/GR may contribute to the opposing effects of stress on memory (i.e., the classic inverted-U-shaped relationship between stress and memory; de Kloet, 1991). During basal or extreme stress conditions, when the MR/GR ratio is low, memory is diminished, but when the ratio is high, during moderate stress conditions, memory is enhanced (de Kloet, Oitzl, & Joels, 1999). Furthermore, GRs selectively encode for information about the stressor that is relevant to survival and, in conjunction with MRs, suppress information that is irrelevant (de Kloet et al., 1999). The regulation of GCs and the expression of GR/MR assume adult-like status shortly after birth (Rosenfeld, Eekelen, Levine, & de Kloet, 1993), with human infants showing adult levels of GR expression in the hippocampus within the first year of life (Perlman, Webster, Herman, Kleinman, & Weickert, 2007).

Acute exposure to GCs generally has been shown to activate two opposing actions in memory processing, where GCs enhance memory consolidation but impair memory encoding and retrieval (de Quervain, Aerni, Schelling, & Roozendaal, 2009; McGaugh, 2000; Roozendaal, 2002). The method behind much of the research on the positive effects of GCs on memory consolidation in human adults have involved injecting GCs into the body shortly after learning (e.g., Abercrombie et al., 2003); however, inducing the release of GCs after learning through physical or emotional challenges has provided similar results (e.g., Andreano & Cahill, 2006). Research on the negative effects of GCs on memory during encoding and retrieval have generated similar results using either exogenous or endogenous methods (e.g., Kirschbaum et al., 1996). Interestingly, one line of experimental research on GCs and memory in children has focused on whether GCs elicited by a stressful event affect the memory of the same stressful event (e.g., Quas, Yim, Edelstein, Cahill, & Rush, 2011). Quas and colleagues (2011) found that 9- to 12-year-olds who showed greater GC reactivity to the psychosocial challenge had better memory when tested after a 2-week delay. In another line of research, a more subtle relationship between memory and GCs was observed. Specifically, Smeekens, Riksen-Walraven, van Bakel, and de Weerth (2010) showed that emotional memories of negative parent–child interactions produced elevations in cortisol in 5-year-old children. This finding illustrates the dynamic relationships existing among stress physiology, relationship disruptions, and memory.

Infants rapidly develop adult-like memory features, as indicated by age-related increases in the length of retention and by the emergence of more sophisticated types of memory, such as explicit memory (Bauer, Chapter 7, this volume). From 2 to 6 months of age, infants demonstrate procedural memory and an exponential increase in their retention of learning on a conditioning task (Fagen & Rovee-Collier, 1983; Rovee-Collier, Sullivan, Enright, Lucas, & Fagen, 1980). However, development of event memory, such as recall of explicit information, emerges as early as 6 months, as indicated by 24-hour memory recall of single events (Barr, Dowden, & Hayne, 1996), but appears more robust at 9 months, when infants demonstrate memory for the order of action sequences for as long as 1 month (Bauer, 1996; Meltzoff, 1988). The maturation of the neural substrates of memory (e.g., the hippocampus, frontal cortices, and limbic-cortical connections) may mediate these age-related changes in recall (Nelson, 1995).

A handful of investigations have examined the associations between GCs and memory performance in infancy (Dettmer, Novak, Novak, Meyer, & Suomi, 2009; Haley, Grunau, Weinberg, Keidar, & Oberlander, 2010; Haley, Weinberg, & Grunau, 2006; Thompson & Trevathan, 2008, 2009). One study found that elevated GCs during learning in 3-month-old infants during a conjugate reinforcement mobile task, in which infants learn to associate leg movement with the movement of an overhead mobile, had a positive effect on memory when tested 24 hours later (Haley, Weinberg, et al., 2006). However, because stress was not manipulated in this study, it remains impossible to infer causal relations between stress and memory. It was speculated that the effect of GC was related to memory consolidation rather than acquisition or retrievals because GC concentrations on day 2 during retrieval and at baseline did not differ between infants who had shown increases or decreases in cortisol on day 1. In contrast, other researchers have found negative effects of GC on memory, but because of differences in design and methods, it is difficult to compare them. Thompson and Trevathan (2008) found that 3-month-old infants who decreased GCs during a preferential-looking paradigm, in which infants learned to associate maternal voice with a visual stimulus, had better memory. These infants showed greater discrimination between blocks paired with mother's voice compared with blocks not paired with mother's voice during the retention phase. In another study, Thompson and Trevathan (2009) found a similar effect in 6-month-olds who were tested in preferential-looking paradigm that presented pictures of the infant's own versus other infant's mother's face. Infants who decreased GCs looked longer at their own mother's face than at other infant's mother's face. In this study, girls who decreased GCs also looked long during a preferential-looking experiment when a recording of a familiar rhyme versus an unfamiliar rhyme was played. Unlike the Haley, Weinberg, and colleagues (2006) study, Thompson and Trevathan tested memory immediately after learning, and so GCs may not have had sufficient time to affect memory consolidation. Finally, in a study of young nonhuman primates, chronic elevations in GCs as measured by hair samples was related to poorer memory processing (Dettmer et al., 2009). Thus, initial reports suggest that the actions of GC on long-term memory consolidation are positive and that the actions of GC on short-term memory retrieval are negative.

Emotion and Stress Interactions in Memory

An important issue that has gained renewed interest in the field of memory research is the role of emotion in stress and memory. In many of the studies just reported, the facilitative effects of GCs on memory consolidation were found only under learning conditions that were emotionally arousing. Although it has long been thought that emotions can enhance memory through activation of adrenergic receptors (Roberts, Flexner, & Flexner, 1970) located in the basolateral amygdala (Quirarte, Roozendaal, & McGaugh, 1997), the pathways have not been clear. It has been shown that noradrenergic activation of the amygdala in rats is a prerequisite condition for the enhancing effects of GC on memory consolidation (Roozendaal, Okuda, Van der Zee, & McGaugh, 2006). There is also some behavioral evidence in adult humans of the synergistic effects of GC and emotional arousal on memory consolidation (Abercrombie, Speck, & Monticelli, 2006), in which subjects who reported negative affect and showed elevations in GC during the posttraining stress induction had better memory recall. This literature raises the question of whether emotional differences in infants during learning or during stress mediate stress–memory relationships, which again points to the regulatory role of the social context in memory formation.

Individual differences in memory recognition or memory recall have been related to temperament (Gunnar & Nelson, 1994), emotion (Fagen & Ohr, 1985; Gunnar & Nelson, 1994), and gender (Carver & Bauer, 1999). Infants showing greater positive affect (based on parent report) had larger brain event-related potentials (ERP) during a visual recognition task (Nelson, 1995) and better memory recall (Gunnar & Nelson, 1994). Research on infant emotions indicates that discrete emotions (e.g., anger, sadness, frustration, surprise, happiness) relate in different ways during HPA and autonomic activation (Lewis & Ramsay, 2005). It was shown that sadness is correlated with greater GC secretion and anger with greater autonomic activity (Lewis & Ramsay, 2005). Whether anger or sadness or frustration enhances the effects of GC on memory consolidation remains unexamined. A second issue concerning the relationship between stress and memory is gender. It has been shown that stress and memory relationships sometimes differ by sex (Wood & Shors, 1998). That sex differences in stress and emotion exist (Haley, Handmaker, & Lowe, 2006; Haley & Stansbury, 2003; Tronick, Als, Adamson, Wise, & Brazelton, 1978) raises the question of whether stress and memory relationships differ between boys and girls.

An indirect pathway that contributes to the synergistic effects of emotion-induced arousal and stress on memory consolidation is the peripheral release of catecholamines, which is triggered by the suppression of parasympathetic activity and activation of the sympathetic adrenal medulla (SAM). Activation of adrenergic receptors on the vagal fibers, which innervates the nucleus of the solitary tract, is associated with the central release of norepinephrine (Flood, Smith, & Morley, 1987). Activity of the vagus nerve, which is indexed by cardiac respiratory sinus arrhythmia (RSA), is used to study emotion and cognition in infants. The brainstem nuclei that underlie the capacity to withdraw parasympathetic tone in response to a challenge (i.e., the "vagal brake") are said to have evolved to support more complex forms of mammalian behavior (Porges, 1995). Activation of the vagal brake is linked to better attention (Porges, 1995), faster habituation to novelty (Bornstien & Suess, 2000), better memory recognition (Linnemeyer & Porges, 1986), and greater expression and regulation of negative affect (Stifter, Fox, & Porges, 1989). We have shown that decreases in RSA predict faster learning and better memory recall (Haley et al., 2006, 2010).

In polyvagal theory, Porges (1995) proposes that parasympathetic activity plays an important role in the coordination of physiological and behavioral response systems, which are needed to maintain homeostasis and enhance growth as well as mobilize energy needed to respond to changes in the environment. Vagal tone is an established autonomic index of parasympathetic activity that reflects RSA, which is assumed to be regulated by the nucleus ambiguus in the brainstem. Studies on human infants have examined basal vagal tone and changes in vagal tone during cognitive tasks in relation to attention (DeGangi, DiPietro, Greenspan, & Porges, 1991; Huffman et al., 1998), habituation (Bornstein & Suess, 2000), memory recognition (Linnemeyer & Porges, 1986), play exploration (DiPietro, Porges, & Uhly, 1992), and contingency learning (Haley, Grunau, Oberlander, & Weinberg, 2008). These studies indicate that higher basal tone and greater suppression of vagal tone during a challenge facilitate cognitive performance. Specifically, we have shown that greater suppression of vagal tone during encoding predicted greater immediate imitation of actions after a brief delay in healthy 6-month-old infants (Haley et al., 2008).

Social Stress

To begin to address the mechanisms by which social stress affects learning and memory, we consider the stress produced by disrupting the parent–infant relationship. We assume that both infants and adults are highly motivated to establish reciprocal interactions with others in which each party recognizes the emotional and spontaneous gestures of the other. These interactions serve interpersonal goals and regulatory functions, which are viewed as reciprocal (Rosenblatt, 1965), hidden (Hofer, 2006), and external (Tronick, 1989) sources of regulation for the infant. When these interpersonal motives are thwarted and expectations are violated, protest behavior is expressed and social reparation processes become necessary. In the case of the parent–infant dyad, play behavior and social expectations are heightened and reinforced when both parties can resume play behaviors after brief violations of social expectation or periods of unresponsiveness. A lack of reciprocity, then, can be a significant source of stress that may affect the ability to learn from others.

The still-face task (Tronick et al., 1978) is thought to violate the infant's expectations of the parent–infant relationship and to disrupt the usually reciprocal and mutual state of parent–infant interactions (see Figure 11.1). Presumably, the violation of expectations is produced by the parent's still-faced unresponsiveness, and the disruption of mutuality results from the infant's failure to reestablish a contingent and reciprocal interaction with the parent. It has been assumed that the stress of the still-face task occurs when the infant's goal of reestablishing this contingent and reciprocal interaction with an unresponsive and still-faced parent is blocked, producing uncertainty, uncontrollability, and therefore distress. In contrast, the reunion

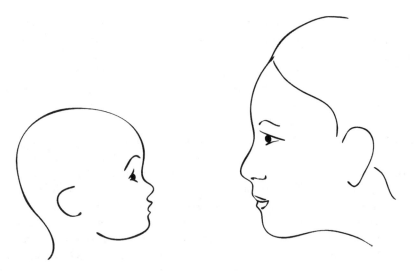

FIGURE 11.1. Still-face condition. Illustrated by Kate Steinmann.

condition offers an excellent opportunity for infants and parents to repair these disruptions to the relationship (see Mesman, IJzendoorn, & Bakermans-Kranenburg, 2009, for a review and discussion of the still-face literature).

Physiological activity recorded during the standard still-face paradigm indicates that infant heart rate levels increase during the still-face condition and, unlike negative affect, show evidence of recovery by returning to pre-still-face levels during the reunion condition. Furthermore, vagal tone levels have shown a similar and expected pattern in the opposite direction of decrease during the still-face condition and return to baseline levels during the reunion episode (Moore & Calkins, 2004; Moore et al., 2009; Weinberg & Tronick, 1996). Infant skin conductance, which is a general measure of arousal, has been shown to increase gradually across the still-face paradigm (Ham & Tronick, 2006). In still-face studies evaluating infant HPA activity, a group elevation from prechallenge to poststress cortisol concentrations has not been observed (Grant et al., 2009; Lewis & Ramsay, 2004); however, elevations in cortisol concentrations have been observed in studies that did not allow any touching during the procedure (Feldman, Singer, & Zagoory, 2010). In addition, elevations in infant cortisol responses have also been reported in studies using an extended or repeated still-face paradigm in which an extra still-face and reunion episode was added (Haley, 2011; Haley & Stansbury, 2003; Haley et al., 2006).

Social Stress and Memory

How well can the infant remember a social stress event like the still-face procedure? In a striking example of the infant's memory for social stress events, Bornstein, Arterberry, and Mash (2004) showed that infants successfully identify the face of an experimenter who had performed a still-face 15 months earlier for the 5-month-old infant as parents do in the typical still-face paradigm. In an effort to understand the mechanisms by which infants remember the stressful event of the still-face paradigm, Tronick and colleagues initiated a new line of work examining the infant cortisol responses to the still face when repeated after a 2-week interval. For example, Montirosso and colleagues (2011) have shown that 4- to 6-month-old infants who show greater stress reactivity to the initial still face at time 1 show greater physiological habituation when the procedure is repeated on the second occasion, suggesting that some of the infants remember the stressful event.

Given that the relationship disruption stress (i.e., the stress produced by the still-face paradigm) is remembered, it becomes possible to consider whether such stressful memories will affect other memories. Initially, we used the still face as a reliable stressor to examine the effects of stress on learning and memory. We have utilized a postlearning stress design (Haley et al., 2010; Haley, Barr, & Condick, 2012) to test the hypothesis that stress hormones can enhance memory consolidation. In one study, healthy 6-month-old infants were randomly assigned to a stress ($n = 15$) or a control ($n = 14$) group immediately after demonstration of a deferred imitation task, and memory was tested 24 hours later (see Figure 11.2). Infants in the stress and non-stress groups performed more target actions (removal of a glove from a puppet, shaking the glove, replacing the glove on the puppet) than infants in the memory control group, who did not see the demonstration. Infants in the stress group participated in a 10-minute double still-face task, and infants in the nonstress group participated in a 10-minute continuous face-to-face task. To evaluate stress responses, saliva samples collected upon arrival to the lab and again 20 and 30 minutes after the start of each

Day 1		Day 2 (24 hours later)
RDS Group (stress group) N = 15		
Puppet Task Demonstration	*Still-Face Paradigm (Stressor, or RDS)*	*Puppet Task Memory Test*
3 target actions	Face to Face / Still Face / Face to Face / Still Face / Face to Face	3 target actions
0–90 secs.	0–2 min. / 2–4 min. / 4–6 min. / 6–8 min. / 8–10 min.	
Non-RDS Group (nonstress group) N = 15		
Puppet Task Demonstration	*Face-to-Face Paradigm*	*Puppet Task Memory Test*
3 target actions	Face to Face	3 target actions
0–90 secs.	0–10 min.	
Control Group N = 8		
(No lab visit on Day 1)		*Puppet Task Memory Test*
		3 target actions

FIGURE 11.2. Schematic of stress and memory study.

stress task were analyzed for cortisol concentrations. Salivary cortisol responses on day 1 were greater in the stress group compared with the nonstress group.

Although there were no group differences in total number of target actions performed 24 hours later, the stress group showed longer latency in the production of target actions than the nonstress group. Specifically, infants in the stress group produced the most target actions of all groups at 90 seconds after testing began. In contrast, infants in the nonstress group performed the most target actions of all groups in the first 30 seconds of testing. Furthermore, the infants in the stress group showed a significant anticipatory stress response when returning to the laboratory (Haley, Cordick, Mackrell, Antony, & Ryan-Harrison, 2011). Presumably, this anticipatory stress response is caused by their memory of the still-face procedure from the day before. The memory of the still face may have interfered with their memory of the target actions.

We also found evidence to support our hypothesis that postlearning stress would enhance memory: Infants who produced two target actions in either the stress or nonstress groups showed the greatest peak cortisol responses on day 1. Regardless of the stress condition, infants who showed elevations in cortisol on day 1 were able to perform more target actions on day 2.

Taken together, these findings shed new light on how stress hormones and stressful memories both enhance and disrupt memory consolidation in infancy and underscore the regulatory function of the parent. In this case, the role of the parents in regulating stress and memory relationships is twofold. First, infants of parents who participated in the still-face procedure, which occurred on day 1 after the puppet demonstration, exhibited an elevation in cortisol secretion on day 1 and day 2, which resulted in a significantly longer latency during memory testing. Second, infants who showed the greatest secretion of cortisol on day 1 (regardless of still-face or non-still-face group assignment) also remembered the most target actions.

Goal Detection and the Mirror Neuron System

One important methodological issue in testing infant memory using a deferred-imitation paradigm in young infants has been identified: It is unclear whether infants' failure to imitate after a delay is due to a failure in memory processing or a failure to understand the purpose of the actions performed. Even if the infants have previously demonstrated their ability to perform the actions, it is unknown whether they understand the actions. The skeptical view of infant imitation is that they merely ape others but do not understand them until they are at least 2 years of age (e.g., Jones, 2005). However, theories of action understanding suggest that infants may be hard-wired to detect the intentions of others (Gallese & Rochat, Chapter 2, this volume). Activation of motor neurons in the mirror neuron system (MNS) is thought to provide an intuitive understanding of others' action (motor resonance), which gives them direct access to and insight into the goals and intentions of others. Although the development of the MNS has been demonstrated in young human infants (Nyström, 2008; Nyström, Ljunghammar, Rosander, & von Hofsten, 2011) and has been linked to immediate imitation in 1-week-old infant rhesus macaques (Ferrari et al., 2012), it remains unknown whether detecting the intention of others is necessary for human infant imitation. Accordingly, we considered whether infants could detect the goal of the actions performed by the experimenter and whether they had the neural capacity to support goal detection and, more importantly, whether this ability to detect the goals of others is necessary for them to remember those actions (i.e., reproduce those actions after a delay). In short, we examined whether motor resonance is present during the observation of target actions and is predictive of imitation.

A wealth of research has contributed to our understanding of infants' early social-cognitive capacities. There has been much interdisciplinary progress in the science of how early relationships affect the developing mind. Research on social-cognitive development supports the biological preparedness and the sophisticated representational capacity of infants, which, taken together, enable them to perceive, respond to, and learn from their relationships. These lines of research include face processing (de Haan & Carver, Chapter 6, this volume), emotional discrimination (Walker-Andrews et al., Chapter 9, this volume), joint attention (Mundy, Chapter 14, this volume), theory of mind (Sabbagh et al., Chapter 13, this volume), event memory (Bauer, Chapter 7, this volume), social loss (Legerstee, Chapter 10, this volume), language, and shared meaning (Trevarthen & Delafield-Butt, Chapter 8, this volume). On other fronts, the discovery of the mirror neuron system (MNS) (Gallese & Rochat, Chapter 2, this volume) provides a new conduit for intersubjectivity, which is likely to affect how we understand the development of the parent–infant relationship as well as the way that relationships affect learning and memory.

The discovery of the MNS in the adult monkey and the possibility of a homologue system in humans has spurred the notion that we understand others' behaviors in part by representing them in our own motor cortex. Mirror neuron activity using noninvasive brain imaging methods can be indirectly measured with electroencephalography (EEG). For example, EEG μ activity is a portion of the alpha frequency band in the 4- to 13-Hz range, and its suppression during observation and execution of goal-directed actions has been linked to the activation of the MNS (Muthukumaraswamy, Johnson, & McNair, 2004; Niedermeyer, 1997; Perry & Bentin, 2009). More recent evidence supports the use of EEG μ suppression as an indirect marker of mirror neuron activity: Coregistration of EEG and functional magnetic resonance imaging data revealed that EEG μ suppression predicted activation of the motor cortex and inferior parietal lobule, regions that have been previously linked to mirror neuron activity (Arnstein, Cui, Keysers, Maurits, & Gazzola, 2011). This is a critical point because it has enabled researchers to use indirect albeit noninvasive methods to study the development of the MNS in humans and primates.

Questions about the development of this system are areas of active investigation. For example, Lepage and Théoret (2006) reported that resting EEG μ rhythm activity displayed by young children (52–133 months) was attenuated during observation and execution of a motor action. More recently, it has been reported that 9-month-old infants who observe goal-directed actions show μ modulation (Southgate, Johnson, El Karoui, & Csibra, 2010), and this was demonstrated in infants who had shown similar μ modulation during execution. Interestingly, Lepage and Théoret (2006) found no association between age and μ modulation, which seems to support the innate modular view of imitation and the MNS. The findings from this study are profoundly similar to findings in adult studies of imitation (Babiloni et al., 2002; Marshall, Bouquet, Shipley, & Young, 2009; Muthukumaraswamy & Johnson, 2004;

Muthkumaraswamy et al., 2004; Perry & Bentin, 2009), leaving open the question of how early the MNS matures. It has been proposed—and recently validated—that neonatal imitation, which has been demonstrated in human and primates, is supported by the activation of the MNS: Ferrari and colleagues (2012) reported EEG μ suppression during observation and execution of facial gestures in newborn rhesus macaques. This provides the evidence for the earliest development of the MNS in primates.

On the basis of evidence that human infants as young as 9 months show μ modulation during observation and execution of actions, we evaluated μ modulation during observation and execution of goal-directed actions in infants younger and older than 9 months. We tested the hypothesis that both younger and older infants would show evidence of goal recognition during observation, but only the older infants would show this capacity when performing the action. We predicted that infants who imitated others would show greater μ power suppression during observation of target actions. In this study, 22 infants (14 female), ages 4–12 months (mean, 8.38 months), were tested to see whether age was a significant factor in μ suppression and whether suppression during observation predicted imitation.

Infants observed a mitten removal, mitten shake, and mitten replacement during a puppet task. Each target action was demonstrated six times. EEG data recorded during the demonstration (Akano, Haley, & Dudek, 2011) were spliced into 1,000-millisecond segments and averaged for each target action. Frequency analysis was conducted to evaluate μ power in the 4–8 Hz range. Mu power suppression scores were created by subtracting μ power during each target action from that during the control phase (stationary puppet).

Analyses of variance were used to test whether μ change differed between imitators and nonimitators and between younger and older infants. Of the 22 participants, 18 had usable EEG and behavioral data. Infant imitators ($n = 11$) showed greater μ change than nonimitators ($n = 7$) during mitten removal, $F(1, 18) = 5.93$, $p < .05$. This finding suggests that the μ power suppression may be a neural marker and perhaps a necessary condition for imitation and memory. Although there were no age differences in imitation behavior per se, older infants showed greater μ power suppression than younger infants during replacement of the mitten, $F(1, 18) = 6.20$, $p < .05$. This is quite consistent with the number of actions young infants perform after a 24-hour delay (i.e., on average 1.5 actions). One practical implication of this work, then, is that the ability to activate the MNS during observation of to-be-remembered actions is a necessary condition for social learning and memory. Overall, these results indicate that imitation is partly mediated by the activation of the MNS and that older infants show greater activation of the MNS during observation, which may explain their ability to remember more actions more faithfully than younger infants, in general, when tested on more complex tasks.

Discussion

While highlighting the parent–infant relationship as a key context through which early learning (e.g., imitation) occurs, we underscore its simultaneous role as a regulator of biological experience. The significance of the relationship in developing regulatory and representational capacities draws attention to the impact of its disruption and thus the impact of social stress on biological development. Here we have focused specifically on the development of memory function, in particular memory consolidation, by examining recent work on the regulatory and representational capacities of the parent–infant dyad.

The model developed in this chapter assumes, then, that the mind has an innate and developing capacity for intersubjectivity, reflected biologically in the MNS. We also examined how the development of the MNS, a mechanism for social learning, contributes to infants' ability to remember the actions of others. The age effects in the activation of the MNS observed suggests that although infants can reproduce the actions of others, their ability to understand the goals of others develops over time and may limit the extent to which they can remember those actions.

Understanding the reciprocal links between relationships and biology and their influence on infants' developing mind remains a major challenge. Animal research has many examples that are helpful for thinking about the complexity of these links. In one fascinating line of research that illustrates the dialectic between stress and learning in the context of an attachment relationship, Sullivan, Landers, Yeaman, and Wilson (2000) provide evidence for a fail-safe system that ensures that rat pups will seek physical proximity to the mother regardless of the standard of care she provides. In an illuminating commentary on this work, aptly titled *Any Kind of Mother in a Storm*, Sapolsky (2009) discusses some of the nuances in the development of the neuroendocrine mechanisms that contribute to Sullivan's findings. Until postnatal day 10, rat pups are stress hyporesponsive, meaning they fail to secrete stress hormones in response to shocks. The secretion of stress hormones is necessary for fear learning to occur, and so these young pups continue to approach the odor that has previously been paired with a shock. After postnatal day 10, however, the pups are able to secrete stress hormones in response to the shocks and so can learn to avoid the odor; however, in the presence of the mother, their stress response is inhibited, thus ensuring that they will continue to approach her and never learn to avoid or fear her smell regardless of her behavior.

Future research should consider how these mechanisms interact and become coordinated. For example, what are the effects of stress on the MNS and the effects of the MNS on stress regulation? What other hormonal, neural, and genetic markers modulate the regulatory functions and representational capacities of the parent–infant dyad? As we gain more knowledge about the regulatory role of parents in human infant development, we will gain greater insight into how the intersubjective mechanisms of human relationships affect memory consolidation.

References

Abercrombie, H. C., Kalin, N. H., Thurow, M. E., Rosenkranz, M. A., & Davidson, R. J. (2003). Cortisol variation in humans affects memory for emotionally laden and neutral information. *Behavioral Neuroscience, 117*(3), 505.
Abercrombie, H. C., Speck, N. S., & Monticelli, R. M. (2006). Endogenous cortisol elevations are related to memory facilitation only in individuals who are emotionally aroused. *Psychoneuroendocrinology, 31*(2), 187–196.

Akano, A. J., Haley, D. W., & Dudek, J. (2011). Investigating social cognition in infants and adults using dense array electroencephalography (dEEG). *Journal of Visualized Experiments, 52,* e2759.

Amini, F., Lewis, T., Lannon, R., Louie, A., Baumbacher, G., McGuinness, T., et al. (1996). Affect, attachment, memory: Contributions toward psychobiologic integration. *Psychiatry—Interpersonal and Biological Processes, 59*(3), 213–239

Andreano, J. M., & Cahill, L. (2006). Glucocorticoid release and memory consolidation in men and women. *Psychological Science, 17*(6), 466.

Arnstein, D., Cui, F., Keysers, C., Maurits, N. M., & Gazzola, V. (2011). μ-supression during action observation and execution correlates with BOLD in dorsal premotor, inferior parietal, and SI cortices. *Journal of Neuroscience, 31,* 14243–14249.

Babiloni, C., Babiloni, F., Carducci, F., Cincotti, F., Cocozza, G., Del Percio, C., et al. (2002). Human cortical electroencephalography (EEG) rhythms during the observation of simple aimless movements: A high-resolution EEG study. *NeuroImage, 17*(2), 559–572.

Barr, R., Dowden, A., & Hayne, H. (1996). Developmental changes in deferred imitation by 6- to 24-month-old infants. *Infant Behavior and Development, 19*(2), 159–170.

Bauer, P. J. (1996). What do infants recall of their lives?: Memory for specific events by one- to two-year-olds. *American Psychologist, 51*(1), 29.

Belsky, J., Spritz, B., & Crnic, K. (1996). Infant attachment security and affective-cognitive information processing at age 3. *Psychological Science, 7*(2), 111–114.

Bornstein, M. H., Arterberry, M. E., & Mash, C. (2004). Long-term memory for an emotional interpersonal interaction occurring at 5 months of age. *Infancy, 6*(3), 407–416.

Bornstein, M. H., & Suess, P. E. (2000). Physiological self-regulation and information processing in infancy: Cardiac vagal tone and habituation. *Child Development, 71*(2), 273–287.

Buchanan, T. W., & Lovallo, W. R. (2001). Enhanced memory for emotional material following stress-level cortisol treatment in humans. *Psychoneuroendocrinology, 26*(3), 307–317.

Carver, L. J., & Bauer, P. J. (1999). When the event is more than the sum of its parts: 9-month-olds' long-term ordered recall. *Memory, 7*(2), 147–174.

Darwin, C. (1871). *The descent of man.* London: Murray.

de Kloet, E. (1991). Brain corticosteroid receptor balance and homeostatic control. *Frontiers in Neuroendocrinology, 12*(2), 95–164.

de Kloet, E. R., Oitzl, M. S., & Joels, M. (1999). Stress and cognition: Are corticosteroids good or bad guys? *Trends in Neurosciences, 22*(10), 422–426.

de Quervain, D. J. F., Aerni, A., Schelling, G., & Roozendaal, B. (2009). Glucocorticoids and the regulation of memory in health and disease. *Frontiers in Neuroendocrinology, 30*(3), 358–370.

DeGangi, G. A., DiPietro, J. A., Greenspan, S. I., & Porges, S. W. (1991). Psychophysiological characteristics of the regulatory disorder infant. *Infant Behavior and Development, 14,* 37–50.

Dettmer, A. M., Novak, M. F., Novak, M. A., Meyer, J. S., & Suomi, S. J. (2009). Hair cortisol predicts object permanence performance in infant rhesus macaques *(macaca mulatta). Developmental Psychobiology, 51*(8), 706–713.

DiPietro, J. A., Porges, S. W., & Uhly, B. (1992). Reactivity and developmental competence in preterm and full-term infants. *Developmental Psychology, 28,* 831–841.

Fagen, J. W., & Ohr, P. S. (1985). Temperament and crying in response to the violation of a learned expectancy in early infancy. *Infant Behavior and Development, 8*(2), 157–166.

Fagen, J. W., & Rovee-Collier, C. (1983). Memory retrieval: A time-locked process in infancy. *Science, 222,* 1349.

Feldman, R., Singer, M., & Zagoory, O. (2010). Touch attenuates infants' physiological reactivity to stress. *Developmental Science, 13*(2), 271–278.

Ferrari, P. F., Vanderwert, R. E., Paukner, A., Bower, S., Suomi, S. J., & Fox, N. A. (2012). Distinct EEG amplitude suppression to facial gestures as evidence for a mirror mechanism in newborn monkeys. *Journal of Cognitive Neuroscience, 24*(5), 1165–1172.

Flood, J. F., Smith, G. E., & Morley, J. E. (1987). Modulation of memory processing by cholecystokinin: Dependence on the vagus nerve. *Science, 236,* 832.

Gillath, O., Bunge, S. A., Shaver, P. R., Wendelken, C., & Mikulincer, M. (2005). Attachment-style differences in the ability to suppress negative thoughts: Exploring the neural correlates. *NeuroImage, 28*(4), 835–847.

Grant, K.-A., McMahon, C., Austin, M.-P., Reilly, N., Leader, L., & Ali, S. (2009). Maternal prenatal anxiety, postnatal caregiving and infants' cortisol responses to the still-face procedure. *Developmental Psychobiology, 51*(8), 625–637.

Gunnar, M., & Quevedo, K. (2007). The neurobiology of stress and development. *Annual Review of Psychology, 58,* 145–173.

Gunnar, M. R., & Nelson, C. A. (1994). Event-related potentials in year-old infants: Relations with emotionality and cortisol. *Child Development, 65*(1), 80–94.

Haley, D. W. (2011). Relationship disruption stress in human infants: A validation study with experimental and control groups. *Stress, 14*(5), 530–536.

Haley, D. W., Barr, R. F., & Cordick, J. A. (2012). *Stress and memory in infancy.* Manuscript submitted for publication.

Haley, D. W., Cordick, J., Mackrell, S., Antony, I., & Ryan-Harrison, M. H. (2011). Infant anticipatory stress. *Biology Letters, 7*(1), 136–138.

Haley, D. W., Grunau, R. E., Oberlander, T. F., & Weinberg, J. (2008). Contingency learning and reactivity in preterm and full-term infants at 3 months. *Infancy, 13*(6), 570–595.

Haley, D. W., Grunau, R. E., Weinberg, J., Keidar, A., & Oberlander, T. F. (2010). Physiological correlates of memory recall in infancy: Vagal tone, cortisol, and imitation in preterm and full-term infants at 6 months. *Infant Behavior and Development, 33*(2), 219–234.

Haley, D. W., Handmaker, N. S., & Lowe, J. (2006). Infant stress reactivity and prenatal alcohol exposure. *Alcoholism: Clinical and Experimental Research, 30*(12), 2055–2064.

Haley, D. W., & Stansbury, K. (2003). Infant stress and parent responsiveness: Regulation of physiology and behavior during still-face and reunion. *Child Development, 74*(5), 1534–1546.

Haley, D. W., Weinberg, J., & Grunau, R. E. (2006). Cortisol, contingency learning, and memory in preterm and full-term infants. *Psychoneuroendocrinology, 31*(1), 108–117.

Ham, J., & Tronick, E. (2006). Infant resilience to the stress of the still-face. *Annals of the New York Academy of Sciences, 1094*(1), 297–302.

Hofer, M. A. (2006). Psychobiological roots of early attachment. *Current Directions in Psychological Science, 15*(2), 84.

Huffman, L. C., Bryan, Y. E., del Carmen, R., Pedersen, F. A., Doussard-Roosevelt, J. A., & Porges, S. W. (1998). Infant temperament and cardiac vagal tone: Assessments at twelve weeks of age. *Child Development, 69,* 624–635.

Ito, R., & Canseliet, M. (2010). Amphetamine exposure selectively enhances hippocampus-dependent spatial learning and attenuates amygdala-dependent cue learning. *Neuropsychopharmacology, 35,* 1440–1452.

Jones, S. S. (2005). Why don't apes ape more? In S. Hurley & N. Chater (Eds.), *Perspectives on imitation: From cognitive neuroscience to social science* (Vol. 1, pp. 297–301). Cambridge, MA: MIT Press.

Kirschbaum, C., Wolf, O., May, M., Wippich, W., & Hellhammer, D. (1996). Stress- and treatment-induced elevations of cortisol levels associated with impaired declarative memory in healthy adults. *Life Sciences, 58*(17), 1475–1483.

Kraemer, G. W. (1992). A psychobiological theory of attachment. *Behavioral and Brain Sciences, 15*(3), 493–511.

LeDoux, J. E. (2000). Emotion circuits in the brain. *Annual Review of Neuroscience, 23,* 155–184.

Lepage, J., & Théoret, H. (2006). EEG evidence for the presence of an action observation-execution matching system in children. *European Journal of Neuroscience, 23*(9), 2505–2510.

Lewis, M., & Ramsay, D. (2004). Development of self-recognition, personal pronoun use, and pretend play during the 2nd year. *Child Development, 75*(6), 1821–1831.

Lewis, M., & Ramsay, D. (2005). Infant emotional and cortisol responses to goal blockage. *Child Development, 76*(2), 518–530.

Linnemeyer, S. A., & Porges, S. W. (1986). Recognition memory and cardiac vagal tone in 6–month-old infants. *Infant Behavior and Development, 9*(1), 43–56.

Lupien, S., Maheu, F., Tu, M., Fiocco, A., & Schramek, T. (2007). The effects of stress and stress hormones on human cognition: Implications for the field of brain and cognition. *Brain and Cognition, 65*(3), 209–237.

Marshall, P. J., Bouquet, C. A., Shipley, T. F., & Young. T. (2009). Effects of brief imitative experience on EEG desynchronization during action observation. *Neuropsychologia, 47*(10), 2100–2106.

McEwen, B. S., Weiss, J. M., & Schwartz, L. S. (1968). Selective retention of corticosterone by limbic structures in rat brain. *Nature, 220,* 911–912.

McGaugh, J. L. (1966). Time-dependent processes in memory storage. *Science, 153,* 1351.

McGaugh, J. L. (2000). Memory—A century of consolidation. *Science, 287,* 248.

Meltzoff, A. N. (1988). Infant imitation and memory: Nine-month-olds in immediate and deferred tests. *Child Development, 59,* 217–225.

Mesman, J., Van IJzendoorn, M. H., & Bakermans-Kranenburg, M. J. (2009). The many faces of the still-face paradigm: A review and meta-analysis. *Developmental Review, 29*(2), 120–162.

Mikulincer, M., & Orbach, I. (1995). Attachment styles and repressive defensiveness—The accessibility and architecture of affective memories. *Journal of Personality and Social Psychology, 68*(5), 917–925.

Montirosso, R., Cozzi, P., Morandi, F., Ciceri, F., Provenzi, L., Borgattil, R., et al. (2011). *Four-month-old infants memory for a stressful social event measured by cortisol reactivity.* Poster presented at the biennial meeting of the Society for Research in Child Development, Montreal.

Moore, G. A., & Calkins, S. D. (2004). Infants' vagal regulation in the still-face paradigm is related to dyadic coordination of mother–infant interaction. *Developmental Psychology, 40*(6), 1068.

Moore, G. A., Hill-Soderlund, A. L., Propper, C. B., Calkins, S. D., Mills-Koonce, W. R., & Cox, M. J. (2009). Mother–infant vagal regulation in the face-to-face still-face paradigm is moderated by maternal sensitivity. *Child Development, 80*(1), 209–223.

Muthukumaraswamy, S. D., & Johnson, B. W. (2004). Changes in rolandic mu rhythm during observation of a precision grip. *Psychophysiology, 41*(1), 152–156.

Muthukumaraswamy, S. D., Johnson, B. W., & McNair, N. A. (2004). Mu rhythm modulation during observation of an object-directed grasp. *Cognitive Brain Research, 19*(2), 195–201.

Nelson, C. A. (1995). The ontogeny of human memory: A cognitive neuroscience perspective. *Developmental Psychology, 31*(5), 723.

Newcomer, J. W., Craft, S., Hershey, T., Askins, K., & Bardgett, M. (1994).

Glucocorticoid-induced impairment in declarative memory performance in adult humans. *Journal of Neuroscience, 14*(4), 2047–2053.

Niedermeyer, E. (1997). Alpha rhythms as physiological and abnormal phenomena. *International Journal of Psychophysiology, 26*(1), 31–49.

Nyström, P. (2008). The infant mirror neuron system studied with high density EEG. *Social Neuroscience, 3*(3–4), 334–347.

Nyström, P., Ljunghammar, T., Rosander, K., & von Hofsten, C. (2011). Using mu rhythm desynchronization to measure mirror neuron activity in infants. *Developmental Science, 14*(2), 327–335.

O'Keefe, J., & Nadel, L. (1978). *The hippocampus as a cognitive map.* Oxford, UK: Clarendon Press.

Perlman, W. R., Webster, M. J., Herman, M. M., Kleinman, J. E., & Weickert, C. S. (2007). Age-related differences in glucocorticoid receptor mRNA levels in the human brain. *Neurobiology of Aging, 28*(3), 447–458.

Perry, A., & Bentin, S. (2009). Mirror activity in the human brain while observing hand movements: A comparison between EEG desynchronization in the µ-range and previous fMRI results. *Brain Research, 1282,* 126–132.

Porges, S. W. (1995). Orienting in a defensive world: Mammalian modifications of our evolutionary heritage. A polyvagal theory. *Psychophysiology, 32*(4), 301–318.

Quas, J. A., Yim, I. S., Edelstein, R. S., Cahill, L., & Rush, E. B. (2011). The role of cortisol reactivity in children's and adults' memory of a prior stressful experience. *Developmental Psychobiology, 53,* 166–174.

Quirarte, G. L., Roozendaal, B., & McGaugh, J. L. (1997). Glucocorticoid enhancement of memory storage involves noradrenergic activation in the basolateral amygdala. *Proceedings of the National Academy of Sciences USA, 94*(25), 140–148.

Roberts, R. B., Flexner, J. B., & Flexner, L. B. (1970). Some evidence for the involvement of adrenergic sites in the memory trace. *Proceedings of the National Academy of Sciences USA, 66*(2), 310–313.

Roozendaal, B. (2002). Stress and memory: Opposing effects of glucocorticoids on memory consolidation and memory retrieval. *Neurobiology of Learning and Memory, 78*(3), 578–595.

Roozendaal, B., Okuda, S., Van der Zee, E. A., & McGaugh, J. L. (2006). Glucocorticoid enhancement of memory requires arousal-induced noradrenergic activation in the basolateral amygdala. *Proceedings of the National Academy of Sciences USA, 103*(17), 6741–6746.

Rosenblatt, J. (1965). The basis of synchrony in the behavioral interaction between the mother and her offspring in the laboratory rat. *Determinants of Infant Behavior, 3,* 3–41.

Rosenfeld, P., Eekelen, J., Levine, S., & de Kloet, E. R. (1993). Ontogeny of corticosteroid receptors in the brain. *Cellular and Molecular Neurobiology, 13*(4), 295–319.

Rovee-Collier, C. K., Sullivan, M. W., Enright, M., Lucas, D., & Fagen, J. W. (1980). Reactivation of infant memory. *Science, 208,* 1159.

Sapolsky, R. (2009). Any kind of mother in a storm. *Nature Neuroscience, 12,* 1355–1356.

Sapolsky, R. M., Romero, L. M., & Munck, A. U. (2000). How do glucocorticoids influence stress responses?: Integrating permissive, suppressive, stimulatory, and preparative actions. *Endocrine Reviews, 21*(1), 55–89.

Smeekens, S., Riksen-Walraven, J. M., van Bakel, H. J. A., & de Weerth, C. (2010). Five-year-olds' cortisol reactions to an attachment story completion task. *Psychoneuroendocrinology, 35*(6), 858–865.

Southgate, V., Johnson, M. H., El Karoui, I., & Csibra, G. (2010). Motor system activation reveals infants' on-line prediction of others' goals. *Psychological Science, 21,* 355–359.

Stifter, C. A., Fox, N. A., & Porges, S. W. (1989). Facial expressivity and vagal tone in 5- and 10-month-old infants. *Infant Behavior and Development, 12*(2), 127–137.

Sullivan, R. M., Landers, M., Yeaman, B., & Wilson, D. A. (2000). Good memories of bad events in infancy. *Nature, 407,* 38–39.

Thompson, L. A., & Trevathan, W. R. (2008). Cortisol reactivity, maternal sensitivity, and learning in 3–month-old infants. *Infant Behavior and Development, 31*(1), 92–106.

Thompson, L. A., & Trevathan, W. R. (2009). Cortisol reactivity, maternal sensitivity, and infant preference for mother's familiar face and rhyme in 6–month-old infants. *Journal of Reproductive and Infant Psychology, 27*(2), 143–167.

Tronick, E. Z. (1989). Emotions and emotional communication in infants. *American Psychologist, 44*(2), 112–119.

Tronick, E. Z., Als, H., Adamson, L., Wise, S., & Brazelton, T. B. (1978). The infant's response to entrapment between contradictory messages in face-to-face interaction. *Journal of American Academy of Child Psychiatry, 17*(1), 1–13.

Weinberg, M. K., & Tronick, E. Z. (1996). Infant affective reactions to the resumption of maternal interaction after the still-face. *Child Development, 67*(3), 905–914.

Wolkowitz, O. M., Reus, V. I., Weingartner, H., & Thompson, K. (1990). Cognitive effects of corticosteroids. *American Journal of Psychiatry, 147*(10), 1297–1303.

Wood, G. E., & Shors, T. J. (1998). Stress facilitates classical conditioning in males, but impairs classical conditioning in females through activational effects of ovarian hormones. *Proceedings of the National Academy of Sciences USA, 95*(7), 4066.

CHAPTER 12

Mother–Infant Attunement

A Multilevel Approach via Body, Brain, and Behavior

MARC H. BORNSTEIN

Bidirectionality. Coaction. Coherence. Concordance. Contingency. Coordination. Coregulation. Covariation. Harmony. Intersubjectivity. Matching. Mirroring. Mutuality. Reciprocity. Responsiveness. Synchrony. For nearly half a century, psychologists, psychiatrists, ethologists, and myriad other students of human behavior and family life have summoned these terms to convey the special character of well-functioning mother–infant relationships—together here referred to as *attunement.*

Parent and child interactions are often described as intricate patterns of sensitive mutual understandings and unfolding synchronous transactions (Bornstein, 2006, 2009; Bugental & Goodnow, 1998; Harris & Waugh, 2002; Kochanska, 1997; Maccoby, 1992; Schaffer, 1991; Stern, Hofer, Haft, & Dore, 1985), and achieving "harmonious dyadic interaction" is considered one of the most significant developmental issues of infancy (Sroufe & Rutter, 1984). Special about human beings, and perhaps one of the most significant characteristics of our species, is developmental plasticity by which biological and psychological structures and processes emerge and come to align in close attunement with their effective environment. Attunement, therefore, consists of the transacting contributions of each partner, but like a gestalt attunement is also more than the sum of its parts. Attunement is dyadic, dynamic, and wholistic.

The Mother's Part in Attunement

Most of theoretical and empirical work relating to parent–child attunement has concerned mothers and their infants. Virgin female and male rats do not readily exhibit parental responses, suggesting that the changes that accompany reproductive experience prime the brain to be sensitive to a new and unique set of stimuli, namely pups (Lambert & Kinsley, 2012). Becoming a parent is a biologically and psychologically

266

transformative experience. Pregnancy heralds adaptations in the hormonal and nervous systems to ensure that fetus(es) are protected, safely delivered, and eventually cared for (Brunton & Russell, 2008). Basic hormonal and neural mechanisms supporting the mother–infant relationship have been conserved throughout mammalian evolution. To maximize the likelihood of survival and well-being of their offspring, mammalian parents, especially mothers, appear to be equipped with motivations to nurture, nurse, thermoregulate, and protect their young. When rat dams are given a choice between a chamber that has been associated with pups and one where they may receive an injection of cocaine, there is a period of time after parturition when new dams prefer pups, spurning even the attraction of narcotics (Mattson, Williams, Rosenblatt, & Morrell, 2001; Pereira, Seip, & Morrell, 2008; Seip & Morrell, 2007). However, simply being exposed to pup-related visual, auditory, or olfactory cues will not sustain maternal behavior (Morgan, Fleming, & Stern, 1992). To ensure their attunement, dams must actively interact with their pups and receive sensory input during that interaction (Morgan, Watchus, Milgram, & Fleming, 1999).

Evolutionary science distinguishes between bringing a new individual into the world and tending to that individual, child*bearing* versus child*caring*. Whereas species lower in the phylogenetic hierarchy are only or principally childbearers, mammals (especially humans) are devoted childcarers. Why? Perhaps because human parents' genetic investment in their small number of progeny is great, or perhaps because very young humans are totally dependent on parents for their survival and early upbringing. Parenting is a job whose primary object of attention and action is the child. Maccoby (1992) observed that, even in the context of bidirectionality of parent–child interactions, there will always be asymmetry in the relationship; caregivers "use their greater interactive skills to adapt themselves to the child's capacities and current states" (p. 1015). Thus, even when participation in interactions is balanced, caregivers are still normally more responsible for facilitating attunement (Kochanska & Aksan, 2004; Vygotsky, 1978).

Mothers are emotionally prepared and positively motivated to engage and care for their children. Parents must be sensitive to infant cues and select those cues for processing in the context of many competing stimuli. To mother appropriately requires harnessing sensory, perceptual, affective, reward, mnemonic, and motor systems as well as learning, and so analysis of parenting's contribution to attunement requires understanding coordinated functions at many levels. Adults' intuitive communicative and empathic behaviors allow for sharing affect and interests (Trevarthen & Aitken, 2001). Human mothers recognize the faces, cries, odors, and tactile characteristics of their newborns (see Corter & Fleming, 2002; Kaitz, Good, Rokem, & Eidelman, 1988; Kaitz, Lapidot, Bronner, & Eidelman, 1992; Kaitz, Rokem, & Eidelman, 1988; Russell, 1983). For example, mothers find infant odors more pleasing than nonmothers (Fleming et al., 1993) and accurately identify the body odors of their own infants over those of unfamiliar infants (Kaitz, Good, Rokem, & Eidelman, 1987; Porter, Cernoch, & McLaughlin, 1983).

Human children do not and cannot grow up as solitary individuals. In Winnicott's (1965, p. 39) memorable phrase: "There is no such thing as an infant." Nonetheless, infants play their part in attunement. Childhood is the time when humans first make sense of the physical world, first learn to express and read emotions, and forge their first social bonds. Parents lead children through all these dramatic firsts.

The fit is neat to a task: The amount of interaction between parent and offspring is greatest in early childhood, and that is just the time in development when human beings are especially susceptible to experience.

The Infant's Part in Attunement

Thinking about parent–child relationships often highlights parents as agents of socialization; however, caregiving is a two-way street. For their part, infants are biologically prepared to engage in and expect attuned interactions with caregivers. Newborns preferentially orient and attend to faces just moments after their birth (Johnson, Dziurawiec, Ellis, & Morton, 1991), and infants as young as 2 months are acutely responsive to the timing and emotional expressions of their partners. This exquisite sensitivity is on plain display in the "still-face" paradigm (Murray & Trevarthen, 1986; Tronick, Als, Adamson, Wise, & Brazelton, 1978). An adult who is interacting naturally with an infant but suddenly becomes nonresponsive elicits demonstrative upsetness in the infant, more than does an adult physically departing the interaction altogether (Field et al., 2007; Goldstein, Schwade, & Bornstein, 2009; Trevarthen & Aitken, 2001; Tronick et al., 1978).

Darwin (1872/1965) originally noted that infants entice adults to care for them (perhaps as a means to increase individual fitness or reproductive success via increased survivorship), and prominent 20th-century ethologists and developmental scientists have followed his lead. Although human infants lack agency per se, they are born with structural and functional characteristics that prompt adult proximity and care and help to ensure survival and wholesome development. Prominent among those characteristics are a physiognomic morphology that adults find irresistible and a suite of communicative signals that adults find undeniable (Bornstein, 2002; Bornstein, Tamis-LeMonda, Hahn, & Haynes, 2008; Bowlby, 1969; Lorenz, 1943, 1971). Little is more compelling to a new parent than the sights, sounds, smells, and somatosensory stimulation of an infant (Barrett & Fleming, 2011). Lorenz (1943) identified physiognomic and morphological infantile features, such as a large head, big eyes, high and protruding forehead, chubby cheeks, small nose and mouth, short and thick extremities, and plump body shape, that serve as *Kindchenschema,* or "innate releasing mechanisms" for affection and nurturing. When infant and adult human and animal faces are balanced for attractiveness, human infant faces are rated cuter than adult human and adult animal faces (Caria et al., 2012). Sensitivity to Lorenz's baby schema can be found in children (Sanefuji, Ohgami, & Hashiya, 2007) and even in infants as young as 4 months themselves (McCall & Kennedy, 1980). Men and women process these baby schema similarly, and higher baby schema faces are perceived as cuter and elicit stronger motivation for caregiving than unmanipulated and lower baby schema faces (Glocker et al., 2009).

A variety of different mechanisms facilitates attunement. Newborn infants prefer their mother's voice: They will suck a nonnutritive nipple to produce their mother's voice more often than a stranger's voice (DeCasper & Fifer, 1980). Breast-fed infants rapidly learn their mother's characteristic olfactory signature (Porter, 2004; Porter & Winberg, 1999). Infants also actively signal and elicit effective parental care by following, clinging, calling, and crying. For example, infant gaze evokes mother gaze and thus leads to "en face" behavior between the two (Messer & Vietze, 1984), and infant cry effectively draws a parent's attention and induces proximity (Bowlby, 1969; Stallings, Fleming, Corter, Worthman, & Steiner, 2001). Mothers experience elevated levels of sympathy and alertness in response to cries of babies, and maternal responses to infant cries are critical for infant survival and the development of mother–infant emotional bonding (Feldman, 2012).

Attunement

Attunement expresses the dynamic adaptation of these two partners, of sensing and reading one another's state and adjusting biology and behavior accordingly. Their mutual attention has been demonstrated from birth (Brazelton, Koslowski, & Main, 1974). Attunement has biological (hormonal and nervous system) and psychological (affective, cognitive, and behavioral) components. Thus, parent–child attunement is best described within the context of a relationship that encompasses individual contributions (Ainsworth, Blehar, Waters, & Wall, 1978; Dunn, 1993; Schaffer, 1991), and attunement is integral to contemporary systems (Bornstein & Sawyer, 2005; Minuchin, 1985), transaction (Bornstein, 2009; Sameroff, 2009), and socioecological frameworks (Bronfenbrenner & Morris, 2006) of development. Each perspective emphasizes influences that cannot be deduced solely from individual parts of the whole, and this conceptualization supplements approaches in which characteristics of the parent and child are assessed separately. Attunement is a property of the dyad that pervades actors in the dyad, and may be defined by those contributions in terms of a close relationships perspective, and is not confined by the contributions of either actor alone.

It has long been recognized that parents and their children exhibit notable biological and psychological similarities, as, for example, in height and facial features, temperament and talent. Attunement transcends these superficial similarities, emerging early and running deep within the relationship. Thus, in attuned interactions, infants and mothers experience mutually positive affective exchanges and transition smoothly between activities (Stern, 1985; Tronick, 1989). Moreover, attunement between mother and infant has come to be acknowledged as a cornerstone of children's biological, socioemotional, and cognitive well-being and adaptation throughout the balance of the life course (Ainsworth, 1989; Bowlby, 1969; Feldman, 2012; Feldman & Eidelman, 2004; Sander, 2000; Sroufe, Egeland, Carlson, & Collins, 2005; van IJzendoorn, Dijkstra, & Bus, 1995).

This chapter focuses on mother–infant attunement and follows a multilevel *behavioral neuroscience* approach. The critical capacities that infants possess in ensuring their own successful development, and adults enact in caring successfully for infants, are expressed in specific behavioral adaptations, and they are supported by specific hormonal, autonomic, and neural circuitry. In elaborating this thesis, the chapter takes up the following topics. First, examples of behavioral attunement between infants and mothers at different levels of analysis are described. The chapter turns then to identify and review selected research on hormonal, autonomic, and central nervous system functioning that likely supports dyadic behavioral attunement and thereby contributes to a more complete multilevel understanding of parent–child attunement. This changing focus on different expressions of attunement follows the synthesis-through-analysis model of science. A summary, conclusions, and final thoughts close the chapter.

Before turning to behavioral attunement, three guiding explanatory words are in order. First, this chapter focuses on mother–infant attunement for several main reasons: Mothers tend to be infants' primary caregivers (Barnard & Solchany, 2002; Bornstein, 2002) and their principal socializers (Greenfield, Suzuki, & Rothstein-Fisch, 2006). So, for example, as de Haan and Carver (Chapter 6, this volume) recount, the majority of infants' facial experience is with their primary caregiver (Rennels & Davis, 2008). Reciprocally, near infrared spectroscopy and evoked-response potential (ERP) studies have recorded increased infant activation to mothers' faces (Carlsson, Lagercrantz, Olson, Printz, & Bartocci, 2008; de Haan & Nelson, 1997, 1999; see also Nakato et al., 2011) and larger ERPs to mothers' faces than strangers' faces (de Haan & Nelson, 1997, 1999). This pattern of findings does not mean, however, that the principles discussed here are limited to biological mothers and do not apply to fathers or other infant caregivers; they may (see Grasso et al., 2009; Leon, 2007; and later discussion).

Second, attunement in mothers and infants is normally investigated in designs that use the same stimuli or tasks with parent and child or that compare own-parent versus other-parent stimuli for child and own-child versus other–child stimuli for parent and then apply concordance (and sometimes sequential) analyses. Concordance describes covariation in the rank-order status of specific mother and infant constructs, structures, functions, or processes. In achieving behavioral concordance, for example, mothers who perform one kind of activity relatively more often, for longer periods, or the like, or who manifest a characteristic to a relatively high degree have infants who perform a specific corresponding activity relatively more often, for longer periods, or the like, or manifest a corresponding characteristic to a relatively high degree. Thus, Karger (1979) operationalized attunement as the correlation between mother and infant communicative behaviors. Although correlations have usually been employed, related regression approaches are useful and common as well (Cohen & Cohen, 1975; DeFries, 1967; DeFries et al., 1978). Thus, DeFries and colleagues (1979) used regression of midchild on midparent values as the principal index of parent–child concordance.

Third, attunement is concerned with mutuality, focusing here on mother–infant associations, and is not (necessarily) concerned with direction of effects that parent and child likely exert on one another. Attunement may also be high or low, independent of content. Furthermore, it may be that attunement is graded or all or none. The ability to achieve attunement may also be relationship specific (see Harris & Waugh, 2002). The conclusion of the chapter returns to how these and other more general issues will shape future directions in attunement theory and research.

Behavioral Attunement

An enduring question in developmental science asks whether lawful relations exist between parent and child, between parent-provided experience and child development, and whether such relations are generalized or specific. As mentioned earlier, parents and their offspring appear to share certain psychological characteristics: They exhibit similarities in engagement in physical activity (Fuemmeler, Anderson, & Mâsse, 2011; Stern, 1985), cognitive functions (Carter, 1932; DeFries et al., 1979; Ditto, France, & Miller, 1989; Williams, 1975; Willoughby, 1927), and even food preferences and disgust or contamination sensitivity (Birch, 1980; Rozin, Fallon, & Mandell, 1984).

Beyond these similarities, quality mother–infant interactions require attunement. Bowlby (1969) underscored the importance of contingent interactions between mothers and infants for survival and appropriate development. Early adult–child dyadic interactions are grounded in mutual regulation as revealed, for example, in video microanalysis (Beebe et al., 2010; Stern, 1985; Trevarthen, 2003). A more patent example of this kind of behavioral reciprocity is observed in "protoconversations," where mother and infant adopt turn-taking patterns when vocalizing.

To investigate mother–infant behavioral attunement, we analyzed data from 796 mother–infant dyads from cultural groups in 11 countries: Argentina, Belgium, Brazil, Cameroon, France, Israel, Italy, Japan, Kenya, South Korea, and the United States (Bornstein, 2012; Bornstein, Park, Haynes, & Suwalsky, 2012). Participating mothers in each country were primiparous, at least 18 years of age, and living in intact families with their healthy, term 5-month-olds. Equal numbers of mother–baby girl and boy dyads participated in each country sample. Of course, substantial differences exist among the different cultural groups in terms of history, beliefs, language, and childrearing values. Central to the concept of culture is the expectation that different peoples possess different ideas and behave in different ways with respect to both their caregiving and their children's development. Indeed, the family is a major conduit for the transmission of culture across generations. However, this range of cultural groups also creates the possibility of identifying universals of childrearing and child development.

Naturally occurring mother–infant interactions at home were video-recorded, and then mutually exclusive and exhaustive coding systems were used to comprehensively characterize frequency and duration of specific mother and infant behaviors. The coding system encompassed primary caregiving tasks appropriate to an infant, from feeding to promoting physical development to expressing affection to encouraging attention to outfitting the surrounding environment. In addition, infant physical development, social engagement, environmental exploration, positive vocalization, and distress communication were coded; they are frequent and prominent infant behaviors, key developmental and performance competencies critical to early ontogenetic adaptation, and they are behaviors that mothers typically monitor closely. In an average hour, mothers and their babies engaged in the full variety of these behaviors. Across cultures, mothers and infants showed noteworthy behavioral attunement as well as specificity. Mothers who encouraged their infants' physical development more had more physically developed infants; mothers who engaged their infants socially more had infants who reciprocated their social attention; mothers who encouraged their infants didactically more had infants who explored properties, objects, and events in the environment more, as did infants whose mothers outfitted their environments in a richer way. In summary, mothers and young infants in a variety of cultures around the world are behaviorally attuned with one another; moreover, correspondences in their behaviors tend to be domain specific.

This study exemplifies behavioral attunement at a microanalytic level. Using similar microanalytic observational techniques, Malatesta and Haviland (1982) uncovered commonalities in the emotional expressiveness of mothers and their 3- and 6-month-old infants. Attunement is also evident from more macroanalytic perspectives on mother–infant interactions. Emotional relationships can be evaluated through observations and ratings of mother–infant interaction using global coding schemes, like the Emotional Availability Scales (Biringen, Robinson, & Emde, 1998). Adult–infant emotional attunement is frequently observed in spontaneous interactions and is widely acknowledged to be a vital ingredient in wholesome infant development (Bornstein, Suwalsky, & Breakstone, 2012). Emotional relationships in infancy help to set the stage for socioemotional regulation in childhood and beyond. Young adults commonly report that their style of emotional expression and skill in communicating emotions developed in the context of the emotional expressiveness of their family environment (Halberstadt, 1986), and meta-analysis confirms associations between family styles of expressing emotion and children's expressive styles and skill in understanding emotion: Positive family expressiveness and positive child expressiveness are consistently associated across age (Halberstadt & Eaton, 2002). Not unexpectedly, therefore, mother and infant Emotional Availability Scales intercorrelate in different cultural groups (see Bornstein, Putnick, et al., 2008, 2012; Bornstein, Suwalsky, et al., 2010).

Consider that infants in the cross-cultural behavioral and emotional relationships studies just discussed are only 5 months old, barely *fetus ex utero*. However, correspondences in mother–infant behavioral and emotional attunement are widespread, specific, and similar in different cultures. Early mother–infant dyadic interactions appear to be accurately characterized by mutually regulated intersubjectivity (Trevarthen & Aitken, 2001), operationalized as intuitive, communicative, and empathic behaviors that allow for sharing of affect and interests. Indeed, mothers of young infants appear to activate the mirror neuron system when interpreting and imitating emotional pictures of their infants (Lenzi et al., 2009). Enhanced ability to encode emotions in faces during late pregnancy may be an evolutionary adaption that prepares women for the protective and nurturing demands of motherhood by increasing their general emotional sensitivity and their vigilance toward emotional signals of threat, aggression, and contagion (Pearson, Lightman, & Evans, 2009). Activation of this empathy system has additional advantages in permitting mothers to share emotions with their still preverbal infants and better understand their needs.

Notably, mother–infant behavioral attunement is robust and appears at least partially refractory to certain dysfunctions. Although the total percentage of time spent in matching behavior states is reduced in depressed relative to nondepressed mother–infant dyads, cross-spectral analyses of mother and infant behavior–state time series indicate comparable coherence in healthy and risk dyads (Field, Healy, Goldstein, & Guthertz, 1990). Mother emotional relationships with their children with Down syndrome or cancer are equally attuned as those mothers of typically developing children (Beeghly, Perry, & Cicchetti, 1989; Bornstein, Scrimin, et al., 2012; Crawley & Spiker, 1983).

In overview, behavioral analyses indicate that infants activate attuned responses in mothers through their face, voice, odor, and gesture. In return, mothers' attuned responsiveness to infants appears to foster children's motivation to interact and has positive predictive effects on child development.

The Behavior and Biology of Attunement

Behavioral attunement appears to have deep roots in evolution and nervous system function. Synchronous behaviors as we interact with others, the thoughts and emotions we experience in relation to others, our perceptions of others' cues and actions, and our abilities to communicate and to share affective experiences are not all necessarily conscious. Papoušek and Papoušek (2002) pointed to behavioral parenting patterns, such as regulation of affective states, responsiveness, structuring, and mirroring of infant experiences, that automatically adjust to the needs of the child. Indeed, some maternal responses to infant cues are believed to occur too quickly (within 200–400 milliseconds) for conscious perception. Mothers respond appropriately to infant behavioral cues (such as different hand positions indicative of different states of infant alertness), even when they report being unaware of such signals (Papoušek, 2000). This kind of observation points to relatively automatic parenting responses to infant-specific sensory and behavioral cues, so-called intuitive parenting, that likely have their origins in biological functioning. Evolution is an organizing principle that has shaped adaptive behavior as well as the structure and function of the hormonal, autonomic, and central nervous systems. Evolutionary forces have molded human behavior and biology, presumably in tandem.

Mother–infant attunement is, on this account, likely a multilevel phenomenon with correspondences to be found in the hormonal, autonomic, and central nervous systems as well as at behavioral levels. Many theorists have contended that parents are biologically preadapted to intuitively attune to their infants (e.g., Brazelton, 1984; Emde, 1984; Papoušek & Papoušek, 2002; Stern, 1985). Parent–offspring biological resemblances for height and weight may be well known (DeFries et al., 1979; Garn & Rohmann, 1966; Livson, McNeill, & Thomas, 1962; Tanner & Israelsohn, 1963; Tiisala & Kantero, 1971), but parent–child correlations are much more pervasive and span total ridge counts on fingers (Holt, 1952, 1955) and the transverseness of palmar main lines (Pons, 1954) to head circumference (Brandt, 1990). Telomeres are protective DNA structures located at the ends of eukaryotic chromosomes. Blood cell analyses in individuals 0 to 102 years of age reveal telomere length correlations in parent–child pairs (Nordfjäll, Svenson, Norrback, Adolfsson, & Roos, 2010). Nutrient intake (dietary cholesterol, total carbohydrate, saturated and polyunsaturated fat, and total calories) is significant and positively related in parent and child (Laskarzewski et al., 1980), and so on.

Hormonal Attunement

Childbearing and early childrearing are accompanied by anatomical, hormonal, and nervous system, in addition to behavioral, adjustments. Together, neurochemical and neuroanatomical adaptations contribute to successful reproduction and adequate maternal care. For example, certain hormones appear to be essential to the acquisition and maintenance of maternal behavior (Bridges, 1990, 2008; Insel, 1990; Numan, Fleming, & Levy, 2006; Pryce, Martin, & Skuse, 1995; Rosenblatt, Olufowobi, & Siegel, 1998). The hormonal profiles of pregnancy, parturition, and parenting involve hormones, neuropeptides, and neurotransmitters, including prolactin, estrogen/estradiol, progesterone, dopamine, oxytocin, and the stress hormone cortisol as well as neural regions that are modified through interactions with these neurochemicals (Lambert & Kinsley, 2012). Hormones activate key brain regions to augment mothers' and fathers' attraction to infant cues, enhance their affective state, and render them attentive and sensitive to infants' needs so that parents learn from their experiences with and behave appropriately toward their infants (Fleming, Ruble, Krieger, & Wong, 1997; Numan et al., 2006; Numan & Insel, 2003).

The neuropeptide oxytocin (OT) is associated with emotional, cognitive, and behavioral aspects of parental (as well as pair and filial) bonding, such as empathy, closeness, and trust (Grewen, Girdler, Amico, & Light, 2005). OT plays a key role in regulating social behavior in mammals (MacDonald & MacDonald, 2010) by augmenting perceptions of cues relevant for social interaction and reducing the impact of socially aversive and threatening cues (Heinrichs, Meinlschmidt, Wippich, Ehlert, & Hellhammer, 2004). For example, OT enhances memory for familiar faces. In one study, adults were given intranasal OT or placebo and then familiarized with a set of faces and a set of nonsocial images (landscapes, sculptures, and houses) in a task where they had to judge how approachable each image was (Rimmele, Hediger, Heinrichs, & Klaver, 2009). In a surprise recognition test 24 hours later, the group that received OT showed better face recognition compared with the placebo group, whereas the two groups showed similar recognition for nonsocial stimuli. Other research has shown that OT biases viewers to focus on the eye region of faces, which may facilitate recognition (Gustella, Mitchell, & Dadds, 2008).

OT is a uniquely mammalian hormone and is observed in brain regions implicated in attachment, and it functions to integrate autonomic states with social behavior. Central OT injection in animals stimulates maternal behavior (Bales & Carter, 2002; Febo, Numan, & Ferris, 2005; Holman & Goy, 1995; Ivell & Russell, 1996; Kendrick, Keverne, & Baldwin, 1987; Pedersen, 1997). In free-ranging rhesus macaques, OT is related to increased nursing and grooming (Maestripieri, Hoffman, Anderson, Carter, & Higley, 2009). OT released in mothers during breastfeeding is associated with more attuned patterns of maternal behavior (Champagne & Meaney, 2001; Heinrichs et al., 2004; MacDonald & MacDonald, 2010; Uvnas-Moberg, 1998; Uvnas-Moberg & Eriksson, 1996). Indeed, generally higher levels of OT are associated with more sensitive and synchronous parental behaviors in human mothers and fathers (Feldman, Weller, Zagoory-Sharon, & Levine, 2007). In a prospective longitudinal study, cohabitating mothers and fathers and their first-born infant were visited at home during the first postpartum weeks and again after 6 months. Maternal OT was related to amounts of typically maternal affectionate parenting, including infant-directed speech, expressions of positive affect, and loving touch (Feldman & Eidelman, 2003, 2007; Feldman, Eidelman, & Rotenberg, 2004; Feldman et al., 2007), whereas paternal OT correlated with behaviors that are more typical of human fathers' interactions with infants, such as proprioceptive contact, tactile stimulation, and object presentation (Feldman, 2003; Parke, 2002). Notably, maternal OT was unrelated to fathering behaviors, and paternal OT was unrelated to maternal behaviors. OT is also released in nursing infants, and OT levels in human 4- to 6-month-olds increase after playful interactions with their caregivers, with higher levels related to greater affective synchrony and social engagement (Feldman, Gordon, & Zagoory-Sharon, 2010). OT is a good example of hormonal attunement in parent (mother or father) and infant. Cortisol is another.

Cortisol levels rise during pregnancy to increase vigilance. German policewomen report enhanced vigilance following the birth of their first child (Fullgrabe,

2002). Higher cortisol levels on postpartum days 3 and 4 are associated with maternal approach behaviors and positive attitudes (Corter & Fleming, 1990; Fleming, Steiner, & Anderson, 1987). Nearly 40% of mothers' cortisol crosses the placenta, and strong relations have been recorded between maternal and fetal cortisol levels (Glover, Teixeira, Gitau, & Fisk, 1999). Gitau, Cameron, Fisk, and Glover (1998) measured plasma cortisol concentrations in paired maternal and fetal venous samples from blood taken for clinically indicated fetal testing at 13 to 35 weeks gestation. Maternal cortisol values were higher than fetal values, with a maternal:fetal ratio of 11:4. Significantly, fetal cortisol concentrations were concordant with maternal cortisol concentrations. Again, mother and infant show hormonal attunement.

Hormonal attunement also seems to be robust and to transcend some developmental dysfunctions. Mothers with depressive symptoms have higher prenatal cortisol levels, and lower dopamine and serotonin levels, than nondepressed mothers (Field et al., 2004, 2006). Newborns of mothers with depressive symptoms also have higher cortisol levels, and lower dopamine and serotonin levels, than newborns of nondepressed mothers. Thus, mothers' and newborns' hormonal levels appear to match one another in typically developing as well as atypically developing populations.

Hormonal attunement is not restricted to females. As noted earlier, OT levels in fathers match their fathering behaviors. Testosterone (T) stimulates the development and maintenance of traits and behaviors that contribute to male mating, including musculature, libido, aggressiveness with conspecifics, and courtship (Archer, 2006; Booth & Dabbs, 1993; Bribiescas, 2001; Hart; 1974). T-driven traits thus factor into mating success and reproductive fitness (Kleiman & Malcolm, 1981; Wingfield, Hegner, Ball, & Duffy, 1990). If T contributes to human male reproductive strategy, high initial T will enhance a man's mating success, but men who have succeeded in securing a mate and/or fathering a child should then down-regulate T, particularly if they frequently engage in child care (Gray & Anderson, 2010; Hirschenhauser & Oliveira, 2006; Wingfield et al., 1990). Consistent with the hypothesis that interacting with a dependent child suppresses T (Alvergne, Faurie, & Raymond, 2009; Gettler, 2010; Muller, Marlowe, Bugumba, & Ellison, 2009), fathers who report 3 hours or more of daily child care have lower T levels compared with fathers not involved in care (Gettler, McDade, Feranil, & Kuzawa, 2011). Men with lower T also report feeling more sympathy and greater need to respond to infant cries compared with men with greater T (Fleming, Corter, Stallings, & Steiner, 2002; Kuzawa, Gettler, Muller, McDade, & Feranil, 2009; Muller et al., 2009). Thus, T levels in males relate to their behavioral attunement with infants.

In overview, human parents (females and males) have evolved neuroendocrine architectures that support committed parenting (Gettler, 2010; Gray & Anderson, 2010; Gray, Kahlenberg, Barrett, Lipson, & Ellison, 2002). Several hormones are implicated in parent–infant attunement.

Autonomic Nervous System Attunement

The autonomic nervous system (ANS) is concerned with the involuntary control of internal organs, including the heart, lungs, and digestive tract. It operates primarily at a subconscious level. Is there attunement between parent and child in autonomic psychophysiological processes when those processes can be measured comparably in both parent and child? In the realm of ANS function, parent–offspring correlations in heart rate and blood pressure responsivity to reaction time tasks have been reported (Hastrup, Kraemer, Hotchkiss, & Johnson, 1986), and significant parent–offspring correlations in heart rate response to a challenging conceptual task (mental arithmetic) and diastolic blood pressure response to physical tasks (isometric handgrip) have also been documented, even if parents and children are tested on different occasions using different procedures (Ditto et al., 1989).

The vagus is the 10th cranial nerve and a major component of the parasympathetic nervous system. The vagus serves as an important bidirectional conduit carrying specialized motor and sensory pathways involved in the regulation of visceral state and affect. Thus, the vagus represents an integrated neural system that communicates in a bidirectional manner between the viscera and the brain. Vagal motor fibers originate in the nucleus ambiguus and regulate striated muscles of the face and head, cardiac and smooth muscles of the heart, and thus cardiovascular activity, digestion, metabolism, and thermoregulation. Polyvagal theory (Porges, 1995, 1996) asserts that the vagal system provides the physiological substrate for regulating arousal, state, and reactivity to stimulation that underlies individual differences in self-regulation, information processing, temperament, and emotion. As Darwin (1872/1965) wrote:

> When the mind is strongly excited, we might expect that it would instantly affect in a direct manner the heart; and this is universally acknowledged and felt to be the case. When the heart is affected it reacts on the brain; and the state of the brain again reacts through the pneumo-gastric [vagus] nerve on the heart; so that under any excitement there will be much mutual action and reaction between these, the two most important organs of the body. (p. 69)

The vagal system functions to maintain homeostasis via a negative feedback system that receives sensory information internally from visceral organs and adjusts its output to maintain target organs at specific functional levels. Cardiac vagal tone reflects the relative and temporal influences of the parasympathetic nervous system, via the vagus, on rhythmic oscillations in heart rate. The vagal system plays an integral role in physiological self-regulation, manifesting its regulatory nature in observable changes in heart rate variability during changing environmental conditions. Cardiac vagal tone has been applied to understand physiological substrates of self-regulation, information processing, temperament, and emotion from infancy through adulthood. In general, mother–infant attunement becomes more understandable when the autonomic nervous system (especially the vagus) is included in an integrated explanatory model.

Vagal efferents to the heart have a characteristic respiratory rhythm ascribable to interneuronal communication between brainstem centers regulating vagal output and respiration (Richter & Spyer, 1990). Rhythmic change in heart rate variability (respiratory sinus arrhythmia; RSA) can be assessed noninvasively from the electrocardiogram (ECG). Estimates of RSA (the natural log of heart period in milliseconds squared) have been used as measures of cardiac vagal tone (Vna) during resting (baseline) states (i.e., in the relative absence of environmental challenge) and during environmental challenge. Resting Vna is theorized to measure the structural organization of the vagal system (e.g., neural feedback mechanisms) and its capacity to maintain homeostasis in the absence of environmental demand. Vagal regulation during environmental challenge—the capacity to engage and disengage vagal outflow—is an appropriate response to stimulation or stress. Baseline-to-task change in Vna, therefore, serves as an index of vagal regulatory function.

Bornstein and Seuss (2000) measured baseline and task Vna in primiparous mothers and their children at 2 months and at 5 years and calculated parent–child attunement in baseline Vna and baseline-to-task change in Vna at each longitudinal wave. ECG activity was separately recorded by chest Ag–AgCl electrodes during a baseline session and then during the administration of an age-appropriate standardized task that required sustained attention. (At 5 years children and their mothers separately participated in the same task.) Children differed from their mothers in baseline Vna at 2 months; by 5 years, however, children and their mothers were similar in baseline levels of Vna. Children and their mothers were also similar in baseline-to-task change in Vna at 2 months and at 5 years. Baseline levels of mother and child vagal tone showed no concordance at 2 months or at 5 years. However, baseline-to-task change in Vna showed marginally significant mother–child concordance at 2 months and significant attunement at 5 years.

In overview, vagal tone, an important component of the autonomic nervous system, assesses self-regulatory physiological processes that function to maintain internal homeostasis. Baseline-to-task change in vagal tone, an indicator of vagal regulation, appears to be concordant in children and their mothers. Children and mothers share characteristic autonomic response styles that are reflected in similar patterns of vagal regulation. The ANS controls physiology-regulating functions, including up-regulation (e.g., arousing) and down-regulation (e.g., soothing). A hypothesized function of dyadic synchrony of the ANS for the infant may be to facilitate physiological and affective homeostatic regulation. Not unexpectedly, vagal tone in some atypically developing dyads (e.g., depressed mothers and their infants) resembles one another as well (Jones, Field, Fox, Lundy, & Hart, 1998).

Central Nervous System Attunement

It is commonly acknowledged that both brain structure and function are plastic to input and experience throughout development. For example, somatosensory cortical representations of the left-hand digits of musicians of string instruments are larger than controls, and cortical reorganization of fingering digits correlates with the age the person began to play (Elbert, Pantey, Wienbruch, Rockstroh, & Taub, 1995). Similar observations have been made about the somatosensory cortex representation of the index finger in blind Braille readers (Pascual-Leone & Torres, 1993). The hippocampus stores long-term memories and spatial representations of the environment. One function of the hippocampus is to serve as a cognitive map or neural representation of the geographical layout of the environment. One group with special long-standing experience with geographical layouts is taxi drivers. Gray matter volume in the posterior of the left and right hippocampi of London taxi drivers is increased relative to controls, and hippocampal volume correlates with the amount of time hacks spent driving taxis (Maguire et al., 2000; Woollett & Maguire, 2011).

The hippocampus is also involved in learning, the formation of new memories, and transfer of information into long-term memory, especially declarative memory that involves verbalization and facts. The size of the hippocampus is related to memory performance. Brain scans of students preparing for a rigorous academic examination 3 months before the test, 1 or 2 days after, and 3 months later revealed increases in the gray matter of the hippocampus between the first scan and the second, suggesting that increases in gray matter accompany abstract learning (Draganski et al., 2006). A significant increase was observed again 3 months after the exam, suggesting that gray matter expansion continues even after learning has ceased. In a nutshell, anatomical representation and specialization in the brain appear to be use dependent, and representation appears to correlate with duration of experience. The adult brain in part attunes itself to specific environmental demands.

There are practical advantages to such plasticity, and plasticity applied to experiences of parenting appears to be one. Both local and general experiences associated with childbearing and childrearing shape brain structure and function. For example, structural magnetic resonance imaging (MRI) of female brains used a contour-and-thresholding technique to establish the size of the brain (as well as the ventricles) before conception, at term, and 24 weeks after delivery; comparisons revealed shrinkages of up to 7% between term and preconception, which recovered postterm (Oatridge et al., 2002). (The investigators hypothesized that intense energy demands of fetal development entail a down-sizing of the maternal brain as the fetus "scavenges" essential fatty acids and thereby alters phospholipid membranes and so morphology of the maternal brain.) Similar shifts in brain density in certain cortical and subcortical structures appear to underlie maternal adaptations to infants in the first few postpartum months: Increases in gray matter volume of the prefrontal cortex, parietal lobes, and midbrain areas, measured via voxel-based morphometry on high-resolution MRI of mothers' brains 2 to 4 weeks postpartum and 3 to 4 months postpartum, have been reported (Kim et al., 2010). Hinting at anatomical bases of behavioral attunement, increases in gray matter volume are also associated with positive maternal perceptions of her baby.

Functional MRI (fMRI) permits examination of brain activity while participants engage in a task. This high-resolution, noninvasive technique assays brain activity by measuring blood oxygenation. The difference between oxygenated and deoxygenated hemoglobin yields characteristic magnetic signals (localized to millimeter resolution) detectable by scanners positioned around the head. fMRI provides information about spatial patterns of brain activation. For example, comparisons of brain activity during baby cry versus control noise that yield greater activation in certain brain regions can then be said to relate to or subserve experiences of a baby cry, and so associated thoughts and behaviors.

The long evolutionary and ontogenetic histories of transactional relations between human parents and offspring support the notion that specific brain circuits might mediate maternal attunement to infants. Based on fMRI methodology, a number of brain regions have been implicated in support of parenting-related emotions, cognitions, and practices: the amygdala in emotions, arousal, and salience detection; the cingulate projection area in attachment, motivation, and reward; the fusiform gyrus in face recognition; the cingulate and insula in empathy and emotional mirroring; and the orbital-frontal cortex supporting positive emotion. Based on the neuroimaging literatures on nonhuman and human parenting, Swain, Lorberbaum, Kose, and Strathearn (2007) hypothesized that human parenting behaviors might be mediated by a complex circuit involving these brain structures.

A burgeoning literature has developed to advance empirically on this modeling. These studies use a variety of infant visual and auditory stimuli in a variety of designs with a variety of parent populations to explore brain structures and their associated functions. This literature had its formative roots in the work of Bartels and Zeki (2000, 2004), who advanced the ideas that parental love may call on the same emotion and reward circuits as romantic love, and that love relationships should be inherently rewarding to ensure the perpetuation of the species. They reported increased activity in certain brain regions in mothers to own-child photographs compared with photographs of age-matched other children. Similar studies of own-baby versus other-baby photographs and videos yield activations in mothers' and fathers' brain circuits with variation by gender, experience, and postpartum time of assessment (Leibenluft, Gobbini, Harrison, & Haxby, 2004; Noriuchi, Kikuchi, & Senoo, 2008; Ranote et al., 2004; Swain, Leckman, Mayes, Feldman, & Schultz, 2006). Exposure to happy, sad, and neutral own-infant versus unfamiliar-infant faces results in more activity in securely attached mothers to their own infants' faces and to own-infant happy faces (Strathearn, Li, Fonagy, & Montague, 2008). Mothers who were scanned at 7 to 17 months postpartum showed activation of dopamine-associated reward-processing regions of the brain when viewing their own infant's face compared with an unknown infant's face. Cries generated by own infant versus a standard cry and control noises matched for pattern and intensity likewise evoke enhanced activity in select regions (Ranote et al., 2004; Swain et al., 2006). Connecting brain activation with cognitions, mothers viewing smiling pictures of their own versus unfamiliar infants yields brain activation that is correlated with pleasant mood ratings and affective responses to their infant (Nitschke et al., 2004). Empathy is key to attuned parenting. Mothers who observe and imitate emotional expressions of their own child versus another activate the mirror neuron system, and insula response correlates with maternal reflective function, conceptualized as a measure of empathy (Lenzi et al., 2009).

The visual and auditory paradigms used to examine differences between own infant and unfamiliar infant suggest that own children excite a complex brain network involved in maternal perception, identification, and emotional responses integral to achieving attunement. Processing of infant cues predisposes adults to sensitively interact with them, an attitude that is readily apparent in parent–infant attuned behavioral interactions. Understanding how a mother responds to her own child's face or voice thereby enriches our understanding of neural bases of attunement.

However, comparing parents' reactions to their own infants versus other infants also cedes stimulus control and misses what may be specific in adult brain responses to human infants generally compared with adults and with infants of other species. To identify brain structures that might underlie adults' propensity to respond in an attuned manner to human infant cues, we recorded fMRI during adults' processing of unfamiliar infant faces compared with adult faces and infrahuman mammal infant and adult faces (Caria et al., 2012). (We included animal faces to clarify whether brain responses relate to a predisposition to build an attachment specifically with human children, a species-specific mechanism, or a more general inclination to infant care and affection, a species-general mechanism.) Human infant faces, compared with human adult faces, revealed a pattern of enhanced activity in the lateral premotor regions, the supplementary motor area (SMA), the thalamo-cingulate circuit, and the left anterior insula. This pattern of activity suggests adults' preparedness to empathic and communicative behavior and reward in the presence of human infants. Two sets of specific results were noteworthy.

First, human infant faces triggered in participants a network involving premotor regions and SMA, which have been implicated in preparation and intention to move and respond and to communicate (Alario, Chainay, Lehericy, & Cohen, 2006; Brendel et al., 2010; Riecker et al., 2005). SMA is activated in preparation for voluntary action (Nachev, Kennard, & Husain, 2008) and to specific objects when they are simply observed without active movement (Grezes & Decety, 2005). SMA, along with lateral premotor areas, generates a "readiness potential" that antecedes movement and is considered the neural correlate of intentional movement planning that can be measured even when people are unaware of their intention to move (Deecke & Kornhuber, 1978; Goldberg, 1985; Haggard & Eimer, 1999; Jahanshahi et al., 1995). Observed premotor activity in participants in our study might reflect implicit preparation to respond to infant faces. The neuroimages suggest that infant faces activate a "readiness" to interact with babies. In accord with this interpretation, a behavioral study of implicit attention to infants reported faster response times to unfamiliar human infant images compared with adult images (Brosch, Sander, & Scherer, 2007).

The SMA is also critical in preparing a verbal utterance and initiating vocal tract movements during speech production (the so-called starting mechanism of speech; Ackermann & Riecker, 2010; Ackermann & Ziegler, 2010; Botez & Barbeau, 1971). In early dyadic interactions, adults readily speak to infants even though they know that babies cannot understand language, and adults even speak to babies in a special speech register called "infant-directed speech" that includes multiple specific prosodic, simplicity, redundancy, lexical, and content modifications from adult–adult or even adult–child speech (Soderstrom, 2007). Infant-directed speech is believed to be intuitive, nonconscious, and virtually universal; indeed, adults in the presence of babies cannot help themselves from using it (Papoušek & Bornstein, 1992). The activations observed in this fMRI study may constitute a biological substrate of the universal propensity to verbally communicate with young infants.

These fMRI findings also parallel behavioral research in adult–infant vocal attunement. Sequential analyses describe patterns of behavior in real time and explain behavior patterns by examining contingency (Bakeman & Quera, 2009). Sequential analysis offers a dynamic approach to the study of attunement in social interaction. So, for example, maternal behavior might (1) precede infant behavior, (2) begin within some predetermined time window following the onset or offset of infant behavior, or (3) follow infant behavior but begin outside that time window. The focus of the following analysis fell on specific maternal (target) behaviors that occur with regularity following (given) infant behaviors within prespecified time windows, and these timed sequences were analyzed. From the cross-cultural behavioral data set described earlier (Bornstein, Park, et al., 2012), we determined whether mothers vocalize contingently in response to their infants' vocalizations and whether infants vocalize in response to their mothers (Bornstein, Putnick, Cote, Haynes, & Suwalsky,

2012). The index of contingency is the odds ratio: the probability that a mother will talk to her infant given that her infant has just stopped vocalizing to her in the last 2 seconds, divided by the mother failing to talk to her infant given that her infant just stopped vocalizing, over the mother having talked to her infant in the absence of her infant having just vocalized divided by the mother's not talking given her infant did not vocalize. With the exception of Cameroon and Kenya, maternal vocalization to infants was contingent on infant vocalization in every country, with medium to large effect sizes. Five-month-old infants' nondistress vocalizations were contingent on their mothers' speech to them in approximately one-half of the countries. Moreover, mothers and infants were approximately equally responsive in most countries. Finally, mothers who were relatively more responsive to infant vocalizations had infants who were relatively more responsive to maternal vocalizations overall and in every group except Brazil. These findings point to the origins of turn-taking in mother–infant vocalization, and these transactions of vocal turn-taking reinforce the culture-general result about mother–infant vocal attunement. In a sense, they reflect a requirement of the nervous system: The nervous system has considerable difficulty processing vocal information at the same time that it is producing vocal information.

The second main result of our fMRI study (Caria et al., 2012) revealed enhanced brain activation patterns that are commonly associated with emotion recognition and evaluation (Carr, Iacoboni, Dubeau, Mazziotta, & Lenzi, 2003; Seitz et al., 2008) as well as simulation of others' emotional experiences (Singer et al., 2004; Wicker et al., 2003). Activation of the thalamocingulate circuit and insula occurs when participants decode another person's emotional states on the basis of facial cues and then evaluate their own emotional responses to those faces (Schulte-Rüther, Markowitsch, Fink, & Piefke, 2007; see also Shamay-Tsoory, Aharon-Peretz, & Perry, 2009). Thus, observed neural activity may subserve adults' readiness to empathize with infants' emotional expressions, a vital constituent of attunement. Together, these areas have been described as the mirror neuron system, and they support spontaneous imitation and intersubjectivity in mother and infant (Gallese & Rochat, Chapter 2, this volume; Killner, Neal, Weiskopf, Frinston, & Frith, 2009; Mukamel, Ekstrom, Kaplan, Iacoboni, & Fried, 2010; Rizzolatti & Sinigaglia, 2010; Schulte-Rüther et al., 2007). Moreover, in response to generic infant faces, the adult brain shows activation of phylogenetically older reward circuits. MacLean (1990) hypothesized that the brain's thalamocingulate division is important in mammalian mother–infant attachment such as infant crying and maternal caregiving. These regions have previously been identified with parental attachment (Glocker et al., 2009; Kringelbach et al., 2008; Ranote et al., 2004), directly linked to "baby schema" features in artificially manipulated infant faces (Goldberg, 1985), and implicated in parents' responses to their own children (Glocker et al., 2009). The results reported previously refine this conclusion to indicate that human infant faces in general appear to constitute trigger features that subserve attunement.

When compared with animal infant faces, human infant faces activated similar brain networks, indicating that adults' brain responses are species specific. These species-specific patterns of brain activity appear to represent the neural correlates of a human adult predisposition to attune with infants, inclinations in adults that are essential to child survival and healthy development. The fMRI findings confirm adults' neural responsiveness to human baby schema, and no differences emerged in brain responses to infant compared with adult nonhuman mammals. This response pattern accords with the view that the human social brain evolved in a situation where alloparenting was common, as has been hypothesized about the human environment of evolutionary adaptation (Bowlby, 1969; Hrdy, 1999, 2005; Lorenz, 1971), that is, where adults acted as cooperative breeders and many adults shared responsibility for infant care.

In overview, the adult human brain appears to respond to human infant faces and voices in a species-specific manner and betrays a predisposition to attunement with the very young of its own species. Many brain regions are also excited by own, relative to other, infant forms. Adults' responses to communicate and empathize with infants stand as complementary to compelling evidence that young infants themselves anticipate that their adult interactants will respond to them. The still-face paradigm reviewed at the start of this chapter validates this expectation on the part of young babies. Indeed, when infants are responsive to strangers, they are more so when strangers' levels of contingent vocalizations and smiles to them emulate those of their mothers, and they are less responsive to strangers who are either more or less contingent than their mothers (Bigelow, 1998). In brief, infants are exquisitely sensitive to levels of (social) contingency and attunement.

Summing Up, Raising Questions, and Looking Forward

The Spanish neuroanatomist and Nobelist Ramon y Cajal (1906) believed that the morphology of the adult brain was essentially fixed. When Nottebohm (1985) reported that the size of certain regions of the bird brain, and the number of neurons in those areas, changed seasonally, this rigid opinion came under question. Nottebohm observed that increases in the number of brain cells also coincided with birds learning new songs. Decades on, research extended the concept of neurogenesis from birds and small mammals to monkeys and eventually to humans (Eriksson et al., 1998; Gould, Cameron, Daniels, Wooley, & McEwen, 1994). We now know that even modest changes in the internal or external world can alter the brain. In fact, the watchword for contemporary neuroscience has become *plasticity*. The adult brain changes morphologically in response to toxins and trauma but also in response to even subtle treatments, conditions, or experiences. Parenting is one.

The human brain evolved to develop and adapt within a social environment, and the "social brain hypothesis" (Dunbar, Chapter 1, this volume) is the inevitable result of subcortical and cortical biases that ensure that human brains attend to and process information about the social world and attune to the tasks of childrearing. Human adults' species-specific behavioral, anatomical, hormonal, autonomic, and brain responses to human infants constitute biological signatures of parenting instincts that are requisite to child survival and the development of human attachments. Pair-bonded species are thought to have significantly larger brains and neocortices than polygamously or promiscuously mating species (Shultz & Dunbar, 2007). Parent–parent pair-bonded mating systems are concerned with provision of biparental care that ensures that they achieve their common goal of successfully rearing offspring (Dunbar, Chapter 1, this volume). Reciprocally, the brains of human offspring evolved and develop to attend to and process information about corresponding social interactions. Internal (hormonal and neural) and external (sensory stimuli) environments converge to induce maternal care.

Attunement is today a key parenting construct (Deater-Deckard & O'Connor, 2000; Harrist & Waugh, 2002). But socialization is a bidirectional enterprise, with parents and children actively assuming reciprocal mutually attuned roles. These two partners co-create their shared history over time and shape their evolving relationship (Collins, Maccoby, Steinberg, Hetherington, & Bornstein, 2000; Maccoby, 1992).

Should we be surprised by the pervasiveness of attunement? Perhaps not. Attunement for most parent–child dyads is expectable. Parents and their children are (usually) genetically related and they reside together, so there are reasons at many levels—from biological to experiential—for the two to be attuned. Moreover, the behavior of each individual influences the behavior of the other. The first 6 months of parenting is associated with a rise in OT, suggesting that OT increases in parents as their relationship with their infant consolidates, and parents typically derive greater reward from interacting with an infant who is a more active and reciprocal social partner (Feldman, 2012; Haith, Bergman, & Moore, 1977; Robson & Moss, 1970; Stern, 1977). Dyads develop and fine-tune characteristic self- and mutual-regulatory patterns through thousands of interactions over the course of development. It is also possible that common fate effects operate, whereby shared third factors (e.g., culture) influence both individuals in a pair in the same ways to reach the same shared goals. More generally, social relationships can themselves promote attunement in people. People who live together, interact, or cooperate, like roommates, romantic couples, teams, and group members, tend to grow emotionally similar (Anderson, Keltner, & John, 2003; Totterdell, 2000). Moreover, emotional similarity in groups further enhances closeness, happiness, and identification (Smith, Seger, & Mackie, 2007; Totterdell, Kellett, Briner, & Teuchmann, 1998), and emotional similarity in dating or married couples is associated with greater relationship satisfaction (Anderson et al., 2003).

Parent–infant attunement appears to contribute to mental and socioemotional development in the child as well as potential for resiliency throughout the balance of the lifespan. Attuned interactions are critically important for establishing a successful relationship and mutual understanding between caregiver and infant (Beebe et al., 2010), which itself provides a foundation for cognitive and socioemotional development (Field et al., 2007; Fullard & Reiling, 1976; Glocker et al., 2009; Hrdy, 1999). Attunement facilitates the growth of a sturdy sense of self in babies (Stern, 1985) and has been linked to a broad spectrum of positive outcomes for children in social development, cognitive maturation, intellectual achievement, and behavioral adjustment (van IJzendoorn et al., 1995; van IJzendoorn, Juffer, & Poelhuis, 2005). More specifically, early mother–infant attunement is associated with attachment security (De Wolff & van IJzendoorn, 1997); positive mood in the child (Lay, Waters, & Park, 1989); child compliance (Rescorla & Fechnay, 1996); delay of gratification and self-control (Feldman, Greenbaum, & Yirmiya, 1999; Raver, 1996); social attentiveness, social problem-solving skills, and nonaggression (Lindsey, Mize, & Pettit, 1997; Mize & Pettit, 1997; Pettit & Mize, 1993); and cooperation, emotional reciprocity, maternal responsiveness, and child responsiveness (Deater-Deckard & O'Connor, 2000). Indeed, these effects appear to be long-lasting—behaviorally and neurally. About the one, in a sample of 3,000 adults, ages 25–74, from the U.S. National Survey of Midlife Development, early parental emotional support—acts of caring, acceptance, and assistance—proved a principal predictor of mental and physical health in adulthood, associations that persisted into the seventh decade of life (Brim et al., 1996). About the other, an fMRI study that examined adults' responses to their mothers' and fathers' faces and the faces of male and female celebrities or strangers showed that mothers' faces overall elicited the most activation in core and extended brain regions involved in familiar face processing (Arsalidou, Barbeau, Bayless, & Taylor, 2010).

Associations between particular forms of parenting and child outcomes are always the same. However, the establishment and maintenance of dyadic, mutually responsive, reciprocal parent–child relationships—attunement—are critically important components of socialization and development. Failures of attunement result in poorly timed, mutually unsatisfying interactions and ultimately undesirable child outcomes: Maternal hyporesponsiveness and hypostimulation at 3 and 9 months predict insecure attachment in children at 12 months (Isabella & Belsky, 1991), aggressive and disruptive behavior at 3 years (Shaw, Keenan, & Vondra, 1994), and externalizing behavior problems at 10 years (Wakschlag & Hans, 1999). Likewise, hyperresponsiveness and hyperstimulation can impede development (Crnic, Ragozin, Greenberg, Robinson, & Basham, 1983) and are associated with decreased attentiveness and increased negative affect in children (Field, 1987). Infants who are over- or understimulated participate in fewer prolonged positive interactions and process less new information (Adamson & Bakeman, 1991; Landry, Smith, Miller-Loncar, & Swank, 1997). When interaction with caregivers becomes mistimed or mismatched, infants experience distress (Tronick, Ricks, & Cohn, 1982).

Parents and infants are strongly motivated to form long-lasting relationships (attachments) described by states of attunement. Understanding different facets of the behavior and neurobiology of attunement is a dawning focus of theory and research in infant and child development and parenting science. Far less empirical research on synchrony-related phenomena has been conducted with dyads beyond the infancy period. Of course, the structure and function of synchrony can be expected to change throughout the course of development (Gross & McCallum, 2000); Smollar and Youniss (1982) noted that ease of communication and maintenance of shared activity are central to young school-age children's friendship interactions, for example. Future research will advantageously concern itself with a developmental perspective on attunement, as it might with the underlying structure and parameters of attunement. Most operationalizations of attunement focus on positive affect (e.g., Censullo, Bowler, Lester, & Brazelton, 1987). Perhaps, however, affect and synchrony are separable components of dyadic interactions. Attuned but affectively negative interactions might function in a maladaptive rather than a positively adaptive way. Patterson (1982; Patterson, Reid, & Dishion, 1992) found that, among families of aggressive children, parent–child dyads tend to engage in elevated rates of "coercive bouts," interactional exchanges that look synchronous in that they are mutually focused (both child and caregiver are highly engaged) and contingent (one partner's behavior follows predictably from the other's) but negatively toned for both partners.

The frontiers of research and theory in attunement in parent–offspring relationships ought also to include connections between a neuroscience of parenting and parental cognitions and practices, parental neuroscience and child neuroscience, parental neuroscience and child development and well-being, and parental cognitions and practices and child neuroscience, as supplements to the much more common approach of relating parental cognitions and practices to child development and well-being. This research agendum in attunement calls for an integration of multiple levels of analysis— genetic, anatomical, hormonal, physiological, behavioral, and cultural—as all levels make critical contributions to a complete and comprehensive understanding of attunement.

It appears from the foregoing survey that key aspects of parent–infant relationships have been conserved throughout the process of evolution: In mammals, they include attuned hormonal, autonomic, and nervous system adjustments along with a repertoire of parental behaviors that sustain infants through an extensive period of dependency and contribute to their long-term health and adjustment (Ellison, 2006; Gerhardt, 2006; Schore, 2005; Sroufe, 2005). Little wonder that Bowlby (1953) contended that a mother's love in infancy and early childhood is as important to child mental health as are vitamins and proteins for the child's physical health.

Acknowledgments

I thank A. Bradley and P. Horn. Preparation of this chapter and research were supported by the Intramural Research Program of the Natioal Institutes of Health, Eunice Kennedy Shriver National Institute of Child Health and Human Development.

References

Ackermann, H., & Riecker, A. (2010). Cerebral control of motor aspects of speech production: Neurophysiological and functional imaging data. In B. Maassen & P. van Lieshout (Eds.), *Speech motor control: New developments in basic and applied research* (pp. 117–134). Oxford, UK: Oxford University Press.

Ackermann, H., & Ziegler, W. (2010). Brain mechanisms underlying speech motor control. In W. J. Hardcastle, J. Laver, & F. E. Gibbon (Eds.), *The handbook of phonetic sciences* (2nd ed., pp. 202–250). Malden, MA: Blackwell.

Adamson, L. B., & Bakeman, R. (1991). The development of shared attention during infancy. *Annals of Child Development, 8*, 1–41.

Ainsworth, M. D. (1989). Attachments beyond infancy. *American Psychologist, 44*, 709–716.

Ainsworth, M. D. S., Blehar, M. C., Waters, E., & Wall, S. (1978). *Patterns of attachment.* Hillsdale, NJ: Erlbaum.

Alario, F. X., Chainay, H., Lehericy, S., & Cohen, L. (2006). The role of the supplementary motor area (SMA) in word production. *Brain Research, 1076*, 129–143.

Alvergne, A., Faurie, C., & Raymond, M. (2009). Variation in testosterone levels and male reproductive effort: Insight from a polygynous human population. *Hormones and Behavior, 56*, 491–497.

Anderson, C., Keltner, D., & John, O. P. (2003). Emotional convergence between people over time. *Journal of Personality and Social Psychology, 84*, 1054–1068.

Archer, J. (2006). Testosterone and human aggression: An evaluation of the challengehypothesis. *Neuroscience and Biobehavioral Reviews, 30*, 319–345.

Arsalidou, M., Barbeau, E. J., Bayless, S. J., & Taylor, M. H. (2010). Brain responses differ to faces of mothers and fathers. *Brain and Cognition, 74*, 47–51.

Bakeman, R., & Quera, V. (2009). GSEQ 5.0 [Computer software and manual]. Retrieved from *www.gsu.edu/~psyrab/gseq* or *www.ub.edu/gcai/gseq.*

Bales, K., & Carter, C. S. (2002). Oxytocin facilitates parental care in female prairie voles (but not in males). *Hormones and Behavior, 41,* 456.

Barnard, K. E., & Solchany, J. A. (2002). Mothering. In M. H. Bornstein (Ed.), *Handbook of parenting* (2nd ed., Vol. 3, pp. 3–25). Mahwah, NJ: Erlbaum.

Barrett, J., & Fleming, A. S. (2011). All mothers are not created equal: Neural and psychobiological perspectives on mothering and the importance of individual differences. *Journal of Child Psychology and Psychiatry, 52,* 368–397.

Bartels, A., & Zeki, S. (2000). The neural basis of romantic love. *NeuroReport, 11,* 3829–3834.

Bartels, A., & Zeki, S. (2004). The neural correlates of maternal and romantic love. *NeuroImage, 21,* 1155–1166.

Beebe, B., Jaffe, J., Markese, S., Buck, K., Chen, H., Cohen, P., et al. (2010). The origins of 12-month attachment: A microanalysis of 4-month mother–infant interaction. *Attachment and Human Development, 12,* 3–141.

Beeghly, M., Perry, B. W., & Cicchetti, D. (1989). Structural and affective dimensions of play development in young children with Down syndrome. *International Journal of Behavioral Development, 12,* 257–277.

Bigelow, A. E. (1998). Infants' sensitivity to familiar imperfect contingencies in social interaction. *Infant Behavior and Development, 21,* 149–162.

Birch, L. L. (1980). The relationship between children's food preferences and those of their parents. *Journal of Nutrition Education, 12,* 14–18.

Biringen, Z., Robinson, J. L., & Emde, R. N. (1998). *Emotional Availability Scales* (3rd ed.). Unpublished manual, Department on Human Development and Family Studies, Colorado State University, Fort Collins.

Booth, A., & Dabbs, J. M. (1993). Testosterone and men's marriages. *Social Forces, 72,* 463–477.

Bornstein, M. H. (2002). *Handbook of parenting* (Vols. 1–5). Mahwah, NJ: Erlbaum.

Bornstein, M. H. (2006). Parenting science and practice. In K. A. Renninger & I. E. Sigel (Vol. Eds.), W. Damon & R. M. Lerner (Eds.-in-Chief), *Handbook of child psychology: Vol. 4. Child psychology in practice* (6th ed., pp. 893–949). Hoboken, NJ: Wiley.

Bornstein, M. H. (2009). Toward a model of culture–parent–child transactions. In A. Sameroff (Ed.), *The transactional model of development: How children and contexts shape each other* (pp. 139–161). Washington, DC: American Psychological Association.

Bornstein, M. H. (2012). Cultural approaches to parenting. *Parenting: Science and Practice, 12,* 212–221.

Bornstein, M. H., Park, Y., Haynes, O. M., & Suwalsky, J. T. D. (2012). *Infancy and parenting in 11 cultures: Argentina, Belgium, Brazil, Cameroon, France, Israel, Italy, Japan, Kenya, South Korea, and the United States.* Unpublished manuscript, Eunice Kennedy Shriver National Institute of Child Health and Human Development.

Bornstein, M. H., Putnick, D. L., Cote, L. R., Haynes, O. M., & Suwalsky, J. T. D. (2012). *Mother–infant vocalizations in eleven cultures.* Unpublished manuscript, Eunice Kennedy Shriver National Institute of Child Health and Human Development.

Bornstein, M. H., Putnick, D. L., Heslington, M., Gini, M., Suwalsky, J. T. D. Venuti, P., et al. (2008). Mother–child emotional availability in ecological perspective: Three countries, two regions, two genders. *Developmental Psychology, 44,* 666–680.

Bornstein, M. H., Putnick, D. L., Suwalsky, J. T. D., Venuti, P., de Falco, S., Zingman de Galperín, C., et al. (2012). Emotional relationships in mothers and infants: Culture-common and community-specific characteristics of dyads from rural and metropolitan settings in Argentina, Italy, and the United States. *Journal of Cross-Cultural Psychology, 43,* 171–198.

Bornstein, M. H., & Sawyer, J. (2005). Family systems. In K. McCartney & D. Phillips (Eds.), *Blackwell handbook on early childhood development* (pp. 381–398). Malden, MA: Blackwell.

Bornstein, M. H., Scrimin, S., Putnick, D. L., Capello, L., Haynes, O. M., de Falco, S., et al. (2012). Neurodevelopmental functioning in very young children undergoing treatment for non-CNS cancers. *Journal of Pediatric Psychology, 37*(6), 660–673.

Bornstein, M. H., & Seuss, P. E. (2000). Child and mother cardiac vagal tone: Continuity, stability, and concordance across the first 5 years. *Developmental Psychology, 36,* 54–65.

Bornstein, M. H., Suwalsky, J. T. D., & Breakstone, D. A. (2012). Emotional relationships between mothers and infants: Knowns, unknowns, and unknown unknowns. *Development and Psychopathology, 24,* 113–123.

Bornstein, M. H., Suwalsky, J. T. D., Putnick, D. L., Gini, M., Venuti, P., de Falco, S., et al. (2010). Developmental continuity and stability of emotional availability in the family: Two ages and two genders in child–mother dyads from two regions in three countries. *International Journal of Behavioral Development, 34,* 385–397.

Bornstein, M. H., Tamis-LeMonda, C. S., Hahn, C. S., & Haynes, O. M. (2008). Maternal responsiveness to young children at three ages: Longitudinal analysis of a multidimensional, modular, and specific parenting construct. *Developmental Psychology, 44,* 867–874.

Botez, M. I., & Barbeau, A. (1971). Role of subcortical structures and particularly of the thalamus in the mechanisms of speech and language. *International Journal of Neurology, 8,* 300–320.

Bowlby, J. (1953). *Child care and the growth of love.* London: Pelican.

Bowlby, J. (1969). *Attachment and loss: Vol. 1. Attachment.* London: Hogarth Press.

Brandt, I. (1990). Growth in head circumference: Parent–child correlation and secular trend. *Arztl Jugendkd, 81,* 321–326.

Brazelton, T. B. (1984). Four early stages in the development of mother–infant interaction. In N. Kobayashi & T. B. Brazelton (Eds.), *The growing child in family and society: An interdisciplinary study in parent–infant bonding* (pp. 19–34). Tokyo: University of Tokyo Press.

Brazelton, T. B., Koslowski, B., & Main, M. (1974). The origins of reciprocity: The early mother–infant interaction. In M. Lewis & L. A. Rosenblum (Eds.), *The effect of the infant on its caregiver* (pp. 49–76). New York: Wiley.

Brendel, B., Hertrich, I., Erb, M., Lindner, A., Riecker, A., Grodd, W., et al. (2010). The contribution of mesiofrontal cortex (SMA) to the preparation and execution of repetitive syllable productions: An fMRI study. *NeuroImage, 50,* 1219–1230.

Bribiescas, R. G. (2001). Reproductive ecology and life history of the human male. *American Journal of Physical Anthropology, 44,* 148–176.

Bridges, R. S. (1990). Endocrine regulation of parental behavior in rodents. In N. A. Krasnegor & R. S. Bridges (Eds.), *Mammalian parenting: Biochemical, neurobiological, and behavioral determinants* (pp. 93–117). New York: Oxford University Press.

Bridges, R. S. (2008). *Neurobiology of the parental brain.* Amsterdam: Academic Press.

Brim, O. G., Baltes, P. B., Bumpass, L. L., Cleary, P. D., Featherman, D. L., Hazzard, W. R., et al. (1996). National survey of midlife development in the United States (MIDUS), 1995–1996 (2nd ICPSR version). Ann Arbor, MI: Inter-university Consortium for Political and Social Research. Retrieved from *http://sodapop.pop.psu.edu/codebooks/midus/1995–96/02760–0001–Codebook.pdf.*

Bronfenbrenner, U., & Morris, P. A. (2006). The bioecological model of human development.

In R. M. Lerner (Vol. Ed.), W. Damon (Ed.-in-Chief), *Handbook of child psychology: Vol. 1. Theoretical models of human development* (6th ed., pp. 793–828). New York: Wiley.

Brosch, T., Sander, D., & Scherer, K. R. (2007). That baby caught my eye . . . Attention capture by infant faces. *Emotion, 7,* 685–689.

Brunton, P. J., & Russell, J. A. (2008). The expectant brain: Adapting for motherhood. *Nature Reviews. Neuroscience, 9,* 11–25.

Bugental, D. B., & Goodnow, J. J. (1998). Socialization processes. In N. Eisenberg (Vol. Ed.), W. Damon (Ed.-in-Chief), *Handbook of child psychology: Vol. 3. Social, emotional, and personality development* (pp. 389–462). New York: Wiley.

Caria, A., de Falco, S., Venuti, P., Lee, S., Esposito, G., Rigo, P., et al. (2012). Species-specific response to human infant faces in the premotor cortex. *NeuroImage, 60,* 884–893.

Carlsson, J., Lagercrantz, H., Olson, L., Printz, G., & Bartocci, M. (2008). Activation of the right fronto-temporal cortex during maternal face recognition in young infants. *Acta Pediatrica, 97,* 1221–1225.

Carr, L., Iacoboni, M., Dubeau, M. C., Mazziotta, J. C., & Lenzi, G. L. (2003). Neural mechanism of empathy in humans: A relay from neural system for imitation to limbic areas. *Proceedings of the National Academy of Sciences USA, 100,* 5497–5502.

Carter, H. D. (1932). Family resemblances in verbal and numerical abilities. *Genetic Psycholoqy Monographs, 12,* 3–10.

Censullo, M., Bowler, R., Lester, B., & Brazelton, T. B. (1987). An instrument for the measurement of infant–mother synchrony. *Nursing Research, 36,* 244–248.

Champagne, F., & Meaney, M. J. (2001). Like mother, like daughter: Evidence for nongenomic transmission of parental behavior and stress responsivity. *Progress in Brain Research, 133,* 287–302.

Cohen, J., & Cohen, P. (1975). *Applied multiple regression/correlation analysis for the behavioral sciences.* Hillsdale, NJ: Erlbaum.

Collins, W. A., Maccoby, E. E., Steinberg, L., Hetherington, E. M., & Bornstein, M. H. (2000). Contemporary research on parenting: The case for nature and nurture. *American Psychologist, 55,* 218 – 232.

Corter, C., & Fleming, A. S. (1990). Maternal responsiveness in humans: Emotional, cognitive and biological factors. *Advances in the Study of Behavior, 19,* 83–136.

Corter, C. M., & Fleming, A. S. (2002). Psychobiology of maternal behavior in human beings. In M. H. Bornstein (Ed.), *Handbook of parenting: Biology and ecology of parenting* (pp. 141–182). Mahwah, NJ: Erlbaum.

Crawley, S. B., & Spiker, D. (1983). Mother–child interactions involving two-year-olds with Down syndrome: A look at individual differences. *Child Development, 54,* 1312–1323.

Crnic, K. A., Ragozin, A. S., Greenberg, M. T., Robinson, N. M., & Basham, R. B. (1983). Social interaction and developmental competence of preterm and full-term infants during the first year of life. *Child Development, 54,* 1199–1210.

Darwin, C. (1965). *The expession of the emotions in man and animals.* Chicago: University of Chicago Press. (Original work published 1872)

de Haan, M., & Nelson, C. A. (1997). Recognition of the mother's face by 6-month-old infants: A neurobehavioral study. *Developmental Psychology, 68,* 187–210.

de Haan, M., & Nelson, C. A. (1999). Brain activity differentiates face and object processing in 6-month-old infants. *Developmental Psychology, 35,* 1113–1121.

De Wolff, M. S., & van IJzendoorn, M. H. (1997). Sensitivity and attachment: A meta-analysis on parental antecedents of infant attachment. *Child Development, 68,* 571–591.

Deater-Deckard, K., & O'Connor, T. G. (2000). Parent–child mutuality in early childhood: Two behavioral genetic studies. *Developmental Psychology, 36,* 561–570.

DeCasper, A. J., & Fifer, W. P. (1980). Of human bonding: Newborns prefer their mothers' voices. *Science, 208,* 1174–1176.

Deecke, L., & Kornhuber, H. H. (1978). An electrical sign of participation of the mesial "supplementary" motor cortex in human voluntary finger movement. *Brain Research, 159,* 473–476.

DeFries, J. C. (1967). Quantitative genetics and behavior: Overview and perspective. In J. Hirsch (Ed.), *Behavior-genetic analysis* (pp. 322–339). New York: McGraw-Hill.

DeFries, J. C., Ashton, G. C., Johnson, R. C., Kuse, A. R., McClearn, G. E., Mi, M. P., et al. (1978). The Hawaii family study of cognition: A reply. *Behavior Genetics, 8,* 281–288.

DeFries, J. C., Johnson, R. C., Kuse, A. R., McClearn, G. E., Polovina, J., Vandenberg, S. G., et al. (1979). Familial resemblance for specific cognitive abilities. *Behavior Genetics, 9,* 23–43.

Ditto, B., France, C., & Miller, S. (1989). Spouse and parent-offspring similarities in cardiovascular response to mental arithmetic and isometric hand-grip. *Health Psychology, 8,* 159–173.

Draganski, B., Gaser, C., Kempermann, G., Kuhn, H. G., Winkler, J., Buchel, C., et al. (2006). Temporal and spatial dynamics of brain structure changes during extensive learning. *Journal of Neuroscience, 26,* 6314–6317.

Dunn, J. (1993). *Young children's close relationships: Beyond attachment.* Newbury Park, CA: Sage.

Elbert, T., Pantev, C., Wienbruch, C., Rockstroh, B., & Taub, E. (1995). Increased cortical representation of the fingers on the left hand in string players. *Science, 270,* 305–307.

Ellison, K. (2006). *The mommy brain: How motherhood makes us smarter* (2nd ed.) New York: Perseus.

Emde, R. N. (1984). The affective self: Continuities and transformations from infancy. In J. D. Call, E. Galenson, & R. L. Tyson (Eds.), *Frontiers of infant psychiatry* (Vol. 2, pp. 38–54). New York: Basic Books.

Eriksson, P. S., Perfilieva, E., Björk-Eriksson, T., Alborn, A.-M., Norberg, C., Peterson, D. A., et al. (1998). Neurogenesis in the adult human hippocampus. *Nature Medicine, 4,* 1313–1317.

Febo, M., Numan, M., & Ferris, C. F. (2005). Functional magnetic resonance imaging shows oxytocin activates brain regions associated with mother–pup bonding during suckling. *Journal of Neuroscience, 25,* 11637–11644.

Feldman, R. (2003). Infant–mother and infant–father synchrony: The coregulation of positive arousal. *Infant Mental Health Journal, 24,* 1–23.

Feldman, R. (2012). Bio-behavioral synchrony: A model for integrating biological and microsocial behavioral processes in the study of parenting. *Parenting: Science and Practice, 12,* 154–164.

Feldman, R., & Eidelman, A. I. (2003). Direct and indirect effects of breast milk on the neurobehavioral and cognitive development of premature infants. *Developmental Psychobiology, 43,* 109 –119.

Feldman, R., & Eidelman, A. I. (2004). Parent–infant synchrony and the social–emotional development of triplets. *Developmental Psychology, 40,* 1133–1147.

Feldman, R., & Eidelman, A. I. (2007). Maternal postpartum behavior and the emergence of infant-mother and infant-father synchrony in preterm and full-term infants: The role of neonatal vagal tone. *Developmental Psychobiology, 49,* 290 –302.

Feldman, R., Eidelman, A. I., & Rotenberg, N. (2004). Parenting stress, infant emotion regulation, maternal sensitivity, and the cognitive development of triplets: A model for parent and child influences in a unique ecology. *Child Development, 75,* 1774 –1791.

Feldman, R., Gordon, I., & Zagoory-Sharon, O. (2010). The cross-generation transmission of oxytocin in humans. *Hormones and Behavior, 58,* 669–676.

Feldman, R., Greenbaum, C. W., & Yirmiya, N. (1999). Mother–infant affect synchrony as an antecedent of the emergence of self-control. *Developmental Psychology, 35,* 223–231.

Feldman, R., Weller, A., Zagoory-Sharon, O., & Levine, A. (2007). Evidence for a neuroendocrinological foundation of human affiliation: Plasma oxytocin levels across pregnancy and the postpartum period predict mother–infant bonding. *Psychological Science, 18,* 965–970.

Field, T. (1987). Affective and interactive disturbances in infants. In J. D. Osofsky (Ed.), *Handbook of infant development* (2nd ed., pp. 972–1005). Oxford, UK: Wiley.

Field, T., Diego, M., Dieter, J., Hernandez-Rief, M., Schanberg, S., Kuhn, C., et al. (2004). Prenatal depression effects on the fetus and the newborn. *Infant Behavior and Development, 27,* 216–229.

Field, T., Healy, B., Goldstein, S., & Guthertz, M. (1990). Behavior-state matching and synchrony in mother–infant interactions of nondepressed versus depressed dyads. *Developmental Psychology, 26,* 7–14.

Field, T., Hernandez-Reif, M., Diego, M., Feijo, L., Vera, Y., Gil, K., et al. (2007). Still-face and separation effects on depressed mother–infant interactions. *Infant Mental Health Journal, 28,* 314–323.

Field, T., Hernandez-Reif, M., Diego, M., Figueiredo, B., Schanberg, S., & Kuhn, C. (2006). Prenatal cortisol, prematurity and low birthweight. *Infant Behavior and Development, 29,* 268–275.

Fleming, A. S., Corter, C., Franks, P., Surbey, M., Schneider, B. A., & Steiner, M. (1993). Postpartum factors related to mother's attraction to newborn infant odours. *Developmental Psychobiology, 26,* 115–132.

Fleming, A. S., Corter, C., Stallings, J., & Steiner, M. (2002). Testosterone and prolactin are associated with emotional responses to infant cries in new fathers. *Hormones and Behavior, 42,* 399–413.

Fleming, A. S., Ruble, D., Krieger, H., & Wong, P. Y. (1997). Hormonal and experiential correlates of maternal responsiveness during pregnancy and the puerperium in human mothers. *Hormones and Behavior, 31,* 145–158.

Fleming, A. S., Steiner, M., & Anderson, V. (1987). Hormonal and attitudinal correlates of maternal behavior during the early postpartum period in first-time mothers. *Journal of Reproductive and Infant Psychology, 5,* 193–205.

Fuemmeler, B. F., Anderson, C. B., & Mâsse, L. C. (2011). Parent–child relationship of directly measured physical activity. *International Journal of Behavioral Nutrition and Physical Activity, 8,* 17–25.

Fullard, W., & Reiling, A. M. (1976). An investigation of Lorenz's "babyness." *Child Development, 47,* 1191–1193.

Fullgrabe, U. (2002). *Psychologie der Eigensicherung: Uberleben ist kein Zufall.* Stuttgart, Germany: Boorberg Verlag.

Garn, S. M., & Rohmann, C. G. (1966). Interaction of nutrition and genetics in the timing of growth and development. *Pediatric Clinics of North America, 13,* 353.

Gettler, L. T. (2010). Direct male care and hominin evolution: Why male-child interaction is more than a nice social idea. *American Anthropologist, 112,* 7–21.

Gettler, L. T., McDade, T. W., Feranil, A. B., & Kuzawa, C. W. (2011). Longitudinal evidence that fatherhood decreases testosterone in human males. *Proceedings of the National Academy of Sciences USA, 108,* 16194–16199.

Gerhardt, S. (2006). *Why love matters: How affection shapes a baby's brain.* New York: Brunner-Routledge.

Gitau, R., Cameron, A., Fisk, N. M., & Glover, V. (1998). Fetal exposure to maternal cortisol. *Lancet, 352,* 707–708.

Glocker, M. L., Langleben, D. D., Ruparel, K., Loughead, J. W., Valdez, J. N., Griffin, M. D., et al. (2009). Baby schema modulates the brain reward system in nulliparous women. *Proceedings of the National Academy of Sciences USA, 106,* 9115–9119.

Glover, V., Teixeira, J., Gitau, R., & Fisk, N. M. (1999). Mechanisms by which maternal mood in pregnancy may affect the fetus. *Contemporary Reviews in Obstetrics and Gynecology, 11,* 1–6.

Goldberg, G. (1985). Supplementary motor area structure and function—Review and hypotheses. *Behavioral and Brain Sciences, 8,* 567–588.

Goldstein, M. H., Schwade, J. A., & Bornstein, M. H. (2009). The value of vocalizing: Five-month-old infants associate their own noncry vocalizations with responses from caregivers. *Child Development, 80,* 636–644.

Gould, E., Cameron, H. A., Daniels, D. C., Wooley, C. S., & McEwen, B. S. (1994). Adrenal hormones suppress cell division in the adult rat dentate gyrus. *Journal of Comparative Neurology, 340,* 551–565.

Grasso, D. J., Moser, J. S., Dozier, M., & Simons, R. (2009). ERP correlates of attention allocation in mothers processing faces of their children. *Biological Psychology, 18,* 95–102.

Gray, P. B., & Anderson, K. G. (2010). *Fatherhood: Evolution and human paternal behavior.* Cambridge, MA: Harvard University Press.

Gray, P. B., Kahlenberg, S. M., Barrett, E. S., Lipson, S. F., & Ellison, P. T. (2002). Marriage and fatherhood are associated with lower testosterone in males. *Evolution and Human Behavior, 23,* 193–201.

Greenfield, P. M., Suzuki, L. K., & Rothstein-Fisch, C. (2006). Cultural pathways through human development. In I. Sigel & K. Renninger (Vol. Eds.), W. Damon & R. Lerner (Eds.-in-Chief), *Handbook of child psychology* (6th ed., Vol. 4, pp. 655–699). Hoboken, NJ: Wiley.

Grewen, K. M., Girdler, S. S., Amico, J., & Light, K. C. (2005). Effects of partner support on resting oxytocin, cortisol, norepinephrine, and blood pressure before and after warm partner contact. *Psychosomatic Medicine, 67,* 531–538.

Grezes, J., & Decety, J. (2002). Does visual perception of object afford action? Evidence from a neuroimaging study. *Neuropsychologia, 40,* 212–222.

Gross, P. H., & McCallum, R. S. (2000). Operationalization and predictive utility of mother–daughter synchrony. *School Psychology Quarterly, 15,* 279–294.

Gustella, A. J., Mitchell, P. B., & Dadds, M. R. (2008). Oxytocin increases gaze to the eye region of human faces. *Biological Psychiatry, 63,* 3–5.

Haggard, P., & Eimer, M. (1999). On the relation between brain potentials and the awareness of voluntary movements. *Experimental Brain Research, 126,* 128–133.

Haith, M. M., Bergman, T., & Moore, M. J. (1977). Eye contact and face scanning in early infancy. *Science, 198,* 853–855.

Halberstadt, A.G. (1986). Family socialization of emotional expression and nonverbal communication styles and skills. *Journal of Personality and Social Psychology, 51,* 827–836.

Halberstadt, A. G., & Eaton, K. L. (2002). A meta-analysis of family expressiveness and children's emotion expressiveness and understanding. *Marriage and Family Review, 34,* 35–62.

Harrist, A. W., & Waugh, R. M. (2002). Dyadic synchrony: Its structure and function in children's development. *Developmental Review, 22,* 555–592.

Hart, B. L. (1974). Gonadal androgen and sociosexual behavior of male mammals: A comparative analysis. *Psychological Bulletin, 81,* 383–400.

Hastrup, J. L., Kraemer, D. L., Hotchkiss, A. P., & Johnson, C. A. (1986). Cardiovascular responsivity to stress: Family patterns and the effects of instructions. *Journal of Psychosomatic Research, 40,* 233–241.

Heinrichs, M., Meinlschmidt, G., Wippich, W., Ehlert, U., & Hellhammer, D. H. (2004). Selective amnesic effects of oxytocin on human memory. *Physiology and Behavior, 83*, 31–38.

Hirschenhauser, K., & Oliveira, R. F. (2006). Social modulation of androgens in male vertebrates: Meta-analyses of the challenge hypothesis. *Animal Behaviour, 71*, 265–277.

Holman, S. D., & Goy, R. W. (1995). Experiential and hormonal correlates of care-giving in rhesus macaques. In C. R. Pryce, R. D. Martin, & D. Skuse (Eds.), *Motherhood in human and nonhuman primates: Biosocial determinants* (pp. 87–93). Basel, Switzerland: Karger.

Holt, S. B. (1952). Genetics of dermal ridges: Inheritance of total finger ridge-count. *Annals of Eugenics, 17,* 140–161.

Holt, S. B. (1955). Genetics of dermal ridges: Parent–child correlations for total finger ridge-count. *Annals of Human Genetics, 20,* 270–281.

Hrdy, S. (1999). *Mother Nature: A history of mothers, infants and natural selection.* New York: Pantheon.

Hrdy, S. B. (2005). Evolutionary context of human development: The cooperative breeding model. In C. S. Carter, L. Ahnert, K. E. Grossmann, S. B. Hrdy, M. E. Lamb, S. W. Porges, et al. (Eds.), *Attachment and bonding: A new synthesis* (pp. 9–32). Cambridge, MA: MIT Press.

Insel, T. (1990). Oxytocin and maternal behavior. In N. A. Krasnegor & R. S. Bridges (Eds.), *Mammalian parenting: Biochemical, neurobiological, and behavioral determinants* (pp. 260–280). New York: Oxford University Press.

Isabella, R. A., & Belsky, J. (1991). Interactional synchrony and the origins of infant-mother attachment: A replication study. *Child Development, 62,* 373–384.

Ivell, R., & Russell, J. A. (1996). Oxytocin: Cellular and molecular approaches in medicine and research. *Reviews of Reproduction, 1,* 13–18.

Jahanshahi, M., Jenkins, I. H., Brown, R. G., Marsden, C. D., Passingham, R. E., & Brooks, D. J. (1995). Self-initiated versus externally triggered movements: I. An investigation using measurement of regional cerebral blood flow with PET and movement-related potentials in normal and Parkinson's disease subjects. *Brain, 118,* 913–933.

Johnson, M. H., Dziurawiec, S., Ellis, H., & Morton, J. (1991). Newborns' preferential tracking of face-like stimuli and its subsequent decline. *Cognition, 40,* 1–19.

Jones, N. A., Field, T., Fox, N. A., Lundy, B., & Hart, S. (1998). Newborns of mothers with depressive symptoms are physiologically less developed. *Infant Behavior and Development, 21,* 537–541.

Kaitz, M., Good, A., Rokem, A. M., & Eidelman, A. I. (1987). Mother's recognition of their newborns by olfactory cues. *Developmental Psychobiology, 20,* 587–591.

Kaitz, M., Good, A., Rokem, A. M., & Eidelman, A. I. (1988). Mothers' and fathers' recognition of their newborns' photographs during the postpartum period. *Journal of Developmental and Behavioral Pediatrics, 9,* 223–226.

Kaitz, M., Lapidot, I., Bronner, R., & Eidelman, A. (1992). Parturient women can recognize their infants by touch. *Developmental Psychology, 28,* 35–39.

Kaitz, M., Rokem, A. M., & Eidelman, A. I. (1988). Infants' face-recognition by primiparous and multiparous women. *Perceptual and Motor Skills, 67,* 495–502.

Karger, R. H. (1979). Synchrony in mother–infant interactions. *Child Development, 50,* 882–885.

Kendrick, K. M., Keverne, E. B., & Baldwin, B. A. (1987). Intracerebroventricular oxytocin stimulates maternal behaviour in the sheep. *Neuroendocrinology, 46,* 56–61.

Killner, J. K., Neal, A., Weiskopf, N., Friston, K. J., & Frith, C. D. (2009). Evidence of mirror neurons in human inferior frontal gyrus. *Journal of Neuroscience, 12,* 10153–10159.

Kim, P., Leckman, J. F., Mayes, L. C., Feldman, R., Wang, X., & Swain, J. E. (2010). The plasticity of human maternal brain: Longitudinal changes in brain anatomy during the early postpartum period. *Behavioral Neuroscience, 124,* 695–700.

Kleiman, D. G., & Malcolm, J. R. (1981). The evolution of male parental investment in mammals. In D. J. Gubernick & P. H. Klopfer (Eds.), *Parental care in mammals* (pp. 347–387). New York: Plenum Press.

Kringelbach, M. L., Lehtonen, A., Squire, S., Harvey, A. G., Craske, M. G., Holliday, I. E., et al. (2008). A specific and rapid neural signature for parental instinct. *PLoS ONE, 3,* e1664.

Kochanska, G. (1997). Mutually responsive orientation between mothers and their young children: Implications for early socialization. *Child Development, 68,* 94–112.

Kochanska, G., & Aksan, N. (2004). Development of mutual responsiveness between parents and their young children. *Child Development, 75,* 1657–1676.

Kuzawa, C. W., Gettler, L. T., Muller, M. N., McDade, T. W., & Feranil, A. B. (2009). Fatherhood, pairbonding and testosterone in the Philippines. *Hormones and Behavior, 56,* 429–435.

Lambert, K. G., & Kinsley, C. H. (2012). Brain and behavioral modifications that accompany the onset of motherhood. *Parenting: Science and Practice, 12,* 74–89.

Landry, S. H., Smith, K. E., Miller-Loncar, C. L., & Swank, P. R. (1997). Predicting cognitive-language and social growth curves from early maternal behaviors in children at varying degrees of biological risk. *Developmental Psychology, 33,* 1040–1053.

Laskarzewski, P., Morrison, J. A., Khoury, P., Kelly, K., Glatfelter, L., Larsen, R., et al. (1980). Parent–child nutrient intake interrelationships in school children ages 6 to 19: The Princeton School District study. *American Journal of Clinical Nutrition, 33,* 2350–2355.

Lay, K. L., Waters, E., & Park, K. A. (1989). Maternal responsiveness and child compliance: The role of mood as a mediator. *Child Development, 60,* 1405–1411.

Leibenluft, L., Gobbini, M. I., Harrison, T., & Haxby, J. V. (2004). Mothers' neural activation in response to pictures of their children and other children. *Biological Psychiatry, 56,* 225–232.

Lenzi, D., Trentini, C., Pantano, P, Macaluso, E., Iacoboni, M., Lenzi, G. I., et al. (2009). Neural basis of maternal communication and emotional expression processing during infant preverbal stage. *Cerebral Cortex, 19,* 1124–1133.

Leon, I. G. (2007). Adoption losses: Naturally occurring or socially constructed? *Child Development, 73,* 652–663.

Lindsey, E. W., Mize, J., & Pettit, G. S. (1997). Mutuality in parent–child play: Consequences for children's peer competence. *Journal of Social and Personal Relationships, 14,* 523–538.

Livson, N., McNeill, D., & Thomas, K. (1962). Pooled estimates of parent–child correlations in stature from birth to maturity. *Science, 138,* 818–820.

Lorenz, K. (1943). Die angeborenen Formen möglicher Erfahrung (Innate form of potential experience). *Zeitschrift für Tierpsychologie, 5,* 235–309.

Lorenz, K. (1971). *Studies in animal and human behavior* (Vol. 2). London: Methuen.

Maccoby, E. E. (1992). The role of parents in the socialization of children: An historical overview. *Developmental Psychology, 28,* 1006–1017.

MacDonald, K., & MacDonald, T. M. (2010). The peptide that binds: A systematic review of oxytocin and its prosocial effects in humans. *Harvard Review of Psychiatry, 18,* 1–21.

MacLean, P. D. (1990). *The triune brain in evolution: Role in paleocerebral functions.* New York: Plenum Press.

Maestripieri, D., Hoffman, C. L., Anderson, G. M., Carter, C. S., & Higley, J. D. (2009). Mother–infant interactions in free-ranging rhesus macaques: Relationships between physiological and behavioral variables. *Physiology and Behavior, 96,* 613–619.

Maguire, E. A., Gadian, D. G., Johnsrude, I. S., Good, C. D., Ashburner, J., Frackowiak, R. S. J., et al. (2000). Navigation-related structural change in the hippocampi of taxi drivers. *Proceedings of the National Academy of Sciences USA, 97*, 4398–4403.

Malatesta, C. Z., & Haviland, J. M. (1982). Learning display rules: The socialization of emotion expression in infancy. *Child Development, 53*, 991–1003.

Mattson, B. J., Williams, S., Rosenblatt, J. S., & Morrell, J. I. (2001). Comparison of two positive reinforcing stimuli: Pups and cocaine throughout the postpartum period. *Behavioral Neuroscience, 115*, 683–694.

McCall, R. B., & Kennedy, C. B. (1980). Attention of 4-month infants to discrepancy and babyishness. *Journal of Experimental Child Psychology, 29*, 189–201.

Messer, D. J., & Vietze, P. M. (1984). Timing and transitions in mother–infant gaze. *Infant Behavior and Development, 7*, 167–181.

Minuchin, P. (1985). Families and individual development: Provocations from the field of family therapy. *Child Development, 56*, 289–302.

Mize, J., & Pettit, G. S. (1997). Mothers' social coaching, mother–child relationship style, and children's peer competence: Is the medium the message? *Child Development, 68*, 312–332.

Morgan, H. D., Fleming, A. S., & Stern, J. M. (1992). Somatosensory control of the onset and retention of maternal responsiveness in primiparous sprague-dawley rats. *Physiology and Behavior, 51*, 549–555.

Morgan, H. D., Watchus, J. A., Milgram, N. W., & Fleming, A. S. (1999). The long lasting effects of electrical simulation of the medial preoptic area and medial amygdala on maternal behavior in female rats. *Behavioural Brain Research, 99*, 61–73.

Mukamel, R., Ekstrom, A. D., Kaplan, J., Iacoboni, M., & Fried, I. (2010). Single-neuron responses in humans during execution and observation of action. *Current Biology, 20*, 750–756.

Muller, M. N., Marlowe, F. W., Bugumba, R., & Ellison, P. T. (2009). Testosterone and paternal care in East African foragers and pastoralists. *Proceedings of the Royal Biological Society, 276*, 347–354.

Murray, L., & Trevarthen, C. (1986). The infant's role in mother–infant communication. *Journal of Child Language, 13*, 15–29.

Nachev, P., Kennard, C., & Husain, M. (2008). Functional role of the supplementary and pre-supplementary motor areas. *Nature Reviews. Neuroscience, 9*, 856–869.

Nakato, E., Otsuka, Y., Kanazawa, S., Yamaguchi, M. K., Honda, Y., & Kakigi, R. (2011). I know this face: Neural activity during mother' face perception in 7- to 8-month-old infants as investigated by near-infrared spectroscopy. *Early Human Development, 87*, 1–7.

Nitschke, J., Nelson, E., Rusch, B., Fox, A. S., Oakes, T., & Davidson, R. (2004). Orbifrontal cortex tracks posititive mood in mothers viewing pictures of their newborn infants. *NeuroImage, 21*, 583–592.

Nordfjäll, K., Svenson, U., Norrback, K.-F., Adolfsson, R., & Roos, G. (2010). Large-scale parent–child comparison confirms a strong paternal influence on telomere length. *European Journal of Human Genetics, 18*, 385–389.

Noriuchi, M., Kikuchi, Y., & Senoo, A. (2008). The functional neuroanatomy of maternal love: Mother's response to infant's attachment behaviors. *Biological Psychiatry, 63*, 415–423.

Nottebohm, F. (1985). Neuronal replacement in adulthood. *Annals of the New York Academy of Sciences, 457*, 143–161.

Numan, M., Fleming, A. S., & Levy, F. (2006). Maternal behavior. In J. D. Neill (Ed.), *Knobil and Neill's physiology of reproduction* (pp. 1921–1993). San Diego, CA: Elsevier.

Numan, M., & Insel, T. (2003). *The neurobiology of parental behavior.* New York: Springer.

Oatridge, A., Holdcroft, A., Saeed, N., Hajnal, J. V., Puri, B. K., Fusi, L., ET AL. (2002). Change in brain size during and after pregnancy: Study in healthy women and women with preeclampsia. *American Journal of Neuroradiology, 23*, 19–26.

Papoušek, H. (2000). Intuitive parenting. In J. D. Osofsky & H. E. Fitzgerald (Eds.), *WAIMH handbook of infant mental health: Vol. 3. Parenting and child care* (pp. 310–321). New York: Wiley.

Papoušek, H., & Bornstein, M. H. (1992). Didactic interactions. In H. Papoušek, U. Jurgens, & M. Papoušek (Eds.), *Nonverbal vocal communication: Comparative and developmental approaches* (pp. 209–220). Cambridge, UK: Cambridge University Press.

Papoušek, H., & Papoušek, M. (2002). Intuitive parenting. In M. H. Bornstein (Ed.), *Handbook of parenting: Vol. 2. Biology and ecology of parenting* (2nd ed., pp. 183–203). Mahwah, NJ: Erlbaum.

Parke, R. D. (2002). Fathers and families. In M. H. Bornstein (Ed.), *Handbook of parenting: Vol. 3. Status and social conditions of parenting* (2nd ed., pp. 27–73). Mahwah, NJ: Erlbaum.

Pascual-Leone, A., & Torres, F. (1993). Plasticity of the sensorimotor cortex representation of the reading finger in Braille readers. *Brain, 116*, 39–52.

Patterson, G. R. (1982). *Coercive family process.* Eugene, OR: Castalia.

Patterson, G. R., Reid, J. B., & Dishion, T. (1992). *Anti-social boys.* Eugene, OR: Castalia.

Pearson, R. M., Lightman, S. L., & Evans, J. (2009). Emotional sensitivity for motherhood: Late pregnancy is associated with enhanced accuracy to encode emotional faces. *Hormones and Behavior, 56*, 557–563.

Pedersen, C. A. (1997). Oxytocin control of maternal behavior: Regulation by sex steroids and offspring stimuli. *Annals of the New York Academy of Sciences, 807*, 126–145.

Pereira, M., Seip, K. M., & Morrell, J. I. (2008). Maternal motivation and its neural substrate across the postpartum period. In R. S. Bridges (Ed.), *Neurobiology of the parental brain.* New York: Academic Press.

Pettit, G. S., & Mize, J. (1993). Substance and style: Understanding the ways in which parents teach children about social relationships. In S. Duck (Ed.), *Understanding relationship processes: Vol. 2. Learning about relationships* (pp. 118–151). Newbury Park, CA: Sage.

Pons, J. (1954). Herencia de las líneas principales de la palma: Contribución a la genética de los caracteres dermopapilares. *Trabajos del Instituto Bernardino de Sahagún de. Antropología y Etnología, 14*, 35–50.

Porges, S. W. (1995). Orienting in a defensive world: Mammalian modifications of our evolutionary heritage. A polyvagal theory. *Psychophysiology, 32*, 301–318.

Porges, S. W. (1996). Physiological regulation in high-risk infants: A model for assessment and potential intervention. *Development and Psychopathology, 8*, 43–58.

Porter, R. H. (2004). The biological significance of skin-to-skin contact and maternal odours. *Acta Paediatrica, 93*, 1560–1562.

Porter, R. H., Cernoch, J. M., & McLaughlin, F. J. (1983). Maternal recognition of neonates through olfactory cues. *Physiology and Behavior, 30*, 151–154.

Porter, R. H., & Winberg, J. (1999). Unique salience of maternal breast odors for newborn infants. *Neuroscience and Biobehavioral Reviews, 23*, 439–449.

Pryce, C. R., Martin, R. D., & Skuse, D. (1995). *Motherhood in human and nonhuman primates: Biosocial determinants.* New York: Karger.

Ramon y Cajal, S. (1906, December). The structure and connexions of neurons. *Nobel Lecture.* Retrieved from *www.nobelprize.org/nobel_prizes/medicine/laureates/1906/cajal-lecture.pdf.*

Ranote, S., Elliott, R., Abel, K. M., Mitchell, R., Deakin, J. F., & Appleby, L. (2004). The neural basis of maternal responsiveness to infants: An fMRI study. *NeuroReport, 15*, 1825–1829.

Raver, C. C. (1996). Relations between social contingency in mother–child interaction and 2–year-olds' social competence. *Developmental Psychology, 32*, 850–859.

Rennels, J. L., & Davis, R. E. (2008). Facial experience during the first year. *Infant Behavior and Development, 31*, 665–678.

Rescorla, L., & Fechnay, T. (1996). Mother–child synchrony and communicative reciprocity in late-talking toddlers. *Journal of Speech and Hearing Research, 39*, 200–208.

Richter, D. W., & Spyer, K. M. (1990). Cardiorespiratory control. In A. D. Loewy & K. M. Syper (Eds.), *Central regulation of autonomic function* (pp. 189–207). New York: Oxford University Press.

Riecker, A., Mathiak, K., Wildgruber, D., Erb, M., Hertrich, I., Grodd, W., et al. (2005). fMRI reveals two distinct cerebral networks subserving speech motor control. *Neurology, 64*, 700–706.

Rimmele, U., Hediger, K., Heinrichs, M., & Klaver, P. (2009). Oxytocin makes a face familiar in memory. *Journal of Neuroscience, 29*, 38–42.

Rizzolatti, G., & Sinigaglia, C. (2010). The functional role of the parieto-frontal mirror circuit: Interpretations and misinterpretations. *Nature Reviews. Neuroscience, 11*, 264–274.

Robson, K. S., & Moss, H. A. (1970). Patterns and determinants of maternal attachment. *Journal of Pediatrics, 77*, 976–985.

Rosenblatt, J. S., Olufowobi, A., & Siegel, H. I. (1998). Effects of pregnancy hormones on maternal responsiveness, responsiveness to estrogen stimulation of maternal behavior, and the lordosis response to estrogen stimulation. *Hormones and Behavior, 33*, 104–114.

Rozin, P., Fallon, A., & Mandell, R. (1984). Family resemblance in attitudes to foods. *Developmental Psychology, 20*, 309–314.

Russell, M. J. (1983). Human olfactory communication. In D. Muller-Schwairze & R. M. Silverstein (Eds.), *Chemical signals in vertebrates* (Vol. 3, pp. 259–273). New York: Plenum Press.

Sameroff, A. (Ed.). (2009). *The transactional model of development: How children and contexts shape each other.* Washington, DC: American Psychological Association.

Sander, L. (2000). Where are we going in the field of infant mental health? *Infant Mental Health Journal, 21*, 1–18.

Sanefuji, W., Ohgami, H., & Hashiya, K. (2007) Development of preference for baby faces across species in humans *(Homo sapiens). Journal of Ethology, 25*, 249–254.

Schaffer, H. R. (1991). The mutuality of parental control in early childhood. In M. Lewis & S. Feinman (Eds.), *Social influences and socialization in infancy: Vol. 6. Genesis of behavior* (pp. 165–184). New York: Plenum Press.

Schore, A. N. (2005). Back to basics: Attachment, affect regulation, and the developing right brain: Linking developmental neuroscience to pediatrics. *Pediatrics in Review, 26*, 204–217.

Schulte-Rüther, M., Markowitsch, H. J., Fink, G. R., & Piefke, M. (2007). Mirror neuron and theory of mind mechanisms involved in face-to-face interactions: A functional magnetic resonance imaging approach to empathy. *Journal of Cognitive Neuroscience, 19*, 1354–1372.

Seip, K. M., & Morrell, J. I. (2007). Increasing the incentive salience of cocaine challenges preference for pup- over cocaine-associated stimuli during early postpartum: Place preference and locomotor analyses in the lactating female rat. *Psychopharmacology, 194*, 309–319.

Seitz, R. J., Schafer, R., Scherfeld, D., Friederichs, S., Popp, K., Wittsack, H.-J., et al. (2008). Valuating other people's emotional face expression: A combined functional magnetic resonance imaging and electroencephalography study. *Neuroscience, 152*, 713–722.

Shamay-Tsoory, S. G., Aharon-Peretz, J., & Perry, D. (2009). Two systems for empathy: A double dissociation between emotional and cognitive empathy in inferior frontal gyrus versus ventromedial prefrontal lesions. *Brain, 132,* 617–627.

Shaw, D. S., Keenan, K., & Vondra, J. I. (1994). Developmental precursors of externalizing behavior: Ages 1 to 3. *Developmental Psychology, 30,* 355–364.

Shultz, S., & Dunbar, R. I. M. (2007). The evolution of the social brain: Anthropoid primates contrast with other vertebrates. *Proceedings of the Royal Society of London: B. Biological Sciences, 274,* 2429–2436.

Singer, T., Seymour, B., O'Doherty, J., Kaube, H., Dolan, R. J., & Frith, C. D. (2004). Empathy for pain involves the affective but not sensory components of pain. *Science, 303,* 1157–1162.

Smith, E. R., Seger, C. R., & Mackie, D. M. (2007). Can emotions be truly group level?: Evidence regarding four conceptual criteria. *Journal of Personality and Social Psychology, 93,* 431–446.

Smollar, J., & Youniss, J. (1982). Social development through friendship. In K. H. Rubin & H. S. Ross (Eds.), *Peer relationships and social skills in childhood* (pp. 279–298). New York: Springer-Verlag.

Soderstrom, M. (2007). Beyond babytalk: Re-evaluating the nature and content of speech input to preverbal infants. *Developmental Review, 27,* 501–532.

Sroufe, L. A. (2005). Attachment and development: A prospective, longitudinal study from birth to adulthood. *Attachment and Human Development, 7,* 349–367.

Sroufe, L. A., Egeland, B., Carlson, E. A., & Collins, W. A. (2005). *The development of the person: The Minnesota study of risk and adaptation from birth to adulthood.* New York: Guilford Press.

Sroufe, L. A., & Rutter, M. (1984). The domain of developmental psychopathology. *Child Development, 55,* 17–29.

Stallings, J., Fleming, A. S., Corter, C., Worthman, C., & Steiner, M. (2001). The effects of infant cries and odors on sympathy, cortisol, and autonomic responses in new mothers and nonpostpartum women. *Parenting: Science and Practice, 1,* 71–100.

Stern, D. N. (1977). *The first relationship: Infant and mother.* Cambridge, MA: Harvard University Press.

Stern, D. N. (1985). *The interpersonal world of the infant.* New York: Basic Books.

Stern, D. N., Hofer, L., Haft, W., & Dore, J. (1985). Affect attunement: The sharing of feeling states between mother and infant by means of intermodal fluency. In T. M. Field & N. A. Fox (Eds.), *Social perception in early infancy* (pp. 249–268). Norwood, NJ: Ablex.

Strathearn, L., Li, J., Fonagy, P., & Montague, P. R. (2008). What's in a smile? Maternal brain responses to infant facial cues. *Pediatrics, 122,* 40–51.

Swain, J. E., Leckman, J. F., Mayes, L. C., Feldman, R., & Schultz, R. T. (2006). Own baby pictures induce parental brain activations according to psychology, experience and postpartum timing. *Biological Psychiatry, 59,* 126S.

Swain, J. E., Lorberbaum, J. P., Kose, S., & Strathearn, L. (2007). Brain basis of early parent infant interactions: Psychology, physiology, and in vivo functional neuroimaging studies. *Journal of Child Psychology and Psychiatry, 48,* 262–287.

Tanner, J. M., & Israelsohn, W. J. (1963). Parent–child correlations for body measurements of children between the ages one month and seven years. *Annals of Human Genetics, 26,* 245–259.

Tiisala, R., & Kantero, R.-L. (1971). Some parent–child correlations for height, weight and skeletal age up to 10 years: A mixed longitudinal study. *Acta Paediatrica, 60,* 42–48.

Totterdell, P. (2000). Catching moods and hitting runs. *Journal of Applied Psychology, 85,* 848–859.

Totterdell, P., Kellett, S., Briner, R. B., & Teuchmann, K. (1998). Evidence of mood linkage in work groups. *Journal of Personality and Social Psychology, 74,* 1504–1515.

Trevarthen, C. (2003). Conversations with a two month-old. In J. Raphael-Leff (Ed.), *Parent–infant psychodynamics: Wild things, mirrors and ghosts* (pp. 25–34). Philadelphia: Whurr.

Trevarthen, C., & Aitken, K. J. (2001). Infant intersubjectivity: Research, theory, and clinical applications. *Journal of Child Psychology and Psychiatry 42*, 3–48.

Tronick, E. Z. (1989). Emotions and emotional communication in infants. *American Psychologist, 44*, 112–119.

Tronick, E. Z., Als, H., Adamson, L., Wise, S., & Brazelton, T. B. (1978). The infant's response to entrapment between contradictory messages in face-to-face interaction. *Journal of the American Academy of Child and Adolescent Psychiatry, 17*, 1–13.

Tronick, E. Z., Ricks, M., & Cohn, J. F. (1982). Maternal and infant affective exchange: Patterns of adaptation. In T. Field & A. Fogel (Eds.), *Emotion and early interaction* (pp. 83–100). Hillsdale, NJ: Erlbaum.

Uvnas-Moberg, K. (1998). Oxytocin may mediate the benefits of positive social interaction and emotions. *Psychoneuroendocrinology, 23*, 819–835.

Uvnas-Moberg, K., & Eriksson, M. (1996). Breastfeeding: Physiological, endocrine and behavioural adaptations caused by oxytocin and local neurogenic activity in the nipple and mammary gland. *Acta Paediatrica, 85*, 525–530.

van IJzendoorn, M. H., Dijkstra, J., & Bus, A. G. (1995). Attachment, intelligence, and language: A meta-analysis. *Social Development, 4*, 115–128.

van IJzendoorn, M. H., Juffer, F., & Poelhuis, C. W. K. (2005). Adoption and cognitive development: A meta-analytic comparison of adopted and nonadopted children's IQ and school performance. *Psychological Bulletin, 131*, 301–316.

Vygotsky, L. (1978). *Mind in society.* Cambridge, MA: Harvard University Press.

Wakschlag, L. S., & Hans, S. L. (1999). Relation of maternal responsiveness during infancy to the development of behavior problems in high-risk youths. *Developmental Psychology, 35*, 569–579.

Wicker, B., Keysers, C., Plailly, J., Royet, J. P., Gallese, V., & Rizzolatti, G. (2003). Both of us disgusted in my insula: The common neural basis of seeing and feeling disgust. *Neuron, 40*, 655–664.

Williams, T. (1975). Family resemblance in abilities: The Wechsler scales. *Behavior Genetics, 5*, 405–409.

Willoughby, R. R. (1927). Family similarities in mental-test abilities. *Genetic Psychology Monographs, 2*, 239–277.

Wingfield, J. C., Hegner, R. E., Ball, G. F., & Duffy, A. M. (1990). The "challenge hypothesis": Theoretical implications for patterns of testosterone secretion, mating systems, and breeding strategies. *American Naturalist, 136*, 829–846.

Winnicott, D. W. (1965). *The maturational processes and the facilitating environment: Studies in the theory of emotional development.* New York: International Universities Press.

Woollett, K., & Maguire, E. A. (2011). Acquiring "the knowledge" of London's layout drives structural brain changes. *Current Biology, 21*, 2109–2114.

PART V

Neural Processes of Mental Awareness

CHAPTER 13

False-Belief Understanding in Infants and Preschoolers

Mark A. Sabbagh
Jeannette E. Benson
Valerie A. Kuhlmeier

Introduction to Controversies in False-Belief Research

A mature, everyday understanding of human behavior rests on having a representational theory of mind—an understanding that observable actions are motivated by internal mental states such as intentions, desires, and beliefs (Wellman, 1990). The term "representational" is used to capture the fact that mental states, in particular the epistemic mental states of knowledge and belief, are representations of some putatively true state of affairs and their formation is due to, and limited by, a person's experience of the world. The term "theory of mind" captures the fact that we use these abstract mental state conceptualizations to both explain and predict others' behavior, just as any theory allows us to explain and predict relevant phenomena. A number of researchers and theorists have suggested that having a representational theory of mind provides the foundation for several important aspects of social-cognitive functioning, such as teaching and learning, lying and pretending, making and keeping friends, and social learning more generally (Tomasello, 2009).

Because of its fundamental importance, cognitive developmentalists have been especially interested in charting the development of representational theory-of-mind abilities in young children. On the basis of suggestions from Dennett (1978), researchers developed a task thought to diagnose a representational theory of mind in children—the false-belief task. In a typical false-belief task (e.g., Baron-Cohen, Leslie, & Frith, 1985; Wimmer & Perner, 1983), a story character puts a desirable object in one hiding place and then leaves the scene. In her absence, a second character moves the object from the original hiding place to another hiding place. Thus, the child observer and second character know where the object really is, but the first character does not. Children are then asked to predict where the first character will look for the object. This is argued to be a clear test of a representational theory of mind because children must reason about the first character's belief as separate and distinct in content from the reality that the mental state is supposed to faithfully represent (Perner, 1991). The typical finding from these studies is that children at about age 3 fail to show an understanding of false belief, predicting that the first character will instead look where the object truly is. Then, sometime between 3 and 5 years, children gradually come to show false-belief understanding by correctly predicting that the first character will look where she left the object originally.

The false-belief literature is large, in part because there has always been a question of whether the false-belief task actually underestimates infants' and young preschoolers' abilities to reason about others' representational mental states (Moses & Chandler, 1992). Early on, researchers noted that there were many things within the everyday behavioral repertoires of even 2-year-olds that entailed a representational understanding of others' minds. Among these everyday behaviors were lying (Chandler, Fritz, & Hala, 1989), teasing (Reddy, 1991), monitoring others' knowledge and ignorance (O'Neill, 1996), and talking about mental states in ways that seemed to demonstrate an understanding of false beliefs (Bartsch & Wellman, 1994; Shatz, Wellman, & Silber, 1983). These researchers (called "boosters" by Chandler et al., 1989) argued that children fail false-belief tasks, perhaps not because they lack a conceptual understanding of representational mental states but rather because false-belief tasks are too complex and unnatural and rely to a great extent on cognitive capacities other than a conceptual understanding of others' minds (such as language, working memory, and executive control). The working hypothesis was that a representational theory of mind might be very early emerging or innate, although its expression across a variety of situations may be quelled by children's slow-maturing abilities in other domains.

On the other side of the debate, another group of researchers argued that these rich interpretations of infants' and young preschoolers' everyday behavior were unwarranted and that such behaviors could be accounted for by mechanisms simpler than a representational understanding of mental states (see, e.g., Perner, 1991). For these researchers, it was not necessarily that infants and younger children had *no* understanding of mind; rather, their understanding early in development was immature and did not encompass a representational understanding of mental states (Gopnik & Wellman, 1994; Wellman, 1990). In line with the results from the false-belief studies and studies that appeared to also require an understanding of misrepresentation, such as the appearance-reality task (Flavell, Green, & Flavell, 1986), researchers argued that a representational theory of mind begins to emerge during the fourth year (see, e.g., Wellman, Cross, & Watson, 2001). Importantly, the underlying ability to think about misprepresentation is described as a new conceptual development that emerges at the end of the preschool period rather than as a change in the ability to express some already present but nascent understanding (Wellman & Gelman, 1998).

Much of the research that came out of this debate involved studies that tweaked the false-belief task to weaken the properties that were theorized to muffle young children's performance. Tasks were designed to increase the naturalism, decrease the memory demands, decrease the linguistic demands, clarify the intention behind the test question, and make the responses less at odds with children's natural tendencies (Carlson, Moses, & Hix, 1998; Lewis & Osborne, 1990; Moses & Flavell, 1990; Perner, Leekam, & Wimmer, 1987). After about 15 years of concentrated interest, Wellman and colleagues (2001) summarized the effects of many of these manipulations in a meta-analysis. Although many types of manipulations affected performance, there was no evidence that any particular manipulation (or even groups of manipulations) improved 3-year-olds' performance to above-chance levels—a clear criterion for demonstrating systematic understanding. The uneasy consensus that appeared to emerge over this period (largely supported by the meta-analysis) was that false-belief tasks constitute valid, robust measures of theory-of-mind understanding for preschool children. Infants' mentalistic understandings, then, were typically thought to be limited to other kinds of mental states and "precursors" of false belief, such as desires (Wellman & Woolley, 1990), intentions (Woodward, 1998), attention (Moore, 1999), emotions (Phillips, Wellman, & Spelke, 2002), and social attributes (Kuhlmeier, Wynn, & Bloom, 2003).

Over the last 5 years, this uneasy consensus has given way in the wake of findings that have assessed infants' understanding of false belief using looking-time methodologies. These methodologies have revealed that 14- to 24-month-olds show the ability to predict the false-belief-based behavior of those around them. In a study by Onishi and Baillargeon (2005), violation-of-expectation methodology was used to test false-belief knowledge in 15-month-olds. During familiarization, infants were shown a scene where an agent hid an object in one of two locations. The object then moved to an alternative location, either while the agent was observing (true-belief condition) or while she was unable to see the object's movements (false-belief condition). A test trial followed during which infants' looking times were measured while observing the agent reaching to either the outdated or current object location.[1] In true-belief conditions, infants looked longer when the agent searched in the outdated location. Infants in false-belief conditions showed the reverse looking-time pattern, looking longer when the agent searched for the object in its current location. Since then, these findings have been replicated and extended to even younger ages, with researchers finding evidence for knowledge of false-belief-based behavior in infants as young as 13 months (Surian, Caldi, & Sperber, 2008).

These findings have catapulted the "booster" hypothesis that a representational theory of mind is either early emerging into or innately in the leading position. This was expressed most clearly in an article by Southgate, Senju, and Csibra (2007), who report that 2-year-olds' eye movements while watching a false-belief scenario show evidence that they correctly predict a protagonists' false belief–based actions. In interpreting these findings, they write:

> Our measure showing that 2-year-olds predicted the behavior of an actor on the basis of a false belief provides compelling evidence for an early-developing reliance on epistemic state attribution in predicting actions, and is incompatible with the position that children are able to attribute false beliefs only after undergoing a conceptual revolution between 3 and 4 years of age. . . . Our data are more consistent with the position that children's difficulties on false-belief tasks stem from performance limitations, rather than competence limitations. (2007, p. 591)

The goal of the rest of this chapter is twofold. First, we briefly outline what we think is the most plausible "performance limitation" account of preschoolers' theory-of-mind failures—the executive function account—and show that this account is not plausible given the extant data that have tested the most direct predictions of the account. Second, we sketch a position in which we argue that the substrate for young infants' success on looking-time false-belief tasks consists not of the same conceptual framework that older children and adults use but rather of an innate and evolutionarily old system that enables infants to perform *sequential episodic encoding* of events. The power of just such a system, we argue, can be seen in the surprisingly sophisticated behavior of a variety of nonhuman species (including birds) that putatively (and in some cases demonstrably) do not have a representational understanding of mental states.

Against a Performance Account of Preschoolers' False-Belief Failures

"Executive functioning" is often used to refer to the suite of cognitive functions that support goal-directed behavior and cognitive control across conceptual domains, including response inhibition (or inhibitory control), working memory, error monitoring, rule representation and use, and attentional control (Zelazo, Carlson, & Kesek, 2009). Researchers have long noted that false-belief tasks place clear demands on executive functioning in at least three ways. First, responding appropriately in a false-belief task requires one to point to where something is *not*. Doing so may require a modicum of executive functioning to overcome a prepotent (or habitual) tendency to point to where something truly is (Carlson et al., 1998). Second, false beliefs, although not uncommon, are likely to be rare occurrences relative to true beliefs. Thus, to think that a given belief might be false, one might need to overcome a habitual tendency to reason that the belief is true (Leslie & Polizzi, 1998; Sabbagh, Moses, & Shiverick, 2006). Finally, the false-belief task requires children to keep two conflicting perspectives on the same situation in mind at once and then determine which is more appropriate given the context of the test question (Frye, Zelazo, & Burack, 1998). For these reasons, researchers have suggested that the executive demands inherent to false-belief tasks may be the root cause of preschoolers' failures on the tasks, not their inability to reason about false beliefs.

Current Support for an Executive Account Is Inconclusive

Currently, evidence in support of the executive account of 3-year-olds' failure comes in two forms. The first is that individual differences in preschoolers' executive functioning, in particular on Stroop-like tasks that pit one habitual or recently learned response against a competitor, predict performance on false-belief tasks (Carlson & Moses, 2001; Hughes, 1998; Perner, Lang, & Kloo, 2002; Sabbagh, Moses, et al., 2006). As a number of researchers and theorists have argued, though, there are many possible interpretations of this relation. Thus, these findings do not provide conclusive evidence for the hypothesis that 3-year-olds' failure is attributable to the surface demands of executive functioning tasks (see, e.g., Moses, 2001; Moses, Carlson, &

Sabbagh, 2004). Moses (2001) argued that an equally plausible alternative hypothesis regarding the relation between false-belief performance and executive functioning is that executive functioning promotes conceptual advances in the ability to reason about false beliefs (Russell, 1996). Indeed, as we discuss in more detail later, a recent review of the now extensive literature on the relation between false belief and executive functioning shows that this alternative hypothesis more comprehensively accounts for the range of findings (Benson & Sabbagh, 2009).

The second line of evidence in support of the executive account is that titrating the executive demands of a false-belief task has highly predictable effects on performance. Leslie and colleagues have clearly demonstrated that raising the executive demands of the false-belief task by, for instance, adding additional locations, leads to poorer performance (Friedman & Leslie, 2004). Conversely, reducing the demands of the task by changing the response modality or by making the true state of affairs less salient leads to improvements in 3-year-olds' performance on the task (though rarely do they show above-chance performance). It is in this light that the false-belief findings with infants are so interesting. On all accounts, the requirement to make a response is the task factor that imposes the most serious executive demands. Because infant looking-time paradigms do not require an explicit response and thus putatively tap only the computation of the false belief, they may constitute false-belief tasks that are essentially free of executive demands (Scott & Baillargeon, 2009).

Over the next few sections, we intend to call this interpretation of the infant data into question. Namely, we review literature showing that straightforward hypotheses of an executive account of young preschoolers' failures in false-belief tasks are either not supported or directly contradicted. In addition, we note that the false-belief task has external validity as a measure of conceptual change in the preschool years, thereby bolstering the case for a qualitative conceptual change in theory-of-mind reasoning over the preschool years.

Cross-Cultural Evidence

The main contention of the executive account of young preschoolers' false-belief failures is that standard false-belief tasks require some level of executive functioning to negotiate the demands of the task. The mechanism for false-belief development, then, is the development of executive functioning. Furthermore, once children's executive functioning skills have matured to some criterion level necessary for negotiating the demands of the task, they will reveal their false-belief knowledge and understanding. Skillful performance on the response–conflict Stroop-like tasks is generally thought to be an index that children's executive skills have matured to that criterion level, which is why their performance on the false-belief task correlates with performance on Stroop-like tasks. However, there is now strong evidence to suggest that attaining a particular level of performance on response–conflict executive functioning tasks does not, in and of itself, lead to correct performance on false-belief tasks. This evidence comes from cross-cultural work on the relation between executive function and false-belief performance.

In East Asian cultures, parents and teachers place particular emphasis on the socialization of self-control in their preschool-age children (Chen et al., 1998; Ho,

1994; Tobin, Wu, & Davidson, 1989). Because of this socialization, and perhaps also cross-cultural differences in the neurotransmitter systems that affect frontal lobe development and executive functioning performance such as dopamine (Chang, Kidd, Kivak, Pakstis, & Kidd, 1996), some researchers have hypothesized that children from East Asian cultures may have earlier-developing executive functioning skills relative to their more Western counterparts (Chen et al., 1998). A critical question, then, concerns whether Chinese preschoolers do indeed have advanced executive functioning skills and, if so, whether they also have advanced theory-of-mind development.

Sabbagh, Xu, Carlson, Moses, and Lee (2006) studied preschool-age children from Beijing, China. The study used the same procedure and assessments that Carlson and Moses (2001) used in their study of the relation between executive functioning and false-belief performance. The comparison of results across the two cultural

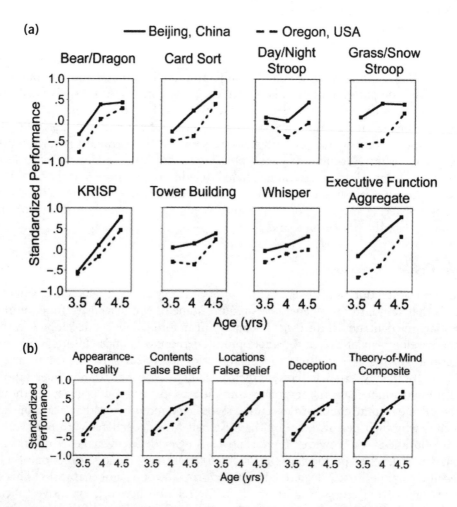

FIGURE 13.1. Standardized performance on (a) executive functioning and (b) false-belief tasks in Chinese and North American preschoolers. From Sabbagh, Xu, Carlson, Moses, and Lee (2006). Copyright 2006 by Sage/American Psychological Society. Reprinted by permission.

groups was striking (see Figure 13.1). On every task of executive functioning that was tested, the Chinese preschoolers outperformed their North American counterparts. In the aggregated data, Chinese preschoolers were roughly 6 months ahead of the North American preschoolers in performance on the executive functioning battery (i.e., on average, 42-month-old Chinese children had scores on a par with 48-month-old North American preschoolers). Yet, despite this striking advantage in executive functioning skills, the Chinese preschoolers were no different from the North American preschoolers in their theory-of-mind development.

If we assume that some criterion level of executive functioning is necessary for performance on the false-belief task, we can assume that many of the 48-month-olds from the North American sample had achieved that level of functioning, given their strong false-belief performance. However, the 42-month-old Chinese children had, on average, achieved the same level of executive functioning performance as the North American children. Thus, many 42-month-old Chinese had reached what should be considered a criterion level of executive maturation, which, if false-belief understanding is indeed early developing, should have allowed them to solve the false-belief tasks. The fact that 42-month-old Chinese remained unsuccessful at false belief despite having executive performance on par with 48-month-old North American children who did do well at false-belief tasks shows that executive maturation alone does not account for preschoolers' false-belief development.

This same pattern of findings has now been replicated in studies with children from Korea (Oh & Lewis, 2008) and Hong Kong (Tardif, So, & Kaciroti, 2007). The findings from all of these studies show that, despite substantially advanced executive functioning skills, 3-year-olds in East Asian cultures show the stereotypical pattern of poor performance on false-belief tasks. Indeed, if anything, children from East Asian cultures may lag behind North American preschoolers in theory-of-mind development (Liu, Wellman, Tardif, & Sabbagh, 2008). These findings provide clear evidence against a simple executive function account of preschoolers' theory-of-mind development; as a group, East Asian preschoolers have a developmentally advanced trajectory of executive functioning but no advantage in false-belief performance.

Developmental Cognitive Neuroscience Evidence

A second line of evidence suggesting that young preschoolers' theory-of-mind development represents bona fide conceptual developments comes from research on the neural bases of these skills in young children. In adults, there is now a substantial body of literature reporting on the neural bases of theory of mind. An exhaustive review of this work is beyond the scope of this chapter. By way of summary, recently published reviews have highlighted the contribution that two areas make to reasoning about one's own and others' mental states, namely circumscribed regions of the dorsal-medial prefrontal cortex (MPFC) (Amodio & Frith, 2006) and the right temporoparietal juncture (rTPJ) (Saxe, 2006). Of these two areas, an emerging body of work from Saxe and colleagues suggests that the rTPJ may be recruited more specifically for reasoning about the representational nature of mental states, whereas the dMPFC may be recruited when reasoning about triadic social-cognitive relations more generally (Perner & Ruffman, 2005; Saxe & Powell, 2006). What is important with respect to the current discussion is that the neural bases of theory of mind are clearly dissociable from those that underlie response–conflict executive functioning skills. In their review analysis, Ridderinkhof, Ullsperger, Crone, and Nieuwenhuis (2004) showed that performance on executive functioning tasks, particularly the Stroop-like tasks that are most strongly associated with false-belief performance, tend to activate a region of the MPFC that is posterior to the region associated with theory-of-mind reasoning and proximal to the cingulate cortex. In another review analysis, Bunge and Zelazo (2006) showed that another, often overlooked, aspect of response–conflict executive functioning that entails keeping in mind and integrating a hierarchy of interrelated rules is associated with the ventral–lateral prefrontal cortex (VLPFC) in adults and perhaps in children.

The dissociation between the neural regions associated with theory of mind and those associated with executive function has been shown perhaps most clearly in research by Saxe, Schulz, and Jiang (2006). In their study, participants were given a pair of tasks that compared the neural activations elicited during theory-of-mind reasoning with those associated with the executive functioning skills required to negotiate theory-of-mind tasks. Indeed, the two tasks were identical except for their instructions: In one case they were encouraged to reason in a rule-like way, whereas in the other they were encouraged to reason mentalistically. Activations in these tasks were compared with activations in localizer tasks that measured executive functioning and theory-of-mind performance independent of the target task. The results showed that when reasoning mentalistically, the usual theory-of-mind areas were activated (i.e., rTPJ), whereas when reasoning in a rule-like way, the usual executive areas were activated (i.e., anterior cingulate cortex and ventral lateral prefrontal cortex). These findings show that even if theory-of-mind tasks have executive demands, reasoning about mental states relies upon a distinct neural substrate.

These findings from adults provide a relatively straightforward framework for making predictions about the neuroanatomical developments that are critical for theory-of-mind reasoning. On the one hand, if executive immaturity was the primary cause of preschoolers' poor performance on theory-of-mind tasks, we would expect individual differences in theory-of-mind performance to be paced by the maturation of regions associated with executive functioning (e.g., posterior MPFC, VLPFC). On the other hand, if preschoolers' poor performance was attributable to theory-of-mind reasoning deficits per se, then we might expect performance to be more related to the maturation of the neural networks that support theory-of-mind reasoning (e.g., dorsal MPFC, rTPJ).

Sabbagh, Bowman, Evraire, and Ito (2009) investigated these questions using dense-array electroencephalography (EEG) measurements combined with tomographic current-source density analyses to assess how individual differences in regional brain maturation predict children's performance on false-belief tasks. A number of researchers have shown that the preschool years see major changes in both the power and coherence of brain electrical activity recorded in the alpha band (for children, between 6–9 Hz) (Marshall, Bar-Haim, & Fox, 2002; Thatcher, Walker, & Guidice, 1987). These changes are attributable to the maturational changes that occur as neural populations become more functionally organized. Advances in EEG analysis techniques have made it possible to use the cross-spectral matrix (essentially a matrix of coherence measures recorded at each electrode) to estimate the extent to which given intracerebral sources contribute to the EEG that is recorded at the scalp. One technique is standardized low-resolution electromagnetic tomography (sLORETA) (Pascual-Marqui, 2002). This allows researchers to assess individual differences in the extent to which any given cortical region is organized. Sabbagh and colleagues used sLORETA measures of regional current-source density estimates to determine what aspects of neurocognitive development make unique contributions to theory-of-mind development during the preschool years.

Children's EEG was recorded with 128 electrodes distributed over the entire scalp (Electrical Geodesics, Inc, Eugene, OR) while children were resting and looking at a static picture of a rocket ship. After EEG recording, children went on to complete batteries of tasks assessing false belief, executive functioning, and language abilities. A series of regression analyses was conducted to determine whether children's theory-of-mind performance could be predicted from sLORETA estimates of brain activity at each voxel while controlling for children's age, vocabulary development, and executive functioning performance. The results clearly showed that preschoolers' false-belief performance was associated with individual differences in the maturation of the theory-of-mind network, including the dMPFC and the rTPJ. In fact, the regions of the dMPFC and rTPJ that were identified as neurodevelopmental predictors of preschoolers' false-belief performance were essentially homologous with the regions that are active when adults make theory-of-mind judgments in experimental tasks.

These findings provide evidence that preschoolers' false-belief performance is associated with the functional maturation of the network of brain areas that are typically associated with theory-of-mind reasoning in adults, not executive function. Within the context of the present discussion, these findings challenge the emerging view that young preschoolers' failures in batteries of false-belief tasks can be attributed to executive immaturity. Instead, these findings support the view that developments in false-belief performance reflect a true qualitative conceptual development, whereby young children gradually acquire the ability to reason about representational mental states over the preschool period (Perner, 1991).

Of course, we do not mean to say that false-belief tasks have no executive demands or that executive functioning is unimportant for both the development and use of theory of mind. Reasoning about false beliefs certainly does require executive functioning, and any challenges that an individual has to executive functioning abilities will affect their false-belief reasoning abilities. Our point is that the cross-cultural findings show that the developmental extension of this argument (i.e., because false-belief tasks require executive function, then executive immaturity is the reason for 3-year-olds' false-belief failure) does not provide a compelling account for the extant developmental data. That is, executive immaturity is not the sole cause of false-belief failures in preschoolers.

This raises an intriguing question: Why is executive functioning correlated with false-belief performance if it is not the case that executive functioning allows children to express a well-formed understanding of beliefs? A full treatment of this question is beyond the scope of this chapter. Briefly, a recent review and summary of the full body of evidence on the question of the relation between executive functioning and false belief suggests that executive functioning may be critical for catalyzing the conceptual developments that themselves enable false-belief performance (Benson & Sabbagh, 2009). This account (sometimes dubbed the "emergence" account) predicts that executive functioning will be associated with theory-of-mind development via its interaction with experiential factors that are known to also contribute to theory-of-mind development, such as parent–child talk about mental states (Ruffman, Slade, & Crowe, 2002) and having siblings (Brown, Donelan-McCall, & Dunn, 1996; Perner, Ruffman, & Leekam, 1994). Several studies have linked executive functioning and experience with conceptual change in domains other than theory of mind, including mathematics (e.g., Bull & Scerif, 2001; Blair & Razza, 2007; Espy et al., 2004; McClelland et al., 2007) and language (e.g., Blair & Razza, 2007; De Bani, Palladino, Pazzaglia, & Cornoldi, 1998; McClelland et al., 2007). Thus, in line with these findings, we believe that the emergence account provides the most coherent current account of the ontogenetic relations between executive functioning and false-belief understanding.

False-Belief Performance Has External Validity

Further support for this view that preschoolers undergo a qualitative conceptual change in their theory-of-mind understanding comes from research showing that false-belief tasks have broad external validity. That is, children's performance on false-belief tasks is associated with just the kinds of real-world behaviors that would seem to require a representational theory of mind. Although the research relevant to this topic is broad, we focus on two examples. In one, Talwar and Lee (2008) argued that the ability to tell a lie to conceal a transgression, particularly one without a serious associated punishment, is predicated on an understanding of false belief. That is, to tell a lie, young children must recognize that they can induce another to believe something that is not true (see Chandler et al., 1989, for a similar analysis). Talwar and Lee (2008) induced children to commit a minor transgression against the rules of game, and then interviewed them to assess whether they would admit the transgression or lie. Children's performance on a small battery of false-belief tasks was an independent, positive predictor of lying to conceal the transgression. In a second part of the study, children were interviewed to determine whether they could "keep up" their lie by concealing the knowledge they had gained during their transgression. Here again, children's performance on advanced (i.e., second-order) false-belief tasks predicted individual differences in maintaining lies. These findings show that the ability to reason about false beliefs is a critical, independent predictor of just the kind of real-world social behaviors that one would expect of theory-of-mind reasoning.

One might counter that lying may only be associated with false-belief reasoning because of a common association with executive functioning abilities. After all, lying almost certainly requires some modicum of executive functioning to overcome one's putatively prepotent tendencies to simply say what is true and known. However, Talwar and Lee (2008) provide evidence against this interpretation. In both of their studies, executive functioning abilities (i.e., performance on a battery of Stroop-like tasks) were assessed and statistically controlled in all of the main analyses. In each case, false-belief reasoning was a unique, independent predictor of children's lying performance. These findings further bolster the claim that it is not simply the task demands but the conceptual advances in understanding of false belief that are associated with lying.

In a similar vein, Peskin and Ardino (2003) argued that children's abilities to participate successfully in games like hide-and-seek and secret keeping might be related to false-belief reasoning because they require children to recognize cases in which others *should* be ignorant of things in the world that they themselves know. Their findings showed that children who were competent at false-belief reasoning were more likely to participate in these games correctly. In the case of hide-and-seek, the children who were better at false belief were better able to hide from a seeker without giving away their location and when playing the seeker role, to allow the hiders to proceed without peeking. Similarly, when keeping a secret, children who were better at false belief were also better at concealing knowledge from a relevant third person. The fact that false-belief reasoning is associated with successful participation in these more real-world behaviors provides support for the idea that children's conceptualizations of mind are maturing over the preschool period, with predictable consequences.

A "Two-System" Approach
to Understanding Infants' and Preschoolers' False-Belief Performance

The bulk of the chapter up until this point has focused on why we do not believe that a "performance account" is an adequate explanation of 3-year-olds' failures at false-belief tasks and why we think the data with preschoolers are more in line with the notion that children's understanding of belief changes over the preschool period. If we are to say that 3-years-olds do not understand false belief, then we are faced with the question of how to explain the findings showing that infants predict people will act on the basis of false beliefs. One possibility is to take strong interpretations of the infant data at face value and then propose that theory-of-mind understanding goes through a sort of U-shaped development. That is, at about 2 years of age, infants understand false belief; then that understanding is lost by the age of 3 years; and it is finally regained over the mid- to late-preschool period. However, there is considerable controversy as to how to best interpret U-shaped patterns of development. More often, researchers argue that U-shaped patterns of development can often be taken as signs of discontinuity in development (Siegler, 2004). That is, the cognitive mechanisms that allow for early competence may be fundamentally distinct from those that support performance later (see Muir & Hains, 2004, for an example from infants' auditory localization).

The same thing may be true of the infant false-belief findings. That is, perhaps infants' predictions in the looking-response paradigms rely on a cognitive substrate that is fundamentally distinct from the substrate that supports preschoolers' reasoning about false beliefs. At least two hypotheses in the extant theoretical literature have attempted to account for infants' skills with mechanisms other than a bona fide understanding of false beliefs (Apperly & Butterfill, 2009; Perner & Ruffman, 2005). These two accounts bear resemblance to theoretical accounts of how social cognition in nonhuman species (such as nonhuman primates and birds) might be distinct from that of humans (at least, preschool-age humans) (Penn & Povinelli, 2007). In what follows, we draw on these accounts to delineate how we think infants might make accurate predictions in false-belief scenarios, even without a bona fide conceptual understanding of false belief.

Empirical Typologies versus Explanatory Concepts

Gopnik and Wellman (1994) began their explication and defense of a "theory theory" approach to theory-of-mind development by raising the distinction between empirical typologies and theoretical constructs. Empirical typologies are generalized descriptions of observable phenomena in any given domain. In the domain of human behavior, including false-belief understanding, an empirical typology might be something like "People look for things where they last put them" or "People look for things where they last saw them." Gopnik and Wellman (1994) made the point that empirical typologies can be very effective constructs for making predictions about future events. This is largely because the content of an empirical typology is based on, and constrained by, the experience of predictable events. There are, however, limitations on empirical typologies. One is that they are merely descriptive and thus provide no causal explanation for the phenomena under consideration. When the task is to explain others' behavior in terms of causal mechanisms, empirical typologies are not sufficient. A second is that empirical typologies are essentially ad hoc—a list of empirical typologies for predicting some general phenomenon like "where people look for things" can be long, but each item in the list bears no necessary relation to another. The ad hoc nature can occasionally lead to incoherence and, as empirical evidence accrues, contradictory predictions about what others will do (see Perner et al., 1987).

Gopnik and Wellman (1994) argued that children's reasoning can go beyond incoherent empirical typologies and rely instead on theoretical constructs, such as a coherent (even if at times incomplete, incorrect, or otherwise developmentally immature) understanding of belief, how beliefs are formed, and how they shape intentional action. Gopnik and Wellman cited both experimental and naturalistic data to argue that even young children are capable of not just predicting but also *explaining* human actions according to their current theories of mind, but that those theories of mind can be developmentally limited; that is, their explanations and explicit predictions are only as good as their current theories. Perner (2009) echoed this conclusion by arguing that preschoolers' performance in a wide variety of tasks that would seem to rest on false-belief understanding (including appearance–reality tasks, level 2 perspective-taking tasks, deception tasks, and the very wide array of false-belief tasks) suggests that preschoolers have a conceptual, theoretical understanding of how beliefs cause intentional behavior.

With Gopnik and Wellman's (1994) distinction in mind, the possibility has been raised that the system that supports infants' predictions in false-belief scenarios may be more like empirical typologies than abstract, conceptual, causal understandings of belief (e.g., Perner & Ruffman, 2005; see also Penn & Povinelli, 2007, for the same argument against claims of mentalistic understandings in nonhuman species). Obviously, this hypothesis is a difficult one to test empirically. As discussed, empirical typologies and theories both allow for correct predictions in false-belief scenarios. Thus, although prediction paradigms can be used with both preschoolers and infants, the phenomenon offers no way of clarifying whether the two groups are using the same mechanisms. Moreover, the types of studies that have been marshaled in support of attributing conceptual knowledge to preschoolers have either not yet been done with infants (e.g., a large number of converging tests) or require peripheral linguistic skills well outside of infants' abilities (e.g., explanation tasks).

There are, perhaps, even more fundamental hurdles facing an "empirical typologies" account of infants' predictions in false-belief scenarios. The empirical typologies that could support the kinds of predictions infants make in false-belief scenarios would have to be fairly sophisticated, including generalizations such as those listed previously, like "People look for things where they last put/saw them" or "People look for things where they told someone to put them." Where might these empirical typologies come from? We can assume that much of the human activity that infants see could provide the relevant data for such a system—after all, people do presumably act in empirically typical (usual) ways with rare exceptions (for instance, they look for things where they leave them). The key question is whether infants can extract the relevant generalizations from these data. In the next sections, we argue that the cognitive prerequisites for these skills are very likely in place for infants, likely from birth.

Sequential Episodic Encoding

Like other researchers in the field (e.g., Apperly & Butterfill, 2009; Perner & Ruffman, 2005), we would like to propose that young infants might be able to develop empirical typologies by relying on two basic perceptual and cognitive mechanisms that are sufficiently sophisticated very early on in development: (1) episodic encoding of intentional action, which allows infants to parse an event representation into its constituent parts and (2) statistical learning and generalization, which allows infants to detect what kinds of intentional actions typically follow in sequence.

Episodic Encoding of Intentional Action

To develop an empirical generalization such as "People look for things where they last put them," infants must first be able to encode actions and their constituent structure. That is, they must have some mechanism that allows them to identify intentional action (i.e., "put") and the constituent structure of that action. The constituent structure of action includes what we call the 4Ws of action: who, what, where, and when. If infants can do this sort of "episodic encoding," then they plausibly possess the ability to encode as a unit such bound events such as "Ruby put her dress in the box last night" and "Ruby is searching for her dress in the box now."

The proposal that young infants encode the constituent structure of action dovetails well with work in the field of infants' event memory (see Bauer, 2006). Although in verbal recall tasks toddlers and young preschoolers sometimes have difficulties recounting past events, they typically perform well on tasks that rely on more implicit measures. In particular, constituent episodic encoding of intentional action can occur on a subconscious or implicit level (Dienes & Perner, 1999). That is, it may be possible to represent and store the 4Ws of a particular episode in a manner similar to a perceptual connectionist network, whereby the experience of the event changes in some small way the neural network dedicated to representing those experiences. The accrual of experiences that activate the same network over time are represented in the stabilization of the connection weights in the network. Over time, this registration would allow for detecting similarity and novelty along the constituent 4W dimensions.

Although there is now a significant amount of data suggesting that infants encode the constituent characteristics of events (see Bauer, 2006, for a review), their abilities might be most neatly described for the present purposes by taking a careful look at paradigms that investigate young children's understanding of intentional action. For instance, in one task developed by Woodward (1998), infants witnessed an actor repeatedly reach and grasp one of two toys until a visual attention habituation criterion was met. Then, in test trials, infants as young as 6 months dishabituated (i.e., showed longer looking) to a scene in which the person reached for and grasped the other toy, suggesting that they detected the change in one of the W's ("what") that was involved in the intentional action. A series of control studies showed that infants did not dishabituate to the change in toy when there was no obvious person involved (i.e., "who"), thereby suggesting that all four W's might be important for encoding episodic representations. Further to this point, subsequent work has shown that when the familiarization episode is followed by a test event in which a *new* person grabs for an object, infants dishabituated strongly irrespective of which object the new person grabbed (Buresh & Woodward, 2007). These findings suggest that even 6-month-olds are sensitive to changes in any of the constituents of intentional actions, a sensitivity that must be made possible by prior constituent encoding of intentional action.[2]

Statistical Learning and Generalization

One straightforward way in which constituent episodic encoding can develop into a broad predictive system is through statistical learning and generalization. Saffran, Aslin, and Newport (1996) showed that infants could parse words out of a continuous speech stream through sensitivity to transitional probabilities. That is, infants judge syllables that have high transitional probabilities (i.e., usually occur in sequence) as constituting a coherent unit, whereas syllables that have low transitional probabilities (i.e., occur in sequence only rarely) are not likely to constitute coherent units. The same kinds of skills have been shown in nonhuman primates as well (Hauser, Newport, & Aslin, 2001). Recently, Baldwin, Anderson, Saffran, and Meyer (2008) showed that these same mechanisms work in the action domain; infants expect aspects of action (see, e.g., Baldwin, Baird, Saylor, & Clark, 2001) that have high transitional probabilities to form coherent units. We suggest that the same system might be at work in helping children to discern patterns of contingent intentional action. That is, if infants notice that constituent-encoded events tend to follow one another in sequence (i.e., "Ruby put her dress in the box last night" and "Ruby is looking for her dress in the box this morning"), then children might be able to develop expectations about how intentional actions typically lead to one another.

Of course, for this system to be very powerful, it must develop general rather than specific rules. For instance, instead of encoding the specific events "Ruby put her dress in the box last night" and "Ruby is looking for her dress in the box this morning," the system would be better off coding these events in a more generalized algebraic structure (Marcus, 1999, 2001), such as "$[X_{agent}]$ put $[Y_{object}]$ at $[Z_{location}]$

in the past," which would then be followed by "[X_{agent}] is looking for [Y_{object}] at [$Z_{location}$] now" where X, Y, and Z can be any agent, object, or location that remains the same across events. We do not know of any work that has investigated infants' or children's abilities to extract this kind of algebraic structure. However, Marcus (1999) has shown that this type of generalized pattern representation occurs when 6-month-old infants process an ongoing speech stream, thereby making it plausible that a similar type of pattern detection could occur in the action domain (Baldwin & Baird, 2001). This kind of learning would be critical to establishing sensitivity to the kinds of patterns that a two-system account suggests is operating when infants show surprise or predictive looking in the false-belief paradigms.

Social Cognition from Sequential Episodic Encoding: Evidence from Nonhuman Species

To illustrate the potential power of sequential episodic encoding, we look to recent work with nonhuman animals. Some corvids, such as the western scrub jay, are socially living, food-storing birds that are thus faced with the challenges of remembering both where their caches are and protecting their caches from thieves. A primary strategy that corvids use to protect their caches is "re-caching," that is, moving their food to another location when the original cache location was observed by a competitor. Work by Clayton and colleagues (e.g., Dally, Emery, & Clayton, 2006) has shown that constituent episodic encoding (i.e., encoding who, what, where, and when) allows scrub jays to engage in strategic re-caching (Dally et al., 2006; Emery, Dally, & Clayton, 2004). In these studies, birds cached food in distinctive trays while observers in an adjoining cage looked on. When subsequently given the opportunity to recover food in private, jays re-cached food items more often if they had been previously observed by a dominant group member than if the observer had been a partner or a subordinate (Dally et al., 2006). A second experiment in this study presented scrub jays with two trays in which to cache, each witnessed by a different observer. When the jays were given the opportunity to recover the caches, one of the two observers was present. Subjects re-cached more items from the tray that this particular bird had previously observed than the tray observed by the other bird.

One might be tempted to assume that the re-caching behavior was a response to the subtle behaviors of an intimidating, competitive observer. That is, perhaps there are ways in which behavior changes once a bird knows where food is. Perhaps it is the sensitivity to these subtle cues (e.g., "evil eye") rather than the memory of the competitor being at the location that is driving behavior. Against this interpretation, Dally, Emery, and Clayton (2006, 2009) showed that subject birds did not re-cache their stores in the presence of a competitor that, instead of observing the subject bird's cache, had seen another bird's caching activity. The authors argued that if re-caching was being motivated primarily by signals from the visible competitor bird, then subject birds would have demonstrated re-caching in both conditions. The study's findings thus confirm that it is the memory of the competitor's location at the time of the initial caching that affected re-caching behavior.

Perhaps most intriguing about this study's findings is that deeper analyses showed that simply encoding the constituent structure events is not alone sufficient to promote re-caching behavior; re-caching was only carried out by older birds that had prior experience with pilfering (Dally et al., 2009; Emery & Clayton, 2005). These findings suggest that re-caching behavior depends on a learning mechanism that enables scrub jays to derive typical action sequences (i.e., what kinds of behaviors typically follow other behaviors). That is, corvids are able to combine their constituent encoding of events with a mechanism that allows them to derive and recognize statistically regular sequences of events, representations of which might drive behavior. Through these mechanisms, scrub jays might develop schema that allow them to expect sequences and combinations such as "Individuals look for food where they last saw it." For the corvids, recognizing this empirical typicality is powerful because it allows for the straightforward strategy of protecting the food by moving it to a location that has not been seen by the competitor.

It seems possible that the same underlying mechanisms might account for the performance of nonhuman primates in similar situations. A full review of this literature is beyond the scope of this chapter, but some studies illustrate that nonhuman primates can be successful in cases where sequential episodic encoding can suffice but not otherwise. For instance, while watching the hiding of a food item in one of two locations in an adjacent cage, a subordinate chimpanzee will encode whether a dominant chimpanzee has also observed the hiding event and later only attempt to retrieve the hidden food in conditions in which the dominant chimpanzee did not previously witness the hiding (Hare, Call, & Tomasello, 2001). As with the scrub jays, it seems sufficient to be sensitive to an empirical typicality like "Agents look for food where they last saw it." A key prediction made by this account is that if the scenario deviated much from this empirical typicality to the extent that the typicality could not be used to make appropriate predictions, then performance might fall apart. It seems as though this might be the case. At least two such tasks may have been complicated by additional processing requirements; here, chimpanzees had to inhibit choosing the same hiding location of food that a misinformed experimenter previously chose (Call & Tomasello, 1999; Krachun, Carpenter, Call, & Tomasello, 2009).

Are There Necessary Connections between Infants' and Preschoolers' Skills?

Apperly and Butterfill (2009) conceptualize the cognitive machinery used by infants a little differently and more subtly than we have here. Nonetheless, they make several points related to their characterization of the infant system that we believe would apply to our characterization of that system as well. Namely, Apperly and Butterfill noted that the system that infants use is highly efficient and may even, at times, be used by adults to make quick predictions about others' actions in particular scenarios. There is plenty of evidence to suggest that adults regularly use behavioral typologies to make predictions about others' actions. For instance, Keysar and colleagues (e.g., Keysar, Lin, & Barr, 2003) have shown across several studies that adults' first rapid guesses about the meanings of words (as detected through eye-tracking measures) are based more on empirical generalizations (how a speaker has used a word in the past) rather than complicated inferences about speakers' beliefs and intentions. Of course, it is not that adults cannot make such complicated inferences; it is only that they take time and may need to be invoked only when our more automatic processing results in a disrupted flow of communication (Kronmüller & Barr, 2007). Apperly and Butterfill (2009) take the position that because of their "job descriptions" over developmental time, the system that infants and adults use to make rapid predictions about others' behavior—based, we think, on generalized empirical models of what people typically do—is fundamentally dissimilar and discontinuous with the system that preschoolers and adults use to *explain* others' actions using theoretical representational constructs.

While we agree with Apperly and Butterfill (2009) that the systems are fundamentally dissimilar, we think it is important to note that there may be ways in which the development of preschoolers' theory of mind may be based on the empirical typologies that are developed early in life. For instance, it could be that emerging conscious awareness of empirical typologies supports the development of abstract theoretical concepts that ultimately provide coherence to the empirical typologies (Karmiloff-Smith, 1994; Zelazo, 2004). There is now emerging evidence suggesting that young infants' performance in social-cognitive paradigms is associated with preschoolers' theory-of-mind development more than 36 months later. For instance, infant looking behavior in social-cognitive tasks at 12 months of age (e.g., intention reading, disposition attribution) has been found to correlate with a battery of theory-of-mind tasks, including false belief, at 4 years (Wellman, Lopez-Duran, LaBounty, & Hamilton, 2008; Wellman, Phillips, Dunphy-Lelii, & LaLonde, 2004; Yamaguchi, Kuhlmeier, Wynn, & vanMarle, 2009). The important point is that the continuities shown across these studies may represent an intriguing developmental relation whereby the empirical typologies that support infant looking behavior in habituation and violation-of-expectation tasks also provide the best data for theory building. Yet, once established, engaging a theory of mind may work on its own cognitive substrate without borrowing from or relying on the persistent empirical typologies that at one time provided a foundation for the theory.

Conclusion

In the first half of our chapter, we argued that young preschoolers' failures on false-belief tasks are unlikely to be due to domain-general performance limitations, namely immature executive functioning. We argued this on two fronts. First, cross-cultural data show that Chinese children with advanced executive functioning do *not* show equally advanced theory-of-mind performance relative to their North American counterparts. Second, EEG studies show that preschoolers' theory-of-mind performance is paced by maturational changes within brain areas that are associated with theory-of-mind reasoning in adults (i.e., MPFC and rTPJ), and not with areas that are associated with executive functioning. Thus, we argue that young preschoolers likely do not have a representational understanding of beliefs. This conclusion is at odds with claims that, in looking paradigms (i.e., preferential looking or predictive gaze), infants seem to have expectations that people will act in accordance with false beliefs. To resolve this discrepancy, we propose, as others have, a "two-system account" whereby infants' behavior in false-belief looking paradigms is supported by a cognitive-perceptual substrate other than a representational theory of mind. In particular, we propose that infants' and toddlers' expectations in looking-paradigm false-belief tasks might be supported by empirical generalizations that are derived through sequential episodic encoding of human intentional action. We note also that these conjectures are difficult to test, but, counter to other claims in the literature, we believe that a two-system account is a necessary, plausible theoretical step in understanding the developmental trajectory of young children's theory of mind.

Acknowledgments

This work was supported by Natural Sciences and Engineering Research Council (NSERC) Discovery Grants to Mark A. Sabbagh and Valerie A. Kuhlmeier and by an NSERC Graduate Award to Benson. We thank members of the Developmental Graduate Program at Queen's University for helpful and patient discussion of issues discussed in the chapter.

Notes

1. Kagan (2008) summarized a number of critiques of the infant looking-time methods that are used in these and other studies. For our part, we take the infant data at face value and go on to offer other empirical and theoretical reasons to doubt their specific conclusions.
2. To those familiar with details of the seminal Woodward (1998) task, our claim may initially seem counterintuitive because the infant observers did not respond to the change of reach position in test trials as long as the reach was to the goal object. However, the position change of the goal object in this task likely would not constitute a change in the "where" constituent as the new space on the stage shares the same boundaries. Actual changes in location of goal-directed activity (e.g., changes in rooms) do appear to be recognized by infants by at least 10 months of age (Sommerville & Crane, 2009).

References

Amodio, D. M., & Frith, C. D. (2006). Meeting of minds: The medial frontal cortex and social cognition. *Nature Reviews Neuroscience, 7,* 268–277.

Apperly, I. A., & Butterfill, S. A. (2009). Do humans have two systems to track beliefs and belief-like states? *Psychological Review, 116,* 953–970.

Baldwin, D. A., Anderson, A., Saffran, J. R., & Meyer, M. (2008). Segmenting dynamic human action via statistical structure. *Cognition, 106,* 1382–1407.

Baldwin, D. A., & Baird, J. A. (2001). Discerning intentions in dynamic human action. *Trends in Cognitive Sciences, 5,* 171–178.

Baldwin, D. A., Baird, J. A., Saylor, M. M., & Clark, M. A. (2001). Infants parse dynamic action. *Child Development, 72,* 708–717.

Baron-Cohen, S., Leslie, A. M., & Frith, U. (1985). Does the autistic child have a "theory of mind"? *Cognition, 21,* 37–46.

Bartsch, K., & Wellman, H. M. (1994). *Children talk about the mind.* Cambridge, UK: Cambridge University Press.

Bauer, P. J. (2006). Event memory. In D. Kuhn & R. S. Siegler (Eds.), *Handbook of child psychology: Vol. 2. Cognition, perception, and language* (pp. 373–425). Hoboken, NJ: Wiley.

Benson, J. E., & Sabbagh, M. A. (2009). Theory of mind and executive functioning: A developmental neuropsychological approach. In P. D. Zelazo, M. Chandler, & E. Crone (Eds.), *Developmental social cognitive neuroscience* (pp. 63–80). New York: Psychology Press.

Blair, C., & Razza, R. P. (2007). Relating effortful control, executive function, and false belief understanding to emerging math and literacy ability in kindergarten. *Child Development, 78,* 647–663.

Brown, J. R., Donelan-McCall, N., & Dunn, J. (1996). Why talk about mental states? The significance of children's conversations with friends, siblings, and mothers. *Child Development, 67,* 836–849.

Bull, R., & Scerif, G. (2001). Executive functioning as a predictor of children's mathematics ability: Inhibition, switching, and working memory. *Developmental Neuropsychology, 19,* 273–293.

Bunge, S. A., & Zelazo, P. D. (2006). A brain-based account of the development of rule use in childhood. *Current Directions in Psychological Science, 15,* 118–121.

Buresh, J. S., & Woodward, A. L. (2007). Infants track action goals within and across agents. *Cognition, 104,* 287–314.

Call, J., & Tomasello, M. (1999). A nonverbal false belief task: The perfomance of children and great apes. *Child Development, 70,* 381–395.

Carlson, S. M., & Moses, L. J. (2001). Individual differences in inhibitory control and children's theory of mind. *Child Development, 72,* 1032–1053.

Carlson, S. M., Moses, L. J., & Hix, H. R. (1998). The role of inhibitory processes in young children's difficulties with deception and false belief. *Child Development, 69,* 672–691.

Chandler, M. J., Fritz, A. S., & Hala, S. (1989). Small-scale deceit: Deception as a marker of 2-, 3-, and 4-year-olds' early theories of mind. *Child Development, 60,* 1263–1277.

Chang, F.-M., Kidd, J. R., Kivak, K. J., Pakstis, A. J., & Kidd, K. K. (1996). The world-wide distribution of allele frequencies at the human dopamine D4 receptor locus. *Human Genetics, 98,* 91–101.

Chen, X., Hastings, P. D., Rubin, K. H., Chen, H., Cen, G., & Stewart, S. L. (1998). Child-rearing attitudes and behavioral inhibition in Chinese and Canadian toddlers: A cross-cultural study. *Developmental Psychology, 34,* 677–686.

Dally, J. M., Emery, N. J., & Clayton, N. S. (2006). Food-caching western scrub-jays keep track of who was watching them. *Science, 312,* 1662–1665.

Dally, J. M., Emery, N. J., & Clayton, N. S. (2009). Avian theory of mind and counter espionage by food-caching western scrub-jays (*Aphelocoma californica*). *European Journal of Development Psychology, 7,* 17–37.

De Beni, R., Palladino, P., Pazzaglia, F., & Cornoldi, C. (1998). Increases in intrusion errors and working memory deficit of poor comprehenders. *Quarterly Journal of Experimental Psychology, 51,* 305–320.

Dennett, D. C. (1978). Beliefs about beliefs. *Behavioral and Brain Sciences, 1,* 568–570.

Dienes, Z., & Perner, J. (1999). A theory of implicit and explicit knowledge. *Behavioral and Brain Sciences, 22,* 735–808.

Emery, N. J., & Clayton, N. S. (2005). Evolution of the avian brain and intelligence. *Cell Press, 15,* R946–R950.

Emery, N. J., Dally, J. M., & Clayton, N. (2004). Western scrub-jays (*Aphelocoma californica*) use cognitive strategies to protect their caches from thieving conspecifics. *Animal Cognition, 7,* 37–43.

Espy, K. A., McDiarmid, M. M., Cwik, M. F., Stalets, M. M., Hamby, A., & Senn, T. E. (2004). The contribution of executive functions to emergent mathematic skills in preschool children. *Developmental Neuropsychology, 26,* 465–486.

Flavell, J. H., Green, F. L., & Flavell, E. R. (1986). Development of knowledge about the appearance-reality distinction. *Monographs of the Society for Research in Child Development, 51*(Serial No. 212).

Friedman, O., & Leslie, A. M. (2004). Mechanisms of belief-desire reasoning: Inhibition and bias. *Psychological Science, 15,* 547–552.

Frye, D., Zelazo, P. D., & Burack, J. A. (1998). Cognitive complexity and control: I. Theory of mind in typical and atypical development. *Current Directions in Psychological Science, 7,* 116–121.

Gopnik, A., & Wellman, H. M. (1994). The theory theory. In L. A. Hirschfeld & S. A. Gelman (Eds.), *Mapping the mind: Domain specificity in cognitionn and culture* (pp. 257–293). New York: Cambridge University Press.

Hare, B., Call, J., & Tomasello, M. (2001). Do chimpanzees know what conspecifics know? *Animal Behaviour, 61,* 139–151.

Hauser, M. D., Newport, E. L., & Aslin, R. N. (2001). Segmentation of the speech stream in a non-human primate: Statistical learning in cotton-top tamarins. *Cognition, 78,* B53–B64.

Ho, D. Y. F. (1994). Cognitive socialization in Confucian heritage cultures. In P. M. Greenfield & R. R. Cocking (Eds.), *Cross-cultural roots of minority development* (pp. 285–313). Hillsdale, NJ: Erlbaum.

Hughes, C. (1998). Executive function in preschoolers: Links with theory of mind and verbal ability. *British Journal of Developmental Psychology, 16,* 233–253.

Kagan, J. (2008). In defense of qualitative changes in development. *Child Development, 79,* 1606–1624.

Karmiloff-Smith, A. (1994). Précis of "Beyond modularity: A developmental perspective on cognitive science." *Behavioral and Brain Sciences, 17,* 693–745.

Keysar, B., Lin, S., & Barr, D. J. (2003). Limits on theory of mind use in adults. *Cognition, 89,* 25–41.

Krachun, C., Carpenter, M., Call, J., & Tomasello, M. (2009). A competitive nonverbal false belief task for children and apes. *Developmental Science, 12,* 521–535.

Kronmüller, E., & Barr, D. J. (2007). Perspective-free pragmatics: Broken precedents and the recovery-from-preemption hypothesis. *Journal of Memory and Language, 56,* 436–455.

Kuhlmeier, V. A., Wynn, K., & Bloom, P. (2003). Attribution of dispositional states by 12-month-olds. *Psychological Science, 14,* 402–408.

Leslie, A. M., & Polizzi, P. (1998). Inhibitory processing in the false belief task: Two conjectures. *Developmental Science, 1,* 247–253.

Lewis, C., & Osborne, A. (1990). Three-year-olds' problems with false belief: Conceptual deficit or linguistic artifact. *Child Development, 61,* 1514–1519.

Liu, D., Wellman, H. M., Tardif, T., & Sabbagh, M. A. (2008). Theory of mind development in Chinese children: A meta-analysis of false-belief understanding across cultures and languages. *Developmental Psychology, 44,* 523–531.

Marcus, G. F. (1999). Rule learning by seven-month-old infants. *Science, 283,* 77–80.

Marcus, G. F. (2001). *The algebraic mind: Integrating connectionism and cognitive science.* Cambridge, MA: MIT Press.

Marshall, P. J., Bar-Haim, Y., & Fox, N. A. (2002). Development of the EEG from 5 months to 4 years of age. *Clinical Neurophysiology, 113,* 1199–1208.

McClelland, M. M., Cameron, C. E., Connor, C. M., Farris, C. L., Jewkes, A. M., & Morrison, F. J. (2007). Links between behavioral regulation and preschoolers' literacy, vocabulary, and math skills. *Developmental Psychology, 43,* 947–959.

Moore, C. (1999). Gaze following and the control of attention. In P. Rochat (Ed.), *Early Social Cognition: Understanding the first months of life* (pp. 241–256). Mahwah, NJ: Erlbaum.

Moses, L. J. (2001). Executive accounts of theory of mind development. *Child Development, 72,* 688–690.

Moses, L. J., Carlson, S. M., & Sabbagh, M. A. (2004). On the specificity of the relation between executive function and children's theories of mind. In W. Schneider, R. Schumann-Hengsteler, & B. Sodian (Eds.), *Young children's cognitive development: Interrelationships among executive functioning, working memory, verbal ability and theory of mind* (pp. 131–145). Mahwah, NJ: Erlbaum.

Moses, L. J., & Chandler, M. J. (1992). Traveler's guide to children's theories of mind. *Psychological Inquiry, 3,* 286–301.

Moses, L. J., & Flavell, J. H. (1990). Inferring false beliefs from actions and reactions. *Child Development, 61,* 929–945.

Muir, D., & Hains, S. (2004). The U-shaped developmental function for auditory localization. *Journal of Cognition and Development, 5,* 123–130.

Oh, S., & Lewis, C. (2008). Korean preschoolers' advanced inhibitory control and its relation to other executive skills and mental state understanding. *Child Development, 79,* 80–99.

O'Neill, D. K. (1996). Two-year-old children's sensitivity to a parent's knowledge state when making requests. *Child Development, 67,* 659–677.

Onishi, K., & Baillargeon, R. (2005). Do 15–month-old infants understand false beliefs? *Science, 308,* 255–258.

Pascual-Marqui, R. D. (2002). Standardized low-resolution brain electromagnetic tomography (sLORETA): Technical details. *Methods and Findings in Experimental and Clinical Pharmacology, 24D,* 5–12.

Penn, D. C., & Povinelli, D. J. (2007). On the lack of evidence that non-human animals possess anything remotely resembling a "theory of mind." In N. J. Emery, N. Clayton, & C. Frith (Eds.), *Social intelligence: From brain to culture* (pp. 393–414). New York: Oxford University Press.

Perner, J. (1991). *Understanding the representational mind.* Cambridge, MA: MIT Press.

Perner, J. (2009). Who took the cog out of cognitive science?: Mentalism in an era of anti-cognitivism. In P. A. Frensch & R. Schwarzer (Eds.), *Cognition and neuropsychology: International perspectives on psychological science* (Vol. 1, pp. 241–261). Hove, UK: Psychology Press.

Perner, J., Lang, B., & Kloo, D. (2002). Theory of mind and self-control: More than a common problem of inhibition. *Child Development, 73,* 752–767.

Perner, J., Leekam, S. R., & Wimmer, H. (1987). Three-year-olds' difficulty with false belief: The case for a conceptual deficit. *British Journal of Developmental Psychology, 5,* 125–137.

Perner, J., & Ruffman, T. (2005). Infants' insight into the mind: How deep? *Science, 308,* 214–216.

Perner, J., Ruffman, T., & Leekam, S. R. (1994). Theory of mind is contagious: You catch it from your sibs. *Child Development, 65,* 1228–1238.

Peskin, J., & Ardino, V. (2003). Representing the mental world in children's social behavior: Playing hide-and-seek and keeping a secret. *Social Development, 12,* 496–512.

Phillips, A. T., Wellman, H. M., & Spelke, E. S. (2002). Infants' ability to connect gaze and emotional expression to intentional action. *Cognition, 85,* 53–78.

Reddy, V. (1991). Playing with others' expectations: Teasing and mucking about in the first year. In A. Whiten (Ed.), *Natural theories of mind* (pp. 143–158). Oxford, UK: Blackwell.

Ridderinkhof, K. R., Ullsperger, M., Crone, E. A., & Nieuwenhuis, S. (2004). The role of the medial frontal cortex in cognitive control. *Science, 306,* 443–447.

Ruffman, T., Slade, L., & Crowe, E. (2002). The relation between children's and mothers' mental state language and theory-of-mind understanding. *Child Development, 73,* 734–751.

Russell, J. (1996). *Agency.* Cambridge, UK: Erlbaum/Taylor & Francis.

Sabbagh, M. A., Bowman, L. C., Evraire, L. E., & Ito, J. M. B. (2009). Neurodevelopmental correlates of theory of mind in preschool children. *Child Development, 80,* 1147–1162.

Sabbagh, M. A., Moses, L. J., & Shiverick, S. M. (2006). Executive functioning and preschoolers' understanding of false beliefs, false photographs and false signs. *Child Development, 77,* 1034–1049.

Sabbagh, M. A., Xu, F., Carlson, S. M., Moses, L. J., & Lee, K. (2006). Executive functioning and theory-of-mind in preschool children from Beijing, China: Comparisons with U.S. preschoolers. *Psychological Science, 17,* 74–81.

Saffran, J. R., Aslin, R. N., & Newport, E. L. (1996). Statistical learning by 8–month-old infants. *Science, 274,* 1926–1928.

Saxe, R. (2006). Uniquely human social cognition. *Current Opinion in Neurobiology, 16,* 235–239.

Saxe, R., & Powell, L. J. (2006). It's the thought that counts: Specific brain regions for one component of theory of mind. *Psychological Science, 17,* 692–699.

Saxe, R., Schulz, L., & Jiang, Y. (2006). Reading minds versus following rules. *Social Neuroscience, 1,* 284–298.

Scott, R. M., & Baillargeon, R. (2009). Which penguin is this? Attributing false beliefs about object identity at 18 months. *Child Development, 80,* 1172–1196.

Shatz, M., Wellman, H. M., & Silber, S. (1983). The acquisition of mental terms: A systematic investigation of the first reference to mental state. *Cognition, 14,* 301–321.

Siegler, R. (2004). U-shaped interest in U-shaped development—and what it means. *Journal of Cognition and Development, 5,* 1–10.

Sommerville, J. A., & Crane, C. C. (2009). Ten-month-old infants use prior information to identify an actor's goal. *Developmental Science, 12*(2), 314–325.

Southgate, V., Senju, A., & Csibra, G. (2007). Action anticipation through attribution of false belief by 2-year-olds. *Psychological Science, 18,* 587–592.

Surian, L., Caldi, S., & Sperber, D. (2008). Attribution of beliefs by 13–month-old infants. *Psychological Science, 18,* 580–586.

Talwar, V., & Lee, K. (2008). Social and cognitive correlates of children's lying behavior. *Child Development, 79,* 866–881.

Tardif, T., So, C. W., & Kaciroti, N. (2007). Language and false belief: Evidence for general, not specific, effects in Cantonese-speaking preschoolers. *Developmental Psychology, 43,* 318–340.

Thatcher, R. W., Walker, R. A., & Guidice, S. (1987). Human cerebral hemispheres develop at different rates and age. *Science, 236,* 1110–1113.

Tobin, J. J., Wu, D. Y. H., & Davidson, D. H. (1989). *Preschool in three cultures: Japan, China and the United States.* New Haven, CT: Yale University Press.

Tomasello, M. (2009). *Why we cooperate.* Cambridge, MA: MIT Press.

Wellman, H. M. (1990). *The child's theory of mind.* Cambridge, MA: MIT Press.

Wellman, H. M., Cross, D., & Watson, J. (2001). Meta-analysis of theory of mind development: The truth about false-belief. *Child Development, 72,* 655–684.

Wellman, H. M., & Gelman, S. A. (1998). Knowledge acquisition in foundational domains. In P. Mussen, W. Damon, & R. S. Siegler (Eds.), *Handbook of child psychology: Vol. 2. Cognition, perception, and language* (5th ed., pp. 523–572). New York: Wiley.

Wellman, H. M., Lopez-Duran, S., LaBounty, J., & Hamilton, B. (2008). Infant attention to intentional action predicts preschool theory of mind. *Developmental Psychology, 44,* 618–623.

Wellman, H. M., Phillips, A. T., Dunphy-Lelii, S., & LaLonde, N. (2004). Infant social attention predicts preschool social cognition. *Developmental Science, 7,* 283–288.

Wellman, H. M., & Woolley, J. D. (1990). From simple desires to ordinary beliefs: The early development of everyday psychology. *Cognition, 35*, 245–275.

Wimmer, H., & Perner, J. (1983). Beliefs about beliefs: Representation and constraining function of wrong beliefs in young children's understanding of deception. *Cognition, 13*, 103–128.

Woodward, A. L. (1998). Infants selectively encode the goal object of an actor's reach. *Cognition, 69*, 1–34.

Yamaguchi, M., Kuhlmeier, V. A., Wynn, K., & vanMarle, K. (2009). Continuity in social cognition from infancy to childhood. *Developmental Science, 12*, 746–752.

Zelazo, P. D. (2004). The development of conscious control in childhood. *Trends in Cognitive Sciences, 8*, 12–17.

Zelazo, P. D., Carlson, S. M., & Kesek, A. (2009). The development of executive function in childhood. In C. Nelson & M. Luciana (Eds.), *Handbook of developmental cognitive neuroscience* (pp. 553–574). Cambridge, MA: MIT Press.

CHAPTER 14

Neural Connectivity, Joint Attention, and the Social-Cognitive Deficits of Autism

PETER MUNDY

By the early 1990s translational developmental research had indicated that key elements of the nosology of autism were incorrect. Children with autism, as a group, did not display "a *pervasive* lack of responsiveness to others," which was the singular description of the social symptoms of autism in the third edition of the *Diagnostic and Statistical Manual of Mental Disorders* (DSM-III; American Psychiatric Association, 1980). Rather, many children with autism responded when others imitated them, some could learn from social modeling, many increased their social output in structured situations, and they varied greatly in their use of gestures and eye contact to communicate (Curcio, 1978; Lewy & Dawson, 1992; Mundy & Sigman, 1989). Perhaps most remarkably, children with autism often displayed levels of attachment behaviors that were commensurate with their mental development and *not atypical* relative to other groups of children with commensurate developmental delays (Shapiro, Sherman, Calamari, & Koch, 1987; Sigman & Mundy, 1989; Sigman & Ungerer, 1984).

Describing the social symptoms of children with autism as "a pervasive lack of responsiveness" not only was inaccurate, but it promoted a constricted view of autism that excluded many children with the syndrome, such as those who frequently make eye contact or display caregiver attachment, from consideration within this nosology. The perseverance of this inaccurate taxonomic prototype over the years likely contributed to a historic underestimation of the prevalence of autism (Wing & Potter, 2002). Indeed, only since the publication of the more recent diagnostic formulations, such as the DSM-IV (American Psychiatric Association, 1994), have we had guidelines with enough precision to begin to appreciate the full range of phenotypic variability expressed across individuals with this syndrome. Prior to this, we limited ourselves to those children who met a very limited and restrictive social criterion.

Empirically based revisions of the descriptions of the social symptoms of autism culminated in diagnostic criteria common to systems used in the United States, in Europe, and worldwide (American Psychiatric Association, 1994, 2000; World Health Organization, 1991). In both systems the qualitative impairment in social interaction in autism became defined as the expression of at least two of the following: (1) a marked impairment in the use of multiple nonverbal behaviors such as eye-to-eye gaze, facial expression, body postures, and gestures to regulate social interaction; (2) a failure to develop peer relationships appropriate to developmental level; (3) a lack of spontaneous seeking to share experience, enjoyment, interests, or achievements with other people (e.g., by a lack of showing, bringing, or pointing out objects of interest); and (4) lack of social or emotional reciprocity.

The criterion of a lack of appropriate peer skills is extremely useful, but not until 3 or 4 years of age. As a result, the early identification and diagnosis of the social deficits of autism relies on observation of the other three social symptoms. This chapter attempts to provide a detailed consideration of why the third symptom, a *lack of spontaneous seeking to share experience, enjoyment, interests, or achievements with other people*, is central to the description of the social pathology of autism. In the research literature, we study the early development of spontaneously seeking to share experience with others with measures of joint attention development. While other domains of social behavior such as imitation face processing, empathy, and pragmatic communication skills are important in the study and understanding of the social deficits of autism (Dawson, 2008; Travis & Sigman, 1998), none of these is as central to the current social nosology of autism. This is because of several features of joint attention.

Research on autism focuses on different levels of biobehavioral processes in trying to understand the nature of autism in the etiology of the syndrome, from genetic through neural growth modulators, to brain functions and ultimately behavioral symptoms (see Figure 14.1). One reasonable goal of research for people with autism is to identify domains of behavioral development that (1) are sensitive to the early expression of autism, (2) display developmental continuity such that variation in early symptom expression is reliable and meaningfully predictive of the subsequent level of expression of the syndrome and/or the responsiveness of individuals with the syndrome to intervention, and (3) the study of the behavior domain facilitates the analysis of the dynamic, developmental interplay between two or more of the processes illustrated in Figure 14.1. The study of joint attention development among people with autism appears to meet all three of these criteria.

Meaningful individual differences in joint attention may be measured reliably in infancy, and infant joint attention is related to subsequent social and cognitive developmental outcomes in children not affected by autism (e.g., Meltzoff & Brooks, 2008; Morales, Mundy, Crowson, Neal, & Delgado, 2005; Mundy et al., 2007; Vaughan et al., 2007; Ulvund & Smith, 2006). Intervention and behavioral research also indicates that individual differences in early joint attention impairment are pivotal to the nature of autism because individual differences predict social symptoms as well as language and cognitive outcomes in these children (e.g., Bruinsma, Koegle, & Koegle, 2004; Charman, 1994; Dawson et al., 2004; Kasari, Freeman, & Paparella, 2006; Mundy & Crowson, 1997; Sigman & Ruskin, 1999). Finally, theory and research suggest that frontal-to-parietal connective neurodevelopmental

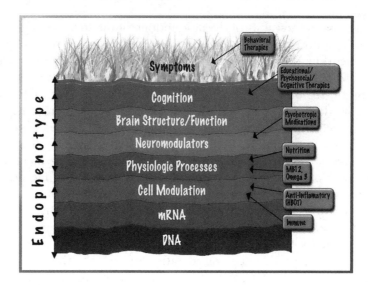

FIGURE 14.1. Different levels of inquiry involved in the multidisciplinary science of autism and the position of joint attention research as bridging studies of behavioral symptom development, cognitive developmental processes, and developmental cognitive neuroscience. The linear arrangement of factors involved in autism is not meant to suggest a linear or deterministic relation among processes. This illustration is a modification of one developed by Robert Hendren to illustrate work at the University of California, Davis, MIND Institute.

vulnerability may play a role in the etiology of autism (e.g., Courschesne & Pierce, 2005). Therefore, early emerging behavior domains that place a high demand on frontal–parietal connectivity may be expected to be especially sensitive and revealing markers of the syndrome of autism. In this regard, cognitive neuroscience has begun to suggest that the adequate development of joint attention may both be a consequence and cause adequate frontal–parietal interconnectivity in the first 3 years of life (Henderson, Yoder, Yale, & McDuffie, 2002; Mundy, 2003; Mundy, Card, & Fox, 2000; Mundy, Sullivan, & Mastergeorge, 2009). Thus, the dynamic neurodevelopmental processes involved in typical join attention development may help us understand why joint attention may be a nexus of autism. The goal of this chapter is to provide an overview of this facet of research and theory on infant joint attention development.

Infants Share Experiences with Other People

Well before infants learn to use symbols and language, they begin to spontaneously share information with other people. They typically do so by coordinating their visual attention with another person and following people's direction of gaze (Scaife & Bruner, 1975) or by using eye contact and gestures to indicate object or events of interest or desire (Bates, Benigni, Bretherton, Camaioni, & Volterra, 1979). This type of social attention coordination is referred to as "joint attention." Infants' ability to follow the direction of another person's gaze (Scaife & Bruner, 1975) is often called responding to joint attention (RJA; Seibert, Hogan, & Mundy, 1982). It can be reliably assessed beginning at about 3 to 6 months of life by determining whether infants correctly process the gaze of others, such as when they turn their head and/or eyes to follow the visual line of regard of another person (see Figure 14.2). Indeed, recent research suggests that discriminant processing of gaze direction and the specific cortical functions associated with this type of joint attention can be measured by 5 months of age (Grossman & Johnson, 2010). Self-initiated joint attention behaviors or simply initiating joint attention (IJA) has been observed as early as 5 months during natural interactions (Legerstee, Markova, & Fisher, 2007), and is firmly established by 8 to 9 months of age (Mundy et al., 2007). It involves infants' use of alternating eye contact with or without gestures (i.e., pointing or showing) to spontaneously direct and coordinate attention to show or share their interest and experience regarding an object or event to a social partner (Bates et al., 1979; Mundy et al., 2007; Figure 14.2). Young infants also learn to direct the attention of other people to request aid in obtaining objects or actions (initiating behavioral requests). In addition, they learn to respond to the attention-directing bids that adults use to request objects or actions from infants or responds to behavioral requests (Figure 14.1).

In the 1970s, theory began to suggest that measures of joint attention could be used in the early identification of children at risk for social, communication, and language disorders. For example, Jeff Seibert and Anne Hogan developed an

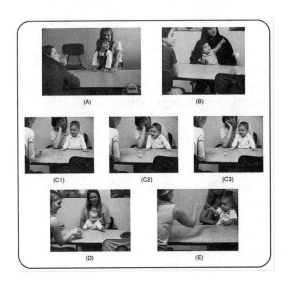

FIGURE 14.2. Different types of infant social attention coordination behaviors. (a) Responding to joint attention (RJA) involving following and other persons' gaze and pointing gesture; (b) initiating joint attention (IJA) involving a conventional gesture "pointing" to share attention regarding a room poster; $(c_{1,2,3})$ IJA involving *alternating eye contact* to share attention with respect to a toy; (d) initiating behavior request involving pointing to elicit aid in obtaining an out-of-reach object; (e) responding to behavior requests involving following an adult's open-palm "Give it to me" gesture.

assessment-based curriculum that focused on joint attention and preverbal communication skill development in an early intervention center for infants and toddlers with cognitive delays and significant motor impairments. The assessment system, called the Early Social Communication Scales (ESCS), organized precise observations of joint attention and social attention coordination into ordinal developmental scales that could be used to evaluate and guide early intervention (Seibert et al., 1982). Along with related measures (Stone, Coonrod, & Ousley, 1997; Wetherby, Allen, Cleary, Kublin, & Goldstein, 2002), a lasting contribution of the infant joint attention scales of the ESCS was that they turned out to be powerful instruments for the study of the social and cognitive developmental pathology of autism.

Joint Attention and Defining the Social Deficits of Autism

Frank Curcio (1978) was the first research scientist to publish the observation that many children with autism capably initiated nonverbal requests but not joint attention bids in social interactions. Fifty percent of the elementary school-age children with autism he observed in classrooms systematically used eye contact and conventional gestures to express their requests. However, few if any displayed evidence of the use of eye contact or gestures to initiate nonverbal "declaratives" (i.e., display an IJA bid). Curcio concluded that impairments in the capacity to initiate declarative communicative functions, or what we now call "initiating joint attention" bids, could be central to the nature of the social impairments of autism.

Subsequent studies have indicated that Curcio was correct (e.g., Charman, 2004; Dawson et al., 2004; Loveland & Landry, 1986; Mundy, Sigman, Ungerer, & Sherman, 1986; Sigman & Ruskin, 1999; Wetherby & Prutting, 1984). Children with autism display deficits in joint attention in interactions with unfamiliar testers as well as their familiar parents compared with both typical and intellectually developmentally disabled (IDD) comparison groups (Mundy et al., 1986; Sigman, Mundy, Sherman, & Ungerer, 1986). However, these studies indicate that 3- to 6-year-old children with autism display levels of requesting that are comparable to those observed in the IDD samples. Consistent with Curcio's observations, the children with autism in these studies were not characterized by a *pervasive* lack of social responsiveness. Even with respect to eye contact, they displayed few differences compared with typical and IDD controls during requesting and social turn-taking games. However, they clearly demonstrated diminished use of alternating gaze to spontaneously initiate sharing of their experience of a mechanical toy with the tester. This type of IJA behavior is illustrated in Figure 14.1, and it alone discriminated over 90% of the autism sample from the typical *and* IDD samples (Mundy et al., 1986). That is to say, there was almost no overlap in the distributions for IJA alternating gaze for the autism and comparison samples.

Additional studies indicated that joint attention deficits were not absolute in children with autism. Rather, they displayed meaningful individual differences; parents of 30 children with autism rated those with better IJA scores as more socially related than children with lower IJA scores (Mundy et al., 1994). Thus, it seemed reasonable to begin to consider the possibility that diminished IJA alternating eye contact was crucial to what Kanner (1943) had characterized as impairments in relatedness and positive affective contact with others in autism (e.g., Mundy & Sigman, 1989). The latter idea was subsequently supported by research showing that about 60% of the IJA bids displayed by typical infants and children with mental retardation involved the conveyance of positive affect (Kasari, Sigman, Mundy, & Yirmiya, 1990; Mundy, Kasari, & Sigman, 1992). However, positive affect was much less frequently part of the IJA bids of children with autism (Kasari et al., 1990). Additional research indicates that the systematic conveyance of positive affect as part of IJA bids begins to develop early in life, at about 8 to 10 months of age (Venezia, Messinger, Thorp, & Mundy, 2004). Thus, joint attention impairments may reflect early arising deficits in the tendency of children with autism to socially share positive affect when playing with objects (Kasari et al., 1990). This, in turn, may involve a disturbance in their early appreciation or sensitivity to the positive social *value* of shared attention. That is, motivation factors may play a role in joint attention disturbance in autism (Mundy, 1995).

The Dissociation of Joint Attention Impairment in Autism

To best interpret the nature of IJA and RJA impairments in autism, it is important to recognize that they dissociate in development. Both RJA and IJA are useful in the early identification and diagnosis of autism (e.g., Lord et al., 2000; Stone, Counrod, & Ousley, 1997). However, RJA impairments are less evident for children with more advanced levels of cognitive development (Mundy, Sigman, & Kasari, 1994). Indeed, across studies of different age groups of children, there is inconsistent evidence of a robust syndrome-specific impairment in the ability to process the direction of gaze or respond to joint attention in people with autism (Nation & Penny, 2008). On the other hand, IJA deficits are observed in children with autism from preschool through adolescence (e.g., Charman, 2004; Dawson et al., 2004; Hobson & Hobson, 2007; Mundy et al., 1986; Sigman & Ruskin, 1999). The correlates of IJA and RJA also diverge as much as they converge in studies of autism. Both IJA and RJA are related to executive inhibition and problems in language development in autism (Bono, Daily, & Sigman, 2004; Dawson et al., 2002, 2004; Griffith, Pennington, Wehner, & Rogers, 1999; Sigman & McGovern, 2005). However, to our knowledge, only IJA is significantly associated with individual differences in social and affective symptom presentation (Charman, 2004; Kasari et al., 1990; Kasari, Freeman, & Paparella, 2007; Lord, Floody, Anderson, & Pickles, 2003; Mundy et al., 1994; Naber et al., 2008; Sigman & Ruskin, 1999). It is also the case that IJA and RJA development appears to dissociate in typical development (e.g., Mundy et al., 2007).

This literature emphasizes that joint attention deficits are neither absolute nor uniform in autism, and the impairment of IJA and RJA may reflect both overlapping and unique developmental processes that contribute to the syndrome. Moreover, although both IJA and RJA deficits are likely to be instrumental in early social and social-cognitive deficits in autism (Mundy et al., 2009), deficits in IJA behavior appear to be the more robust feature of autism (Mundy, 1995). In line with the latter observation, intervention and sibling research also emphasizes that vulnerability for autism is characterized by a disturbance of the spontaneous *generation* of social behaviors, as much as or more than it is characterized by a disturbance of perception and *response* to the social behaviors of others (Koegel, Carter, & Koegel, 2003; Zweiganbaum et al., 2005). Indeed, the centrality of initiating deficits, especially IJA, is highlighted in current nosology, where it is "a lack of *spontaneous seeking* to share enjoyment, interests, or achievements with other people (e.g., by a lack of showing, bringing, or pointing out objects of interest to other people)" that is described as one of the primary social symptoms of autism (American Psychiatric Association, 1994). Furthermore, the gold standard diagnostic observation instrument, the Autism Diagnostic Observation Schedule, recognizes the robust nature of IJA symptoms. Measures of IJA and RJA are used in module 1 diagnostic algorithms for the youngest children. However, modules for older children only include IJA measures in their diagnostic criteria (Lord et al., 2000). These observations imply that the nature of the differences as well as commonalities between IJA and RJA may be a key to conceptualizations of the joint attention impairments of autism.

IJA Behaviors and Autism

IJA impairments in autism are often equated with problems with pointing and showing gestures. However, diminished alternating gaze behavior (see Figure 14.1) is a more powerful measure of IJA impairment in autism. This type of measure, rather than pointing and showing, correctly identified 94% of 54 preschool children with autism, mental retardation, and typical development (Mundy et al., 1986). Most of the variance in ESCS-IJA scores is carried by alternating gaze behavior (Mundy et al., 2007), and Dawson and colleagues (2004) have observed that IJA measured with the ESCS had a sensitivity of 83 to 97% and a specificity of 63 to 67% in discriminating 53 3- to 4-year-olds with autism from controls (Dawson et al., 2004). Observations also indicate that IJA alternating gaze of 2-year-olds predicts symptom outcomes at 4 years of age in children with autism (Charman, 2004) as well as social-cognition in typical 4-year-old children (Charman et al., 2000).

These details provide important information for understanding joint attention disturbance in autism. Often joint attention problems are viewed as growing out of developmental antecedent or successor processes that are considered to be more fundamental, such as affective processes, reward sensitivity, executive attention control, social orienting, identification, imitation and mirror neurons, intersubjectivity, and most prominently social cognition (e.g., Baron-Cohen, 1989; Charman, 2004; Dawson et al., 2004; Mundy et al., 1986; Williams, 2008). This has led to a paradox wherein joint attention deficits are viewed as pivotal to autism but also as an outgrowth of more basic processes. Charman (2004) recognized this paradox in noting that we often think of joint attention not as "a starting point [for autism], but merely a staging post in early social communicative development, and hence a 'postcursor' of earlier psychological and developmental processes . . . [which may] underlie the impaired development of joint attention skills in autism" (p. 321).

There are at least three problems with the idea that joint attention grows out of earlier, primary developmental processes. First, stable individual differences in IJA alternating gaze are well established by 8 to 9 months in typical development (Mundy et al., 2007; Venezia, Messinger, Thorp, & Mundy, 2004), and the onset of cortical control of the types of eye movements that may be involved in alternating gaze begins between 4 to 6 months (Mundy, 2003; Striano, Reid, & Hoel, 2006). Thus, it is likely that joint attention precursors would need to be present and well-established domains of behavior prior to 6–9 months (see Legerstee et al., 2007). Second, there is little evidence that the association of joint attention with the etiology or outcomes of autism is mediated by more basic antecedent or successor processes. Eleven studies have observed that joint attention accounts for significant portions of variance in the language, symbolic play, and symptom development of children with autism above and beyond variance associated with measures of executive functions, imitation, knowledge about others' intentions, or global measures of mental development, social relatedness, or attachment (e.g., Capps, Sigman, & Mundy, 1994; Charman 2004; Dawson et al., 2004; Kasari et al., 2007; Naber et al., 2008; Royers, Van Oost, & Bothutne, 1998; Rutherford, Young, Hepburn, & Rogers, 2007; Sigman & Ruskin, 1999; Smith, Mirenda, & Zaidman-Zait, 2007; Thurm, Lord, Lee, & Newschaffer, 2007; Toth, Munson, Meltzoff, & Dawson, 2006).

A third issue is that precursor and successor process hypotheses do not explicitly account for the dissociation of IJA and RJA (Mundy et al., 2007). Social-cognitive hypotheses suggest that RJA and IJA should be highly related because they are both precursors of a common "mentalizing" ability involved in perceiving the intentions of others (e.g., Baron-Cohen, 1995; Tomasello, 1995). In autism the development of IJA and RJA dissociate such that IJA deficits are more pervasive than RJA deficits (Mundy, Gwaltney, & Henderson, 2010). However, neither the very creditable social-orienting nor executive function accounts of autism clearly recognize and address this phenomenon (e.g., Dawson, Meltzoff, Osterling, Rinaldi, & Brown, 1998; Landry & Bryson, 2004). Imitation and mirror neuron theory emphasizes the role of deficits in processing and responding to the behavior of other people in the development of autism (e.g., Williams, 2008). Hypothetically, though, this should be more applicable to explanations of responsive joint attention deficits in autism rather than deficits in the spontaneous initiation of joint attention bids. So what other type of model may be useful in understanding joint attention and its role in autism? An answer may be provided by considering joint attention as integral to human social learning (e.g., Bruner, 1975, 1995).

Learning and the Importance of Joint Attention

Early language learning often takes place in unstructured, incidental situations where parents spontaneously refer to a new object (Figure 14.3). How do infants know how to map their parents' vocal labels to the correct parts of the environment amidst myriad potential referents? Baldwin (1995) suggested that they use RJA and the direction of their parent's gaze to guide them to the correct area of the environment, thereby reducing "referential" mapping errors. Infants' use of IJA also reduces the chance of referential mapping errors. IJA serves to denote something of immediate interest to the child. This assists parents in following their child's attention to provide new information in a context when the child's interest and attention are optimal for learning (Tomasello & Farrar, 1986). Hence, joint attention may be conceived of as a self-organizing system that facilitates information processing in support of social learning (Mundy, 2003). This "learning function" is fundamental to joint attention (Bruner, 1975) and continues to operate throughout our lives (e.g., Bayliss, Paul, Cannon, & Tipper, 2006; Nathan, Eilam, & Kim, 2007). Without the capacity for joint attention, success in many pedagogical contexts would be difficult. Imagine the school readiness problems of a 5-year-old who enters kindergarten but is not facile with coordinating attention with the teacher. Similarly, children, adolescents, and adults who cannot follow, initiate, or join with the rapid-fire exchanges of shared attention in social interactions may be impaired in any social learning context as well as in their very capacity for relatedness and relationships (Mundy & Sigman, 2006).

If joint attention helps self-organize social learning, then the more children engage in joint attention, the more optimal social learning opportunities they help create for themselves. This may help to explain why the frequency with which infants engage in joint attention is positively related to their language acquisition and childhood IQ status (e.g., Mundy et al., 2007; Smith & Ulvund, 2003; Ulvund & Smith, 1996). More direct evidence of the links between joint attention and early learning is provided by the observation that coordinated social attention to pictures elicits electrophysiological evidence of enhanced neural activity (Striano, Reid, & Hoel, 2006) and recognition memory associated with greater depth of processing in 9-month-olds (Striano, Chen, Cleveland, & Bradshaw, 2006).

In light of the assumption that joint attention is basic to early learning, reconsider the observation that IJA and RJA dissociate in development. Theory and research suggest that this occurs because these forms of joint attention involve functions of two distinct neural networks, and that practice with and the exchange of information across these systems is vital to optimal joint attention development (Mundy & Newell, 2007; Mundy et al., 2009). An analogy here might be the dorsolateral frontal

FIGURE 14.3. The referential mapping problem encountered by infants in incidental social word-learning situations. From Baldwin (1995). Copyright 1995 by Erlbaum. Reprinted by permission.

guidance of expressive language (Broca's area) and the temporal guidance of receptive language (Wernicke's area). Just as practice with receptive language processing (outside-in processing) and with the expression of words (inside-out processing) may be expected to be synergistic with respect to functional language development, we have suggested that practice with both RJA and IJA is necessary for the development of a fully informative and functional joint attention system (Mundy et al., 2009, 2010). This notion, of course, is consistent with tenets of cognitive theory of parallel and distributed processing, which suggests that learning occurs best in the context of the simultaneous activation of multiple neural networks during encoding (e.g., Munakata & McClelland, 2003; Otten, Henson, & Rugg, 2001). Taken together, these ideas raise the hypothesis that joint attention may involve the early development of a form of social information processing across multiple distributed neural networks. A corollary hypothesis is that joint attention may reflect deficits in the development of this parallel and distributed activation of cortical neural networks in autism

The Two Neural Systems of Joint Attention and Social Cognition

Research has indicated that IJA is associated with frontal-cortical activity (Caplan et al., 1993; Henderson et al., 2002; Mundy et al., 2000; Torkildsen, Thormodsen, Syvensen, Smith, & Lingren, 2008) while RJA and related gaze-following behaviors are more closely tied to parietal and temporal cortical processes (e.g., Emery, 2000; Frieschen, Bayliss, & Tipper, 2007; Materna, Dicke, & Thern, 2008; Mundy et al., 2000). One interpretation of these data is that joint attention involves developments of functions of both the anterior and posterior cortical attention networks that have been described by Posner and Rothbart (2007).

The functions of the posterior network are common to many primates, but the anterior network is not well represented in primates other than humans (Astafiev et al., 2003; Emery, 2000; Gilbert & Burgess, 2008; Jellema, Baker, Wicker, & Perrett, 2000). RJA appears to be most closely associated with the posterior system, which regulates relatively involuntary attention, begins to develop in the first 3 months of life, and prioritizes orienting to biologically meaningful stimuli. It is supported by neural networks of the parietal/precuneous and superior temporal cortices (Figure 14.4). These neural networks are active in the perception of the eye and head orientations of others as well as the perception of spatial relations between self, other, and the environment. The posterior system is especially involved in control of orienting on a trial-by-trial basis and the development of cognitive representations about the world built from information acquired through external senses (Cavana & Trimble, 2006; Dosenbach et al., 2007; Fuster, 2006).

IJA is supported by a later developing anterior attention network involved in the cognitive processing, representation, and regulation of self-initiated goal-directed action. This network includes the anterior cingulate; rostral-medial superior frontal cortex, including the frontal eye fields; anterior prefrontal cortex; and orbital frontal cortex (e.g., Dosenbach et al., 2007; Fuster, 2006). The development of the intentional control of visual attention begins at about 3 to 4 months of age, when a pathway from the frontal eye fields (BA 8/9) that releases the superior colliculus

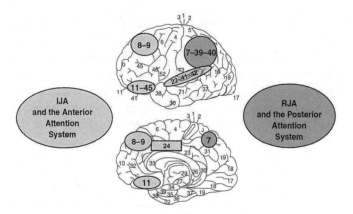

FIGURE 14.4. Lateral (top) and medial (bottom) illustrations of Brodmann's cytoarchitectonic areas of the cerebral cortex associated with initiating joint attention and the anterior attention system as well as RJA and the posterior attention systems. The former include areas 8 (frontal eye fields), 9 (prefrontal association cortex), 24 (anterior cingulate), 11, and 47 (orbital prefrontal and insula association cortices [not illustrated]). The latter include areas 7 (precuneous, posterior parietal association area), 22, 41, and 42 (superior temporal cortex), and 39 and 40 (parietal, temporal, occipital association cortex). From Mundy and Newell (2007). *www.ncbi.nlm.nih.gov/ pmc/articles/PMC2663908.*

from inhibition begins to be actively involved in the prospective control of saccades and visual attention (Canfield & Kirkham, 2001; Johnson, 1990). The function of this pathway may underlie 4-month-old infants' ability to suppress automatic visual saccades in order to respond to a second, more attractive stimulus (Johnson, 1995) and 6-month-olds' ability to respond to a peripheral target when central, competing stimuli are present (Atkinson, Hood, Wattam-Bell, & Braddick, 1992). We assume that the functions of this pathway also enable intentional gaze alternation between interesting events and social partners (Mundy, 2003).

Differences in the functions and developmental timing of the anterior and posterior attention networks help to explain why IJA and RJA dissociate in development (Mundy et al., 2000, 2007). However, although IJA and RJA follow distinct biobehavioral paths of development, it is also likely that they integrate in development. Indeed, EEG data indicate that activation of a distributed anterior and posterior cortical system predicts IJA development in infants (Henderson et al., 2002), and functional magnetic resonance imaging data indicate that activation of a distributed anterior-posterior cortical network is associated with the experience of joint attention in adults (Williams et al., 2005). These observations, among others, have motivated the description of a parallel and distributed information-processing model (PDPM). In this model, the integrative processing internal self-referenced information about one's own visual attention, with the processing of external information about the visual attention of other people, is a defining feature of joint attention (Mundy et al., 2009, 2010). Indeed, one hypothesized function of the human rostral-medial frontal cortex is the capacity to switch attention between self-generated and perceptual information in support of social cognition (Gilbert & Burgess, 2008). The PDPM suggests that this utility is "allocated" to the rostral-medial frontal cortex with development, in part, as a function of the adequate biobehavioral exercise of joint attention in infancy.

An assumption of the PDPM of joint attention is that the integrated processing of information about self-attention and the attention of others is a form of parallel processing that occurs across a distributed cortical network. It is first practiced in infancy and contributes to an information synthesis that plays a crucial role in human social cognition. The basic idea here is that human levels of self-awareness cannot develop without bidirectional interactive processing of information about self and others (e.g., Piaget, 1952). The potential role of the synthesis (parallel processing) of self–other information in human social cognition and its relations to self-awareness has previously been recognized (Decety & Sommerville, 2003; Keysers & Perrett, 2006). However, the developmentally primary role of joint attention in this synthesis is less well recognized.

Social Cognition, Joint Attention, and the PDPM

Social-cognitive models often describe joint attention in terms of incremental stages of knowledge about the intentionality of other people. Baron-Cohen (1995) described a sequence of cognitive modules, which included the intentionality detector, a dedicated cognitive facility that attributes goal-directed behavior to objects or people, and the eye direction detector, which senses and processes information about eyes. These combine to form the shared attention mechanism (SAM), a cognitive module that represents self and other as attending to the same referent *and* attributes volitional states (intentionality) to direction of gaze of other people. As infancy ebbs, the theory-of-mind mechanism replaces SAM and allows for the representation of the full range of mental states of others and the ability to make sense of others behaviors.

Tomasello, Carpenter, Call, Behne, and Moll (2005) more explicitly described joint attention development in terms of three stages of what infants know about other people. In *understanding animate action*, 3- to 8-month-old infants can perceive contingencies between their own animate actions and emotions relative to the animate actions and affect of others. However, they cannot represent the internal mental goals of others that are associated with these actions. In the next stage—*understanding of pursuit of goals*—9-month-olds become capable of shared action and attention on objects (e.g., building a block tower with parents).

Tomasello and colleagues (2005) suggest this stage involves joint perception, rather than joint attention, because the social-cognitive capacity to represent others' internal mental representations necessary for true joint attention is not yet available. However, this ability emerges between 12–15 months in the *understanding choice of plans* stage. This stage is heralded when infants become truly active in initiating episodes of joint engagement by alternating their eye contact between interesting sights and caregivers (Tomasello et al., 2005). This shift to active alternating gaze indicates infants' appreciation that others make mental choices about alternative actions that affect their attention. Infants also now know themselves as agents that initiate collaborative activity based on their own goals. Hence, the development of "true" joint attention at this stage is revealed in the capacity to adopt two perspectives analogous to speaker-listener.

The capacity to adopt two perspectives is also assumed to be an intrinsic characteristic of symbolic representations. In this regard, Tomasello and colleagues (2005) raise a truly seminal hypothesis that symbolic thought is a *developmental transformation* of joint attention. They argue that symbols themselves serve to socially coordinate attention so that the intentions of the listener align with those of the speaker. In other words, linguistic symbols both lead to and are dependent upon the efficient social coordination of covert mental attention to common abstract representations among people. This hypothesis fits well with the PDPM of joint attention, but the PDPM places it in a substantially different developmental framework.

The PDPM does not emphasize functional segregation of cognitive systems implicit to modular perspectives but, rather, the cortically multidetermined nature of human cognition because of the "massively parallel nature of human brain networks and the fact that function also emerges from the flow of information between brain areas" (Ramnani, Behrens, Penny, & Matthews, 2004, p. 613). Furthermore, cognitive development need not be construed only in terms of changes in discontinuous stages of knowledge. It can also be modeled as a continuous change in the speed, efficiency, and combinations of information processing that give rise to knowledge (Hunt, 1999). Specifically, the PDPM envisions joint attention development in terms of increased speed, efficiency, and complexity of processing of (1) internal information about self-referenced visual attention, (2) external information about the visual attention of other people, and (3) the neural networks that integrate processing of self-generated visual attention information with processing of information about the visual attention behavior of other people (Mundy & Newell, 2007; Mundy et al., 2009).

Consequently, the notion that *true* joint attention does not emerge until requisite social-cognitive knowledge emerges at 12–15 months (Tomasello et al., 2005) is not germane to the PDPM. Rather, consistent with a growing empirical literature, the PDPM holds that the true joint processing of attention information begins to be practiced by infants by 3 to 4 months of age (D'Entremont, Hains, & Muir, 1997; Farroni, Massaccesi, & Francesca, 2002; Hood, Willen, & Driver, 1998, Morales, Mundy, & Rojas, 1998; Striano et al., 2006; Striano & Stahl, 2005). Indeed, even the types of active alternating gaze behaviors thought to mark the onset of true joint attention at 12–15 months (Tomasello et al., 2005) develop no later than 8–9 months of life and quite possibly earlier (Mundy et al., 2007; Venezia et al., 2004).

Equally important, the PDPM assumes that joint attention is not replaced by the subsequent development of social-cognitive processes. Instead, joint attention is thought to remain an active system of information processing that supports cognition through adulthood (Mundy & Newell, 2007; Mundy et al., 2009). As an example, recall the hypothesis that linguistic symbols enable the social coordination of covert attention to common mental representations across people (Tomasello et al., 2005). According to the PDPM, symbolic thinking *involves* joint attention but does not *replace* joint attention. Just as 12-month-olds can shift eye contact or use pointing to establish a common visual point of reference with other people, 4-year-olds can use symbols to establish a common reference to covert mental representations with other people. Symbolic representations are often, if not always, initially encoded during the joint processing of information about the overt attention of self and of others directed toward some third object or event (Adamson, Bakeman, & Dekner, 2004;

Baldwin, 1995; Werner & Kaplan, 1963). The PDPM combines that hypothesis with the connectionist notion that "representations can take the form of patterns of activity distributed across processing units" that occurred during encoding (Munakata & McClelland, 2003, p. 415). Together, these two ideas lead to the assumption of the PDPM that symbol acquisition incorporates the distributed activation of the joint self-attention and other-attention neural processing units, which were engaged during encoding, as part of their functional neural representational mappings. Hence, the distributed joint attention processing system may always be activated as a network that encodes and contributes to the intersubjectivity (i.e., shared attention and meaning) of symbolic thought.

In infancy, the distributed joint attention processing system is initially effortful. With development, and multiple episodes of practice, the joint information processing of self–other attention becomes more efficient (i.e., less effortful) and can even be automatically activated in social engagement. As this occurs, joint attention becomes a social-executive "subroutine" that runs in support of symbolic thought, capable of maintaining a shared focus in social interactions and in social cognition (Mundy, 2003). The distributed neural activation patterns associated with joint attention are part of infants' developing sense of relatedness to others (Mundy & Hogan, 1994; Mundy, Kasari, & Sigman, 1992). Moreover, the distributed neural activation associated with joint attention can be thought of as an enduring stratum of a more *continuous spiral* of human social-neurocognitive development that supports, if not enables, later emerging human symbolic, linguistic, and social-cognitive facilities (see Mundy et al., 2009).

Inside-Out Processing and the PDPM

In addition to parallel and distributed processing, the PDPM may be distinguished from other models by its constructivist perspective on development. Rather than focusing on the development of knowledge about others, the PDPM gives equal footing to the significance of infants' development of their own intentional visual behavior in joint attention and social-cognitive development (Mundy et al., 1993). The assumption here is that neonates and young infants receive greater quantities and fidelity of information about self-intended actions (e.g., active looking) through proprioception than about others' intended actions through exteroceptive information processing. Thus, infants have the opportunity to learn as much or more about intentionality from their own actions as from observing the actions of others. A corollary of this assumption of the PDPM is that joint attention is an embodied form of cognition (Feldman & Narayanan, 2004). Its development is a constructivist process that involves self-perception as a foundation for the attribution of meaning to the perception of others' behaviors. We have referred to this as the "inside-out" processing assumption of the PDPM (Mundy & Vaughan Van Hecke, 2008).

The general tenor of this constructivist assumption is nothing new. Bates and colleagues (1979) suggested that a sense of self-agency was basic to joint attention. More generally, Piaget (1952) argued that infants do not learn through the passive perception of objects (or others) in the world. Rather, infants take action on objects and learn from their (causal) actions. They then modify their actions, observe changes in causal relations, and learn new things about the physical world.

Thus, Piaget viewed the processing of self-initiated actions on objects as a singularly important fuel for the engines of cognitive development. Not only is the constructivist viewpoint central to the PDPM, it is also a mainstay of contemporary connectionist biological principles of typical and atypical neurocognitive development (e.g., Blakemore & Frith, 2003; Elman, 2005; Mareschal et al., 2007; Meltzoff, 2007; Quartz, 1999).

The vast number of functional neural connections that are made in early postnatal brain development are thought to be too numerous to be specified by genes alone. Instead, genes specify relatively wide channels of potential neurodevelopmental architecture (e.g., Quartz, 1999). Within these prescribed channels, the specifics of important functional connections in the developing nervous systems are sculpted by our experience. Because most of us experience relatively similar environments and experiences in early life, developmental brain organization displays significant similarities across most people (Mareschal et al., 2007). Greenough, Wallace, and Black (1987) refer to this gene–environment interaction in the ontogeny of neural connections as "experience-expectant" neurodevelopment. Greenough and colleagues also explicitly noted that infants' generation of actions, and observations of social reactions, likely play a role in experience-expectant processes specific to the neurodevelopmental basis of human social behavior. So just as Piaget envisioned that infants learn about the physical world from their self-generated actions on objects, it is reasonable to think that a significant portion of what infants learn about the social world comes from their self-generated actions with people.

Dynamic Systems, Integrated Processing, and the PDPM

The PDPM emphasizes inside-out processing, constructivism, and the role of active vision (Findlay & Gilchrist, 2003) in the development of joint attention. Active vision in infancy involves the goal-directed selection of information to process, which begins to develop at 3–4 months (e.g., Canfield & Kirkham, 2001; Johnson, 1990, 1995). It is one of the first types of volitional actions that infants use to control stimulation in order to problem solve and to self-regulate arousal or affect (Posner & Rothbart, 2007). It can also elicit contingent social behavior responses from other people, such as parental smiles, vocalizations, and gaze shifts.

Vision and looking have unique properties. Vision provides information regarding the relative spatial location of ourselves and other people. Moreover, direction of vision (gaze) conveys the distal and proximal spatial direction of our attention to others, and vice versa (Butterworth & Jarrett, 1991). Comparable information on the spatial direction of attention is not as clearly available from the other senses, such as audition. This is especially true in the first 9 months of life, before locomotion, and for distal information. Precise information about the spatial direction of attention is available from human eyes, relative to the eyes of other primates, because of the highlighted contrast between the dark coloration of the pupil and iris versus the light-to-white coloration of the sclera. These observations have led to the suggestion that the ease of processing the direction of attention of other people's eyes contributed to the human phylogenetic and ontogenetic development of social cognition (e.g., Tomasello, Hare, Lehman, & Call, 2006).

It is also the case, though, that these same characteristics of the human eye just as likely allow the saccades of infants to be readily observed by other people. Consequently, infant saccades can effectively act as elicitors of contingent social feedback. When infants shift attention to an object, their parents may pick up and show them the object. When infants shift attention to their parents' eyes, they may also receive a vocal, affective, or physical parental response. Thus, just as the characteristics of eyes make it easier for infants to perceive the attention of others, the signal value of eyes makes the active control of vision a likely nexus of infants' developing sense of agency. A corollary here is that proprioceptive and interoceptive processing of visual attention relative to processing of changes in state or responses to one's own attention from the social world contributes to a sense of *visual self-agency,* which may play a role in joint attention and social development (see Mundy et al., 2009, for elaboration).

While emphasizing the foregoing constructivist point of view, the PDPM does not maintain that the inside-out processing of self-attention is more important for social-cognitive development than outside-in processing of other's attention. This is because the PDPM holds that social meaning, and even conscious self-awareness, cannot be derived from processing either self attention or other's attention in isolation (cf. Decety & Sommerville, 2003; Keysers & Perrett, 2006; Vygotsky, 1962). Ontogeny may be best viewed as a dynamic system through which interactions of multiple factors over time and experience coalesce into higher order integrations, structures, and skills (e.g., Smith & Thelen, 2003). The development of joint attention, or the joint processing of the attention of self and other, is such a dynamic system. Indeed, the pertinence of joint attention for human development derives in no small part from the unique synthesis that arises from the rapid, parallel processing of self attention and other attention across distributed neural networks. Consequently, it is not possible to account for the role of joint attention in typical or atypical development with an inquiry about only one of its elements in isolation.

The dynamic system of joint attention begins to synergize as frontal executive functions increasingly enable the infant to attend to multiple sources of information. According to one definition, executive functions involve the transmission of bias signals throughout the neural network to selectively inhibit comparatively automatic behavioral responses in favor of more volitional, planned, and goal-directed ideation and action in problem-solving contexts (Miller & Cohen, 2001). These bias signals act as regulators for the brain affecting visual processes and attention as well as other sensory modalities and systems responsible for task-relevant response execution, memory retrieval, emotional evaluation, and so on. *The aggregate effect of these bias signals is to guide the flow of neural activity along pathways that establish the proper mappings between inputs, internal states, and outputs needed to perform a given task* more efficiently (Miller & Cohen, 2001). According to this definition, joint attention development may be thought of as reflecting the emergence of frontal bias signals that establish the proper mappings across (1) outside-in posterior cortical (temporal-precuneous) processing of inputs about the attention behaviors of other people and (2) rostral-medial-frontal (BA 8-9, anterior cingulate) inside-out processing of internal states and outputs related to active vision. This mapping results in the integrated development of a distributed anterior and posterior cortical joint attention system.

It is conceivable that the early establishment of this mapping of the joint processing of attention is formative with respect to the shared neural network of representations of self–other that Decety and Grezes (2006) suggest is essential to social cognition. It also may play a role in what Keysers and Perrett (2004) have described as a Hebbian learning model of social cognition. Neural networks that are repeatedly active at the same time become associated, such that activity (e.g., re-presentations) in one network triggers activity in the other (Hebb, 1949). Keysers and Perrett suggest that *common* activation of neural networks for processing self-generated information and information about conspecifics is fundamental to understanding the actions of others. This Hebbian learning process is fundamental to the hypothesized functions of simulation (Gordon, 1986) and mirror neurons (i.e., Decety & Sommerville, 2003; Williams, 2008) that are commonly invoked in current models of social-cognitive development.

The PDPM is consistent with these interrelated ideas *and* suggests that Hebbian mapping in social cognition begins with integrated rostral-medial-frontal processing of information about self-produced visual attention and posterior processing of the attention of others. Moreover, the PDPM specifically operationalizes the study of development of this dynamic mapping system in terms of psychometrically sound measures of early joint attention development (Mundy et al., 2007). Indeed, IJA assessments may be relatively powerful in research on social-cognitive development and autism because they measure variance in the whole dynamic system rather than any one of its parts alone.

Once well practiced, the joint processing of attention information requires less mental effort. As the basic joint attention process is mastered and its "effort to engage" subsides, it can become integrated as an executive function that contributes to the initial development and increasing efficiency of social-cognitive problem solving. Thus, joint attention development may be envisioned as shifting from "learning to do joint attention" in the first 6 to 9 months to "learning from joint attention" in the second year of life (Mundy & Vaughan Van Hecke, 2008; Figure 14.5). In the "learning from" phase, the capacity to attend to multiple sources of information in "triadic attention" deployment becomes more common (Scaife & Bruner, 1975). Triadic attention contexts provide infants with rich opportunities to compare information gleaned through processing internal states associated with volitional visual attention deployment and the processing of the visual attention of others in reference to a common third object or event. Through simulation (Gordon, 1986), infants may begin to impute that others have intentional control over their looking behavior that is similar to their own.

The role of simulation in the "learning from" phase of joint attention development is well illustrated by a recent sequence of elegant experimental studies. Twelve-month-olds often follow the gaze direction of testers even if their eyes are closed. After 12 months, though, infants discriminate and follow the gaze of testers whose eyes are open only. This suggests that infants' understanding of the eye gaze of others may improve in this period, leading older infants to inhibit looking in the "eyes-closed" condition (Brooks & Meltzoff, 2002).

To examine this interpretation, Meltzoff and Brooks (2008) conducted an experimental intervention. They provided 12-month-olds with the experience of blindfolds that occluded their own looking behavior. After gaining that experience,

12-month-olds did not follow the head turn of blindfolded testers, but did follow the head turn and gaze of non-blindfolded testers. Meltzoff and Brooks also provided 18-month-olds with experience with blindfolds that looked opaque but were transparent when worn. After this condition, the 18-month-olds reverted to following the gaze of blindfolded social partners. These data strongly suggest that the infants demonstrated inside-out learning and constructed social-cognitive awareness about others' gaze based on the experience of effects of blindfolds on their own active vision.

The PDPM and Intervention for Autism

The utility of any model, including the PDPM, is based on how well it deepens understanding of phenomenon in a science. In previous reports, we have examined how the PDPM helps to bridge theory and data on the social deficits of autism with phenomenon observed in genetic, neurodevelopmental, and neurocognitive research on autism (Mundy & Jarrold, 2010; Mundy et al., 2009, 2010). In this chapter, we consider the utility of the PDPM model for explaining why joint attention is a pivotal skill in early intervention for children with autism (Bruinsma et al., 2004; Charman, 2004; Mundy & Crowson, 1997).

Improvements in pivotal skills, by definition, lead to positive changes in a broad array of *other* problematic behaviors. This appears to be the case with joint attention. It can be improved with early intervention (e.g., Kasari et al., 2006, 2007; Pierce & Schreibman, 1995; Rocha, Schreibman, & Stahmer, 2007; Yoder & Stone, 2006), and joint attention improvement has collateral benefits on language, cognitive, and social development (Jones, Carr, & Feeley, 2006; Kasari et al., 2007; Whalen & Schreibman, 2006). Joint attention also appears to mediate responsiveness to early intervention among children with autism (Bono et al., 2004; Yoder & Stone, 2006).

According to the PDPM, joint attention is a pivotal skill in autism because its improvement has multiple effects on social learning. Recall that joint attention facilitates the self-organization of information processing to optimize incidental as well as structured social learning opportunities (Baldwin, 1995). Hence, impairment in joint attention may be viewed as part of a broader social constructivist learning disturbance in autism. By the same token, effective intervention likely improves social constructivist learning in autism.

Second, the PDPM proposes that joint attention serves as a foundation for social-cognitive development. Social-cognitive development is defined in terms of advances in the processing of information about self and other rather than singularly in terms of changes in knowledge about intentionality. Following connectionist cognitive theory (McClelland & Rogers, 2003; Otten et al., 2001), the PDPM assumes that information encoded during learning is stored as a distributed neural network activation pattern that involves parallel activation of networks of related semantic information. Additionally, whenever information is acquired during social learning and joint attention, it is also encoded in parallel with the activation of a frontal-temporal-parietal neural network that maps relations between representations of information about self-directed attention and information about the attention of other people. Thus, every time we process information in social learning, we encode it as an activation pattern in a distributed semantic network in conjunction with an activation pattern of the anterior-posterior cortical joint attention network (see Figures 14.4 and 14.5). Recall that deeper information processing and learning occur best in the context of the simultaneous activation of multiple neural networks during encoding (Otten et al., 2001). If so, joint attention may lead to deeper processing because it adds activation of the distributed social attention network (a form of episodic encoding) to the network activation associated more directly with semantic information. This conjecture provides one interpretation of the observation that joint attention facilitates depth of processing in 9-month-olds (Striano, Chen, et al., 2006; Striano, Reid, & Hoel, 2006). It also suggests that part of the learning disability of autism occurs because children with this disorder do not reap the full benefits of encoding semantic information in conjunction with episodic memory encoded within the integrated processing of self and other attention. This, in turn, may help to explain the attenuation of self-referenced memory effects in autism (Henderson et al., 2009).

Third, the PDPM argues that overt joint attention becomes increasingly internalized as a social executive function that supports the social coordination of covert

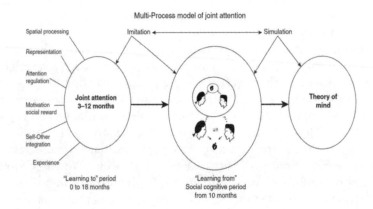

FIGURE 14.5. In the first year, the development of joint attention involves the "learning to" integration of executive, motivation, and imitation processes to support the routine, rapid, and efficient (error free) execution of patterns of behavior that enable infants to coordinate processing of *overt* aspects of visual self-attention with processing of the social attention of other people. In the latter part of the first year and into the second year, infants can better monitor their own experiences and integrate it with information about the social partners during joint attention events. This provides a critical multimodality source of information to the infants about the convergence and divergence of self and others' experience and behavior during sharing information in social interactions. Theoretically, this sets the stage for the "learning from" phase of joint attention development. In this stage, infants can control their attention to self-organize and optimize information processing in social learning opportunities. The integration of anterior and posterior self–other attention processing provides a neural network that enriches encoding in social learning. The internalization of the overt joint processing of attention to the covert joint processing of attention to representations is part of an executive system that facilitates symbolic development and the social cognition. Indeed, both symbolic thought and social cognition may be characterized by a transition from learning to *socially coordinate overt attention* to the capacity to *socially coordinate covert mental representations of the attention of self and others.*

mental attention to cognitive representations. The spontaneous coordination of mental attention cognitive representations is an essential element of symbolic thought (Tomasello et al., 2005). The PDPM assumes that months of practice of the social coordination of overt attention (i.e., joint attention) in the first years of life are required before this function can be internalized and transformed to an executive facility for the socially coordinated covert mental attention and symbolic thought. Thus, symbolic thought processes incorporate but do not replace activation of the self–other joint attention system. Joint attention, on the other hand, does not necessarily involve symbolic process (Mundy, Sigman, Ungerer, & Sherman, 1987).

These assumptions of the PDPM are consistent with two recent observations. Joint attention is a unique predictor of pretend-play development in children with autism relative to measures of imitation or executive functions (Rutherford, Young, Hepburn, & Rogers, 2008). Moreover, successful symbolic-play intervention, which according to the PDPM must involve effects on joint attention, *is* associated with parallel collateral improvements in joint attention in autism. However, intervention with joint attention has less immediate impact on symbolic-play behavior (Kasari et al., 2006).

Fourth, the joint processing of attention information also plays a fundamental role in social-cognitive development defined in terms of the development of knowledge about intentions in self and other (Mundy & Newell, 2007). The assumption here is that when infants or primates practice monitoring others' attention (RJA), statistical learning ultimately leads to the associative rule *"Where others' eyes go, their behavior follows"* (Jellema et al., 2000). Similarly, anterior monitoring or *self-awareness* of control of visual attention likely leads to awareness of the self-referenced associative rule *"Where my eyes go, my intended behavior follows"* (Mundy & Newell, 2007). An integration of the development of these concepts leads to the logical cognitive output *"Where others eyes go → their intended behavior follows,"* which is a building block of social-cognitive development (Mundy & Newell, 2007). Social cognition of this kind is thought to enable new and more efficient levels of social or cultural learning atypical in autism.

Finally, the constructivist assumptions of the PDPM stress that motivation factors are part of a crucial fifth path of association between joint attention and social learning. IJA requires "choosing" between behavior goals, such as fixated looking at an event or alternating looking to the event and another person. Choosing among behavior goals is thought to involve frontal and medial cortical processing of the relative reward associated with different goals (Frank & Claus, 2006; Holroyd & Coles, 2002). Therefore, IJA impairment in autism may be expected to be related to deficits in biobehavioral processes associated with reward sensitivity and motivation (Dawson, 2008; Kasari et al., 1990; Mundy, 1995). Such a deficit, however, could take several forms.

Social stimuli could be aversive in some way for children with autism. However, the aversion hypothesis is complicated by observations of behaviors indicative of relatively intact caregiver attachment in many children with autism and a willingness to engage in playful physical interactions with strangers (e.g., Mundy, Fox, & Card, 1986; Sigman & Underer, 1984). Thus, it seems that social stimuli may not be aversive. Rather, they may simply not be sufficiently positive to compel social orienting and joint attention early in the life of children with autism (Dawson et al., 1998; Mundy, 1995). Finally, social stimuli could have a positive valence for children with autism, but be overshadowed by an atypically strong visual preference that make objects, rather that social elements of the world, more "interesting" (Karmel, Gardner, Swensen, Lennon, & London, 2008; McCleery, Allman, Carver, & Dobkins, 2007; Mundy & Crowson, 1997).

The construction of effective empirical approaches to address these alternatives is one of the outstanding challenges in the science of autism (Dawson, 2008; Koegel et al., 2003). Research on joint attention in relation to motivation and the perceived valence of objects in adults (Bayliss et al., 2006) offers one potential route for developmental and functional neurocognitive studies on this topic. For now, though, the literature on early intervention may be the best source of information in this regard. Early interventions studies offer some of the most systematic investigations to date of how to structure social engagements with young children with autism to modify and increase their motivation to initiate episodes of shared attention and shared experience with others (e.g., Kasari et al., 2006, 2007).

Conclusions

Only in its most expansive interpretation can the PDPM be viewed as an explanatory model of joint attention, or autism. Nevertheless, the PDPM does serve a purpose. It presents a new perspective on joint attention that suggests its impairment in autism is more than an epiphenomenon associated with other fundamental precursor or successor processes. This alternative perspective can be summed up in terms of several general principles. First, autism is as much about impairments in self-generated activity as it is about problems in perceiving or responding to the behavior of others. Hence, we need to consider the neurodevelopmental processes and networks involved in initiating behavior and attention control as well as those involved in perceiving and responding to the behaviors of others to understand this disorder (Mundy, 2003). Second, joint attention is a form of information processing that gives rise to social-cognitive knowledge. Third, joint attention is a form of parallel and distributed processing that involves the conjoint analysis of information from the anterior cortical system for guidance of goal-directed attention and behavior, with posterior cortical processing external information about the attention-related behavior of other people. Ultimately, joint attention becomes a social executive process that supports all subsequent cognition and learning that demands the rapid social coordination of mental attention to internal representations of object and events. Thus, neural network activation associated with joint attention is an enduring substrate that plays a role in the unique characteristics of human cognition throughout the lifespan (Mundy & Newell, 2007). Indeed, it may be one example of the type of "hot" executive functions that Zelazo, Qu, and Müller (2005) theorize are central to social cognition. Such "hot" functions are those that entail motivation processes and affect regulation specific to the support of successful goal-directed behavior in social engagements. It follows from this notion that individual differences in the operation of the social-executive function of joint attention, including the extreme variation displayed by people with autism, may be an expression of variance in motivation process.

Acknowledgments

The research and theory development reported in this chapter were supported by National Institutes of Health Grant Nos. HD 38052, MH 071273, and MH085904, as well as the generous support of Marc Friedman and Marjorie Solomon for the Lisa Capps Endowment to the University of California, Davis, Department of Psychiatry and the M.I.N.D. Institute.

References

Adamson, L., Bakeman, R., & Dekner, D. (2004). The development of symbol infused joint engagement. *Child Development, 75,* 1171–1187.

American Psychiatric Association. (1980). *Diagnostic and statistical manual of mental disorders* (3rd ed.). Washington, DC: Author.

American Psychiatric Association. (1994). *Diagnostic and statistical manual of mental disorders* (4th ed.). Washington, DC: Author.

American Psychiatric Association. (2000). *Diagnostic and statistical manual of mental disorders* (4th ed., text rev.). Washington, DC: Author.

Astafiev, S., Shulman, G., Stanley, C., Snyder, A., Essen, D., & Corbetta, M. (2003). Functional organization of human intraparietal and frontal cortex for attending, looking and pointing. *Journal of Neuroscience, 23,* 4689–4699.

Atkinson, J., Hood, B., Wattam-Bell, J., & Braddick, O. (1992). Changes in infants' ability to switch attention in the first three months of life. *Perception, 21,* 643–653.

Baldwin, D. (1995). Understanding the link between joint attention and language. In C. Moore & P. Dunham (Eds.), *Joint attention: Its origins and role in development* (pp. 131–158). Hillsdale, NJ: Erlbaum.

Baron-Cohen, S. (1989). Joint attention deficits in autism: Towards a cognitive analysis. *Development and Psychopathology, 3,* 185–190.

Baron-Cohen, S. (1995). *Mindblindness.* Cambridge, MA: MIT Press.

Bates, E., Benigni, L., Bretherton, I., Camaioni, L., & Volterrra, V. (1979). *The emergence of symbols: Cognition and communication in infancy.* New York: Academic Press.

Bayliss, A., Paul, M., Cannon, P., & Tipper, S. (2006). Gaze cuing and affective judgments of objects. I like what you look at. *Psychonomic Bulletin and Review, 13,* 1061–1066.

Blakemore, S., & Frith, C. (2003). Self awareness and action. *Current Opinion in Neurobiology, 13, 219–224.*

Bono, M., Daley, T., & Sigman, M. (2004). Joint attention moderates the relation between intervention and language development in young children with autism. *Journal of Autism and Related Disorders, 34,* 495–505.

Brooks, R., & Meltzoff, A. (2002). The importance of eyes: How infants interpret adult looking behavior. *Developmental Psychology, 38,* 958–966.

Bruinsma, Y., Koegle, R., & Koegle, L. (2004). Joint attention and children with autism: A review of the literature. *Mental Retardation and Developmental Disabilities Research Reviews, 10,* 169–175.

Bruner, J. S. (1975). From communication to language: A psychological perspective. *Cognition, 3,* 255–287.

Bruner, J. S. (1995). From joint attention to the meeting of minds: An introduction. In C. Moore & P. J. Dunham (Eds.), *Joint attention: Its origins and role in development* (pp. 1–14). Hillsdale, NJ: Erlbaum.

Butterworth, G., & Jarrett, N. (1991). What minds have in common is space: Spatial mechanisms in serving joint visual attention in infancy. *British Journal of Developmental Psychology, 9,* 55–72.

Canfield, R., & Kirkham, N. (2001). Infant cortical development and the prospective control of saccadic eye movements. *Infancy, 2,* 197–211.

Caplan, R., Chugani, H., Messa, C., Guthrie, D., Sigman, M., Traversay, J., et al. (1993). Hemispherectomy for early onset intractable seizures: Presurgical cerebral glucose metabolism and postsurgical nonverbal communication patterns. *Developmental Medicine and Child Neurology, 35,* 574–581.

Capps, L., Sigman, M., & Mundy, P. (1994). Attachment security in children with autism. *Development and Psychopathology, 6,* 249–261.

Cavanna, A., & Trimble, M. (2006). The precuneus: A review of its functional anatomy and behavioural correlates. *Brain, 10,* 1–20.

Charman, T. (2004). Why is joint attention a pivotal skill in autism? *Philosophical Transactions of the Royal Society of London, 358,* 315–324.

Charman, T., Baron-Cohen, S., Swettenham, J., Baird, G., Cox, A., & Drew, A. (2000). Testing joint attention, imitation, and play infancy precursors to language and theory of mind. *Cognitive Development, 15,* 481–498.

Courschesne, E., & Pierce, K. (2005). Why the frontal cortex in autism might be talking only to itself: Local over connectivity but long distance disconnection. *Current Opinion in Neurology, 15,* 225–230.

Curcio, F. (1978). Sensorimotor functioning and communication in mute autistic children. *Journal of Autism and Developmental Disorders, 8,* 281–292.

Dawson, G. (2008). Early behavioral intervention, brain plasticity and the prevention of autism spectrum disorders. *Development and Psychopathology, 20,* 775–804.

Dawson, G., Meltzoff, A., Osterling, J., Rinaldi, J., & Brown, E. (1998). Children with autism fail to orient to naturally occurring social stimuli. *Journal of Autism and Developmental Disorders, 28,* 479–485.

Dawson, G., Toth, K., Abbott, R., Osterling, J., Munson, J., Estes, A., et al. (2004). Early social attention impairments in autism: Social orienting, joint attention, and attention in autism. *Developmental Psychology, 40,* 271–283.

Dawson, G., Webb, S., Schellenberg, G., Dager, S., Friedman, S., Ayland, E., et al. (2002). Defining the broader phenotype of autism: Genetic, brain, and behavioral perspectives. *Development and Psychopathology, 14,* 581–612.

Decety, J., & Grezes, J. (2006). The power of simulation: Imagining one's own and other's behavior. *Social Cognitive Neuroscience* [Special issue: Cognitive Brain Research], *1079,* 4–14.

Decety, J., & Sommerville, J. (2003). Shared representations between self and other: A social cognitive neuroscience view. *Trends in Cognitive Sciences, 7,* 527–533.

D'Entremont, B., Hains, S., & Muir, D. (1997). A demonstration of gaze following in 3- to 6-month-olds. *Infant Behavior and Development, 20,* 569–572.

Dosenbach, N., Fair, D., Miezin, F., Cohen, A., Wenger, K., Dosenbach, R. A. T., et al. (2007). Distinct brain networks for adaptive and stable task control in humans. *Proceedings of the National Academy of Sciences USA, 104,* 11073–11078.

Elman, J. (2005). Connectionist models of cognitive development: Where next. *Trends in Cognitive Science, 9,* 111–117.

Emery, N. (2000). The eyes have it: The neuroethology, function, and evolution of social gaze. *Neuroscience and Biobehavioral Reviews, 24,* 581–604.

Farroni, T., Massaccesi, S., & Francesca, S. (2002). Can the direction of gaze of another person shift the attention of a neonate? *Giornole-Italiano-di-Psicologia, 29,* 857–864.

Feldman, J., & Narayanan, S. (2004). Embodied meaning in a neural theory of language. *Brain and Language, 89,* 385–392.

Findlay, J., & Gilchrist, I. (2003). *Active vision: The psychology of looking and seeing.* New York: Oxford University Press.

Frank, M. J., & Claus, E. D. (2006). Anatomy of a decision: Striatoorbitofrontal interactions in reinforcement learning, decision making, and reversal. *Psychological Review, 113*, 300–326.

Frieschen, A., Bayliss, A., & Tipper S. (2007). Gaze cueing of attention: Visual attention, social cognition and individual differences. *Psychological Bulletin, 133*, 694–724.

Fuster, J. (2006). The cognit: A network model of cortical representation. *International Journal of Psychophysiology, 60*, 125–132.

Gilbert, S., & Burgess, P. (2008). Social and nonsocial functions of rostral prefrontal cortex: Implications for education. *Mind, Brain and Education, 2*, 148–156.

Gordon, R. (1986). Folk psychology as simulation. *Mind and Language, 1*, 158–171.

Greenough, W., Black, J., & Wallace, C. (1987). Experience and brain development. *Child Development, 58*, 539–559.

Griffith, E., Pennington, B., Wehner, E., & Rogers, S. (1999). Executive functions in young children with autism. *Child Development, 70*, 817–832.

Grossman, T., & Johnson, M. (2010). Selective prefrontal cortex response to joint attention in early infancy. *Biology Letters, 6*, 540–543.

Hebb, D. (1949) *The organization of behaviour.* New York: Wiley.

Henderson, H., Zahka, N., Kojkowski, N., Inge, A., Schwarz, C., Hileman, C., et al. (2009). Self referenced memory, social cognition and symptom presentation in autism. *Journal of Child Psychology and Psychiatry, 50*, 853–861.

Henderson, L., Yoder, P., Yale, M., & McDuffie, A. (2002). Getting the point: Electrophysiological correlates of protodeclarative pointing. *International Journal of Developmental Neuroscience, 20*, 449–458.

Hobson, J., & Hobson, R. P. (2007). Identification: The missing link between joint attention and imitation. *Development and Psychopathology, 19*, 411–431.

Holroyd, C., & Coles, M. (2002). The neural basis of human error processing: Reinforcement learning, dopamine and the error related negativity. *Psychological Review, 109*, 679–709.

Hood, B., Willen, J., & Driver, J. (1998). Adult's eyes trigger shifts of visual attention in human infants. *Psychological Science, 9*, 131–134.

Hunt, E. (1999). Intelligence and human resources: past, present and future. In P. Ackerman, P. Kyllonen, & R. Roberts (Eds.), *Learning and individual differences* (pp. 97–114). Washington, DC: American Psychological Association.

Jellema, T., Baker, C., Wicker, B., & Perrett, D. (2000). Neural representation for the perception of intentionality of actions. *Brain and Cognition, 44*, 280–302.

Johnson, M. (1990). Cortical maturation and the development of visual attention in early infancy. *Journal of Cognitive Neuroscience, 2*, 81–95.

Johnson, M. (1995). The inhibition of automatic saccades in early infancy. *Developmental Psychobiology, 28*, 281–291.

Jones, E., Carr, E., & Feeley, K. (2006). Multiple effects of joint attention intervention for children with autism. *Behavior Modification, 30*, 782–834.

Kanner, L. (1943). Autistic disorder of affective contact. *Nervous Child, 2*, 217–250.

Karmel, B., Gardner, J., Swensen, L., Lennon, E., & London, E. (2008, March). *Contrasts of medical and behavioral data from NICU infants suspect and non-suspect for autism spectrum disorder (ASD).* Paper presented at the International Conference on Infant Studies, Vancouver.

Kasari, C., Freeman, S., & Paparella, T. (2006). Joint attention and symbolic play in young children with autism: A randomized controlled intervention study. *Journal of Child Psychology and Psychiatry, 47*, 611–620.

Kasari, C., Freeman, S., & Paparella, T. (2007, April). *The UCLA RCT on play and joint attention.* Paper presented at the biennial conference of the Society for Research on Child Development, Boston.

Kasari, C., Sigman, M., Mundy, P., & Yirmiya, N. (1990). Affective sharing in the context of joint attention interactions of normal, autistic, and mentally retarded children. *Journal of Autism and Developmental Disorders, 20,* 87–100.

Keysers, C., & Perrett, D. (2006). Demystifying social-cognition: A Hebbian perspective. *Trends in Cognitive Science, 8,* 501–507.

Koegel, L., Carter, C., & Koegel, R. (2003). Teaching children with autism self-initiations as a pivotal response. *Topics in Language Disorders, 23,* 134–145.

Landry, R., & Bryson, S. (2004). Impaired disengagement of attention in young children with autism. *Journal of Child Psychology and Psychiatry, 45,* 1115–1122.

Legerstee, M., Markova, G., & Fisher, T. (2007). The role of maternal affect attunement in dyadic and triadic communication. *Infant Behavior and Development, 2,* 296–306.

Lewy, A., & Dawson, G. (1992). Social stimulation and joint attention in young autistic children. *Journal of Abnormal Child Psychology, 20,* 555–566.

Lord, C., Floody, H., Anderson, D., & Pickles, A. (2003, April). *Social engagement in very young children with autism: Differences across contexts.* Paper presented at the meeting of the Society for Research in Child Development, Tampa, FL.

Lord, C., Risi, S., Lambrecht, L., Cook, E. H., Jr., Leventhal, B. L., DiLavore, P. C., et al. (2000). The Autism Diagnostic Observation Schedule-Generic: A standard measure of social communication deficits associated with the spectrum of autism. *Journal of Autism and Developmental Disorders, 30,* 205–223.

Loveland, K., & Landry, S. (1986). Joint attention and language in autism and developmental language delay. *Journal of Autism and Developmental Disorders, 16,* 335–349.

Mareschal, D., Johnson, M., Sirois, S., Spratling, S., Thomas, M., & Wasserman, G. (2007). *Neuroconstructivism. I: How the brain constructs cognition.* New York: Oxford University Press.

Materna, S., Dicke, P., & Thern, P. (2008). Dissociable roles of the superior-temporal sulcus and the intraparietal sulcus in joint attention: A functional magnetic resonance imaging study. *Journal of Cognitive Neuroscience, 20,* 108–119.

McCleery, J., Allman, E., Carver, L., & Dobkins, K. (2007). Abnormal magnocellular pathway visual processing in infants at risk for autism. *Biological Psychiatry, 62,* 1007–1014.

McClelland, J., & Rogers, T. (2003). The parallel distributed processing approach to semantic cognition. *Nature Reviews. Neuroscience, 4,* 310–322.

Meltzoff, A. (2007). "Like me": A foundation for social cognition. *Developmental Science, 10,* 126–134.

Meltzoff, A., & Brooks, R. (2008). Self experiences: A mechanism for learning about others. A training study in social cognition. *Developmental Psychology, 44,* 1–9.

Miller, E., & Cohen, J. (2001). An integrative theory of prefrontal cortex functioning. *Annual Review of Neurosciences, 24,* 167–2002.

Morales, M., Mundy, P., Crowson, M., Neal, R., & Delgado, C. (2005). Individual differences in infant attention skills, joint attention, and emotion regulation behavior. *International Journal of Behavioral Development, 29,* 259–263.

Morales, M., Mundy, P., & Rojas, J. (1998). Following the direction of gaze and language development in 6-month olds. *Infant Behavior and Development, 21,* 373–377.

Munakata, Y., & McClelland, J. (2003). Connectionist models of development. *Developmental Science, 6,* 413–429.

Mundy, P. (1995). Joint attention and social-emotional approach behavior in children with autism. *Development and Psychopathology, 7,* 63–82.

Mundy, P. (2003). The neural basis of social impairments in autism: The role of the dorsal medial-frontal cortex and anterior cingulate system. *Journal of Child Psychology and Psychiatry and Allied Disciplines, 44,* 793–809.

Mundy, P., Block, J., Vaughan Van Hecke, A., Delgadoa, C., Venezia Parlade, M., & Pomares, Y. (2007). Individual differences and the development of infant joint attention. *Child Development, 78,* 938–954.

Mundy, P., Card, J., & Fox, N. (2000). EEG correlates of the development of infant joint attention skills. *Developmental Psychobiology, 36,* 325–338.

Mundy, P., & Crowson, M. (1997). Joint attention and early social communication: Implications for research on intervention with autism. *Journal of Autism and Developmental Disorders, 27,* 653–676.

Mundy, P., Fox, N., & Card, J. (2003). Joint attention, EEG coherence and early vocabulary development. *Developmental Science, 6,* 48–54.

Mundy, P., Gwaltney, M., & Henderson, H. (2010). Self-referenced processing and neurodevelopment in autism: Perspectives from joint attention research. *Autism, 14,* 408–429.

Mundy, P., & Hogan, A. (1994). Intersubjectivity, joint attention and autistic developmental pathology. In D. Cicchetti & S. Toth (Eds.), *Rochester symposium of developmental psychopathology: Vol. 5. A developmental perspective on the self and its disorders* (pp. 1–30). Hillsdale, NJ: Erlbaum.

Mundy, P., & Jarrold, W. (2010). Infant joint attention, neural networks and social-cognition. *Neural Networks, 23,* 985–997.

Mundy, P., Kasari, C., & Sigman, M. (1992). Nonverbal communication, affective sharing, and intersubjectivity. *Infant Behavior and Development, 15,* 377–381.

Mundy, P., & Newell, L. (2007). Attention, joint attention and social cognition. *Current Directions in Psychological Science, 16,* 269–274.

Mundy, P., & Sigman, M. (1989). Theoretical implications of joint attention deficits in autism. *Development and Psychopathology, 1,* 173–184.

Mundy, P., & Sigman, M. (2006). Joint attention, social competence and developmental psychopathology. In D. Cicchetti & D. Cohen (Eds.), *Developmental psychopathology: Vol. 1. Theory and methods* (2nd ed., pp. 293–332). Hoboken, NJ: Wiley.

Mundy, P., Sigman, M., & Kasari, C. (1994). Joint attention, developmental level, and symptom presentation in children with autism. *Development and Psychopathology, 6,* 389–401.

Mundy, P., Sigman, M., Ungerer, J., & Sherman, T. (1986). Defining the social deficits of autism: The contribution of nonverbal communication measures. *Journal of Child Psychology and Psychiatry, 27,* 657–669.

Mundy, P., Sigman, M., Ungerer, J., & Sherman, T. (1987). Nonverbal communication and play correlates of language development in autistic children. *Journal of Autism and Developmental Disorders, 17,* 349–364.

Mundy, P., Sullivan, L., & Mastergeorge, A. (2009). A parallel and distributed processing model of joint attention and autism. *Autism Research, 2,* 2–21.

Mundy, P., & Vaughan Van Hecke, A. (2008). Neural systems, gaze following and the development of joint attention. In C. Nelson & M. Luciana (Eds.), *Handbook of developmental cognitive neuroscience* (pp. 819–837). New York: Oxford University Press.

Naber, F., Bakermans-Kranenburg, M., van IJzendoorn, M., Dietz, C., Daalen E., Swinkels, S. H., et al. (2008). Joint attention development in toddlers with autism. *European Child and Adolescent Psychiatry, 17,* 143–152.

Nathan, M., Eilam, B., & Kim, S. (2007). To disagree we must all agree: How intersubjectivity structures and perpetuates discourse in a mathematics classroom. *Journal of Learning Sciences, 16,* 523–563.

Nation, K., & Penny, S. (2008). Sensitivity to eye gaze in autism: Is it normal? Is it automatic? Is it social? *Development and Psychopathology, 20,* 79–97.

Otten, L., Henson, R., & Rugg, M. (2001). Depth of processing effects on neural correlates of memory encoding. *Brain, 125,* 399–412.

Piaget, J. (1952). *The origins of intelligence in children.* New York: Norton.

Pierce, K., & Schreibman, L. (1995). Increasing complex social behaviors in children with autism: Effects of peer implemented pivotal response training. *Journal of Applied Behavior Analysis, 28,* 285–295.

Posner, M., & Rothbart, M. (2007). Research on attention networks as a model for the integration of psychological science. *Annual Review of Psychology, 58,* 1–23.

Quartz, S. (1999). The constructivist brain. *Trends in Cognitive Science, 3,* 48–57.

Ramnani, N., Behrens, T., Penny, W., & Matthews, P. (2004). New approaches for exploring anatomical and functional connectivity in the human brain. *Biological Psychiatry, 56,* 613–619.

Rocha, M., Schriebman, L., & Stahmer, A. (2007). Effectiveness of training parents to teach joint attention with children with autism. *Journal of Early Intervention, 29,* 154–172.

Royers, H., Van Oost, P., & Bothutne, S. (1998). Immediate imitation and joint attention in young children with autism. *Development and Psychopathology, 10,* 441–450.

Rutherford, M., Young, G., Hepburn, S., & Rogers, S. (2008). A longitudinal study of pretend play in Autism. *Journal of Autism and Developmental Disorders, 37,* 1024–1039.

Scaife, M., & Bruner, J. (1975). The capacity for joint visual attention in the infant. *Nature, 253,* 265–266.

Seibert, J. M., Hogan, A. E., & Mundy, P. C. (1982). Assessing interactional competencies: The Early Social-Communication Scales. *Infant Mental Health Journal, 3,* 244–258.

Shapiro, T., Sherman, M., Calamari, G., & Koch, D. (1987). Attachment in autism and other developmental disorders. *Journal of the American Academy of Child and Adolescent Psychiatry, 26,* 480–484.

Sigman, M., & McGovern, C. (2005). Improvements in cognitive and language skills from preschool to adolescence in autism. *Journal of Autism and Developmental Disorders, 35,* 15–23.

Sigman, M., & Mundy, P. (1989). Social attachments in autistic children. *Journal of the American Academy of Child and Adolescent Psychiatry, 28,* 74–81.

Sigman, M., Mundy, P., Sherman, T., & Ungerer, J. (1986). Social interactions in autistic, mentally retarded, and normal children and their caregivers. *Journal of Child Psychology and Psychiatry, 27,* 647–656.

Sigman, M., & Ruskin, E. (1999). Continuity and change in the social competence of children with autism, Down syndrome, and developmental delays. *Monographs of the Society for Research in Child Development, 64*(1, Serial No. 256).

Sigman, M., & Ungerer, J. (1984). Attachment behaviors in autistic children. *Journal of Autism and Related Disabilities, 14,* 231–244.

Smith, V., Mirenda, P., & Zaidman-Zait, A. (2007). Predictors of expressive vocabulary growth in children with autism. *Journal of Speech, Language and Hearing Research, 50,* 149–160.

Smith, L., & Thelen, E. (2003). Development as a dynamic system. *Trends in Cognitive Science, 7,* 343–348.

Smith, L., & Ulvund, L. (2003). The role of joint attention in later development among preterm children: Linkages between early and middle childhood. *Social Development, 12,* 222–234.

Stone, W., Coonrod, E., & Ousley, C., (1997). Screening tool for autism in two year olds (STAT): Development and preliminary data. *Journal of Autism and Developmental Disorders, 30,* 607–612.

Striano, T., Chen, X., Cleveland, A., & Bradshaw, S. (2006). Joint attention social cues influence infant learning. *European Journal of Developmental Psychology. 3,* 289–299.

Striano, T., Reid, V., & Hoel, S. (2006). Neural mechanisms of joint attention in infancy. *European Journal of Neuroscience, 23*, 2819–2823.

Striano, T., & Stahl, D. (2005). Sensitivity to triadic attention in early infancy. *Developmental Science, 8*, 333–343.

Thurm, A., Lord, C., Lee, L., & Newschaffer, C. (2007). Predictors of language acquisition in preschool children with autism spectrum disorders. *Journal of Autism and Developmental Disorders, 37*, 1721–1734.

Tomasello, M. (1995). Joint attention as social cognition. In C. Moore & P. Dunham (Eds.), *Joint attention: Its origins and role in development* (pp. 129–146). New York: Erlbaum.

Tomasello, M., Carpenter, M., Call, J., Behne, T., & Moll, H. (2005). Understanding sharing intentions: The origins of cultural cognition. *Brain and Behavior Sciences, 28*, 675–690.

Tomasello, M., & Farrar, M. J. (1986). Joint attention and early language. *Child Development, 57*, 1454–1463.

Tomasello, M., Hare, B., Lehman, H., & Call, J. (2006). Reliance on head versus eyes in the gaze following of great apes and humans: The cooperative eyes hypothesis. *Journal of Human Evolution, 52*, 314–320.

Torkildsen, J., Thormodsen, R., Syvensen, G., Smith, L., & Lingren, M. (2008, March). *Brain correlates of nonverbal communicative comprehension in 20–24 month olds.* Paper presented at the International Conference on Infant Studies, Vancouver.

Toth, K., Munson, J., Meltzoff, A., & Dawson, G. (2006). Early predictors of communication development in young children with autism spectrum disorders: Joint attention, imitation and toy play. *Journal of Autism and Developmental Disorders, 36*, 993–1005.

Travis, L., & Sigman, M. (1998). Social deficits and interpersonal relationships in autism. *Mental Retardation and Developmental Disabilities Research Reviews, 4*, 65–72.

Ulvund, S., & Smith, L. (1996). The predictive validity of nonverbal communicative skills in infants with perinatal hazards. *Infant Behavior and Development, 19*, 441–449.

Vaughan (Van Henke), A., Mundy, P., Acra, C. F., Block, J., Delgado, C., Parlade, M., et al. (2007). Infant joint attention, temperament, and social competence in preschool children. *Child Development, 78*, 53–69.

Venezia, M., Messinger, D., Thorp, D., & Mundy, P. (2004). Timing changes: The development of anticipatory smiling. *Infancy, 6*, 397–406.

Vygotsky, L. (1962). *Thought and language.* Cambridge, MA: MIT Press.

Werner, H., & Kaplan, B. (1963). *Symbol formation.* Oxford, UK: Wiley.

Wetherby, A., Allen, L., Cleary, J., Kublin, K., & Goldstein, H. (2002). Validity and reliability of the communication and Symbolic Behavior Scales developmental profile with very young children. *Journal of Speech, Language, and Hearing Research, 45*, 1202–1218.

Wetherby, A., & Prutting, C. (1984). Profiles of communicative and cognitive-social abilities in autistic children. *Journal of Speech and Hearing Research, 27*, 367–377.

Whalen, C., & Schreibman, L. (2006). The collateral effects of joint attention training on social initiations, positive affect, imitation, and spontaneous speech for young children with Autism. *Journal of Autism and Developmental Disorders, 36*, 655–664.

Williams, J. (2008). Self-other relations in social development and autism: Multiple roles for mirror neurons and other brain bases. *Autism Research, 1*, 73–90.

Williams, J., Waiter, G., Perra, O., A., Perrett, D., Murray, A., & Whitten, A. (2005). An fMRI study of joint attention experience. *NeuroImage, 25*, 133–140.

Wing, L., & Potter, D. (2002). The epidemiology of autistic spectrum disorders: Is the prevalence rising? *Mental Retardation and Developmental Disabilities Research, 8*, 151–161.

World Health Organization. (1991). *The international classification of diseases, ninth revision.* Geneva: Author.

Yoder, P., & Stone, W. (2006). Randomized comparison of two communication interventions for preschoolers with autism spectrum disorders. *Journal of Consulting and Clinical Psychology, 74,* 426–435.

Zelazo, P. D., Qu, L., & Müller, U. (2005). Hot and cool aspects of executive function: Relations in early development. In W. Schneider, R. Schumann-Hengsteler, & B. Sodian (Eds.), *Young children's cognitive development: Interrelationships among executive functioning, working memory, verbal ability, and theory of mind* (pp. 71–93). Mahwah, NJ: Erlbaum.

Zwaigenbaum, L., Bryson, S., Rogers, T., Roberts, W., Brian, J., & Szatmari, P. (2005). Behavioral manifestations of autism in the first year of life. *International Journal of Neuroscience, 23,* 143–152.

Index